ROUTLEDGE HANDBOOK OF SPORT MANAGEMENT

The *Routledge Handbook of Sport Management* is the most up-to-date and comprehensive guide to theory and practice in sport management ever published. It provides students and scholars with a broad-ranging survey of current thinking in contemporary sport management, exploring best practice in core functional areas and identifying important future directions for new research.

Key topics covered in the book include:

- Managing performance
- Marketing
- Human resource management
- The economics and finance of sport
- Strategy
- Managing change
- Governance of sports organizations
- Customer relations
- Branding and retail

With contributions from leading scholars and professionals from around the world, the book illustrates the global nature of contemporary sport business and highlights the opportunities and challenges for managers operating in an international marketplace. Representing a definitive survey of contemporary issues in sport management, this is an essential reference for all students, scholars and practitioners working in sport.

Leigh Robinson is Professor of Sport Management at the University of Stirling, Scotland. Her principal research interest is in the management and measurement of performance, governance and quality in Olympic sport organizations.

Packianathan Chelladurai is Professor of Sport Management at The Ohio State University, USA. He is an internationally recognized scholar of management science, specializing in organizational theory and organizational behaviour in the context of sport.

Guillaume Bodet is a lecturer in Sport Marketing and Management within the Institute of Sport and Leisure Policy, at the University of Loughborough, England. His research primarily deals with consumer behaviour regarding sport organizations, sporting events and sport brands.

Paul Downward is Director of the Institute of Sport and Leisure Policy, University of Loughborough, England. He is currently embarked on a study of the economic determinants and impacts of sports participation in the UK.

ROUTLEDGE HANDBOOK OF SPORT MANAGEMENT

Edited by Leigh Robinson, Packianathan Chelladurai, Guillaume Bodet and Paul Downward

LONDON AND NEW YORK

First published 2012
by Routledge
2 Park Square, Milton Park, Abingdon, Oxon OX14 4RN

Simultaneously published in the USA and Canada
by Routledge
711 Third Avenue, New York, NY 10017

Routledge is an imprint of the Taylor & Francis Group, an informa business

British Library Cataloguing in Publication Data
A catalogue record for this book is available from the British Library

Library of Congress Cataloging in Publication Data
Routledge handbook of sport management / edited by Leigh Robinson
. . . [et al.].
 p. cm.
1. Sports administration. 2. Sports—Management. I. Robinson, Leigh, 1965–
GV713.R68 2012.
796.8—dc23

2011029795

ISBN: 978–0–415–58788–4 (hbk)
ISBN: 978–1–138–77725–5 (pbk)

Typeset in Bembo
by RefineCatch Limited, Bungay, Suffolk

CONTENTS

List of figures   ix
List of tables and boxes   xi
Notes on contributors   xiii
Preface: The field of sport management   xix

PART I
Managing the performance of sport organizations   **1**
Edited by Leigh Robinson

1 Contemporary issues in the performance of sport organizations   3
   Leigh Robinson

2 From daily management to high politics: the governance
   of the International Olympic Committee   7
   Jean-Loup Chappelet

3 The contingent and standards governance framework for
   national governing bodies   26
   Denis Mowbray

4 The planned development of sport organizations   42
   Brian Minikin

5 Managing customer expectations of sport organizations   57
   Leigh Robinson

6 Approaches to managing performance in sport organizations   69
   Peter Taylor

Contents

7 Forecasting the performance of nations in elite sport 86
Simon Shibli, Veerle De Bosscher, Maarten van Bottenburg and Jerry Bingham

8 Corporate social responsibility in sport 101
Stephen Morrow

9 Theoretical approaches and practical strategies for
change management 116
Peter McGraw, Tracy Taylor and Daniel Lock

PART II
Managing human resources in sport organizations **135**
Edited by Packianathan Chelladurai

10 Contemporary issues in the management of human resources 137
Packianathan Chelladurai

11 Human resource management in sport: a service-based approach 145
Solha Husin

12 Volunteer management in sport 159
May Kim and Hyejin Bang

13 Sources of support for employees in sport organizations 178
Boyun Woo and Claudio Rocha

14 Psychological contract in the context of sport organizations 193
Gonzalo Bravo, David Shonk and Doyeon Won

15 Managing contingent workers in sport 214
Kyungro Chang

PART III
The marketing of sport **221**
Edited by Guillaume Bodet

16 Contemporary issues in sport marketing 223
Guillaume Bodet

17 Consumer loyalty in sport participation services 227
Guillaume Bodet

Contents

18 Relationship marketing: from theoretical issues to its application
    by sport organizations   238
    Alain Ferrand

19 Sport spectators' segmentation   254
    Guillaume Bodet and Iouri Bernache-Assollant

20 Sporting goods brands and retail store dramatization   267
    Patrick Bouchet

21 Sport promotion through communication: a mass media perspective   281
    Daniel C. Funk and Kevin Filo

22 Sport sponsorship: definitions and objectives   296
    Pascale Quester and Charles Bal

23 Ambush marketing   311
    Benoit Séguin and Dana Ellis

PART IV
The economics of sport   **325**
Edited by Paul Downward

24 Contemporary issues in the economics of sport   327
    Paul Downward

25 The economic analysis of sport participation   331
    Paul Downward, Fernando Lera-López and Simona Rasciute

26 Expenditures on sport products and services   354
    Tim Pawlowski and Christoph Breuer

27 Do sport clubs maximize wins or profits? And does it
    make any difference?   373
    Stefan Kesenne

28 International sport league comparisons   388
    Helmut Dietl, Rodney Fort and Markus Lang

29 Attendance and broadcast demand for professional team
    sport: the case of English league football   405
    Babatunde Buraimo

Contents

30 The labor market in professional team sport: the case of
   football players in Europe   419
   Bernd Frick

31 The economic benefits to cities from hosting major sport events   441
   Chris Gratton

32 The future of sport management   457
   Leigh Robinson, Packianathan Chelladurai,
   Guillaume Bodet and Paul Downward

   Index   462

FIGURES

2.1	Organization chart of the IOC	10
3.1	Governance lifecycle	27
3.2	Contingency model	32
4.1	Development assessment of Fiji Swimming	53
5.1	The management of customer expectations	62
6.1	Benchmarks and quartiles	82
6.2	Grid analysis of importance and satisfaction scores	82
7.1	Australia's performance in the summer Olympic Games (1976–2008)	90
7.2	The nine pillars used in elite sport development systems	91
7.3	China's performance in the Olympic Games (1984–2004)	94
7.4	Extrapolating China's gold medals in 2008 based on past performance	95
7.5	Host nation performance compared with the Games immediately prior to hosting	96
9.1	Schein/Lewin model	124
9.2	The Dunphy and Stace change matrix	125
10.1	Contingency approach to HRM practices	141
10.2	Three domains of sport	142
10.3	Vertical differentiation of three subsystems of an organization	143
12.1	Stages of volunteer management	173
14.1	Psychological contract analytical framework	198
18.1	Marketing strategies typology	241
18.2	The three categories of relationship	245
18.3	The steps in implementing the principles of relationship marketing in a sport organization	246
18.4	Direct and indirect relationships between BNL and Internazionali BNL d'Italia primary stakeholders	249
22.1	The sponsorship actors and their relationships	298
26.1	Results of the second survey for the Council of Europe	361
26.2	Results of miscellaneous surveys on private consumer spending on attending sport events	362

26.3	Results of miscellaneous surveys on private spending on services for active sport consumption	363
27.1	Marginal and average revenue curves	374
27.2	Market equilibrium	375
27.3	Transfer system under win maximization	377
27.4	Monopsony under profit and win maximization	378
27.5	Revenue sharing under profit maximization	380
27.6	Revenue sharing under win maximization	381
27.7	Salary cap	382
27.8	ECA payroll cap under profit maximization	384
27.9	ECA payroll cap under profit maximization (bis)	384
27.10	ECA payroll cap under win maximization	385
29.1	Revenue sources by season	410
29.2	Economic fundamentals of the professional team sport market	416
30.1	The development of transfer fees in the German Bundesliga (1981/82–2009/10)	425
30.2	Mean and standard deviation of transfer fees in the German Bundesliga (1981/82–2009/10)	425
30.3	Percentage of movers with transfer fee in the German Bundesliga (1981/82–2009/10)	426
30.4	The development of player salaries in the German Bundesliga (1995/96–2009/10)	428
30.5	The development of player salaries by position in the German Bundesliga (1995/96–2009/10)	428
31.1	Towards an event evaluation model	444

TABLES AND BOXES

Tables

2.1	Five levels of management and governance	8
2.2	The basic universal principles of good governance of the Olympic Movement	22
2.3	The five levels of governance of the IOC	23
4.1	Recommendations for Fiji Swimming	54
5.1	Knowledge of the work of the ASA	64
5.2	Overall satisfaction with membership	65
6.1	Criteria for a good performance indicator	73
6.2	Performance ratios for commercial organizations	75
6.3	Public sector national indicators relevant to sport services in the UK	76
6.4	Performance indicators for Sport England's National Benchmarking Service (2010)	79
7.1	Bernard forecast medals compared with actual in Beijing	89
7.2	Actual versus predicted gold medals outside the range of +/− 2	89
7.3	Shibli/Bingham forecast gold medals compared with actual in Beijing	97
7.4	Factors influencing improved elite sport performance	98
8.1	Examples of CSR activities undertaken by SPL clubs	111
9.1	A schematic overview of different change issues	119
11.1	Sources of service-based HRM practices	149
18.1	Definitions of relationship marketing	240
18.2	Definitions of relationship	242
25.1	Summary of empirical studies on sport participation	335
25.2	Variable description	346
25.3	Regression results	349
26.1	Macroeconomic oriented studies on sport expenditures	355
26.2	Microeconomic oriented studies from Europe	356
26.3	Microeconomic oriented studies from Asia, America and Oceania	357
26.4	Households with expenditures on specific sport and recreational services	358
26.5	Private households' expenditure on sport and recreational services in PPP	360

26.6 Most frequently analyzed factors influencing consumer expenditure
      on SAR services   364
26.7 Signs of the significant Tobit estimates for 18 different expenditure categories 366
29.1 Rights fees paid from 1983–84 to 2013–14   407
29.2 Seasonal EPL attendance   409
29.3 Distribution of televised matches in 2006–07 season   411
30.1 Market values of first division teams in the "Big 5" European leagues
      (2005/06–2010/11)   421
30.2 Estimation results I: various methods   431
30.3 Estimation results II: quantile regressions   432
31.1 Economic impact of 16 major sport events   448
31.2 Legacy benefits of the Barcelona Olympic Games   452

Boxes

9.1   New technologies – a changing sport landscape   117
9.2   Kotter's eight-step model   127

CONTRIBUTORS

Leigh Robinson PhD (Editor)   Leigh is Professor of Sport Management at the University of Stirling, Scotland. Her principal research interest is in the management and measurement of performance, governance and quality in Olympic sport organizations. She works extensively with the Olympic Solidarity funded MEMOS network and is a member of the Steering Committee for their advanced sport management courses. Leigh is author of *Managing Public Sport and Leisure Services* and co-editor of *Managing Olympic Sport Organisations* and *Managing Voluntary Sport Organisations*.

Pakianathan Chelladurai PhD (Editor)   Chella is Professor of Sport Management at The Ohio State University, USA. He is an internationally recognized scholar of management science, specializing in organizational theory and organizational behaviour in the context of sport. He is the first recipient of the Earle F. Zeigler Award from the North American Society for Sport Management. Chella has authored three books: *Sport Management: Macro Perspectives*; *Human Resource Management in Sport and Recreation*; and *Managing Organizations for Sport and Physical Activity*, two monographs: *Leadership in Sports* and *Cohesion in Sport*, and contributed over 90 articles and over 25 chapters to sport management literature.

Gillaume Bodet PhD (Editor)   Guillaume is a lecturer in Sport Marketing and Management within the Institute of Sport and Leisure Policy at the University of Loughborough, England. His research primarily deals with consumer behaviour regarding sport organizations, sporting events and sport brands. He has published several papers in peer-reviewed journals such as *European Sport Management Quarterly, Journal of Retailing and Consumer Services, International Journal of Sport Management and Marketing, Sport Management Review* and *Psychology and Marketing*.

Paul Downward PhD (Editor)   Paul is Director of the Institute of Sport and Leisure Policy, University of Loughborough, England. He has recently published *The Economics of Sports: Theory, Evidence and Policy* following up an earlier monograph, *The Economics of Professional Team Sports*. He is currently embarked on a study of the economic determinants and impacts of sports participation in the UK. He is a member of UK Sport's research advisory group, and UEFA's Research Grants Committee.

Charles Bal PhD   Charles is head of brandRapport France, a sponsorship and associative marketing consultancy owned by QobliQ Group, where he has developed an approach of sponsorship taking into account the highly emotional nature of sport. He has already presented at marketing conferences in Europe and Asia-Pacific, and has published his work in several international reviews such as *Journal of Sponsorship*, *Asia-Pacific Journal of Marketing and Logistics* and *Admap*.

Hyejin Bang PhD   Hyejin is with the faculty of Recreation and Sport Management in the Department of Leadership and Professional Studies at Florida International University. Her research area is examining the psychological attitudes and motivations of human resources in a sport context. Her research works have been published in academic journals such as *Journal of Sport Management*, *Sport Marketing Quarterly* and *International Journal of Sport Management and Marketing*. She has also presented her research at numerous international and national conferences.

Iouri Bernache-Assollant PhD   Iouri is a Lecturer in Social Psychology within the Marketing Techniques Department at the University of Franche-Comté (France) and a member of the psychology laboratory of Besançon. His research expertise and interests focus on social psychology and sport fan behaviours. He has published several papers on sport fanship in such peer-reviewed journals as *International Journal of Sport Management and Marketing*, *International Journal of Sport and Exercise Psychology*, *Journal of Language and Social Psychology* and *Journal of Sport and Social Issues*.

Patrick Bouchet PhD   Patrick is Professor of Sport Management within the Sport Sciences Faculty at the University of Bourgogne, Dijon (France) and a member of the Socio-Psychology and Sport Management (SPMS) research group. He is widely interested in actors' behaviours (consumers, groups and organizations) linked to the consumption of sport (events, tourism and retailing). He has edited *Sport Management and Marketing: from Local to Global* and *Francophone Africa and Sport Development: From myth to reality* and co-authored two books on Sport Brands (Economica, 2008; Broché, 2009).

Gonzalo Bravo PhD   Gonzalo is an Assistant Professor of sport management at West Virginia University. His research interests include organizational behavior in sport organizations, consumer choice, and sport management education. He is the co-editor of the book *International Sport Management* (Human Kinetics, 2011).

Christoph Breuer PhD   Christoph is Full Professor of Sport Management at German Sport University, Cologne and Research Professor at the German Institute of Economic Research (DIW Berlin). His main research fields are in sport systems, sponsorship and the methodology of sport management research.

Babatunde Buraimo PhD   Tunde is a Senior Lecturer in Sport Management and Sport Economics at the University of Central Lancashire. He is a sport economist who has published widely on the economics of sport and broadcasting. He has published ground-breaking research on the uncertainty of outcome hypothesis and competitive outcomes in sport using previously unavailable data. He is currently working on several topics within sport management and sport economics including television audience demand for sport, the impact of televised sport on stadium attendance and wage discrimination in male and female sport.

Kyungro Chang PhD   Kyungro is a Professor of Sport Management at the School of Sport Sciences, Sungkyunkwan University, Korea. He researches human resources management with a special focus on contingent workers in sport organizations. His research has been published in the *Journal of Sport Management*, *Sport Management Review*, *Service Industries Journal* and *Journal of Marketing Management*.

Jean-Loup Chappelet PhD   Jean-Loup is a Professor of Public Management and Director of the Swiss Graduate School of Public Administration associated with the University of Lausanne. Prof. Chappelet specializes in sport management and sport policy with a particular emphasis on the organizations of Olympic Games and other sport events. He has written several books on sport organizations, is on the editorial boards of two sport management journals and is a member of the board of the Lausanne-based International Academy of Sport Sciences and Technology (AISTS).

Veerle De Bosscher PhD   Veerle works at the Department of Sports Policy and Management in the Faculty of Physical Education at the Vrije Universiteit Brussel (VUB), Belgium. In 2007 she obtained her doctorate cum laude on the topic 'Sports Policy Factors Leading to International Sporting Success (SPLISS),' which led to the publication of the *Global Sporting Arms Race*. Her research interests are related to sport and elite sport systems, international comparisons, measuring competitiveness, youth and sport development and quality management in sport. She is an advisor for elite sport policies in Flanders (Belgium).

Helmut Dietl PhD   Helmut is Chairman of the Board for the Center for Research in Sports Administration (CRSA) at Universitat Zurich. Professor Dielt is an economist with interests in a wide-ranging set of areas including professional teams sports, competition policy and business strategy.

Dana Ellis MA   Dana is a PhD candidate in Human Kinetics, Sport Management, at the University of Ottawa, Canada. Her main research interests include ambush marketing, sport sponsorship, branding, organization theory and mega-event management. She has published articles in peer-reviewed journals such as the *Journal of Sponsorship* and *Sport Management Review*.

Alain Ferrand PhD   Alain is Professor of Marketing at the Sport Sciences Department at the University of Poitiers (France) and leads the Research Centre in Business Administration (CEREGE). He has published several books such as the *Routledge Handbook of Sport Sponsorship: Successful Strategies* and *Marketing of Olympic Sport Organisations*. He has published several articles in journals such as *European Journal of Marketing*, *Journal of Sport Management* and *European Sport Management Quarterly*.

Kevin Filo PhD   Kevin is a Lecturer at Griffith University, Australia in the Department of Tourism, Leisure, Hotel and Sport Management where his primary research interests focus on the synergy that exists between sport and charity in the sport event context. He has published his research in *Journal of Sport Management*, *Journal of Leisure Research*, *Sport Marketing Quarterly* and *International Journal of Sport Management and Marketing*.

Rodney Fort PhD   Rod is a professor in the Division of Kinesiology at the University of Michigan. He has wide-ranging interests in sport economics and is the author of a best-selling US textbook on *Sports Economics*.

Bernd Frick PhD   Bernd works at the University of Paderborn, Germany. He is an economist with a particular interest in the economics of sports labour markets, tournaments and individual sports.

Daniel C. Funk PhD   Dan is a Professor and Washburn Senior Research Fellow in the School of Tourism and Hospitality at Temple University, Philadelphia and the Professor of Sport Marketing in the Griffith Business School, Australia. His research examines the personal, psychological and environmental factors that explain sport involvement. Professor Funk has published three books, more than 65 articles in peer-reviewed journals, and currently works with various industry and government partners to provide marketing and management solutions to enhance the commercial sustainability of sport and related industries.

Chris Gratton PhD   Chris is Professor of Sport Economics at Sheffield Hallam University, UK. Chris is the UK representative in the EU Workshop on Sport and Economics. He is also chair of Sport England's Active People Expert Advisory Group. Professor Gratton has published widely on all aspects of sport economics.

Solha Husin PhD   Solha is a senior lecturer and the coordinator of the sport management programme at the University of Malaya Sport Center. Her research interests revolve around service quality, sport employee behavioural attributes (e.g. commitment and motivation) and sport tourism. She has published or has in press articles in journals such as *Journal of Sport Management* and *Journal of Physical Education and Sport in Malaysia*.

Stefan Kesenne PhD   Stefan is a Professor at the University of Antwerp, Belgium. He is a sports economist whose primary interests are in the theoretical economic analysis of professional sports leagues. He is the author of *Economic Theory of Professional Team Sports: An Analytic Approach*.

May Kim PhD   May is an Associate Professor in the Department of Physical Education, College of Education, Korea University. Her research focus is on human resource management in sport, volunteer management, and volunteering as leisure. She has published several research articles in journals such as *Journal of Sport Management*, *European Sport Management Quarterly* and *Sport Management Review*.

Markus Lang PhD   Markus works at the Institut für Betriebswirtschaftslehre – Services and Operations Management, Universitat Zurich. He is a microeconomist with interests in sports economics, game theory, contest theory and regulation.

Fernando Lera-López PhD   Fernando is a Senior Lecturer in Economics in the Department of Economics at the Public University of Navarra (Spain). He is an economist with a variety of research interests, with a particular interest in the economics of the household, leisure and sport.

Daniel Lock PhD   Dan is a Lecturer in the Griffith Business School at Griffith University, Australia. His research expertise lies in social identification, consumer behaviour and sport fan development. He has published several papers in peer-reviewed journals such as *European Sport Management Quarterly*, *Sport Management Review* and *Soccer and Society*.

Peter McGraw MA   Peter McGraw is Director of the Labour-Management Studies Foundation and a faculty member in the Department of Business at Macquarie University,

Sydney, Australia. He is the author of many academic papers on a broad range of HR issues and is a well-known consultant and executive educator.

Brian Minikin MSc   Brian is a Research Associate at the University of Stirling, Scotland, responsible for research investigating capacity building in national federations. Prior to this he was the Regional Sport Development Manager for the Oceania National Olympic Committees, where he was responsible for supporting the development and professionalization of the Oceania Island Nations Olympic Committees. He is the author of a number of papers and chapters on strategic development and planning.

Stephen Morrow ICAS   Stephen is a Senior Lecturer in the School of Sport at the University of Stirling, Scotland. Stephen is a Chartered Accountant and trained with the international firm of accountants, Ernst & Young. His research concentrates on financial aspects in sport, particularly in the football industry. He is the author of *The People's Game? Football, Finance and Society* and *The Business of Football: Image Management in Narrative Communication*.

Denis Mowbray PhD   Denis Mowbray has gained extensive experience through his practice as a board advisor and strategist for corporate and not-for-profit clients. Enhancing this experience is his practical experience gained through roles as chairman and director for both corporate and not-for-profit organizations. These practical experiences combine with his doctoral research to give Denis an insight and knowledge in governance and strategy that is difficult to replicate.

Tim Pawlowski PhD   Tim is a sports economist at the Institute of Sport Economics and Sport Management, German Sport University Cologne. He has wide-ranging research interests in both professional and non-professional sport.

Pascale Quester PhD   Pascale is currently Deputy Vice Chancellor and Vice President (Academic) at the University of Adelaide (Australia). She also holds the inaugural Chair in Marketing in the Business School. Her research focuses on several aspects of consumer behaviour, most notably sponsorship, as well as country-of-origin effects and wine marketing. Her work has been widely published with over 130 journal articles appearing in titles such as *Journal of Consumer Research, Psychology and Marketing, Journal of Advertising Research, Journal of International Business Studies* and *European Journal of Marketing*.

Simona Rasciute PhD   Simona is a Lecturer in Economics at the School of Business and Economics at Loughborough University, UK. She is an economist who is interested in the application of discrete-choice models to economics and has published in a variety of areas including Foreign Direct Investment and Sport and Subjective Well Being.

Claudio Rocha PhD   Claudio is with the School of Physical Education and Sport of Ribeirao Preto, University of Sao Paulo, Brazil. His research interests include human resources practices in sport organizations, international sport consumer behavior and the organization of sport mega events.

Benoît Séguin PhD   Benoît is an Associate Professor of Sport Marketing in the School of Human Kinetics at the University of Ottawa (Canada). His research primarily deals with sport sponsorship, ambush marketing and major sporting events. He has published his work in several peer-reviewed journals including *Journal of Sport Management, European Journal of Sport Management, Sport Management Review, International Journal of Sport Marketing and Sponsorship* and *Asian Business and Management*. He has also co-written a book titled *Sport Marketing: A Canadian Perspective*.

Simon Shibli CIMA   Simon is the Director of the Sport Industry Research Centre (SIRC) at Sheffield Hallam University, UK. Simon is a Chartered Institute of Management Accountants (CIMA) qualified management accountant whose specialist areas of interest are the finance and economics of the sport and leisure industries. He has been involved in research and consultancy relating to the economics and finance of the sport industry and has authored a number of books and papers in this field.

David Shonk PhD   David is an Assistant Professor in the School of Hospitality, Sport and Recreation Management at James Madison University, Virginia, USA. His primary research has focused on understanding client perceptions of quality in the various dimensions of sport spectator services, especially within the context of sport tourism. He has published articles in the *Journal of Sport Management, International Journal of Sport Management and Marketing, Journal of Sport and Tourism* and *Recreational Sports Journal*.

Peter Taylor MA   Peter is Professor of Sport Economics and Co-Director of the Sport Industry Research Centre (SIRC) at Sheffield Hallam University, UK. He is technical consultant to Sport England's National Benchmarking Service for sport and leisure centres. Peter is the Editor in Chief of *Managing Leisure: An International Journal* and has written widely on sport management. He has recently edited the sixth edition of *Torkildsen's Sport and Leisure Management*.

Tracy Taylor PhD   Tracy is currently the Deputy Dean in the Faculty of Business at the University of Technology, Sydney, Australia. Professor Taylor has a significant research profile in the area of sport management and is on the editorial boards of several international sport management journals; she is Associate Editor of *Sport Management Review*. Her most recent book is *Managing People in Sport Organizations: A Strategic Human Resource Management Perspective*.

Maarten van Bottenburg PhD   Prof. van Bottenburg is a professor of sports development at Utrecht University in The Netherlands. He is a member of the SPLISS consortium and is the author of *Global Games*, a key work in the historical sociology of sport.

Doyeon Won PhD   Doyeon is on the faculty in the Department of Sport and Leisure Studies at Yonsei University in Seoul, South Korea. His current research interests focus on issues relating to the management of organizations and individuals within sport.

Boyun Woo PhD   Boyun is an assistant professor in sport management at Endicott College, Massachusetts, USA. Her research interests include organizational behaviour, consumer behaviour, and cross-cultural studies in sport management. Dr Woo has previously published research articles in *Sport Marketing Quarterly* and *International Journal of Sports Marketing and Sponsorship*. In addition, she has made research presentations at various conferences, such as those of the North American Society for Sport Management, Association for Consumer Research, Sport Marketing Association, and Alliance for Health, Physical Education, Recreation and Dance.

PREFACE: THE FIELD OF SPORT MANAGEMENT

Management can be considered as a formal process that occurs within organizations in order to direct and organize resources to meet stated objectives. It is an activity that utilizes the internal strengths and weaknesses of an organization in order to take advantage of the opportunities in the external environment and to minimize potential threats. Thus, managers need to be simultaneously internally focused and outward looking.

The nature of the sport context makes these dual aspects of management even more pertinent. First, most sport organizations provide a service and services have a number of characteristics that make their delivery complex. Sport services are intangible and perishable and thus cannot be seen, or stored; they are inseparable in that they are simultaneously produced and consumed and finally, they are heterogeneous in that each time the service is delivered it is different and each customer's experience of it is different. These characteristics have implications for performance management, marketing and human resources. Second, sport services are discretionary in that people do not have to take part in sport the way they need food, clothing and shelter. This means that sport organizations are competing for income that remains after customers have met their costs of living. Consequently, sport management is carried out in a highly competitive environment, both within the industry and with other industries. Thus, the outward focus is paramount.

Finally, the delivery of sporting opportunities tends to fall into three main sectors, which are characterized by different principles, different objectives and different governance methods. The first sector is the public or state sector, which mainly encompasses the work of local authorities, municipalities and schools. The second is the private or commercial sector, primarily consisting of the health and fitness industry and professional sport leagues. The third is the voluntary sector, primarily made up of clubs and national federations. It is, however, more complex than this as it is often difficult to determine what sector an organization operates within. For example, many sport leagues operate on a commercial basis; however, the teams that participate within them are usually part of the voluntary sector. The public sector provides sport facilities that are increasingly operated by commercial organizations or trusts – which are part of the voluntary sector. The Olympic Games is a commercial event; however, some of the sports in the Games are professional, while others are still considered to be amateur. All athletes compete under the banner of their National Olympic Committee, which is part of the voluntary sector. This "mixed economy" of sport emphasizes the need for planned and careful sport management.

The field of sport management has changed significantly over the past few decades, becoming more formalized, better planned and, arguably, more professional. Much of this change can be related to a growing interest in "good" management that has emerged among practitioners, policy-makers, funding agencies and, of course, researchers. This interest is reflected in the extensive body of research and literature that has emerged in the field of sport management. This *Handbook* makes a unique contribution to this field as it provides a definitive account of current academic and professional knowledge in relation to key aspects of sport management. It does this by bringing together a range of researchers and practitioners who discuss diverse topics across the key management disciplines of performance, human resources, marketing and economics.

In reflection of its contemporary nature, the *Handbook* contains contributions from internationally established researchers, as well as contributions from those emerging in their fields. There are chapters which discuss the concepts associated with a particular activity, framework or function and chapters that set out seminal or innovative research that demonstrates the range of academic activity in the field of sport management. As a consequence, there is variety in the focus, structure and writing styles within sections and between sections as the *Handbook* sets out what is required for sport management to be inwardly focused and outward looking. Two principles, however, underpin all chapters. The first is a focus on sport and the second is a focus on research and its application to sport management. Thus, the *Handbook* takes stock of progress in this field and "maps the territory" of sport management as an activity.

The *Handbook* is arranged in four substantive sections containing 31 chapters. Details on the four sections are set out below and the *Handbook* concludes with a consideration of the future of sport management as a discipline and area of research.

Part I: Managing the performance of sport organizations
(Editor: Leigh Robinson)

This section considers aspects related to the management of performance in sport organizations from two perspectives: it presents the key functions of managing a sport organization in contemporary times. The section considers those more traditional functions such as governance, planning and change and then focuses on more recent concerns such as the management of expectations and corporate social responsibility. Second, it sets out a number of key techniques for managing the performance of sport organizations themselves. As this is a new and growing field of academic study, this section contains contributions from both established and emerging researchers, and presents research from both academics and practitioners.

Part II: Managing human resources in sport organizations
(Editor: Packianathan Chelladurai)

This section considers a fundamental area of sport management in addressing different aspects of the management of human resources (HRM) in sport organizations. The aim of this section is not simply to confirm existing knowledge of the practices of HRM, but rather to provide an overview of contemporary issues and thinking within this field. As such it attempts to "signpost" future research focus in the field and contains contributions primarily from emerging researchers.

Part III: The marketing of sport
(Editor: Guillaume Bodet)

This section considers different aspects of sport marketing. The aim of this section is to provide an extended overview of the different sport marketing dimensions from both *business to consumer* and *business to business* perspectives, encompassing sport services, goods and brands, sport participation and sport spectatorship, at the local and global level.

Part IV: The economics of sport
(Editor: Paul Downward)

In this section each of the main contexts of sport, mass participation, professional sports and sport events, are addressed by authorities in the field. Each has a substantial and seminal research profile that embraces both research monographs, textbooks and peer-reviewed papers. The section focuses on the unifying concept that all sport competitions can be presented as economic tournaments, which each have different features but are linked by common principles. The different features and detail of these tournaments are explored in detail.

PART I

Managing the performance of sport organizations

Edited by Leigh Robinson

1

CONTEMPORARY ISSUES IN THE PERFORMANCE OF SPORT ORGANIZATIONS

Leigh Robinson

The current economic environment throws a sharper focus on sport management and the performance of sport organizations than ever before. In a context of severe cuts in public funding, significant reductions in the discretionary expenditure of many customers and the daily battle for survival faced by many organizations, sport organizations have to perform with increasing efficiency and effectiveness, with the second of these gaining in importance. In addition, there is growing public intolerance of unethical and unprincipled behavior by those responsible for managing the major organizations that deliver sport. These two environmental factors are responsible for the key themes that underpin and drive contemporary practice and research in the performance of sport organizations. The first is a need for *accountability, transparency and ethical behavior* in sport organizations, while the second theme is a need for *greater organizational competitiveness* across the industry as a whole.

Accountability, transparency and ethical behavior

FIFA – football's governing body – has recently been rocked by scandal. Details that emerged following the award of the 2022 World Cup to Qatar have revealed activities that can only be described as improper or unethical and a number of key people within the organizations have been investigated and/or censured, including Sepp Blatter, FIFA's president. The suspension of presidential candidate Mohamed Bin Hammam is arguably a direct result of the need for sport organizations to be seen to be accountable to those stakeholders that have an interest in the organization. In addition, the fact that these activities have become known is also a direct result of the desire for transparency amongst the public that has to be part of the management of sport organizations. This shows that it is no longer possible for sport organizations to be run as a "closed book." There is a need for openness and transparency in the management of sport organizations, who also need to "behave" in a way that is acceptable to the public at large. As a consequence, the principles of accountability, transparency and ethical behavior have become fundamental aspects of the performance of sport organizations and are driving research in this field.

Accountability has become an increasingly complex issue as the stakeholders of many sport organizations are growing. For example, it is possible to argue that even though they are membership organizations, National Governing Bodies (NGBs) of sport should not be primarily accountable to their membership given the funding resource that comes from outside of the membership base. For example, in many countries the vast majority of funding that is available to an NGB comes from government or some government agency. In this instance, why should the needs of the members outweigh the needs of the funding agency? In addition, different stakeholders may result in conflicting objectives such as those often faced in the public sector, where managers have to balance the provision of low-cost "sport for all" with the need to generate revenue to support activities. This too brings challenges to accountability.

The delivery of accountability, transparency and ethical behavior underpins the management activities set out in this section. First, the good governance of sport organizations, discussed in Chapters 2 and 3, is based on accountability and transparency as these principles are considered to be the main pillars of governance. In Chapter 2, Jean-Loup Chappelet sets out and discusses a framework of governance (Pérez, 2009) that he illustrates using the example of the International Olympic Committee (IOC). From his discussion it becomes clear that governance is a complex and often structure-led process, particularly in an organization as multifaceted as the IOC. More importantly, his discussion establishes how governance processes are necessary in order to overcome the potential for unethical behavior within sport organizations. The *Contingent and Standards* model of governance proposed by Denis Mowbray in Chapter 3 has emerged from his research with sport organizations. This has led to the development of the CaS template that can be used to shape the governance of sport organizations. This practical application of the theory of governance is an example of how research into the performance of sport organizations results in tools that can then be used to guide organizational performance.

The second set of techniques that allow managers to deliver expectations of accountability, transparency and behavior are those associated with performance management and these are addressed in the subsequent four chapters. In Chapter 4, Brian Minikin argues strongly for the planned development of sport organizations. This chapter is not simply about strategic planning as his argument is that organizations should understand what they are capable of, and what they need to be capable of, and their planning should focus on closing this gap. This makes the organization more accountable for its resources and involves stakeholders in the process of developing the organization. He illustrates this argument by showing how the Readiness Assessment Tool (Minikin, 2009) has informed the planning of Fiji Swimming as the organization aims to improve its performance on the international stage.

The argument set out by Leigh Robinson in Chapter 5 focuses on the need to understand what stakeholders expect of organizations. This information can be used in the planning process and demonstrates to stakeholders that the organization understands the need to consult and to be accountable. She presents research carried out with the Amateur Swimming Association, which shows a need to inform members more widely of the work of the organization. In Chapter 6, Peter Taylor sets out the principles and techniques associated with performance management, demonstrating how they can be applied in the three main sectors that make up the sport industry. He considers the performance management process in its entirety, which highlights how this process can support the planned development argued for by Minikin in Chapter 4. In concluding his arguments, Taylor presents the National Benchmarking Service (NBS), which is a performance measurement framework developed from the research of Taylor, Bovaird, Gratton, Robinson and Kung (2000). The NBS provides managers of UK public facilities with information that makes them accountable, more transparent, and allows the planning process to be more effectively informed.

In Chapter 7, Simon Shibli, Veerle De Bosscher and Maarten van Bottenburg discuss the ultimate assessment of the performance of elite sport systems – that of Olympic medals won. They set out a technique that has been developed to forecast the performance of nations at Olympic Games and in this chapter they focus on the performance of China at the Beijing Olympics. The value of this technique in informing performance and thus accountability is discussed, showing how the information from forecasting can inform planning and set realistic expectations of performance. It can also be used to justify investment in particular activities. This chapter also discusses the SPLISS project, research that has determined the dimensions of an elite sport system perceived to be necessary in order to manage high-level performance (De Bosscher, De Knop, van Bottenburg, Bingham and Shibli, 2008).

Finally, and in line with public desire for ethical behavior, comes the concept of corporate social responsibility (CSR), which is an attempt by sport organizations to "give back," through community-focused activities, to society some of the value (profit) they have created. In Chapter 8, Stephen Morrow sets out the concept of CSR and its application to sport organizations. This chapter is a "taking stock" of the concept as CSR is a relatively new activity within sport management, and has only recently emerged as being of research interest. Morrow's review of corporate social responsibility concludes with a discussion of the CSR activities by the Scottish Premier League football clubs and highlights how CSR engagement was primarily motivated by financial objectives, immediate and/or longer-term, which is arguably contradictory to the concept of CSR.

Greater organizational competitiveness

The drive for efficiency and effectiveness that has been part of the sport management environment for the past two decades has gained further momentum during the current period of financial constraint. Organizations across all three sectors are expected to deliver more, with fewer resources and in an environment where competition is growing for three main reasons. First, not only do sport organizations compete with other industries for discretionary income, but there are more and more alternatives for people seeking a sport experience. Non-competitive, recreational activities in particular appear to be becoming more popular, particularly amongst younger people, as they do not require a commitment or effort from participants. Responding to this intra-industry competition is a growing challenge for sport management.

Second, the cost of either watching an event or taking part in sport is becoming a significant factor in the management of sport organizations. Traditionally sport has been a cheap or even free form of activity. However, as business principles evolve and there is an increase in pressure to package sport in a more entertaining way, so the cost of participating in, and spectating at, sport events also increases. This puts sport in a position where the consumer market, the spectators and participants may be attracted to the idea of spending their money elsewhere, bringing pressure to bear on sport organizations to provide value for money. The principles of planning and performance management set out in Chapters 4, 6 and 7 are integral to organizations becoming more competitive as the planning process should ensure that objectives are appropriate and the performance management process should ensure efficiency and effectiveness. The managerial tools developed by the research set out in the chapters by Minikin and Taylor provide examples of how academic activity in the field of sport management informs and improves the performance of organizations.

In addition, customer expectations of sport organizations continue to increase. This is being driven by improvements in service quality within all aspects of society, an increasing culture of seeking and providing feedback to organizations and a strong belief in the concept of value for money. The ultimate dilemma facing sport management is to understand what level of service to provide, what this costs and what the customer base is willing to pay for it in order for the organization to remain competitive. Robinson (2004) argued that public sector providers needed to manage expectations of sport services to make sure that they were attainable for the organization. This argument is made again in Chapter 5, but the focus in 2011 is on all sport organizations as expectations of services are now at a point where it is becoming extremely difficult for managers to meet them. Robinson's argument is that expectations of customers should be known by the organization as not only does this help to demonstrate accountability (see above) but also it will allow managers to work with stakeholders to prevent an unrealistic rise in expectations from occurring. In Chapter 5 she sets out a framework that can facilitate this process and she argues that the key to expectations management is information exchange between the organization and its stakeholders so that the organization understands what is required and can set out what is possible within its current resources.

Finally, a changing operating environment is one of the constant factors that affects the management of sport organizations. The factors set out above require "things to be different," leading to a focus on the management practices, procedures and services that need to change in order for organizations to continue to perform competitively. The management of change is one of the omni-present and ongoing activities associated with the performance of sport organizations and the final chapter in this section sets out the principles and techniques associated with this management activity. In Chapter 9, McGraw and Taylor consider approaches to change that explain why change is necessary and how it can be implemented. Of key importance to the process is the need to overcome resistance and they discuss why resistance arises and how it can be overcome. The chapter ends with a case study by Dan Lock setting out the complete restructuring of the Australian Soccer Association into the Football Federation of Australia (FFA) in response to stakeholder discontent.

References

De Bosscher, V., De Knop, P., van Bottenburg, M., Bingham, J. and Shibli, S. (2008) *The Global Sporting Arms Race: Sport Policy Factors Leading to International Success*, Brussels, Meyer and Meyer.

Minikin, B. (2009) 'A Question of Readiness', *Unpublished MEMOS Project*. Lausanne, Olympic Solidarity.

Pérez, R. (2009) *La gouvernance de l'entreprise*, Paris, La Découverte. Nouvelle édition.

Robinson, L.A. (2004) 'Public leisure facilities: managing customer expectations', *Municipal Engineer*, 157(ME2), 129–33.

Taylor, P., Bovaird, A., Gratton, C., Robinson, L.A., and Kung, S. (2000) *Performance measurement for local authority sports halls and swimming pools*, London, Sport England.

2

FROM DAILY MANAGEMENT TO HIGH POLITICS

The governance of the International Olympic Committee

Jean-Loup Chappelet

For over a century, international sport has been primarily governed by a network of non-profit associations centered round the Olympic Games and the World Championships, in around forty sports. This network has the name of 'The Olympic Movement' and its leading actor is the International Olympic Committee (IOC). This is an association of individuals that chooses its own members, and that was founded in 1894 by Pierre de Coubertin. Since the IOC's foundation, the main task of the members has been to perpetuate the Modern Games. Despite the considerable evolution of sport during the twentieth century and the increasing scale of the Summer and Winter Games, the IOC continued to exist without major changes to its structure throughout the twentieth century. It was only in 1999 that the very foundations of the IOC suddenly trembled, as a result of around twenty of its members being involved in a corruption scandal related to the awarding of the Olympic Winter Games to Salt Lake City. It was also around this time that doping and violence at sport events began to constitute a serious concern for governments, who realized that the Olympic Movement was unable to keep these issues under any real control. Therefore, at the end of the last century, primarily due to the media, the IOC suddenly found itself confronted with doubts regarding its legitimacy and governance.

The emergence of the term governance within Olympic circles was around this same period, notably due to the influence of American journalists and sponsors. It was officially introduced within the Olympic Charter in 2004. Governance deals with the high-level issues of strategy and policy direction, transparency, and accountability and is not concerned with daily operations, which are the responsibility of management. Corporate governance refers to the systems and processes for ensuring proper accountability, probity and openness in the conduct of an organization. This might include the processes by which committees are selected, monitored and replaced; the capacity of committees to effectively formulate and implement sound policies; and the respect of members for the structures and the procedures that govern economic and social interactions amongst them. This focus on governance is a result of the dysfunctions mentioned above, but also because of growing professionalism within Olympic sport organizations and the increasing interest on the part of the various stakeholders, in particular, nation states, the European Union and the sponsors, in how the

Olympic System functions (Chappelet and Kübler, 2008). Although the IOC characterized one of the oldest ways of self-government by means of a network, with consensual, horizontal co-ordination mechanisms, its fragile equilibrium became threatened at the end of the 1990s, as a result of new public and commercial actors who wished to take part in its governance.

The question of the functioning of the IOC remained central within the new organization of world sport that commenced at the beginning of the twenty-first century. This chapter is devoted to the governance of the IOC, and, more precisely, the corporate governance of the enterprise that has become the IOC. As a non-profit association, the IOC is not, of course, a commercial enterprise in the usual sense, but it nevertheless owns several limited companies (see below) and regularly deals with multinationals that are in turn subject to the rules of corporate governance. The IOC has no shareholders, but is responsible for numerous contracted parties and, above all, it is accountable for its management of the Olympic ideal in the eyes of the public. Coubertin saw the IOC members as the trustees of the Olympic Games and the Olympic ideal. Today the IOC must draw inspiration from the rules of good governance: rules that are to an increasing extent required by those national or supranational governments with which it must co-operate in order to organize the Olympic Games, and to promote its philosophy of sport, known as 'Olympism'.

There are a number of approaches regarding corporate governance and, over the last decade, these have been applied to sport organizations (Thoma and Chalip, 1996; Caiger and Gardiner, 2000; Katwala, 2000; Chaker, 2004; EOC and FIA, 2001; Hums and MacLean, 2004; Zölch, 2004; Hoye and Cuskelly, 2007; Bayle and Chantelat, 2008; King, 2009; Robinson, 2010). The work of Pérez (2009) will be used to structure this chapter. Pérez identifies five successive levels in the systems of management and devices of governance of an organization, ranging from the management of the organization to the legal and societal framework in which it operates (see Table 2.1).

These levels will be applied to describe and analyse the current governance of the IOC. The specific organizational characteristics of the IOC and other entities related to its governance will be presented in five successive sections corresponding to the five Perez (2009) levels. A conclusion will summarize the structures and policies put in place for the governance of the IOC and the Olympic System over the twentieth century and will show the shift occurring from corporate governance to political governance.

Level one: the management of the IOC

The IOC's daily management is carried out by its *Administration*, which includes all of the organization's salaried staff and has been located in Lausanne (Switzerland) since 1915. Somewhat simplistic in the 1960s, the Administration developed during the 1970s thanks to a boost by a strong director, Frenchwoman Monique Berlioux, and as a consequence of

Table 2.1 Five levels of management and governance

Level	Level name
1	Management (strategic and operational management)
2	Management of management (governance)
3	Management of governance (regulation)
4	Governance of governance (harmonization)
5	Meta-governance (legal and societal framework)

Source: Pérez, 2009: 29

the arrival of income from television broadcasting rights for the Olympic Games. This development gained impetus under Juan Antonio Samaranch's Presidency of the IOC, from 1980 until 2001, and the Administration grew from a staff of approximately thirty to around one hundred, with the arrival of specialists in various fields. From a managerial point of view, however, the most important development was Samaranch's decision to live and work in Lausanne, and use the Administration as a base for his work. Thus, he became a full-time, executive President, which, with the exception of Coubertin, was not the case for his predecessors. This decision led to the departure of Berlioux in 1985.

However, the President remained a non-remunerated official even though all the expenses related to carrying out his mission and his residence costs in Lausanne (notably his hotel suite, living expenses, insurance and residence taxes) were borne by the IOC. This arrangement continued with the election of Jacques Rogge to the presidency in 2001. In 2008, the latest figures available, the presidential residence costs amounted to US$556,000 and those for the Honorary President for Life, as Samaranch became in 2001 until his death in 2010, totaled US$310,000 (IOC, 2009: 98).

With the arrival of Rogge, the growth of the Administration continued, and in 2010 reached around 425 persons from 43 countries. This spectacular growth was partly due to incorporating the staff of the Olympic Museum and those of other entities (limited companies) which were previously not included in the Administration as a ploy to remain below the arbitrary threshold of 100 employees laid down for the Administration by Samaranch.

Following several internal and external audits that were commissioned by Rogge over the first years of his presidency, the Administration has been restructured into 15 departments or entities, each headed by a Director (all men in 2011) and listed below in the order as published in the Olympic Movement Directory (IOC, 2010b):

- Executive Office of the President
- Office of the Director General
- International cooperation and development
- Finance and administration
- Olympic Games
- Sport (or relations with international sport federations (IFs))
- Relations with the National Olympic Committees (NOCs)
- Technology
- Communication
- Information Management
- Marketing (IOC Television and Marketing Services)
- Legal Affairs
- Medicine and Science
- Olympic Solidarity
- Olympic Museum.

On a hierarchical level, the Directors report to a Director General, who in turn reports to the President. Two Directors, however, occupy particularly key positions and these are the Chief of Staff, who handles all political questions and relations with the IOC members, and the Executive Director of the Olympic Games, who is in charge of the IOC's principal 'product'. The executive management of the IOC is considered to be the President, the Director General, the President's Chief of Staff and the Executive Director of the Olympic Games. As stated above, the President is not remunerated; however, the salaries and short-term benefits of the other three members of the executive management amounted to USD 1,627,000 million (IOC, 2009: 98). The Director of Communication also plays an important role as the President's spokesman. No organization chart of the Administration is published officially, but that shown in Figure 2.1 below was printed in the IOC Administration Guide. The President's Chief of Staff, over the years, has gained a lot of power as the President's right-hand man and became Director General in 2011.

The Director General is appointed by the IOC Executive Board, and the other Directors are appointed by the IOC President, who informs the Executive Board accordingly. The Former Director General was appointed in 2003. Most of his Directors had already been in place for some time. The Directors hold a monthly Management Committee meeting, sometimes with the President, and have regular, external one-day management seminars. Otherwise, they run their departments in a fairly autonomous manner. Staff units are, however, attached to the Director General for Human Resources and Corporate Development (formerly known as Strategic Planning). The first corporate plan was adopted for the period 2009–12 (Chappelet, 2010a). The Directors of the Olympic Museum and of Olympic Solidarity, the department that redistributes the sums due to the NOCs, have a greater degree of autonomy because they are geographically located outside the main headquarters in Vidy,

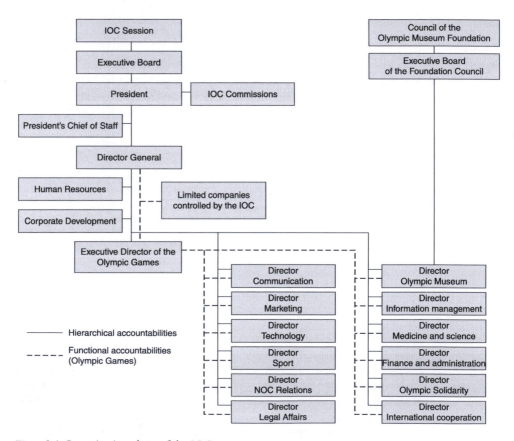

Figure 2.1 Organization chart of the IOC

Source: Chappelet and Kübler, 2008: 32

and because of the nature of their activities. The Director of Olympic Solidarity also heads the NOC Relations Department.

In 2008, the operating costs for the IOC and its Administration amounted to approximately US$115million (IOC 2009: 69). For a detailed analysis of how the IOC is financed see Chappelet (2006). The great majority of the IOC's assets are shared between two foundations subject to Swiss law that the IOC controls. These are the Olympic Foundation and the Olympic Museum Foundation, which are managed by the IOC Administration. The latter owns the Olympic Museum, which is located in Lausanne and houses two of the IOC's departments: the Museum and Information Management.

The Olympic Foundation holds the IOC's financial assets and owns several limited companies that are subject to Swiss law. Two of these have a large number of employees: IOC Television and Marketing Services and Olympic Broadcasting Services (OBS SA). The former, which provides services contractually promised to the IOC's sponsors, is managed by the IOC's Television and Marketing Director and the second, in charge of producing the basic televised images of the Games, is headed by a former executive of the European Broadcasting Union. The two companies have a Board of Directors that is chaired respectively by the member of the IOC who is Chairman of the Marketing Commission and the honorary member of the IOC who was chairman of the Commission for the Co-ordination of the 2008 Games. The Foundation Boards (the supreme governing bodies) of the IOC's two Foundations mainly consist of members of the IOC Executive Board. The Olympic Foundation is chaired by the IOC President and the Museum Foundation is chaired by the Honorary President for Life. All these legal entities, foundations and limited companies, under the aegis of IOC are known internally by the term 'IOC Group'.

There can be no doubt that the arrival of Jacques Rogge as the IOC President constituted a major turning point for the IOC on a management level, with the introduction of more solid structures and procedures and, above all, a change to a more technocratic style of management that was far more sensitive to questions of governance and risk management yet less entrepreneurial and paternalist than that of the former President. A consolidation phase followed a strong period of expansion. At the same time, the role of the Director General became far less political in order to focus on operational issues and the management of the structure. Under Samaranch the former Director General was, in fact, flanked by a Secretary General who handled administrative issues. However, that post has not been filled since the last holder resigned in 2002.

Level two: the management of the IOC's management

The second level of the governance of an enterprise according to Pérez (2009) begins with reflection on the management of the top management. At the IOC, this level is handled by the institutional authorities elected by the members of the IOC, which as mentioned above is an association under Swiss law. These authorities are, in order of importance, the Session, which is the Annual General Assembly of the members, or the legislative body; the Executive Board, which is a committee or sub-entity of the Session that plays an executive role, and the IOC President, who is the IOC's permanent representative.

These structures and their functions are laid down in the Olympic Charter (IOC, 2010). This document sets out the principles and values and also the rights and obligations of the components of the Olympic Movement. At the same time, it serves as the statutes of the IOC (notably its Chapter 2). The Charter is drawn up and modified according to the wishes of the IOC, by its Session and based on proposals by the Executive Board. It is made up of the fundamental principles of Olympism and 59 Rules, at times accompanied by Bye-Laws. Modifying a Rule requires a two-thirds majority vote by the members, while a simple majority is sufficient for the By-Laws. The text of the Charter was entirely reviewed and refined in 2004, as had happened in 1986. The Rules concerning the members and the election of the Olympic cities was considerably revised in 1999.

The IOC members assemble once a year for their Session. During Olympic years, the meeting is held just prior to the Games in the Olympic city. Its decisions are sovereign regarding all issues concerning the running of the IOC and of the Olympic Movement, which are brought to its attention by the Executive Board. The decisions include the awarding of the host cities for the Games. The members also elect, from among their number, a President, four Vice Presidents and ten other members of the Executive Board (15 persons). Four seats on the Executive Board are reserved for the Presidents of the ANOC (Worldwide Association of the NOCs), the Athletes Commission, the Association of the IFs whose sport is on the programme of the Summer Games (ASOIF) and its counterpart for the Winter Games (AIOWF). The terms of office are of four years, with the exception of the President who is elected for eight years and who can be re-elected for a further four (a maximum of 12 years). Samaranch remained in office as the President for 21 years, which was a major criticism levelled against the IOC in 1999. Rogge was elected in 2001 and re-elected in 2009 for a second term ending in 2013. The elections do not all take place simultaneously, meaning that the IOC members are constantly occupied with election campaigns within their number and/or for host cities. Since 1999, with a view to transparency, the proceedings of the Session have been broadcast by closed circuit television to interested journalists.

Below the sovereignty of the Session, the Executive Board (created in 1921) enjoys extensive powers. '[It] assumes the general overall responsibility for the administration of the IOC and the management of its affairs. [. . .] it approves all internal governance regulations relating to its organization' (Rule 19.3.2 of the Olympic Charter). It also controls the Boards of the Olympic Foundation and the Olympic Museum Foundation, since these Boards mainly consist of its members. In comparison to the Administration, which deals with daily operational issues, it has a strategic function, although it is extremely difficult to separate the two dimensions. The Executive Board is thus at the heart of the IOC's 'management of the management', since it meets far more regularly than the annual Session. It usually meets four times a year, or if specially convened by the President, or by a majority of its members. In 2011, only two women were members of the Executive Board. IOC Presidents always were men.

According to the Olympic Charter, the IOC President has far fewer powers than the Executive Board. The 1999 reform enhanced this characteristic, which constitutes a strong difference between the IOC and a classical enterprise. Thanks to his presence and his daily involvement in management issues, however, the President is able to make all kinds of decisions, not only those that are urgent, as the Charter states he should. He must, however, in principle submit such decisions as rapidly as possible to the Executive Board or to the Session, both of which he chairs. His main autonomous power is that of appointing the Directors of the Administration (to be confirmed by the Executive Board) and the persons who make up the various IOC Commissions. The exceptions to this are the Executive Board, the Athletes Commission and the Nominations Commission, whose members are elected. He may also create commissions or dissolve non-statutory ones. The role of commissions, consisting of IOC members and external experts, is to make recommendations to the Executive Board and the Session. Each is assisted by an IOC Director and serves, in a sense, as that Director's supervisory board for his department. Some Commissions form an official part of the governance authorities. These are statutory, mentioned as such by the Charter and designated below by the letter 'S'. The other thematic commissions play roles of less importance within the management of the IOC management.

In 2010, the IOC had some 25 Commissions for the following areas, uniting over 350 persons (IOC, 2010b):

- Athletes (S)
- Audit Committee
- Co-ordination of the Games in Preparation (4 to 5 commissions)
- Culture and Olympic Education
- Entourage
- Ethics (S)
- Evaluation of the Candidate Cities
- Finance (S)
- International Relations
- Juridical
- Marketing
- Medical
- Nominations (S)
- Olympic Programme
- Philately and Memorabilia
- Olympic Solidarity (S)
- Press, Radio and Television
- Sport and Environment
- Sport and Law
- Sport for All
- TV Rights and New Media
- Women and Sport.

When taking office as President in 2001, Rogge attempted to reduce the number of Commissions that had existed at the time of his predecessor, but without real success. The 2009 Olympic Congress recommended the creation of the Entourage Commission. The Commissions in fact permit their chairs, who are all IOC members, to focus on a topic of interest to them and to increase their seniority. Rogge did, however, significantly reduce the number of meetings, which today, in principle, take place in Lausanne and only once per year.

Certain Commissions are far more important than others: the Ethics, Nominations, Athletes, Finance, TV Rights and Solidarity Commissions. The first three will be presented in the following section since they relate to the IOC's regulatory processes or the management of its governance. The three others are presented below.

Finance Commission

The Finance Commission is a long-standing one, and its chairmanship is one of the most prestigious offices. It supervises the IOC's accounts and the management of its financial assets. It is assisted by professional auditors (PricewaterhouseCoopers have carried out this role for nearly 20 years, as a result of several renewed mandates). The Chairman co-signs the contracts with the elected Host Cities. Following the 1999 reforms, the IOC has published three reports covering four years of activity (with the somewhat strange name of 'Final Reports') – for the periods 1997–2000, 2001–04 and 2005–08 (IOC, 2009). These public documents contain relatively detailed financial information (balance sheet and accounts) that contributes towards a certain degree of transparency from the institution. The most recent report in particular provides consolidated figures for the 'IOC Group' for the first time. We note that the IOC under Rogge has adopted a policy of constituting financial reserves and of risk management thanks to insurance taken out against the cancellation of the Games, which is a policy clearly inspired by good governance practices for an enterprise.

Since 2006, the Finance Commission has been supported by an Audit Committee that has the same Chairman but whose secretariat is provided by the IOC President's Chief of Staff – not the Director of Finance. This Committee functions as an internal control unit. A small group devoted to the issue of remuneration also existed from 2001 until 2005. Like their President, the IOC members are not remunerated for their work, but the expenses involved in accomplishing their mission are reimbursed and, at times, a fee is paid to them for a particular task. This group was set up following the discovery by Rogge that large amounts had been paid as remuneration under Samaranch's presidency, notably to the Chairman of the Marketing Commission. Since 2005, each member has received a lump sum of US$5,000 per year for office expenses, and the special remunerations appear to have disappeared, although per diems for attending IOC meetings are generous.

TV Rights and New Media Commission

The TV Rights and New Media Commission was created and is chaired by Jacques Rogge, thus demonstrating its importance. Today, it negotiates the broadcasting rights on the basis of public tenders for the two consecutive editions of the Games. This practice differs considerably from that under the previous President, who proceeded in a far less transparent manner and granted rights spanning several Olympiads. A description of the former and current approaches, and of the IOC's managerial practices relating to marketing, is provided by Payne (Payne, 2005: 49–74).

Olympic Solidarity Commission

The Olympic Solidarity Commission is also extremely important because of the budget it controls (US$311 million for the period 2009–12). This amount represents the portion due to the NOCs from the IOC's various revenues, mainly broadcasting rights and from the marketing of the Games. The funds are used to assist the NOCs to accomplish their mission, and in particular, funding goes to those whose needs are the greatest. The eminence of this statutory Commission was reinforced by the Olympic Charter, which, until its revision in 2004, specified that its Chairman should be the IOC President (Rule 8.2). Perhaps to avoid any potential conflict of interest, Jacques Rogge preferred, from the outset of his period in office, that the responsibility be borne by the President of the ACNO (Worldwide Association of the NOCs). Olympic Solidarity publishes full annual and four-yearly reports on how the funds are allocated, but the main question that remains is that of how the money is accounted for at the sites receiving it. Controlling that aspect is extremely difficult for an administration located in Lausanne.

We thus note that, with its annual Session and its Executive Board assisted by other Commissions, the IOC has mechanisms that permit it to manage its management. These mechanisms have been strengthened since 1999, and to a large extent are based on the IOC members. But who appoints and monitors the IOC members, and how? This central question for the governance of the institution is the subject of the following section.

Level three: the IOC's regulatory mechanisms

The main reforms implemented by the IOC in 1999, following the crisis that arose as a result of the Salt Lake City scandal, were focused on its members. Until that point, few rules applied regarding their recruitment and their behaviour. That state of affairs was severely criticized by the media, the sponsors and governments as it was perceived to be the very source of the IOC's governance problems, since the guardians of the Olympic temple were not guarded by anyone. To use the structure set out by Pérez (2009), what 'management of governance' or what regulatory mechanisms could be proposed for the IOC in the new century?

Under pressure from the media, Samaranch created an ad hoc Commission by the name of 'IOC 2000' to reflect on the issue. It consisted of around 50 members, with a balance between IOC members and individuals from outside the Olympic Movement, such as Henry Kissinger and Giovanni Agnelli. It worked at a rapid pace from March to December 1999, and its conclusions, symbolically united in the form of 50 recommendations, were all adopted by the IOC's (extraordinary) Session held in Lausanne in mid-December 1999 (IOC, 1999). Those relating to the composition, structure and the organization of the IOC (numbered 1–12) and to the designation of the Host City of the Olympic Games (49–50) have been fully implemented. Recommendations 13–48, concerning the role of the IOC, have only been partially put in place (Sport in Society, 2011). We shall now describe those that are directly related to regulatory mechanisms for the IOC members.

First of all, the number of members was fixed at a maximum of 115. The number had risen to around 100 by the IOC's centenary in 1994, and then rose to 130 toward the end of the Samaranch presidency. In mid-2010, the IOC had 112 members (17 women) from 79 countries. It is worth noting that the IOC suggested that, by the end of 2005, there should be a quota of 20 per cent of women in all the decision-making structures of the Olympic Movement – a suggestion that is not respected by the IOC itself.

Of these maximum 115 members, 15 are selected by an International Sport Federation (IF), and 15 by a National Olympic Committee (NOC). The members admitted to these 'reserved seats' lose their membership if they leave office, most often that of President. A further 15 members are 'active' athletes, those having taken part in the Olympic Games less than eight years previously. For the other 70 members not subject to such a quota, it was decided that there could not be more than one per country, as opposed to two per country until 1999. Many countries, in fact, have no members, although in 2010, Italy and Switzerland each had five! This is because no such restrictions regarding nationality exist for members who are athletes or represent the IFs or NOCs. There has also been a case where an IOC member for his country (Un-Yong Kim) was also the President of an IF (Taekwondo) and of his NOC (South Korea).

The IOC stresses that its members do not represent their country, IF, or NOC at the IOC, but the IOC within their country and the institutions from which they come. This stance sometimes puts IF and NOC Presidents in a difficult position as they might have to choose between the IOC's interests and their own organization's interests. Since 1999, the Olympic Charter has stipulated that members do not take part in votes concerning their countries or one of its citizens (By-Law to Rule 18). For the rest, 'Rules relating to conflicts of interest' were adopted in 2002 after difficult discussions during the Session held in Salt Lake City.

Since 1999, each member is elected for eight years, and membership is renewable. Each member leaves office at age 70, and if they have served for at least ten years they become an honorary member, but with no right to vote. In the past, a member was elected on a permanent basis until age 75, which was extended to 80 in 1995 to allow for the re-election of Samaranch. Moreover, a seven-member Nominations Commission was created in 1999. It is composed of three members chosen by the Ethics Commission (see below), three by the Session and one by the Athletes Commission (see below). It examines the quality of potential candidates who may be proposed by an existing member or by an organization recognized by the IOC, including the IFs and the NOCs. The Commission then recommends several individuals to the IOC Executive Board each year, and the Executive Board may propose them for individual election at the Session. Elections are now held by secret ballot and by simple majority. Prior to 1999, the IOC President proposed a list of names, and a genuine vote at the Session rarely took place. One of the objectives of the 1999 reform was to renew the IOC membership more often. However, all the IOC members elected since 1999 have been almost automatically re-elected by list vote after their first eight-year mandate, if they had not reached the age limit. This included Rogge in 2008.

Athletes Commission

Twelve active athletes from the quota of 15 in the membership are subject to an election by their peers, by secret ballot at the Olympic Village (four at the Summer Games and two at the Winter Games, over two Olympiads). The remaining three are proposed to the session by the IOC President from members of the Athletes Commission, whom he nominates, to guarantee a certain degree of balance regarding gender and geographical distribution and to include types of member who would not necessarily be elected. Candidate athletes are presented by their NOC if they are taking part at the current Games or if they took part in those preceding them, and if they have never been found guilty of doping. There were nine candidates at the Vancouver Winter Games for two places, and 75.3 per cent of the Olympic athletes voted. The elected athletes form part of the Athletes Commission, which comprises 19 members, with the others being appointed by the IOC President. The elected athletes are confirmed as members by the Session, at the end of the Games, and then presented to the public at the Closing Ceremony.

Ethics Commission

The IOC members have a series of rights and obligations that are laid down in the Olympic Charter. They must take an oath whereby they make a commitment to serve the Olympic Movement, to respect the Charter, to comply with the Code of Ethics, to remain free from any political or commercial influence and to refrain from appealing IOC decisions (Rule 16.1.3). Apart from voting for a colleague wishing to become a member of the Executive Board, the main power of a member resides in their vote for a candidate city for the organization of the Games. In 1999, a few members wished to reduce this power drastically by entrusting the IOC Executive Board with this designation, or by imposing a single round of voting with a relative majority. In the end, however, the members retained their main prerogative. The reforms relating to the designation process for the Olympic city in 1999 nevertheless led to a reduction in the number of candidate cities proposed to the session. This is due to a pre-selection by the Executive Board one year before the final vote. Members are also prohibited from visiting the cities concerned and representatives of the cities are prohibited from visiting members in their countries. In principle, the only contact now authorized is at pre-designated Olympic meetings.

The IOC's Ethics Commission is tasked with investigating whether the members and the candidate cities respect these clauses. More generally, it is responsible for evaluating ethical behaviour, with the exception of doping and judging issues, on the part of the staff and members of the IOC, of athletes and officials taking part in the Games, of the NOCs, of the

Organising Committees and of Candidature Committees for the Games. To do so, it applies a Code of Ethics that was adopted in 1999 and revised in 2010 (IOC, 2010d). Four members have been excluded since 2000 upon its recommendations, or have tendered their resignation. The Commission was created in March 1999, before the other reforms relating to governance were set in motion, and its creation was in response to enormous pressure on the IOC by the media and the American sponsors at the time. It consists of nine persons, of whom a majority are non-IOC members. The Ethics Commission has taken on considerable importance since its creation, notably since the election of Jacques Rogge in 2001. It has improved the governance of the IOC but there is still room for progress to be made with respect to the Commission's transparency and independence from the IOC.

The 1999 reforms made it possible to guarantee that a certain number of IOC members come from the main stakeholders of the Olympic Movement, i.e. the athletes, the IFs and the NOCs. It would be possible to go even further, by imagining that all Olympians (those who have taken part in the Games at least once) or Olympic fans could vote, for example via the internet. In 2002, the IOC launched an online system for finding ideas with a view to reducing the gigantism of the Games, and in 2007 launched a virtual Olympic Congress to gather suggestions prior to the real congress in 2009. A World Olympian Association was founded in 1995 but so far has no particular role in IOC governance, except for a seat on the Athletes Commission. In order for their voices to be better heard within the IOC's reform process, Canadian athletes founded OATH (Olympic Advocates Together Honorably) in 1999. The organization, financed by the Magna Corporation, has since disappeared. Ten years later, a European Elite Athletes Association was founded to unite 15 professional independent athletes' federations. It now plays an important role in the fight against some anti-doping procedures such as the 'whereabouts rules'.

Certain authors, moreover, believe that the Olympic sponsors and the media that broadcast the Games should have a say regarding how the IOC is regulated. Based on agency theory, Mason et al. (2006) propose incorporating all these stakeholders within a board that would supervise the Session. The IOC members could not, of course, be in agreement with such a proposal, which would reduce their personal interests in being agents of the IOC. Having said that, the President of Samsung (an Olympic sponsor) and a Vice-President of NBC Sport, the broadcaster of the Games in the USA, have been IOC members for many years. Other members are also closely connected with sponsors.

Level four: harmonizing the regulatory mechanisms

As we have just seen, the Ethics Commission is, with the Nominations Commission, the IOC's main mechanism for managing its governance. But its authority goes well beyond the IOC members and staff, since the Code of Ethics is also applied to the NOCs, the Organising Committees and the Candidature Committees for the Games. Curiously, the IFs are not officially among the 'Olympic parties' (*sic*) subjected to the Code of Ethics. Moreover, the sanctions stipulated by the Olympic Charter only relate to the participation of individuals or organizations in the Games. They do not affect other areas of sport not directly related to the Games, such as championships, leagues and clubs. Several IFs and NOCs do, in fact, have their own Ethics Commissions and Code of Ethics, or regulations concerning conflicts of interest, or even rules of good governance, such as those of the International Cycling Union. This is also the case for the IFs of football, volleyball and wrestling (Chappelet, 2005) and the NOCs of Italy, the Netherlands, the USA, Slovenia and Switzerland (Chaker, 2004: 29). Some national sport federations also have their own regulatory bodies, such as the French Football Federation's National Ethics Council.

We could therefore imagine that an IF or NOC President who is a member of the IOC would be sanctioned with regard to ethics by the IOC but not by his IF or NOC. This is as a result of the disparities between the various regulatory texts or simply because of different interpretations among the regulatory entities concerned. Such a case almost arose with the International Volleyball Federation (FIVB) in 2004. The problem is one of harmonizing the regulatory mechanisms, or the 'governance of the governance' to use Pérez's (2009) expression.

This type of problem has already been encountered by international sport, in connection with doping. In 1999, it led to the creation of the World Anti-Doping Agency (WADA), a private foundation subject to Swiss law, controlled in equal parts by the Olympic Movement and the public authorities (Chappelet, 2002). One of the main objectives of the Agency is to harmonize the various sporting rules and legislative mechanisms related to doping. At the time, the case of a cyclist from Sydney was frequently cited: he took part in the Tour de France cycling race that started in Ghent, Belgium, and was thus subject to four or five different sets of regulations: Australian, French, Belgian (and Flemish), as well as those of the International Cycling Union. The beginning of a solution to this problem was reached, in 2003, with the adoption of the World Anti-Doping Code, signed by the IOC and all the IFs.

This Code has now been accepted by more than 150 states within their respective national legislation via the signature and ratification of an International Anti-Doping Convention, adopted by the United Nations Educational, Scientific and Cultural Organization (UNESCO) in 2005. WADA is empowered by the Code and is independent from the IOC despite half its budget coming from the broadcasting and sponsorship rights for the Games and the fact that several IOC members and Olympic Movement representatives play a leading role on the WADA board. For example, for the first seven years of WADA, its chairman was an IOC member. WADA therefore provides a private form of regulating the IOC's governance for the cases of doping it handles – those identified at the Games.

On a more global level, WADA constitutes an international public–private partnership that symbolizes a new and better governance of doping in sport for the twenty-first century. In 2010, its President called for a similar organization to fight corruption in sport. A similar idea had been voiced before by Chappelet (2002) and Play the Game (Andersen, 2007), a Danish organization which acts as a watchdog for the sport movement and calls for the creation of a 'Global Coalition for Good Governance in Sport'. Citing WADA as a good example, Bourg and Gouguet (2004) believe that, beyond codes and specialized agencies, a supranational organization could be tasked with protecting and regulating international sport, including the Olympic Games as a 'global public good'.

In addition to the lack of harmonization and the divergences of sporting rules that can exist within the sport movement, we also note a harmonization problem between the IOC's governance rules and the national laws of the states where it operates and where its members live. On several occasions, the IOC Ethics Commission has been forced to suspend its recommendations until national courts take decisions. This was the case, for example, for Guy Drut, a French IOC member and Olympic gold medal winner. In 2004 Drut was found guilty of abusing public funds in an affair that was not related to sport and which took place before he was elected to the IOC. He appealed against the court's decision and was finally granted a pardon by the French President. Subsequently, the Ethics Commission recommended a reprimand for having tarnished the reputation of the Olympic Movement and an interdiction to chair IOC commissions for five years. Until a final decision is taken by the competent national court or authority, the Ethics Commission prefers not to make a final decision for fear of reaching opposing conclusions. It simply proposes that the member be provisionally suspended. All that is legal is not, however, necessarily ethical. As the above example shows, the Commission has (slightly) sanctioned a member who was pardoned by his country, but would have probably not done so if he had been judged to be innocent.

Contradictions between the IOC's rules of governance and Swiss law – under which it mainly operates as well as many IFs – can also occur. Two cases can be cited in this connection. The first dates from 1979 and concerns the problem of the 'two Chinas'. The Taiwanese IOC member at the time lodged a complaint before a court in the Swiss Canton of Vaud against the decision by the IOC's Executive Board to impose a change of name and of emblem on the NOC of his country so that it could be allowed to continue taking part in the Games. The plaintiff also took advantage of his legal prerogatives as a member of a Swiss association to contest a decision that violates its statutes, according to him. The problem resolved itself two years later when the complaint was withdrawn. Following the incident, the members' oath was modified to indicate that they considered the IOC's decisions as being without appeal on their part. This clause is probably not valid before a Swiss court, but for the time being has avoided other complaints being filed by members against 'their' IOC.

The second affair dates from 2003, and has not yet been resolved in the Swiss courts. It concerns an Association by the name of 'Gibraltar National Olympic Committee', which has been requesting recognition by the IOC as an NOC in its own right since the end of the 1980s. The Association fulfils the conditions that were required at the time of its application, notably before the IOC demanded that the territory concerned be 'an independent State recognized by the International Community' (Rule 31 of the Olympic Charter). It criticizes the fact that the decision by the IOC has been so slow in coming; the IOC does not want to take a positive decision, which would not be accepted in Spain, or a negative one, which risks a negative outcome in a Swiss court because of the Charter that was in force at the time.

In its Olympic Charter, the IOC states that its decisions 'are final'. Any dispute relating to their application or interpretation may only be resolved by the IOC Executive Board and in certain cases by arbitration before the Court of Arbitration for Sport (CAS) (Rule 15.4). Since arbitration before the CAS is, however, subject to agreement by both parties concerned, it is clear that this clause by no means prevents the case from being brought before the Vaud courts and, if necessary, to the Federal Court (Switzerland's highest court) if the party opposing the IOC does not wish to resort to the CAS or if the IOC does not wish to do so.

Nonetheless, the CAS has in the past provided the IOC, and more widely sport organizations and athletes, with the possibility of avoiding state courts in Switzerland and elsewhere (Blackshaw et al., 2006). It has frequently been used by athletes who contest decisions by the IOC or the IFs in relation to doping, sometimes to the athletes' advantage. The World Anti-Doping Code has, moreover, declared the CAS its supreme court once all internal appeal mechanisms have been exhausted. The IOC, on the other hand, has rarely been able to impose recourse to the CAS within the contracts it signs with its commercial partners.

The CAS arbitrators are appointed by an International Council of Arbitration for Sport (ICAS), which itself is a foundation subject to Swiss law, and of which the IOC only designates one-fifth of the board members. The structure functions within the framework of Swiss public order, and in particular the Swiss Federal Private International Law, which regulates questions of arbitration even though the parties can decide, jointly, to apply another national law. The CAS's independence has been acknowledged on several occasions by the

Swiss Federal Court, which may nevertheless intervene in the case of an alleged procedural error.

During its activity over more than 25 years, the CAS has incontestably contributed towards aligning sport regulations with natural law, and towards a certain degree of harmonization of the rules of the Olympic sport organizations, which use it regularly and designate it as their supreme court. Even FIFA, football's governing body, which wished to create its own court of arbitration, accepted in 2005 the role of the CAS. In this sense, the CAS indeed constitutes a mechanism for the governance of the IOC's governance, and that of the IFs and any sport organization that wishes to use it. However, questions have been raised about the way CAS arbitrators are selected by ICAS and about the fact that few arbitrators keep up to date with the evolution of sport governance (Baddeley, 2004). Thus, the choice of competent arbitrators is limited.

Level five: the meta-governance of the IOC

The IOC receives no subsidies from public authorities, which protects it from governmental pressure. As already stressed, however, the IOC functions within the framework of Swiss legislation as an Association in accordance with Articles 60 to 79 of the Swiss Civil Code, or through its foundations and limited companies (SA) that are also subject to Swiss law. Admittedly, it was granted a special agreement with the Federal Council (Swiss Government) in 2000 regarding its status which, according to Latty (2001), makes it an actor of international law. The fact remains, however, that the IOC, even if it benefits from certain privileges concerning its direct taxes and the recruitment of its staff, is not a fully fledged international organization and does not benefit from a Headquarters Agreement that would provide it with the classical diplomatic privileges.

This situation could change in the future thanks to a recent Federal Law on the Host State which entered into force in 2008. The law permits the Swiss Government, without having to refer to its Parliament, to grant certain 'other international entities' privileges, immunities and other special waivers of Swiss law (Article 2.1.m of the law). From a governance point of view, this could permit the IOC to avoid any cases being filed against it in Swiss courts.

The IOC enjoys no specific protection in other jurisdictions or under other national legislations. It is mentioned every two years, within the Resolutions of the General Assembly of the United Nations (UN), with reference to the Olympic Truce (UNIC, 2005). Since 2009, it has had an observer seat at the UN and it has been mentioned in UNESCO resolutions concerning doping. It is recognized by the Treaty of Nairobi (1981) as being the owner of the Olympic symbol – the interlaced rings. All that, however, does not give the IOC international legal status or the Olympic Charter any legal power. There are even other, lesser-known texts that have greater legal scope: for example the International Charter for Physical Education and Sport (adopted by UNESCO in 1978) or the European Charter for Sport and the Code of Ethics for Sport (adopted by the Council of Europe in 1992). The aforementioned texts are considered to be recommendations for the Member States. It should be noted that the European Code of Ethics for Sport has virtually nothing in common with the Olympic Code of Ethics. The problem is again one of harmonization.

There are also international conventions that have a significant role in sporting matters and can sometimes constrain the IOC's or the Olympic Movement's decisions. Examples of these are the European Convention for the Protection of Human Rights and Fundamental Freedoms (Council of Europe, 1950); the European Convention on Spectator Violence and

Misbehaviour at Sport Events (Council of Europe, 1985); the Anti-Doping Convention (Council of Europe, 1989); the United Nations Convention against Corruption (2003), as well as similar conventions passed by the Council of Europe and the Organisation for Economic Cooperation and Development; the International Convention against Doping in Sport (UNESCO, 2005). In 2005, the Council of Europe sport ministers adopted recommendations for effective policies and measures of good governance in sport which are considered to be a response to inadequate behaviours by sport organizations (COE, 2005). Moreover, European Community law has often been invoked to successfully contest some sporting rules, the most famous example being the Bosman ruling in 1995.

In 2006, the Court of Justice of the European Communities declared that the IOC's rules on doping control fall within the scope of the Community competition law (CJEC, 2006). This prompted the IOC and IFs to organize two brainstorming meetings on the autonomy of sport organizations (Chappelet, 2010b). The conclusion of the second meeting in 2008 was to propose 'Basic universal principles of good governance of the Olympic and Sport Movement' which were formally adopted at the Olympic Congress in Copenhagen in 2009 (IOC, 2010c, point 41 of the Final document: 250). These principles must now be respected by all Olympic Movement constituents according to the IOC Code of Ethics as amended in 2010 'in particular, transparency, responsibility and accountability' as stated in the Code. The principles are organized in seven sections, outlined in Table 2.2.

The rationale for the adoption of such 'basic universal principles' was to emphasize good governance as the fundamental basis to secure the autonomy of Olympic and sport organizations. Beyond its own governance, the IOC wants to impose better governance on the whole Olympic and sport movement, i.e. on the Olympic System to secure its full autonomy or self-governance. Rogge highlighted this aim in his speech at the opening of a conference on the governance of sport in January 2001, a few months prior to his election as IOC President, saying: 'Since sport is based on ethics and competition on fair play, the governance of sport must comply with the highest standards in terms of transparency, democracy and accountability' (Rogge, 2001). We can see here a shift from corporate governance of sport organizations to the governance of sport as a social and political object worthy of public policies and constitutional support.

Sport is indeed mentioned as an object of public interest within numerous national constitutions (for instance in Greece, France and Switzerland) and in articles 16 and 165 of the Lisbon Treaty adopted in 2009 as a form of constitutional law for the European Union. Such legislation is the fundamental framework for the life of a nation's citizens, from which neither sport nor the IOC can exclude itself. The IOC President, in his speech to a gathering of NOC representatives and sport ministry officials which took place in Acapulco in 2010, admitted that the IOC 'fully recognizes and accepts the need to act within the framework of national and local laws, which when approved, must take into consideration the international sport law (in accordance with the Olympic Charter) in order to avoid any potential future conflict' (Rogge, 2010). Here the IOC President refers to the necessary harmonization between sporting rules and laws of the lands where sport is practised.

The IOC states, moreover, in the preamble to the Olympic Charter, several principles that can be found in constitutional texts and the recommendations of inter-governmental organizations. It refers, for instance, to respect for 'universal fundamental ethical principles', the preservation of human dignity, the right to practise sport being a human right, friendship, solidarity, fair play, non-discrimination and the educational value of sport. This highly general framework of social and political responsibility remains at the base of the IOC's meta-governance.

Table 2.2 The basic universal principles of good governance of the Olympic Movement

1. Vision, mission and strategy	1.1. Vision
	1.2. Mission
	1.3. Strategy
2. Structures, regulations and democratic process	2.1. Structures
	2.2. Clear regulations
	2.3. Governing bodies
	2.4. Representative governing bodies
	2.5. Democratic processes
	2.6. Attribution of the respective bodies
	2.7. Decision-making
	2.8. Conflicts of interests
	2.9. Duration of the terms of office
	2.10. Decisions and appeals
3. Highest level of competence, integrity and ethical standards	3.1. Competence of the members of the executive body
	3.2. Power of signature
	3.3. Internal management, communication and coordination
	3.4. Risk management
	3.5. Appointment of the members of the management
	3.6. Code of Ethics and ethical issues
4. Accountability, transparency and control	4.1. Accountability
	4.2. Processes and mechanisms
	4.3. Transparency and communication
	4.4. Financial matters – applicable laws, rules, procedures and standards
	4.5. Internal control system
	4.6. Education and training
5. Solidarity and development	5.1. Distribution of resources
	5.2. Equity
	5.3. Development
6. Athletes' involvement, participation and care	6.1. Right to participate and involvement of the athletes in the Olympic and Sport Movement and governing bodies
	6.2. Protection of athletes
	6.3. Health
	6.4. Fight against doping
	6.5. Insurance
	6.6. Fairness and fair play
	6.7. Athletes' education and career management
7. Harmonious relations with governments while preserving autonomy	7.1. Cooperation, coordination and consultation
	7.2. Complementary missions
	7.3. Maintain and preserve the autonomy of sport

Source: IOC, 2008

Conclusion

As we have noted, the IOC's governance has evolved considerably since the end of the twentieth century. This is partly due to the influence of the media and of public opinion that in 1999 forced the IOC to carry out drastic reforms, but also to the determination of the new President who, as of 2001, introduced classical principles of corporate governance that had previously been virtually ignored. Table 2.3 summarizes the IOC structures, external entities or instruments for the governance of the IOC and the Olympic System, some of which have been in place since its origin in 1894, but most of which were introduced more recently, in 1999, as a consequence of the corruption scandal concerning the awarding of the Olympic Winter Games to Salt Lake City.

At the beginning of the twenty-first century, the IOC is clearly more professionally managed than it was in the 1980s and 1990s when it rose from a club in charge of ensuring the regular celebration of the Olympic Games to a major transnational organization trying to lead sport on a worldwide basis. The entrepreneurial expansion years of the Samaranch presidency (1980–2001) had to be followed by a management consolidation period under the Rogge presidency (2001–13). Improvements can still be made (see Chappelet, 2011), but the corporate governance mechanisms of the IOC are now in place and the main challenge is to use them properly for the 'good governance' of the IOC.

However, the focus of attention has now moved from the governance of the IOC to the governance of the Olympic System and of world sport. Here the challenge is to make sure that the basic universal principles of good governance as defined by the IOC in 2009 are accepted, adopted and implemented by all Olympic organizations. The preservation of the autonomy of sport organizations at the national and international level rests on such an implementation.

Table 2.3 The five levels of governance of the IOC

Level	Level name	IOC structures, external entities and instruments
1	Management (strategic and operational)	IOC President and Directors with IOC Administration
2	Management of management (governance)	IOC Session Executive Board (since 1921) Statutory and Thematic Commissions (since 1968)
3	Management of governance (regulation)	IOC Nominations Commission (since 1999) Athletes Commission (since 1981) Ethics Commission (since 1999)
4	Governance of governance (harmonization)	WADA (since 1999) CAS (since 1984) National courts
5	Meta-governance (legal and societal framework)	Swiss legislation National constitutions and laws related to sport International conventions and treaties concerning sport

References

Andersen, J. S. (2007) *Towards a global coalition for good governance in sport*, Play the Game Press Release, 26 January, [online] available at <www.playthegame.org/knowledge-bank/articles/towards-a-global-coalition-for-good-governance-in-sport-1096.html> (accessed 28 December 2010).

Baddeley, M. (2004) *Thoughts on Swiss Federal Tribunal decision 129 III 445*, CausaSport 1/2004, 91 et seq.

Bayle, E. and Chantelat, P. (2008) *La gouvernance des organisations sportives*, Paris, L'Harmattan.

Blackshaw, I. S., Siekmann, R. C. M. and Janwillem, S. (eds) (2006) *The Court of Arbitration for Sport, 1984–2004*, Cambridge, Cambridge University Press.

Bourg, J.-F. and Gouguet, J.-J. (2004) 'L'économie des Jeux olympiques', *Revue juridique et économique du sport*, 72, September, 107–26.

Caiger, A. and Gardiner, S. (eds.) (2000) *Professional Sport in the European Union: Regulation and Re-regulation*, The Hague, Time Asser.

Chaker, A. N. (2004) *Good Governance in Sport: A European Survey*, Strasbourg, Council of Europe Publishing.

Chappelet, J.-L. (2002) 'L'Agence mondiale antidopage, un nouveau régulateur des relations internationales sportives', *Relations Internationales*, 111, 381–401.

—— (2005) 'Une commission d'éthique pour la gouvernance du mouvement olympique', *Ethique publique*, 7(2), 132–43.

—— (2006) 'Chapter 22: The economics of the International Olympic Committee', in W. Andreff and S. Szymanski (eds), *Handbook on the Economics of Sport*, London, Edward Elgar.

—— (2010a) 'Chapter 4: Strategic management in voluntary sport organisations' in L. Robinson and R. Palmer (eds), *Managing Voluntary Sport Organisions*, London, Routledge.

—— (2010b) *The Autonomy of Sport*, Strasbourg, Council of Europe Publishing.

—— (2011) *Towards Better Olympic Accountability*, Sport in Society, 3, March.

Chappelet, J.-L. and Kübler, B. (2008) *The International Olympic Committee and the Olympic System: The governance of world sport*, London, Routledge.

CJEC (2006) *The International Olympic Committee's rules on doping control fall within the scope of Community competition law*, Press Release {65/06}, Luxembourg, 18 July.

COE (2005), *Recommendation Rec(2005)8 of the Committee of Ministers to member states on the principles of good governance in sport*. 20 April. [Online] Available at <www.coe.int/t/dg4/sport/resources/texts/sprec05.8_en.asp> (accessed 28 December 2010).

EOC and FIA (2001) *The Rules of the Game: Conference Report and Conclusions*. [Online] Available at <www.fia.com/public/fia_structure/resources/governance_sport.pdf> (accessed 28 December 2010).

Hums, M. A. and MacLean, J. C. (2004) *Governance and Policy in Sport Organizations*, Scottsdale, Arizona, Holcomb Hathaway.

Hoye, R. and Cuskelly, G. (2007) *Sport Governance*, Oxford, Elsevier.

IOC (1999) *Report by the IOC 2000 Commission to the 110th IOC Session*, Lausanne, 11 and 12 December.

—— (2008) *Basic universal principles of good governance of the Olympic and Sport Movement. Preliminary document*, Lausanne, 1st February. [Online] Available at <www.olympic.org/Documents/Reports/EN/fr_report_1292.pdf> (accessed 28 December 2010).

—— (2009) *The Olympic Movement in Society: IOC Final Report 2005–2008*, Lausanne, IOC.

—— (2010) *Olympic Charter: Version in force as from 11 February 2010*, Lausanne, IOC.

—— (2010a) *Presentation to the AIST students*, Lausanne, 16 April 2010.

—— (2010b) *Olympic Movement Directory*, Lausanne, IOC Communication Department.

—— (2010c) *XIII Olympic Congress: Proceedings*, Lausanne, IOC.

—— (2010d) *IOC Code of Ethics: Text adopted by the IOC Executive Board on 26 October 2010, in Acapulco*. [Online] Available at <www.olympic.org/en/content/The-IOC/Commissions/The-ethics-commission/?Tab=2> (accessed 28 December 2010).

Katwala, S. (2000) *Democratising Global Sport*, London, The Foreign Policy Centre.

King, N. (2009) *Sport Policy and Governance: Local Perspectives*, Oxford, Elsevier.

Latty, F. (2001) *Le Comité international olympique et le droit international*, Paris, Montchrestien.

Mason, D. S., Thibault, L. and Misener, L. (2006) 'An Agency Theory Perspective on Corruption in Sport: The Case of the International Olympic Committee', *Journal of Sport Management*, 20(1), 52–73.

Payne, M. (2005) *Olympic Turnaround*, Twyford, London Business Press.

Pérez, R. (2009) *La gouvernance de l'entreprise*, Paris, La Découverte. Nouvelle édition.

Robinson, L. (2010) 'Chapter three: The governance of voluntary sport organisations' in L. Robinson and R. Palmer, (eds.) *Managing Voluntary Sport Organisations*, London, Routledge.

Rogge, J. (2001) 'Governance in sport, A challenge for the future' in EOC and FIA (Eds), *The Rules of the Game: Conference Report and Conclusions*.

—— (2010) *Speech from the IOC President*, First World Olympic Sport Convention, Acapulco, 23 October. [Online] Available at <www.olympic.org/Documents/Conferences_Forums_and_Events/2010-ACNO-Acapulco/ANOC2010-First-World-Olympic-Sport-Convention-Acapulco-eng-final-2010.pdf> (accessed 28 December 2010).

Sport in Society (2011) *Special issue: Olympic Reform – 10th Year Anniversary*, Volume 15, February.

Thoma, J. E. and Chalip, L. (1996) *Sport Governance in the Global Community*, Morgantown, WV, FIT.

UNIC (2005) *United Nations and Olympic Truce*, Athens, United Nations Information Centre and International Olympic Truce Centre.

Zölch, F. A. (2004) Corporate Governance im Sport' in U. Scherrer and F. A. Zölch (Hrsg.), *Sportveranstaltungen – im Fokus von Recht und Wirtschaft*, Zürich, Orell Füssli, 93–112.

3

THE CONTINGENT AND STANDARDS GOVERNANCE FRAMEWORK FOR NATIONAL GOVERNING BODIES

Denis Mowbray

Introduction

Governance and what constitutes good or bad governance of sporting organisations continues to be a topic as hotly debated today as it has been for the last decade. One need only review the sporting or financial sections of almost any newspaper to see examples of poor governance in the sporting sector. An important point that bears repeating is that there is no model of governance that will transform a poor-performing organisation into a pillar of high performance. The performance of the board is almost entirely dependent on the people involved; models or frameworks can only help them by providing tools to work with.

With this in mind, this chapter starts by briefly discussing a concept called the governance lifecycle and its relevance before moving on to review the current literature. This is followed by a discussion of the methodology, participant selection process, data gathering and analysis methods used to produce a flexible framework of governance for sport organisations. The core of the chapter discusses the Contingent and Standards (CaS) framework of governance that has emerged from the above research. This is in two sections: first, the contingency section discusses the driving governance role (DGR) of the board and how a board knows which role to use; and the second section discusses the standards that underpin the whole operation of the board. This discussion of standards is divided into four sections:

- Structural: describes the core documents and regulations of the standards;
- Partnership and Communication: outlines the core requirements and responsibilities of the board in this area;
- Planning: a key role of the board which includes the strategic and annual plans;
- Transparency: essential to successful boards.

The chapter closes by outlining the anticipatory mechanisms of the CaS framework that the board can use, which enable the board to understand and predict which driving governance role the board should be using.

The governance lifecycle

Organisations need to build and develop a governance structure that suits their organisation's stage of development as it moves through its lifecycle. Figure 3.1 shows how the governance lifecycle is characterised by a change in emphasis from being predominantly focused on operations during the start-up phase of the organisation (point A) through to a greater emphasis on governing as the organisation reaches maturity (point B).

Organisations need a governance framework that is adjustable and develop with the organisation, not one that is rigid. Stages of the governance lifecycle follow the lifecycle of the organisation – start, growth, maturity, decline, near death and death – highlighting that, as an organisation develops, the requirements of the governance structure will vary. Therefore, a model of governance that is simultaneously rigid in its methods and prescriptive in their application is unsustainable for the dynamic environment sport boards operate in.

Literature review

Modern corporate governance was first put under the microscope of public review with the release of the Cadbury Report (1992) in the United Kingdom. Commissioned by the Financial Reporting Council and the London Stock Exchange, the report investigated concerns regarding the financial reporting standards and the (in)ability of auditors to stand up to dominant boards. Highlighting these concerns were cases such as the Bank of Credit and Commerce International (BCCI). This was followed by the Hilmer Report (1998) and the two King Reports (2001, 2002). These reports have been further advanced with writings by Conger, Lawler and Finegold (2001), Carver and Oliver (2002), Matheson (2004) and Monks and Minow (2004).

The Cadbury Report made a number of recommendations, including prescriptions for board structure and composition, such as recommending the proportion or numbers of independent directors. The theoretical underpinning for these and other such recommendations is agency theory, which derives from the disciplines of economics and law. Agency theory focuses on two main organisational players: the executives (management), who are the agents, and the owners (principal). The role of the board is to act on behalf of the ownership to ensure that agency costs are minimised, i.e. to minimise or eliminate managerial opportunism and expropriation. Agency theory has guided the development of most of the governance regulations and remedies that have been proposed, including prescribing numbers

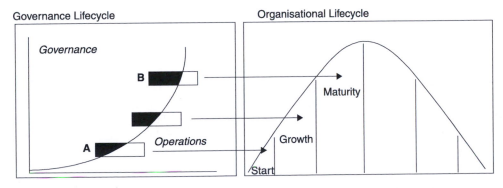

Figure 3.1 Governance lifecycle

of independent or non-executive directors and the separation of the CEO and Chair roles. The expected outcomes from adoption of these and other remedies were improved board oversight and performance, leading to improved organisational performance. Unfortunately, researchers have shown that this is not the case (Bhagat and Black, 1999; Baliga, Moyer and Rao, 1996; Finkelstein and Mooney, 2003).

Roberts, McNulty and Stiles (2005) stated that a widely held belief exists that independently structured boards, with a majority of non-executive directors, are associated with higher financial performance and better shareholder returns. While this belief is popular with regulators and the market, the Finkelstein and Mooney (2003) research into organisations that suffered high-profile collapses or scandal (Enron, WorldCom, Global Crossing, Quest Communications and Tyco International) showed no evidence supporting this belief. In addition, a meta-analysis of 159 studies covering a 40-year time frame found no evidence of a relationship between board composition and firm financial performance (Dalton, Daily, Ellstrand, and Johnson, 1998). Finkelstein and Mooney (2003: 102) described this best when concluding that the 'benefits of board independence seem to be rather illusory'.

These and other corporate governance standards, such as the need for independent directors and set director tenure, have become the norm by which Not for Profit (NFP) organisations are measured. The blind adoption of corporate governance standards with their focus on profit and shareholder return raises questions specifically in relation to sport. For example: are corporate governance standards and best practice relevant in sport? If so, what are they? What is good governance? How is best practice defined? Is best practice in one sport or country applicable to another? Once defined, how do we implement these standards? How is performance and/or conformance against standards measured?

These questions, and incidents of poor governance, such as corruption allegations associated with the voting process for the 2018 and 2022 Fifa World Cups, have ignited intense interest in the governance of sport organisations. Governance as applied to sport organisations is essentially normative, meaning it is founded on common elements such as performance, conformance, policy, operations and social responsibility. The corporate governance environment is evidence of this normative approach and although some elements may vary, Ferkins, Shilbury and McDonald (2005) found that the substantive elements remain similar. This fits a critical observation of Nadler and Tushman (1980) that it is not how to find the 'best way' to govern that is crucial, but it is rather what the effective combination of elements is that leads to congruence that is critical.

A major influence on the development of governance best practice as it affects sport has been the policy governance model developed by Carver (1997) combined with additional influences from the corporate governance environment. Carver (1997) describes the Board as a servant leader and owner representative which uses systematic delegation of power via carefully crafted policies to guide the Executive in their work. The assumption underpinning this model is that it is applicable to organisations of all sizes. While agreeing that Carver (1997) has made a useful, if prescriptive, contribution to sport governance, Ingles (1997) noted that none of Carver's assumptions regarding board practice have been tested empirically. Indeed, Gill (2001) and Hoye and Cuskelly (2003) found the Carver (1997) model assertions to be at odds with their own findings. Plumptre and Laskin (2003: 3) said claims made regarding the model's universality were 'seriously over-inflated and worked better in theory than in practice'.

This assertion of Plumptre and Laskin's (2003) is supported by Gill (2001), who found evidence of seven different governance models in use by sporting organisations with 75 per cent using a mixture of governance models. Organisations applied these different governance models to different aspects of their governance processes and practices. These findings support the earlier contention that the governance needs of an organisation change as they progress through their organisation's governance lifecycle. Herman, Renz and Heimovics (1997) also found a wide variation in the use of prescribed board practices, finding that the perception of board effectiveness varied dramatically. Herman and Renz (1998) identified a correlation between the board and organisational effectiveness, leading to the development of five points which are applicable to sport organisations:

- Organisational effectiveness is multidimensional and not reducible to a single factor.
- Boards do make a difference to organisations, but how they do this is unclear.
- Effective organisations are more likely to implement best practice standards and practices, such as strategic development and/or review, CEO reviews, than non-effective organisations.
- Organisational effectiveness is a social construction.
- Programme outcomes, as key performance indicators of organisational effectiveness, are limited in their use.

The general dissatisfaction with the Carver model combined with the incidents of poor governance and the questions raised earlier have resulted in significant country-specific research into the governance of sport organisations, which include the Australian Sport Commission whose research led to the release of its 'principles of best practice'. UK Sport, in conjunction with Deloitte and Touche, produced the *Investing in Change* (2003) report, which included the recommendation that a specific model for governance best practice be developed for national governing bodies (NGBs). A *UK Sport Good Governance Guide for National Governing Bodies* has also been developed by the Institute of Chartered Secretaries and Administrators with the purpose of supplementing existing governance publications tailored to small voluntary organisations. Deloitte and Touche also developed the *National Governing Bodies of Sport Success Criteria/Model Framework* (2003), which measured success based on turnover, value of grants, number of paid staff, number of clubs and personal members. Criteria developed on these metrics were categorised as one through five. NGBs were cat-egorised according to which criteria they fitted and where that placed them in the categories, with level one being the highest ranking.

Like the countries above, New Zealand, following poor performances at international events, notably the 2000 Olympics, embarked on a programme of development and research into various aspects of sport organisation development including governance. One of the outputs from this focus was the development of the *Nine Steps to Effective Governance* (SPARC, 2004) which are:

- Prepare the job description;
- Develop the work plan;
- Review the standard and content of the standard board meeting;
- Recast the strategic plan;
- The chief executive – recruitment, performance, measures and evaluation;
- Enhance the board's monitoring effectiveness;
- Regularly review the board's performance;
- Ensure active succession planning;
- Effective induction process.

This guideline details the key steps an organisation should initiate in developing good governance practices and the document provides policy and other templates for organisations. All these developments aspire to bring consistency, professionalism, transparency and accountability into the governance practices of sporting organisations, while achieving sporting success and governments' social imperatives of health and well-being for their citizens.

The influence of the Carver (1997) model is evident in all these developments. However, Gill (2001) noted that a 'one size fits all' approach could well be counterproductive, especially for those smaller organisations where the interaction between board, CEO, staff and stake-holders may need to be more collaborative due to factors such as size and resources. This denunciation of the one size fits all approach is also supported by Hoye (2002), who found the roles of the board and paid executive are interrelated and subject to ongoing role design and as such the prescriptive nature of the Carver (1997) model would be problematic.

In summary, this review reinforces the need to develop a governance framework that adapts to the changing needs of sport organisations as they progress through their governance lifecycle. What follows is a brief description of the research methodology used to develop such a framework.

The development of the Contingent and Standards governance framework (CaS)

The development of the CaS framework was based on mixed methods of data collection, so that the final research processes were complementary in their strengths while eliminating overlapping weaknesses. The research was carried out in New Zealand, Australia, Canada and the United Kingdom for the following reasons:

- Developed sporting structures, highly developed national sporting federations;
- Well-developed sport management structures;
- Wide range of experiences concerning governance of sport organisations, from inception to those who have undergone significant change;
- Ease of communication;
- Access to a significant amount of data;
- Consistency of selected sport codes across all countries.

The federations chosen from these countries were swimming, cycling, athletics and yachting because of:

- Diversity of social and cultural mixes;
- A mix of professional and volunteer executive and board members;
- A significant national governing body in these sports;
- Consistency across countries;
- Strong international organisations;
- A diversity of experience with the implementation of best practice governance standards.

Data was collected using the following methods:

- Questionnaires: these went to 32 participants (CEO and Chairman/President) from the organisations selected. The return rate was 50 per cent.

- Existing or secondary data: three types of existing data were used – documents, physical and archived. Using a wide range of externally gathered and collated data available on the selected sport lessened the impact of the lack of observational data.
- Interviews: construction of the questions for the interviews followed analysis of the completed questionnaires. This allowed development of new themes of investigation not previously identified. The questions typically dealt with the personal views and opinions of the interviewee.

The results and subsequent analysis led to the development of the CaS framework, which is described in the following section. The framework allows organisations to adapt their governance style and practices dependent on their position within their governance lifecycle.

The Contingent and Standards framework

Participants in the interviews repeatedly asked this question:'There are times when circumstances call for us to be involved in the operations of the organisation; how can I tell when that is?' While seemingly complex, this question has an elegant yet simple solution. In an article discussing contingent governance, Strebel (2004) said that boards, in dealing with external and internal forces, must emphasise a particular focus in decision-making and resource allocation, referring to this as the *driving governance role* (DGR).

This role changes as the importance and nature of external forces (externalities) that shape the organisation's future, current operations or planning needs change. Internal forces (internalities) have their own impact, as well as adding to those external factors. For example, when management is ineffective and the organisation's functionality is affected by internal or external factors, a board will generally become involved in execution, taking a steering or coaching role (see discussion below). Boards alternate between the four principal roles of governance (Figure 3.2), depending on the macro and micro implications that events have on their internal and external environments and the effectiveness or ineffectiveness of management.

A board works within four governing roles – coaching, auditing, supervising and steering – and each is dependent on three factors. The first is internal – is management ineffective or effective? The second is the board perspective – is it long or short term? Third are external conditions – are they significant or insignificant? This focuses a board on what its behaviour should be in terms of monitoring policy or involved with execution.

The ability to adapt their governance style allows a board to move between roles as necessitated and changes in role can occur during a board meeting. For example, an NGB hired a CEO with extensive knowledge of the sport and skilled at public relations yet his governance knowledge was limited. The interviewee described how the board dealt with this and agreed that the board oscillated between *auditing* in those areas of strength and *coaching* in the areas of weakness (governance). They were using the CaS model without even knowing.

For the board to identify changes in externalities that may influence the DGR, it must have an excellent line of communication with its constituents. A board that is reliant on the CEO and executives for information will be ineffectual, as they may hear only what the CEO and executive believe is important, or want them to hear. There are two key indicators that assist a chairman and board members in anticipating when to change their DGR. The first is a review of the agenda items and papers in order to note which DGR the board may need to adopt, and the second is an intuitive recognition of the need to change, which relies on the

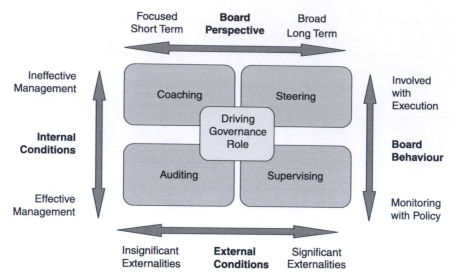

Figure 3.2 Contingency model

Source: Strebel, 2004

chair's skills in reading the mood of the directors, its proceedings and the relative importance or not of the topic or item under discussion.

Definitions of driving governing roles

The four DRG roles are:

- *Coaching:* The coaching role is undertaken when the externalities concerned are of an insignificant nature; the impact from the board's perspective is short term, and the management is ineffective. This role sets out to develop the required skill with the executive concerned and the coach should be the director with the greatest expertise or, if unavailable, the board should access these skills from training providers or consultants. Coaching and developing the skills of the executive is one of the great contributions a board can make towards the success of their NGB.
- *Auditing:* The board takes on an auditing role when the externalities are insignificant and the management is effective. The dominant activity is one of fiduciary responsibility – monitoring the agreed key performance indicators (KPIs) for the organisation. This relies heavily on the reporting structures initiated through the anticipatory mechanisms. Conceivably boards may work within both the auditing and coaching styles, with the auditing style being dominant. The auditing role is appropriate in a stable environment, where the need to make dramatic changes or decisions or deal with high-impact situations is unlikely.
- *Supervising:* The supervising role is appropriate when an NGB with effective management undertakes strategic decisions aimed at creating value over the longer term, or which carry a measure of risk more significant than normal. It occurs when the externalities or internalities are significant but the management *is* effective. This is the most difficult for boards to grasp, due to the culture of the volunteer, which is 'to roll their sleeves up and get stuck in'. Boards working within this DGR must go beyond the fiduciary duties of an auditing

role and include oversight and policy in order to accommodate the risk effects of the externalities or internalities impacting on the NGB.

- *Steering:* In this role, the board goes beyond coaching or supervising and becomes an active player in the management of the organisation. In extreme cases, such as the replacement of the CEO, the board may have to support a director as they fulfil the role of CEO. In the situation where a board member (or external consultant) replaces the CEO, the board needs to ensure it remains apprised of, and agrees with, the major decisions affecting the organisation.

Anticipatory mechanisms for the driving governance role

The research identified five key aspects required to aid a board in identifying what driving governance role it should be using. These are referred to as the anticipatory measures and they are:

- *Board reviews*: These should be carried out bi-annually and preferably with an outside facilitator, inclusive of all directors (including the chair). While this was a contentious subject when discussed with chairmen, the CEOs all agreed it would be a good thing, saying that their performance was influenced by the board's performance.
- *Meeting without the CEO*: Board meetings may be the only opportunity a board has to discuss in private any issues concerning the organisation's performance and any other matters that should remain private amongst board members.
- *Agenda, meeting management*: The board (chair) must control the agenda detail in consultation with the CEO and executive. This includes the reports and other informational mechanisms required for meetings. Not surprisingly with these two aspects, CEOs were more reluctant to see these implemented than the chairmen were. The management of the agenda is practically important as this is one method by which CEOs control their boards. This inhibits a board's ability to perform and undertake the governance role required.
- *Communication*: However it is managed it is essential to have excellent channels of communication across the organisation.
- *Statutory and governance committees*: The only committee recommended no matter the size of the organisation is an audit and risk committee. After this, the number and types of committees to be constituted and that report directly to the board can be adjusted to suit the needs, size and cultural and other drivers of the NGB. A significant number of NGBs indicated they had no audit/risk committee. Given the large amount of public funding channelled through these organisations this is a significant oversight. Roles for the audit and risk committee include reviewing financial results, planning, reporting, and overseeing risk and risk minimisation and this committee is an essential component of all NGBs' governance structure.

An outline of CaS standards

The CaS framework is not prescriptive in its application, therefore neither are the standards that underpin the DGR. The CaS framework encourages a board to look at its role as complementary to the CEO, executive and staff, not as a replacement for them. When the governance of an organisation is working well, the board should display a combination of intangible and tangible qualities that add significant value to their organisations, while making a discernible contribution to the accomplishment of their vision and strategic plan.

Board members link organically to the NGB, not by formula and rules but by the feeling that they, as volunteer board members, are contributing to the success of the NGB.

What follows are the standards of the CaS framework and their associated sub-components. These are the structures, policies and activities that will help the board to become more effective. This offers readers the opportunity to reflect on their board's conformance with them, while allowing NGB boards, CEOs, constituents and major funders a view of how an empowered board may operate so as to add lasting value to their organisation.

Structural standards

There are nine components associated with the structural standards of CaS:

Framework: The existence of a sound governance framework is imperative for the board of an NGB. This 'governance framework' comprises a core set of documents including:

- Articles of incorporation;
- Registered company status (in some cases);
- By-laws and regulations;
- Policies: i.e. executive limitations, conflicts of interest;
- Board charter: including code of conduct, chairman's role, and induction of new board members;
- Practices.

These guide and define how the governance processes will work, who takes decisions and the limitations of power in various circumstances. The size and complexity of the by-laws, regulations and policies are in part determined by the complexity of the organisation. They must reflect the core values, objectives and essential mission of the NGB.

Purposeful structure: Boards should purposefully structure their activities in order to fulfil essential governance duties, making the governance process intentional in design rather than accidental. High-performing boards invest in structures and systems that are dependable and flexible enough to accommodate the changing requirements of the organisation.

Process-based: Whatever the design of the governance system, it is imperative it is process-based, not people-based, and the governance of the NGB should not be reliant on an individual or their skills. The governance system should have strong processes, policies and procedures. While acknowledging the importance of strong leadership, in the event of the loss of a strong leader, the organisation's processes and policies will ensure it continues to function well.

Induction: A new board member must be given a proper induction into the processes, policies and workings of the board. Those involved will typically be the chairman, CEO, divisional heads and CFO. The process should include:

- A full briefing by the chair regarding the board and its policies;
- An induction pack that includes meetings minutes, financials, board regulations, letter of commitment, current papers before the board, any supplementary papers, annual work plan and meeting plan;
- A full contact list of directors and executives as required;

- Copy of the constitution and strategic plan;
- A CEO and executive briefing outlining the organisation's progress on deployment of the strategic plan;
- A detailed analysis of issues currently on the board's agenda.

Purpose: The board should be core-driven. It is the board's responsibility to help develop, shape and uphold a compelling core purpose for the NGB. The board must articulate this and ensure integrity between decisions and core values. Whenever deliberations take place these should acknowledge how possible decisions may fit within the purpose and core values of the organisation and how the final decision will embody these core components.

Board size: The board's size should reflect the complexity, activity and needs of the organisation. Where possible a mix of appointed and elected board members gives the best results. Ten is the largest suggested board size with five being the smallest. If an NGB can appoint outside directors, it should appoint directors only when they bring the skill sets identified in the developed skills matrix.

Tenure: Board rotation and replenishment should aim to invigorate the board with new members while not losing the board's corporate memory and the skills of experienced members. Revitalisation cannot happen if the same board members are sitting for lengthy periods so a maximum term of office should be determined.

Chairman selection: The chair's role is pivotal to the success of the board as a whole and should not be left to the vagaries of a general election. It is recommended the chair is elected by the board (his peers). The tenure of the chair should be the same as the elected period of other board members. The reasons for, and process required, if a board wishes to remove a chair or director should be clearly defined in its regulations.

Policy: Boards spend considerable time developing policy, which is often unused or not required. Policies are living documents; they should be at hand at every meeting and have a review date, at which time each policy's relevance and usefulness is discussed. Following this, any changes or deletions to the policy should be actioned.

Partnership and communication standards

There are four components associated with the partnership and communication standards of CaS:

Partnership: A board's role is to advance and protect the interests of the organisation and its constituents. Exceptional boards undertake this through a constructive partnership with the CEO, remembering that the board and CEO's effectiveness are independent but still intrinsically linked. This is not, however, a partnership of equals as the board is the ultimate authority. To facilitate this, this partnership must be built through trust, candour and mutual respect for each other's role and, foremost of all, must operate within an environment of honest communication. The CEO and board chair should have a strong relationship as this is critical to the NGB's success and the way the board–CEO relationship manifests itself. If for whatever reason either feels that this relationship is dysfunctional in any way, they should immediately take steps to correct it, either through discussion among themselves or, if necessary, with other members of the board.

Relationships: NGBs have, by their very nature, a complex set of relationships with an extremely diverse group of organisations and individuals, including members, regional and local clubs and associations, volunteers and funders. Maintaining good relationship with stakeholders is essential as these provide valuable input and expertise, which allows the NGB to identify new opportunities, challenges and methods or means of dealing with a crisis. The board is not personally responsible for the management of all these relationships; however, it plays a pivotal role in ensuring that the CEO, and through them the organisation, manage these relationships to maximise the benefit. Relationships with major stakeholders are a form of insurance for the future of the NGB. Relationship building is a key task of the board and should be managed with the same careful approach used in managing the finances of the organisation.

Communication: Perhaps the least understood, most neglected and yet one of the most important roles that NGB boards undertake is communication. The board's ability to communicate well with its constituents and stakeholders will be the measure of success or failure. Importantly, the NGB must purposely set out to communicate all that it does to those it affects, in a timely and honest manner. Communication outside board meetings between individual board members should be encouraged. This allows informal discussion to take place and further develops collegiality within the board.

Advocacy: Advocacy undertaken by the board on behalf of the organisation was identified as a key role of governance and could be within their local area or at local government level. While not denying the benefits gained from having strong advocates, especially in the form of board members, the limitations on this advocacy must be clearly defined within policy, regarding members advocating on behalf of the board. The board should take a specific interest in ensuring that the key relationships are well managed, particularly with major funders, regional associations and other major stakeholders. This is achieved through the CEO reporting regularly on events that have taken place and inviting major stakeholders to meet with the board or board chair and CEO alone if desired.

Planning standards

There are four components associated with the planning standards of CaS:

Strategy: The board must ensure that it allocates sufficient time and resources to thinking strategically about the organisation. This will aid in the development of agendas and goals that are aligned with the strategic plan. Once per year the board and selected staff should meet for a strategic review process. The length of this meeting will be governed by the NGB's structure and complexity, but will, however, involve a complete review of the strategic plan and the accomplishments to date and a review of the following year's strategic plan to ascertain its validity.

Annual Plan: This is a key working document through which the chair, in consultation with the CEO and board members, sets out major action points for the following year.

Meeting plans: From the Annual Plan, the board will develop their meeting plans. These allow the chair and CEO to put in place the structure and content for the meeting while also ensuring matters deemed as essential in the Annual Plan are dealt with in a timely manner. This should be a board meeting, not the CEO's meeting, and the chair and board should drive the agenda *in consultation* with the CEO.

Resources: Boards of NGBs should be reminded constantly that resources are not infinite and most NGBs rely heavily on grants and subsidies to undertake and complete their work. Boards of NGBs should ensure strategic and operational plans link to the resource allocation plan. It is only by linking budgeting to the strategic plan via a resource plan that NGBs can realistically finance and plan within the existing or procurable resources. This should be balanced against the need to ensure the NGB has the infrastructure and internal capacity required to sustain its core operations.

Performance standards

There are six components associated with the partnership and communication standards of CaS:

Performance: For a board to judge if the organisation has performed well it must ask the right questions. To do this it must first know what good performance is and what that means for their NGB, e.g. financial, sport performance, increased membership. Therefore boards must spend time detailing and defining good performance, and how and when it will be measured.

Financial: A principal role of the board is to ensure the financial health of the NGB and this role is more encompassing than just making sure money is spent in the right way. It is, in fact, financial stewardship. This includes a number of important components, such as adopting a budget, appointing a reputable auditor, measuring performance against the budget and understanding and receiving the necessary financial reporting monthly, including a cash flow statement and if required a cash flow forecast.

Results: The board should regularly review the organisation's achievements against its stated strategic objectives by measuring the NGB's progress towards the achievement of its strategy. The board should be able to measure the achievement level through the 'anticipatory measures' that it has in place and the reporting that it receives. These measures should not only look at the core activities – 'Did we provide X service or run Y programmes? – they should also look at the quality of service, effectiveness and impact. Benchmarking is difficult for NGBs, so unless it is easily achievable great effort should not be put into measuring the success of the NGB against others. Each structure and sport body is unique and comparisons of success between sporting bodies are almost irrelevant. The board, executive and constituents will know if the NGB is successful or not.

Learning: NGBs should develop a culture of continuous learning, championed by the board, as they themselves evaluate their own performance and measure the value they add. Through their actions, the board leads the NGB in accessing opportunities for learning, in both their internal and external board activities.

Meeting attendance: Board members should prepare for and attend meetings regularly. If there are continued absences, the chair should speak to the board member and if necessary they should be asked to reconsider their position. Members should prepare for meetings by ensuring that they have fully read all the papers and are fully versed in the issues that are on the agenda.

Risk minimisation: Risk minimisation is a key component of good governance. The role of a director is to ensure that the NGB has fully identified and assessed all risks that are associated with its operations. There are two parts to this assessment. One is operational, for which the CEO is responsible; the other is strategic, which the board is responsible for. The strategic assessment includes the review of the CEO's plan. The board and CEO should each prepare a risk assessment and minimisation plan for their respective areas. Both should be reviewed twice yearly by the board to ensure they are current as risk changes over time. Appropriate actions must be taken to minimise risk and reviews of the risk minimisation plans should form part of the work undertaken by the audit committee as part of its statutory duties.

Transparency standards

There are eight components associated with the transparency standards of CaS:

Board committees: As well as the permanent audit and risk committees others will be needed to provide a level of closer scrutiny as the DGR changes or as the need dictates. It is imperative that all committees have as a minimum the following:

- Clear terms of reference (TOR), including, powers, budgetary allowance, responsibility, selection of members and chair;
- Clearly defined reporting guidelines;
- A date for disestablishment if not a standing committee such as audit;
- All committees' TOR should be reviewed annually as this ensures the TOR are current and reflect the mission, vision and strategic plan while fulfilling the role required by the board.

Compliance with integrity: Through the actions of each member of the board, the board as a group should demonstrate strong ethical values and a disciplined approach to compliance. The board should establish mechanisms, such as the anticipatory mechanisms discussed above, to ensure accountability, with sufficient controls so that the opportunities for waste, fraud and abuse of position in any form are minimised.

Conflict of interest: There are two minimum standards that an NGB board should have in place. The first is *conflict of interest* policy, which every board member signs up to when they join, and the second is a *register of interests* which requires board members and the CEO to list all the connections, outside interests or other relevant associations that may have some bearing on the NGB. This register should be available at each meeting and should be an agenda item to ensure that it is kept up to date. The policy must be clear and concise and used as required and the actions taken listed in the minutes of the meeting.

Culture of inquiry: The board's role is one of a 'loyal opposition' and this requires a culture of mutual respect and constructive debate that takes the board and CEO through a sound and shared decision-making process. When required, the board should seek more information, and challenge and question assumptions and conclusions. This ensures the solutions or decisions are tested and based on analysis rather than a blind acceptance of the information given.

Transparency: It would be easy for the board to be led by the CEO because the locus of power rests with the CEO. The board must therefore promote a culture of transparency both for their own benefit and for all other stakeholders. The board does this by ensuring that the appropriate levels of access and the accuracy of information are maintained for all stakeholders and individual directors in such areas as finance, operations and results. The culture of inquiry discussed above is unattainable if there is not transparency and access to information. These two important standards are inextricably linked.

Board members: Alongside selection of the CEO, selection of board members is a key step in the development of a board committed to good governance. No matter the process used, prospective board members should be recruited and selected in the same manner as a senior member of staff. There are three major criteria a board can use to ensure the right people are elected or selected and these are:

- The board develops a skills matrix, detailing strengths, weaknesses and needs;
- The board undertakes development and publication of a role description and expectations document;
- Candidates are interviewed by the chair and one other senior director or, if available, an independent director.

Selection is a key step in the development of good governance, yet often it is left to chance. NGBs can improve the odds of appointing a good director by ensuring all involved understand the needs and expectations required of the successful candidate. A well-planned succession process will energise the board as they see the emerging relationship between a dynamic board, its composition and the successful development and deployment of the NGB's strategy.

Equal opportunity: The board should openly and continuously reinforce its commitment to equal opportunities for all those involved in the organisation. This is achieved not only by the adoption of equal opportunity policies, but also by these being reflected in the organisation's activities and the board's own mix of technical expertise and the geographical, gender and cultural backgrounds of its members.

Independence: Members of the board should put the interests of the NGB ahead of any other interest when making decisions. There is a need for honest reflection by each director when an issue arises in which they have an interest. It is preferable to declare the interest and decide its relevance, followed by a decision on what if any actions are required, rather than have the decision process and its outcome called into question.

Summary

The CaS framework recognises that organisational effectiveness is multidimensional and cannot be reduced to a single factor. The CaS framework's flexibility allows the development of best practice governance standards in smaller organisations where by necessity the interaction between the CEO, stakeholders and staff may need to be more interactive due to factors such as size and resources.

The non-prescriptive nature of the CaS framework allows organisations to develop governance standards that account for the different governance requirements associated with the recreational and elite/competitive elements of the sport. The conflicts that occur between these sectors were evident in the research in a number of sports but specifically in cycling where the reality is that, for the great majority of participants, their participation does not require the help or services of the NGB.

The CaS governance framework provides an alternative for those NGBs who are dissatisfied with their current structure and who do not want to adopt models that are not reflective of the culture of the sport or its constituents or the volunteers that govern it. Boards can attain a level of excellence through the application of the CaS framework that will reflect the success of the organisation. Finally, it does not matter what standards, policies or rules are implemented or developed; good governance is totally dependent on the quality of the people that participate and are involved in it, combined with the synergy, trust and communication that exists between the board and executive teams of the organisation.

For a full description of the framework please visit <www.sportgovernance.org>.

References

Baliga, B. R., Moyer, N. C. and Rao, R. S. (1996) 'CEO duality and firm performance: What's the fuss?', *Strategic Management Journal*, 17, 41–53.

Bhagat, S. and Black, B. (1999) 'The uncertain relationship between board composition and firm performance', *Business Lawyer*, 54(3), 921.

Carver, J. (1997) *Boards That Make a Difference: A New Design for Leadership in Nonprofit and Public Organizations* (2nd edn). New York, Jossey-Bass, John Wiley.

Carver, J. (2002) *On Board Leadership*, New York, Jossey-Bass, John Wiley.

Carver, J. and Oliver, C. (2002) *Corporate Boards That Create Value: Governing Company Performance from the Boardroom*, San Francisco, Jossey-Bass, John Wiley.

Conger, J. A., Lawler, E. E. and Finegold, D. L. (2001) *Corporate Boards: New Strategies for Adding Value at the Top*, San Francisco, Jossey-Bass, John Wiley.

Committee on Financial Aspects of Corporate Governance (1992). *The Financial Aspects of Corporate Governance*, London, The Committee and Gee Publishing, Dec 1992 [Foreword by Adrian Cadbury, chairman] (The Cadbury Report).

Dalton D. R., Daily C. M., Ellstrand A. E. and Johnson J. L. (1998) 'Meta-analytic reviews of board composition leadership structure and financial performance', *Strategic Management Journal*, 19(3), 269–90.

Finkelstein, S. and Mooney, A. C. (2003) 'Not the usual suspects: How to use board process to make boards better', *Academy of Management Executive*, 17(2), 101–13.

Ferkins, L., Shilbury, D. and McDonald, G. (2005) 'The role of the board in building strategic capability: towards an integrated model of sport governance research', *Sport Management Review*, 8, 195–225.

Ferkins, L., Shilbury, D., and McDonald, G. (2009) 'Board involvement in strategy: Advancing the governance of sport organizations', *Journal of Sport Management*, 23(3), 245–77.

Gill, M. (2001) *Governance Do's and Don'ts: Lessons from Case Studies on Twenty Canadian Non-profits, Final Report*, Ottawa, Canada, Institute on Governance.

Heracleous, L. (2001) *What is the Impact of Corporate Governance on Organisational Performance?* Presentation, The 3rd International Conference on Corporate Governance and Direction, Henley Management College, July 2001.

Herman, R. D. and Renz, D. O. (1998) 'Nonprofit organizational effectiveness: contrasts between especially effective and less effective organizations', *Nonprofit Management & Leadership*, 9(1) 23–38.

Herman, R. D., Renz, D. O. and Heimovics, R. D. (1997) 'Board practices and board effectiveness in local nonprofit organizations', *Nonprofit Management and Leadership*, 7, 373–85.

Hilmer, F. G. (1998) *Strictly Boardroom: Improving Governance to Enhance Company Performanc.* (2nd edn), Melbourne, Information Australia.

Hoye, R. (2002) 'Board performance of Australian voluntary sport organisations'. Unpublished thesis. Griffith University, Sydney.

Hoye, R. and Cuskelly, G. (2003) 'Board–executive relationships within voluntary sport organisations', *Sport Management Review*, 6(1), 53–74.

Ingles, S. (1997) 'Roles of the board in amateur sport organisations', *Journal of Sport Management*, 11(2), 160–76.

King, M. E. (2001) 'King committee on corporate governance', Research Paper, South Africa, Institute of Directors in Southern Africa.

—— (2002) 'King committee on corporate governance', Research Paper, South Africa. Institute of Directors in Southern Africa (King II).

Matheson, D. (2004) *The Complete Guide to Good Governance in Organizations and Companies*, Auckland: Profile Books.

Mizruchi, M. S. (1983) 'Who controls whom? An examination of the relationship between management and boards of directors in large American corporations', *Academy of Management Review*, 8, 426–35.

Monks, R. A. G. and Minow, N. (1995) *Corporate Governance*, Oxford, Blackwell Business.

Monks, R. A. G. and Minow, N. (2004) *Corporate Governance* (3rd edn), Oxford, Blackwell Publishing.

Nadler, D. and Tushman, M. L. (1980) 'A Model for Diagnosing Organisational Behaviour', *Organizational Dynamics*, 9(2), 35–51.

Plumptre, T. and Laskin, B. (2003) *From Jeans to Jackets: Navigating the Transition to More Systematic Governance in the Voluntary Sector*, Ottawa, Institute of Governance.

Roberts, J., McNulty, T. and Stiles, P. (2005) 'Beyond agency conceptions of the work of the non-executive director: creating accountability in the boardroom', *British Journal of Management*, Supplement 1, 16, 5–26.

Sport and Recreation New Zealand (SPARC) (2004) *Nine Steps to Good Governance*, [online], available at <http://www.sparc.org.nz/Documents/Sector%20Capability/effective_govt_2nd.pdf> (accessed 30 June 2011).

Strebel, P. (2004) 'The case of contingent governance', *MIT Sloan Management Review*, 45(2), 1532–9194.

Walsh, J. P. and Seward, L. K. (1990) 'On the efficiency of internal and external corporate control mechanisms', *Academy of Management Review*, 15, 421–58.

4

THE PLANNED DEVELOPMENT OF SPORT ORGANIZATIONS

Brian Minikin

Planning happens at all levels of a sport organization. Athletes plan what they are going to do today. Coaches think through training routines and strategies for the next competition. Officials review their performances and look at ways of improving their accuracy and interpretation of the rules. Administrators analyze what they are doing and look for a way forward to improve the capacity of the organization to support all of its activities. Planning may happen naturally as information is processed and decisions are made either consciously or unconsciously. The nature of planning, however, often means that it occurs within a specific context and more usually within a specific frame of activity or perspective.

Planned development in sport is something else altogether. The challenges that face sport administrators today revolve largely around making the best use of planning as a tool for achieving results on the field of play, while at the same time planning for the growth of the organization. The ultimate aim is to grow the organization so that its capacity to deliver effective sport programs improves steadily over time. Planned development is taking a proactive approach to growing the sport by assessing the available alternatives and taking the best possible strategic direction to achieve outcomes that are within the capacity of the organization to obtain.

A sport organization naturally grows in size and complexity, from "kitchen table" to boardroom (Kikulis, Slack and Hinings, 1995), from volunteer administration to professional management (Chelladurai and Madella, 2006), from a pastime to a serious endeavor. Sustained growth in a sport organization requires an understanding of what its core business is and what structures or pillars have been put in place to execute its core business. An example of one such pillar might be governance, or human resources. We then need to know what components make up each pillar and what relationship between these components exists, if any, as the organization grows. By taking this approach we can identify readily what impact changes in one pillar of the organization have on another and this in turn should lead to better planning outcomes. Effective planning for growing a sport organization needs to be fundamentally holistic, but leading to specialized planning as it focuses on the specific pillars of the organization.

This chapter will discuss the rationale for planned development in sport organizations and examine some of the assumptions that are accepted as the norm in the development of sport from an organizational perspective. Its intention is to offer some clarity and focus to planning the development of a sport organization and its capacity to deliver successful sport programs and activities. The focus of the chapter is on the planned development of National Governing Bodies (NGBs), also known as National Federations, National Sport Associations or National Sport Organizations. However, the principles and processes addressed in the chapter are applicable to all sport organizations. The chapter will address three main aspects of planning for sport. It will define planned development, set out the necessity to plan effectively and discuss the creation of plans that have practical, managerial value.

Readers of this chapter will hopefully gain a better understanding of the need to plan as well as the process of planning, learning to appreciate planning as a tool that will enhance how a sport organization does its work and, in particular, make the life of its human resource base, whether voluntary or professional, more effective and satisfying. The chapter ends with a case study of the internal analysis of Fiji Swimming.

Planned development

The measure of success for national sport organizations is often reflected in either medal-winning performances at multi-sport games such as the Olympic Games or Commonwealth Games or recorded success in leagues or championships. To achieve success on the field of play requires a great deal of effort and consistency and sport organizations not only need to compete with others with the same interests but also with organizations that encompass other disciplines or activities as well, as they attempt to lure members and support from the public and sponsors alike. As sport organizations grow to support successful "on-field" performances, they develop in a manner that enables the organization to be managed in a more efficient and effective way and this in turn leads to a need for planning for future growth and development.

Most national sport organizations have been formed according to guidelines that satisfy the recommendations of their respective International Sport Federation (IF). These guidelines provide an adequate platform on which to establish a functional organization that lends itself to a planned and proactive approach to development. Proponents of planning such as government departments and sport funding agencies urge the view that success in sport should be a result of the environment created by the organization rather than a goal in itself. The challenge then, for all sport organizations, is to get their infrastructure properly established so that the output from it is successful performance.

Single-outcome planning, such as supporting a national team, while ignoring other aspects of the organization's activities might achieve this. However, if there are elements of development missing from the organization's overall operational structure it is unlikely that such performance will be sustained. A simple example of this is investing all of the organization's financial resources to support an athlete to win a medal at a major event. While this might be good for the athlete, the short-term gain that might be made will have meant that other areas of the organization have had to forgo their development through lack of finances. In the medium to long run this will further compromise the ability of the organization to support the effort of future athletes.

Success in sport requires multi-dimensional planning and, more importantly, the successful execution of plans. In particular, this means having an understanding of what influence the various managerial functions or pillars that make up the organization have on the overall performance of its administrators, coaches, officials and athletes.

The logic that underlies the planning method described in this chapter accepts the need for organizations to:

- establish a firm base or a foundation from which to build or grow;
- expand gradually within the limits of their human and physical resources;
- take advantage of opportunities as they arise and evolve from current and past achievement;
- strive for perfection and ensure that what is achieved is of the highest quality;
- ensure every step taken leaves a viable legacy that can be expanded upon at a later date.

In essence, organizations need to develop their existing resources and work with what is available before new opportunities present themselves. This is the purpose of planned development.

The temptation for many sport organizations is to aim straight for the top, to "shoot for the stars" without establishing a proper base. The end result is usually disappointing and it will either have cost a lot of money and left very little to show for it, or achieve success without having the capacity to be able to capitalize on it. Some symptoms of this might include:

- establishing a national squad before establishing a national competition framework in the sport;
- spending vital development funds on sending athletes to where they can access facilities for training and competition because they are not available at home;
- employing foreign coaches or human resources at rates well beyond the economic viability of the organization in a bid to gain early success.

Taking short cuts to achieve aspirations that the organization is not ready to take on may retard the growth of the organization and ultimately compromise the overall development of the sport itself. Many sport managers are in favor of gambling on a results-based outcome, in the hope that the outcome will stimulate the development required. The problem with this approach, however, is that if the organization does achieve a successful outcome, it might not be in a position to take advantage of the opportunities for development that arise from it.

For example, if a basketball club invests heavily in a team to win promotion to a higher league it might be unable to accommodate the extra demands placed by the higher level of competition if it hasn't accounted for factors such as the standard of coaching, recruitment of new players, the court the club uses and the competence of those who run the club. By attracting more interest in the team, the club will need access to a court that can hold more spectators and also has a playing surface that meets the expectations of the next level of competition. Without this in place, the opportunities gained by investing in a successful team in isolation from the rest of the club will very likely be lost. This scenario can be avoided with effective planning. Effective planning must ensure that the key components of the organization do not work independently of each other but develop in coordination with the rest of the organization. It is this tenet that should form the basic rationale for planned development.

The need for planned development

Sport organizations operate in an environment that is constantly growing and changing. There is increasing pressure on sport organizations to run their sport professionally in order to maintain or improve their position in the community. National Federations (NFs), associations and clubs face multiple challenges such as increasing costs, rising demand for volunteers/personnel, public liability and a preference for non-sport or activity-based lifestyles among younger people. In addition to competing with other sport disciplines to attract participants and spectator interest, sport organizations also face increasing competition from the entertainment industry and a booming recreation industry that includes electronic games, as well as non-competitive activities and adventure sport.

Consequently sport organizations need to plan strategically if they are to survive and thrive in the modern environment. Boyd (2005) provides the following examples of a strategic thinking approach to specific problems:

- A national federation faces financial difficulties and needs to develop strategies that generate new long-term income sources and minimize costs. Potential strategies could focus on sponsorship from the public and private sector, increasing revenue through membership fees, government grant applications, fundraising events and activities, more accountable financial control and ultimately, commercializing their activities so that they earn revenue and add to the overall asset value of the organization.
- A football club had 39,545 members in 2011. However, the club estimated that it had 1.1 million supporters throughout the country – making the club's nationwide supporter base a major strength. Club management identified that in order to capitalize on this strength, they need to convert these supporters to members by identifying as many of these supporters as possible and developing a greater sense of involvement between them and the club.

The benefits of planning

There are a number of benefits to planning (Chappelet and Bayle, 2005; Gollwitzer, 1996) and some of these include:

- *Increasing the awareness of the operating environment both within the organization and outside of it.* By understanding the forces that are working within and around the organization, volunteers have a better chance of becoming more efficient and more productive with the limited but valuable time that they are contributing.
- *Coping with change in the environment.* As an organization undertakes projects that develop areas of its operating environment, it is likely that these changes will impact other areas of the organization. For example, running a new competition may require the addition of new personnel and access to new facilities. This in turn may impact on the financial procedures and the skills required of volunteers, which will in turn require additional training and preparation and a better communications strategy. Effective planning will assist the organization with these rolling changes.
- *Exerting more control over the organization's destiny.* This means members can decide where they want the organization to be in the future and how to get there. This will provide members with a clear picture of their own roles and responsibilities and enable more effective contribution to the common goal by the members as a whole.
- *Improving the financial performance of the organization.* This engenders confidence by assuring staff and volunteers that monies are being handled responsibly and spent effectively. An organization in a healthy financial position is more likely to provide for the needs of its members.

- *Improving organizational control and coordination of activities.* This will reduce duplication of effort and create an environment that members are happy to operate in. A sign that governance is not achieving this is when a "them and us" mentality develops within the organization, resulting in a lack of respect for decision-makers and the administrative processes that exist within the organization.
- *Providing a sound platform for decision-making and forming other plans.* This should be based on an effective monitoring and evaluation process that provides information accurately and in a timely fashion to the decision-makers.

In more simple terms, Boyd (2005) suggests that strategic planning will assist a sport organization by:

- identifying and building a broad framework that allows an organization to achieve its mission and vision;
- matching the strengths of an organization to available opportunities that arise within the internal and external environment of the organization;
- providing a set of guidelines that guides an organization in the pursuit of its mission and objectives.

These outcomes are usually only achieved with effective planning. The larger and more diverse the organization becomes, the more critical the level of planning needs to become to support it and maintain beneficial outcomes. Many sport organizations prefer not to spend the time planning and still manage to achieve results that are satisfactory to members. However, it is likely that there will come a time when this is no longer the case as the volume of challenges generated by reactive activity becomes unmanageable and difficult to direct effectively. The planning process, however, needs to be as simple as possible so that volunteers are not put off the thought of undertaking this vital activity. The first step in the process of planning often starts with the establishment of a vision and a mission. This will now be discussed.

The benefit of establishing a vision and mission statement

An NGB will have a constitution or administrative rulebook to guide its governance. Furthermore, the majority of sport clubs and associations have a well-established product: the sport itself, which comes with an established set of rules and code of conduct that has been formed and promulgated by its peak body, the International Federation. Armed with these fundamental processes, the organization can quickly establish its mission and vision, around which the actual planning process is driven.

Unfortunately, many sport organizations often become bogged down in trying to develop these and occupy more time working out their vision and mission than actually deciding what it is they are trying to do and how best to achieve it. Some organizations avoid this by keeping to a very simple vision and mission to get the planning process started and then revise these statements with the benefit of hindsight once the planning process is under way.

The vision statement is generally written as an ideal and ultimate long-term outcome or goal for the organization and may be so general that it is never actually achieved. However, a good vision statement establishes the "big picture" for the organization and if properly derived will provide the basis for the branding and market positioning of the organization as it grows and becomes more influential within the community.

Developing the vision can be very difficult, simply because it attempts to bring together the ideas of many and encapsulate them into a simple statement that appeals to everyone. For the majority of sport organizations, a simple concise statement is all that is needed. For example, the Vision for the World Anti Doping Agency (WADA) is "A world that values and fosters doping-free sport." This was adapted by the Oceania Regional Anti Doping Agency, a subset of WADA, to read, "An environment in which doping-free sport is valued and fostered in the Oceania Region." By taking its vision from WADA, the Oceania agency was able to commence its planning process quickly and easily and over time has been able to modify its vision and mission to suit the evolution of its core business specifically for its own operating environment.

Having stated what the organization stands for in its vision, it can then establish its mission. The mission statement is a clear, brief statement of the organization's long-term purpose, core business and values. It is an action statement rather than an outcome statement and should be geared toward attaining the vision of the organization. An example of this might be a mission statement that reads something like this:

> To provide opportunities for the young people of our community to take part in regular competition and training programs, run by well-trained and caring sport leaders.

Once the organization has a clear vision and mission in place it is ready to undertake the planning process.

The planning process – a staged approach

The nature of planning has been well described in planning handbooks and guidelines (Chappelet and Bayle, 2005; Boyd, 2005; SPARC, 2004). However, the planning process in itself can be a long and arduous one, especially for national governing bodies that are volunteer governed and managed (see Chapters 2 and 3). The primary aim of the planning process for a sport organization is to produce a strategic plan that will guide its development and provide a framework for the day–to-day operations of the organization.

A strategic plan is a document that presents a strategic direction, lists objectives, and records the actions that will be taken to meet these objectives. In theory, a strategic plan helps an organization to identify its desired future direction and goals, and then map out a way to achieve them within the constraints of its internal and external environment. For sport organizations these generally cover a three- to five-year period. In the case of Olympic sport organizations, planning tends to occur around the four-year Olympic cycle from one summer Olympic Games to the next. Planning processes for sport organizations are well established (Chappelet and Bayle, 2005). However it is very tempting to make the process a complex and difficult one to manage and implement. The challenge is to keep the process as straightforward as possible.

Essentially it requires four simple stages that refer to the established vision and mission for the organization, which are diagnosis, setting the direction, putting into action and monitoring and evaluation. These are set out below.

Stage one: Diagnosis

This stage focuses on generating an understanding of where the organization is positioned with respect to its internal and external environment and should determine what it can and cannot undertake in order to develop further and achieve results. An important part of any analysis is to review the current strengths, weaknesses, opportunities and threats (SWOT) facing the organization (Morrison, 2008). The SWOT has also been expanded to SCORE (Graves, 2006), an acronym for determining the strengths, challenges, options, responses and effectiveness of an organization. In sport planning the SCORE acronym has been applied to reflect the strengths, constraints, opportunities, risks and expectations surrounding a sport organization. The SCORE approach to organizational analysis has the added benefit of understanding the expectations that lie within the organization.

While a traditional SWOT analysis can be applied to almost any component of an organization, a SWOT or SCORE analysis by itself is not of much use. A good environmental analysis should provide knowledge from which to develop an organization's strategic direction, by identifying what the organization does well, the challenges it faces, and by providing background on the factors that influence the organization's functions and performance. A solid understanding of environmental circumstances will help the organization to think strategically and ultimately survive and prosper.

One good example of a tool that assists with this is the Readiness Assessment Tool (RAT) established by Minikin (2009). This tool attempts to identify and recognize the current level of development of a sport organization across eight pillars and compare this to the level of internal development required for that organization to undertake the activity in question. The tool, in essence, assesses what a sport organization has in place already and what an organization needs to have in place in order to undertake a particular activity. An example of its use in Fiji Swimming is set out at the end of this chapter.

Stage two: Setting the direction

This stage focuses on establishing goals and objectives that take the organization to where it wants to go. Determining the direction that the organization wants to take is based on the establishment of objectives that reflect the current capacity and level of development of an organization and provide a framework for a staged development process that will advance the development of the organization in a systematic and manageable way. It is therefore essential that the first stage of the planning process is completed thoroughly.

When confronted with lists of issues that might need to be addressed the planning process can easily become chaotic. For this reason, planners tend to group issues that cover similar areas affecting the organization into Key Result Areas (KRA) (Minikin, 2009). By categorizing the many issues that are to be considered in planning under a set of pillars it is possible for a sport organization to effectively identify a primary objective for each pillar and then list a set of objectives that will direct the achievement of the mission.

The term "SMART objectives" is used widely in the planning process, and is an acronym used to describe objectives constructed as follows:

- *Specific* objectives detail a specific outcome to be achieved within a pillar. They are characterized by a clearly defined scope and time frame.
- *Measurable* objectives are those that can be quantified in some way so as to gauge whether or not it has been achieved.
- *Achievable* objectives are those that the organization has the necessary resources in place to meet.
- *Realistic* objectives are those that are set within the capabilities of the organization to deal with them.

- *Time* bound objectives clearly set out a time frame by which an expected outcome is to be achieved.

An example of a SMART objective might be:

To enhance the performance of the national team and improve international ranking by taking part in six official ranking tournaments by 2013.

In order for objectives to be considered as SMART, each one will need to be evaluated to determine whether or not it is specific enough, has measurable outcomes, is achievable given the current capacity of the organization, is realistic given the current capabilities of the organization and meets a defined time period or deadline.

If this part of the planning process is done in haste and fails to refer to the analysis carried out earlier in the process, objectives are then set that sound appropriate but are no longer SMART as they become unrealistic or out of touch with the realities of the organization itself. It is essential that once the objectives have been agreed they are referred back to earlier assessments to determine if the organization is ready to pursue these objectives and that the right environmental conditions exist that make it possible to pursue them.

Stage three: Putting into action

This stage focuses on taking the objectives that have been determined and implementing them in a way that will achieve the defined strategies within the limits of the resources available. The aim of stage three is to develop an action plan. The action plan will consist of a number of specific actions that will contribute towards the achievement of the stated objectives within a functional pillar of the organization. This is the 'How To' part of the strategic plan and addresses all the key tasks/actions, including:

- What is to be achieved?
- How will it be achieved?
- How much will it cost?
- When will it be achieved?
- Who will achieve it?
- Why has it to be achieved?
- What will be measured to indicate that it has been achieved?

For each objective listed, planners should consider their options and agree on a strategy that will enable the organization to achieve the objective within the constraints it has identified and the time frame that has been established.

Actions need to be detailed in their construction, be costed, have appropriate resources identified and assigned and the required human resources to complete them. Usually there will be someone from within the organization who is responsible for supervising the completion of each action. In a well-established sport organization this is likely to be done by professional managers or, at the very least, specialized volunteers. For more simple organizations, it is more likely to be a member of the elected board or executive committee.

It is necessary to use verbs when developing a strategy and this language continues through all of the action statements that are to be included. For example, when setting objectives and actions for governance:

- Objective 1: Review the structure of the board of management to reflect changes in the scope of activities being undertaken by the organization, by April 2013.
- Action 1: Complete an internal audit of the organization by November 2012.
- Action 2: Complete an assessment of activity across all aspects of the organization by December 2012.
- Action 3: Conduct a workshop involving board members and other key stakeholders to review the audit and current activity level to determine if the current functions of the board match activities, by January 2013.
- Action 4: Complete a proposal that recommends changes to the structure of the board of management and have this circulated to members by 1 March 2013.
- Action 5: Present any changes proposed to the 2013 Annual General Meeting, along with necessary amendments to the Constitution, if required.

For each of the actions prescribed there needs to be an assessment to ensure that the order and time lines will achieve the objective. This requires the establishment of measurable Key Performance Indicators (KPIs). Generally there are two or three KPIs assigned to any action, but there is no limit provided that the measure being undertaken is specific to the action and relevant to the overall objective being addressed. The KPIs need to:

- reflect the desired end results and outcomes of the action to be measured and the overall objective that the action is working towards;
- target what the organization wants to achieve in quantifiable terms;
- be measurable and quantifiable and must relate directly to the stated outcomes.

Once this is done then the plan should go back to the board and ultimately the Annual General Meeting for approval, be signed off formally and approval given to those responsible to proceed.

Examples of KPIs for an objective that relates to improving the performance of the National Team might be:

The national senior and junior squads to have completed, at minimum:

- twelve sessions with top-level international coaches during the period 2012–2014;
- four sport science sessions (one video analysis and three fitness testing) by qualified sport/exercise science professionals throughout the same period of time;
- one international tour by the end of 2013.

The process of developing action plans for each stated objective under each key result area is complex and needs to follow a logical sequence. However, once in place the reporting and function of the organization should proceed in a clear and efficient way.

It is worthy of note that action plans are established based on the objectives provided but often within the framework of an organizational pillar. This provides a means of developing job descriptions or work plans, but runs the risk of targeting individual organizational pillars so that they are developed in isolation from the rest of the organization. A simple example of this might be the classification of an organization's performance on the basis of its team's competitive performance, as reflected by medal-winning performances or standings on a premiership ladder. Such an approach might ignore or disregard important advances that have been made in other areas of their operations, such as human resource development, facilities and equipment, sponsorship and marketing, all of which were stimulated by a successful strategic delivery of a medal-winning team. Furthermore, for sport organizations with limited resources, the temptation to concentrate on one or two organizational pillars while ignoring the rest can lead to an imbalance in the organization's development. Minikin (2009) proposes that such imbalances may eventually compromise the achievements made by the organization, because they become unsustainable.

Consequently, balanced planning across all of the organizational pillars is necessary. This is best achieved by planning the progress in each pillar in accordance with an understanding of the influence of elements within one pillar on the elements that exist across the rest of the pillars. For example, in planning to establish a national league competition, it is important to understand how the establishment of this sport activity will impact on the demand for human resources, physical resources, finance and communications and ensure that these pillars have or will have what is needed to be able to support the establishment and maintenance of a national league. Planning for a national league without taking into account the pressures on the organization as a whole may well lead to failure of both the establishment of the national league and the effective development of the organization itself. It is for this reason that the final stage in the planning process becomes essential.

Stage four: Monitoring and evaluation

This stage focuses on determining if the established objectives are being achieved and if the strategies chosen are effective in achieving them. The overall effectiveness of the planning process for sport is often difficult to determine if only quantitative evaluation frameworks are applied. These tend to measure the implementation of programs such as coaching courses for sport organizations and the parameters measured usually include quantitative measures such as:

- Number of courses held
- Number of coaches achieving certification
- Funds distributed.

While these measures might tell us whether or not programs have been implemented, they do not address the more important indicators of how much improvement in the quality of coaching has occurred, or whether or not the funds could have been spent more effectively. It is reasonable to suggest that as part of the planning process, a more comprehensive monitoring and evaluation framework will be constructed that will enable the sport organization to not only measure its performance against specific KPIs but also determine whether, as a result of the action completed, there has been a measurable improvement in the overall performance of the sport organization. (See Chapter 6 for more information on performance management and measurement.)

Implementation of the plan

For many organizations, the planning process is an end in itself. It is one thing to develop a plan and quite another to implement it. Before embarking on the planning process, sport organizations must commit themselves to follow it and work to it, otherwise the document will become no more than window dressing. The following six points are essential to the effective implementation of a strategic plan.

First, all decision-making and reporting should link to the strategic plan. Progress reports for actions occurring in each of the organizational pillars must be included on the agenda for board meetings and reported to the Annual General Meeting. The plan itself should be readily available to all members and stakeholders, and reports need to refer to the relevant section of the plan at all times. In doing so, the plan will become a "living document" and achieve its purpose of bringing together the members for a common cause. It also means that if projects are being entered into that have not been addressed in the plan, appropriate questions can be asked and the accountability of board members is guaranteed.

Second, the allocation of financial, human and physical resources to the strategies outlined in the plan needs to be a formal process that is reported during the monitoring and evaluation phase. This should be agreed to at the Annual General Meeting when budgets are passed. A well-functioning organization will find this process very easy to do once the plan is in place and being implemented.

Third, key stakeholders must all agree and sign off on the relevant sections of the strategic plan that relate to them. This is particularly important for sponsors, who need to know exactly how their contributions are to be used in the organization and what outcomes they will achieve.

Fourth, it is important that all strategies chosen are in line with the ethics and values being promoted within the organization. For example, the organization may promote healthy living as part of its values and this would be compromised if funds were accepted from a tobacco company to support their activities.

Fifth, risk management strategies should be incorporated into the management of the organization and these need to consider the risks involved with implementing and managing the strategies. By undertaking this additional level of thinking, sport organizations become aware of the potential consequences of actions they undertake and can anticipate problems if and when they arise.

Finally, policies and procedures will change as a consequence of development and managers must be ready to address these and ensure that changes are made to the organization's constitution or statutes, in line with the strategies outlined in the plan.

Case study

Fiji Swimming Association and the use of a Readiness Assessment Tool (RAT)

The Fiji Swimming Association has made major strides in its development over the past ten years, lifting its membership by many hundreds of active swimmers, educating its coaches and officials and improving its overall performances at regional competitions. After reviewing the current plan, it was agreed that a fresh approach was needed to assessing the planning needs of the association.

The RAT is a tool that has emerged from a program of mixed methods research carried out with those within the Olympic Movement familiar with the key activities undertaken by NGBs (Robinson and Minikin, 2011). The research, carried out between 2008 and 2009, comprised focus groups, workshops and scenario testing with senior sport administrators and managers from the Oceania region. The RAT is based on eight functional pillars of performance that contain a number of organizational elements that become increasingly complex as an organization develops. The pillars identified were:

- Governance: including rules and regulations, policies and strategic planning.
- Management: including organizational structure and role development.
- Physical resources: including equipment (sport and administrative), facilities access and availability.
- Human resources: including type and diversity as well as planning and management practices.
- Finance: including record keeping, marketing and planning.
- Communication: including methods used, responsiveness and technology available.
- Sport activity: including competition or preparing for competition, development programs and training.
- Values: cultural, attitudinal and behavioral values that are most essential at any given point of development.

In the case of Fiji Swimming, the RAT was employed to identify the current level of development of the association and what areas needed to be prioritized in terms of organizational development in order for the association to achieve its stated ambition of being successful at regional competition. The application of the RAT to Fiji Swimming is set out in Figure 4.1, which summarizes the scores on the NF Assessment. This averages the stage of development on a scale of 1–4 within each of the above eight pillars. Fiji Swimming shows an average of 2.29, which indicates a moderately well-developed organization overall with its sport activity more developed than its remaining pillars. The results of the assessment indicated balanced development, and specific weaknesses were identified within the pillars of finance, human resources and physical resources.

A readiness assessment of the organization indicates that there are programs being undertaken by Fiji Swimming that it does not appear to be ready to undertake. These include advanced coach training, attendance at world championships and even successful attendance at regional championships.

In order to bring the association up to a level where it could theoretically be able to undertake the activities it aspires towards, the elements set out in Table 4.1 were identified as needing attention.

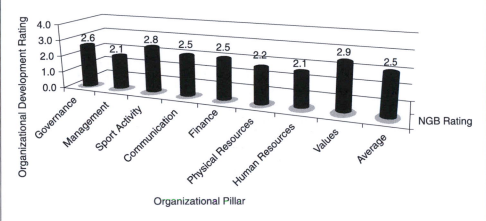

Figure 4.1 Development assessment of Fiji Swimming

Table 4.1 Recommendations for Fiji Swimming

Pillar	Recommendation
Governance	Revise the constitution in order to better cope with the increasing demands being placed on Fiji Swimming.
	Improve the structure of the board by assigning specific portfolios to board members that address the established key result areas of the organization.
	Revise the membership criteria for the national body and determine if it is feasible to move from club affiliation to Association or Regional affiliation (groups of clubs).
	Establish a written strategic plan that specifically addresses the aspirations of the organization based on the needs identified in the RAT analysis.
	Revise the "code of conduct" to include all areas of the Association's operation and ensure that it is fully understood by the members of the Federation.
Management	Establish formal subcommittees that oversee activities of the Association conducted under each of the organization's pillars.
	Construct an operations manual that reflects the current structure of the Board (urgent).
	Put in place a specialized competition management team that separates coaches from officials.
	Establish a coordinated Risk Management Plan that addresses areas of potential litigation against the Association.
	Improve the reporting structure for all meetings held and ensure that all Executive Board decisions are verified by the AGM.
Finance	Apply significant attention to fundraising strategies. Need to generate significant and reliable income that can provide a platform for meeting the costs of the Association's aspirations.
	Establish consistent income from competitions and at least aim to break even.
	Improve the merchandising program and target people from outside Fiji Swimming.
	Establish income streams from investments and/or term deposits.
Sport activity	Establish regular high-level training programs for athletes under the supervision of specialized coaches.
	Establish a competition program that schedules events to be held all year round and that are appropriately graded by age and standard.
	Ensure that Fiji Swimming is positioned so that it can take part in "sport for development" initiatives, such as HIV awareness, drowning awareness and prevention, and boating safety programs.
	Introduce a more sophisticated incentive system for members including recognition, awards, scholarships, career development opportunities and cash prizes.
Physical resources	Acquire sufficient equipment that is fully compliant with IF standards that will support the competition framework required to meet the Association's aspirations.
	Acquire IF standard competition and training uniforms.
	Own or lease simple club facilities for the Association.
	Acquire a dedicated and reasonably well-equipped office.

	Acquire secure access to dedicated training facilities that meet national standards.
Human resources	Group Clubs into associations or regions that conduct their own regular competitions and training programs.
	Implement a graded education program for developing Technical Officials that are specialized with some formal training in place.
	Review gender equity policies and ensure that equal opportunities for competition and training are provided.
	Review the gender demographics in administration and coaching to see if they reflect athlete ratios of male and female swimmers.
Communication	Produce regular media releases by dedicated public relations volunteers.
	Establish a high-quality periodical membership publication.
	Establish an email and text messaging contact network among members.
	Initiate regular features in all forms of media.

With the information gained from the RAT, Fiji Swimming are now in a better position to review their current objectives and plan towards the implementation of programs that would assist the organization to further develop. The RAT assessment and its recommendations are intended only to be a guide to the overall development planning for Fiji Swimming. By establishing objectives that systematically put into place within the organization the criteria considered necessary for it to achieve its mission, Fiji Swimming could now plan with confidence, knowing that the actions it was taking would ultimately lead it to be in a state of readiness to achieve its stated mission.

Summary

This chapter has discussed the way that sport managers can go about the planned development of their organizations. In summary, the planning process should be simple and easy to follow and the following elements contribute towards the construction of a plan that will lead to a better organization:

- Make the plan achievable: Develop a realistic planning document that defines achievable objectives for the sport.
- Carry out a thorough analysis: Develop a plan based on a thorough analysis of the sport's current situation, its internal strengths and weaknesses and external opportunities and threats.
- Get stakeholder buy-in: Make sure that planning processes are inclusive of, and agreed to by, key stakeholders such as associations, clubs and other members.
- Develop a professional document: The strategic plan should be comprehensive, relevant, manageable, logically presented and easy to follow.
- Plan for implementation: The roles and responsibilities of who, how, when and where the plan will be implemented are clearly defined and agreed to by all involved.

If these principles are followed, managers will be able to carefully plan the development of their organizations and achieve strategic success.

References

Boyd, P. (2005) *Forging Future Success: A Strategic Planning Guide for Fiji's National Sport Federations*, Fiji, Fiji Association of Sport and National Olympic Committee.

Chappelet, J. L. and Bayle, E. (2005) *Strategic and Performance Management of Olympic Sport Organisations*, Champaign, Human Kinetics.

Chelladurai, P. and Madella, A. (2006) *Human Resource Management in Olympic Sport Organisation.* Champaign, Human Kinetics.

Gollwitzer, P. M. (1996) 'The volitional benefits of planning', in M. Gollwitzer and J. A. Barch (eds.) *The Psychology of Action: Linking Cognition and Motivation to Behavior*, New York, The Guilford Press.

Graves, T. (2006) *An introduction to SCORE. Beyond SWOT analysis: strategy, capability and effectiveness*, Colchester, Teradian Consulting.

Kikulis, L. M., Slack, T. and Hinings, C. R. (1995) 'Toward an understanding of the role of agency and choice in the changing structure of Canada's national sport organizations', *Journal of Sport Management*, 9, 135–52.

Minikin, B. (2009) 'A Question of Readiness', *Unpublished MEMOS Project*. Lausanne, Olympic Solidarity.

Morrison, M. (2008) 'History of the SWOT Analysis', *RapidBi's Weblog – OD, L&D*, http://rapidbi. wordpress.com/2008/12/29/history-of-the-swot-analysis/, accessed April 2011.

Peters, M. (2005) 'Editorial comment', *AusSport*, 2(3), 1.

Robinson, L. and Minikin, B. (2011) 'The strategic capacity of Olympic Sport Organisations', *Sport, Business and Management: An International Journal*, 1(3).

Slack, T. and Parent, M. (2004) *Understanding Sport Organizations: The Application of Organization Theory* (2nd edn), Champaign, Human Kinetics.

SPARC (2004) *Strategic and Business Planning*, Sport and Recreation New Zealand. [online] available at <www.sparc.org.nz>, accessed 22 April 2011.

Theodoraki, E. I. and Henry, I. P. (1994) 'Organizational structures and contexts in British national governing bodies of sport', *International Review for the Sociology of Sport*, 26, 83–97.

5

MANAGING CUSTOMER EXPECTATIONS OF SPORT ORGANIZATIONS

Leigh Robinson

Introduction

Over the last three decades the management of service quality has been of paramount importance to managers of sport organizations. However, more recently the concept of customer expectations has grown in prominence for a number of reasons. First, in many countries there has been a sustained government drive for improved satisfaction with public services amongst the general public. Second, sport funding agencies such as Sport England have become increasingly concerned with stakeholder satisfaction with National Governing Bodies. Satisfaction, as we will see below, is based on expectations. Finally, expectations of some sport organizations have grown to such an extent that they may be impossible to meet and thus need to be carefully managed (Robinson, 2006). Therefore understanding customer expectations is an issue of importance to contemporary sport managers. This is because expectations impact both on assessments of the quality of a sport organization and on customers' satisfaction with the organization.

This chapter begins by setting out the relationship between expectations, satisfaction and quality. It goes on to discuss the types of expectations that customers have and how these are formed. The chapter then sets out a framework to assist with the management of customer expectations. Finally, the chapter presents a case study of research carried out with the membership of the Amateur Swimming Association, in England, which demonstrates how important it is to manage customer expectations.

Expectations, service quality and customer satisfaction

Coye (2004) has argued that expectations are beliefs about a future event that are developed from information received from a variety of sources. These expectations then act as comparators in the evaluation of the service received (Coye, 2004; Niedrich et al., 2005; Parasuraman et al., 1985). Walker (1995) has suggested that expectations are predictions about what is likely to happen in the service exchange and that these are used as a reference against which comparisons of performance are carried out. Thus they are used by customers to evaluate whether they are happy with the service or not.

Customers have two different types of expectation for services. First, customers expect services to provide certain attributes and use these expectations to make judgments about service quality (Bolton and Drew, 1991; Boulding et al., 1993; Grönroos, 1984; Parasuraman et al., 1985, 1994a, 1994b). Knowledge of what customers expect from sport organizations allows managers to identify what is important to customers when they use these services. For example, if a customer expects a facility to provide activities for children and these are not provided, the customer will be unhappy with the service no matter how good other aspects are.

Second, customers have expectations of each service encounter and these shape feelings of satisfaction with the service (Coye, 2004; Murray and Howat, 2002; Wong, 2004). These expectations are perceptual in nature, as satisfaction with a service is determined by the customer's perception of how well the service encounter has met their expectations of it, rather than by any attributes provided by the service. For example, although a facility may provide a car park, if a customer has to park at the far end of the car park and misses the start of their activity, they are likely to feel dissatisfied with the service, perceiving the car park not to have met their expectations. Alternatively, if they do not miss the start of their activity the fact that they had to park at the far end of the car park is likely to have little or no impact on their satisfaction with the service.

The distinction has been made between the two concepts by arguing that expectations leading to satisfaction consist of what a customer thinks a service firm *has* to offer, while expectations leading to perceptions of service quality are what a customer thinks a service firm *should* offer (Parasuraman et al., 1994b) Alternatively, satisfaction can be considered as an outcome that emerges from the experience of the service, while service quality is concerned with the attributes of the service itself (Crompton and MacKay, 1989). Using the example above, a car park has been provided to meet expectations of quality, but whether a customer is satisfied with the car park is determined by the impact of car parking on their service encounter. Perceived service quality is generally accepted as a long-run, overall evaluation of the service and customer satisfaction as a transaction-specific measure of the experience (Cronin and Taylor, 1994; Parasuraman et al., 1994a; Wong, 2004).

Types of customer expectations

Research carried out by Boulding et al. (1993) demonstrated that expectations are not one-dimensional. They argued that expectations can be divided into *will* expectations and *should* expectations. Will expectations refer to what customers perceive will happen in their next service encounter, while should expectations are what customers expect should occur. For example, when watching an international rugby match, spectators expect that they will be able to see the entire pitch, but will also expect that other spectators will be able to as well. Walker (1995) differentiated between *active* expectations that are consciously anticipated by the customer and *passive* expectations that customers are not aware of until they are not met. In this instance, a spectator would actively expect to be able to buy refreshments at the match, but only become aware of their expectations about the range of refreshments if this range was either limited or extensive.

A more detailed typology of expectations has been developed by Ojasalo (2001) through research carried out with recruitment services. Ojasalo (2001) has argued that customers have six types of expectations: fuzzy, implicit, unrealistic, precise, explicit and realistic. Customers have *fuzzy* expectations when they expect the service provider to deliver 'something', but they do not have a precise picture of what this may be. For example, customers consider that the service is not value for money, but are not sure why. *Implicit* expectations are rarely thought about by customers as these refer to situations or characteristics of the service that are perceived to be so self-evident that they are only noted if they are missing. This type of expectation, which is similar in concept to passive expectations (Walker, 1995), is difficult to manage as they often become obvious when something has gone wrong. *Unrealistic* expectations cannot be met and these are the main reason why managers need to establish what customers expect of their sport services.

On the positive side, *precise* expectations are the opposite of fuzzy expectations, as customers know exactly what they expect to be delivered. *Explicit* expectations, similar in nature to those Walker (1995) called active, can be identified and expressed. Most importantly, *realistic* expectations are those that sport providers can actually deliver to customers. In his discussion of the management of customers' expectations Ojasalo (2001: 210) concluded that managers need to 'focus fuzzy expectations, reveal implicit expectations and calibrate unrealistic ones'.

Influencing and shaping customer expectations is a complex process (Boulding et al., 1993; Coye, 2004; Ojasalo, 2001; Robinson, 2006). However, the delivery of required levels of service relies upon customers having expectations of services that are precise, explicit and realistic, rather than fuzzy, implicit and unrealistic (Ojasalo, 2001; Robinson, 2006). The following section discusses the ways in which customer expectations are formed.

Influences on customer expectations

A number of arguments have been made for attempting to influence customer expectations. Parasuraman et al. (1988) proposed that perceptions of services could be improved either by increasing perceptions or by managing expectations to a lower level. As mentioned earlier, Boulding et al. (1993) also supported the need for the management of expectations in order to improve perceptions of services. Ojasalo (2001) suggested that expectations management would allow the creation of long-term customer relationships through the provision of long-term high quality, while Coye (2004), Robinson (2006) and Robledo (2001) have all argued for the need to influence expectations to ensure that they remain realistic.

Perhaps the most compelling argument for attempting to influence expectations is that not only do customers expect more than they perceive they get, but they are becoming increasingly demanding of service providers (Douglas and Connor, 2003; Donnelly and Shiu, 1999). Arguably, quality management strategies have been responsible for increasing customer expectations of services. Robinson (1999) found that as quality management techniques raised the level of service offered to customers, they began to expect ongoing improvements. Walsh (1991) also identified that as people become used to a service they begin to expect more. The current level of quality becomes the norm, forcing levels of quality to increase to align themselves with rising expectations. For example, if a health and fitness facility supplies members with clean towels, this is initially seen as adding value, and thus quality, to the service. Over time, however, this becomes the expectation and instead of valuing the towels, members may begin to complain about their colour, texture or size. Managers then have to respond to these complaints in order to meet expectations.

In order to prevent this from occurring, managers need to be able to work with expectations in order to prevent or to slow down this rise in expectations. Control of customer expectations is arguably unrealistic (Robinson, 2006) and therefore what managers should do is attempt to manage, influence and shape customer expectations of service quality to bring these into line with the levels of service they are able to deliver. In order to do this, managers need to understand how expectations are created and updated. Although the process of expectation formation is not clearly understood (Coye, 2004; Robledo, 2001) there are a number of other factors that are believed to be instrumental in influencing customer expectations.

Past experience

ıe organization is considered to be the main factor that shapes experience
ıd Drew, 1991; Boulding et al., 1993; Coye, 2004; Douglas and Connor,
ͻ2; Kang and James, 2004; MORI, 2002; Parasuraman et al., 1994a;
ͻ01). Familiarity with the service will increase the likelihood of realist expecta-
ıııs, although O'Neil and Palmer (2003) have identified that prior users of a service have
more complex expectations of it than those without prior use. It would appear that more
detailed knowledge of a service promotes multifaceted expectations, although these may be
more realistic due to experience.

Previous experience of similar services is also useful in forming expectations, particularly
if a customer has no prior experience of the service (Bolton and Drew, 1991; Boulding et al.,
1993; Coye, 2004; Douglas and Connor, 2003; Grönroos, 1982; Kang and James, 2004;
O'Neil and Palmer, 2003; Robledo, 2001). The assumption is that the service to be received
will reflect that experienced elsewhere. From a service provider perspective this is not always
beneficial as high levels of service experienced elsewhere create high expectations for all
similar services (Boulding et al., 1993).

Customer needs

Ojasalo (2001) considers customer needs to be the natural trigger for expectations as needs
provide the reason for choosing to make use of a service. It is also suggested that the more
important the need, the higher the expectation of the service (Bolton and Drew, 1991;
Grönroos, 1982; MORI, 2002; Parasuraman et al., 1994b; Ting and Chen, 2002). Arguably,
if sport providers are able to identify the most important needs of their customers they can
influence expectations (Ting and Chen, 2002). However, the impact of needs on expectations may not be this simple, as O'Neil and Palmer (2003) have established that not only do
customers have diverse needs, but the relative priority of their needs may change, causing a
change in expectations. This may occur over time, or because of a change in circumstances
such as visiting with friends or children.

Word of mouth

Word of mouth communications from family, friends, staff or other credible sources
allows people to form an expectation of services they have yet to use. Word of mouth
also acts to change or reinforce existing expectations (Bolton and Drew, 1991; Boulding
et al., 1993; Coye, 2004; Grönroos, 1982; Parasuraman et al., 1994a). Indeed, Robledo
(2001) has argued that this is the most influential source of expectations, an argument
supported by Clow et al. (1997) and Grace and O'Cass (2005), who noted that consumers
rely heavily on this type of communication when forming impressions about an
organization.

Due to the personal nature of this type of communication (Clow et al., 1997; Grace and
O'Cass, 2005), customers are more likely to believe information they are told from sources
they perceive to be credible than information they read. In some cases word of mouth
information will override a customer's past experience of an organization. Consequently,
Ojasalo (2001) and Grace and O'Cass (2005) have argued that word of mouth has the highest
potential of all antecedent factors to generate unrealistic expectations.

Market communications

Advertisements, publicity material, personal selling and contracts make explicit promises to customers about the attributes of the service the organization will deliver (Grace and O'Cass, 2005; Ojasalo, 2001; Zeithaml et al., 1993). Implicit promises are also made about quality, value for money, reliability and reputation through the image, branding and price communicated in market communications. As promises are antecedents to expectations (Ojasalo, 2001; Zeithaml et al., 1993) customers use these promises in the formation of their expectations.

In their discussion of expectations Boulding et al. (1993) outlined the importance of market communications on expectations, arguing that if the communications of an organization promise high quality, or to increase services, then customers will expect this to happen, raising their expectations in anticipation. Rosen et al. (2003) noted that if the marketing function promises too much, expectations are likely to exceed perceptions of the service delivered. Thus, market communications impact on the formation of expectations by establishing how services can be accessed, what will be experienced and at what level of quality (Boulding et al., 1993; Coye, 2004; Grönroos, 1982; Parasuraman et al., 1994b; Robledo, 2001).

Image

Research carried out by Clow et al. (1997) found that image was an important antecedent of customer expectations and for some service organizations it was the most important influence. Clow et al. (1997) argued that this is because image allows customers to 'see and perceive' an organization and thus has a significant impact on expectations. This argument had been previously made by Grönroos (1982, 1984, 1988), who argued that the positive or negative view of an organization created by its image impacts on what customers expect. In addition, the research carried out by Ojasalo (2001) showed that image is particularly important in terms of unrealistic expectations as it can both create and overcome this type of expectation.

The management of expectations

In terms of sport organizations, a number of these factors act and interact on customer expectations and allow them to develop a framework that they then use to evaluate the service in terms of service quality and customer satisfaction. Figure 5.1 outlines these and proposes a number of areas where managers can intervene in an attempt to influence customer expectations of their service.

It is important to note that managers will not necessarily want to lower expectations. Coye (2004: 63) noted that the management of expectations may have the intention of 'raising, lowering or making salient, initial expectations' of a service. Ojasalo (2001) argued that expectations should be realistic, neither too high nor too low. Boulding et al. (1993) discussed the need to manage *will* expectations upwards and *should* expectations downwards in order to improve perceptions of service quality. In addition, low expectations of services may lead customers to choose other providers and therefore managers may wish to raise expectations in order to be considered competitive. For example, UK public sport providers offering health and fitness services have had to raise customer expectations of their services in order to be perceived as a viable alternative to the high-quality commercial market.

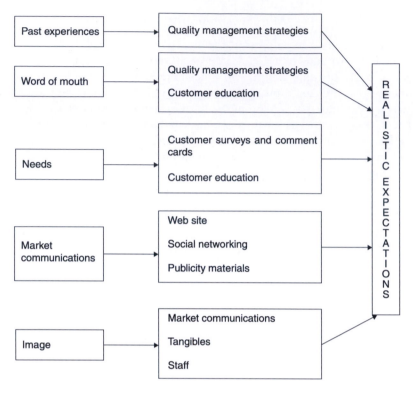

Figure 5.1 The management of customer expectations

Past experience

As can be seen from Figure 5.1, managers have the opportunity to directly influence expectations formed by past experience of the organization through their quality management strategies, although they have no control over past experiences of competitor organizations. Quality management strategies can also influence expectations formed by word of mouth, as can organizational image (Grönroos, 1984; Ojasalo, 2001). Determining the needs of customers by market segment is an activity that most sport organizations carry out as a matter of course (Chelladurai, 2005; Nichols and Robinson, 2000; Taylor, 2011), although this may be an area that the voluntary sector needs to address more fully (Weed et al., 2005). Research that allows the needs of different segments to be established makes it more likely that customer expectations will be met as, first, managers can establish what the needs are and second, they can tailor services to meet these.

Customer education

In addition to this type of customer research, direct intervention in the formation of expectations is required. Described by Robledo (2001) as a consumer education programme and by Robinson (2004) as dialogue, strategies that expose customers to the realities of what can be offered will facilitate the development of realistic expectations (Ojasalo, 2001). It is apparent that customer education strategies can take a variety of forms. Douglas and Connor (2003) discuss the need for a partnership between provider and consumer so that both understand the needs of the other. Nichols and Robinson (2000) have provided evidence of UK public sport and leisure providers using focus groups to ask customers to make choices about the funding of certain services, while Zeithaml and Bitner (1996) propose communicating the realities of the industry to the customer.

What is clear is that customer education is more than the collection of customer opinions. The goal of this intervention is to increase customer understanding of the constraints facing the organization and the impact of expectations on this. In sport organizations this may be accomplished by 'encouraging a customer to increase his/her level of participation in the delivery system so that he/she understands better the capabilities of the delivery process' (Coye, 2004: 66).

Market communications

Managers can use marketing communications to directly influence expectations. (Yu, 2007). Material on websites or social media, such as Facebook and Twitter, as well as printed materials such as leaflets allows managers to set realistic expectations of the service. These provide an opportunity for pricing policies to be stated, programming objectives to be communicated and standards of service to be set. They also provide the opportunity to provide information about the attributes of the service provided and to highlight future service changes and the rationale for these.

Image

Finally, it is also apparent that managing the image of the organization allows providers to influence expectations as an organization's image creates expectations of what a customer can expect. Clow et al. (1997: 241) argued that managing image is a critical function as

> Customers with a high image of a service firm will tend to believe they are being treated well by the firm's personnel. They will also tend to believe the service outcome either meets or exceeds what they expected. The reverse is true for firms or organizations for which consumers have a low image.

Therefore the careful management of an appropriate image appears to allow providers to influence expectations. In her paper evaluating models of corporate identity, Stuart (1999) noted that organizational image can be constructed by the careful control of the messages that are delivered by market communications and brand, strategic documents, the physical tangibles of the organization (i.e. facilities, equipment, logos or mascots) and staff (Stuart, 1999; Ojasalo, 2001). Clow et al. (1997) highlight how price, advertising and tangible cues will have an impact on how customers view and use a service and therefore what they expect.

For example, as mentioned earlier, in order to compete in the health and fitness market, UK public providers had to raise expectations of the service they could offer. In order to do this, providers created an image of the service that was intended to be perceived by customers as being as good as that of commercial providers. This was done by a number of mechanisms. First, the service was offered on a membership basis only; second, state of the art equipment was purchased or leased; third, the ABC1 market was targeted; and finally, managers created a physical or conceptual separation of the health and fitness service from other services offered by the public facilities.

Case study

Member expectations of the Amateur Swimming Association (ASA)

Stakeholder satisfaction is of natural concern to all organizations that wish to function effectively. It is of greater concern to those organizations, such as the ASA (the governing body for swimming in England), which need to consider the satisfaction of both member and non-member groups, as this often leads to diverse and conflicting stakeholder objectives. It is therefore important that solid research evidence is available regarding stakeholder satisfaction to understand stakeholder requirements and to plan effectively.

In order to do this, the ASA commissioned a five-year, longitudinal assessment of satisfaction with its services, which is intended to understand satisfaction with and knowledge of the organization's activities and to generate recommendations for improvements in performance. The findings of the first stage of the research are set out below, and primarily constitute a benchmarking of levels of member satisfaction in order to identify areas for development and to provide a standard against which to assess future levels of satisfaction.

The research was carried out via an online questionnaire survey made available to all members. Members were asked about themselves (age, gender, length of membership), their knowledge of the activities of the ASA and their satisfaction with the organization. The sample completing this questionnaire was 1,142, which means the findings are statistically representative of the current ASA membership. The findings of the questionnaire were subject to SPSS analysis and the results below focus on knowledge and satisfaction.

Knowledge of ASA activities

Respondents were asked to indicate how much they knew about the work of the ASA across various areas. Table 5.1 shows that there is a limited understanding of some areas of the ASA and thus a need

Table 5.1 Knowledge of the work of the ASA

Area of work	I know about it	I've heard about it	I haven't heard about it
With pool providers to improve the swimming experience	28	39	33
Learn to swim	39	44	17
Developing and education of teachers, coaches, volunteers and officials	59	31	10
Young volunteers	35	37	28
Equality	36	35	29
Child safeguarding and protection	67	24	9
Promotion of health for the government	34	45	21
Facility advice and expertise	24	41	35
Lifelong participation and recreational swimming	38	44	18
Developing talent	61	29	9
Fundraising to support activities	22	39	39
Developing clubs	46	37	17
Staging competitions	64	25	11
Pool operators and local authorities	28	39	33

for greater information and communication about the work of the ASA. There is familiarity with the work that directly impacts on members, such as child safeguarding and competitions, but there are a number of aspects that are less well known that are important to the objectives of the ASA, such as work with pool providers. Increasing awareness of all of the activities of the ASA seems important to ensure that members understand the activities their membership supports. In addition, this lack of knowledge of the work of the ASA makes it difficult for members to assess satisfaction with their membership as they lack expectations that can be used for comparison.

Satisfaction with membership

Respondents were asked to indicate their overall level of satisfaction with their membership. Table 5.2 shows that only 40 per cent of members were satisfied with their membership, although only 19 per cent were dissatisfied. Interestingly, a significant percentage of members rated themselves as neutral in terms of satisfaction, a finding that was replicated when asking in more detail about specific services.

There are a number of possible reasons for these findings. First, members may not know what to expect of their membership and therefore have not considered in any detail whether they are satisfied or not. Once again, this suggests a need to create member expectations so that they have a comparison for assessing satisfaction with the service. Second, it is possible that many members do not consider their membership to be with the ASA, but with their club. Therefore, they have no strong feelings about their ASA membership and thus are neither satisfied nor dissatisfied. Finally, as Table 5.1 suggests, the work of the ASA is not particularly well known or understood and therefore some respondents may have been cautious about assessing satisfaction in light of a perception of limited knowledge.

Discussion and recommendations

This research indicates that a significant number of members are neutral about their satisfaction with the ASA services, opportunities and their membership. When this is considered alongside the number of respondents who did not know about aspects of the ASA, it is clear that there is a need to create expectations, which provides an opportunity for the organization to actively manage them. Converting the 'neutrals' and 'don't knows' to 'satisfied' appears a more worthwhile strategy than trying to make those who are dissatisfied more satisfied.

Table 5.2 Overall satisfaction with membership

Level of satisfaction	Percentage
Very dissatisfied	4
Dissatisfied	15
Neutral	37
Satisfied	33
Very satisfied	7
Don't know	3

N = 1142

In line with this, the main recommendation that emerges from the above results is a need for much greater communication, information and education about the work of the ASA, particularly its activities with external stakeholders. This will raise awareness of what the organization does and allow members to create expectations that can be used to assess satisfaction. Most importantly, this will create expectations that reflect the reality of the current operating context of the organization.

Conclusion

This chapter has argued that managers need to take a proactive approach to the management of customer expectations of sport organizations. Although *a posteriori* measures of service quality are common, managers should seek to influence customer expectations of service quality prior to service experience. This will facilitate the formation of realistic customer expectations of the level of service quality to be offered by the organization.

The model discussed in this chapter proposed a number of ways in which managers can seek to influence expectations prior to experience. Quality management activities form an important part of this process; however, consultation needs to become educational so that service issues can be debated and resolved to the satisfaction of both customers and the organization. In addition, although no doubt already considered by many managers, more attention should be paid to creating and/or maintaining a good image of the organization. The interventions proposed will lead to levels of service that are appropriate for both the customer and the organization.

References

Bolton, R. N. and Drew, J. H. (1991) 'A multistage model of customers' assessments of service quality and value', *Journal of Consumer Research*, 17 (March), 375–84.

Boulding, W., Kalra, A., Staelin, R. and Zeithaml, V. (1993) 'A dynamic process model of service quality: from expectations to behavioural intentions', *Journal of Marketing Research*, Feb, 7–27.

Burns, R. C., Graefe, A. R. and Absher, J. D. (2003) 'Alternate measurement approaches to recreational customer satisfaction: satisfaction-only versus gap scores', *Leisure Sciences*, 25, 363–80.

Chelladurai, P. (2005) *Managing Organizations for Sport and Physical Activity* (2nd edn), Arizona, Holcomb Hathaway Publishers.

Chen, I., Gupta, A. and Rom, W. (1994) 'A study of price and quality in service operations', *International Journal of Service Industry Management*, 5(2), 23–33.

Clow, K. E., Kurtz, D. L., Ozment, J., and Soo Ong, B. (1997) 'The antecedents of consumer expectations of services: an empirical study across four industries', *Journal of Services Marketing*, 11(4), 230–48.

Coye, R. W. (2004) 'Managing customer expectations in the service encounter', *International Journal of Service Management*, 15(1), 54–71.

Crompton, J. L. and MacKay, K. J. (1989) 'Users perceptions of the relative importance of service quality dimensions in selected public recreation programs', *Leisure Sciences*, 4, 367–75.

Cronin, J and Taylor, S. (1992) 'Measuring service quality: A re-examination and extension', *Journal of Marketing*, 56 (July), 55–68.

—— (1994) 'SERVPERF versus SERVQUAL: Reconciling performance-based perceptions-minus-expectations measurement of service quality', *Journal of Marketing*, 58, Jan, 125–31.

Donnelly, M. and Shiu, E. (1999) 'Assessing service quality and its link with value for money in a UK local authority's housing repairs service using the SERVQUAL approach', *Total Quality Management*, 10(4), 498–506.

Douglas, L. and Connor, R. (2003) 'Attitudes to service quality – the expectations gap', *Nutrition and Food Science*, 33(4), 165–72.

Grace, D. and O'Cass, A. (2005) 'Examining the effects of service brand communications on brand evaluation', *Journal of Product and Brand Management*, 14(2), 106–16.

Grönroos, C. (1982) *Strategic Management and Marketing in the Service Sector*, Swedish School of Economics Finland, Helsingfors (cited in Grönroos, 1988).

—— (1984) 'A service quality model and its marketing implications', *European Journal of Marketing*, 18, 36–44.

—— (1988) 'Service quality: the six criteria of good perceived service quality', *Review of Business*, 3, 10–13.

Kang, G. and James, J. (2004) 'Service quality dimensions: an examination of Grönroos' service quality model', *Managing Service Quality*, 14(4), 266–77.

Murray, D. and Howat, G. (2002) 'The relationships among service quality, value, satisfaction, and future intention of customers at an Australian sport and leisure centre', *Sport Management Review*, 5, 25–43.

MORI (2002) 'Public service reform: measuring and understanding customer satisfaction', *MORI Review*, London, MORI.

Nichols, G. and Robinson, L. (2000) *The Process of Best Value: Further Lessons from the Leisure Pilots*, Melton Mowbray, Institute of Sport and Recreation Management.

Niedrich, R., Kiryanova, E. and Black, W. (2005) 'The dimensional stability of the standards used in the disconfirmation paradigm', *Journal of Retailing*, 81(1), 49–57.

Ojasalo, J. (2001) 'Managing customer expectations in professional services', *Managing Service Quality*, 11(3), 200–12.

Oliver, R., Rust, R. and Varki, S. (1997) 'Customer delight: foundations, findings, and managerial insight', *Journal of Retailing*, 73, 3, 311–36.

O'Neil, M. and Palmer, A. (2003) 'An exploratory study of experience on consumer perceptions of the service quality construct', *Managing Service Quality*, 13, 187–96.

Parasuraman, A., Zeithaml, V. and Berry, L. (1985) 'A conceptual model of service quality and its implications for future research', *Journal of Marketing*, 49(Fall), 41–50.

—— (1988) 'SERVQUAL: A multiple item scale for measuring consumers perceptions of service quality', *Journal of Retailing*, 64(1), 13–40.

—— (1994a) 'Alternative scales for measuring service quality: a comparative assessment based on psychometric and diagnostic criteria', *Journal of Retailing*, 70(3), 201–30.

—— (1994b) 'Reassessment of expectations as a comparison study in measuring service quality: implications for further research', *Journal of Marketing*, 58, 111–24.

Robinson, L. (1999) 'Following the quality strategy: the reasons for the use of quality management in UK public leisure facilities', *Managing Leisure: An International Journal*, 4(4), 201–17.

—— (2004) 'Public leisure facilities: managing customer expectations', *Municipal Engineer*, 157, ME2, 129–33.

—— (2006) 'Customer expectations of sport organisations', *European Sport Management Quarterly*, 6(1), 67–84.

Robledo, M. (2001) 'Measuring and managing service quality: integrating customer expectations', *Managing Service Quality*, 11(1), 21–31.

Rosen, L. D., Karwan, K. and Scribner, L. (2003) 'Service quality measurement and the disconfirmation model: taking care in interpretation', *Total Quality Management*, 14(1), 3–14.

Rust, R. and Oliver, R. (2000) 'Should we delight the customer?' *Journal of the Academy of Marketing Science*, 28(1) 86–94.

Stuart, H. (1999) 'Towards a definitive model of the corporate identity management process', *Corporate Communications: An International Journal*, 4(4), 22–207.

Taylor, P. (ed.) (2011) *Torkildsen's Sport and Leisure Management* (6th edn), London, Routledge.

Teas, R. (1993) 'Expectations, performance evaluation and consumer's perceptions of service quality', *Journal of Marketing*, 57(Oct), 18–34.

Ting, S. and Chen, C. (2002) 'The asymmetrical and non-linear effects of store quality attributes on customer satisfaction', *Total Quality Management*, 13(4), 547–69.

Tse, A. (2001) 'How much more are consumers willing to pay for a higher level of service? A preliminary survey', *Journal of Services Marketing*, 15(1), 11–17.

Walker, J. L. (1995) 'Service encounter satisfaction: conceptualized', *Journal of Services Marketing*, 9(1), 5–14.

Walsh, K. (1991) 'Quality and public services', *Public Administration*, 69 (Winter), 503–14.

Weed, M., Robinson, L., Green, M., Henry, I., Houlihan, B., Downward, P. and Argent, E. (2005) 'Academic review of the role of voluntary sports clubs'. Research report. Loughborough: Institute of Sport and Leisure Policy.

Wong, A. (2004) 'The role of emotional satisfaction in service encounters', *Managing Service Quality*, 14(5), 365–76.

Yu, C. C. (2007) 'Professional sports marketers' perceptions regarding the use of web advertising', *European Sport Management Quarterly*, 7(2), 213–26.

Zeithaml, V., Berry, L. L. and Parasuraman, A. (1993) 'The nature and determinants of customer expectations of services', *Journal of the Academy of Marketing Science*, 21(1), 1–12.

Zeithaml, V. and Bitner, M. (1996) *Services Marketing*, Singapore, McGraw–Hill.

6

APPROACHES TO MANAGING PERFORMANCE IN SPORT ORGANIZATIONS

Peter Taylor

Introduction

How do you know how your organization is doing if you don't have accurate performance evidence? How do you know what to aim for if you don't know what your current position is? Or what other similar organizations achieve? These questions demonstrate that performance management is not some abstract notion. It is a logical procedure through which improvements in organizational performance can be sought and achieved. It focuses on performance measurement and consequent actions. It informs management decisions with appropriate planning, objectives, targets, performance measurement and review. In contemporary management it represents information as power, because through appropriate performance information, management has the power to change its organization's achievements.

The first part of this chapter summarizes essential principles underlying performance management, in a modified version of the author's analysis in Taylor (2010). The second part of the chapter focuses on a current, practical UK example of a performance management tool, Sport England's National Benchmarking Service. The service is for UK sports centres, with either or both of a swimming pool and a main sports hall.

Performance management and measurement

Performance management is a cyclical, continuous process which relies on:

- specifying objectives for the organization such that their achievement or not can be identified by performance information;
- employing appropriate performance indicators to ensure that these objectives are measurable;
- measuring baseline performance using the selected performance indicators;
- setting challenging but realistic management targets for the performance indicators, using data benchmarks for similar organizations;
- taking the required management actions to realize these targets, with reference to process benchmarks from best-practice organizations;
- measuring performance, using the selected performance indicators;

- reviewing performance achievements; and
- reconsidering objectives, indicators, targets and actions.

Performance management has not always been undertaken by sport managers, particularly in the public and voluntary sectors. The Audit Commission in Britain, for example, exposed weaknesses in public leisure management in a series of seminal reports on sport (1989), entertainments and the arts (1991a) and museums and art galleries (1991b). However, since these reports were published, a variety of performance management systems have been devised in the UK to help public sector managers achieve continuous improvement.

The Audit Commission (2000a) has made clear why performance measurement is central to performance management.

- What gets measured gets done
- If you don't measure results, you can't tell success from failure
- If you can't see success, you can't reward it
- If you can't reward success, you're probably rewarding failure
- If you can't see success, you can't learn from it
- If you can't recognize failure, you can't correct it
- If you can demonstrate results, you can win public support.

However, before measuring performance, an essential first step is to specify organizational objectives in a manner which can be measured.

Objectives

An objective is a desired future position, so it makes sense to start the process of performance measurement by specifying objectives in a way that makes the organization accountable to them. There are a number of desirable attributes for organizational objectives, often summarized in the acronym SMART (see Chapter 4), but it is also useful to add a letter and use the acronym MASTER:

- *Measurable*: At the end of an appropriate period, the extent to which objectives have been achieved or not is clear. Each objective requires appropriate performance indicators, by which measurement of performance is possible.
- *Achievable*: If an objective is unrealizable it quickly falls into disrepute and is not taken seriously. Therefore objectives need to be achievable within the resources of the organization. It would be better to amend or abandon an unachievable objective, because it has no practical value.
- *Specific*: Often, particularly in the public and voluntary sectors, organizational objectives are expressed vaguely or generally, so that it is difficult if not impossible to identify whether or not they have been achieved. Examples of such mis-specified objectives include 'achieving sport for all' and 'serving the community's needs'. These are 'aims' rather than objectives – they are broadly based and non-measurable. They require more specific, measurable objectives to be monitored through performance indicators and used for management decision-making.
- *Time-specific*: This requires a deadline by which the objective has to be achieved. Without this, the objective is too open-ended to be of value and an organization can always suggest they are aiming for it, even when they never achieve it!

- *Ends not means*: For example, it is not an objective to 'set low prices for disadvantaged groups in the community'; rather, the objective here is 'to increase visits to the service by people from disadvantaged groups'.
- *Ranked*: The prioritization of objectives is important, because sometimes objectives may conflict. For example, 'increase revenue' might conflict with 'increase usage of a sport facility by disadvantaged groups'. Where trade-offs between conflicting objectives are apparent, priorities need to be identified. Otherwise, managers are put in a situation where some kind of failure is inevitable.

Performance

Performance for sport organizations can mean any number of things, depending on what objectives are specified. This section identifies different aspects of performance that are referred to in relevant literature and which sport managers will be most likely to be interested in. They are not all mutually exclusive.

Economy: This is concerned only with costs, i.e. inputs to the production process. Economy improves if costs are reduced, e.g. by acquiring inputs at lower unit cost. Overemphasis on economy, of course, carries some risk – for example, 'false economy' when the inputs are of lower quality, adversely affecting service quality or quantity. For example, a major input in sport services is typically labour and to reduce the costs of labour risks such problems as higher labour turnover or lower-skilled labour and consequently poorer service quality.

Effectiveness: This is concerned entirely with outputs, outcomes and impacts, particularly reaching specified targets. It is not concerned with the resources taken to achieve these outputs.

Efficiency: This is concerned with achieving objectives and targets at minimum cost, so it simultaneously takes into consideration both outputs and inputs. It is sometimes given the terms 'cost effectiveness' or 'cost efficiency', and is also what is meant by the terms 'productivity' and 'value for money'. A contemporary term in much use in recent years, particularly in public sector services, is 'efficiency savings'; which typically means maintaining service outputs whilst cutting costs – a very difficult thing to achieve.

Equity: This means measuring fairness in the distribution of services to different types of customers, e.g. by age, gender, ethnicity and ability. It is particularly relevant to public sector services, where there are important policy and management issues concerning equity. One is horizontal equity, the extent to which all people of the same socioeconomic status are treated the same. Another is vertical equity, the extent to which people of different socioeconomic status are treated the same or differently – e.g. positive discrimination favours selected types of people. A third issue is whether or not equity concerns opportunities or actual participation – it is not uncommon to have equal opportunity in principle but very unequal participation in practice. A fundamental problem with equity is that it can be interpreted in a number of ways – everyone has a different vision of what a 'fair' distribution of public sport services would look like. It is therefore an important performance dimension for political decision-making.

Customer or member satisfaction: This can be measured directly by methods such as questionnaire surveys, comments slips or complaints, although the last two of these tend to concentrate on customer dissatisfactions rather than satisfaction. A survey provides the opportunity for more comprehensive satisfaction scoring by customers/members, for an array of service attributes – an example is shown later. Measuring customer satisfaction alone, however, is 'anomic' – it lacks a reference point. It is increasingly the case, in the design of customer surveys, that respondents are asked to score something else to compare with their satisfaction scores. This something else is typically either customer expectations of the service attributes, or the importance of the attributes to customers. Either of these will lead to the measurement of a 'gap' score – i.e. either expectations score minus satisfaction score, or importance score minus satisfaction score. A positive gap indicates satisfaction is falling short of either customer expectations of an attribute or the importance of an attribute (see Chapter 5).

Citizen satisfaction: Particularly in the public sector, it can be important to measure the satisfaction with services by local citizens, whether or not they have actually used the service. This is because public services such as sport are typically subsidized by local and national tax revenue, which taxpayers contribute to even though they may not benefit from the services. Also, even non-participants in public sport services may have a vested interest in, and knowledge of, these services. An example is sport services for disaffected or vulnerable young people. A wide range of people in local communities will have a view on whether or not such services are satisfactory, from parents and neighbours to anyone with a fear of nuisance and vandalism from bored young people.

Finance: This is the most conventional dimension to performance found in the private sector and it is also very important in the public and voluntary sectors. It is often specified simply as profits, but in fact financial performance covers much wider ground, such as growth in sales, organizational security and liquidity – see examples below.

Social performance: This is most typically identified with the public sector and involves non-financial performance, for example increased usage by ethnic minorities or disabled people, or improved health in the local community as a result of participation in physical activities.

Outputs: These measure the immediate results of a service, such as the number of visitors in a given time period, the sales revenue, or the profit or loss results. They are the most basic and limited measure of effectiveness. A good example is throughput of visitors, often recorded as the number of visits in a week. It contains no indication of the types of visitors that have been attracted, nor the extent to which the service has met the needs of the visitors – both of which can easily be measured by market research of customers.

Outcomes: These measure the consequences of the outputs for customers, e.g. the improved health of sport participants which results from their use of sport services, and the improved achievements of elite athletes which result from their use of facilities and coaching. Such outcomes are not normally measured by the standard monitoring procedures at the facility or service level. They require specific evaluation methods, such as surveys or qualitative research.

Impacts: These are the effects of a service which go beyond the customers and reach a broader community. Three impacts have become well recognized in recent years, not just in respect of sport but in a wide variety of contexts. Economic impact assesses the full effects on a local, regional and/or national economy of a given activity. There are many examples of economic impact studies for sport and sport events, such as the economic impact of the London Marathon and the European Football Championships. Environmental impact assessment identifies the short- and long-term effects of an activity on the immediate environment in which it takes place. Examples in sport are environmental assessments of skiing on mountain environments, and the effects of football stadia on noise, litter and congestion in specific neighbourhoods. Social impact assessment considers issues such as the changes in the welfare or behaviour of selected groups of people as a result of an activity, a sport example being the impact of a major event such as the Olympic Games on deprived local communities in the host city.

Performance indicators

A performance indicator is a measure which is constructed from empirical data and can be repeated at time intervals or in different organizations. It is used to identify the performance of an organization. The UK Audit Commission (2000b) has identified criteria for good performance indicators (Table 6.1). Although designed for the public sector, these criteria are transferable to other sectors.

It is also important that performance indicators should be capable of being disaggregated to separate parts of an organization's structure, since it is likely that different objectives and different targets are applicable to different parts of the service, even within one facility. For example, a health suite might have different targets from a sports hall. The Audit Commission criteria present a very challenging list of requirements and it is often the case that a performance indicator does not meet all of them. In recognition of this the Audit Commission (2000b) advised that at the national level a performance indicator should be clearly defined,

Table 6.1 Criteria for a good performance indicator

Criteria	Explanation
Relevant	Indicators should be relevant to the organization's strategic goals and objectives and cover all relevant performance dimensions.
Clear definition	The performance indicators should have a clear and intelligible definition in order to ensure consistent collection and fair comparison.
Easy to understand and use	Performance indicators should be described in terms that the user of the information will understand.
Comparable	Indicators should be comparable on a consistent basis between organizations and this relies on there being agreement about definitions. They should also be comparable on a consistent basis over time.
Verifiable	The indicator also needs to be collected and calculated in a way that enables the information and data to be verified. It should therefore be based on robust data collection systems, and it should be possible for managers to verify the accuracy of the information and the consistency of the methods used.
Cost effective	There is a need to balance the cost of collecting information with its usefulness. Where possible, an indicator should be based on information already available and linked to existing data collection activities.
Unambiguous	A change in an indicator should be capable of unambiguous interpretation so that it is clear whether an increase in an indicator value represents an improvement or deterioration in service.
Attributable	Service managers should be able to influence the performance measured by the indicator.
Responsive	A performance indicator should be responsive to change. An indicator where changes in performance are likely to be too small to register will be of limited use.
Avoid perverse incentives	A performance indicator should not be easily manipulated because this might encourage counter-productive activity.
Allow innovation	Indicators that focus on outcome and user satisfaction are more likely to encourage such innovation to take place than indicators that are tied into existing processes.
Statistically valid	Indicators should be statistically valid and this will in large part depend on the sample size.
Timely	Data for the performance indicator should be available within a reasonable timescale.

Source: adapted from Audit Commission, 2000b

comparable, verifiable, unambiguous and statistically valid; whilst at the local community level it is important that indicators are relevant and easy to understand. For example, a national indicator might include participation rates in sport for a number of different sub-groups of the population, whilst at the local level the number of visits to sport facilities would be more easily measured and understood.

Reliable performance information needs good-quality data, otherwise there is a danger of the clichéd 'rubbish in, rubbish out' problem. The Audit Commission (2007) defined six key characteristics for the quality of data used to construct performance indicator scores – accuracy, validity, reliability, timeliness, relevance and completeness. Most of these replicate and therefore reinforce the criteria stipulated for performance indicators in Table 6.1. The additional consideration for performance data, which could equally apply to performance indicators, is completeness. Validity and reliability of data and indicators are as much dependent on what is missing as on what is collected.

As with the criteria for performance indicators above, the desired qualities for performance data are difficult to achieve in practice. In both cases it is important for sport managers to be open about the limitations of the data and indicators that they use. A common set of missing data, for example, at national and local levels, is data on young people's participation in and attitudes towards sport. This is because most surveys are conducted with adults – surveying young people requires different survey techniques and parental permission. When examining survey data on participation data and satisfaction with sport facilities, therefore, it is important to acknowledge that this data is for adults, not younger people.

Private or commercial sector

For a private, commercial organization, performance is largely specified in financial terms, although there are other important considerations. Business accounting ratios are designed principally for planning purposes (strategic appraisal) and control purposes (operational appraisal). The largely financial ratios are concerned not just with profit, but also with growth, liquidity, asset utilization, defensive position and investment performance. Examples of commonly used business ratios are given in Table 6.2.

These ratios, and many more, are detailed for individual companies and industry sectors by commercial sources such as ICC British Company Financial Datasets, a part of Dialog's company and industry intelligence, which covers nearly half a million companies worldwide.

The reason for using ratios rather than absolute values is that they offer a better perspective and one which is more likely to be comparable across time and between organizations. Ratios, however, have to be interpreted very carefully. Many are more appropriate for comparing a single firm's performance over time than comparing different firms, particularly if the firms are from a different industry or sector. Some ratios involve estimates which can be done in various ways, so comparing like with like can be problematic – for example valuing inventories and intangible assets. Some ratio values are annual averages, so getting the information from balance sheets is unreliable, merely averaging the beginning and end of the year situations, when more observations during the year are really required – e.g. liquidity ratios.

It is a mistake to think that private commercial firms are only interested in financial ratios. Non-financial performance of interest includes market share and customer market research results. Market share is normally measurable, even at the local or regional level, and is one of a number of possible indicators of the demand for the product. It is vital for any organization to be informed about the nature of, and changes in, demand for the service they are providing. Market research is a typical means of generating demand evidence.

Table 6.2 Performance ratios for commercial organizations[1]

Growth	Explanations
$\dfrac{\text{(This year} - \text{last year)}}{\text{Last year}} \times 100$	Year-on-year percentage changes in key variables, e.g. income, expenditure, profit, assets, liabilities.
Profitability	
$\dfrac{\text{Either Gross or Net Profit}}{\text{Sales}}$	Gross profit ratio or net profit ratio. No rules of thumb. It varies widely between industries and firms.
$\dfrac{\text{Net Profit after tax}}{\text{Total Assets}}$	'Return on Capital Employed'. No standard definitions, so care is needed in making comparisons between firms and industries.
Liquidity	
$\dfrac{\text{Current Assets}}{\text{Current Liabilities}}$	'Current Ratio'. Rule of thumb = at least 1:1 and preferably higher.
$\dfrac{\text{Current Assets} - \text{Inventories}}{\text{Current Liabilities}}$	'Acid Test', 'Quick' or 'Liquidity' Ratio. A more discriminating test of ability to pay debts.
$\dfrac{\text{Cash}}{\text{Current Liabilities}}$	'Cash ratio'. A more conservative measure which ignores less liquid assets such as stock
$\dfrac{\text{Balance Sheet Trade Debtors}}{\text{Total Credit Sales}} \times 365$	Average collection period of trade debts, i.e. average number of days before accounts are paid.
Asset Utilization	
$\dfrac{\text{Sales}}{\text{Fixed Assets}}$	Indicates the effectiveness in using fixed plant to generate sales.
$\dfrac{\text{Cost of Goods Sold}}{\text{Inventories}}$	'Stock Turnover'. Varies a lot between industries.
$\dfrac{\text{Sales}}{\text{Number of Employees}}$	Indicates revenue productivity of labour.
Defensive position	
$\dfrac{\text{Net Worth}}{\text{Total Assets}}$	Indicates shareholders' interest in the business. (Net Worth is ordinary shares + preference shares + reserves)
$\dfrac{\text{Borrowing}}{\text{Net Worth}} \times 100$	'Gearing ratio'. An indication of the riskiness of the capital structure.
$\dfrac{\text{Total debt}}{\text{Total assets}} \times 100$	'Debt ratio'. An indication of the powers of creditors over an organization.
Investment	
$\dfrac{\text{Dividend per Share}}{\text{Market Price per Share}}$	'Dividend Yield'. Indicates rate of return on investment in shares.
$\dfrac{\text{Net profit} - \text{Preference Share Dividend}}{\text{Number of Ordinary Shares}}$	Earnings per ordinary share.
$\dfrac{\text{Market Price per Share}}{\text{Earnings per Share}}$	'Price/Earnings Ratio'. Indicates the market's evaluation of a share.

Note: Details of the use of these ratios can be found in any good accounting text.
Sources: Gratton and Taylor, 1988; Wilson and Joyce, 2008, 2010

Most large private sport organizations have marketing departments, with market research functions. As well as continual monitoring of demand for their goods and services by this means, they regularly employ outside market research agencies or consultancies to conduct specialist market research. In addition, some consultancies produce regular reports with market research information alongside financial data for different industries. The 2010 reports from Mintel, for example, include reports on Bicycles, Children's Sporting Activities, Snowsports, and Sports Goods Retailing. Key Note's recent market reports for the UK include Football Clubs and Finance, Health Clubs and Leisure Centres, and Sports Equipment.

Public sector

Public sector services have been subject to increasing pressure for accountability in recent decades. Accountability does not just mean spending money correctly rather than fraudulently, it also refers to achieving value for money from public spending. This requires appropriate performance indicators and in particular efficiency indicators rather than simple economy indicators. In the UK the process of reporting to standard performance indicators has been driven in recent years by Best Value legislation and particularly by Comprehensive Performance Assessment (CPA), and more recently Comprehensive Area Analysis (CAA). These government requirements have obliged local authorities to publish performance information for a set of national performance indicators.

Table 6.3 shows the indicators relevant to public sector sport services at the time of writing, for the CAA, with two being specific to sport and physical activity but the other two being broader in concept. The final column in Table 6.3 shows that the adoption by local authorities of these indicators is variable, with two indicators quite commonly adopted (sport and active recreation participation, young people's participation in positive activities) but the other two being selected by fewer authorities.

At the individual service level, much more comprehensive lists of performance indicators can be found, as we will see later with Sport England's National Benchmarking Service, which has 47 performance indicators across four dimensions of performance. It is the responsibility of each organization to choose a manageable array of indicators to reflect its objectives. For a public sector provider, this may include throughput indicators for particular groups of clients, such as women, the elderly, lower socioeconomic groups, and the disabled, since this would monitor the effectiveness of the organization in dealing with such target groups. It may also include very conventional indicators of financial performance such as some of those relevant to the commercial provider in Table 6.2, particularly for parts of the service which have no particular 'social service' function, such as the bar, cafe, vending machines and other merchandise sales.

Table 6.3 Public sector national indicators relevant to sport services in the UK

National indicators	Number of local area agreements including each indicator	Rank in popularity, out of 152 indicators
Adult participation in sport and active recreation	82	16
Young people's participation in positive activities	75	22
Participation in regular volunteering	42	43
Children and young people's participation in high-quality PE and sport	24	65=

NB: The ranks are according to how many local area agreements include each indicator. For example, adult participation in sport and recreation is in 82 agreements, which makes it the 16th most popular indicator in such agreements.

Source: IDeA (http://www.idea.gov.uk/idk/core/page.do?pageId=8399555)

Although a top-down government requirement to report on national performance indicators appears to require performance measurement for reporting and accountability purposes, in fact reporting performance to an organization's stakeholders is a secondary, albeit important function of performance measurement. The primary purpose of performance measurement is to help management decisions – i.e. to service performance management.

Voluntary sector

Voluntary sector organizations are accountable primarily to their members but there may also be an array of funders, stakeholders and partners to whom performance needs to be communicated, especially at the national level. Voluntary sport organizations are typically non-profit but they have to break even financially to survive. Therefore, many of the performance indicators reviewed for the commercial sector above may be relevant. However, finance is only one of a number of performance dimensions relevant to the voluntary sector.

Arguably, performance measurement and management in the voluntary sport sector is most likely at the national level. Robinson and Palmer (2011) provide two examples. First, Chappelet and Bayle (2005) identify six performance dimensions for national Olympic sport organizations:

- Sport: e.g. sporting results; changing number of members;
- Internal/social: e.g. member satisfaction;
- Societal: e.g. economic and social impacts;
- Financial: e.g. financial independence; value of volunteer inputs;
- Promotional: e.g. image and reputation;
- Organizational: e.g. use of quality assurance procedures.

Second, Deloitte and Touche (2003) provide 30 key performance indicators for national governing bodies of sport in the UK, including revenue per member, number of affiliated clubs, number of volunteers contributing more than 12 hours a year, number of elite athletes in the top 100 UK/World rankings, and number of schools affiliated to an accredited training scheme.

At the local level, voluntary sport clubs are less likely to engage in systematic measurement of performance for use in the management of clubs. Nevertheless, local clubs are typically in the province of national governing bodies and as such may be encouraged by these bodies to generate appropriate performance information. Of relevance to local voluntary sport clubs would be 'internal' indicators of finance, sporting success, volunteers' utilization, and members' and volunteers' satisfaction. More outward-facing clubs may also be interested in awareness of, and attitudes to, the club in the local community and the local authority.

Targets

Targets give objectives specificity, because they are precise statements of what is to be achieved, and by when. They support the process of performance management because they are the key reference points against which improvement can be monitored. A target is typically quantitative, e.g. to increase profits by 5 per cent in the next year.

How is a target decided? The most appropriate basis is evidence of previous performance by the organization, and evidence of the performance of similar organizations elsewhere – i.e. data benchmarks (see below). Such evidence enables the target setter to reach the difficult but necessary balance between ambition and realism. Targets need to be challenging but they also need to be achievable. If they are too easily reached, or if they are impossible to reach, they quickly fall into disrepute. Targets can and do change in the course of time. They need to remain under continual scrutiny for their relevance to the operating circumstances of the organization.

Benchmarking

When performance of an organization has been measured, it is likely that managers will want comparisons to be made with other similar organizations, to put their own performance into perspective. Benchmarking is a process which provides such comparisons. There are two main types.

- Data benchmarking involves comparison with numerical standards (e.g. averages) calculated for performance indicators in a particular service. The benchmarks are typically organized into relevant 'families' of similar organizations. An example of this which is detailed below is the National Benchmarking Service (NBS) for indoor sports and leisure centres in the UK.
- Process benchmarking involves comparison of different procedures adopted in different organizations. Used in conjunction with performance data, process benchmarking helps a manager understand how to improve performance. It is often facilitated by 'benchmarking clubs' of similar organizations.

Comparative performance information is available in both the private sector and the public sector. In the private sector, for example, ICC British Company Financial Datasheets provide detailed evidence for individual companies, including industry comparisons for a number of key business ratios. Similarly, Key Note provides Business Ratio Reports for each UK industry sector.

In the public sector in the UK, benchmarks are provided for sport and leisure in two annual publications by the Chartered Institute of Public Finance and Accountancy (CIPFA). These are *Culture, Sport and Recreation Statistics* and *Charges for Leisure Services*. The former in the main contains financial statistics, which are estimates for the year, rather than outturns. Three other explicit benchmarking services can be identified for sport and leisure – one in Australia and New Zealand (CERM), the other two in the UK (APSE Performance Networks and NBS). The rest of this chapter focuses on the NBS to provide a detailed insight into the structure and processes of a benchmarking service.

Case study

Sport England's National Benchmarking Service

The National Benchmarking Service (NBS) began in 2000, utilizing substantial research on indoor sports and leisure centres commissioned by Sport England. The national government of the time was intent on pursuing more consistent performance measurement in public services and Sport England's research provided the data with which benchmarks could be estimated for these particular public sport facilities. This evidence was important because these facilities consumed about two-thirds of local authorities' subsidy for sport. The benchmarks provided reference points against which individual facilities could compare, as well as a national picture of industry performance standards for sports and leisure centres. The performance indicators (PIs) measured by the NBS are identified in Table 6.4.

Table 6.4 Performance indicators for Sport England's National Benchmarking Service (2010)

---

a) Access

Key

% visits 11–19 years ÷ % catchment population 11–19 years
% visits from NS-SEC classes 6&7 ÷ % catchment population in NS-SEC classes 6&7[1]
% visits 60+ years ÷ % catchment population 60+ years
% visits from black, Asian & other ethnic groups ÷ % catchment population in same groups
% visits disabled, <60 years ÷ % catchment population disabled, <60 years

Other

% visits 20–59 years ÷ % catchment population in same group
% of visits which were first visits
% visits with discount card
% visits with discount cards for 'disadvantage'[2]
% visits female
% visits disabled, 60 years+ ÷ % catchment population disabled, 60+ years
% visits unemployed

Notes:
1 NS-SEC classes 6 & 7 are the two lowest socioeconomic classes in the official classification used in the UK.
2 Disadvantage eligibility for discount cards includes over-50s, students, unemployed, disabled, single parents, government support, government funded trainees, widows, exercise referrals, and elite performers

---

b) Utilization

Key

annual visits per sq. m (of usable space, i.e. excluding offices and corridor space)

Other

annual visits per sq. m (of total indoor space, including offices and corridor space)
% of visits casual, instead of organized
weekly number of people visiting the centre as % of catchment population

---

c) Financial

Key

subsidy per visit

Other

% cost recovery
subsidy per resident
subsidy per sq. m.
total operating cost per visit
total operating cost per sq. m.
maintenance and repair costs per sq. m.
energy costs per sq. m.
total income per visit
total income per sq. m.
direct income per visit
secondary income per visit

(Continued overleaf)

Table 6.4 Continued

---

d) Service attributes for customer satisfaction and importance scoring

---

Accessibility
Activity available at convenient times
Ease of booking
The activity charge/fee
The range of activities available

Quality of facilities/services
Quality of flooring in the sports hall
Quality of lighting in the sports hall
Quality of equipment
Water quality in the swimming pool
Water temperature of swimming pool
Number of people in the pool
Quality of car parking on site
Quality of food and drink

Cleanliness
Cleanliness of changing areas
Cleanliness of activity spaces

Staff
Helpfulness of reception staff
Helpfulness of other staff
Standard of coaching/instruction

Value for money
Value for money of activities
Value for money of food/drink

Overall satisfaction only
Overall satisfaction with visit

The NBS indicators cover four dimensions of facilities' performance, designed to help inform decisions such as pricing, marketing, resourcing and investing in sport services at the centres. These four dimensions are as follows.

- *Access*: representing the extent to which facilities are used by specific market segments, including disadvantaged groups and new users. These are indicators of effectiveness, particularly in the context of social inclusion.
- *Financial*: representing subsidy, cost and income performance. These are indicators of efficiency and economy.
- *Utilization*: representing the scale and nature of usage of facilities. These are indicators of effectiveness and efficiency.
- *Satisfaction and importance*: representing the extent to which users are satisfied with different service attributes of the facility and how important these attributes are to them. These are indicators of effectiveness.

The main criteria for the selection of the performance indicators in Table 6.4 were that it is relatively easy to interpret either changes in them, or differences between the facility's score and the benchmarks for the performance indicator; they are relevant to policy and management of sports facilities generally; they embrace as wide a variety of facilities' performance as is feasible; and predominantly, they concern outputs rather than inputs.

However, the NBS indicators do not cover other aspects of public facilities' performance that managers and politicians would like information on. For example, the indicators do not measure many of the wider social impacts of such facilities, such as improvements in health, improved quality of life, reduced crime and vandalism, or education benefits – these are considered too difficult to measure regularly in the specific context of these facilities. The NBS also does not record the profiles, behaviour and attitudes of young people under 11 years old, who are not considered suitable for the questionnaire survey employed. These exclusions demonstrate the compromise that is often necessary in practical performance measurement systems between what indicators are desirable and what indicators can be measured reliably and at reasonable cost.

The NBS results for access, finance and utilization performance are compared with benchmarks for four 'families' of centres, which have been empirically tested and proven to have structural effects on performance:

- Type of centre – wet; dry (with/without outdoor facilities); and mixed (with/without outdoor facilities). There are good reasons to suggest that many aspects of performance vary by the type of facility, e.g. many costs are known to be higher for swimming pools than sports halls; specific market segments are known to use some types of facility more than others. In addition, the presence of outdoor pitches is known to have a distinctive effect on user profiles, finances and other performance variables.
- The socioeconomics of a centre's location – high deprivation; medium deprivation; low deprivation – measured by the percentage of the catchment population in the bottom two socioeconomic classes. It is highly likely that many aspects of both policy and performance in facilities will be heavily influenced by the type of neighbourhood in which the facility is located. The socioeconomics of the catchment population is important to issues of market segmentation and pricing – key principles underlying policy and performance in access/social exclusion.
- Size of the centre – large; medium; and small. Studies have indicated that the size of facility may have a significant impact on performance. In particular large facilities may benefit from economies of scale.
- Management type at the centre – in-house local authority; trust; commercial contractor. The different types of management complicate the objectives of the facilities concerned, particularly their prioritization of different objectives, and consequently lead to differences in performance.

Three benchmarks are employed. The 25 per cent, 50 per cent and 75 per cent benchmarks are the quarter, half and three-quarters points in the distribution of scores for a PI, if all the centres' scores were organized from the lowest score at the bottom end of the distribution to the highest score at the top end (Figure 6.1). The 50 per cent benchmark is the median and is an appropriate mid-range score when, as is often the case, the distribution of performance scores in a family category is skewed or unduly influenced by unusually high or low scores. A mean (average) score would be distorted by these influences and would therefore be unreliable.

For the importance and satisfaction attributes (Table 6.4), the NBS reports in four ways:

- the satisfaction scores in comparison with industry averages for different facility types – wet, dry and mixed centres;
- the gaps between importance and satisfaction mean scores from customers – the largest gaps being the strongest indication of problems;
- grid analysis of the importance and satisfaction scores, whereby each service attribute is positioned in one of four quadrants, each with different implications for interpretation and action – see Figure 6.2; and
- the percentage of customers dissatisfied with each attribute.

Reasons for using NBS

In qualitative research with ten NBS clients in 2003, several major reasons were given for undertaking it. First, NBS informs public policy requirements for public services to consult with customers and compare their performance with other similar services. Furthermore, NBS achieves these with independent and nationally credible evidence from a national agency. Some respondents suggested that without NBS data there would have been a large gap in their Best Value information, particularly on social objectives/access.

Second, NBS provides comparative industry performance information for centres of a broadly sim-

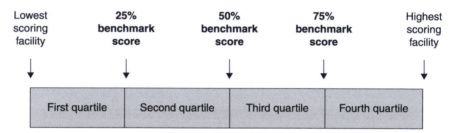

| Lowest scoring facility | 25% benchmark score | 50% benchmark score | 75% benchmark score | Highest scoring facility |

| First quartile | Second quartile | Third quartile | Fourth quartile |

Figure 6.1 Benchmarks and quartiles

S A T I S F A C T I O N	*HIGH SATISFACTION AND LOW IMPORTANCE* Possible over-resourcing? Check for potential efficiency gains.	*HIGH SATISFACTION AND HIGH IMPORTANCE* Good correlation. Maintain this performance.
	LOW SATISFACTION AND LOW IMPORTANCE No need for action unless satisfaction is particularly low or there are other implications (e.g. financial).	*LOW SATISFACTION AND HIGH IMPORTANCE* In most urgent need of action to increase satisfaction.
	IMPORTANCE	

Figure 6.2 Grid analysis of importance and satisfaction scores

ilar type, which is not obtainable on this scale and in this detail by other means. One client suggested that other services in leisure were sorely in need of a parallel service (e.g. museums, arts, parks). Third, NBS facilitates service improvement – its results inform management plans and decisions in order to provide a better service for customers. Fourth, a few clients at the time of the qualitative research were about to contract out the management of their centres to trusts/contractors and they wished to have performance data in order to set terms and possibly targets for the funding agreement/contract.

Other reasons for undertaking NBS were more general – simply wanting to improve services with the expectation that the results would enable the identification of strengths and weaknesses; or information for defending against any questions of the facilities by the local authority or external parties; or in readiness with performance information which was not available by other means, such as customer satisfaction and access by target groups.

Uses of NBS

According to the qualitative research with NBS clients, the most common uses of the NBS results were to inform strategies and business plans; inform action plans and short-term decisions; report facilities' performance to the local authority; and inform performance reviews and inspections. In three authorities the NBS results had fed directly into new sport strategies. In others there was clear intent to inform strategy development. A few respondents had concentrated on their centres' weaknesses according to their NBS reports, and acted as quickly as possible on those weaknesses. One respondent had used the NBS data in negotiations with the client authority about threatened reduced funding, pointing out that this would probably cause increased user charges at the expense of access performance.

In a couple of cases the local authorities received the full NBS report; in other cases the authority received key performance results only, often with careful interpretation of the NBS data for members. In these latter cases it was apparent that the main use of the performance data was located at the centre or the contract operation level rather than the client local authority. In the UK, management contracts for public sports centres are most commonly held by one of three types of organization – in-house local authority teams, independent and often charitable trusts, or commercial contractors. NBS was seen to provide valuable information for performance reviews and in two cases the use of NBS results was seen by Best Value inspectors as a positive contribution. All respondents used the NBS data selectively, prioritizing data which was important to their objectives, or particular weaknesses or strengths.

Benefits of benchmarking using NBS

NBS clients have demonstrated a number of general learning responses to the processes of performance management, i.e. generating the right information, interpreting the results meaningfully, and utilizing the results in performance planning. In addition, benefits described by NBS clients in feedback workshops include the following.

- *Awareness of performance*: Facility managers are provided by NBS with an objective, externally validated set of performance measures, with the authority of Sport England and Sheffield Hallam University behind them. This is important for reporting to stakeholders. Local managers can add explanations of strengths and weaknesses identified in the NBS report, using their knowledge of local circumstances.

- *Education of stakeholders*: The NBS data helps to educate stakeholders, particularly politicians, about the realities of performance at the sports and leisure centres. It is very easy to become overambitious in setting targets, for example. NBS benchmark data identifies what is achievable, which is often different to what is ideal. For practical management purposes it is the achievable which is most useful, rather than the ideal.
- *Challenges*: Managers and stakeholders, again particularly politicians, often have preconceived ideas about the performance of their facilities. These ideas are from their own personal experiences of encounters with the public or with customers – but these experiences can be very different to the average situation. The NBS performance data is more objectively determined and more a reflection of normality for the centres. This data may confirm preconceived ideas but it can also throw up some unexpected surprises, both negative and positive. In such cases it is important to recognize the difference between subjective experiences and objective evidence, and for management decisions to reflect the latter.
- *Expectations and targets*: NBS data helps managers and other stakeholders to form realistic expectations about what performance is possible, given not only the performance of their own centres but also comparisons with national benchmarks. In turn, these expectations help to determine targets which are not too safe and not too ambitious.
- *Evidence-based management culture*: Experience of collecting data and receiving benchmarking reports helps to develop an awareness of further information needs. An example is qualitative research needed to identify exactly why customers have given a relatively weak satisfaction score to a particular service attribute. Another example is conducting research in the local community around the facility, to complement the views of the centre's customers.
- *Process benchmarking*: Benchmarking data facilitates the selection of partners, with whom to discuss how to generate better performance for specific performance indicators. From 2010, the NBS is publishing the top quartile centres for each performance indicator, giving other centres the opportunity to contact these top quartile performers to discuss how they did it. NBS also holds an annual conference which includes workshops with best-performing managers in access, finance and customer service discussing how they achieved their strong performance.

Conclusions

Performance management is an outcomes-led approach to good management. Measuring performance accurately and comparing it with other similar services and facilities can be the starting point in a logical approach to service improvement. It identifies strengths and weaknesses, asks questions about how to improve services, helps identify appropriate targets for improvement, and gives a consistent framework through which strategic decisions are taken in future.

Performance management and measurement is also an approach which invests power at the level of the individual service or facility, because it is here that the performance data is owned and where decisions are made about the use of the data. This then determines not only how the performance information is reported to others, but more importantly how it can be used to change services for the better. If these processes are owned and driven by the individual service, there are fewer unpleasant surprises from stakeholders and others asking difficult questions. Even if they do, there is a greater likelihood of having the right information with which to answer the questions.

The National Benchmarking Service is a good example of a performance measurement and benchmarking service for sport. Analysis of how it is used and the benefits clients derive from its use demonstrates many of the essentials of performance management. It makes considerable demands in terms of data collection, particularly in terms of surveying customers, but the rewards are the scope and depth of performance data which can then be used to make plans and take actions to improve services.

References

Audit Commission (1989) *Sport for Whom? Clarifying the local authority role in sport and recreation*, London, HMSO.

—— (1991a) *Local Authority Entertainments and the Arts*, London, HMSO.

—— (1991b) *The Road to Wigan Pier? Managing local authority museums and art galleries*, London, HMSO.

—— (2000a) *Aiming to Improve: The principles of performance measurement*, London, Audit Commission.

—— (2000b) *On Target: The practice of performance indicators*, London, Audit Commission.

—— (2007) *Improving Information to Support Decision Making: Standards for better quality data*, London, Audit Commission.

Chappelet, J-L. and Bayle, E. (2005) *Strategic and Performance Management of Olympic Sport Organisations*, Champaign, Human Kinetics.

Deloitte and Touche (2003) *Investing in Change*, London, Deloitte and Touche.

IDeA (2008) *Culture and Sport Improvement Toolkit*, London, IDeA.

Gratton C. and Taylor P.D. (1988) *Economics of Leisure Services Management*, Harlow, Longman.

Robinson, L. (2004) *Managing Public Sport and Leisure Services*, London, Routledge.

Robinson, L. and Palmer, D. (2011) *Managing Voluntary Sport Organizations*, Abingdon, Routledge.

Taylor, P.D. (1996) 'Chapter 18: The role of management information systems in sport', in G. Ashworth and A. Dietvorst (eds) *Policy and Planning for Sport and Tourism*, London, CAB International.

—— (ed.) (2010) *Torkildsen's Sport and Leisure Management*, London, Routledge.

Wilson, R. and Joyce, J. (2008 and 2010) *Finance for Sport and Leisure Managers: An Introduction*, London, Routledge.

7

FORECASTING THE PERFORMANCE OF NATIONS IN ELITE SPORT

Simon Shibli, Veerle De Bosscher, Maarten van Bottenburg and Jerry Bingham

Introduction

The purpose of this chapter is to give an insight into how the performance of nations in elite sport can be forecast with what appears to be a reasonable degree of accuracy. Forecasting performance is an essential part of the performance management process as it allows managers to anticipate the resources they might need and the strategies they might follow. It also sets out the areas in which performance must be managed within elite sport systems in order to produce medal-winning athletes – arguably the main area of performance and indicator of success for these sport organizations. The chapter is concerned with looking at the effectiveness of nations at using the resources at their disposal (inputs), the techniques they use to produce athletes (processes), and the results they achieve as a result (outputs). The research upon which the chapter is based is from the summer Olympic Games of 2008. For this event, a forecast had been made of the host nation's performance against which actual performance achieved is reviewed.

The use of the Olympic Games as a case study is quite deliberate as it represents a broad portfolio of sports and disciplines that act as a proxy for a nation's success in sport. In the case of the 2008 Beijing Olympic Games, performance is measured over 28 sports, 41 disciplines (for example the sport of cycling has four disciplines, namely track, road, mountain bike and BMX), and 302 events. The focus on a large-scale multi-sport event with high numbers of medal-winning opportunities is deliberate because, unlike the FIFA Football World Cup where there is only one winner, it is possible to calculate a nation's "share" of overall success in the summer Olympics. In a single sport, such as football or rugby, where there can be only one world champion and therefore there is only one winning opportunity, the techniques described in this chapter are not really appropriate.

Why should we bother ourselves with measuring success in sport? After all, the International Olympic Committee (IOC) does not recognize the Olympic medal table as an order of merit and simply presents the number of medals won by each nation in descending order of gold, silver and bronze medals, for information purposes only (De Bosscher et al., 2008a). The answer to this question lies in part in the investment made by national governments in elite sport systems. Governments are required to account for their use of public funding, which is a scarce resource and therefore needs to be justified. A good example of how return on investment can be measured is the report made by the National Audit Office (NAO) in the UK after the 2004 Athens Olympics which found that on average each medal won by athletes representing Great Britain and Northern Ireland "cost" £2.4m (NAO, 2005). Following the award of the 2012 summer Olympic Games to London there has been a considerable increase in public funding for elite sport and with this a continued scrutiny of how the investment is being used. In its 2008 report (NAO, 2008), which pre-dated the Beijing Olympic Games, the National Audit Office (NAO, 2008: 7) made the recommendation cited below.

> UK Sport should agree firm medal targets with each sport for 2012 as soon as possible after the Beijing Games and in time to inform funding decisions for the start of the 2012 Olympic cycle in April 2009. It should then confirm the level of funding it will provide until 2012 for each sport it expects to win medals, subject to achieving their performance targets at major events in the years leading up to the Games.

The message from the NAO is that there must be a clear link between the medal-winning prospects of a specific sport and the level of funding provided by UK Sport for that sport. Thus, regardless of the IOC's position, it is certainly the case in the UK, and probably in many other nations, that the Olympic medal table is more than just for information only in the context of national performance in elite sport. So how can performance in the Olympic Games be measured and how can future performance be forecast? In the remainder of this chapter these questions are tackled by looking at macro-economic forecasts of performance and the processes that nations use to give themselves a competitive advantage in elite sport, and we conclude by looking at an alternative forecasting technique using China, the last hosts of the summer Olympic Games, as a case study.

Macro-economic measures of performance

The use of macro-economic measures to forecast the performance of nations in the Olympic Games has been an area of considerable interest for researchers since the 1950s, for example Jokl et al. (1956), Jokl (1964), Shaw and Pooley (1976), Colwell (1982), Baimbridge (1998) and Johnson and Ali (2002). The rationale for this type of analysis is that athletic talent is evenly distributed across the globe and will inevitably rise to the top. It is for this reason that population is such an important macro-economic variable because, in theory, the more people a nation has, the more athletic talent it will have. On its own, population explains around 20 percent of nations' sporting success. Perhaps the key flaw with population-based measures is that they overestimate the expected performance of highly populated, but relatively economically poor, nations such as India. Similarly, nations with relatively small populations, but high wealth, tend to have their performance underestimated, for example Norway. However, it is not surprising that a country's population will be a determining factor for sporting success as the bigger the population, the greater the talent pool from which athletes can be selected. Furthermore, all things being equal, there will be greater opportunities to organize training and competition from which to filter talented athletes upwards to the highest level. There are also plausible explanations as to why relatively wealthy countries perform better than their poorer counterparts. Richer countries can invest more in sport generally and elite sport specifically; individuals have the opportunity to participate in a wide range of sport; and a higher living standard may improve their general fitness and ability to perform at the top level. Den Butter and Van der Tak (1995) found that the number of medals won correlates strongly with income (GDP) as well as with more general welfare indicators.

In the literature it has been the trend over the last 60 years for economists to use models that are based upon the two key variables of population and wealth. In her doctoral thesis, De Bosscher (2007) reviewed 33 studies which sought to compare actual performance in the Olympic Games with what macro-economic variables such as population and wealth might predict. Many of these studies show that population and wealth are the two most important socio-economic determinants of success (see, for example, Bernard and Busse, 2004; De Bosscher, De Knop and Heyndels, 2003; Johnson and Ali, 2002; Kiviaho and Mäkelä, 1978; Levine, 1974; Morton, 2002; Novikov and Maximenko, 1972; Suen, 1992; and van Bottenburg, 2000). These two variables typically account for, or "explain," over 50 percent of a nation's success in the Olympic Games where success is measured by either total medals or medal points (for example gold = 3 points, silver = 2 points and bronze = 1 point). For these reasons, success has also sometimes been reported in terms of medals per head of population, or in terms of per capita GDP, as a measurement of wealth.

Taking into account one determinant such as population size or wealth in isolation is crude in two regards. First, it ignores other potentially important determinants. Second, it assumes that there is a linear relationship between the factor concerned and success. This approach can create a biased view as a nation that has twice as many inhabitants as another country might not be able to win twice as many Olympic medals. For example, in the 2008 Olympic Games there were 11 boxing events and 44 medals available (four per event as both losing semi-finalists receive a bronze medal). However, nations are only allowed to enter one boxer per weight category and thus, regardless of the size of a nation, a maximum of 11 boxing medals could be contested by any one nation. Add to this a complex continental qualifying system and we find that a relatively small nation such as Cuba is able to contest as many boxing medals as a larger nation such as the UK.

The techniques commonly used to include more than one variable into a forecast of sporting success are multiple regression and econometric modeling. For an overview of the subject in the context of the Olympic Games see De Bosscher et al. (2008b), who found that 52.4 percent of success could be explained by the three variables: population; wealth as measured by gross domestic product (GDP) per head; and whether or not a country had or had previously had a communist government. These findings were broadly similar to the work of Bernard and Busse (2004), who derived four key variables in their highly accurate econometric forecasting model, namely population, GPD per capita, past performance and a host nation effect. Whilst regression analysis and econometric modeling provide a useful context in which to compare a nation's performance in the Olympic Games, the two key determinants of such success, population and wealth, are not really controllable in the short term for the purposes of elite sport. That is, it would be hard to imagine a nation making the policy decision to pursue population growth or economic growth in order to drive ambitions in elite sport.

To conclude this section we review the July 2008 forecast of performance in the Beijing Olympic Games made by Andrew Bernard using his model based on population, GDP, past performance and the host nation effect (Bernard, 2008). The Bernard forecast was confined to the top five nations as shown in Table 7.1.

As can be seen in Table 7.1, the Bernard model was exactly right for the USA; within two gold medals for Russia and Australia; overestimated Japan's score by 8 gold medals; and underestimated China's score by 14 gold medals. Across the top five nations the accuracy of the model was within two gold medals out of 133 actually won, or a 98 percent accuracy rating. The purpose of a model of this type is to set realistic expectations of what nations might reasonably anticipate achieving using an objective measure (Chapter 6 has discussed

Table 7.1 Bernard forecast medals compared with actual in Beijing

Nation	Forecast gold medals	Actual gold medals	Variance
China	37	51	+14
USA	36	36	0
Russia	25	23	−2
Japan	17	9	−8
Australia	16	14	−2
Total	131	133	+2

Source: Bernard, 2008

Table 7.2 Actual versus predicted gold medals outside the range of +/− 2

Nation	Predicted gold medals 2004	Actual gold medals 2004	Variance
Netherlands	9	4	−5
Greece	10	6	−4
Australia	14	17	+3
Hungary	5	8	+3
Brazil	1	5	+4
Norway	1	5	+4
China	27	32	+5
Ukraine	1	9	+8
Japan	6	16	+10

the need for realistic expectations). However, the nature of sport is that people and nations are competitive and seek to perform better than an objective measure of performance might otherwise forecast. These nations often take what is known as a "strategic approach to elite sport development," which in broad terms can be defined as adopting a set of policies designed to enable the nation concerned to achieve success at a greater rate than would be expected ordinarily. Good examples from history include East Germany and the then Soviet Union, while more contemporary examples include Australia, China and currently the United Kingdom. Nations that are successful in their efforts to implement a strategic approach to elite sport development tend to have their performance underestimated by models based on macro-economic variables. To illustrate this point, for the Athens Olympics Bernard and Busse (2004) produced forecasts of how they expected nations to perform. Following the event, these forecasts were reviewed by Shibli and Bingham (2008), who found that where the actual medals won differed from the forecast by more than two gold medals, the data was characterized by two key points. First, the variance was mainly actual gold medals won exceeding the forecast, which was true in seven out of nine cases as shown in Table 7.2. Second, all seven of these nations were known to be investing in elite sport development systems, or taking a strategic approach to achieve elite sport success.

For nations achieving more elite sport success than might be expected on the basis of macro-economic variables, we would cite two plausible explanations. First, the variance between actual and forecast performance could be entirely random and due to a chance event such as the emergence of an exceptional athlete who is capable of winning medals single-handedly. A good example of this phenomenon is Zimbabwe, which until 2004 had only ever won one Olympic medal. The emergence of the Zimbabwean swimmer Kirsty Coventry who won one gold, one silver and one bronze medal in 2004 and one gold medal and three silver medals in 2008, is an example of how an athlete can create the illusion that a nation as a whole is "punching above its weight" in the Olympic Games. Kirsty Coventry was not the product of a system in Zimbabwe and indeed had done most of her training at an American university. Second, nations that seemingly overachieve in elite sport could have effective elite sport development systems in place whereby success is driven by proactive policy factors rather than by passive factors such as population and wealth. This point is particularly pertinent where a nation's overachievement occurs on a consistent basis. Australia is a good example in this regard. Following the perceived disappointment of Montreal 1976, when Australia was ranked in 32nd place in the medal table with one silver and four bronze medals, the Australian Institute of Sport was established, which enabled large-scale investments to be made in infrastructure, personnel and systems to improve Australia's future performance. The impact of these investments has been impressive, as demonstrated by the performance of Australia in the summer Olympic Games subsequently, which is shown in Figure 7.1.

Following the establishment of the Australian Institute of Sport in the 1980s, Australia enjoyed continuous improvement from 1988 to 2000, when it was the host nation and finished fourth in the medal table. Since the peak of 2000 there has been a decline in the number of medals won by Australia but the achievements of 2004 and 2008 exceed all preceding editions in the time series except 2000. There is no random pattern to Australia's performance and it would be appropriate to attribute the nation's success to the impact of the investment in its elite sport development systems. Hogan and Norton (2000) even found there was a linear relationship between money spent and total medals won by Australia since the 1980s, which in turn reinforced an Australian saying in elite sport which is "more money in equals more medals out." An overview of the components most commonly found in an elite sport development system is provided in the following section.

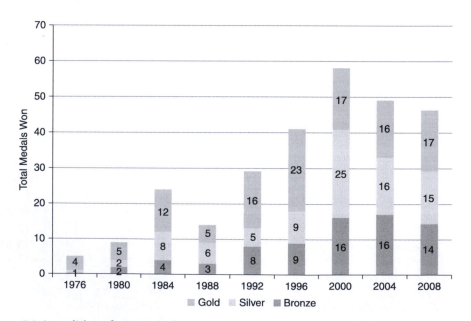

Figure 7.1 Australia's performance in the summer Olympic Games (1976–2008)

Managing performance in elite sport development systems

Since the 1960s the competition between nations to win medals in major international competitions has increased. This has led to governments across the world spending increasing sums of money on elite sport. In their quest for international success in a globalizing world, the elite sport systems of leading nations have become increasingly homogeneous. More than ever before, they are based around what appears to be a single model of elite sport development with only marginal cultural variations (Oakley and Green, 2001a, 2001b; Clumpner, 1994; Krüger, 1989). The premise of what Oakley and Green (2001b) describe as "a global sporting arms race" is that international sporting success can be produced by investing strategically in elite sport. Based on the previous research reviewed above, De Bosscher et al. (2008a) concluded that the factors leading to success which are influenced by policy can be distilled down to nine key factors or "pillars." These nine pillars along with the notions of the processes found in a system, namely "input," "throughput" and "output" are illustrated in Figure 7.2.

The term "input" refers primarily to money and "output" refers to the production of elite athletes and the winning of medals. Consequently, these concepts are easily understood. The more interesting and more complex concepts to understand are the techniques that are used to convert the inputs into outputs, that is, the processes used or "throughput."

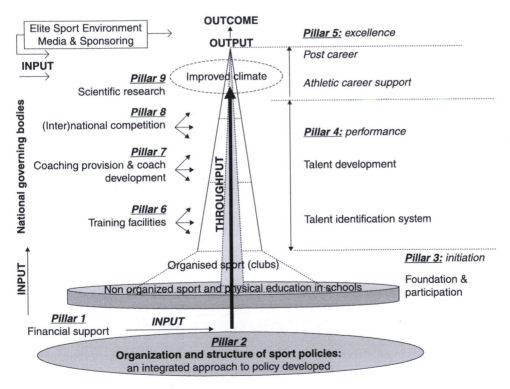

Figure 7.2 The nine pillars used in elite sport development systems

Source: De Bosscher et al., 2008a: 24

Input

Pillar 1: Financial support

Financial resources are measures of input because countries that invest more in elite sport are able, in theory, to create more opportunities for athletes to train under ideal circumstances. Although the link between expenditure on elite sport and success (output) is rare in the literature, there are many examples of countries that have performed better after increasing their investment in elite sport, notably Australia as discussed earlier.

Throughput

Pillar 2: An integrated approach to policy development

The amount of resource devoted to elite sport is important, but it is the organization and structure of sport in a particular country and its relationship to society that enables efficient use of these resources to further the chances of elite sporting success (SIRC, 2002). As Clumpner (1994) notes, it is important to have a good communication system and clear task descriptions as well as financial resources.

Pillar 3: Participation in sport

Most elite athletes tend to originate from grass roots participation. Van Bottenburg (2003) found a significant correlation between mass participation and medals won during the Barcelona 1992 and Sydney 2000 Olympic Games, especially when sport was "intensive and competitive." A broad base of sport participation is not always a condition for success, but it may influence success to a large extent because it provides a supply of young talent and the opportunity for training and competing at various levels of ability and in various sports.

Pillar 4: Talent identification and development system

Pillar four begins when a talented athlete is "discovered" and starts to receive special attention, normally from a national governing body for sport. From a recognized best practice perspective, there is the necessity for monitoring systems to identify talent characteristics; for robust talent detection systems that minimize drop-out; and for well-organized scouting systems. The second phase of the pyramid is where athletes follow a period of intensive training during which they develop a mastery of their sport. This is the phase of talent development. Many nations have established national coordinated programs to support governing bodies to set up high-level training and competition programs and to support athletes to combine their academic careers with a career in sport.

Pillar 5: Athletic and post-career support

The logical extension of the talent identification and development phase is the production of athletes capable of competing at the highest level. This stage is often coordinated by the national governing bodies or by elite sport clubs. In only a few sports can athletes make a living from their earnings and pay for all the costs they incur. Therefore some countries provide financial support for athletes to meet their living costs and to fund support programs to give them access to the services needed to help them realize their potential. Finally, athletes also need to be prepared for life after sport while they are still engaged in their athletic careers.

Pillar 6: Training facilities

Training facilities are an important success factor enabling athletes to train in a high-quality environment. Facility provision also supplies a link between participation and excellence. For example, De Bosscher and De Knop (2002) showed that in tennis the number of courts was highly correlated with the international success of tennis playing nations ($r^2 = 0.858$).

Pillar 7: Coaching provision and coach development

The quality and quantity of coaches is important at each level of the sport development continuum. At the highest level it is recognized that the best athletes will only reach their potential if they have access to the best coaches. For this reason a global market has been created for the services of the world's top coaches. In the same way that athletes need to be developed, so too sport should have in place mechanisms to produce the coaches of the future so that a system is dependent upon its structures and procedures and not key individuals.

Pillar 8: (Inter)national competition

It has been shown consistently in sport that the staging of international events provides nations with a positive home advantage effect. Athletes performing in their home country have the benefit of low travel costs, limited disorientation caused by traveling, familiar weather conditions and facilities, as well as crowd support. Internally, the national competition structure is also an important ingredient as competition is a necessary factor in player development and helping talent to be filtered upwards.

Pillar 9: Scientific research

Scientific research concerns the systematic gathering and dissemination of scientific information in areas such as talent identification and development, medicine, nutrition, psychology, physiology and biomechanics. These factors were typical in the former communist nations and are now commonplace as nations use research to innovate and to achieve performance gains.

Output

Outputs in elite sport can be clearly defined in terms of actual performance, both in terms of the production of elite athletes and the success they achieve in international sporting competition. In any national level elite sport development system some, or all, of the nine pillars will be present to a greater or lesser extent. There will, however, be variations in how effectively the nine pillars are implemented and in the range of sports to which they are applied. In the search for processes that will provide nations with a competitive advantage in international sport, it is not a case of what nations do, as most nations are doing essentially the same, but rather how effectively nations carry out the processes (Böhlke and Robinson, 2009). Some nations try to achieve success in a relatively narrow range of sport and are said to be taking a "priority" ' approach, whereas others pursue success in a broader portfolio of sport and are said to take a "diversification" approach.

Nations taking a strategic approach to elite sport provide an interesting context in which to experiment with alternative models that might forecast their likely results with a comparable degree of accuracy to those based on macro-economic variables. In the next section we demonstrate how the use of linear regression analysis on past performance, plus making an adjustment for host nation effect (where relevant), has produced credible results that are a relatively simple alternative to those based on macro-economic variables.

An alternative forecasting technique

Forecasting using macro-economic variables in a regression model is beyond the abilities and resources of most people with an interest in how nations might perform at the Olympic Games. Shibli and Bingham (2008) forecast that China would win 46 gold medals at the Beijing Olympic Games by simply regressing China's historical performance over time and factoring in a home advantage effect. Casual observation of the data since 1984 when China first took part in the Olympic Games revealed that the nation was on something of an upward trajectory, particularly in terms of gold medals won, as shown in Figure 7.3.

When China took part in the 1984 Los Angeles Olympics it won 32 medals in total, of which 15 were gold medals. However, this edition of the event was marred by the Eastern Bloc boycott, which had the effect of reducing the level of competition and thereby enabling nations to win more medals than they would have done had there been no boycott. Perhaps not surprisingly, in Seoul 1988, when normal order was restored, after the various boycotts of 1976, 1980 and 1984, China performed less well than it had done in 1984. To the ruling party of China the Seoul 1988 performance was perceived as being a huge humiliation to national pride and the government "took steps" to improve performance for the future. These can be summarized as: first; making success in international sport an explicit government priority; and, second, implementing most of the nine pillars discussed earlier in a culturally relevant manner. Chalip (1995: 5) states that changes in policy follow what can be described as being

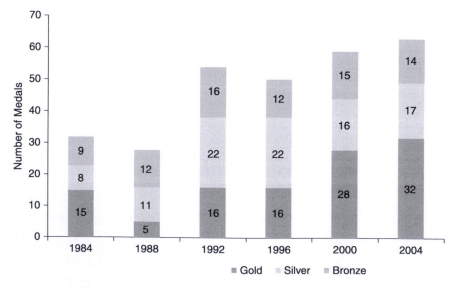

Figure 7.3 China's performance in the Olympic Games (1984–2004)

"focusing events," which are "nationally traumatic events that can symbolize an issue and focus policy makers' attention on proposals to redress the issue." Some focusing events in national sporting performance have led to increased investment in elite sport, often as a means of overcoming perceived failures. In the same way that Montreal 1976 was a focusing event for Australia, so too Seoul 1988 was a focusing event for China. From a forecasting perspective it was clear that 1984 probably overstated China's performance and that consequently, for the post-boycott era, 1988 was probably a better starting point. The end result produced a very strong correlation of 0.97 ($r^2 = 0.94$) as shown in Figure 7.4 and suggested that China would win 39 gold medals.

The forecast of 39 gold medals did not factor in any host nation effect, which historical evidence indicated was likely to be positive. In the case of China, there were three factors which suggested the potential for a positive home nation effect. First, China had been bidding to host the summer Olympic Games since the early 1990s, when Beijing was a candidate city for the 2000 Olympic Games. In preparation for eventually hosting the event China had made a massive investment in its sport infrastructure and elite sport development systems. The Association for Asian Research (2004) estimated that in the Athens Olympiad alone China invested US$2.4 billion in the China General Administration of Sport (CGAS), the central government body for sport related affairs in China.

Second, and perhaps most significantly, being host nation enabled China to contest more events and more medals than it had ever done before. According to Hong et al. (2005), in 2004 China contested 203 out of 301 events and took part in 26 out of 28 sports. In most of the 28 sports contested (swimming and athletics excluded), the host nation is afforded preferential qualifying rights for its athletes and teams. A good example to illustrate this point is boxing, in which the number of nations from any given continent taking part is rationed by a continental quota system. The quotas used for boxing revealed that under normal circumstances China would have had to compete with the rest of the Asian continent

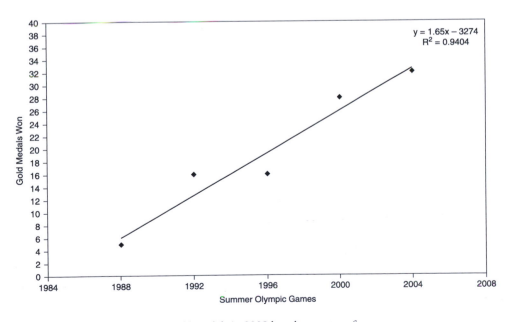

Figure 7.4 Extrapolating China's gold medals in 2008 based on past performance

for a restricted number of qualification places. However, being the host nation under the qualification criteria in place at the time, China was guaranteed places in six weight categories of its choice. In addition, China had the right to contest as many additional weight categories as it could by securing such rights on merit in the normal round of qualifying tournaments. In Athens 2004 China contested five boxing events, and favorable qualifying conditions alone enabled China to contest more boxing medals in 2008 than it did in 2004. These favorable qualifying conditions for the host nation are replicated in most other sports, enabling the host nation to contest more events and more medals than would be the case typically.

Third, China enjoyed an advantage in sport where familiarity with the venue was a source of competitive advantage. In the case of sailing, for example, Chinese competitors had four years to become familiar with winds and currents on the regatta waters, which was much greater access than for competitors from other nations. In the five editions of the Summer Olympic Games before Beijing (1988–2004) the host nation has performed better than it did in the previous edition of the event. This point can be demonstrated clearly by plotting the change in gold medals won against the change in medals table rank for the five nations concerned as shown in Figure 7.5.

All host nations since 1988 have won more gold medals and improved their medal table ranking relative to the Games prior to being host. For example, in 2004 Greece won two more gold medals than it did in 2000 and in so doing improved its medal table ranking by two places. In 1992 Spain won twelve more gold medals than in 1988 and improved its medal table ranking by nineteen places. The most pragmatic way of computing the host nation effect was simply to take the average of the increase in gold medals won by the last five host nations relative to their tally in the edition prior to being host. This average was seven gold medals. On the basis of the home nation effect data we revised our forecast by proposing that

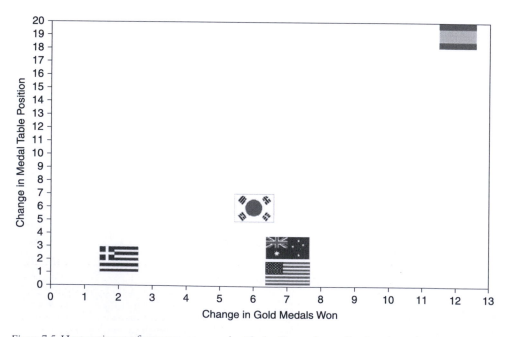

Figure 7.5 Host nation performance compared with the Games immediately prior to hosting

China would win 46 gold medals in 2008, that is, 39 based on the past performance regression and an additional seven for the host nation effect. This forecast proved to be five gold medals fewer than China actually won, but more accurate than Bernard (38) and also than a form-based forecast made by former head of the Italian Olympic Committee Luciano Barra, who stated that China would win 37 gold medals (see Williams, 2008).

When this forecasting approach is applied to other nations the results remain encouragingly accurate. If we replicate Table 7.1 using the methods employed by Shibli and Bingham (2008) we achieve results that are broadly comparable to those achieved by Bernard (2008) as shown in Table 7.3.

Despite the weakness in the Russia forecast, the total number of gold medals forecast for the five nations in Table 7.3 was 139, which in total was six more than actually achieved by the nations concerned. The overall accuracy of the approach was 96 percent, which is comparable to the Bernard model of 98 percent accuracy (minus two gold medals between the forecast and the actual). The point of comparing the accuracy of models is not to come up with a judgment about which is the best. A more constructive purpose is to illustrate the relative importance of the various components of a forecasting model. What the findings discussed in this chapter seem to indicate is the importance of past performance and host nation effects as factors that are likely to impact upon future success. As increasing numbers of nations take a strategic approach to elite sport development, it is likely that factors such as population and wealth will reduce in importance and policy factors such as the nine pillars will increase in importance. Past performance seems to have a useful role in acting as a proxy for the efficacy of policy factors.

Money alone does not buy success and there may be other factors at play. First, there are positive psychological effects for the host nation. Many people believe that playing at home gives athletes a lift and enables them to perform at their best. This is unproven scientifically and is equally likely to hinder athletes, who may become riddled with self-doubt under the weight of national expectation. Crowds do help, but it tends to be the more subtle impact of crowds on officials in subjectively scored events that creates benefits for the host nation. Judges might be subconsciously influenced to award higher marks to host nation athletes and referees inadvertently tend to favor home teams. The second key benefit of home advantage was highlighted earlier in that Chinese athletes had the opportunity to train in the facilities that were actually used during competition. Finally, the favorable qualifying conditions

Table 7.3 Shibli/Bingham forecast gold medals compared with actual in Beijing

Nation	Forecast gold medals	Actual gold medals	Variance
China	46	51	+5
USA	36	36	0
Russia[1]	29	23	−6
Japan	11	9	−2
Australia	17	14	−3
Total	139	133	−6

[1] The forecast for Russia is based on three data points as Russia has only competed in the Olympic Games in its own right since 1996. In 1992 Russia competed as part of a Unified Team and up until 1988 Russia was part of the Union of Soviet Socialist Republics' team (URS), which was an amalgamation of 15 different nations. It is not really appropriate to conduct a linear regression on three data points, so for the purposes of this exercise a simple average of Russia's three most recent scores has been taken (26 gold medals in 1996, 32 in 2000 and 28 in 2004).

offered to the host nation mean that qualification for the host nation may be easier than it is for other nations.

What can we learn from the performance of China?

The findings about the performance of China in Beijing 2008 provide an improved insight into the potential causes of improved performance in international sporting competition. What are the ingredients that contribute to improved sporting performance and to what extent were they present in the case of China? Table 7.4 provides a summary of the key factors that we have discussed in this chapter and it demonstrates that all were present to a greater or lesser extent in China.

Where the policy factors outlined in Table 7.4 are present, that is excluding population and GDP, it is likely that forecasting performance will be more accurate using techniques that rely more on variables that can be influenced in the short term by policy decisions rather than macro-economic variables. This can then feed directly into the performance management process as these are factors that can be included in organizational plans. Increased population and wealth do not of themselves cause improved sporting performance. They are, however, building blocks that can be used in the sense that increased population may increase the pool of talent from which to produce athletes; and extra wealth may provide the resources required to fund policy decisions. Once a decision to develop elite sport has been taken, it is highly likely that some or all of the nine pillars will be implemented to a greater or lesser extent. In managerial and policy terms this is in effect to adopt the principles and procedures of performance management rather than passively waiting to see what happens in the end. The forecasting set out in this research provides a rationale for pursuing investment in elite sport systems, which can then be managed using the performance management processes set out in the previous chapter.

Table 7.4 Factors influencing improved elite sport performance

Factor	China 2008
Increased population[1]	✓ +3%
Increased wealth (GDP)[2]	✓ +124%
Evidence of a "focusing event"	✓ Seoul 1988
Central government support for elite sport	✓ (Hong et al., 2005)
Increased funding for elite sport	✓ (Hong et al., 2005)
Previous track record of improvement	✓ See Figure 7.3
Evidence of the nine pillars in use	✓ (Hong et al., 2005) not Pillar 3

[1] China 2004 population 1.295 billion; 2008 1.330 billion; increase +3%
[2] China 2004 GDP US$1.93 trillion, 2008 US$4.33 trillion; increase 124%

References

Association for Asian Research, (2004) 'Beware of the financial black hole of the Olympic Games', [online] available at <http://www.asianresearch.org/articles/2346.html> (accessed 15 June 2007).

Baimbridge, M. (1998) 'Outcome uncertainty in sporting competition: the Olympic Games 1896–1996', *Applied Economics Letters*, 5, 161–64.

Bernard, A. (2008) *Going for the gold: Who will win the 2008 Olympic Games in Beijing*, Tuck School of Business, New Hampshire, USA.

Bernard, A. and Busse, M. (2004) 'Who wins the Olympic Games? Economic resources and medal totals', *Review of Economics and Statistics*, 86, 413–17.

Böhlke, N. and Robinson, L. (2009) 'Benchmarking of elite sport systems', *Management Decision*, 47(1), 67–84.

Chalip, L. (1995) 'Policy Analysis in Sport Management', *Journal of Sport Management*, 9, 1–13.

Clumpner, R. A. (1994) '21st century success in international competition', in R. Wilcox (ed.), *Sport in the Global Village* (298–303). Morgantown, WV, FIT.

Colwell, J. (1982) 'Quantity or quality: Non-linear relationships between extent of involvement and international sporting success', in A. O. Dunleavy, A. W. Miracle, and C. R. Rees (eds.), *Studies in the Sociology of Sport* (101–18). Fort Worth, TX, Christian University Press.

De Bosscher, V. (2007) 'Sport policy factors leading to international sporting success', unpublished dissertation, Brussels, Free University.

De Bosscher, V. and De Knop, P. (2002) 'The influence of sport policies on international success: An international comparative study', in IOC, *Proceedings of the 9th World Sport for All Congress. 'Sport for All and Elite Sport: rivals or partners?* (31). Arnhem (Netherlands), International Olympic Committee.

De Bosscher, V., De Knop, P. and Heyndels, B. (2003) 'Comparing relative sporting success among countries: Create equal opportunities in sport', *Journal of Comparative Physical Education and Sport*, 3(3), 109–20.

De Bosscher, V., De Knop, P., van Bottenburg, M., Bingham, J. and Shibli, S. (2008a) *The Global Sporting Arms Race: Sport Policy Factors Leading to International Success*, Brussels, Meyer and Meyer.

De Bosscher, V., Heyndels, B., De Knop, P., van Bottenburg, M. and Shibli, S. (2008b) 'The paradox of measuring success of nations in elite sport', *Belgeo*, 9(2), 1–18.

Den Butter, F. A. G. and Van der Tak, C. M. (1995) 'Olympic medals as an indicator of social welfare', *Social Indicators Research*, 35, 27–37.

Hogan, K. and Norton, K. (2000) 'The price of Olympic Gold', *Journal of Science and Medicine in Sport*, 3(2), 203–18.

Hong, F., Ping, W. and Xiong, H. (2005) 'Beijing Ambitions: An analysis of the Chinese elite sport system and its Olympic strategy for the 2008 Olympic Games', *The International Journal of the History of Sport*, 22(4), 510–29.

Johnson, K. N. and Ali, A. (2002) 'A tale of two seasons: participation and medal counts at the summer and winter Olympic Games', Wellesley College Department of Economics Working Paper 2002–02. [Online] Available at SSRN: <http://ssrn.com/abstract=297544> (accessed 26 August 2011).

Jokl, E. (1964) 'Health, wealth, and athletics', in E. Simin (ed.) *International Research in Sport and Physical Education* (218–22), Springfield, IL, Thomas.

Jokl, E., Karvonen, M., Kihlberg, J., Koskela, A. and Noro, L. (1956) *Sport in the Cultural Pattern of the World*. Helsinki, Institute of Occupational Health.

Kiviaho, P. and Mäkelä, P. (1978) 'Olympic Success: A sum of non-material and material factors', *International Review of Sport Sociology*, 2, 5–17.

Krüger, A. (1989) 'The sportification of the world: are there any differences left?' *Journal of Comparative Physical Education and Sport*, 2, 5–6.

Levine, N. (1974) 'Why do countries win Olympic medals: Some structural correlates of Olympic Games success', *Sociology and Social Research*, 58, 353–60.

Morton, R. H. (2002) 'Who won the Sydney 2000 Olympics? An allometric approach', *The Statistician*, 51, 147–55.

National Audit Office (NAO), (2005) *UK Sport: Supporting Elite Athletes*, London, National Audit Office.

National Audit Office (NAO) (2008) *Preparing for Sporting Success at the London 2012 Olympic and Paralympic Games and Beyond*, London, National Audit Office.

Novikov, A. D. and Maximenko, A. M. (1972) 'The influence of selected socio-economic factors on the level of sport achievements in the various countries', *International Review of Sport Sociology*, 7, 22–44.

Oakley, B. and Green, M. (2001a) 'Still playing the game at arm's length? The selective re-investment in British sport, 1995–2000', *Managing Leisure: An International Journal*, 6(2), 74–94.

Oakley, B. and Green, M. (2001b) 'The production of Olympic champions: international perspectives on elite sport development system', *European Journal for Sport Management*, 8, 83–105.

Shaw, S. and Pooley, J. (1976) 'National success at the Olympics: an explanation', in C. Lessard, J. P. Massicotte and E. Leduc (eds.) *Proceedings of the 6th International Seminar: History of Physical Education and Sport* (1–27), Trois Rivieres, Quebec.

Shibli, S. and Bingham, J. (2008) 'A forecast of the performance of China in the Beijing Olympic Games 2008 and the underlying performance management issues', *Managing Leisure: An International Journal*, 13(4), 272–92.

SIRC (2002) *European Sporting Success: A study of the development of medal winning elites in five European countries*, Sheffield, Sheffield Hallam University.

Suen, W. (1992) 'Men, money and medals: an econometric analysis of the Olympic Games', *Discussion Paper*, Hong Kong, The University of Hong Kong.

van Bottenburg, M. (2000) *Het topsportklimaat in Nederland (The elite sport climate in the Netherlands)*, Diopter-Janssens and van Bottenburg BV, 's Hertogenbosch, the Netherlands.

—— (2003) 'Sport for All and Elite Sport: Do they benefit one another?', in IOC, *Proceedings van het 9e World Sport for All Congress: Sport for all and elite sport: rivals or partners*, (25), Arnhem (Netherlands), IOC.

Williams, O. (2008) 'GB "to meet" Olympic medal target', BBC Sport, 5 August, [online] available at <http://news.bbc.co.uk/sport1/hi/olympics/team_gb/7534962.stm> (accessed 26 August 2011).

8

CORPORATE SOCIAL RESPONSIBILITY IN SPORT

Stephen Morrow

Introduction

In the last two decades or so, many sport teams, leagues, organizations and athletes have embraced the principles and practices of corporate social responsibility (CSR). There are numerous instances of diverse community and social initiatives, at local, national and global levels, associated with a range of different sports in different countries. The following examples illustrate that diversity:

- In South Africa, FirstGolf is working with the Government of the Western Cape to create a multi-stakeholder corporate social initiative, providing facilities which will broaden the base of golf to include previously disadvantaged communities.
- Football for Hope is a strategic alliance between world football governing body, FIFA, and streetfootballworld, which promotes sustainable social and human development programmes focused on football in areas like health promotion, peace building, children's rights and education, anti-discrimination and social integration and the environment.
- At English FA Premier League Club, Arsenal, the Arsenal Double Club is a programme run in school curriculum time through which 'Arsenal teachers' are employed in schools, working on literacy, numeracy, science and language programmes.
- In the United States, the Golden State Warriors NBA team has promoted a number of diversity initiatives in its communities, including LGBT evenings.
- In England, the Bright Sparks social inclusion programme run by Bristol Rugby Club combines rugby union skills, drills and games, with team building and leadership workshops, with the aim of re-engaging designated young people from schools in high-risk areas back into the educational process.

The purpose of this chapter is to provide an insight into CSR in sport. The chapter begins by considering the social responsibility of organizations in general, before going on to consider whether sport organizations have a particular social responsibility and/or particular opportunity to engage in socially responsible activities. This is followed by an overview of research that has focused on CSR in sport and in sport organizations, concluding with a more detailed description of a recently completed research project in the area.

The social responsibility of organizations

While interest in CSR has become more apparent in the last two or three decades in business, in the wider political and social context and also in academia (see Kakabadse et al., 2007 for an overview), relationships between business and society have been matters of concern for a couple of centuries. For example, the writings and actions of the industrialist and philanthropist, Andrew Carnegie, the Quaker tradition of major companies like Barclays and Cadbury and the pioneering co-operatives established by Robert Owen in New Lanark in Scotland all demonstrate, in different ways, long-standing concerns about how business impacts on people and society.

While no single widely accepted definition of CSR exists, a number of generally accepted characteristics are presented in the literature in terms of an organization's obligations to society or furthering some social good extending beyond its narrow economic, technical and legal requirements (McWilliams and Siegel, 2000; Ullman, 1985; Wood, 1991). Carroll (1979, 1999) provides an important framework which recognized the multifaceted complexity of corporations' responsibilities in society, where CSR is presented as consisting of four elements:

- *Economic*: of paramount importance as only profit-making enterprises will be able to continue in business and hence benefit society;
- *Legal*: the duty to follow the rules and regulations created for the good of everyone;
- *Ethical*: responsibilities going beyond economic and legal responsibilities which are consistent with societal expectations;
- *Discretionary*: activities that go beyond societal expectations.

In addition to the definition of social responsibility, the framework identified social issues to which these responsibilities are tied (consumerism, environment, discrimination, product safety, occupational safety and shareholders) and a consideration of the philosophy or strategy behind business response to social responsibility and social issues (reaction, defence, accommodation and proaction). One example which highlights different elements involved in CSR was the decision by the football club Celtic plc in 2003 to remove its then sponsor's logo, the brewer Carling, from children's versions of its replica jersey. This decision demonstrated how an ethical issue (the product and the sponsorship were legal) could turn into an economic one (i.e. the risk that protests and pressure from supporters' groups and others could turn into a product boycott). Another example was the decision taken by the broadcaster BSkyB to terminate the contract of its FA Premier League football analyst Andy Gray, when evidence of his sexist behaviour and attitudes came to light in early 2011. BSkyB has invested heavily in corporate sport-based social responsibility initiatives, the benefits of which could have been undermined by any perception that the attitudes of Gray and fellow presenter Richard Keys were widespread.

More fundamentally, opinions about the nature of CSR derive from how one believes the world to be and indeed how one would like the world to be. For example, Gray et al. (1996) provide one illustration of the diversity of views on the relationships that exist between organizations and society, and hence on the nature of social responsibility. At one extreme are those who seek social change, or at the very least a diminution of the dominance of financial capital within social, economic and political life. At the other are those wedded to an unspoiled view of capitalism, where liberal economic democracy is considered a good approximation of how the world works and of how it should work. This latter view underpins

Friedman's (1970) famous contribution on the legitimacy of CSR, where he argued that the social responsibility of business is to make profits and hence any activity, social or otherwise, is only justifiable when it is in the organization's self-interest. A less extreme view suggests that longer term economic welfare and stability is achievable only if organizations accept that certain (usually minimum) social responsibilities require to be met.

This can be characterized as enlightened self-interest; recognition that some moral content requires to be added to the organization–society relationship in order to moderate the risk of unacceptable excesses that might otherwise occur (Gray et al., 1996). Both of these latter views rely on the separation thesis in which business is considered apart from ethical or social dimensions, reinforcing the pre-eminence of capitalism being about business with CSR as an add-on to ameliorate the worst excesses of business capitalism (Freeman et al., 2010: 262). CSR is thus conceptualized as a residual activity through which social responsibility is organizations giving back to society some of the value (profit) they have created, but CSR is not itself integrated with the organization's value-creating activities. As Freeman et al. (2010) note, this residual view of CSR remains predominant today, particularly in the United States. Under this approach, the distribution of profits can be normatively motivated, e.g. where an organization believes that the welfare of society is more important than its own financial performance and hence profits are a means of improving society. Alternatively it can be instrumentally motivated, where CSR strategies sanction the firm to continue to make its profit. In the latter case the CSR activities need not be integrated into an organization's activities or even entered into for well-principled reasons, but instead could simply be used as a defence mechanism, for example against campaigning stakeholders or constituencies.

Alternatively, companies and other organizations can be characterized as existing at society's will and hence beholden to the wishes of society. In other words, all organizations, including businesses, are social institutions which operate in society via a social contract. Here the survival and growth of organizations is dependent on their ability to demonstrate both their legitimacy and their relevance, i.e. does society require the organization's services and do the groups benefiting from its rewards have society's approval? Wood's (1991) work arises out of this view. In this, CSR is used as a basis to challenge the purpose of organizations, suggesting that they need to encompass larger and wider social interests and to consider the interests of stakeholders, including but not restricted to shareholders. The explicit identification of stakeholders, rather than the abstract interests of society, is an important development in this process. Moreover, in making explicit the link between the social of CSR and stakeholder theory, this work acted as a catalyst in promoting an integrated approach to CSR; the assimilation of social, ethical and environmental concerns into corporate strategy adopted by management. This approach parallels those early nineteenth-century co-operative industrial organizations promoted by social reformers like Robert Owen in New Lanark, in which the emphasis was on productivity, profit and the person (Claeys, 1992). As such CSR is not seen as the imposition of additional duties on a 'business as usual model', but rather it is about widening the understanding of a corporation's status and of its management's responsibilities.

The social responsibility of sport organizations

In the last two decades or so, professional sport has become increasingly concerned with financial matters, with its clubs and leagues becoming more business oriented. But notwithstanding what could be termed the incorporation of sport, the very structure of professional sport and sport leagues – market interventions like promotion and relegation, transfer systems, redistribution of league-wide revenues, salary caps and player drafts – emphasizes the inap-propriateness of adopting an unfettered market approach to strategy and decision-making in sport and sport organizations. Professional sport continues to exist in a highly institutional-ized structure, which inevitably has implications for how we understand the relationship between CSR and sport (Godfrey, 2009).

A more politically informed approach can be adopted where sport organizations are char-acterized as having distinctive characteristics which emphasize their societal and community significance, as well as their economic importance. Indeed, in some sports like professional football, the characterization of its clubs as social institutions as well as financial and sporting ones is something that dates back to their origins as one of the principal agents through which collective social identities were created and reinforced (Holt, 1989). Moreover, sport has advantages not enjoyed by other areas of activity.

In one of the key contributions to the sport CSR literature, Smith and Westerbeek (2007) put forward a powerful argument for the potential role that sport can play in bridging the gap between economic and social issues. In their paper they identify seven unique features of sport CSR. The importance of the first two features – 1) mass media distribution and commu-nication power and 2) youth appeal – is the opportunity these provide to implement sport CSR initiatives that might be expected to have a greater impact than conventional CSR activities. Sport is a powerful vehicle for social messages and engagement, not least with youth.

The next four features – 3) positive health impacts, 4) social interaction, 5) sustainability awareness and 6) cultural understanding and integration – emphasize claims made for aspects of sport which, if accepted, hence provide a basis for developing sport CSR in pursuit of some or all of them. The final feature – 7) immediate gratification benefits – suggests that sport CSR can offer those involved in it fun and satisfaction, providing attractive, if imprecise, social advantages. In a similar vein, Babiak and Wolfe (2009) identify unique elements of the professional sport industry that may contribute to the practice of CSR, as well as increasing its impact, specifically: a greater responsiveness to CSR messages arising from the passion that sports teams and events generate among supporters and/or customers; the economic structure and funding of sports leagues and teams where the protection, real and perceived, afforded to leagues and teams by governments and others may encourage some stakeholders to expect a higher level of social and community responsibility from sport organizations in compensa-tion; the high degree of transparency in professional sport which leads to higher levels of scrutiny and demands for accountability; and the stakeholder nature of professional sport organizations. In a broader context, the importance of sport as a vehicle for international development, particularly at recreational and grassroots level, also relies on some of these features, coupled with its portrayal as a non-political vehicle which has the ability to send out messages to communities in a value-neutral manner, untainted by association with develop-ment institutions and politicians (Levermore, 2010).

Accepting the distinct features of sport and the dual financial and social orientation of many sport organizations, the relevance of CSR principles and practices and the opportuni-ties for sport become clear (Brown et al., 2010; Giulianotti, 2005; Godfrey, 2009; Morrow, 2003; Sheth and Babiak, 2009; Smith and Westerbeek, 2007). But at the same time caution is required. Sport is often portrayed unproblematically as something people believe is inher-ently good. It is frequently presented as a means of alleviating a variety of social problems and of improving individuals and communities, for example in increasing social inclusion, in engaging with diverse population groups in communities and in diverting young people from crime and anti-social behaviour; as well as contributing to international development in areas including empowerment, health awareness, peace building and conflict prevention or resolution (Beutler, 2008; Bridgewater, 2010; Coalter, 2007; Kidd, 2008; Levermore, 2010). However, the evidence available to back up some of the claims made for sport and hence for the impact of some of the community, social and development initiatives remains weak (Coalter, 2007; Levermore, 2010; Tacon, 2007), not least because research into the precise contribution of sport faces substantial methodological problems (Coalter, 2007). There is also a need to prioritize improved monitoring and evaluation of projects and initiatives.

Other critical perspectives on sport CSR highlight its conflicting images or messages. Athletes are portrayed as role models, despite numerous high-profile misdemeanours involving alcohol, drugs and/or sex. Focusing on sport-for-development, Levermore (2010) contrasts its putative virtuous potential for promoting various forms of development with its tarnished image as a site for cheating, corruption and financial inequality. Blumrodt et al. (2010) and Hamil et al. (2010) observe the paradox that despite numerous scandals in professional football, ranging from match fixing to what has been described as 'financial doping', it remains the most popular sport entertainment activity and hence a powerful social vehicle. Drawing on sport's institutional structure and actors, Godfrey (2009) poses a series of thought-provoking questions to focus attention on CSR issues that may be unique to sport as a social and economic institution. These include:

- What social obligations or responsibilities do athletes, teams and sport organizations have toward the communities in which they are based?
- Do professional teams and leagues have obligations to stay in communities under less than optimal economic conditions?
- Do sport organizations have an obligation to promote values like participation and fair play rather than winning?
- Does the escalation of athlete salaries have non-economic effects on different stakeholders?

Review of CSR in sport

While almost all of the papers on aspects of CSR in sport comment on the lack of attention that CSR has received in sport management, there is now a growing body of literature on the subject. In 2009, a special edition of the *Journal of Sport Management*, a leading journal in the area, was given over to CSR in sport, the aim of which was to enhance and expand the literature by examining research and issues related to CSR within the sport context. This was followed the following year, 2010, by a special issue of the *Journal of Management and Organization*, devoted to CSR, philanthropy and entrepreneurship in sport. Previously, in 2007 both the North American Society of Sport Management Conference and the Academy of Management Annual Meeting included symposia on CSR in professional sport.

Three broad themes dominate the wider CSR literature: 1) conceptual/theoretical papers; 2) motives-oriented work; and 3) outcomes-oriented work. Unsurprisingly sport CSR research studies are concentrated in the second and third of these themes (though as discussed in the previous section, a small number of papers such as Smith and Westerbeek (2007) have focused or touched on conceptual issues such as the distinctiveness of the sport setting and hence its significance to the CSR debate).

The majority of sport CSR papers thus rely on conceptual frameworks developed in the mainstream literature. One exception to this, however, is Breitbarth and Harris's (2008) paper, which, using a blend of induction and deduction reasoning processes, proposes a conceptual model outlining the role that football can play in creating value for its external shareholders, while at the same time positioning itself as an influential social, economic and political agent. Four distinct areas are identified: football as an agent in the creation of humanitarian value, for example through the support of supra-national organizations concerned with nation building; football as a business agent in the creation of financial value for other industries; football as a social agent fostering cultural value, for example through social and personal identification; and football as a functional agent in the creation of reassurance value, which the authors indicate as being the game's ability to bring together commercial and political actors with people, for example through social marketing campaigns. The paper also provides empirical evidence to support the model from case studies of football clubs in four countries: England, Germany, Japan and the United States. At the same time a number of papers which are primarily outcomes-oriented or motives-oriented also contain a conceptual element (see, for example, Lachowetz and Gladden, 2003; Walker and Kent, 2009).

The brief review below sets out some of the principal contributions organized around these two themes, as well as a number of other less easily classified papers.

Outcomes-oriented

Papers in this section include those that focus on the link between CSR and financial performance, as well as studies which consider the impact, effects and influence of CSR actions from a consumer or customer perspective. Prominent here are examinations of sport CSR from a marketing perspective, where the emphasis is on organizational activities that are designed to benefit the organization and society such as cause-related marketing and sponsorship, where the marketing activities are characterized by contributing a specific sum to a designated not-for-profit activity, that in turn encouragers customers to enter into revenue-providing exchanges (Mullen, 1997). More simply it can be thought of as the marketing strategy an organization uses to associate itself with a good cause (Kim et al., 2010).

Lachowetz and Gladden (2003) introduce a framework for evaluating and understanding the effectiveness of cause-related marketing programmes in the spectator sport industry. The conditions necessary for optimal implementation of a cause-related sport marketing programme are identified as: a cause that resonates with consumers and organization; complete and genuine organizational commitment to the cause; evidence of a tangible transfer to the not-for-profit activity; and promotion of the cause-related sport marketing programme. The extent to which these conditions are met will determine the extent to which the following outcomes will result: enhanced brand image, enhanced brand loyalty and consumer brand switching. What emerges in several studies is the suggestion that increasingly sport organizations are strategically deploying their CSR activities in order to contribute to the organization's financial performance while simultaneously making a contribution to society, hence ensuring the sustainability of cause-related marketing (Irwin et al., 2003; Lachowetz and Irwin, 2002; Roy and Graeff, 2003; Walker and Kent, 2009, 2010). In terms of major sport events, an ongoing study at Cambridge University's Judge Business School is seeking to provide a more rigorous view of the supposed return on investment from CSR and grassroots marketing activities, in conjunction with the London 2012 Olympics and other major sport sponsors.

A small body of work has focused on the effects of CSR actions on consumers. Irwin et al. (2003) examined the attitudes, beliefs and purchase intentions of consumers exposed to a firm's sponsorship of a professional golf tournament. They examined the effect that sponsorship of an event, the FedEx St Jude Classic, had on the image of a major US company as well as on consumers' propensity to purchase from that company. (The FedEx St Jude Classic was a PGA Tour event which had raised in excess of $13m for the beneficiary, the St Jude Children's Research Hospital, 90 per cent of which had arisen following FedEx's sponsorship). Their findings were consistent with previous studies, indicating that individuals believe cause-related marketing to be an important and positive component of a company's activities. They also reported that positive attitudes towards sport-themed cause-related sponsorships had the potential to positively impact consumer/spectator impressions. Perhaps of most interest was that female respondents rated all cause-related marketing the same or higher than male respondents, indicating that it would be beneficial for marketers of sport targeting female consumers to consider developing partnerships with appropriate and significant causes.

Walker and Kent (2009) were concerned with the benefits that might accrue to organizations from CSR, specifically the reputational assessment and patronage intentions of consumers in response to various CSR activities within the National Football League (NFL) in the United States. Overall they found a general positivity in sport consumers' responses, with CSR activities found to have a strong and positive impact on the team's reputation. In developing an overall reputational assessment of the team, respondents were concerned not just with sporting performance, but also with non-product dimensions of the organization – in this case CSR – which explained 16 per cent of organizational reputation in their study. At the same time, however, the authors called for future research to be more incisive about the nature of sport fans and how they interpret information about activities related to their team/ club, in particular the use of non-product dimensions by highly identified fans as a way of rationalizing their behavior. In terms of patronage intentions, they found that CSR was a significant predictor of word of mouth and merchandise consumption behaviour; a positive reaction to CSR allowing team fans to show their affiliation by buying team-related products and discussing their team. The authors identify this as a particularly important finding as where consumers perceive an organization as having a good reputation, this is likely to encourage them to talk in positive terms about the team and to demonstrate their affiliation by buying team-related products.

In another study, Walker and Kent (2010) focused on golf and the PGA Tour, long recognized as an industry leader in the area of CSR, seeking to explore whether discretionary/ philanthropic CSR activities might have positive strategic outcomes for the Tour, beyond those pertaining to the direct corporate beneficiaries. They found that PGA Tour consumers' faith in CSR was much broader than had previously been conceptualized. In addition to benefits that organizations would gain as a result of increased standing in the community, they also found that CSR had a substantial strategic role which can provide 'value' for the Tour. Specifically, consumers' patronage intentions towards the Tour were significantly related to their belief in the CSR agenda, suggesting that social responsiveness can also lead to market competitiveness. Moreover, it was found that the most effective way to achieve secondary value for the organization was by integrating the core product (the PGA Tour) and social responsibility.

Another study concerned with CSR actions on consumers' perceptions and opinions was that carried out by Giannoulakis and Drayer (2009). Here the focus was on the way consumer perceptions of NBA (National Basketball Association) players were influenced by league CSR initiatives like the NBA Cares program, an outreach initiative designed to address social issues with an emphasis on programmes that support education, youth and family development and health-related activities. Player image had been a major problem for the NBA following a number of controversies, including a brawl between players representing Detroit

Pistons and Indiana Pacers and various instances of steroid, drug and alcohol abuse. Consequently, questions about the authenticity of the NBA Cares programme and the motivations of the league and players in introducing it had been raised. Findings from the exploratory study suggested that while concerns about player image were still evident, the NBA Cares programme did appear to strengthen the image of the league and its players. This finding was considered to be of particular significance to the league given the impact players' images have on financial outcomes like ticket sales, merchandising and sponsorship deals. A further interesting comment in this paper was its appeal to entities like the NBA to prioritize the monitoring and evaluation of social and community initiatives.

Motives-oriented

A small number of studies on CSR in sport have focused on motivations for sport organizations to engage in CSR, as well as on related issues like perspectives and understandings of CSR. One such paper is Babiak and Wolfe (2009), who, in response to a call from Margiolis and Walsh (2003) for researchers to look beyond the relationship between financial and social performance, sought to broaden the focus, instead concentrating on contextual forces that encourage sport organizations to become more socially responsible. Based on a sample of US professional sport teams in the NFL, MLB (Major League Baseball), NHL (National Hockey League) and NBA that had demonstrated a commitment to CSR initiatives, they adopted a qualitative approach involving the analysis of organizational documents, followed up by semi-structured interviews with mid- to high-ranking individuals working for professional sport teams.

The interviews were used to ascertain the motives for the organization's CSR involvement, based around the key question: 'Why is your organization involved in CSR?' The data showed that external drivers of CSR (i.e. strategic responses to institutional pressures such as from the league, or the interconnectedness of the organizational field) play a more important role in determining the adoption of CSR by professional sport teams than internal drivers (resources like supporter passion and identification, media access and profile, or celebrity employees). They comment on the difficulties in both sustaining socially beneficial CSR initiatives that are driven by external factors due to poor alignment with internal values and core competencies, and conversely, in ensuring that internally driven CSR initiatives, appropriately aligned with internal values and competencies, reflect wider societal needs. Based on this they propose a framework that considers both external pressures and internal resources to explain the adoption and focus of CSR in professional sport organizations.

The perception and practice of CSR in North American professional sport franchises, in the shape of executives in those organizations, was the focus of a paper by Sheth and Babiak (2009). (The paper discussed in more detail in the final section of this chapter also explores similar themes in professional football in one part of the UK.) The Sheth and Babiak study found that professional sport executives view CSR as a strategic imperative for their business. The philanthropic nature of CSR in sport was emphasized by nearly all the respondents. Beyond philanthropy as an altruistic activity, it was also seen as a strategic tool to advance business interests, to improve the organization's image and to help the community in which the team operated. Related to this last point, the importance of developing and maintaining partnerships and network was also stressed, these being seen as an effective way to work for the betterment of a community.

Ethical and philanthropic responsibilities were found to be viewed as more important than legal or economic ones, a finding the authors attributed, in part at least, to the prevalence of ethical concerns in US professional sport at that time (cf. Carroll, 1979, 1999). They suggest that the most interesting relationships uncovered in their study were between organizational variables investigated and CSR perceptions and reporting. In particular they found that teams that are successful on the field may not require the image–enhancing function or community relationship building that socially responsible efforts might provide, while a team that is enjoying less on–field success may want to maintain its name and brand in the community. This was in line with the ranking of CSR priorities by executives, where they found that those who placed more of a priority on ethical/philanthropic CSR came from teams with lower winning percentages, suggesting perhaps that CSR is being used as a tool to enhance team/brand image in communities in which teams operate.

Looking beyond the United States, a number of studies, particularly around professional football, have considered CSR from a corporate governance-type perspective, broadening the issue of motivation to include issues of organizational form, ownership and organizational objectives. The majority of these studies around professional football have used some version of the stakeholder theory of the firm as the basis for analysis and discussion. This work has been most prominent in the United Kingdom, where there has been considerable attention devoted to the appropriateness of the limited liability corporate ownership model prevalent in most British football clubs to organizations grounded in society and community (Brown et al., 2010; Hamil, 1999; Morrow, 2003). The study carried out by Brown et al. (2010) was commissioned by Supporters Direct, an organization set up by the UK government to encourage greater supporter involvement in and ownership of British football clubs. The specific aims of the research were to:

- investigate ways in which we might measure or account for the social and community value of football clubs;
- identify evidence of the added value that alternative fan or community ownership structures might bring;
- outline how the community role of football clubs relates to wider regulatory issues.

The final and summary reports are all available on the Supporters Direct website, along with the working papers which sought to provide a broader framework in which to consider the social and community value of football by relating it to wider debate around areas like social accounting (Ashton, 2008), social value (New Economics Foundation, 2008), the valuation of public goods (Barlow, 2008), and measuring the social impact of football (Casey-Challies, 2008). The report concludes that football as a whole has a great deal to gain from promoting an improved understanding of its social value, developing an appropriate framework through which it can be assessed and reporting its activities. In terms of motivations, it observes that 'there are good business reasons as well as those of an enlightened self-interest in taking [the promotion and reporting of the social value of football] more seriously' (p. 56). The report concludes by making a number of recommendations directed at clubs, football authorities, supporter agencies and governments, the aim of which is to make football a modern and responsible business.

Other CSR themes

In other papers focusing on professional football in the UK, Walters and Tacon (2010) use stakeholder theory to examine three key CSR issues around stakeholder definition and salience, firm actions and responses, and stakeholder actions and responses. Their study was based on interviews with senior stakeholder representatives from a number of different clubs, supporter bodies and football agencies and illustrated how stakeholder management strategies could be used to implement CSR. In a further paper, Walters (2009) uses Smith and Westerbeek's (2007) framework to consider the potential role that community sport trusts can play in helping commercial organizations meet their CSR objectives.

CSR has also been considered at the level of major events and event hosting. For example, in a paper focused on the Super Bowl, Babiak and Wolfe (2006) outlined the CSR activities undertaken by the NFL and the Super Bowl committee, as well as discussing how these activities could be used to build the NFL's image as a socially responsible professional sport league. Misener and Mason's (2009, 2010) studies focus on sporting events and community development, as well as considering how sport and non sport organizations can develop socially responsible programmes in conjunction with event hosting. Seguin et al.'s (2010) study was based on the use of CSR (or corporate support) rather than event sponsorship for a one-off major sporting event, the 2005 FINA World Aquatic Championships. The authors distinguish corporate support from event sponsorship by emphasizing that it is motivated by concerns related to civic engagement and social responsibility, rather than potential return on investment. The paper used stakeholder theory to determine how the organizing committee went about gaining corporate support and to consider how transferable this strategy would be for other events. The data analysed in their study re-affirmed the notion that a community as a whole benefits from hosting major events. Comparing their findings to Carroll's (1979, 1999) CSR aspects, they reported that these were most clearly associated with the economic aspect (securing corporate funding for the event), but that legal and also discretionary aspects were also in evidence. Leadership and political and networking skills were also important in acquiring corporate support, along with the positioning of the event/sport as a cause.

Corporate social responsibility in the Scottish Premier League: context and motivation

In the final section of this chapter a description is provided of a study of CSR carried out by Hamil and Morrow (2011) in a very specific professional sporting context, the Scottish Premier (Football) League (SPL). The study involved all twelve clubs that were members of the SPL in season 2007/08. The project was concerned with a number of aspects of CSR among the SPL clubs, including types of engagement, mechanisms of structure and delivery, and motives and orientation, the latter being analysed in the context of Donaldson and Preston's (1995) explanatory framework of the firm. Drawing on previous work in this area by both authors, the stakeholder theory of organizations was used to interpret the implications for football clubs.

The SPL provides an interesting research site within which to consider CSR for a number of reasons: the high public and media profile of football in Scotland (and in the UK); the high degree of stakeholder engagement in Scottish football clubs; the depiction of Scottish football clubs as being embedded in their communities – both geographical and cultural communities – and hence favourably positioned to influence society in general and specific communities; and the historical emphasis on relationships between business and society in Scotland's political and social structure, in particular the emphasis of social democratic communitarianism.

Football clubs in the SPL vary markedly in size and status. The two largest SPL clubs have annual turnovers which range anywhere from £45 million to £70 million depending on on-field success, in particular qualification for the lucrative UEFA Champions' League, and average weekly home attendances of around 50–60,000 people. At the other end of the scale the SPL is home to a number of clubs where turnover is in the region of £3–4m, with average weekly home attendances of 4–5,000. All the clubs are structured as shareholder-owned limited liability companies and the majority have concentrated ownership structures, i.e.

where one or a few individuals own a large percentage of shares in the club. But notwith-standing their corporate status, the majority of the clubs behave as not-for-profit organiza-tions, focusing on utility maximization rather than on the maximization of shareholder wealth. Few clubs make a financial profit. Indeed over the last 21 years, a combined profit has been reported for clubs in the SPL in only two seasons (2006/07 – £3m; 2007/08 – £23m) (PricewaterhouseCoopers, 2010).

Publicly available information including annual financial reports over a three-year period (financial years ending in 2005–07) and clubs' official websites was used to provide a picture of CSR activity, both descriptive and strategic, among the SPL's clubs. Content analysis was used to code the information disclosed under a number of pre-defined themes encompassing elements of social and community activity: education-related activities, charitable activities, youth development-/gender-related activities, environmental initiatives, health initiatives, supporter-related initiatives, economic/regeneration issues and social inclusion/exclusion. Some examples of the types of initiatives currently undertaken by SPL clubs are set out in Table 8.1.

Table 8.1 Examples of CSR activities undertaken by SPL clubs

Club(s)	Project	Background
Celtic and Rangers	Vibrant Glasgow	Seeks to engage asylum seekers and refugees. The project aims to improve employability skills and self-confidence, developing a strong, fair and inclusive community.
Heart of Midlothian	Onside	Seeks to engage Young Offenders, focusing on education, employment and social responsibility exercises within a football setting.
Hibernian	Kick for Kids	Young people from Edinburgh-based charities engaging with local businesses to purchase season tickets for the benefit of those less fortunate.
Kilmarnock	Killie Cheerleaders	Focusing on girls from 8 to 18 years old, the project aims to encourage healthier and more physically active lifestyles and to encourage greater social inclusion through the presence of more females in and around the club.
Motherwell	Give Learning a Sporting Chance	Aims to use sport as the hook to encourage participants back into learning. The programme covers literacy and numeracy skills, healthy eating, report writing, presentations and business skills within a football environment.
St Johnstone	'Plus' – Mental Health Project	Football coaching sessions aimed at bringing people with mental health problems together to reduce the stigma of poor mental health, facilitate recovery through increased physical activity and encourage confidence and self-esteem.
St Mirren	Panda Club Diary	Focused on primary school children, the project delivers creative writing lessons using football as the hook and aims to increase literary skills.

Source: Scottish Premier League, 2011

111

Semi-structured interviews were then held with representatives of all twelve SPL clubs, consistent with Breitbarth and Harris's (2008) call for interviews covering entire leagues. The primary purpose of the interviews was to establish the motivation for clubs' engagement in CSR. To that end, the target interviewees were managers with responsibility for CSR policy and practice. The interviews also focused on establishing the purpose and forms of CSR communication, the structures of clubs' community departments, their links with public/private agencies and the extent to which clubs involved stakeholders in their CSR activities.

In terms of communication, little or no disclosure is provided by most clubs in their annual reports, while limited use is made of electronic communication via club websites. The most likely explanation for this is that the small size of most of the organizations limits their opportunities to devote resources to prioritizing CSR communication. Another explanation is that the concentrated ownership structures prevalent in most of the clubs, where one or a few individuals own a large percentage of shares in the company, encourages club executives to see the annual report as simply a legal reporting requirement, rather than also as a vehicle through which to communicate with wider groups of interested stakeholders.

Notwithstanding this, given clubs' corporate status, improved communication would be potentially advantageous in terms of helping to legitimize their CSR orientation and activities, as well as addressing agency issues which could arise from perceptions of directors or executives pursuing private interests.

CSR activities are delivered by the football club itself (or some division thereof) in just over half the clubs and through a separate foundation or company in the other clubs. Those clubs which kept the activities in-house emphasized the benefits this provided in terms of retaining control of the activities the club was associated with. It was also seen as important by some clubs from a public relations perspective, allowing the club to make a statement that community activities were central to its activities. An important argument advanced in favour of a separate structure was that this reduced dependence on the inevitably unpredictable on-field performance of clubs, hence lessening the risk that expenditure on social and community activities might be seen as discretionary. At the same time it was acknowledged that this approach carried with it the risk that social and community activities could be ghettoized.

For some clubs involvement in CSR was normatively motivated, philanthropic behaviour which benefits the recipient only and demonstrates the donor's social conscience. For others it was instrumentally motivated, used as a strategic tool through which to secure competitive advantage. At one small club, ostensibly all community activity was motivated by a philanthropic desire on the part of the majority owner to give something back to the community. (This was an unusual case, where a very small club was transformed on the field of play through the owner's investment. The structure was not, however, sustainable and the club went into liquidation after the owner became terminally ill.) A small number of clubs talked in terms of their commitment to CSR reflecting the ethos of their club and of CSR providing a means by which their obligations to, and expectations of, their community of stakeholders could be fulfilled. At other clubs the embeddedness of highly engaged stakeholders (supporter groups) in the management of the organization was a contributory factor in motivating CSR engagement and in ensuring congruence in terms of prioritizing community and social activities.

The last decade or so has been financially challenging for Scottish football with clubs reporting sustained losses, record levels of indebtedness and several clubs having been placed in administration. In view of this it was unsurprising that at several clubs an instrumental approach was evident, with CSR engagement being motivated by financial objectives, immediate and/or longer term. This could be characterized as a form of enlightened self-interest: club executives recognizing the fundamental importance of the club's communities in sustaining it as a business. In this context it is important to note that television income in Scotland is markedly lower than in countries like England or other major television markets: £13m per annum for the SPL, compared to approximately £600m per annum in the English Premier League. Hence for Scottish clubs, the direct community of supporters remains the principal source of revenue.

Irrespective of the motivations espoused, one pervasive feature of the interviews was an absolute and unquestioning belief that football clubs were uniquely positioned to deliver CSR in Scotland. The views of the interviewees and their justification for those views reflected the arguments made by authors like Smith and Westerbeek (2007) and Babiak and Wolfe (2009), who had identified features which contribute to making professional sport an ideal vehicle through which to deliver CSR. Several clubs were seeking to take advantage of football's putative special community role in an instrumental way to secure external funding; most noticeably by seeking to align their CSR activities with broader public sector or government social agendas. Linking this to previous comments, a further benefit of improved CSR communication by clubs would be to increase awareness of their activities, which in turn may increase their opportunities to engage in other funded social partnerships. At the same time, however, there was limited evidence of clubs undertaking monitoring and/or evaluation of their CSR projects, something which one would expect to see improve as a result of receiving public funding.

Scottish football clubs are an enduring presence in their communities, a reflection on their continuing reinterpretation of how they interact with and affect their communities, both economically and socially. The challenge is to harness the potential and the commitment within the clubs around CSR. Opportunities exist to improve the communication of clubs' CSR activities, one benefit of which may be to facilitate partnership working in pursuit of wider social agendas. At the same time, greater engagement with clubs' stakeholders and improved monitoring and evaluation of projects were identified as requirements within the SPL.

Summary

Sport is a prominent social and economic institution across the world. For many years sport organizations and athletes have been active in community development initiatives. In recent years, however, there has been evidence of a more formalized approach to CSR among sport organizations. Sport-related CSR is seen by some as having characteristics which distinguish it from CSR in other areas of activity, in particular its media profile and attractiveness to youth; characteristics which make it an ideal vehicle through which to promote CSR. These dimensions contribute to the effectiveness of sport CSR programmes and of their ability to generate awareness of social problems. The impact and power that sport has with respect to its CSR-related practices is also reflected in the growing body of academic literature on the subject. There continue to be opportunities for further development of this literature, including issues as diverse as stakeholder congruence around CSR motivation and engagement; the connection between 'doing good' and the public relations function and role of leagues, teams and clubs; cost–benefit analysis of sport CSR; and the relationship between organizational form and effective delivery of sport-related CSR.

References

Ashton, A. (2008) *Playing with a standard formation: social accounting for football clubs and supporters trusts – towards a unified approach*, Manchester, Substance.

Babiak, K. and Wolfe, R. (2009) 'Determinants of corporate social responsibility in professional sport: External and internal factors', *Journal of Sport Management*, 23: 717–42.

——— (2006) 'More than just a game? Corporate social responsibilities and the Super Bowl XL', *Sport Marketing Quarterly*, 15, 214–22.

Barlow, A. (2008) *Do we know the true value of football? A review of the methodologies used to value public goods*, Manchester, Substance.

Beutler, I. (2008) 'Sport serving development and peace: Achieving the goals of the United Nations through sport', *Sport in Society*, 11(4), 359–69.

Blumrodt, J., Desbordes, M. and Bodin, D. (2010) 'The sport entertainment industry and corporate social responsibility', *Journal of Management and Organization*, 16(4), 514–29.

Breitbarth, T. and Harris, P. (2008) 'The role of corporate social responsibility in the football business: Towards the development of a conceptual model', *European Sport Management Quarterly*, 8(2), 179–206.

Bridgewater, S. (2010) *Football Brands*, Basingstoke, Palgrave.

Brown, A., McGee, F., Brown, M. and Ashton, A. (2010) *The social and community value of football. The final report*, London, Supporters Direct.

Carroll, A. B. (1999) 'Corporate social responsibility: Evolution of a definitional construct', *Business and Society*, 38(3), 268–96.

——— (1979) 'A three-dimensional conceptual model of corporate performance', *Academy of Management Review*, 4(4), 497–505.

Casey-Challies, R. (2008) *Measuring the social impact of football*, Manchester, Substance.

Claeys, G. (1992) 'After "Socialism": Mr Owen, democracy, and the future' in C. Tsuzuki (ed.) *Robert Owen and the World of Co-operation*, Tokyo, Robert Owen Association of Japan, 3–28.

Coalter, F. (2007) *A Wider Social Role for Sport: Who's keeping the score?* London, Routledge.

Donaldson, T. and Preston, L. (1995) 'The stakeholder theory of the modern corporation: Concepts, evidence and implications', *Academy of Management* Review, 20, 65–91.

Freeman, R. E., Harrison, J. S., Wicks, A. C., Parmar, B. L. and De Colle, S. (2010) *Stakeholder Theory: The state of the art*, Cambridge, Cambridge University Press.

Friedman, M. (1970) 'The social responsibility of business is to increase profit', *New York Times Magazine*, September 13, 33.

Giannoulakis, C. and Drayer, J. (2009) ' "Thugs" versus "Good Guys": The impact of NBA cares on player image', *European Sport Management Quarterly*, 9(4), 453–68.

Giulianotti, R. (2005) *Sport: A Critical Sociology*, Cambridge, Polity Press.

Godfrey, P.C. (2009) 'Corporate social responsibility in sport: an overview and key issues', *Journal of Sport Management*, 23, 698–716.

Gray, R., Owen, D. and Adams, C. (1996) *Accounting and Accountability: Changes and challenges in corporate social and environmental reporting*, London, Prentice Hall.

Hamil, S. (1999) 'A Whole New Ball Game: Why Football Needs a Regulator' in S. Hamil, J. Michie and C. Oughton (eds) *The Business of Football: A Game of Two Halves*, Edinburgh, Mainstream, 23–39.

Hamil, S. and Morrow, S. (2011) 'Corporate Social Responsibility in the Scottish Premier League: Context and Motivation', *European Sport Management Quarterly*, 11(2), 143–70.

Hamil, S., Morrow, S., Idle, C., Rossi, G. and Facchendini, S. (2010) 'The governance and regulation of Italian football', *Soccer and Society*, 11(4), 373–413.

Holt, R. (1989) *Sport and the British: A modern history*, Oxford, Oxford University Press.

Irwin, R. L., Lachowetz, T., Cornwell, T. B. and Clark, J. S. (2003) 'Cause-related sport sponsorship: An assessment of spectator beliefs, attitudes, and behavioural intentions', *Sport Marketing Quarterly*, 12(3), 131–39.

Kakabadse, A. P., Kakabadse, N. K. and Rozuel, C. (2007) 'Corporate Social Responsibility: Contrast of Meanings and Intents' in A. Kakabadse and N. Kakabadse (eds) *CSR in Practice: Delving deep*, Basingstoke, Palgrave, 9–45.

Kidd, B. (2008) 'A new social movement: Sport for development and peace', *Sport in Society*, 11(4), 370–80.

Kim, K. T., Kwak, D. H. and Kim, Y. K. (2010) 'The impact of cause-related marketing (CRM) in spectator sport', *Journal of Management and Organization*, 16(4), 515–27.

Lachowetz, T. and Gladden, J. (2003) 'A framework for understanding cause-related sport marketing programs', *International Journal of Sport Marketing and Sponsorship*, December/January, 313–33.

Lachowetz, T. and Irwin, R. (2002) 'FedEx and the St. Jude Classic: An application of a cause-related sport marketing program (CRMP)', *Sport Marketing Quarterly*, 11(2), 114–16.

Levermore, R. (2010) 'CSR for development through sport: Examining its potential and limitations', *Third World Quarterly*, 31(2), 223–41.

McWilliams, A. and Siegel, D. (2000) 'Corporate social responsibility and financial performance: Correlation or misspecification?', *Strategic Management Journal*, 21(5), 603–18.

Margiolis, J. D. and Walsh, J. P. (2003) 'Misery loves companies: Rethinking social initiatives by business', *Administrative Science Quarterly*, 48(2), 268–305.

Misener, L. and Mason, D. (2010) 'Towards a community centred approach to corporate community involvement in the sporting events agenda', *Journal of Management and Organization*, 16(4), 495–514.

—— (2009) 'Fostering community development through sporting event strategies: An examination of urban regime perceptions', *Journal of Sport Management*, 23, 770–94.

Morrow, S. (2003) *The People's Game? Football, finance and society*, Basingstoke, Palgrave.

Mullen, J. (1997) 'Performance-based corporate philanthropy: How "giving smart" can further corporate goals', *Public Relations Quarterly*, 42(2), 42–48.

New Economics Foundation (2008) *Football, ownership and social value*, Manchester, Substance.

PriceWaterhouseCoopers (2010) *The 21st annual financial review of Scottish Premier League football*, Glasgow, PWC.

Roy, D. P. and Graeff, T. R. (2003) 'Consumer attitudes towards cause-related marketing activities in professional sport', *Sport Marketing Quarterly*, 12(3), 163–72.

Scottish Premier League (2011) *Football clubs and the community: SPL Community Report 2011*, Glasgow, SPL.

Seguin, B., Parent, M. and O'Reilly, N. (2010) 'Corporate support: a corporate social responsibility alternative to traditional event sponsorship', *International Journal of Sport Management and Marketing*, 7(3/4), 202–22

Sheth, H. and Babiak, K. M. (2009) 'Beyond the game: Perceptions and practices of corporate social responsibility in the professional sport industry', *Journal of Business Ethics*, 91(3), 433–50.

Smith, A. and Westerbeek, H. (2007) 'Sport as a vehicle for deploying corporate social responsibility', *Journal of Corporate Citizenship*, 25, 43–54.

Tacon, R. (2007) 'Football and social inclusion: Evaluating social policy', *Managing Leisure*, 12(1), 1–23.

Ullman, A. H. (1985) 'Data in search of a theory: A critical examination of the relationship among social performance, social disclosure and economic performance in US firms', *Academy of Management Review*, 10(3), 540–57.

Walker, M. and Kent, A. (2010) 'CSR on tour? Attitudes towards corporate social responsibility among golf fans', *International Journal of Sport Management*, 11, 179–206.

—— (2009) 'Do fans care? Assessing the influence of corporate social responsibility on consumer attitudes in the sport industry', *Journal of Sport Management*, 23, 743–69.

Walters, G. (2009) 'Corporate social responsibility through sport: The community sport trust model as a CSR delivery agency', *Journal of Corporate Citizenship*, 35, 81–94.

Walters, G. and Tacon, R. (2010) 'Corporate social responsibility in sport: Stakeholder management in the UK football industry', *Journal of Management and Organisation*, 16(4), 566–86.

Wood, D. (1991) 'Corporate social performance revisited', *Academy of Management Review*, 15(4), 691–718.

9

THEORETICAL APPROACHES AND PRACTICAL STRATEGIES FOR CHANGE MANAGEMENT

Peter McGraw, Tracy Taylor and Daniel Lock

Introduction

The ways in which people play, train, coach, manage and engage in sport are constantly changing. The changing nature of sport is driven by a complex array of social, economic, technological and political factors. Consequently, managers of sporting organizations, both professional and non-professional, are confronted with the challenge of leading change initiatives whilst other members and associates of these organizations are faced with the rigors of the implementation of, and adaptation to, these change initiatives.

As in the broader business world, the pace of change for sporting organizations has increased sharply in recent times. Some of the reasons for this increasing pace can be broadly classified into the following areas: social changes which incorporate demographic and cultural aspects; economic changes linked to the globalization of markets; the rapid development of new technologies (see Box 9.1); and changes in the political environments which organizations operate in. Changes in one area will more than likely stimulate changes in other areas, the interconnected nature of which is illustrated below.

As modern society has become more commercially focused, consumer driven and globalized, so has sport. The amateur, locally-based leisure pastime of sport and its organization has evolved, in many instances, into a professional, highly competitive and lucrative industry with international exposure. Increasing globalization and competitive pressures in professional sport have also led to professional sport generating substantial revenue through media rights, sponsorship and merchandising, which in turn leads to escalating salaries for players and coaches and the globalization of the marketplace for talent.

For professional sport the ever-expanding earning power of athletes, the cult of the sport superstar, and the rise of the player agent, greatly facilitated by an ever-expanding media and sponsorship reach, has changed the very nature of the business of sport. Professional sport has spawned a myriad of associated services and large multinational sport giants such as Octagon and IMG are no longer just sport agents but now deal in event management, hospitality, league development, licensing, media distribution and sponsorship.

At the community level local sports that do not have professional leagues or competitions have to compete with sports that have access to greater funds and sponsorship revenue. At the same time there has been increasing pressure on community sport organizations to deliver

Box 9.1 New technologies – a changing sport landscape

Sport organizations worldwide continually grapple with a myriad of new technologies that seem to emerge on a daily basis. One technology that has been embraced almost universally is what is generically termed 'new media', that is the development of interactive websites, streaming audio and video, chat rooms, online communities, web advertising, and virtual reality environments among others (Santomier and Shuart, 2008).

YouTube is increasingly used by sport governing bodies, clubs and fans to distribute audiovisual coverage of sporting events. The National Hockey League (NHL) in North America was one of the first governing bodies of sport to launch its own YouTube channel in 2006. This enabled the NHL to bypass traditional television outlets, open up other revenue streams through advertising and subscription and get direct editorial control over how the sport is produced (Boyle and Haynes, 2009). In 2007, this model was followed by Chelsea Football Club, which launched their own YouTube channel to showcase news and interviews with players and the manager.

Another example is technology-based ticketing systems that have been introduced by all major sport stadia around the globe. The technologies most commonly used are magnetic stripes tickets/cards, electronic tickets via internet, smart cards and mobile ticketing systems. Most systems are a cheaper and more effective way to handle ticket sales for organizations and allow 24/7 purchasing, last-minute discounts and other benefits. These systems have radically changed the way stadia and sport organizations operate. Currently ticketing is often outsourced to ticket seller and distributer companies, such as Ticketed and Ticketmaster, which reduces operational issues and costs (Karaiskos, Kourouthanassis and Giaglis, 2007).

New technologies are now prominent in the development of sport equipment and clothing. This is a challenge for many sport organizations that must continuously adapt competition rules and policies. A recent example that caused much public attention and challenged all parties involved was the revolutionary Arena swimsuits used at the 2009 World Swimming Championships in Rome, where dozens of records were broken due to the use of polyurethane (a form of plastic) in the suits. The suits were consequently banned on the grounds that they artificially enhanced performance (Ross, 2010). As this example illustrates, the introduction of new technology forces sport organizations to constantly adapt to technological developments.

Modern technologies have changed the world of sport. Technological developments and innovations not only create opportunities for new organizations to enter the marketplace but create whole new markets – such as new sport (Boyle and Haynes, 2009). Also, modern technologies have changed the structure of organizations (Slack and Parent, 2006), the way they operate and their inter-organizational relationship (for example between sport producer and sport broadcaster). On the one hand, sport organizations have become more regulated and interdependent, as is shown by the symbiotic relationship between sport and the media (Lange, Nicholson and Hess, 2007; Turner and Shilbury, 2010). On the other hand, modern technologies make organizations more independent and self-regulated as new communication channels such as the internet enable them to communicate directly with fans, participants and others (Hutchins, 2008; Webb, 2007).

Many sport organizations have become highly professional as they embrace new technologies (Webb, 2007). Whether these imply more benefits than costs for an organization depends on many factors. With the right skills and knowledge, sport organizations can definitely benefit from modern technologies in many ways such as through a more efficient operation or more communication channels that reach out internationally (Slack and Parent, 2006; Santomier and Shuart, 2008;

Kriemadis, Terzoudis and Kartakoullis, 2010) or other business-generating opportunities (Webb, 2007). However, modern technologies often imply additional costs as they can be very expensive and qualified staff are needed (Santomier and Shuart, 2008; Slack and Parent, 2006). Therefore, it is often a challenge for sport organizations to embrace modern technologies, especially when resources are scarce (Santomier and Shuart, 2008).

The rapid development of technologies in sport also forces sport organizations and clubs to acquire more high-tech and sophisticated training and athlete development methods in order to stay competitive. This often implies high costs but opens up new avenues of revenue as athletes can be better developed and assessed (Chadwick, 2009). Regardless of the nature of innovations, sport organizations must seek to quickly adapt to modern technologies to manage their ongoing activities and operations (Turner and Shilbury, 2010).

'professional' services, from facilities to coaching, with limited resources; and to top it off there has been a worldwide decline in the numbers of citizens volunteering in sport organizations. Government policy, regulations and reporting requirements have led to an increased bureaucratization of sport and escalating safety requirements have meant that even non-professional sport organizations have to develop ever-widening organizational capabilities to manage risk and liability.

A country's political regime and approach to sport through policy and funding can also be major change drivers. For example, after the demise of the USSR many of the newly independent states were left with a sporting system that had to be completely restructured and reorganized. In other countries a change of government or its policy platform has meant either a discontinuation of funding or the requirement to meet certain targets and management standards to attain support.

In addition to change stemming from external sources, organizations also need to manage change from internal sources. Internal change comes from the need to adapt and innovate organizational strategies, structures and processes to the changing external environment either in response to external change stimuli or in anticipation of them. For example, the introduction of web-based data systems requires managers, employees and volunteers to learn new ways of responding to simple administrative matters such as membership applications, funding requests and human resource matters.

In short, there are many reasons why sport organizations have to change and equally there are many types of organizational responses to the need for change. The stimulus for change may come from broad structural changes in the macro level, external social and economic environment but the response is always initiated at the micro level of human agency (i.e. how managers of sport organizations interpret the changing external environment and their responses to it). Such responses will vary depending on the context of the organization as defined by its external and internal environment, the content of the particular change initiative being introduced and the process adopted to introduce change (Pettigrew, 1997).

Types and characteristics of change

The way that change is managed will relate to the nature of the change, its origins and the extent to which the change impacts on the everyday activities of those involved. There are many different types of organizational change, ranging from minor changes in systems or

Table 9.1 A schematic overview of different change issues

Characteristic/Issue	Alternatives from each end of spectrum	
Stimulus	External	Internal
Scale and Scope	Revolutionary	Evolutionary
Strategy and Timing	Planned	Emergent
Language	Rational	Non-rational
Drivers/Leaders	Top down	Bottom up
Environmental determinants and duration	Equilibrium (single issue and non-continuous)	Non-equilibrium (continuous change and multiple issues)
Power and resources	Non-political, e.g. improving internal efficiency	Political, e.g. power struggle between different stakeholders over organizational mission, resource allocations, etc.
Direction	Linear	Non-linear
Emphasis	Macro-organizational strategy/ structure/systems and processes	Micro-behavioural change at the level of individuals

work practices that only affect a small number of people, to major shifts in the way sport organizations do business which require total organizational restructures. Table 9.1 provides a schematic overview of some of the different characteristics of change with examples from each end of a possible spectrum of alternatives.

As can be seen from Table 9.1 the contours of change can vary enormously, depending first on the mix of characteristics and issues involved in any particular change and secondly on the point of focus for any particular characteristic. These are discussed in the following sub-sections.

External and internal

At the most fundamental level change can be regarded as inevitable and ubiquitous for all organizations, although the requirements and pace may vary depending on a range of contingencies. As discussed in the introduction to this chapter, organizational change can result from changed external circumstances or internal adaptation and innovation. External factors are typically viewed to be the most powerful of the forces driving change but internal adaptation should also be acknowledged. Two academic perspectives are helpful in better understanding the relationship between external and internal change.

First, the economic perspective outlines the core assumption that in a competitive world the survival of all organizations depends on their ability to respond to changing external competitive circumstances. The examples already given in the introduction illustrate how changing external circumstances require organizations to respond to large-scale change in external environments. Second, from an organizational learning perspective organizations can be viewed as having an internal capability for adaptation which will be higher in successful organizations. From this perspective change is not always directly precipitated by an external event but may occur in anticipation of the need to respond to external events. Thus, in the first instance organizational change is viewed more as a direct and largely reactive response to external stimulus whereas in the second it is viewed more as a proactive internal capability to pre-empt the need for chaotic responses.

Both perspectives are useful in theorizing how change occurs and clearly point to the key role of managers and leaders in correctly interpreting the signals of the need for change and responding in an appropriate and timely manner. Managers, in their role as key players in assessing the strengths and weaknesses of organizations and the need to respond to opportunities and threats, take centre stage in the change management process.

Environmental opportunities and threats can come from many directions, such as:

- Increasing market competition, e.g. HD sport telecasts;
- Possibilities offered by new markets, e.g. soccer in Asia and Africa;
- External regulatory mandates, e.g. public liability insurance;
- Pressure to conform to what other organizations are doing, e.g. social media;
- Reputational risk and credibility pressures, e.g. FIFA's decision-making processes in allocating host countries for football World Cups.

In anticipating and responding to environmental change by building appropriate internal capabilities and taking appropriate actions/decisions, managers must take account of the strengths and weaknesses of the organization in areas such as:

- Organizational learning capacity, i.e. how ready is the organization to learn new behavioral responses and techniques?;
- Organizational capacity for change in terms of e.g. systems flexibility;
- The forces for stability and continuity and the views of key stakeholders;
- Strategic clarity (or lack of it) around vision, mission and values that may prevent the organization from over-responding to short term environmental turbulence;
- The balance of power between different managers and units within the organization and whether there is a consensus on the need for and direction of change.

Evolution and revolution

The scale and scope of change is another major variable influencing the impact on sport organizations. Evolutionary change is an incremental process whereby organizations make minor changes to their strategy, structure or practices over time in relatively stable external environments. Revolutionary change, as suggested by the name, occurs when the organization engages in a monumental shift in its focus, structure or culture and changes the essence of the organization. Such a dramatic change is typically driven by a need to respond to radically significant events in the sport organization's operating environment. A well-documented example of revolutionary change can be found in the work of Slack, Kikulis and colleagues (cf. Kikulis, Slack and Hinings, 1995: Amis, Slack and Hinings, 2002) in their description and analysis of the changes in Canadian national sport organizations (NSOs) in the 1980s when federal government funding requirements necessitated the introduction of systems and structures that moved the NSOs from an amateur to a professional approach to their operations. A more recent example of a revolutionary change is evidenced in the complete restructuring of the Australian Soccer Association into the Football Federation of Australia (FFA). This process of wide-ranging structural change was instigated following a Federal Government inquiry into the governance structure of the sport (Lock et al., 2009) and is discussed at the end of this chapter.

Other factors

Change can also be viewed as *planned* or *emergent*. Much of the managerialist literature on change, stemming back to the earliest work on the subject, presents management as concerned with planning, co-ordinating, controlling and implementing to ensure that intended changes are translated into realized changes within the organization. From this perspective change is viewed primarily as a *top-down, non-political* and largely *linear* activity. Emergent change perspectives generally recognize that unforeseen and unintended consequences will arise as change is implemented and that the final change outcome will be influenced by either unforeseen issues or political processes driven by opponents of the planned change, particularly resistance from people within the organization who will be most affected by it. From this perspective change can also be viewed as *bottom up* and *political* and *non-linear*. Related to the degree to which change is implemented as originally planned is the issue of whether the outcome of change is *rational* (efficiency related only) or *non-rational*, whereby change can be driven by wider political agendas of various stakeholders which often result in compromise positions.

In this chapter the focus will be on change that is generally within the rational and contextual approaches. *Rational* models of organizational change suggest that change occurs through following a systematic programme led by organizational strategists and leaders such as directors and managers. *Contextual* approaches to change differ from rational perspectives in that change is seen as the outcome of non-linear, multilevel and incremental processes that are shaped by competing group interests, organizational power and politics (Caldwell, 2005). An insightful perspective explaining non-rational, contextual and emergent organizational change can be found in the explanations contained within institutional theory.

The underlying idea within institutional theory is that an organization's governance structures are based on rules, norms, values and systems of cultural meaning and that decisions are institutionally aggregated. Historical institutionalism suggests that organizations keep equilibrium through the maintenance of the status quo, while sociological institutionalism suggests that organizations seek consolidation of institutional legitimacy in a changing environment (DiMaggio and Powell, 1983).

Change and innovations can be introduced to improve performance in one organization which are modelled on successful techniques used in other organizations. Or changes may be introduced to 'keep up with the Joneses', that is, to be seen as up to date with global trends or by switching to what is believed to be best practice. Much of the early theorizing in relation to institutional theory focused on those organizations that adopted or copied the practices of market leaders and examined the dynamics that lead to conformity among organizations. These institutional researchers found that the 'first in market' differentiation of leading-edge innovating organizations shifted over time to reflect homogeneity of approaches when the organization entered later stages of the diffusion process. McDonald's is frequently cited as a prime example of this: their business model of fast food was unique when first introduced but eventually, through franchising of the brand and with the emergence of a plethora of competitors into the marketplace, what was once a point of difference and thus an advantage, over time lost its edge and further eroded when consumers began to demand healthier, more flexible food choices. In the sport world the same points are often made about Nike, a business started by an athlete and coach who made a limited number of athlete-friendly shoes sold out of the back of co-founder Phil Knight's car. As Nike's business grew and moved beyond the track athlete to the sport shoe for everyone, so did the business model; the business outsourced production offshore which brought greater financial success and led to direct competitors and others copying this approach.

This propensity to copy or imitate successful organizations is reflected in the premise of isomorphism (DiMaggio and Powell, 1983, 1991), which has been explained as occurring when

Organizations are driven to incorporate the practices and procedures defined by prevailing rationalized concepts of organizational work . . . organizations that do so increase their legitimacy and their survival prospects, independent of the immediate efficacy of the acquired practices and procedures.

(Meyer and Rowan, 1977: 340)

DiMaggio and Powell (1983, 1991) noted two types of isomorphism: competitive isomorphism that emerges from market forces, and institutional isomorphism that develops from competition for political and organizational legitimacy. The latter encompasses three elements: coercive, mimetic and normative.

Coercive pressures are the elements that push organizational procedures and structures to conform to best practices, influenced by the factors that the organization is dependent on for resources. A pervasive coercive isomorphic pressure for all organizations is the need to conform to changing laws. Mimetic pressures relate to the drive to reduce uncertainty whereby imitating successful peer organizations is seen as a safe strategy. The whole 'best practice' movement has this principle at its heart. Normative isomorphic pressures are a response to professionalization, where certain types of structure and process are viewed as more legitimate than others.

In relation to normative isomorphic pressures, the emergence of managerialism in the running of sport organizations, especially in voluntary organizations, has assumed dominance in the last two decades. While in professional and for profit sport organizations this focus on business acumen, target setting, performance indicators, responsibility and accountability has been underpinned by commercial viability drivers, in the non–profit and community sport arena the changes have primarily been driven by government policy and funding. For example, in analysing recent UK sport policy Phillpots, Grix and Quarmby (2011: 278) found that the imposition of County Sport Partnerships (CSPs) with highly controlled governance arrangements introduced another level of bureaucracy with tightly imposed targets and that 'the use of PSAs [public service agreement] and KPIs [key performance indicator] has strengthened Sport England's control over the agencies involved in CSPs'. They concluded that 'despite notions of decentralization, new governance arrangements for CSPs appear relatively top-down and managerial' (Phillpots et al., 2011: 278). This finding follows on from Houlihan and Green's (2009: 678) evaluation of the impact of New Labour's 'modernization project' on Sport England and UK Sport, which they argued resulted in the objectives of both organizations being narrowed and the adoption of 'business–like principles and a "command and control" regime in relationships with key frontline delivery partners'.

Models of change

There are a number of different models that explain and explore the nature of organizational change and how best to manage it. These typically comprise five key aspects:

- Motivating for change, creating readiness to accept change and dealing with any resistance;
- Building a shared vision to which the organization can gain commitment;
- Developing a support base that includes key stakeholders;
- Managing the transition, locking in commitment;
- Sustaining and embedding the change through support and alignment of rewards and recognition (Waddell, Cummings and Worley, 2000).

One of the most commonly cited change frameworks is Lewin's (1951) classic change model. Lewin identified three stages involved in changing organizations and people, which were:

- Establishment of the rationale and motivation to change (unfreeze);
- Empowerment of stakeholders to embrace new ways of thinking about the organization and of working (change);
- Finally returning the organization to stability (refreeze).

In the first stage of change Lewin believed that the equilibrium needs to be challenged (unfrozen) before old behaviours are left behind (unlearnt) and new behaviours are adopted. In this stage the organization should be primed to accept that change is necessary; this means challenging the existing way of operating. One way to do this is to articulate how the change is aligned with achieving the organization's vision and strategy. This may be prefaced by a documentation of the key issues underpinning the need for change, such as declining club membership or sport participation figures, unsatisfactory financial performance, member or customer dissatisfaction, or poor onfield performance results. This first stage may also involve challenging current organization values, attitudes and behaviours if these are likely to block change. These stimuli then create a (planned) crisis which in turn can facilitate the buy-in and engagement context for meaningful change. Stakeholder analysis and management mapping can assist with identifying and gaining the support of key people within the organization for the change process.

The second stage is characterized by change, as organizational staff and stakeholders start to reconsider the future and accept and support the new direction. This transitory stage may stretch over a period of time, as those affected grapple to understand how the changes can benefit them. A good communication strategy is critical to keeping everyone informed about the changes and feeling connected to the organization. This stage should also include the provision of opportunities for employee and key stakeholder involvement.

The organization enters the refreeze stage when equilibrium is reached and aspects such as the organization structure are agreed upon, new roles are filled or new ways of operating have been fully documented. To support the change it is useful to identify actions to reinforce the new elements, such as implementing reward systems aligned with the changes, and to establish explicit feedback systems to address any barriers to sustaining the change. As a component of the refreezing process it is important to commemorate the success of the change, reinforcing associated benefits and outcomes.

Edgar Schein (1996) extended Lewin's model by embedding a greater focus on psychology and group dynamics termed cognitive redefinition and depicted in Figure 9.1.

In this model **Stage 1** suggests that the motivation to change (unfreezing) is linked to the premise that past observational learning and cultural influences drive behavior. Schein (1996: 27) felt that change was 'a profound psychological dynamic process.' Therefore, he suggested that new forces for change need to be introduced or some of the existing aspects that are perpetuating the behaviour need to be removed. Three sub-processes underpin readiness and motivation to change.

- Disconfirmation: where present conditions lead to dissatisfaction.
- Pressure to change: creates survival anxiety, which may take several forms from fear of incompetence to fear of loss of personal identity or group membership.
- Learning anxiety: learning something new can trigger defensiveness and/or denial, scapegoating, and manoeuvring.

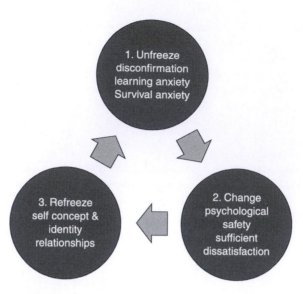

Figure 9.1 Schein/Lewin model

Those involved in the change need to feel safe before they engage with the process and move to accept new ways of thinking and/or doing things. If the survival anxiety is greater than the learning anxiety or, preferably, the learning anxiety is reduced, then unfreezing proceeds. Learning anxiety can be reduced by increasing psychological safety through training, performance coaching, support groups and other such mechanisms.

In **Stage 2** change is facilitated when there is adequate dissatisfaction with the current conditions and there is acceptance to change. The disparity between the present state and that being proposed should be clear. Activities that assist in making the change include replication of role models and using trial-and-error learning to devise individualized solutions.

To lock in the change as permanent (refreezing, **Stage 3**), new behaviour should become habitual, and include developing a new self-concept and identity and instituting new inter-personal relationships. Refreezing seeks to provide an environment where the change is aligned with the changed organizational culture, policies and practices.

Another way of looking at change is embodied in **contextual or processual change theory**, which emerged in the 1980s as a rejection of rational, planned change. It was argued that the latter was too prescriptive and failed to recognize the inherent complexity of change. According to this perspective Pettigrew (1997) and his colleagues saw change as involving complex, dynamic and non-linear politically and culturally influenced processes. This approach also notes the importance of understanding the sequencing and pacing of different types of changes. The reality of change in sport organizations being complex and non-linear is evident in the 12-year study of change in 36 Canadian sport organizations by Amis, Slack and Hinings (2004). These researchers found that revolutionary change was accomplished by pacing the changes so that after each change the organization had time to settle into the new way of doing things, establish trust and relationships and then engage in the next change.

Another change approach is outlined in the work of Dunphy and Stace (1990) and Stace and Dunphy (2001). This influential model combined internal and external factors into a contingency theory matrix. This model seeks to explain how organizations adjust to their external environments and the scale and scope of change required (from fine tuning to

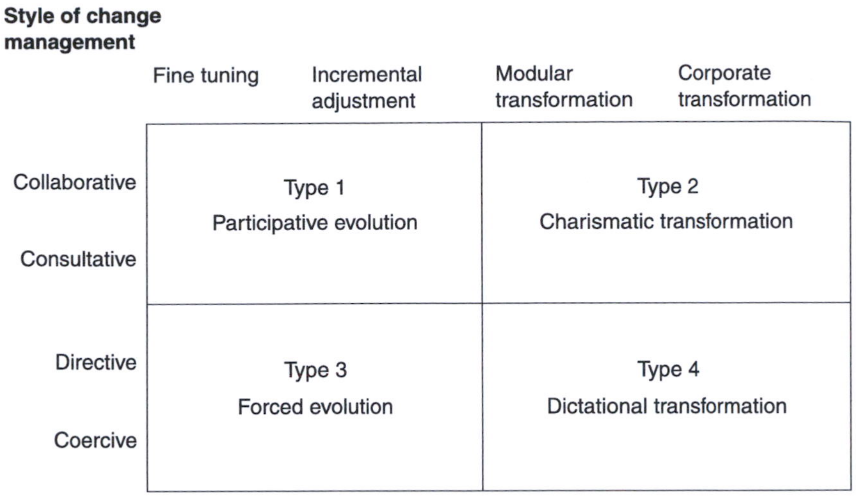

**Style of change
management**

	Fine tuning	Incremental adjustment	Modular transformation	Corporate transformation
Collaborative	Type 1 Participative evolution		Type 2 Charismatic transformation	
Consultative				
Directive	Type 3 Forced evolution		Type 4 Dictational transformation	
Coercive				

Figure 9.2 The Dunphy and Stace change matrix

Source: Stace and Dunphy, 2001: 109

corporate transformation) via a standardized, but comprehensive, list of managerial styles ranging from collaborative to coercive. In total the model canvasses 16 possible styles of change but five main approaches are highlighted (see Figure 9.2):

- In *developmental transitions* there is regular change as organizations adapt to their external environments. Here the leadership style is most appropriately consultative where the leader acts to gain shared commitment from organizational stakeholders on the need for continual improvement.
- In *task-focused transitions* the management style is most appropriately directive with managers seeking compliance from organizational stakeholders about changes to operational requirements in certain areas. Although strongly directed from the top there is scope in this type of change for a more consultative approach as change is implemented lower down the organization.
- In contrast, in *charismatic transformations* the need for radical transformation is led by an inspiring leader who can symbolically mobilize the emotional commitment of staff and in so doing lead the organization in a new direction.
- *Turnarounds* are situations where organizational survival is perceived to be at stake and radical transformations are led by command and control-oriented leaders who force change via coercive and directive commands with limited emphasis on employee engagement or commitment.
- The fifth category of *Taylorism* is associated with *fine tuning* and paternalistic approaches to change.

Each of the approaches noted above is associated with a consequent 'path of change' (Stace and Dunphy, 2001: 108–93) that takes account of the long-term consequences of different approaches. For example, organizations that rely a lot on *fine tuning* may also have to contemplate *turnarounds* or *charismatic transformations* at times to reinvigorate themselves and where *charismatic transformations* occur they may need to be supported over time by *developmental* or *task-focused transitions* to maintain momentum. In related empirical work Stace and Dunphy (2001) found that the most commonly used change processes were hybrid forms that combined directive and consultative styles, although the exception to this was turnarounds, which were more likely to be directive and/or coercive in style. In addition, the empirical research suggested that the most successful organizations used consultative and directive change management styles and the least successful were more likely to use Tayloristic fine tuning. Overall, the main conclusions were that more effective managers and organizations tended to be comfortable using different approaches depending upon the prevailing circumstances.

Resistance to change

Whilst it would be an overstatement to say that people always resist change, it is certainly a commonly reported response from those who are presented with the need to change without being involved in the initial decision. People tend to be resistant to change because they have an investment in the status quo (position, prestige, rewards, comfort level, status, etc.) but change, especially when imposed by others, also offers an unbalanced 'psychological bargain'. In effect the change leaders are asking organizational members to trust them in relation to an uncertain future where many known and hard-won things may be jeopardized. Resistance can come from a number of sources, from the requirement for new skills, changed norms or perceived loss of status, power or conditions.

This can lead to individual or group feelings of frustration, insecurity or anger, and result in employee or volunteer turnover or regressive aggressive behaviours. Stages in the response to change process have been suggested to encompass psychological reactions such as denial, resistance, exploration and commitment. Also, uncertainty about the future can create fear and a perception of threat associated with lack of control. The most commonly asked question in relation to change processes is 'What does this mean for me?' Therefore anticipating and dealing with resistance is paramount and the organization should have a communications plan for keeping people informed as a key part of managing change processes.

Planning for change and thus minimizing resistance can be tackled in a number of ways. A change plan should clearly state why change is needed and how it will impact groups of people and, at some stage, each individual. Also, change responsiveness can be facilitated by creating a climate of trust through supporting and involving affected staff and volunteers in the change process and allowing them to have some input into either the direction or the implementation of change.

One of the best-known and influential prescriptive models of managing change to overcome resistance can be found in Kotter's eight-step model (see Box 9.2). This model emerged from Kotter's (1995) research-based observations of why change programmes fail, which was further developed by Kotter (1996) and Kotter and Cohen (2002).

The Kotter model is a classic example of a top-down change management process and is likely to work best for change projects that are driven by the top leadership of an organization. Kotter acknowledges that his somewhat linear model tends to oversimplify what is often a more complex reality and that even successful change processes are subject to surprising and unforeseeable developments that can make them messy. However, Kotter maintains that all elements of the eight steps must be addressed and that skipping steps will only create the illusion of speed and progress and lead eventually to poorer results.

In terms of management style Kotter suggests that managers follow a 'see-feel-change' pattern in which problems are presented in a way which captures the attention of stakeholders and taps into their feelings about the need for change at a profound level. An example of this

---

Box 9.2 Kotter's eight-step model

1. Establishing a sense of urgency: Examining market and competitive realities, identifying and discussing crises, potential crises, or major opportunities.
2. Forming a powerful guiding coalition: Assembling a group with enough power to lead the change effort. Encouraging the group to work together as a team.
3. Creating a vision: Developing strategies for achieving that vision. Creating a vision to help direct the change effort.
4. Communicating the vision: Using every vehicle possible to communicate the new vision and strategies. Teaching new behaviours by the example of the guiding coalition.
5. Empowering others to act on the vision: Getting rid of obstacles to change. Changing systems or structures that seriously undermine the vision. Encouraging risk taking and non-traditional ideas, activities and actions.
6. Planning for and creating short-term wins: Planning for visible performance improvements. Creating those improvements. Recognizing and rewarding employees involved in the improvement.
7. Maintaining focus and momentum: Beware of declaring victory too early and recognize that fundamental change requires a long time before new behaviours become embedded.
8. Institutionalizing new approaches: Articulating the connections between the new behaviours and corporate success. Developing the means to ensure leadership development and succession.

---

is given in relation to step 1 (creating a sense of urgency), where Kotter recommends 'bringing the outside in' so that stakeholders such as employees come face to face directly with the nature of the external issue driving change.

The major strengths of the Kotter model are that it outlines clear and well-researched steps which provide guidance on how to manage change, focuses on the importance of getting buy-in from employees, acknowledges the need to build a political consensus with key stakeholders and combines the need to change systems with the need to manage the reactions of groups and individuals impacted by change. The limitations of the model are that it is best suited to top–down change processes and that it does not provide room for participation inputs which fundamentally challenge the initial strategy. In this sense the genuineness of the participation mechanisms can be questioned.

Case study

Change or die: reforming football governance practice in Australia

DANIEL LOCK

Introduction

In Australia, association football (previously known as soccer and now simply football) has endured a turbulent history, marred by corruption, hooliganism, nationalistic rivalry and mismanagement (Crawford, 2003). Despite boasting the highest participation figures of any team sport in Australia

(Australian Sport Commission, 2002, 2003, 2004, 2005, 2006), football has consistently failed to attract a sufficient supporter base to lure the sponsors and media coverage required for a solvent and competitive professional sporting code and national competition (Lock, 2009). To compound the issues with national-level governance, Australia's national team, the Socceroos, failed to qualify for the FIFA World Cup finals between 1975 and 2005 and the National Soccer League (NSL) floundered, which served to further marginalize football from mainstream Australian sporting culture.

In 2003, following increasing public pressure for change, the Australian Federal Government intervened, commissioning a report into 'The Structure, Governance and Management of Soccer in Australia' (Crawford, 2003). This report sought to address the issue of providing a suitable figurehead to oversee a revolutionary change process to improve existing management practices of football governance in Australia. The Crawford Report instigated a pronounced process of change to Australian football governance. It was, as Lynch (2003: 19) asserted, time for change: 'The game can no longer be held back by a management and organizational culture historically characterized by deal making, factionalism and politics.' The chosen figurehead, Frank Lowy, and his newly constituted board headed quickly into a process of organizational change, founded specifically around enacting a new and meticulously prepared strategic plan. In the strategic business plan unveiled by the Australian Soccer Association (ASA) (2004: 2–3) four areas of change were identified. These were:

- People and organizational culture
- Stakeholder management
- Game and core product
- Commercial and marketing.

These areas of change sought to act on clearly identified and widely agreed problems within football in Australia. As incoming CEO John O'Neill (2006) summarized the situation (in his address to the Australian Press Club) when he became incumbent:

> Relations with players were strained and unworkable, sponsorship and media deals flawed and untenable, relations between the various stakeholders were dysfunctional, and Australian Soccer had a somewhat justified reputation for nepotism, parochialism, jingoism and shoddy practices, and was constantly under attack in the media.

Change agenda

To address the recommendations of the Crawford Report, the ASA developed a plan which outlined a strategy to: create a new league; improve international performances; attract credible corporate partners; and reform the factionalized organizational structure of the ASA to better serve its stakeholders (ASA, 2004). For the purposes of this case study, the reformation of stakeholder management processes and creating a positive new organizational culture are the focus. The reformation of the game and core product and the development of commercial and marketing relationships are briefly covered as these were key to improving perceptions of the ASA in Australia following the changes to organization structure and culture.

Calls for radical changes to football in Australia were not a novelty. The Bradley Report had outlined a blueprint for changes to football's administrative structure in 1990. However, the decision-making process associated with previous incarnations of football governance in Australia allowed individuals and clubs with vested interests to block reform (Solly, 2004). When the Australian Federal

Government intervened in 2003 to reform football in Australia, they offered AU$15 million in grant and loan funding to administer the first steps of change. To secure this money the recommendations of the Crawford Report were to be adopted in full, which circumnavigated the previous issues associated with change processes being blocked by bureaucracy (Solly, 2004). To initiate the process of radical changes, the ASA itself was required to change fundamentally. These changes are defined below.

People and organizational culture

To reform the governance structure at the ASA, it was evident that a shift in personnel was required. The existing board of the ASA, despite attempts to resist, was removed soon after the Crawford Report was published (Solly, 2004). The Crawford Report identified that 'appropriately skilled' individuals were required as change agents and that the current administration was not fit to implement the changes delegated (Crawford, 2003: 4). Initially a suitable figurehead was sought to oversee the changes and remove the existing board. The review committee recommended Australian business tycoon and property magnate Frank Lowy as a suitable figurehead to supervise the change process at the ASA. His recruitment was based on three factors. First, Lowy had the backing of the Federal Government to initiate the changes and override attempts to block the process as had been encountered during previous attempts for reform (Solly, 2004). Second, Lowy had global networks and respect that would be vital in improving Australia's standing within Oceania, Asia and FIFA. Third, Lowy was an extremely well-respected businessman and capable of recruiting high-profile administrators as appropriately skilled change agents to transform football in Australia (Solly, 2004).

On assuming the role of Chairman, Lowy began a widespread search for a skilled administrative team to develop and carry through the strategic objectives outlined in the Crawford Report (ASA, 2004; Crawford, 2003). Extensive research was undertaken before recruiting ex-Australian Rugby Union (ARU) aficionado John O'Neill as CEO (Cockerill, 2004). O'Neill had a formidable record in the administration of the ARU having been involved in the bid for the 2003 Rugby World Cup and the day-to-day running of a top-level Australian sport. In addition, the ASA's Strategic Plan also sought to establish an outstanding commercial team (ASA, 2004). This was formed to introduce best practice into the ASA and to shift the organizational culture away from the nepotism and other dubious practices of the past (O'Neill, 2006).

Moving beyond the poor practices of previous governance required considerable strategic planning and a thorough adherence to the recommendations of the Crawford Report. To introduce best governance practice at a national governance level, the Crawford Report required that the ASA clearly define, differentiate and separate the duties of board members and employees (Crawford, 2003). This involved articulating a clear organizational plan to improve the efficiency and effectiveness of the ASA. In addition to the recommendations of the Crawford Report, the ASA's Strategic Plan sought to develop a clear succession management process so the new organizational structure and culture was not reliant wholly on people, but on sound practice instead (ASA, 2004). Beyond the scope of the internal function of the ASA, the Crawford Report was specific that relationships with stakeholders in Australia and internationally should be improved. This facet of change is discussed here.

Stakeholder management

Two key weaknesses in current stakeholder management practices were identified in the Crawford Report and targeted in the ASA's strategic plan (ASA, 2004). These were the need to improve relationships with and management of state-based organizations and to develop relationships with international stakeholders at continental and global levels (ASA, 2004).

First, the Crawford review committee presented findings showing that the ASA did not have the support of the majority of its domestic stakeholders, including state and local football associations (Crawford, 2003; Solly, 2004). John O'Neill (2006) articulated the problems this caused: 'For too long, this sport [football] has been fractured with local committees, mostly with the best of intentions, developing their own regulations.' Therefore, there was no consistency of delivery from the national governing body through to the state and local football associations (Crawford, 2003). Delivery was determined at state and local levels, which was ad hoc and reliant on the expertise of individuals present in localities, which is not a sound management framework.

The Crawford Report recommended that the ASA develop a coherent strategy for national, state and local delivery and management of football and that all state and local associations should be members of the national governing body (Crawford, 2003). The ASA Strategic Plan acted on this recommendation by introducing service contracts between the ASA and each state and territory of Australia (ASA, 2004). A specific point of strategic change was to 'ensure that state members' administration and football structures mirror those of the ASA' (ASA, 2004: 25). By ensuring that each state and local association shared a common purpose with the ASA and had a similar organizational structure, O'Neill (2006) hoped that 'new national regulations would provide the framework for all clubs and districts to administer the game correctly.' By 'correctly', O'Neill was referring to states and localities delivering football based on best practice observed from around the globe and disseminated by the ASA.

Second, the ASA set out to develop a more prominent relationship with international football stakeholders, namely FIFA and the Asian Football Confederation (AFC) (ASA, 2004). Both attempts to develop international stakeholder relationships were conceived to promote Australia's marginalized position in the administration of football globally (ASA, 2004). Strategic conversations with the AFC were used to generate a potential shift into the AFC from the Oceanic Football Confederation (OFC). Shifting to the AFC was preferential for two reasons. One, the AFC provided a far more powerful, influential and organized confederation within FIFA's structure. Two, the OFC included minimal competitive fixtures, which were played against weak opposition, which failed to garner public attention. The AFC offered four or five places (dependent on the host) to the OFC's one in the FIFA World Cup qualifying procedure and the potential for participation in the Asian Cup (International) and the Asian Champions League (Club), which offered a renewed international appeal for the ASA and an increase in the number of high-profile competitive fixtures hosted in Australia (ASA, 2004). The broader impact of the changes to governance structure and stakeholder management practices is discussed now.

The immediate impact of change

The change processes described during this case study created a period of considerable success for football in Australia between 2005 and 2006. The ASA was renamed the Football Federation Australia (FFA) in 2004, to create a clean break from 'old soccer', thus launching 'new football' to tap into the global nature of the sport (Cockerill, 2005). In 2005, the A-League was launched and the Socceroos qualified for the FIFA World Cup. The following year saw Australia join the AFC, which gave the Socceroos access to an improved pathway to FIFA World Cup qualification and the Asian Cup, and all A-League teams the opportunity to qualify for the Asian Champions League (FFA,

2010a). Additionally, it provided Australia with a far stronger standing within the FIFA structure and an opportunity to develop better networks with international stakeholders. In 2010 the Socceroos again participated in the FIFA World Cup.

Off the field, the FFA secured a media-rights deal with FOX Sport Television to broadcast A-League and international matches exclusively on pay television (which was renegotiated shortly before the FIFA World Cup in 2006 for a significant increase in value). Additionally the FFA attracted the support of high-profile corporate sponsors including Hyundai, Qantas, Optus, Nike, Solo, Westfield and NAB (FFA, 2010b). The accrual of a significant group of corporate sponsors was aided by the FFA's decision to join the AFC as it provided corporate partners with access to the lucrative Asian business market through support of an Australian sport.

Notwithstanding the on and off field success, the management of stakeholders at a state and local level has continued to trouble the FFA. The culture of mismanagement that preceded 2004 led to state organizations holding considerable autonomy, which they have fought hard to maintain. Slowly the FFA has been able to pull the organizations into their structure, first through the changing of their titles to reflect 'football' not 'soccer', and second through each state and territory becoming a member of the FFA, as stipulated in the Crawford Report (2003) and ASA Strategic Plan (ASA, 2004). This process has been arduous, with some state associations resisting membership until as recently as 2010.

Despite the radical changes that were implemented from 2004 to 2006, the process of change has not been straightforward since. The FFA has endured a revolving door of staff, with John O'Neill and the majority of the commercial team departing soon after the FIFA 2006 World Cup in Germany. Although Frank Lowy remains as Chairman of the FFA, the turnover of staff has tested the succession planning processes (ASA, 2004). Lowy has continued to oversee the recruitment of a high-profile commercial team and CEO, but football has undoubtedly entered a period of consolidation since 2006.

Linking the case to key chapter concepts

The FFA case illustrates many of the concepts discussed in the body of the chapter and provides a vivid illustration of large-scale, managerially led change in an important sporting organization. In relation to the types of change discussed in Table 9.1 and the associated commentary, the FFA case is a clear example of organizational change that is 'root and branch' in scale and scope. The drivers for change in the FFA case were a widespread recognition that the pre-change administrative structures and processes were flawed beyond redemption and required a transformational turnaround led by a new and powerful management team with a clear mandate. Clearly, the key engine of the reform was economic with government funding being conditional on the implementation of new structures and new TV and commercial contracts supporting the rationale for the revised operations once established. Although the change had an overt and highly public political agenda to improve Australian football and rid it of 'shoddy practices', once under way the language of change was primarily concerned with professionalism, administrative efficiency, implementing globally accepted managerial systems and becoming economically self-sustaining by providing a high-quality and attractive product. Additionally the change process in the FFA case was linear in that it was managed over time in accordance with a clearly envisioned set of goals and outcomes and not allowed to deviate from these, it was long run (and continues at the time of writing), and it involved many factors traversing the spectrum of macro-related systems and structures and micro aspects relating to the way individuals were expected to behave.

The management approach in the FFA case is an interesting illustration of the managerial actions required to overcome resistance as espoused by Kotter (1995). A sense of urgency was created by the economic incentives for successful change and a clear articulation of the opportunity cost of continuing without reform. A powerful guiding coalition was established to oversee the change, starting at the board level and continuing with the appointment of a new CEO and new managerial team. The vision for the new organization was articulated very strongly and communicated consistently as a reference point during the long-term change implementation process as a way of overcoming resistance along the way. Short-term wins to show that change was working were delivered through the success of the A League and the national team in qualifying twice for the FIFA World Cups of 2006 and 2010. Lastly, momentum was maintained through the introduction of new managerial systems and the longer-term establishment of a different culture for the FFA.

This case has outlined both the necessity for change and the strategic planning processes that underpinned the reformation of football in Australia. Although the governance of football has developed markedly since 2003, the sport still faces significant challenges as it continues to overcome the mismanagement of previous governance. The future of football in Australia has been given a lifeline by the Australian Federal Government's intervention; however, the process of change is incomplete and will provide an ongoing challenge to the management team at the FFA to satisfy the needs of those domestic stakeholders that are responsible for ensuring the coherent and best-practice delivery and management that is fundamental to the ongoing management of football in Australia.

Summary and conclusion

This chapter has provided an overview of some of the key issues driving change in sport organizations incorporating economic, demographic, technical, social and political sources. The chapter has outlined key characteristics and types of change that may be required in sport organizations in response to different change drivers and suggested that change management competence is essential for organizations adapting to rapidly changing environments.

Key change models that are widely regarded in the academic and practitioner literature have been discussed and reviewed. These models provide a useful template for managers confronted with the need to effectively manage change, as well as recommendations to evaluate context-related strategy choices. Some of the key components of the approaches discussed have concerned the ways in which people typically react to change and the way that sport organizations and their managers can best facilitate the introduction of changed ways of working to maximize benefit and to overcome the likely resistance that is often central to the reactions of other organizational members.

In conclusion, we suggest that an understanding of the forces driving change and a sensitivity to the alternative approaches outlined in this chapter are critical for managers of modern sport organizations. Equally, well-developed change management skills, especially those related to overcoming resistance, are also vital. We noted at the start of this chapter that the pace of change has increased dramatically in sport organizations during the last two decades. In closing we note no sign of a reduction in either the scale or scope of change or the need for managers to be skilled in handling it.

References

Amis, J., Slack, T. and Hinings, C. R. (2002) 'Values and organizational change', *The Journal of Applied Behavioural Science*, 38, 436–65.

—— (2004) 'The pace, sequence, and linearity of radical change', *The Academy of Management Journal*, 47, 15–39.

Australian Soccer Association (2004) *Strategic Business Plan: Creating a sustainable, flourishing game*, Canberra, Australian Sport Commission.

Australian Sport Commission (2002) *Exercise, Recreation and Sport Survey (ERASS)*, Canberra, Australian Sport Commission.

—— (2003) *Exercise, Recreation and Sport Survey (ERASS)*, Canberra, Australian Sport Commission.

—— (2004) *Exercise, Recreation and Sport Survey (ERASS)*, Canberra, Australian Sport Commission.

—— (2006) *Exercise, Recreation and Sport Survey (ERASS)*, Canberra, Australian Sport Commission.

Boyle, R. and Haynes, R. (2009) *Power play: Sport, the media and popular culture*, Edinburgh, Edinburgh University Press.

Caldwell, R. (2005) *Agency and change: Rethinking change agency in organizations*, New York, Routledge.

Chadwick, S. (2009) 'From outside lane to inside track: sport management research in the twenty-first century', *Management Decision*, 47, 191–203.

Cockerill, M. (2005) 'Lowy targets young, welcomes old', *Sydney Morning Herald*, 9 August, 35.

—— (2004) 'O'Neill taking off without enough baggage', *Sydney Morning Herald*, 13 March, 74.

Collins, D. (1998) *Organizational change: Sociological perspectives*, London, Routledge.

Collis, J. and Hussey, R. (2009) *Business research: A practical guide for undergraduate and postgraduate studies* (3rd edn), Basingstoke, Palgrave-McMillan.

Crawford, D. (2003) 'The structure, governance and management of soccer in Australia', *Report of the Independent Soccer Review Committee*, Canberra, Australian Sport Commission.

DiMaggio, P. J. and Powell, W. W. (1983) 'The iron cage revisited: Institutional isomorphism and collective rationality in organizational fields', *American Sociological Review*, 48, 147–60.

—— (1991) *The new institutionalism in organizational analysis*, Chicago, University of Chicago.

Dunphy, D. and Stace, D. (1990) *Under new management: Australian organizations in transition*, Sydney, McGraw-Hill.

Football Federation Australia Limited (FFA) (2010a) 'About the FFA', [online] available at <http://www.footballaustralia.com.au/2009InsideFFA/default.aspx?s=insideffa2009_about_new> (accessed 10 November 2010).

—— (2010b) 'Partners', [online] available at <http://www.footballaustralia.com.au/2009InsideFFA/default.aspx?s=insideffa_ffa_partners_new (accessed 10 November 2010).

Houlihan, B. and Green, M. (2009) 'Modernization and sport: The reform of Sport England and UK Sport', *Public Administration*, 87(3), 678–98.

Hutchins, B. (2008) 'Signs of meta-change in second modernity: the growth of e-sport and the World Cyber Games', *New Media and Society*, 10, 851.

Kikulis, L. M., Slack, T. and Hinings, C. R. (1995) 'Toward an understanding of the role of agency and choice in the changing structure of Canada's national sport organizations', *Journal of Sport Management*, 9, 135–52.

Kotter, J. P. (1995) 'Leading change: Why transformational efforts fail', *Harvard Business Review*, 59–67.

—— (1996) *Leading change*, Boston, MA, Harvard Business School Press.

Kotter, J. P. and Cohen, D. S. (2002) *The heart of change: Real life stories of how people change their organizations*. Boston, MA, Harvard Business School Press.

Kriemadis, T., Terzoudis, C. and Kartakoullis, N. (2010) 'Internet marketing in football clubs: a comparison between English and Greek websites' *Soccer and Society*, 11, 291–307.

Lange, K., Nicholson, M. and Hess, R. (2007) 'A new breed apart? Work practices of Australian internet sport journalists', *Sport in Society*, 10, 662–79.

Lewin, K. (1951) *Field theory in social science: Selected theoretical papers*, ed. D. Cartwright, New York, Harper and Row.

Lock, D. (2009) 'Fan perspectives of change in Australia's A-League', *Soccer and Society*, 10, 109–23.

Lock, D., Darcy, S. and Taylor, T. (2009) 'Starting with a clean slate: Analysis of member identification with a new sport team', *Sport Management Review*, 12, 15–25.

Lynch, M. (2003) 'There's only one way forward', *The Age*, 9 April, 19.

Meyer, J. and Rowan, B. (1977) 'Institutionalized organizations: Formal structures as myth and ceremony', *American Journal of Sociology*, 83, 340–63.

O'Neill, J. (2006). *National Press Club Address*, [online] available at <http://www.footballaustralia.com.au/default.aspx?s=insideffa_newsfeature_features_itemandid=10252> (accessed 30 October 2007).

Pettigrew, A. (1997) 'What is processual analysis?' *Scandinavian Journal of Management*, 13, 337–48.

Phillpots, L., Grix, J. and Quarmby, T. (2011) 'Centralized grassroots sport policy and "new governance": A case study of County Sports Partnerships in the UK – unpacking the paradox', *International Review for the Sociology of Sport*, 46(3), 265–81.

Ross, S. (2010) *Sport technology*, London, Evan Brothers Limited.

Santomier, J. and Shuart, J. (2008) 'Sport new media', *International Journal of Sport Management and Marketing*, 4, 85–101.

Schein, E. H. (1996) 'Kurt Lewin's change theory in the field and in the classroom: notes towards a model of management learning', *Systems Practice*, 9, 27–47.

Slack, T. and Parent, M. (2006) *Understanding sport organizations: The application of organization theory*, Champaign, IL, Human Kinetics.

Solly, R. (2004) *Shoot out: The passion and the politics of soccer's fight for survival in Australia*, Milton, John Wiley and Sons.

Stace, D. and Dunphy, D. (2001) *Beyond the boundaries: Leading and recreating the successful enterprise* (2nd edn), Sydney, McGraw-Hill.

Turner, P. and Shilbury, D. (2010) 'The impact of emerging technology in sport broadcasting on the predictions for interorganizational relationship (IOR) formation in professional football', *Journal of Sport Management*, 24, 10–44.

Waddell, D., Cummings, T. and Worley, C. (2000) *Organisation development and change*, Melbourne, Nelson Thompson Learning.

Webb, T. (2007) 'How European sport has changed the way it sells its sponsorship packages', *Journal of Sponsorship*, 1, 20–27.

PART II

Managing human resources in sport organizations

Edited by Packianathan Chelladurai

10

CONTEMPORARY ISSUES IN THE MANAGEMENT OF HUMAN RESOURCES

Packianathan Chelladurai

Introduction

One perspective on organizations would hold that the human resource at the disposal of the organization is the most important resource because it is the human resource that puts into use all the other resources of the organization. Given this level of significance, it is not surprising that every organization strives to increase the caliber of its employees and enhance their productivity. Concomitantly, scholars in human resource management and/or organizational behavior have been engaged in intensive research spanning a myriad of topics including, for example, individual differences in personality, perceptions, attitudes, motivation, commitment, and satisfaction; managerial practices aimed at the commitment and satisfaction of employees; and employee reactions to these practices. While this section on human resource management could cover any subset of human resource topics, we have confined ourselves to those topics that are more pertinent to sport organizations. Further, as is fitting for a book mapping the territory of sport management, we have focused on those topics that have not been given due attention in the sport management literature.

As the products of most sport organizations are services instead of goods, human resource management should reflect, and be consistent with, the imperatives of service operations. Hence, the section begins with Solha Husin's chapter titled "Human resource management in sport: a service-based approach." In her chapter, Solha Husin notes that the service employee is the key to creating the perceptions of service quality among clients or customers. Therefore, managing the human resources based on the exigencies of a service operation is strategically important. She describes the critical factors in such human resource management, which include support at work, training, reward system, supervisory assistance, and performance appraisal.

It is also acknowledged that most sport organizations rely on the contributions of volunteers both at the policy level and at the service level. So it is only appropriate that Chapter 12 deals with volunteer management in sport. May Kim and Hyejin Bang begin their chapter on volunteering in sports by outlining the extent to which sport organizations depend on volunteers to achieve their goals. As an aside, Chelladurai (2006) estimated the value of volunteer contributions to sport in America to be around US$50 billion, which is nearly one-fourth of the most liberal estimate of $207.503 billion in 2005 (Milano and Chelladurai, 2011). Kim and Bang explain the management of human resources focusing on three important stages of recruitment and selection, training, and retention. It must be added that retaining the current volunteers is more efficient and cost-effective than recruiting new volunteers. Another important contribution of the Kim and Bang chapter is that they juxtapose these managerial practices within four different sport settings – non-profit sport organizations, youth sports, mega/international sporting events, and community sport.

One of the factors that sustain the motivation, involvement, and productivity of both paid workers and volunteers is what is termed organizational support. The chapter by Boyun Woo and Claudio Rocha is focused on this critical component of human resource management – the support workers get in performing their assigned activities. Woo and Rocha explain that such support can emanate from the three different sources of co-workers, supervisor, and the organization itself. After elaborating on the definitions of various forms of support a worker can get, in Chapter 13 Woo and Rocha discuss the antecedents and consequences of such support.

Another topic that has not been addressed adequately in sport management literature is psychological contract. In Chapter 14, Gonzalo Bravo, David Shonk, and Doyeon Won address the topic of psychological contract and its ramifications. Their essential argument is that while workers may be attuned to the elements contained in their formal work contract, they are equally sensitive to the unwritten and tacit understandings between the worker and the organization. After defining the construct of psychological contract, Bravo, Shonk, and Won discuss the psychological contract theory and describe the two major forms of psychological contract – transactional psychological contract and relational psychological contract. They explain the issues related to the breach, violation, and fulfillment of the psychological contract. They also discuss psychological contract in the context of four relational contexts: administrators–volunteers; administrators–coaches; coaches–players; and administrators–graduates. Finally, they report on methodological issues and future research on the psychological contract in sport management.

Finally, one of the realities of modern-day organizations and their management is the tendency of organizations to rely more and more on contingent workers. The technological advances that facilitate accomplishment of varieties of work and the tendency among organizations toward downsizing (the reduction in workforce as a cost-saving strategy) have resulted in a growing number of contingent workers. Employment of contingent workers is also a necessity for those sport organizations whose service operations are seasonal. For example, golf courses are out of use in the winter months in places where there is heavy snowfall. Many professional sport franchises whose competitive seasons are limited to a few months in a year need to turn to contingent workers. Given this imperative, in Chapter 15, Kyungro Chang deals with the emergent phenomenon of contingent workers which includes part-time workers, temporary workers, employee leasing (i.e., one organization lending the service of its own workers to another organization), and self-employed workers. He concludes the chapter with a discussion of the strategy of outsourcing which has become common among organizations.

HRM as a social responsibility

One of the continuing difficulties faced by management is the balancing of the concerns for people on the one hand and task accomplishment on the other. Any and every legitimate organization is sanctioned and sustained by society because its stated objectives are expected to serve society well. Therefore, the most important social responsibility of any organization is to try its best to achieve its stated goals (Chelladurai, 2010a). While achieving organizational goals is serving society, it must also be understood that doing good by the employees of the organization and their welfare is also serving society. After all, the employees are members of the society! The exciting aspect of this phenomenon of goal attainment versus employee welfare is that they need not be antithetical to each other. Good human resource management should yield benefits to both the organization and its workers.

Principle of fit

While the following chapters address some of the critical issues associated with human resource management, there is an underlying principle that should guide all HRM practices – the fit. The principle of fit deals with two types of fit – the fit between the person and the task (i.e., person–task fit) and the fit between the person and the organization (i.e., person–organization fit).

Person–task fit

The authors of the following chapters have identified recruiting the right person for a job, training the person in the task responsibilities, appraising the performance of the individual, and then rewarding the person accordingly. The notion of the right person for a job has been emphasized, with a greater focus on the person and the person's attributes such as personality, ability, and aptitudes. In the process, the significance of the task and its attributes are largely overlooked.

While differences among tasks are varied and numerous, a useful schema can be derived from the distinctions made among consumer services, professional services, and human services (Hasenfeld and English, 1974; Sasser, Olsen, and Wyckoff, 1978). Sasser et al. (1978: 400) defined consumer services as "a limited range of services delivered by a relatively low-skill workforce to a large aggregate market." An example of such a service in sports is that of a ticket checker in a football stadium who simply confirms that the tickets are valid for the specific game and punches or tears the tickets and directs the spectators to the appropriate seat. On the other hand, professional services are "individualized for each customer and delivered by a relatively high-skill workforce" (Sasser et al., 1978: 400). In the case of our football stadium, the engineers who ensure the safety of the seats – and the proper functioning of the lighting systems and the scoreboards – are providing professional services. The third class of services are the human services in which human beings with specific attributes are processed and changed into persons of higher levels of those attributes or with different attributes (Hasenfeld and English, 1974). In our example of a football game, the coaches who enhance the abilities of the players, assign them specific roles, and mold them into a well-coordinated team are providing human services.

It must be noted that sport management and sport managers are mostly concerned with consumer services and human services. In the case of consumer services, the sport managers are largely concerned with efficiency of operations. Such efficiency is enhanced by breaking down the task to simple routines, stating specific rules for each routine, and monitoring those who carry out those routines. The ticketing operation in a professional sport franchise is a good example of an efficient consumer service. From the time a fan calls in for tickets to the time the fan attends a specific game, all the actions of the franchise and its employees are scripted. This process is akin to the assembly line in a manufacturing firm where the activities at every station of the assembly line are simplified and specified.

In contrast, the coach and assistant coaches can routinize only a few things like setting the practice times and ensuring that the equipment is in place for those practice sessions and that the field is marked. But their major task of developing the players and molding them into an effective team cannot be simplified or routinized because the inputs (i.e., the players) are characterized by a multitude of individual differences among them, their reactions to practice regimens are varied, the interactions among them during practices and games are mixed, and the opposing teams come with differing personnel, strategies, and tactics. Given this extensive variability, the coaching job cannot be scripted. In other words, the coaches must be left alone to decide on what, when, and how they would do to make a winning team but within the rules of the game, the league, and the land.

Empowerment

An often cited human resource strategy is empowerment. According to Schneider and Bowen (1995), the empowerment of employees can best be achieved by:

- redesigning the jobs to permit more autonomy and more room to make decisions,
- management sharing the power with the employees;
- sharing of information about the organization, its units, and their performances;
- sharing task-relevant knowledge; and
- sharing of rewards based on organizational and individual performance.

From a different perspective, Spreitzer (1995: 1444) defines psychological empowerment as:

> a motivational construct manifested in four cognitions: meaning, competence, self-determination, and impact. Together, these four cognitions reflect an active, rather than a passive, orientation to the work role.

Meaning refers to the value of a work goal. It is a fit between the requirements of a work role and one's personal beliefs, values, and behaviors. For example, a person who values including everyone in a program may be comfortable in mass sport and not in an elite program which tends to exclude the not-so-gifted individuals. Competence refers to an individual's belief in his or her capability to perform activities with skill. For example, some people feel competent to work in the recreational setting while others are competent in the coaching of elite athletes. Self-determination refers to an individual's sense of having choice in initiating and regulating actions. It reflects autonomy in the initiation and continuation of work behaviors and processes. For example, individual workers in both the recreational and elite settings may be permitted relatively more autonomy to decide on how they will carry out their responsibilities. Impact refers to the degree to which an individual can influence strategic, administrative, or operating outcomes at work. This attribute refers to whether the volunteers and paid workers are permitted to have a voice in determining the policies and strategies of the sport's governing body.

It is expected that empowered frontline workers would (a) respond quickly to customer needs during service delivery, (b) handle dissatisfied customers through service recovery, (c) interact with customers with more warmth and enthusiasm, and (d) feel better about their jobs and about themselves. Thus, empowered employees can be a great source of service ideas, word-of-mouth advertising, and customer retention. The process of empowerment releases hidden resources that would otherwise remain inaccessible to both the individual and the organization.

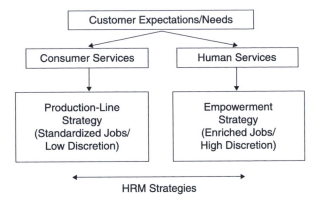

Figure 10.1 Contingency approach to HRM practices

Reprinted, with permission, from P. Chelladurai, 2006, *Human resource management in sport and recreation*, 2nd ed. (Champaign, IL: Human Kinetics), 310.

While empowering employees is a laudable strategy, such a practice is not tenable in highly simplified and routinized consumer services where rational and efficient processes are paramount. On the other hand, empowerment is the most rational strategy in human services. Given this dichotomous nature of tasks in sport organizations and based on Bowen and Lawler (1992), Chelladurai (2006) has advanced a contingency approach to human resource management in sport organizations. His scheme shown in Figure 10.1 begins with the idea that consumer expectations can be met by either consumer services or human services as defined above. If it is a consumer service, the production-line strategy would be most appropriate where the jobs are specialized and standardized and where the service provider does not have much discretion. In a human service, however, the empowerment strategy would be most fruitful with the jobs fully enriched and where the service provider is given a greater degree of autonomy in carrying out the task.

Person–organization fit

The next level of fit discussed in the literature is the fit between the person and the organization. What is meant here is that a worker in the organization needs to share the goals and values of the organization for that person to feel comfortable in it and to also be productive. In the context of sports, the goals and values of a professional sport franchise and the recreation department of a city government are divergent. It is only reasonable to expect that the personal goals and values of a person may steer that person toward either professional sports or community recreation. By the same token, it is also reasonable to expect that a person's commitment to the organization, satisfaction with the job, and actual performance in the job will be a function of the fit between the individual and the organizational goals and values.

We can extend this line of thinking to different manifestations of sport and the services thereof. Chelladurai (2010b) has distinguished among egalitarian sport, elite sport, and entertainment sport as illustrated in Figure 10.2. Egalitarian sport is variously labeled as mass sport or participant sport or recreational sport. In such a venture, the organization facilitates the participation of all interested persons. It is an inclusionary process where the pleasure in participation is the ultimate aim. Elite sport refers to the domain where talented and dedicated individuals are in pursuit of excellence by engaging in a well-planned practice and

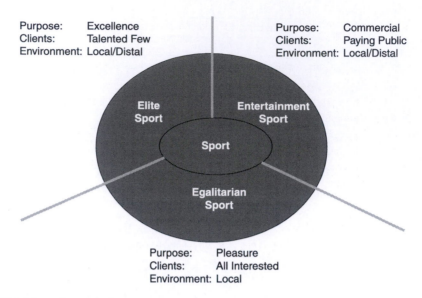

Figure 10.2 Three domains of sport

Reprinted, with permission, from P. Chelladurai, Human Resource Management in the Sport Industry. Opening Keynote Paper at the 6th Congress of the Asian Association for Sport Management. 13–16 October 2010, Kuala Lumpur, Malaysia.

competitive regimen. It is an exclusionary process whereby those not talented enough or dedicated enough are excluded from the organizational process designed for excellence. Finally, entertainment sport is concerned with generating revenue by offering competitions among elite teams as entertainment. Professional sports franchises attempt to make a profit over the expenses, which include paying the players. In non-professional sports, the organization does not pay the players but still attempts to raise money through the provision of sport as entertainment. The surplus in such efforts is used to cover the costs and to support other organizational efforts as in the case of North American university athletics.

The point here is that as these three domains of sport have differing goals and processes, the people who are hired to carry out the tasks associated with each domain must have the skills and competencies to create the person–task fit. More importantly, they must also share the goals and values associated with each manifestation of sport. The problem becomes more acute in those organizations that provide all three forms of sport services. A good management strategy would be to differentiate the operation of these three domains in terms of structure and processes. Equally important is recruitment and retention of the right people in each domain.

Vertical differentiation

The above discussion of staffing of the consumer service operations versus human service operations, and the differential staffing of the egalitarian, elite, and entertainment sports represents the differentiation of units offering different services. Differentiation occurs when an organization is divided into units according to environmental exigencies, and those units are then staffed with people of the appropriate aptitude and skills. Note that differentiation is not identical to the concept of departmentalization. The emphasis in differentiation also extends to staffing the units with the requisite abilities, competencies, aptitudes, and dispositions.

The foregoing differentiation among the three domains of sport and between consumer and human services is horizontal in the sense that they are all equally important without any hierarchy among them. We should also look at vertical differentiation in management of these domains of sport. Figure 10.3 illustrates a model drawn from Parsons' (1960) thinking. In his view, an organization consists of distinct hierarchical sub-organizations – the technical, the managerial, and the institutional subsystems. The technical subsystem is concerned with those activities that are directly associated with the major tasks of the organization. The nature of the technical task and the processes involved define its fundamental requirements. The managerial subsystem is a higher-order system that both administers and serves the technical system. The two major areas of responsibility of the managerial subsystem are to (a) mediate between the technical organization and those who use its "products" – the customers – and (b) procure the resources necessary for carrying out the technical functions (i.e., financial resources, personnel, and physical facilities). In essence, the managerial subsystem spans the boundaries and secures the necessary resources for the production of its products as well as for the exchange of its products with the environment. In the process, the technical system is unencumbered by environmental turbulences.

The function of the institutional subsystem is to interact with the wider environment with which the organization must deal. It works to legitimize the existence of the focal organization and justify the societal support extended to it. It is responsible to set the objectives and policies of the organization, to recruit the top managers, and to influence the wider economic and political systems in support of the organization. In essence, the institutional system first charts the major course for the organization and then deals with the larger environment with a view to securing necessary resources and legitimizing the organization in the eyes of the public.

From a human resources perspective, it is imperative that those who will occupy positions within each of the three subsystems described above must have those aptitudes and skills to perform. For example, individuals who are elected to the institutional system (e.g., the board of directors of a sport governing body) must have the capacity and inclination to influence the external groups.

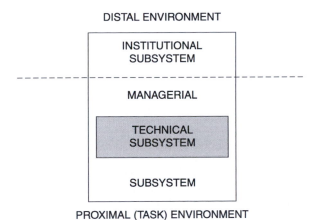

Figure 10.3 Vertical differentiation of three subsystems of an organization

Reprinted, with permission, from P. Chelladurai, 2009, *Managing organizations for sport and physical activity: A systems perspective.* 3rd ed. (Scottsdale, AZ: Holcomb Hathaway Publishers), 213.

In summary, three contingent factors to be kept in mind when instituting and implementing human resource strategies have been outlined. First, the differences between consumer services and human services clearly indicate the extent to which a given human resource practice would be effective in the two distinct service operations. As an example, the empowerment strategy would be more effective in human service operations than in consumer service operations. The second contingent factor is the conceptual distinctions among egalitarian, elite, and entertainment sport. These three enterprises have differing goals and processes and, therefore, the staffing of them should be consistent with the exigencies posed by them. Finally the vertical differentiation among the institutional, managerial, and technical subsystems of an organization has been highlighted. Accordingly, those who are recruited and hired for any of the subsystems must have the requisite abilities, competencies, and aptitudes to suit the requirements of each subsystem.

References

Bowen, D. E., and Lawler, E. E. III. (1992) 'The empowerment of service workers. What, why, how and what?', *Sloan Management Review*, 33, 33–39.

Chelladurai, P. (2006) *Management of human resources in sport and recreation* (2nd edn), Champaign, IL, Human Kinetics.

—— (2009) *Managing organizations for sport and physical activity: A systems perspective* (3rd edn), Scottsdale, AZ, Holcomb Hathaway.

—— (2010a) 'The twin edges of corporate social responsibility and irresponsibility: A synthesis and application to sport', paper presented at the 18th Congress of the European Association of Sport Management, Prague, Czech Republic. September 15–18, 2010.

—— (2010b) 'Human resource management in the sport industry', opening keynote paper at the 6th Congress of the Asian Association for Sport Management. 13–16 October 2010, Kuala Lumpur, Malaysia.

Hasenfeld, Y., and English, R. A. (1974) 'Human service organizations: A conceptual overview', in Y. Hasenfeld and R. A. English (eds.), *Human service organizations: A book of readings*, Ann Arbor, University of Michigan Press pp. 1–23.

Milano, M., and Chelladurai, P. (2011) 'Gross domestic sport product: the size of the sport industry in the United States', *Journal of Sport Management*, 25(1), 24–35.

Parsons, T. (1960) *Structure and process in modern societies*, New York, The Free Press of Glencoe.

Sasser, W. E., Olsen, R. P., and Wyckoff, D. D. (1978) *Management of service operations*, Rockleigh, NJ, Allyn and Bacon.

Schneider, B., and Bowen, D. E. (1995) *Winning the service game*, Boston, Harvard Business School Press.

Spreitzer, G. M. (1995) 'Psychological empowerment in the workplace: Dimensions, measurement, and validation', *Academy of Management Journal*, 38, 1441–65.

11

HUMAN RESOURCE MANAGEMENT IN SPORT

A service-based approach

Solha Husin

Introduction

All organizations including sport firms depend on human resources to run their businesses and achieve their organizational goals. For example, the state-of-the-art Yankee Stadium in New York will not be profitable to the Yankee Club if the majority of the 52,000 seats are not filled up by baseball fans every time there is a tournament being held there. The attendance of fans depends so much on the work contributed by the Yankee staff, which includes not only the Yankee baseball players, but other employees such as the stadium manager, marketers, public relation officers, promoters and so forth. Even the staff who sell tickets at the ticket counter, janitors who clean the premises, security guards who look after the safety of the crowd and stadium are also responsible for the spectators' turning out as their work performance will influence the intention of these clients to repeat their visits to the stadium as well as spread good word of mouth to other potential spectators. In short, an organization may have very sophisticated and high-technology facilities. However, these resources will not be able to generate any income for the organization should there be no human resources with the right knowledge, skills and attitudes to make use of them for the organization's advantage. This has been clearly summarized by Chelladurai (1999: 1) in the following statement.

> While sufficient importance needs to be placed on the material resources, it is equally, if not more, important that the organization gives attention to the human resources because the human resources put the material resources into use and convert them into wealth.

Apart from being able to transform inanimate resources from being useless into something worthwhile and valuable to the organization, human resources are the only asset that cannot be copied by competitors. Barney (1991: 110) posits that "physical technology, whether it takes the form of machine tools or robotics in factories or complex information management systems, is by itself typically imitable." Hence, should these imitable resources be the reason for the firms' successes, it will not be too long before other competing firms outsmart them with the same and even better duplicates. Human resources, on the other hand, are unique creatures. Because of issues related to scarcity, specialization, and tacit knowledge, the work

145

qualities of human beings are impossible to be cloned (Lippman and Rumelt, 1982; Teece, 1982). Coff (1997: 374) has simply concluded that human resources are "difficult to understand and observe."

Being the organization's most valuable assets (as compared to other duplicable resources such as machinery and physical facilities), human resources are even more critical in sport. Athletes or sport players, for example, have their own unique skills which cannot be duplicated by other sport individuals. David Beckham, for instance, has his own reputation for his phenomenal skills as a football player. Instead of trying to do the impossible, which is to create a "second copy of David Beckham", LA Galaxy was willing to pay Real Madrid 25 million Euros in order to "buy" this player. Such an expensive decision as that made by LA Galaxy indicates the precious worth of human resources in sport. Take a look at the list of top 10 Premier League transfer payments which demonstrate the monetary value placed on human resources (<http://soccerlens.com/top-10-most-expensive-transfers-in-football/5244>, accessed September 7, 2011) as illustrated below,

Top 10 Premier League transfers

1. Fernando Torres: Liverpool to Chelsea – £50m (2011)
2. Sergio Aguero: Atletico Madrid to Manchester City – £35m (2011)
3. Andy Carroll: Newcastle United to Liverpool – £35m (2011)
4. Robinho: Real Madrid to Manchester City – £32.5m (2008)
5. Andriy Shevchenko: AC Milan to Chelsea – £30.8m (2006)
6. Dimitar Berbatov: Tottenham to Manchester United – £30.75m (2008)
7. Rio Ferdinand: Leeds to Manchester United – £29.1m (2002)
8. Juan Sebastian Veron: Lazio to Manchester United – £28.1m (2001)
9. Edin Dzeko: Wolfsburg to Manchester City – £27m (2011)
10. Wayne Rooney: Everton to Manchester United – £25.6m (2004)

Within the study of human resource management (HRM), it is insisted that the way human resources are managed must be tailored to the demands of the organization's business strategy (Khatri, 2000; Lawler, 1992). For instance, if a firm is pursuing innovation as its strategy, its HRM must be oriented towards making its people work differently; if the strategy is to reduce costs, the employees have to work harder; and for an organization targeting achieving excellent quality, the aim of its HRM is at developing a smarter workforce (Schuler and Jackson, 1987). This idea originates from the theory of contingency and is further supported by the theory of role behavior.

The proponents of contingency theory state that "a structure which is consciously adapted to the task, to expectations of personnel, to the size and complexity of the operation, and to pressures for change from the environment will promote higher effectiveness" (Child, 1974: 175). The alignment between an HRM policy and the organization's ultimate goals also becomes the premise of a role behavior perspective (Katz and Kahn, 1978) which specifically focuses on the behaviors of individuals within the system's behavioral requirements. It is believed that the effectiveness of an organization will be heightened if employees are performing behaviors that are in accordance with the needs of the organization's requirements, such as the organization's business strategy and the nature of industry (Jackson and Schuler, 1992).

In a nutshell, the more congruent the approach of HRM is with the goals of organizations, the more likely productivity is increased. Using this as the formula for success, this chapter will discuss the HRM approach that a sport organization needs to adopt in order to ensure it is aligned with the demands of its business.

Service-based human resource management in sport

In service firms, customer perceived service quality is the pillar of the business (Strong and Harris, 2004). It is suggested that service companies strive towards providing quality services that meet customers' expectations and satisfactions (Dean and Bowen, 1994; Noble, Rajiv, and Kumar, 2002). Evidence from empirical research has verified the significant relationship between the customer orientation of a firm and its financial and market performance (e.g., Ambler, 1999; Day, 2000; Doyle and Wong, 1998).

Schneider, who is pioneering work on the climate for service research (e.g., Parkington and Schneider, 1979; Schneider, 1980; Schneider, Wheeler, and Cox, 1992; Schneider, White, and Paul, 1998), has a special interest in looking at service-oriented HRM as a critical determinant of service quality. He believes that "a business is not in the business of service quality if its HRM practices are not suffused with a focus on service quality" (Schneider, 2004: 148). What he means is that, if the objective of the firm is to provide quality service to customers, the corresponding values and cultures must be reinforced and communicated to the deliverers of the service. Otherwise stated, in any service-based organizations, the HRM practices must be service-oriented or service-based.

Ground-breaking research on the climate for service or customer satisfaction was first conducted by Parkington and Schneider (1979) in bank branches. In that particular research, it was discovered that customers base their perceptions of service quality not only on their interactions with the customer-contact staff but on the whole process of service experiences, ranging from the appearances of physical facilities to the rules and procedures of the organizations. This points to the fact that, besides those whose jobs are attending to customers at the counter, the contributions of non-customer-contact employees, such as the technicians, clerical staff and janitors, are also crucial in the overall service quality impressions of customers. Although there are no direct employee–customer interface activities, the resulting work of the non-customer-contact employees in making the customers' service experiences satisfactory, such as providing a clean and safe environment or ensuring all the electrical equipment and machinery is functioning well, is critical in this context. As mentioned earlier, these favorable outcomes of work performances will have great impacts on customers' evaluations of service quality.

Another important finding from the study (Parkington and Schneider, 1979) is about the spill-over effect of employee behaviors on the customers. The conclusion that is made based on this finding is that employee and customer perceptions of service quality are highly correlated. In the subsequent series of research and conceptual papers, Schneider and his colleagues started accumulating a conclusive body of knowledge on the relationship between employee and customer experiences of service climate and service quality (e.g., Schneider, 1980; Schneider and Bowen, 1993; Schneider, Parkington, and Buxton, 1980; Schneider et al., 1992, 1998).

In line with Schneider's idea of the climate for service, other service scholars begin to recognize the need to change the traditional managerial functions of service employee management (e.g., Bowen and Schneider, 1985; Grönroos, 1983). Some of the given recommendations include getting the employees involved in the planning and organizing of service activities; acknowledging the influence of employee work environments on customer experiences of service quality; and recognizing that the way employees are managed can predict customer perceived service quality (Chebat, Babin, and Kollias, 2002; Hartline and Ferrell, 1996). The tenet of these recommendations is that in service companies, the role of HRM must also be service-focused.

In a nutshell, service-based HRM is materialized when the design of HRM practices is geared towards achieving the service-related goals. This objective can be accomplished by focusing on satisfying the needs and wants of employees, through the implementation of HRM practices. The underlying premise for this strategy is that a positive treatment given by the management to the employees will be reflected or mirrored in the quality of performances exhibited by the employees (Grönroos, 1983; Zerbe, Dobni and Harel, 1998). Based on the author's literature review, a number of HRM practices have been found to be empirically influential in fostering service-related behaviors among employees (Table 11.1). All these practices are conceptually integrated and classified into their respective groups. Five groups have emerged and they are considered as the practices that are crucial in the development of employees with service-based behaviors. These particular HRM practices will be used as the bases for the following discussions for HRM managers in sport organizations. These practices are believed to be facilitative in inculcating service-based values in the attitudes and behaviors of sport employees.

Support at work

Regarded as fundamental in the effort to foster service climate for the organizations, *support at work* is an HRM practice that refers to the physical aspects of the organization and workplace environment that potentially hinder or aid employees' efforts in accomplishing the given tasks. It is deduced from the integration of scales discovered in previous studies (e.g., Johnson, 1996; Little and Dean, 2006; Lux, Jex, and Hansen, 1996; Rogg, Schmidt, Shull, and Schmitt, 2001; Schneider and Bowen, 1985; Wiley, 1991). In the case of sport organizations, support at work may include organizational rules, policies and procedures, job descriptions, workload distributions, work demands, safety measures, work design, scheduling system, and others.

The idea that the dimension of support at work can affect productivity is inferred from the principle of scientific management introduced by an industrial engineer, Frederick Taylor (1911). The premise of Taylor's theory is that employee performances can be increased by providing them opportunities to earn more financial returns. Although this philosophy can be considered narrow by contemporary standards (Schneider, 1994), the fact that employee motivation and productivity go hand in hand has made organizations begin to find ways to motivate their workforce.

Soon after the initiation of Taylor's theory, the idea of work design, time-and-motion technique and many other industrial engineering devices began to be applied to each facet of a job. It is believed that once employees are fully equipped with the appropriate work equipment and environment, they will be prompted to produce more (Griffin and Ebert, 2006). Extending this concept to the sport context, employees can be expected to be committed in doing their jobs if, for example, all necessary equipment works efficiently, the workplace is secured with adequate safety measures, the rules and procedures are easy to understand and follow, and there are always enough people to ask for assistance.

Empirical evidence has also shown that support at work is found to be generally positive in the promotion of high service-related outputs. For example, in Schneider and Bowen's (1985) seminal study, the correlation is revealed between work facilitation and customer perceptions of service quality. Adopting and modifying Schneider and Bowen's scale, a similar result has been depicted in the study carried out by Little and Dean (2006).

Table 11.1 Sources of service-based HRM practices

	Support at work	Supervisory assistance	Reward system	Performance appraisals	Training
Browning (2007)		Management support		Performance appraisal	
Elmadağ et al. (2008)		Coaching	Rewarding		Training
Johnson (1996)	Service strategy Service support Service system	Management service orientation	Reward and recognition		Training
Little and Dean (2006)	Work facilitation				
Lux et al. (1996)	Work environment Work design		Reward and recognition		Training
Lytle et al. (1998)					Training
Rogg et al. (2001)	Policy Job description		Rewards	Performance review	Training
Schneider and Bowen (1985)	Work facilitation	Supervision			
Schneider et al. (1992)			Internal equity compensation	Performance feedback	Training
Schneider et al. (1998)		Leadership	Rewards Compensation	Performance appraisal	Training
Strong and Harris (2004)				Evaluation	Training
Tornow and Wiley (1990)	Work group climate	Managerial practices	Rewards for performance		
Tsaur and Lin (2004)			Compensation and benefit	Performance appraisal	Training
Wiley (1991)	Working conditions Work scheduling Processes and procedures	Supervisory practices	Benefits Pay practices	Performance feedback	Training emphasis
Yoon et al. (2001)		Supportive mgt			
Zerbe et al. (1998)		Leadership	Rewards Career opportunity	Performance appraisal	Training

Tornow and Wiley (1990) also provide substantiation when they find that work rules and policies, health conditions and safety are highly associated with customer satisfaction. In a somewhat similar study, Wiley (1991) reveals that employee perceptions of the support at work, characterized by problems related to the physical work context and safety level at the workplace, and work obstacles, demonstrated by priority issues such as deadlines, keeping costs down and providing quality services, have been found to be significantly correlated with various dimensions of customer satisfaction.

Training

Training serves to furnish employees with certain sets of knowledge, skills and behaviors related to the goals espoused by the organizations (Swanson and Holton, 2001). Another purpose of training is to hint to employees that organizations are committed to take care of their well-being (Elmadağ, Ellinger, and Franke, 2008) and value them as their priceless assets (Moreland and Levine, 2001). There are two types of training; formal (off-the-job) and informal (on-the-job) (Liu and Batt, 2007). Formal training typically requires employees to be relieved from work routines and the training program is conducted systematically based on a standardized curriculum. Meanwhile, informal training occurs in the context of daily work and expects employees to learn independently by observing how their co-workers or supervisors do their jobs. Both formal and informal training have been found to be related to organizational productivity (e.g., Bartel, 1994; Liu and Batt, 2007).

Human resource professionals have long acknowledged the importance of employee training in boosting the efficiency of service processes and outcomes (Yoo and Park, 2007), the organization's competitive ability (Frabotta, 2000), and overall performance (Colbert, 2004). It has also been argued that training allows service firms to "provide a better class of quality of service, or to develop a competitive niche market" (Davies, Taylor, and Savery, 2001: 367), which ultimately promotes repeat purchases from customers. In fitness clubs, for instance, examples of training may range from acquiring basic skills in performing their jobs to making decisions in solving customer-related problems or complaints as well as learning about the clubs' new service-related policies and procedures. Lytle, Hom, and Mokwa (1998) observe that leading service providers are investing substantial resources in implementing their service training programs which include advanced quality-based team training, problem-solving training, inter-personal skills training, and other advanced training purported to empower employees with excellent work performance skills.

Training is exceptionally critical to organizations whose main orientation is to delight customers (Johnson, 1996; Schneider and Bowen, 1985). Hence, for service quality purposes, training is claimed to be an essential facet of HRM practices (Ueno, 2008). Based on Heskett, Jones, Loveman, Sasser Jr., and Schlesinger's (1994) model of the service-profit-chain, it can be implied that the achievement of customer loyalty and customer satisfaction is heavily dependent on an efficient service provision, which certainly includes the capability, know-ledge and motivation of service employees. Wexley and Latham (1991) also add that employee behavior can be influenced through the behavior modeling process of thorough training programs.

Where employees are sufficiently trained and committed to providing a good quality of service, there is evidence to suggest that customer perceptions of service quality are increased significantly (Armistead and Kiely, 2003). Studies related to service quality, for example, have shown that training is a significant contributor in the employees' own perceptions of customer orientation (Strong and Harris, 2004), employee role-prescribed (prosocial) behaviors

(Chebat et al., 2002) and extra-role (prosocial) behaviors (Chebat et al., 2002), job satisfaction (Elmadağ et al., 2008), commitment to firm (Elmadağ et al., 2008), two aspects of service quality measures, namely, responsiveness and assurance (Tsaur and Lin, 2004), and employee perceived service quality (Yoo and Park, 2007). Training has also been shown to be highly correlated with four service climate variables (Rogg et al., 2001), service behavior (Browning, 2006), organizational commitment (Lux et al., 1996), customer service climate (Lux et al., 1996), customer satisfaction (Wiley, 1991) and service culture (Zerbe et al., 1998).

Reward system

People do not work for free. Even volunteers expect *rewards*, except that their rewards are typically more intangible, intended to satisfy their intrinsic needs. In the context of human resource management, the reward system constitutes an economic exchange, thereby representing a key element of the employment relationship. In this exchange, employees "undertake a certain amount of physical and mental effort and accept the instructions of others" (Bratton and Gold, 2003: 277). For these reasons, it is natural for employees to expect their organizations to reciprocate what they have given and done for the management with some form of rewards.

A reward system in this chapter refers to all monetary and non-monetary compensations and incentives provided by the organizations to employees as a kind of appreciation for the contributions which have been expended by the employees to the organization. According to Bau and Dowling (2007), there are five categories of rewards or incentives. The first one is the incentives provided by the work itself, such as autonomy and growth through career development and the recognition of individual performance. The second type of reward is called social incentives and this is characterized by information distribution and communication with employees. The third category is the incentives related to the internal organizational environment, such as the size of the company, organizational structure and leadership style. The next two reward categories are monetary oriented, classified as direct and indirect financial groups. Direct incentives are pay-for-performance while indirect incentives include things such as free access to phone and internet at the office, recreational facilities such as cafeterias or pantries, and payment of hospital bills (with certain limitations).

The importance of rewards in eliciting desired performances from employees can be justified by using the reinforcement theory (Skinner, 1953). Its basic assertion is that "employee behavior is a function of its contingent consequences" (Luthans and Stajkovic, 1999: 50). When this premise is applied to the workplace, it yields a concept of *you get what you reinforce*. Building on the same foundation, a reward system can be seen as an approach to promote employees' commitment towards helping the organizations in achieving their business goals (Bowen and Johnston, 1999). That is because, when it is strategically designed with certain purposes, a reward system is able to motivate the behaviors and actions of employees accordingly (Elmadağ et al., 2008) The employees' high motivations to engage in service-related behaviors are assumed to result from fair (Dubinsky and Levy, 1989; McFarlin and Sweeney, 1992), conspicuous and specific compensation practices and programs (Hartline and Ferrell, 1996; O'Connor and Shewchuck, 1995). Establishing rewards contingencies and recognizing employees' superior service deliveries as well as rewarding them in a timely manner are also found to be significant indicators of employee commitment to service quality (Schneider and Bowen, 1993).

In general, the reward system has been found to be highly instrumental in stimulating the causal chain from employee behaviors to service quality (Elmadağ et al., 2008; Schneider and

Bowen, 1985). Specifically, there is an existence of a high correlation value in the relationship between rewards and a climate for service (Schneider et al., 1992), organizational commitment (Lux et al., 1996), service culture (Zerbe et al., 1998), customer satisfaction (Johnson, 1996), service behavior (Browning, 2006), and extra-role behavior (Tsaur and Lin, 2004).

Supervisory assistance

Supervisors are leaders or persons whom employees are answerable to. With their leadership, supervisors are potentially influential in shaping positive service orientation within an organization (Lytle et al., 1998). Supervisors' roles are often associated with providing assistance in terms of physical and emotional supports necessary in the successful accomplishment of the given tasks (Goleman, 2000). In short, it is believed that *supervisory assistance* can be considered as a critical component in the dissemination of organizational strategies to employees and a productive approach for affecting changes in their attitudes (Den Hartog and Verburg, 2002).

A similar concept of supervisory assistance is seen in Schneider and Bowen's (1985) study. In this study, the dimension is labeled as supervisory behaviors and they are described by the supervisors' or managers' acts of providing feedback, establishing rewards contingencies, and sharing information. In some other studies, this dimension is known as managerial practices (Schneider et al., 1998; Tornow and Wiley, 1990), supervisory practices (Wiley, 1991), management service orientation (Johnson, 1996), leadership (Schneider et al., 1998; Zerbe et al., 1998), supportive management (Yoon, Beatty, and Suh, 2001) and coaching (Elmadağ et al., 2008).

Effective supervisors are able to influence the attitudes and actions of their subordinates for the betterment of the organization (Bovee, Thill, Wood, and Dovel, 1993). Employees believe supervisors to be supportive when the supervisors allow them "to fail without fear of reprisal" (Yoon et al., 2001: 504). If positively perceived by employees, supervisor supportive assistance can be a catalyst for employees to develop the right attitudes and behaviors towards quality service. In golf clubs for example, employees who are unwell will feel cared for when their supervisors give them a day off or let them go out to see a doctor. In addition, if the supervisors recognize them for their involvements in successful golf competitions and make this known to everybody else in the clubs, the esteem needs of the employees will likely be heightened and this consequently will enhance their motivations to give greater performances in the future. Being supportive and appreciative of the workers' work efforts has been shown to be strongly related to employees' willingness to provide good services (Schneider and Bowen, 1993). Singh (2000) also finds that with supervisory assistance, service employees perceive their roles to be less stressful and their burnout tendencies to be less likely, and thus their performances and perceived commitment level are prone to be elevated.

Most of the studies demonstrate that supervisory assistance is facilitative in the organizational achievement of high service quality. Examples can be extracted from Schneider and Bowen's (1985) study, where supervision is found to be strongly related to customer perceptions of service quality. Similarly, significant correlations are found in Johnson's (1996) study (between managerial service orientation and overall service climate), in Tornow and Wiley's (1990) (between managerial practices and customer satisfaction), in Zerbe et al.'s (1998) (between leadership and culture and service behavior), in Elmadağ et al's (2008) (between coaching and employee service quality commitment) and in Yoon et al.'s (2001) (between supportive management and job satisfaction and work effort).

Performance appraisals

Performance appraisals or evaluations of employees' current performances are another crucial component in the management of human resources as this procedure is considered very facilitative in the administration of various human resource activities such as staffing, training, compensation and so forth (Boswell and Boudreau, 2002). This particular HRM practice refers to an "observation and assessment of employee performance against pre-determined job-related standards, for purpose(s) delineated by the organization" (Cheung and Law, 1998: 404). In line with this definition, Bratton and Gold (2003) add that the objectives of performance appraisals are to judge and develop the qualities of employees' performances. According to Dixon (2002), performance appraisals work on two levels. First, they facilitate employee efficiency by making employees understand that they are responsible for their own performances. Second, if properly conducted, performance appraisals can help direct employees on how to improve their current performances.

The need to evaluate the performances of employees is a conclusion that can be drawn from the famous Hawthorne Study. In 1925, a group of researchers conducted a study at the Hawthorne Works of Western Electric outside Chicago. These researchers discovered that the productivities of the workers involved in the study increased and this outcome is attributed to the attention that was given to the workers throughout the experiment process (Griffin and Ebert, 2006). This study shows that human beings appreciate attentions because, through those attentions, they are motivated to demonstrate their maximum capabilities to the observers. This sequence of events is used to explain the high productivity that was revealed in the study.

In the case of sport settings, performance appraisals are believed to work in much the same way. Performance appraisals can be used as an avenue for employees to know the standard of their work performances, particularly in terms of serving and satisfying their customers. A formal, structured and periodical evaluation system communicates a message to employees that the club management makes a serious effort to pay considerable attention to them. Based on the Hawthorne Study, such a message will encourage employees to upgrade their current work performance levels.

Research in general has proven that performance appraisals are linked to firms' performances (e.g., Delery and Doty, 1996). Work in the area of performance management has confirmed that appraisals from multiple sources or upward feedback from subordinates are contributive to individual high performance (e.g., Sanwong, 2008; Walker and Smither, 1999). In their meta-analysis study, Kluger and DeNisi (1996) found that groups that receive feedback give higher performances than those that do not. While a significant link has been produced by many studies in the literature, some organizations are still unhappy with their evaluation schemes due to complaints from employees regarding the process of performance appraisals, which some of them perceived as unfair (Fletcher, 1997). It is therefore suggested that in order for performance appraisal to be supportive of employee behaviors, employees must first be satisfied with the way performance appraisals are implemented (Kuvaas, 2007).

Jawahar (2007: 736) has noted that

in practice, perceived fairness of evaluation, the procedures used to evaluate performance, and the manner in which performance-related information is communicated likely play an integral role in shaping ratees' reactions to critical elements of the appraisal process.

The same author has also provided empirical evidence that shows satisfaction with appraisal feedback is related to job satisfaction and organizational commitment. In short, performance appraisal can be a powerful HRM tool to influence the attitudinal behaviors of the sport employees, as long as they accept or are satisfied with the management of that performance appraisal process (Pettijohn, Pettijohn, and D'Amico, 2001).

According to the social exchange theory, employee behavior at the workplace is actually a form of reciprocation of the treatment he or she receives from the organization (Rousseau and Parks, 1993). Inferentially, this theory implies that there is a relationship between organizational practices such as HRM and employee behavior. This also means that the kind of behaviors that organizations hope their employees will possess depend on the kind of treatment that organizations are willing to extend to their employees. Thus, using the social exchange theory as the theoretical foundation, it can be logical to assume that HRM practices which place a strong emphasis on employee well-being are bound to produce employees with the desired behaviors. In other words, customer-focused or service-based HRM practices will correspondingly unearth service-focused behaviors from the employees.

In short, in service-based businesses, the practices of HRM must also be service-based. According to Schneider (2004: 147), "generic HRM will not suffice in an increasingly competitive marketplace; organizations must, to use a phrase from marketing, focus or falter." What he means by that is that having good HRM practices such as a high-performance work system is not enough. These seemingly profitable sets of practices evidently help to produce a talented and inimitable workforce (e.g., Becker and Huselid, 1998; Delery and Shaw, 2001; Huselid, 1995). However, a much greater competitive advantage can be achieved if those HRM practices are designed with a focus on superior service and service quality delivery, especially in a context of high intangibility where the performance of employees becomes an indicator of quality service. Furthermore, the socio-political, national culture and economic situation in the country within which the service organization is operating should be taken into consideration when determining the relevancy of specific HRM practices that are geared towards fostering service climate (Browning, 2006).

Hence, for a purpose of achieving high service quality, sport managers are advised to instill customer-focused values in the attitudes and behaviors of employees. Otherwise stated, the match between the goals of the service organizations and the design of their HRM practices is very fundamental in securing high levels of service-related outcomes (e.g., perceived service quality) (Furunes, 2005; Grönroos, 2000; Zeithaml and Bitner, 2003).

Conclusion

Employees are the responsible factors that determine the worth of all other non-human resources to the organization. The cutting-edge quality of any resources that the organization may possess will be of little value if the available employees do not perform their respective jobs well. The indispensable role of human resources is further amplified when their inimitable nature is considered. Unlike inanimate resources (e.g., money, machines, materials, information), humans are complex creatures and their capabilities and experiences cannot be duplicated and, as such, can be used as an asset to help an organization achieve competitive advantage.

In service-based businesses, human resources serve as the link to profit. That is because their work performance determines the quality of service as evaluated by customers. If their mindsets are oriented towards satisfying the customers, the outcomes of their performance are more likely to be perceived as favorable by the customers. Hence, producing employees with customer or service focused behaviors is the key to success in service-based organizations.

Accustoming human resources to behave according to the needs of service organizations is also the fundamental principle of contingency and role behavior theory. These two theories strongly suggest that a close alignment between the internal business operations (e.g., human resource management) and the goals of their organizations will always produce good productivity results. This belief provides an additional support to the call for a service-based approach in the management of human resources in any service-based organizations, including sport. As proposed by these theories and verified by a number or empirical studies, the more service-based the HRM practices of the organization, the more service-focused the employees will be, and the tendency for organization to achieve high customer perception of service quality will also be higher. As service quality-driven businesses, sport companies must have human resources whose work mentalities are service-oriented. Based on the integration of service-based HRM practices from previous empirical findings, human resources with service behaviors can be developed through such HRM practices as support at work, training, rewards system, supervisory assistance and performance appraisals.

In conclusion, in service-based businesses such as sport, the human resources will be more effective if they are service-oriented; that is, customer satisfaction is the goal of their every given task. Human resources with such orientation are those which are satisfied with the way they are managed by the organization. The underlying theme of this chapter is that when employees' commitments to perform well are made easier by the management's positive employment-related treatment, "both employees and consumers are likely to react positively – that is, employees should have feelings of satisfaction, not frustration, and so on; customers should feel good about the quality of the service they receive" (Schneider, 1980: 54).

References

Ambler, T. (1999) 'Where Does the Cash Flow from?' *Journal of Marketing Management*, 15, 705–10.

Armistead, C., and Kiely, J. (2003) 'Creating Strategies for Managing Evolving Customer Service', *Managing Service Quality*, 13(2), 164–70.

Barney, J. (1991) 'Firm Resources and Sustained Competitive Advantage', *Journal of Management Studies*, 17(1), 99–120.

Bartel, A. P. (1994) 'Productivity Gains from the Implementation of Employee Training Programs', *Industrial Relations Review*, 33, 411–25.

Bau, F., and Dowling, M. (2007) 'An Empirical Study of Reward and Incentive Systems in Germany Entrepreneurial Firms', *Schmalenbach Business Review*, 59, 160–75.

Becker, B. E., and Huselid, M. A. (1998) 'High Performance Work Systems and Firm Performance: A Synthesis of Research and Managerial Implications', in G. R. Ferris (ed.) *Research in Personnel and Human Resource Management* (16), Greenwich, CT, JAI Press, pp. 53–101.

Boswell, W. R., and Boudreau, J. W. (2002) 'Separating the Developmental and Evaluative Performance Appraisal Uses', *Journal of Business and Psychology*, 16, 391–412.

Bovee, C., Thill, J., Wood, M., and Dovel, G. (1993) *Management*, New York, McGraw-Hill.

Bowen, D. E., and Johnston, R. (1999) 'Internal Service Recovery: Developing a New Construct', *International Journal of Service Industry Management*, 10(2), 118–31.

Bowen, D. E., and Schneider, B. (1985) 'Boundary Spanning Role Employees and the Service Encounter: Some Guidelines for Management Research', in J. A. Czepiel, M. R. Soloman and C. F. Surprenant (eds.) *The Service Encounter*, Lexington, MA, Lexington Books.

Bowen, J., and Ford, R. C. (2002) 'Managing Service Organizations: Does Having a "Thing" Make a Difference?' *Journal of Management Studies*, 28(3), 447–69.

Bratton, J., and Gold, J. (2003) *Human Resource Management: Theory and Practice* (3rd edn), New York, Palgrave Macmillan.

Browning, V. (2006) 'The Relationship between HRM Practices and Service Behavior in South African Service Organizations', *International Journal of Human Resource Management*, 17(7), 1321–38.

Chebat, J., Babin, B., and Kollias, P. (2002) 'What Makes Contact Employees Perform? Reactions to Employee Perceptions of Managerial Practices', *International Journal of Bank Marketing*, 20(7), 325–32.

Chelladurai, P. (1999) *Human Resource Management in Sport and Recreation*, Champaign, IL, Human Kinetics.

Chelladurai, P., Scott, F. L., and Haywood-Farmer, J. (1987) 'Dimensions of Fitness Services: Development of a Model', *Journal of Sport Management*, 1(2), 159–72.

Cheung, C., and Law, R. (1998) 'Hospitality Service Quality and the Role of Performance Appraisal', *Managing Service Quality*, 8(6), 402–6.

Child, J. (1974) 'Managerial and Organizational Factors Associated with Company Performance: Part 1', *Journal of Management Studies*, 11, 175–89.

Coff, R. W. (1997) 'Human Assets and Management Dilemmas: Coping with Hazards on the Road to Resource-Based Theory', *Academy of Management Review*, 22(2), 374–402.

Colbert, B. A. (2004) 'The Complex Resource-Based View: Implications for Theory and Practice in Strategic Human Resource Management', *Academy of Management Review*, 29(3), 341–58.

Davies, D., Taylor, R., and Savery, L. (2001) 'The Role of Appraisal, Remuneration and Training in Improving Staff Relations in the Western Australian Accommodation Industry: A Comparative Study', *Journal of European Industrial Training*, 25(7), 366–73.

Day, G. (2000) 'The Market-Driven Organization', *Direct Marketing*, 62(10), 20–30.

Dean, J., and Bowen, D. (1994) 'Management Theory and Total Quality: Improving Research and Practice through Theory Development', *Academy of Management Review*, 19(3), 392–418.

Delery, J. E., and Doty, D. H. (1996) 'Modes of Theorizing in Strategic Human Resource Management: Tests of Universalistic, Contingency, and Configurational Performance Predictions', *Academy of Management Journal*, 39, 802–35.

Delery, J. E., and Shaw, J. D. (2001) 'The Strategic Management of People in Work Organizations: Review, Synthesis and Extension', *Research in Personnel and Human Resource Management*, 20, 165–97.

Den Hartog, D. N., and Verburg, R. M. (2002) 'Service Excellence from the Employees' Point of View: The Role of First Line Supervisors', *Managing Service Quality*, 12(3), 159–64.

Dixon, M. A. (2002) *The Relationship between Human Resource Management and Organizational Effectiveness in Non-Profit Sport Organizations: A Multi-Level Approach*. Ph.D. thesis, Ohio State University. Retrieved from ProQuest Dissertation and Theses Database (UMI 3039465).

Doyle, P., and Wong, V. (1998) 'Marketing and Competitive Performance: An Empirical Study', *European Journal of Marketing*, 32(5/5), 514–35.

Dubinsky, A. J., and Levy, M. (1989) 'Influence of Organizational Fairness on Work Outcomes of Retail Salespeople', *Journal of Retailing*, 65(Summer), 221–52.

Elmada, A. B., Ellinger, A. E., and Franke, G. R. (2008) 'Antecedents and Consequences of Frontline Service, Employee, Commitment to Service Quality', *Journal of Marketing Theory and Practice*, 16(2), 95–110.

Fletcher, C. (1997) *Appraisal: Routes to Improved Performance* (2nd edn), London, Institute of Personnel and Development.

Frabotta, D. (2000) 'Human Resources Director Praises Culture at Marriot', *Hotel and Motel Management*, 215(19), 136–39.

Furunes, T. (2005) 'Training Paradox in the Hotel Industry', *Scandinavian Journal of Hospitality and Tourism*, 5(3), 231–48.

Goleman, D. (2000) 'Leadership that Gets Results', *Harvard Business Review*, Mar–Apr, 78–88.

Griffin, R. W., and Ebert, R. J. (2006) *Business: International Edition* (8th edn), Pearson Higher Education.

Grönroos, C. (1983) *Strategic Management and Marketing in the Service Sector*, Cambridge, MA, Marketing Science Institute.

—— (2000) *Service Management and Marketing: A Customer Relationship Management Approach* (2nd edn), Chichester, John Wiley.

Hartline, M. D., and Ferrell, O. C. (1996) 'The Management of Customer-Contact Service Employees: An Empirical Investigation', *Journal of Marketing*, 60(October), 52–70.

Heskett, J. L., Jones, T. O., Loveman, G. W., Sasser Jr., W. E., and Schlesinger, L. A. (1994) 'Putting the Service-Profit Chain to Work', *Harvard Business Review*, 72(2), 164–75.

Huselid, M. A. (1995) 'The Impact of Human Resource Management Practices on Turnover, Productivity, and Corporate Financial Performance', *Academy Management Review*, 38(3), 635–72.

Jackson, S. E., and Schuler, R. S. (1992) 'HRM Practices in Service-Based Organizations: A Role Theory Perspective', *Advances in Services Marketing and Management*, 1, 123–57.

Jawahar, I. M. (2007) 'The Influence of Perceptions of Fairness on Performance Appraisal Reactions', *Journal of Labor Research*, 28, 735–54.

Johnson, J. W. (1996) 'Linking Employee Perceptions of Service Climate to Customer Satisfaction', *Personnel Psychology*, 49, 831–51.

Katz, D., and Kahn, R. L. (1978) *The Social Psychology of Organizations*, New York, Wiley.

Khatri, N. (2000) 'Managing Human Resources for Competitive Advantage: A Study of Companies in Singapore', *The International Journal of Human Resource Management*, 11(2), 336–65.

Kluger, A. N., and DeNisi, A. (1996) 'The Effects of Feedback Interventions on Performance: Historical Review, a Meta-Analysis and a Preliminary Feedback Intervention Theory', *Psychological Bulletin*, 119, 254–84.

Kuvaas, B. (2007) 'Different Relationships between Perceptions of Developmental Performance Appraisal and Work Performance', *Personnel Review*, 36(3), 378–97.

Lawler, E. (1992) *The Ultimate Advantage: Creating the High-Involvement Organization*, San Francisco, Jossey-Bass.

Lippman, S. A., and Rumelt, R. P. (1982) 'Uncertain Imitability: An Analysis of Interim Differences in Efficiency under Competition', *The Bell Journal of Economics*, 13, 803–39.

Little, M. M., and Dean, A. M. (2006) 'Links between Service Climate, Employee Commitment and Employees' Service Quality Capability', *Managing Service Quality*, 16(5), 460–76.

Liu, X., and Batt, R. (2007) 'The Economic Pay-Offs to Informal Training: Evidence from Routine Service Work', *Industrial and Labor Relations Review*, 61(1), 75–89.

Luthans, F., and Stajkovic, A. D. (1999) 'Reinforce for Performance: The Need to Go Beyond Pay and Even Rewards', *Academy of Management Executive*, 13(2), 49–57.

Lux, D. J., Jex, S. M., and Hansen, C. P. (1996) 'Factors Influencing Employee Perceptions of Customer Service Climate', *Journal of Market-Focused Management*, 1, 65–86.

Lytle, R. S., Hom, P. W., and Mokwa, M. P. (1998) 'SERV*OR: A Managerial Measure of Organizational Service-Orientation', *Journal of Retailing*, 74(4), 455–89.

McFarlin, D. B., and Sweeney, P. D. (1992) 'Distributive and Procedural Justice as Predictors of Satisfaction with Personal and Organizational Outcomes', *Academy of Management Journal*, 35(August), 626–37.

Moreland, R. J., and Levine, J. M. (2001) 'Socialization in Organizations and Work Groups', in M. E. Turner (ed.), *Groups at Work: Theory and Research*, Mahwah, NJ, Lawrence Erlbaum Associates, pp. 69–112.

Noble, C. H., Rajiv, K. S., and Kumar, A. (2002) 'Market Orientation and Alternative Strategic Orientations: A Longitudinal Assessment of Performance Implication', *Journal of Marketing*, 66(4), 25–40.

O'Connor, S. J., and Shewchuck, R. M. (1995) 'Service Quality Revisited: Striving for a New Orientation', *Hospital and Health Services Administration*, 40(4), 535–52.

Parkington, J. P., and Schneider, B. (1979) 'Some Correlates of Experienced Job Stress: A Boundary Role Study', *Academy of Management Journal*, 22, 270–81.

Pettijohn, C. E., Pettijohn, L. S., and D'Amico, M. (2001) 'Characteristics of Performance Appraisals and their Impact on Sales Force Satisfaction', *Human Resource Development Quarterly*, 12, 127–46.

Rogg, K. L., Schmidt, D. B., Shull, C., and Schmitt, N. (2001) 'Human Resource Practices, Organizational Climate, and Customer Satisfaction', *Journal of Management*, 27, 431–50.

Rousseau, D. M., and Parks, J. M. (1993) 'The Contracts of Individuals and Organizations', in L. L. Cummings and B. M. Staw (eds.) *Research in Organizational Behavior*, vol. 15, Greenwich, CT, JAI Press, pp. 1–43.

Sanwong, K. (2008) 'The Development of a 360-degree Performance Appraisal System: A University Case Study', *International Journal of Management*, 25(1), 16–22.

Schneider, B. (1980) 'The Service Organization: Climate is Crucial', *Organizational Dynamics*, 9(2), 52–65.

—— (1994) 'HRM – A Service Perspective: Towards a Customer-Focused HRM', *International Journal of Service Industry Management*, 5(1), 64–76.

—— (2004) 'Welcome to the World of Services Management', *Academy of Management Executive*, 18(2), 144–50.

Schneider, B., and Bowen, D. E. (1985) 'Employee and Customer Perceptions of Service in Banks: Replication and Extension', *Journal of Applied Psychology*, 70, 423–33.

—— (1993) 'The Service Organization: Human Resources Management is Crucial', *Organizational Dynamics*, 21(4), 39–52.

Schneider, B., Bowen, D., Ehrhart, M., and Holcombe, K. (2000) 'The Climate for Service: Evolution of a Construct', in N. Ashkanasy, C. Wilderom and M. Peterson (eds.) *Handbook of Organizational Culture and Climate*, London, Sage, pp. 21–36.

Schneider, B., Parkington, J. P., and Buxton, V. M. (1980) 'Employee and Customer Perceptions of Service in Banks', *Administrative Science Quarterly*, 25, 252–67.

Schneider, B., Wheeler, J. K., and Cox, J. F. (1992) 'A Passion for Service: Using Content Analysis to Explicate Service Climate Themes', *Journal of Applied Psychology*, 77(5), 705–16.

Schneider, B., White, S. S., and Paul, M. C. (1998) 'Linking Service Climate and Customer Perceptions of Service Quality: Test of a Causal Model', *Journal of Applied Psychology*, 83(2), 150–63.

Schuler, R. S., and Jackson, S. E. (1987) 'Linking Competitive Strategies with Human Resources Management Practices', *Academy of Management Executive*, 1, 207–19.

Singh, J. J. (2000) 'Performance Productivity and Quality of Frontline Employees in Service Organizations', *Journal of Marketing*, 64 (April), 15–34.

Skinner, B. F. (1953) *Science and Human Behavior*, New York, Free Press.

Strong, C. A., and Harris, L. C. (2004) 'The Drivers of Customer Orientation: An Exploration of Relational, Human Resource and Procedural Tactics', *Journal of Strategic Marketing*, 12, 183–204.

Swanson, R. A., and Holton, E. F. (2001) *Foundations of Human Resource Development*. San Fransisco, Berrett-Koehler.

Taylor, F. W. (1911) *Principles of Scientific Management*, New York, Norton.

Teece, D. (1982) 'Towards and Economic Theory of the Multiproduct Firm', *Journal of Economic Behavior and Organization*, 3, 38–63.

Tornow, W. W., and Wiley, J. W. (1990) 'Service Quality and Management Practices: A Look at Employee Attitudes, Customer Satisfaction, and Bottom-Line Consequences', *Human Resource Planning*, 14(2), 105–15.

Tsaur, S., and Lin, Y. (2004) 'Promoting Service Quality in Tourist Hotels: The Role of HRM Practices and Service Behavior', *Tourism Management*, 25, 471–81.

Ueno, A. (2008) 'Which Management Practices are Contributory to Service Quality?' *International Journal of Quality and Reliability Management*, 25(6), 585–603.

Walker, A. G., and Smither, J. W. (1999) 'A Five-year Study of Upward Feedback: What Managers Do with Their Results Matters', *Personnel Psychology*, 52, 393–423.

Wexley, K. N., and Latham, G. P. (1991) *Developing and Training Human Resources in Organisations* (2nd edn), New York, HarperCollins.

Wiley, J. W. (1991) 'Customer Satisfaction: A Supportive Work Environment and Its Financial Cost', *Human Resource Planning*, 14(2), 117.

Yoo, D. K., and Park, J. A. (2007) 'Perceived Service Quality: Analyzing Relationships among Employees, Customers, and Financial Performance', *International Journal of Quality and Reliability Management*, 24(9), 908–26.

Yoon, M. H., Beatty, S. E., and Suh, J. (2001) 'The Effect of Work Climate on Critical Employee and Customer Outcomes', *International Journal of Service Industry Management*, 12(5), 500–521.

Zeithaml, V., and Bitner, M. J. (2003) *Services Marketing: Integrating Customer Focus across the Firm* (3rd edn), New York, McGraw-Hill.

Zerbe, W. J., Dobni, D., and Harel, G. H. (1998) 'Promoting Employees Service Behavior: The Role of Perceptions of Human Resource Management Practices and Service Culture', *Canadian Journal of Administrative Science*, 15(2), 165–79.

12

VOLUNTEER MANAGEMENT IN SPORT

May Kim and Hyejin Bang

Sport and recreation organizations and events often rely on volunteer labor when providing services to their clients. Approximately 21 percent of all volunteers in Australia (Australian Bureau of Statistics, 2008) and 26 percent of all volunteers in the United Kingdom (Institution for Volunteering Research, 2007) volunteer in sport and recreation areas. The numbers of volunteers in large and well-established sport organizations and events can easily reach hundreds and even thousands. For example, approximately 60,000 volunteers worked at the Athens Olympic Games in 2004 (Kennett, 2005) and 1,700,000 people volunteered at the Beijing Olympic Games and hosting communities in 2008 (Beijing Organizing Committee for the Olympic Games, 2008). Volunteer labor has been a critical labor source in youth sport organizations. A Report of the Department of Health and Human Service and Department of Education (2000) indicated that approximately 2.5 million volunteers work annually as coaches of youth sport programs in the US. In the case of the American Youth Soccer Organization (AYSO, 2004), nearly 250,000 individuals participated in volunteer activities to run the youth soccer programs of the organization.

Although varying in service frequency and duration, the levels of skill and knowledge, and volunteer motivation, these sport volunteers provide indispensible services in various positions and levels of responsibility. However, according to the Corporation for National and Community Service (Grimm, Dietz and Foster-Bey, 2006), the rate of adults volunteering for sport and cultural organizations in the U.S. significantly dropped from 1989 to 2005. This calls managers' special attention to developing strategies to recruit, manage, and retain quality volunteers. Cuskelly, Taylor, Hoye, and Darcy (2006) suggested that sound human resources practices (i.e. planning, recruitment, screening, orientation, training and support, performance management, and recognition) should be applied to manage volunteers in sports. In this chapter, based on previous research and human resources practices used, volunteer management practices are reviewed in four different sport settings: non-profit sport organizations, youth sport settings, mega sporting events, and local community events.

Volunteer management in non-profit sport organizations

Recruitment and selection

For non-profit sport organizations, recruiting volunteers is a constant challenge since volunteers receive non-monetary benefits but are preferred to volunteer for a long term. Although finding the right person with the right skills for a job is important for effective volunteer recruitment, finding the perfect candidate who is highly qualified and experienced may not always be the case in non-profit organizations. Thus, managers can rank potential candidates based on how well the candidates meet the minimum or required qualifications and then select the best person for the job.

The first stage of the volunteer recruitment process should involve determining what benefits current volunteers perceive from their contributions, then identifying a target market of potential volunteers who desire those benefits the organization provides (Mitchell and Taylor, 1997). That is, it is important to recognize and understand why individuals choose to volunteer with their chosen non-profit sport organization. Moreover, Munro (2001) noted that in order to maintain a viable volunteer base, one of the most important issues facing non-profit-sector programs and services is to know what specifically motivates individuals to participate. Hoy and Miskel (1982: 137) stated that volunteer motivation involves "the complex forces, drives, needs, tension states, or other mechanisms that start and maintain voluntary activity toward the achievement of personal goals." Caldwell and Andereck (1994) adopted the conceptual approach developed by Knoke and Prensky (1984) and categorized motivations of volunteers in recreational-related volunteer associations into three categories of incentives: purposive, solidary, and material incentives.

- Purposive incentives: doing something useful and contributing to society.
- Solidary incentives: dealing with social interactions and networking opportunities.
- Material incentives: tangible benefits provided by the host organization utilizing the volunteers.

Of these three categories, purposive incentives were identified as the strongest volunteer motivation, whereas material incentives were often the least important (Caldwell and Andereck, 1994).

Furthermore, organizations can focus on improving volunteer recruitment efforts by employing the following approaches (Kolnick and Mulder, 2007).

- Conveying a clear message that highlights local service involvement;
- Demonstrating proficient leadership;
- Providing one-hour information sessions for prospective volunteers;
- Targeting corporations, college/high school students, and sport teams;
- Identifying a champion to serve as a spokesperson;
- Accentuating flexibility and friendship in volunteering;
- Underlining the benefits of volunteering.

With regard to the recruitment advertising, utilizing internet job boards has become important today. Sixty percent of respondents indicated that they used the internet to search for information about volunteer activities (Kolnick and Mulder, 2007). In-house recruitment can also be effective. Current volunteers within an organization can be a great source of volunteer recruitment and recommend strong candidates. Given that current volunteers are already committed to the organization, its goals, and its processes, they may have a good grasp of who will cope with the organization (Chelladurai, 2006) and, particularly, who can carry out a job that comes with non-monetary rewards effectively.

Training

Cuskelly et al. (2006) found that sports clubs using training and support practices extensively were less likely to have problems related to volunteer retention. These days, non-profit sport organizations provide an orientation for new volunteers, as an initial program of training, which can help the volunteers understand the organization's mission, main goals, policies, and procedures. The goals in the orientation are to provide a favorable impression of the organization for the volunteers, to help them get used to the demands of their job, and to create a good atmosphere to enhance their acceptance in the agency (Rossman and Schlatter, 2003). Rossman and Schlatter (2003) proposed three types of information that organizations should provide during the orientation:

- Outlining the nature of the organization and the volunteers' role to help the organization accomplish its goals. (Who are they working for? What is this organization trying to accomplish, e.g. organizational mission?)
- Explaining about the nature of a typical workday and then making them anticipate what they need to do in a typical workday. (What is a typical order of events in a workday? What kinds of tasks will they do in a typical day?)
- Covering the work rules, policies, procedures, and special skills that are needed. (Provide the volunteers an opportunity to know some details of agency operation.)

Training plays an essential role in enhancing the fit between the individual and the organization (Chelladurai, 2006). Different from most paid positions, many volunteer roles will be performed by individuals who do not have prerequisite skills or knowledge for the job, so specific on-the-job training for volunteers may need to be offered to provide the information and skills necessary to effectively accomplish the volunteer role (Taylor, Doherty, and McGraw, 2008).

The training period can range from a few hours of training to a couple of weeks of training depending on the difficulty and requirements of the position and the experience of the volunteer. Holding daytime volunteer training sessions during the working week may be an unwise strategy (Kolnick and Mulder, 2007). However, one-hour information sessions at an organization during the lunch hour could be an efficient means of enticing potential volunteers to participate in a full training session (Kolnick and Mulder, 2007). During the training sessions, volunteers should learn their role in the non-profit sport organization. Volunteers in basic and reutilized positions can be given only fundamental information about the organization and job, while those in highly responsible or complex positions might be required to take extensive ongoing training about organizational policies and procedures.

Retention

Volunteer retention is a significant organizational outcome (Cuskelly et al., 2006) and is often considered to be as challenging as volunteer recruitment in the first place. By reducing volunteer turnover and absenteeism while increasing the effectiveness and satisfaction of volunteers, at the same time organizations can save the time and money associated with recruiting and training new volunteers (Clary, 2004). Frequently, withdrawal behaviors, such as absenteeism and turnover intention, can be influenced by organizational commitment (Freund, 2005; Worrall, Cooper and Campbell-Jamison, 2000). In human resource management studies, it has been suggested that employees with high levels of commitment improve work performance and a wide range of other positive organizational outcomes such as reduced absenteeism and turnover (Cuskelly and Boag, 2001; Griffeth, Horn, and Gaertner, 2000; Meyer and Herscovitch, 2001; Riketta, 2002). Volunteers who are more committed to a sporting organization may be less likely to leave than volunteers who are less organizationally committed (Cuskelly and Boag, 2001). That is, organizational commitment seems to discriminate more between those who stay and those who leave in comparison with other components such as job satisfaction (Griffeth et al., 2000).

Social exchange theory is one of the most influential conceptual paradigms for understanding workplace behavior (Cropanzano and Mitchell 2005); specifically, most commitment literature has been grounded in social exchange theory (Bishop, Scott, Goldsby and Cropanzano, 2005). The social exchange theory proposed by Thibaut and Kelley (1959) considers that voluntary relationships depend on the rewards and costs that satisfy the values of outcomes in different situations for an individual. Social exchange relationships evolve over time into trusting, loyal, and mutual commitments (Bishop et al., 2005). However, the individuals need to find out who is supporting them (e.g. organizational support vs. team support) and distinguishing their commitment to a social entity from the social entity's support for them (Bishop et al., 2005). This is because when an individual or entity makes a contribution, the obligations of the individual or entity develop into an expectation of a return at a future time.

To increase volunteers' organizational commitment, there are many factors that non-profit sport organizations and managers need to consider in return for volunteers' contribution to the organization. Organizations can induce a feeling of obligation by treating volunteers satisfactorily. When an individual has made a decision to volunteer, volunteerism generally takes place in an organizational context (Penner, 2002). This means organizational variables seem to be the determinant of an individual's volunteering behavior (Penner, 2002). One element of organizational variables is an individual member's perceptions of an organization and feelings about the way he or she is treated by the organization (Penner, 2002). Although volunteers pursue their own goals and values in contributing their time and effort to non-profit organizations, the length of volunteer involvement may be accounted for by the organizations' treatment of the volunteers. Volunteers' satisfaction is usually made up by their motivation and by the emotional support provided by the organization (Jiménez and Fuertes, 2005).

Organizations should pay attention to meeting the motivational needs of their volunteers. According to the social exchange theory, people inquire about the degree that they are being rewarded for their efforts, and if an imbalance of reciprocity is conceived, an individual moves toward a better equilibrium (Zafirovski, 2003). Volunteers exchange their time and labor for some sort of psychological gain (Green and Chalip, 1998). That is, individuals who believe that their needs and goals were fulfilled through volunteering are more likely to engage in the service than those with no such belief (Clary, 2004). For example, volunteers may stay with the organization because they believe their personal needs, such as doing something worthwhile, having social interactions, and developing their personal career, are satisfied by their volunteering experience in the organization.

Non-profit sport organizations need to focus on leader–member relations to enhance volunteers' organizational commitment as well. Given that leaders are volunteers, they may be motivated by a truthful interest in members and a desire to assist in their advance. In a sport setting, the roles that people play or their standardized patterns of behavior as part of a given functional relationship are inherent (Case, 1998). Thus, an active role from both leaders and members is a part of required behavior within a non-profit sport organization, and both parties must share a commitment to the mission and goals of the organization in providing sport and recreational services. High-quality relationships between leaders and members indicate that leaders exchange advice, social support, feedback, decision-making latitude, and opportunities for interesting and high-visibility assignments with members (Sparrowe and Liden, 2005). From the members' viewpoint, members provide high levels of contribution in return, such as commitment to the leader and cooperation in group tasks (Sparrowe and Liden, 2005).

In addition, organizations should consider ways to evaluate and publicly praise volunteer performance (Preston, 2006). Presenting a volunteer appreciation luncheon where organizations can provide certificates of service and speeches highlighting individuals' contributions, or nominating special volunteers for community service awards, can be a good way to make volunteers feel appreciated and recognized (Preston, 2006). Increasing responsibility that includes longevity and positive contributions to the organization can accelerate the committed volunteers' motivation as well (Preston, 2006). If organizations possess a large volunteer staff, providing opportunities for volunteers whose performance was highly evaluated to move up the hierarchy into management roles might make the volunteers feel valued (Preston, 2006). Therefore, performance appraisal can be an effective tool to reward the contributions of volunteers and encourage the volunteers' participation and involvement, which has a positive impact on volunteer retention in non-profit sport organizations.

Volunteer management in youth sport settings

Recruitment and selection

Recruiting and selecting qualified volunteers is also important in youth sport settings like non-profit youth sport organizations. However, somewhat different approaches and practices should be considered based on the context of youth sport settings. Participation in organized youth sport has always been a popular activity of American youth (Coakley, 2007; Hedstrom and Gould, 2004; Seefeldt and Ewing, 1997). In the United States, more than 60 million young people participate in organized youth sport (Coakley, 2007; National Council of Youth Sport, 2008; Pennington, 2003). These organized youth sport activities are run by adult volunteers who play various roles such as coaches, officials, and administrators of youth sport. Although varying in service frequency and duration, volunteers provide youth sport organizations with needed services in various positions and levels of responsibility (AYSO, 2004). Scholars agree that effective involvement of these adults is a crucial factor in providing high-quality sport experiences of children (Hedstrom and Gould, 2004; Seefeldt and Ewing, 1997; Wiersma and Sherman, 2005).

As youth sport participation increases (NCYS, 2008; Seefeldt and Ewing, 1997), the demand for sport volunteers also increases. Thus, most youth sport organizations face challenges in recruiting and retaining volunteers. Similarly they rely on the support of volunteers who are parents of youth sport participants (Doherty, 2005). Some youth sport organizations even require a parent of each youth sport participant to volunteer for a league (personal conversation with Patti Atchison, the manager of Gainesville Soccer Association). In the late 1970s, volunteer coaches in youth sport were more likely to be male, married, and to have started coaching with the participation of their children (Gould and Martens, 1979). Today, the characteristics of volunteer coaches are not much different. Messner and Bozada-Deas (2009) found in their investigation on coaching staffs of 1,490 youth soccer teams and 538 youth baseball/softball teams in a regional area from 1999 to 2007 that about 90 percent of head coaches were male volunteers while female volunteers often worked as team managers, and often were called team parents or "team moms" (Coakley, 2007; Messner and Bozada-Deas, 2009).

Although parents of youth sport participants serve as volunteers, youth sport organizations have often experienced a lack of personnel to work for the organizations. Thus, researchers have been interested in understanding the motivation of youth sport volunteers (Eley and Kirk, 2002; Kim, Zhang, and Connaughton, 2010a, 2010b) because volunteer motivation involves the reasons, purposes, plans, and goals which lead individuals to get involved and stay in volunteer positions (e.g. Clary et al., 1998; Cuskelly, Hoye, and Auld, 2006; Kim and Chelladurai, 2008; MacLean and Hamm, 2007). Kim et al. (2010a) explored the motivation of youth sport volunteers using the Modified Volunteer Function Inventory for Sport (MVFIS), which was modified from the Volunteer Function Inventory (VFI, Clary et al., 1998). The VFI and MVFIS applied a functional approach to volunteers' motives and indicated that involvement in volunteer work is a function of the joint effects of individuals' motives for volunteering and the opportunities provided in the volunteer work environment to meet their needs. They identified six broad functions served by volunteering: values, understanding, social, career, protective, and enhancement (Clary et al., 1998).

- Values: the opportunities that volunteerism presents to express one's values related to altruistic and humanitarian concerns for others;
- Understanding: the opportunities for new learning experiences, and to exercise one's knowledge, skills, and abilities;
- Social: a functional motivation to be with one's friends or to engage in an activity viewed favorably by important others;
- Career: a function that may be obtained from participation in volunteer work;
- Protective: traditional concerns that may serve to reduce guilt over being more fortunate than others and addressing one's own personal problems;
- Enhancement: a function of volunteering that involves the ego's growth and development.

Allison, Okun, and Dutridge (2002) stated that volunteers generally consider the values, understanding, and enhancement functions as more important motives than career, social, and protective functions. However, motivation functions usually vary among individuals with different backgrounds; one volunteer can possess multiple motivations (Clary and Snyder, 1999) and the order of importance among the motivation dimensions may differ among organizations, settings, and volunteer groups (Allison et al., 2002). In the case of youth sport leagues where most volunteers were parents of participants, the values and understanding functions of volunteer motivation were the highest and second-highest ranked motivation of volunteers and the career and protective functions were the lowest and second-lowest ranked functions (Kim et al., 2010a). However, among teenager volunteers in youth sport organizations, understanding, career, and values were ranked as the highest volunteer functions (Eley and Kirk, 2002).

Training

The contribution of volunteers in youth sport leagues, mainly volunteer coaches, is significant; however, their knowledge and skills in youth sport have been continuously questioned. Although most volunteers get involved in sports and tasks (e.g. coaching, refereeing, or administrating) which they feel comfortable to perform or are, at least, interested in, many of them do not have adequate knowledge and skills regarding communication, first aid, risk management, and other coaching and administration practices (Missing, 1995). The poor coaching of volunteers often leads to serious physical or mental injuries to youth participants, sometimes brings lawsuits, and causes financial damage to youth sport organizations or leagues (e.g. Ashcroft, 1997; *Byrne v Boys Baseball League*, 1989; *Hills v Bridgeview Little League Association*, 2000).

Farmer and Fedor (1999) noted that adequate organizational control, performance standards, appraisals, and support/training would diminish various issues including low quality or high variability of volunteers' performances/coaching. Thus, many youth sport organizations and leagues require their volunteers to participate in volunteer training as well as the initial orientations. While a few large youth sport organizations create and provide their own training programs to volunteer coaches, (e.g. AYSO's volunteer training program, Safe Haven), many youth sport leagues rely on training programs created and distributed by umbrella organizations like the National Alliance for Youth Sport (NAYS), National Youth Sport Coaches Association (NYSCA) and the American Sport Education Program (ASEP), which include coaching essentials, safety basics, practice, game-day tips, and sport specific skills (ASEP, 2009; NAYS, 2011). For instance, NYSCA has trained more than 2.5 million volunteer coaches through 3,000 community-based agencies and organizations since 1981 (NAYS, 2011). These volunteer training programs include series of courses on various topics to provide quality sport programs to youth sport participants and protect both participants and volunteers (AYSO, 2004; NAYS, 2011). Also, federal and state laws (e.g. the Volunteer Protection Act of 1997) reinforce the importance of adequate volunteer training or risk management programs.

However, the training requirement of most youth sport leagues is to take an initial one-day (or a few hours) training course, probably more appropriately called orientation (NAYS, 2011). Volunteer coaches in various youth sport leagues reported that their previous volunteer training experiences did not positively influence their self-efficacy on volunteer responsibility (Kim, 2009). Moreover, although volunteers prefer hands-on training, these initial volunteer training courses are more likely to be in-class or online courses (Kim and Chelladurai, 2008). Thus, sport leagues should be more interested in providing adequate training for youth sport volunteers to provide better sport experiences for youth participants and protect both youth participants and adult volunteers.

Retention

Retaining a skilled and experienced coach is far more beneficial than searching for and replacing one (Turner and Chelladurai, 2005). It is the same for volunteer coaches in youth sport settings. However, most volunteers are parents of youth sport participants and the majority of those volunteers leave the organization or league when their children stop playing. Thus, retaining volunteer coaches is extremely difficult although retention of them is a critical issue for youth sport organizations and leagues.

Kim, Chelladurai, and Trail (2007) found in their study on youth sport volunteers that when a volunteer's skills and knowledge fit well with the volunteer's responsibilities (person–task fit) and a volunteer's value matched the organization's mission (person–organization fit), the volunteer was empowered and eventually intended to continue volunteering. That is, youth sport organizations and leagues should carefully recruit volunteers and place them based on the fit between the volunteers' interests, values, knowledge, and abilities and their volunteer roles.

Also, Kim et al. (2007) found that managerial treatments positively influenced the level of empowerment which led to a high level of intention to remain as volunteers. The managerial treatments Kim et al. (2007) studied included proper supervision and rewards (e.g. recognition and appreciation). That is, to retain quality volunteers in youth sport, volunteer managers should be interested in volunteers and volunteer duties and performances and show appreciation of volunteer services. Probably, providing appreciation and recognition gifts (e.g. thanks card and plaque) and promoting high-performing and experienced volunteers to highly responsible positions might be effective to retain quality volunteers in youth sport.

Volunteer management in mega events

Recruitment and selection

Episodic volunteers also bring the power that keeps mega/international sporting events running. Without doubt, volunteers have been the crucial labor source for mega sporting events requiring several thousand individuals in a relatively short time (a few days to a couple of weeks). Such organizations as the International Olympic Committee (IOC) consider volunteer involvement as a key element for its summer and winter Olympic Games (IOC, 2000). Thus, volunteer recruitment and the selection of massive numbers of volunteers for mega sporting events have been a big challenge for event managers.

No different from other sport settings, mega/international sporting event organizations and their volunteer managers have paid attention to the motivations of volunteers when recruiting. However, the motivations of episodic volunteers at mega international sporting events could be qualitatively different from those of continuous volunteers who provide services for regularly scheduled programs for two reasons: (a) the short duration of commitment for episodic volunteering, and (b) the high status and prestige associated with special events. This view is supported by a study by Saleh and Wood (1998) on volunteer motivations in multicultural festival events. Their findings indicated that, although some conventional motivations were significant to the volunteers, other special event-related motivations, such as a pride in one's culture and a desire to maintain links with one's ethno-cultural group, were also important. Moreover, Manzenreiter and Horne (2005: 30) stated that "major international sporting events have an extraordinary capacity to generate emotionally powerful and shared experiences." As international events such as the Olympic Games and FIFA World Cup, reveal both the mass appeal of sport and the symbolic power embodied in the sport competitions (Manzenreiter and Horne, 2005), individuals and nations attach bigger meanings to these events. Consequently, volunteers at mega international sporting events might have more specific and unique motives because of the nature of these international events.

Given that most mega/international sporting events rely heavily on volunteers, event organizations or volunteer managers need to focus on meeting the volunteers' motivational needs. Williams, Dossa, and Tompkins (1995) found in their study on the motivation of volunteers in a mega ski event that supporting the community and the national team were considered most important by volunteers; whereas free tickets and souvenirs were considered least motivating. Later, by modifying Knoke and Prensky's (1984) three-factor concept, Farrell, Johnston, and Twynam (1998) developed the Special Event Volunteer Motivation

Scale (SEVMS) with four dimensions to study volunteer motivations for working at an elite women's curling competition event: purposive (i.e. contribution to society or doing something useful), solidary (i.e. social interactions and networking), external traditions (i.e. family tradition and external influence), and commitments (i.e. the need of personal skills and external expectations for volunteering). In that study, the researchers found that purposive and solidary incentives were primary motives when compared to external traditions and commitments.

More recently, Bang and colleagues (Bang and Chelladurai, 2009; Bang, Alexandris, and Ross, 2010) developed the Volunteer Motivations Scale for International Sporting Events (VMS-ISE) in the contexts of the 2002 FIFA World Cup, 2002 Asian Games, and 2004 Athens Olympic Games, which includes seven factors: expression of values, patriotism, interpersonal contacts, personal growth, career orientation, extrinsic rewards, and love of sport.

- Expression of values: concern for others, the success of the event, and society;
- Patriotism: pride in and love of the country, and allegiance to the country;
- Interpersonal contacts: meeting and interacting with people and forming friendships;
- Personal growth: gaining new perspectives, as well as feeling important and needed;
- Career orientation: career development such as gaining experience and career contacts;
- Extrinsic rewards: getting tangible rewards such as free uniforms, food, and admission;
- Love of sport: loving sport and any event related to sport.

Among volunteers in the FIFA World Cup and Asian Games, the expression of values and interpersonal contacts factors were the highest and second-highest ranked whereas the extrinsic rewards and career orientation factors were the lowest and second-lowest ranked (Bang and Chelladurai, 2009). On the other hand, among volunteers in the Athens Olympic Games, expression of values and patriotism were found to be the highest and the second-highest ranked factors (Bang, Alexandris and Ross, 2010). However, similar to the previous study at the FIFA World Cup and Asian Games, extrinsic rewards and career orientation factors were the lowest and second-lowest ranked factors. These different motives imply that when event organizations or managers seek volunteers for their events, they should identify the various volunteer motives in order to develop strategies to satisfy volunteers' needs and expectations (Farrell et al., 1998).

Therefore, volunteer managers may need to adapt volunteer recruitment strategies by developing recruitment messages and/or approaches that can play on each of the motivations of volunteering. Although it depends on the nature of the mega/international sporting event, sources of volunteers for consideration can vary such as sponsors; universities, schools, and colleges; service, social, and sport clubs; special interest groups; previous volunteers; religious groups; and professional organizations and unions (Salem, Jones and Morgan, 2003). Once news of the event is out, individuals may volunteer immediately if it is a mega/international event in which one of the most important motivations would be "being there" (Catherwood and Van Kirk, 1992). Thus, effective marketing strategies for a mega/international sporting event would also help run a recruitment campaign to attract individuals to volunteering.

Unlike other events or organizations, another big challenge for mega sporting events is to screen and select adequate volunteers. Often, not only local residents but also volunteer applicants from other regions or countries want to volunteer. In the case of the 2008 Beijing Olympic Games, 1.126 million domestic and foreign individuals applied and only 100,000 were selected as volunteers at the Beijing Olympics and Paralympics (Xinhua News Agency, 2008). In fact, it is very common for most mega sporting events to have more volunteer applicants than the positions available because it is such a unique opportunity. Thus, mega event managers often spend several months or years recruiting and screening volunteers based on knowledge, skills, and experiences. Specifically, the 2010 South Africa FIFA World Cup recruited volunteers in two groups: specialist volunteers with expert knowledge and skills (e.g. language, information technology, and media skills) and general volunteers performing customer service duties, and selected volunteers in a three-stage process including application-based initial screening, security screening based on each volunteer position requirement, and face to face interviews (FIFA, 2007).

More generally, with regard to the staffing process in the context of events, Getz (2005: 222) proposed a three-stage process:

- Identify all tasks associated with event creation, delivery and shutdown (e.g. game management, administration, access control, accreditation, language services, marketing, medical and health, transportation, telecommunication, IT, media, accommodation, and logistics);
- Determine the number of people that are needed to accomplish a range of tasks regarding conducting the event (e.g. do all the tasks have to be done in order, by the same work group, or all at once by a larger group? What level of supervision will be required? What tasks can be outsourced and what must be done by the event team? Will more staff than normal be required to perform tasks such as security, as a result of some specific circumstance such as a visit by a celebrity to the event?);
- List the numbers of volunteers and supervisors and the skills/experiences/qualifications needed to create the "ideal'" workforce for the event.

Moreover, providing a clear and complete description of the duties and responsibilities for each volunteer position is important. All the position descriptions need to be developed before any recruitment activities take place. The position descriptions must include the purpose and responsibilities of the position, job qualifications, a designated supervisor and worksite, a timeframe for all activities of the job, and a description of job benefits.

Training

Due to the complexity of organizing and managing various events and functions, the responsibilities of volunteers in mega events are functionally specialized (IOC, 2000). Thus, training volunteers can be a big challenge. A large number of volunteers from different backgrounds are involved in mega/international sporting events for a variety of job positions. Sometimes, the core management team starts work months or even years prior to the event, so many different types of training may be necessary (Van der Wagen, 2006). Often, event organizing committees develop a volunteer training manual (such as the Manual for Beijing Olympic Volunteers) based on experience from previous events and specific situations of the host country or city. Then, volunteer leaders of the event, who are often selected earlier and go through additional training, deliver or support training for general volunteers of the event based on the volunteer training manual (Beijing Olympic Games Volunteer Work Coordination Group, 2006).

For mega/international event managers, it is very important to educate volunteers about the spirit and mission of the mega/international event as well as the specialized functions and organization standards and rules (IOC, 2000). Thus, mega/international event managers provide orientation and training sessions to instruct volunteers about the event and its mission.

For example, the volunteer training programs for the FIFA World Cup also include fundamental and core knowledge about the event along with protocol/rules, venue-specific training, customer service, etc. (FIFA, 2007).

From the perspective of volunteers, training is one of two key components of volunteer experiences along with volunteer task execution (Costa, Chalip and Green, 2006), and quality of volunteer training plays a critical part in the evaluation of volunteer experience (Green and Chalip, 2004). Thus, to increase the effectiveness of volunteer training and volunteer satisfaction, it can be useful to measure volunteers' motivations when event managers and/or volunteer managers assign and schedule the volunteers. Consideration should be given by event managers and/or volunteer managers in planning volunteer training and orientation to:

(a) what information is needed about each volunteer; and
(b) how to utilize the information in deciding where to assign a volunteer.

If the orientation and/or training are well planned, volunteers should certainly be able to understand what their role, duties, and schedules are. Given that orientation and training not only directly influence a volunteer's satisfaction but also impact the overall success of the event (Stevens, Connolly, Adams and Bradish, 2008), carefully planned orientation and training should be provided to the volunteers.

Retention

Compared to paid employees, event volunteers mostly have a shorter commitment to their job; the commitment may not even be noticed if they leave before their allocated time has finished, especially in a large-scale event (Van der Wagen, 2006). Therefore, ongoing communication at all stages, from recruitment to the end of an event, is fundamentally essential in order to increase the retention of volunteers (Byrne, Houen and Seaberg, 2002). Costa et al. (2006) noted that satisfaction plays a significant role in employees' retention in general, so identifying the antecedents that influence volunteers' satisfaction would be worthwhile. According to Costa et al. (2006), the sense of community and commitment both affect job satisfaction. Volunteers who have opportunities to share opinions and experiences during training sessions tend to build their sense of community at the event and the sense of community positively influences the volunteers' commitment to the event, which leads to increased satisfaction with the job (Costa et al., 2006). In addition to satisfaction, Van der Wagen (2006: 237) emphasized that an event's organizational culture has an impact on volunteer retention and proposed the elements of the event organizational culture as follows.

- Feedback: encouragement and a sense of direction;
- Cohesion: everyone wants to feel part of a team that has a positive dynamic, as dysfunctional teams fall apart very rapidly. Shared goals leads to developing a sense of cohesion;
- Resources: lack of resources to do the job proficiently or properly would discourage volunteers, while being well equipped helps productivity;
- Support: being neglected by team members or supervisors makes volunteers feel unhappy, especially those left isolated at distant spots with a lack of relief or encouragement;
- Fairness: like permanent employees, volunteers would be uncomfortable with inequitable treatments;

- Improvement: in the ongoing event operational environment, suggestions for improvements should be taken seriously and acted upon;
- Information provision: to provide high–quality services, volunteers should be in the information loop, which contributes to a sense of collaborative teamwork as well.

Therefore, volunteers' propensity to continue volunteer activities at a mega/international sporting event comes from the opportunity of being part of the subculture, which is represented experientially in the sense of community gained through their volunteering role, rather than the job itself (Costa et al., 2006). This sense of commitment the volunteers have built then contributes to increasing volunteer retention.

While individual volunteers are satisfied with their volunteer experiences and cherish their memories at mega/international events, retention efforts by mega/international events have been very rare (Kim, Lee, Chon and Chae, 2008). The mega/international sporting event organizers and managers may provide appreciation gifts and awards and throw volunteer social parties; however, their efforts are very limited because the mega/intentional sporting event is not routinely hosted. However, recently, researchers, practitioners, and policy-makers have realized the significance of the mega/international sporting event volunteers and put efforts into retention. Host countries and cities now try to utilize these experienced volunteers in their other mega/international events. Further, the United Nations (UN) helped volunteer training for the 2008 Beijing Olympic Games and supported retention of these volunteers because the UN believed the volunteerism of the Beijing Olympic Games could be a great opportunity to promote volunteerism in China (United Nations, 2007). In general, the effort to retain mega/international event volunteers for other events or areas has been increased.

Volunteer management in community sporting events

Recruitment and selection

Similar to mega/international sporting events, episodic volunteers are the main source of service delivery in community sporting events. Volunteer labor may be more beneficial in small, regional, and participant sport events which do not receive the sponsorship money and benefits of popular mega-events. Although some local sporting events get sponsorship money, much of it is used for other administrative expenses or contributed to charity; thus, volunteers' free labor is an indispensable factor in the running of community sporting events (Coyne and Coyne, 2001). However, for community sporting events which are not well known to the public, recruiting enough volunteers and filling essential volunteer positions is not simple. Thus, managers of community sporting events must work even harder to recruit volunteers than those in other sport settings.

As discussed in the previous sections, researchers and practitioners have tried to recruit more volunteers through understanding demographic characteristics and the motivation of volunteers. Kim et al. (2010b) found in their study on local Special Olympic event volunteers that the average mean age of volunteers was 39.17 years old and the majority of them were highly educated and had full-time jobs. These volunteers indicated the values and understanding functions of MVFIS as the highest and second-highest motivation while the career and protective functions were the lowest and second-lowest motivations.

Strigas and Jackson (2003) found from volunteers in a local marathon event that the predominant group was volunteers who were Caucasian, mid-aged (35–50 years old), and full-time-employed. In the study, Strigas and Jackson explored five motivation factors of these volunteers: (a) purposive (i.e. humanitarian, beneficial to the community/event), (b) leisure, (c) external influences (i.e. family tradition or for significant others), (d) material (i.e. utilitarian and career-related incentives), and (e) egoistic (i.e. social or networking) and indicated that egoistic motivations were the most important reason for volunteer decision. Similarly, Hardin, Koo, King, and Zdroik (2007) surveyed volunteers at a golf tournament and identified four motivational factors: (a) self-interest, which is similar to Strigas and Jackson' egoistic, (b) external influences, (c) purposive, and (d) escapism, identical to the leisure factor of Strigas and Jackson.

Although motivation and demographic characteristics might be major antecedents of volunteer involvement, the individual's role identity is another factor influencing an individual's intention to engage in volunteering. Kim and Trail (2007) found among college students regarding their intention to volunteer in different local events that university students with high levels of university athletic team identity and sport identity indicated a higher level of intention to volunteer for university sporting events. That is, fans of a specific team or sport are more likely to volunteer for an event relevant to that specific team and sport. Specifically, in the context of the sport of golf, Coyne and Coyne (2001) found that "love of golf" was a very critical motivation of volunteers. Actually, many golf and tennis events attract volunteers with free tickets to events (Kim, Won, and Harrolle, 2009). Thus, contacting university or local sport clubs or sport fans would be helpful to effectively recruit volunteers.

Training

Sporting event volunteers often start their volunteer experiences at the training session and meet other volunteers and supervisors; then, by doing so, volunteers can develop the sense of community which enhances training effectiveness, fosters continuous learning environment, and eventually improves volunteer systems (Costa et al., 2006). Also, the impact of volunteer training goes beyond the individual level to enhance community partnerships and social cohesion and foster local sports clubs by increasing the interests of local residents (Sport and Recreation Victoria, 2008). However, volunteer training for local sporting events has not been the main area of event managers' interest because of the situations of community sporting events. Except for a few well-known events, community sporting events which are held over a few days need several hundred to a thousand individuals but do not have enough money to pay these individuals. Accordingly, just filling the volunteer positions is a big challenge. Thus, in this situation, it is hard to focus on quality training for volunteers. In most cases, volunteer training in community sporting events is replaced with a day's or even an hour's orientation program. A few big-name professional sporting events (e.g. Professional Golf Association or International Tennis Federation events) require their volunteers to participate in a volunteer training session prior to working for the events. However, some events just provide a brief introduction before placing volunteers in their positions on the event day. Although it is practically hard, community event managers should care more about volunteer training and provide training including introduction of the event and its mission, sport and event-related rules and protocol, customer services, and risk management. By doing so, they will help to provide better service for event participants and spectators and protect volunteers and participants from any possible physical injuries and lawsuits.

Retention

Due to the difficulty of recruiting volunteers in community sporting events, it is extremely beneficial to retain existing volunteers and let them come back to subsequent events. Also, returned volunteers need less training and help new volunteers learn about the system and event; thus, successful retention of experienced volunteers minimizes the problems of volunteer training in community sporting events. Indeed, some individuals volunteer for the same event for several years, which is not common in most community sporting events, despite the benefits of experienced volunteers. Thus, researchers and practitioners have suggested various practices to retain volunteers.

Kim, Trail, Lim, and Kim (2009) found that volunteers in a local Special Olympics event felt empowered and intended to return for the next event because they felt that their values and ability matched well with the event mission and volunteer requirement (good fit) and their volunteer experiences were similar to their expectation (fulfilled psychological contract). That is, recruiting volunteers fitting well with the event and the volunteer position may be a good way to retain volunteers. However, for many community sporting events it is not realistic to rigorously screen volunteer applicants for good task and organization fit. Instead of screening and hiring well-matched volunteers, if the event managers provide accurate information about the event and volunteer responsibilities during recruiting and orientation or initial training, volunteers can create realistic expectations toward the organization and the required duties, and thus construct realistic psychological contracts. Accordingly, it is more likely that the psychological contract will be fulfilled and the volunteers will be empowered and willing to return for the next event.

Further, Andrew et al. (2009) found that when volunteers perceived adequate organizational supports (i.e. personal care for and interest in volunteers and their performance) by the event organizer, volunteers were likely to be satisfied and return for the next event. Thus, it is an effective means to retain volunteers if event managers are interested in the needs of volunteers and appreciate volunteer services. Specifically, expressing appreciation and rewarding good performance are a key but relatively simple practice as a volunteer retention effort. Giving out free gifts, sending a post-event thank you postcard, and recognizing volunteers' names in local newspapers or pamphlets are some effective examples (Forsyth 1999; Martinez and McMullin, 2004). Also, Kim et al. (2009) found that free gifts (e.g. free game entrance tickets, food, volunteer uniforms, chances to play sport, chances to meet athletes, discount coupon for sponsored products, and social events) could be a significant factor for college students to return as volunteers. Therefore, community event managers who experience difficulty in filling their volunteer positions should put more effort into these effective retention practices.

Summary

Figure 12.1 shows the significant elements of the three stages of recruitment/selection, training, and retention in the management of volunteers in sport. These elements were discussed in the context of four different sport settings (non-profit sport organizations, youth sport, mega/international sporting events, and community sporting events). Although volunteer management practices are somewhat different due to unique characteristics of each sport setting, all sport organizations and leagues and their volunteer managers should keep in mind the following important things in volunteer management:

- Managers should not forget that volunteers are a crucial labor source of volunteer service delivery (Green and Chalip, 1998).
- Managers should understand motivations of potential volunteer groups.
- Managers should match the knowledge and skills of volunteers and their job requirements, if possible.

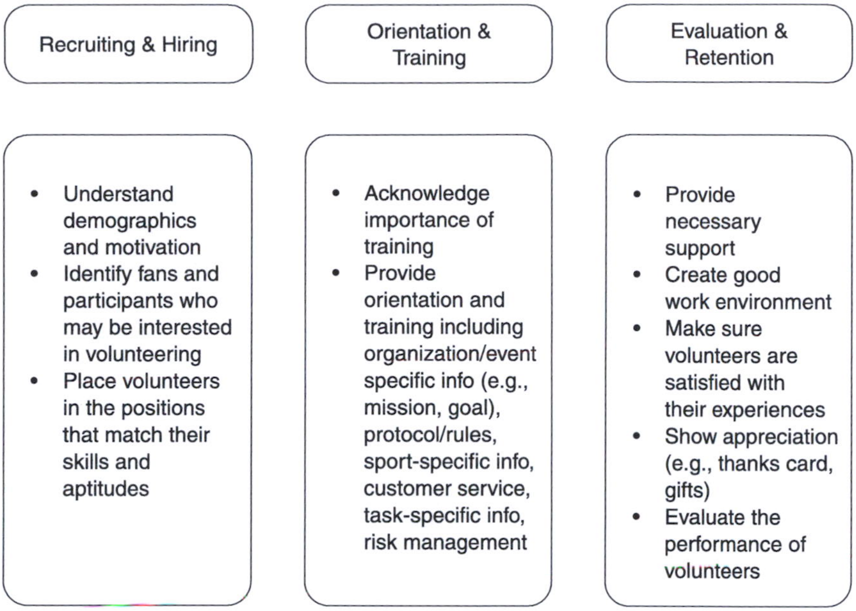

Figure 12.1 Stages of volunteer management

- Although the labor of volunteers is free, managing volunteers should be professionally done because the client's evaluation of the service and image of the organization or event are caused by the service given by volunteers (Kim and Trail, 2007). Thus, managers should provide proper orientation and training including sport-specific, organization/event-specific, and task-specific knowledge and skills, risk management, and customer service information.
- Mangers should express personal interest in volunteers and their performance and create a good volunteer environment.
- Managers should show appreciation for volunteer services through various practices such as thank-you cards, plaques, free gifts, and volunteer social parties.
- Managers should try to satisfy volunteers' motivational needs.
- Managers should evaluate the performance of volunteers and try to retain quality volunteers.

References

Allison, L.D.C., Okun, M.A. and Dutridge, K.S. (2002) 'Assessing volunteer motives: a comparison of an open-ended probe and Likert rating scales', *Journal of Community and Applied Social Psychology*, 12, 243–55.

America Youth Soccer Organization (2004) *A history of AYSO*, AYSO Website. Online. Available HTTP: <http://soccer.org/AboutAYSO/history.aspx> (accessed 1 March 2009).

American Sport Education Program (2009) *About ASEP*. Online. Available HTTP: <http://www.asep.com/about.cfm> (accessed 5 April 2009).

Andrew, D.P.S., Kim, M. and Kim, S.M. (2009) 'The influence of leader-member exchange and organizational support on volunteer satisfaction and retention', paper presented at the 24th Annual Conference of the North American Society for Sport Management, Columbia, SC.

Ashcroft, J. (1997) *Testimony by U.S. Senator John Ashcroft on Volunteer Liability Reform*.

Austrian Bureau of Statistics (2008) *Australian Social Trends, 2008: Volunteer work*. Online. Available HTTP: <http://www.abs.gov.au/AUSSTATS/abs@.nsf/Lookup/4102.0Chapter4102008> (accessed 10 February 2009).

Bang, H. and Chelladurai, P. (2009) 'Development and validation of the volunteer motivations scale for international sporting events (VMS-ISE)', *International Journal of Sport Management and Marketing*, 6, 332–50.

Bang, H., Alexandris, K. and Ross, S. (2010) 'Validation of the revised volunteer motivations scale for international sporting events (VMS-ISE) at the Athens 2004 Olympic Games', *Event Management*, 12, 119–31.

Beijing Olympic Games Volunteer Work Coordination Group (2006) *Manual for Beijing Olympic Volunteers, Series of Beijing Olympiad Training Brochures*, Beijing, China Renmin University Press.

Beijing Organizing Committee for the Olympic Games (2008) *1,700,000 volunteers welcome Olympic Guests*. Online. Available HTTP: <http://en.beijing2008.cn/volunteers/news/n214527376.shtml> (accessed 17 September 2008).

Bishop, J.W., Scott, K.D., Goldsby, M.G. and Cropanzano, R. (2005) 'A construct validity study of commitment and perceived support variables: A multi-foci approach across different team environments', *Group and Organization Management*, 30, 153–80.

Byrne v Boys Baseball League (1989) *NJ 236*.

Byrne, C., Houen, J. and Seaberg, M. (2002) 'One team: Communicating to unite a growing, disparate workforce under one umbrella', *Communication World*, April, 28–32.

Caldwell, L. and Andereck, K. (1994) 'Motives for initiating and continuing membership in a recreation-related voluntary association', *Leisure Sciences*, 16, 33–44.

Case, R. (1998) 'Leader member exchange theory and sport: Possible applications', *Journal of Sport Behavior*, 21, 387–95.

Catherwood, D.W. and Van Kirk, R.L. (1992) *The complete guide to special event management: Business insights, financial advice, and successful strategies from Ernst and Young, advisors to the Olympics, the Emmy Awards, and the PGA tour*, New York, John Wiley and Sons.

Chelladurai, P. (2006) *Human resource management in sport and recreation*, Champaign, Human Kinetics.

Clary, E.G. (2004) 'Volunteer sustainability: How nonprofits can sustain volunteers' commitment', *Snapshots 36*, 1–6.

Clary, E.G. and Snyder, M. (1999) 'The motivation to volunteer: Theoretical and practical consideration', *Current Directions in Psychological Sciences*, 8, 156–59.

Clary, E.G., Snyder, M., Ridge, R.D., Copeland, J., Stukas, A.A., Haugen, J. and Miene, P. (1998) 'Understanding and assessing the motivations of volunteers: a functional approach', *Journal of Personality and Social Psychology*, 74, 1516–30.

Coakley, J.L. (2007) *Sport and society: Issues and controversies* (9th edn), St. Louis, Times Mirror/Mosby.

Costa, C.A., Chalip, L. and Green, B.C. (2006) 'Reconsidering the role of training in event volunteers' satisfaction', *Sport Management Review*, 9, 165–82.

Coyne, B.S. and Coyne Sr, E.J. (2001) 'Getting, keeping, and caring for unpaid volunteers for professional golf tournament events: A study of the recruitment/retention of unpaid volunteers for staging large, mass-attended, high-profile Professional Golf Association (PGA) golf tournaments', *Human Resource Development International*, 4, 199–216.

Cropanzano, R. and Mitchell, M.S. (2005) 'Social exchange theory: An interdisciplinary review', *Journal of Management*, 31, 874–900.

Cuskelly, G. (1998) 'Organisational commitment and committee turnover of volunteers in sport', *Australian Journal on Volunteering*, 3, 4–14.

Cuskelly, G. and Boag, A. (2001) 'Organizational commitment as a predictor of committee member turnover amongst volunteer sport administrators: Results of a time-lagged study', *Sport Management Review*, 4, 65–86.

Cuskelly, G., Hoye, R. and Auld, C. (2006) *Working with volunteers in sport: Theory and practice*, New York, Routledge.

Cuskelly, G., Taylor, T., Hoye, R. and Darcy, S. (2006) 'Volunteer management practices and volunteer retention: A human resource management approach', *Sport Management Review*, 9, 141–63.

Department of Health and Human Services and Department of Education (2000) *Promoting better health of young people through physical activity and sport*. Online. Available HTTP: <http://www.ed.gov/offices/OSDFS/physedrpt.pdf> (accessed 16 September 2002).

Doherty, A. (2005) *A profile of community sport volunteers, Ontario: Parks and Recreation Ontario and Sport Alliance of Ontario*. Online. Available HTTP: <http://www.sportalliance.com/Images/Resource%20Documents/Volunteer%20Resources/Phase1_execSummary.pdf> (accessed 5 February 2009).

Eley, D. and Kirk, D. (2002) 'Developing citizenship through sport: The impact of a sport-based volunteer programme on young sport leaders', *Sport, Education, and Society*, 7, 151–66.

Farmer, S.M. and Fedor, D.B. (1999) 'Volunteer participation and withdrawal: a psychological contract perspective on the role of expectations and organizational support', *Nonprofit Management and Leadership*, 9, 349–67.

Farrell, J.M., Johnston, M.E. and Twynam, G.D. (1998) 'Volunteer motivation, satisfaction, and management at an elite sporting competition', *Journal of Sport Management*, 12, 288–300.

FIFA (2007) *2010 FIFA World Cup Organising Committee South Africa Volunteer Policy*. Online. Available HTTP: <http://www.docstoc.com/docs/5388175/FIFA-World-Cup-Organising-Committee-South-Africa-Volunteer-Policy> (accessed 5 September 2011).

Forsyth, J. (1999) 'Volunteer management strategies: Balancing risk and reward', *Nonprofit World*, 17, 40–44.

Freund, A. (2005) 'Commitment and job satisfaction as predictors of turnover intentions among welfare workers', *Administration in Social Work*, 29, 5–22.

Getz, D. (2005) *Event management and event tourism* (2nd edn), New York, Cognizant Communication Corp.

Gould, D. and Martens, R. (1979) 'Attitudes of volunteer coaches toward significant youth sport issues', *Research Quarterly*, 50, 369–80.

Green, B.C. and Chalip, L. (1998) 'Sport volunteer: Research agenda and application', *Sport Marketing Quarterly*, 7, 14–23.

—— (2004) 'Paths to volunteer commitment: Lessons from the Sydney Olympic Games', in R.A. Stebbins and M. Graham (eds.) *Volunteering as Leisure. Leisure as Volunteering. An International Assessment*, Wallingford, CABI Publishing.

Griffeth, R.W., Horn, P.W. and Gaertner, S. (2000) 'Meta-analysis of antecedents and correlates of employee turnover: Update, moderator tests, and research implications for the next millennium', *Journal of Management*, 26, 463–88.

Grimm Jr, R., Dietz, N. and Foster-Bey, J. (2006) *Volunteer growth in America: A review of trends since 1974*. Online. Available HTTP: <http://www.nationalservice.gov/pdf/06_1203_volunteer_growth.pdf> (accessed 1 March 2009).

Hardin, R., Koo, G., King, B. and Zdroik, J. (2007) 'Sport volunteer motivations and demographic influences at a nationwide tour event', *International Journal of Sport Management*, 8, 80–94.

Hedstrom, R. and Gould, D. (2004) *Research in Youth Sport: Critical Issues Status*. Online. Available HTTP: <http://www.educ.msu.edu/ysi/project/CriticalIssuesYouthSports.pdf> (accessed 1 March 2009).

Hills v. Bridgeview Little League Association (1996) Nos. 1–98–0630 House Judiciary Committee. Online. Available HTTP: <http://www.state.il.us/court/opinions/appellatecourt/1999/1stdistrict/june/html/1980620.htm> (accessed 5 September 2011).

Hoy, W.K. and Miskel, C.G. (1982) *Educational administration: Theory, research, and practice* (2nd edn), New York, Random House.

Institution for Volunteering Research (2007) *Helping out: A national survey of volunteering and charitable giving*. Online. Available HTTP: <http://www.volunteering.org.uk/NR/rdonlyres/BFC9C41E-7636-48FB-843C-A89D2E93F277/0/OTS_Helping_Out.pdf> (accessed 5 September 2011).

International Olympic Committee (2000) 'Conclusion and Recommendations: International symposium on volunteers, global society and the Olympic movement', *IOC Olympic Studies Centre*. Online. Available HTTP: <http://doc.rero.ch/lm.php?url=1000,10,38,20100507110340-MT/IOC_Symposium_1999.pdf> (accessed 1 October 2007).

Jiménez, M. and Fuertes, F. (2005) 'Positive emotions in volunteerism', *The Spanish Journal of Psychology*, 8, 30–35.

Kennett, C. (2005) 'Helping hands', *Olympic Review*, 34–37.

Kim, M. (2009) 'Training effectiveness: The relationship between training experience and volunteer coaches' self-efficacy', *Journal of Youth Sport*, 4, 27–30.

Kim, M. and Chelladurai, P. (2008) 'Volunteer preferences for training: Influences of individual difference factors', *International Journal of Sport Management*, 9, 233–49.

Kim, M., Chelladurai, P. and Trail, G.T. (2007) 'A model of volunteer retention in youth sport', *Journal of Sport Management*, 21, 151–71.

Kim, M., Lee, C.W., Chon, T.J. and Chae, J.H. (2008) 'What can we learn from former Olympic volunteers? Interview with 1988 Olympic volunteers', paper presented at the 23rd Annual Conference of the North American Society for Sport Management, Toronto, Canada, June.

Kim, M., Won, D. and Harrolle, M.G. (2009) 'The influences of gifts on perspective volunteers: A conjoint analysis', *International Journal of Sport Management*, 10, 1–17.

Kim, M. and Trail, G.T. (2007) 'Influence of role identities on volunteer intentions', *International Journal of Sport Management*, 8, 1–15.

—— (2010) 'The effects of service provider gender on technical and relational service quality', *International Journal of Sport Management*, 11, 55–70.

Kim, M., Trail, G.T., Lim, J. and Kim, Y.K. (2009) 'The role of the psychological contract in intention to continue volunteering', *Journal of Sport Management*, 23, 549–73.

Kim, M., Zhang, J.J. and Connaughton, D.P. (2010a) 'Comparison of volunteer motivation in three different types of sport organizations', *European Sport Management Quarterly*, 10, 343–65.

—— (2010b) 'Modification of volunteer functions inventory for sport settings', *Sport Management Review*, 13, 25–38.

Knoke, D. and Prensky, P. (1984) 'What relevance do organization theories have for volunteer associations?', *Social Science Quarterly*, 65, 3–20.

Kolnick, L. and Mulder, J. (2007) 'Strategies to improve recruitment of male volunteers in nonprofit agencies', *American Journal of Hospice and Palliative Medicine*, 24, 98–104.

MacLean, J. and Hamm, S. (2007) 'Motivation, commitment, and intentions of volunteers at a larger Canadian sporting event', *Leisure/Loisir*, 31, 151–83.

Manzenreiter, W. and Horne, J. (2005) 'Public policy, sport investments and regional development initiatives in contemporary Japan', in J. Nauright and K. Schimmel (eds.) *The political economy of sport*, London, Palgrave.

Martinez, T.A. and McMullin, S.L. (2004) 'Factors affecting decisions to volunteer in nongovernmental organizations', *Environment and Behavior*, 36, 112–36.

Messner, M.A. and Bozada-Deas, S. (2009) 'Separating the men from the mom: The making of adult gender segregation in youth sport', *Gender and Society*, 23, 49–71.

Meyer, J.P. and Herscovitch, L. (2001) 'Commitment in the workplace: Toward a general model', *Human Resource Management Review*, 11, 299–326.

Missing, R. (1995) 'Training volunteer sport coaches', *Illinois Parks and Recreation*, 46–48.

Mitchell, M.A. and Taylor, S.L. (1997) 'Adapting internal marketing to a volunteer system', *Journal of Nonprofit and Public Sector Marketing*, 5, 29–42.

Munro, J. (2001) 'Motivations and enduring involvement of leisure program volunteers: A study of the Waterloo region Track 3 ski school', paper presented at the 9th Annual Graduate Leisure Research Symposium, '2001: A Leisure Odyssey', Waterloo, Ontario, May, 2001.

National Alliance for Youth Sport (2011) *Volunteer Coaches*. Online. Available HTTP: <http://www.nays.org/Coaches/index.cfm> (accessed 5 September 2011).

National Council of Youth Sport (2008) *Reports on trends and participation in organized youth sport*. Online. Available HTTP: <http://www.ncys.org/pdf/2008/2008-market-research.pdf> (accessed 7 October 2008).

Penner, L.A. (2002) 'Dispositional and organizational influences on sustained volunteerism: An interactionist perspective', *Journal of Social Issues*, 58, 447–67.

Pennington, B. (2003) 'As team sport conflict, some parents rebel', *New York Times. Online*. Available HTTP: <http://query.nytimes.com/gst/fullpage.html?res=9904E7DA1638F931A25752C1A9659C8B63> (accessed 5 June 2008).

Preston, A. E. (2006) 'Volunteer resources', in D. R. Young (ed.) *Financing nonprofits: Putting theory into practice*, Lanham, AltaMira Press.

Riketta, M. (2002) 'Attitudinal organizational commitment and job performance: A meta-analysis', *Journal of Organizational Behavior*, 23, 257–66.

Rossman, J.R. and Schlatter, B.E. (2003) *Recreation programming: Designing leisure experiences* (4th edn), Champaign, Sagamore Publishing.

Saleh, F. and Wood, C. (1998) 'Motives of volunteers in multicultural events: The case of the Saskatoon FolkFest', *Festival Management and Events Tourism*, 5, 59–70.

Salem, G., Jones, E. and Morgan, N. (2003) 'An overview of events management', in I. Yeoman, M. Robertson, J. Ali-Knight, S. Drummond and U. McMahon-Beattie (eds.), *Festival and events management: an international arts and cultural perspective*, Oxford, Elsevier Butterworth-Heinemann.

Seefeldt, V.D. and Ewing, M.E. (1997) *Youth sport in America: An overview*. Online. Available HTTP: <http://www.fitness.gov/youthsport.pdf> (accessed 1 March 2009).

Sparrowe, T.S. and Liden, R.C. (2005) 'Two routes to influence: Integrating leader-member exchange and network perspectives', *Administrative Science Quarterly*, 50, 505–35.

Sport and Recreation Victoria (2008) *Volunteer training for future participation and events: Outcomes from Yachting Victoria's Go Sailing and Boating Project*. Online. Available HTTP: <http://www.dpcd.vic.gov.au/__ data/assets/word_doc/0006/39084/Volunteer_Training_for_Future_Participation_and_Events_ Outcomes_from_Yachting_Victoria_-_website_version_-_kt_-_15jan08.doc> (accessed 20 April 2009).

Stevens, J., Connolly, M., Adams, L.J. and Bradish, C. (2008) 'The event planning model: The event development phase, Part II' in C. Mallen and L. Adams (ed.) *Sport, recreation and tourism event management: Theoretical and practical dimensions*, Burlington: Butterworth-Heinemann/Elsevier.

Strigas, A. and Jackson, E.N. (2003) 'Motivating volunteers to serve and succeed: Design and results of a pilot study that explores demographics and motivational factors in sport volunteerism', *International Sport Journal*, 7, 111–23.

Taylor, T., Doherty, A. and McGraw, P. (2008) *Managing people in sport organizations: A strategic human resource management perspective*, Oxford, Elsevier.

Thibaut, J.W. and Kelley, H.H. (1959) *The social psychology of groups*, New York, John Wiley and Sons.

Turner, B.A. and Chelladurai, P. (2005) 'Organizational and occupational commitment, intention to leave and perceived performance of intercollegiate coaches', *Journal of Sport Management*, 19, 193–211.

United Nations (2007) *Partners launch Beijing Olympics volunteering project*. Online. Available HTTP: <http://www.unv.org/en/news-resources/news/doc/partners-launch-beijing-olympics.html> (accessed 10 October 2007).

Van der Wagen, L. (2006) *Human resource management for events: Managing the event workforce*, Oxford, Elsevier Butterworth-Heinemann.

Volunteer Protection Act of 1997 (1997) *One hundred fifth Congress of the United State of America*.

Wiersma, L.D. and Sherman, C.P. (2005) 'Volunteer youth sport coaches' perspectives of coaching education/certification and parental codes of conduct', *Research Quarterly for Exercise and Sport*, 76, 324–38.

Williams, P.W., Dossa, K.A. and Tompkins, L. (1995) 'Volunteerism and special event management: A case study of Whistler's Men's World Cup of Skiing', *Festival Management and Event Tourism*, 3, 83–95.

Worrall, L., Cooper, C.L. and Campbell-Jamison, F. (2000) 'The impact of organizational change on the work experiences and perceptions of public sector managers', *Personnel Review*, 29, 613–36.

Xinhua News Agency (2008) *Olympics volunteer office gets 22,000 foreign applications*. Online. Available HTTP: <http://www.china.org.cn/olympics/news/2008-04/04/content_14273265.htm> (accessed 10 April 2009).

Zafirovski, M. (2003) 'Some amendments to social exchange theory: A sociological perspective', *Theory and Science*, 4, 1–22.

13

SOURCES OF SUPPORT FOR EMPLOYEES IN SPORT ORGANIZATIONS

Boyun Woo and Claudio Rocha

Introduction

What makes an organization successful? One would agree that employees of the organization play a key role in the overall success of the organization since employees' positive work attitudes and behaviors are essential to maintaining an organization. This may be particularly true for organizations that provide services. As a matter of fact, service organizations greatly base their performance on employees because the employees are the ones who have direct contact with the customers and influence shaping the image of the organization in consumers' minds. Since many sport organizations deal with service, keeping employees' work attitudes and behaviors positive is essential for them.

So what would influence employees' attitudes and behaviors at work? One factor that is considered to have a great influence on employees' overall work experience is the amount of support available in the workplace. According to Sundin, Bildt, Lisspers, Hochwalder, and Setterlind (2006), support in the workplace is important for two reasons. First, support helps employees to create a sense of belonging to the organization on individual and emotional levels. Second, on external and collective levels, support serves as a tool to meet the needs of the environment.

In general, when dealing with support available at work, the literature has focused on three different sources of support in the organizational context: coworker support, supervisor support, and organizational support. This chapter elaborates different sources of support available in the workplace and the measurement of each source of support. In addition, previous studies that have investigated the antecedents and consequences of these sources of support are discussed. Finally, the chapter concludes with some suggestions on possible future studies in relation to the sources of support.

Definitions

Coworker support

Coworker support has been defined in several ways. According to Ellis and Miller (1994), coworker support is defined as the degree to which coworkers provide emotional, instrumental, and informational support to their fellow employees. Ko, Price, and Mueller (1997: 963) defined coworker support as the "degree to which employees have close friends in their immediate work unit." In addition, Susskind, Kacmar, and Borchgrevink (2007: 372) defined coworker support as "the extent to which employees believe their coworkers provide them with work-related assistance." Among these definitions, Ellis and Miller's definition is the most comprehensive since it includes various aspects of support, whereas Ko et al.'s and Susskind et al.'s definitions are limited to a single aspect, such as social and work-related aspects respectively.

Supervisor support

Supervisor support has been defined in various ways. In fact, many researchers have used the same definition of coworker support by substituting the word "coworker" with "supervisor." For example, Ellis and Miller (1994) and Susskind et al. (2007) defined supervisor support in the same way as coworker support but with a different entity providing support. Ellis and Miller's (1994) definition indicated that supervisor support is emotional, instrumental, and informational support that comes from supervisors. According to Susskind et al. (2007: 372), supervisor support represents "the extent to which employees believe that their supervisors offer them work-related help in performing their jobs as service workers." On the other hand, Ko et al. (1997: 963) referred to it as the "degree to which superiors are helpful in job-related matters." Also, Bhanthumnavin (2003: 79) defined supervisor support as "the positive work interaction between a supervisor and a subordinate." Similar to coworker support, while Ellis and Miller encompassed all the aspects of support, Ko et al. and Susskind et al. focused only on work-related support from supervisors. Therefore, Ellis and Miller's definition is more comprehensive.

Organizational support

Regarding organizational support, Eisenberger, Huntington, Hutchison, and Sowa's (1986) definition has been widely accepted and used by many researchers. According to Eisenberger et al., organizational support refers to employees' perception about the degree to which the organization values their contributions and cares about their well-being. In other words, it involves how an employee feels about their work being appreciated by the organization and how much the organization shows concern for and cares about the individual.

Measure of support

To date, coworker support, supervisor support, and organizational support have been measured using subjective self-reporting scales. In other words, rather than measuring the actual support provided, researchers have measured the employees' perception of the support received. There are various measures that are used to measure perceived coworker, supervisor, and organizational support. These measures are discussed further in this section.

Various scales have been proposed to measure coworker support. Coworker exchange scales, which measure the quality of exchange between coworkers, have been largely used in investigations of coworker support. Many researchers have used Graen and Uhl-Bien's (1995) leader-member exchange scale after changing the word "supervisor" to "coworker" (e.g., Sherony and Green, 2002; Wikaningrum, 2007). Other researchers (e.g., Lee and Gao, 2005) have used the satisfaction with coworker component from the Job Descriptive Index, which was developed by Smith, Kemdall, and Hulin (1969). Yet many researchers have also developed scales that directly measure coworker support (Ducharme and Martin, 2000; Poulin, 1995). These scales have all usually shown high internal consistency in previous usage. As such, researchers have used various scales when measuring coworker support.

Similarly, various measures for perceived supervisor support have been proposed in the literature. Among them, the most popular method is using Eisenberger et al.'s (1986) perceived organizational support scale by substituting the word "organization" with "supervisor". In fact, many researchers have used this scale when measuring employees' level of perceived supervisor support (e.g., Rhoades et al., 2001; Shore and Tetrick, 1991; Yoon and Lim, 1999). However, researchers have also suggested that this may be problematic when measuring supervisor support and organizational support together (e.g., Rhoades and Eisenberger, 2002). These researchers claim that respondents, many times, have had a hard time distinguishing between support that comes from the supervisor and from the organization. And this distinction becomes more unclear when the supervisors are higher in the hierarchical system and when organizational support and supervisor support are measured at the same time (Rhoades and Eisenberger, 2002; Rhoades, Eisenberger, and Armeli, 2001)

Meanwhile, other researchers have measured supervisor support by the related measure of leader-member exchange (e.g., Hofmann and Morgeson, 1999; Settoon et al., 1996; Sherony and Green, 2002; Wayne, Shore, and Liden, 1997; Wikaningrum, 2007). Leader-member exchange scales include Scandura and Graen's (1984) 7-item scale, Graen and Uhl-Bien's (1995) 7-item scale, Liden and Maslyn's (1993) scale with subscales of loyalty, respect, contribution, and affect, and Anderson, Coffey, and Byerly's (2002) 6-item scale. These scales all have been reported to have a good internal consistency ($\alpha = .70 - .96$) in the previous usages. Among them, Graen and Uhl-Bien's (1995) scale has been the most widely used in recent studies (e.g., Hofmann and Morgeson, 1999; Sherony and Green, 2002; Wikaningrum, 2007).

Different from coworker support and supervisor support, which have been measured on various distinct scales, one common measure has been used to measure perceived organizational support. That is Eisenberger et al.'s (1986) perceived organizational support scale. The original scale consists of 36 items that measure two factors: employees' perceptions about the degree to which the organization values their contributions and cares about their well-being. However, many researchers have used shortened versions of the scale, which have included different number of items ranging from three to 17 (e.g., Eisenberger et al., 2001; Eisenberger et al., 1997; Settoon et al., 1996; Shore and Tetrick, 1991; Yoon and Lim, 1999). These shortened versions of the scale have been frequently used in the studies because the internal consistency of the shortened versions has been shown to be as high as the original 36-item version (e.g., Harris, 1995; Pack, Jordan, Turner, and Haines, 2007; Rhoades and Eisenberger, 2002; Shore and Tetrick, 1991).

Antecedents of support

Understanding what influences the level of support is important to find out how support operates. Identifying the factors that predict employees' perception of support is crucial since it could help the organization to develop a strategy that can enhance the ways to provide support. However, despite the importance of identifying predictors for support, few studies have investigated the antecedents of perceived support. In the limited research, researchers have focused on different variables for different sources of support. In this section, the antecedents of different sources of support are discussed separately.

Coworker support

While some researchers have investigated the antecedents of organizational and supervisor support, few researchers have investigated what predicts the level of coworker support. One exception is Bowling, Beehr, Johnson, Semmer, Hendricks, and Webster (2004), who examined whether physical attractiveness and sense of humor could trigger support from coworkers. They hypothesized that when someone is deemed to be attractive, people would like that person and offer them more support. Based on the principle of reciprocity (Gouldner, 1960), Bowling et al. (2004) hypothesized that physical attractiveness and sense of humor might make coworkers want to be close and to feel positively attached to the person, thus increasing the odds for them to provide social support. However, their result revealed that physical attractiveness and sense of humor were not significant predictors of coworker support.

In general, antecedents of coworker support have been understudied. In particular, to the authors' knowledge, no studies have examined the antecedents of coworker support in sport contexts. More studies are definitely needed in this area in the future.

Supervisor support

Some researchers have claimed that the amount of support provided by supervisors is determined by coworker support and organizational support provided to an employee (e.g., Yoon and Thye, 2000). In other words, an individual who is already receiving coworker and organizational support is more likely to receive supervisor support as well. The notion is well explained by Dornbusch and Scott's (1975) theory of organizational authority. According to this theory, social support is viewed as the transfer of positive sanctions among employees. Therefore, when one is already receiving support from other parties, it is deemed that the activities and positions of the employees are validated. There are two ways that one's activities and positions could be validated: authorization and endorsement. In authorization, positive sanction comes from a higher authority. On the other hand, positive sanction comes from someone at the same or lower level in endorsement (Dornbusch and Scott, 1975). In this sense, when someone is already receiving support from the organization and peers, his or her position is validated. Thus, the supervisor is more likely to view the individual in a positive manner and provide more support.

This notion has been empirically tested. Yoon and Thye (2000) examined whether coworker support, organizational support, and positive affectivity predicted the amount of supervisor support provided to hospital employees. The results showed that both variables were significant predictors for supervisor support. However, the amount of supervisor support was the strongest when coworker support, organizational support, and positive affectivity were present at the same time. Meanwhile, there was no significant effect of positive affectivity alone on supervisor support.

Other constructs, such as job demands, job control, and job content, have been considered to influence supervisor support. Based on a demand–control–support model (Karasek and Theorell, 1990), researchers have supported the theory that job demand and job control are significant predictors of supervisor support (e.g., Johnson, 1991; Sundin et al., 2006). For example, Sundin et al. (2006) investigated whether organizational variables (i.e., job demands, job control, and job content), individual variables (i.e., self-esteem, mistrust), and socio-demographic variables (i.e., type of employer, occupational position, age, gender, and educational level) were associated with supervisor support. They found that these variables all together explained 22 percent of variance in supervisor support. However, the majority of the variance was explained by organizational variables, indicating that individual and socio-demographic variables did not explain a significant amount of variance. In particular, job control explained the largest variance in supervisor support (10 percent).

Organizational support

There are two antecedents of organizational support that are frequently discussed in the literature: organizational justice and perceived supervisor support. Researchers have argued that perception of organizational justice is an important antecedent of organizational support (e.g., Eisenberger, Stinglhamber, Vandenberghe, Sucharski, and Rhoades, 2002; Fasolo, 1995; Masterson et al., 2000; Shanock and Eisenberger, 2006). The notion is that justice perceptions may be one aspect of an employee's assessment of discretionary action taken by the organization or its agents (Rahim, Magner, and Shapiro, 2000). This discretionary action perception plays an axiomatic role in the degree of support employees perceived from their organization (Moorman, Blakely, and Niehoff, 1998; Wayne, Shore, Bommer, and Tetrick, 2002). In particular, researchers have found that procedural justice and distributive justice positively influence employees' perceived organizational support (e.g., Fasolo, 1995; Moorman et al., 1998; Wayne et al., 2002).

Another antecedent frequently discussed for organizational support is supervisor support. Eisenberger et al. (2002) observed that perceived supervisor support was positively related to temporal change in perceived organizational support, suggesting that supervisor support leads to organizational support. Additionally, they noted that the supervisor support–organizational support relationship rose with perceived supervisor status, suggesting that the higher the perceived standing of a supervisor within the organization, the more likely it would be that an employee perceived his or her supervisor as the organization representative. Also, Shanock and Eisenberger (2006) found that employees' perceived supervisor support was positively associated with perceived organizational support.

In sport settings, there is little research that has been performed on the antecedents of perceived organizational support. One exception is Kim and Cunningham's (2005) study. They examined whether job autonomy, job variety, and job feedback could work as antecedents of perceived organizational support among college coaches of various sports. Their results showed that job feedback was significantly related to perceived organizational support whereas job autonomy and job variety were not related to organizational support. Kim and Cunningham's (2005) findings showed the importance of job feedback in predicting perceived organizational support.

Consequences of support

Although some studies have investigated the antecedents of support, many times support has been examined as an independent variable (Sundin et al., 2006). In other words, research on different sources of support has been largely geared towards the outcomes of support. Many researchers have, in fact, investigated how the sources of support impact employees' work attitudes and behaviors, such as organizational commitment, job satisfaction, and turnover intention. The relationships between the outcome variables are explained by social exchange theory (Blau, 1967). According to Blau (1967: 89), "an individual who supplies rewarding services to another obligates him. To discharge this obligation, the second must furnish benefits to the first in turn." In other words, the key notion of social exchange theory is reciprocity. When one person supports another, the norm of reciprocity (Gouldner, 1960) foresees the return of such support. For example, if someone feels that she is receiving some-thing valuable from her coworkers, she will repay something valuable to them so that she can receive the benefits continuously. This way the relationships of reciprocity become stronger.

However, the reciprocal relationship goes beyond the individual level. Although the norm of reciprocity is commonly found between individuals, it is also developed between individuals and organizations (Shore, Sy, and Strauss, 2006; Rousseau, 1989). Therefore, when someone perceives that he is receiving benefits from the organization, he finds a way to repay the organization by providing something valuable to the organization. Many times, this would be something that enhances the organization's performance. In this sense, social exchange theory well explains the relationships between sources of support and the outcome variables. This section focuses on previous studies that have investigated the consequences of three different sources of support in the workplace.

Coworker support

As outcomes of coworker support, organizational commitment (e.g., Chiaburu and Harrison, 2008; Ko et al., 1997; Lee and Gao, 2005; Simons and Jankowski, 2008), work effort (e.g., Chiaburu and Harrison, 2008), turnover intention (e.g., Chiaburu and Harrison, 2008) and job satisfaction (e.g., Simons and Jankowski, 2008) have been discussed frequently in the literature.

To begin, regarding coworker support, Chiaburu and Harrison (2002) conducted a meta-analysis on how employees' perception about coworker support and coworker antagonism were linked to employees' outcomes, such as role perceptions, work attitudes, withdrawal, and effectiveness. The researchers used 161 independent samples, which included 77,954 employees in various business organizations. The results showed that employees' perception of coworker support was significantly related to organizational commitment ($r = .34$), effort reduction ($r = -.23$), and intention to quit ($r = -.27$). In addition, employees' perception about coworker antagonism was closely associated with organizational commitment ($r = -.25$) and intention to quit ($r = .26$). Regarding job satisfaction, McCalister, Dolbier, Webster, Mallon, and Steinhardt's (2006) study that included 310 high-tech employees and 745 government employees indicated that those with high levels of perceived coworker support had high levels of job satisfaction.

Although there is much evidence that coworker support is related to organizational behav-iors, coworker support has been mostly linked with physical and psychological well-being. In fact, many researchers have supported the idea that perceived coworker support elicits the benefits for physical health (e.g., Dean and Ensel, 1982; Holahan and Moos, 1981; Rosenfeld and Richman, 1997), mental health (e.g., Luszczynska and Cieslak, 2005), stress (e.g., Fletcher and Hanton, 2003; McCalister et al., 2006; Woodman and Hardy, 2001), and burnout (e.g., Beehr, Jex, Stacy, and Murray, 2000). For example, Luszczynska and Cieslak (2005) found that coworker support was significantly associated with employees' stress reduction and well-being. Similarly, Beehr et al. (2000) discovered that coworker support was significantly related to psychological strains, but weakly related to job performance among door-to-door book dealers.

In a sport context, Rosenfeld and Richman (1997) investigated whether student athletes' sources of social support were related to their physical and emotional well-being. The sources of support included in the study were support from coaches and teammates. It was revealed that both sources of support were significant predictors of the athletes' physical and emotional well-being. Rosenfeld and Richman also claimed that one's perception about support results in team-building intervention. According to the researchers, individual benefits, such as mental health and reduced stress, can have a positive impact on the quality of relationships among athletes, therefore increasing their ability to work together. In other words, through support, members (i.e., athletes) learn about each other and come to the realization of how to work with each other.

However, Rook (1992) points out that there are certain situations where perception of support would not provide any benefits at either individual nor team level. These include (a) when a member does not need support; (b) when the support provided to a member is too much or too little; or (c) when the support gives a false sense of self-efficacy.

Supervisor support

Similar to coworker support, supervisor support is discussed much as a predictor of various work-related outcomes. In fact, Pastore, Goldfine, and Riemer (1996: 374) stated, "by being supportive, athletic administrators may encourage coaches to stay." This statement points to the link between supervisor support and employees' intention to stay. Yet, there are many other behavioral outcomes that result from supervisor support. The outcomes frequently discussed regarding supervisor support include organizational commitment (e.g., Kidd and Smewing, 2001; Ko et al., 1997; Lee and Gao, 2005; Shore, Sy, and Strauss, 2006; Simons and Jankowski, 2008), job satisfaction (e.g., Simons and Jankowski, 2008), organizational citizenship behavior (e.g., Shore et al., 2006), turnover intention (e.g., Shore et al., 2006), and job performance (e.g., Shore et al., 2006).

In business settings, Kidd and Smewing (2001) investigated whether supervisor support was a predictor of employees' commitment to the organization. The data were collected from employees in various organizations. The measure for supervisor support was developed specifically for the study and it included support about career promotion, interpersonal skills and commitment, feedback and goal setting, and trust and respect. It was found that only trust and respect and feedback and goal setting were significant predictors of organizational commitment. Considering overall supervisor support, the results were different based on gender. For females, as perceived supervisor support increased their commitment to the organization increased as well. However, for male participants, there was a certain point in the middle where organizational commitment decreased as perceived support increased. A possible explanation for this finding would be that employees have perceived a moderate level of support as "routinized"; therefore, they consider it to be not sincere.

Shore et al. (2006) examined the influence of perceived supervisor support on work attitudes and behaviors of organizational commitment, job satisfaction, organizational citizenship behavior, turnover intention, and job performance among managers and subordinates. They additionally examined the moderating role of employees' equity sensitivity in the relationships. It was discovered that leader responsiveness to employee request explained 25 percent of the variance in affective commitment. Also, it explained a significant amount of variance in job satisfaction (15 percent), organizational citizenship behavior (9 percent), turnover intention (8 percent), and job performance (9 percent). Employees' equity sensitivity only moderated the relationship between perceived supervisor support and job satisfaction.

Ko et al. (1997) conducted two studies to examine the influence of perceived support on organizational commitment among Korean research institute and airline company employees. In this study, the researchers included three forms of organizational commitment suggested by Meyer and Allen (1991) as outcomes of coworker and supervisor support. These included affective commitment, continuance commitment, and normative commitment. The results of the study were slightly different for sample 1 and sample 2. For sample 1, which was composed of 278 employees of a research institute, supervisor support and coworker support were significantly and positively related to affective commitment, while only supervisor support was significantly correlated with continuance commitment and normative commitment. For sample 2, which was composed of 589 employees of the head office of an airline company, supervisor support was highly associated with affective commitment and normative commitment, whereas coworker support was significantly correlated with continuance commitment.

Simons and Jankowski (2008) developed a model of quitting intention. Modifying Price's (2000) model, these researchers proposed that positive affect, negative affect, job involvement, stress, autonomy, distributive justice, promotional chances, routinization, coworker support, and supervisor support were the antecedents of job satisfaction. In addition, job satisfaction influences organizational commitment, which in turn has an impact on job-searching behavior and quitting intent. The model was well supported, and showed that coworker support and supervisor support had a significant impact on job-searching behavior and quitting intention through job satisfaction and organizational commitment.

Job performance has also been supported as an important outcome of supervisor support. In a study of health center employees in Thailand, Bhanthumnavin (2003) compared the employees' perception of supervisor support with their objective job performance ratings that came from their supervisors. The study results confirmed that emotional, information, and material support that comes from supervisors leads to higher supervisor ratings of job performance. This finding seems to indicate that when the employees perceived they were receiving support from the supervisors, they perfomed better in their jobs.

Studies have also supported that supervisor support is closely associated with the employees' psychological well-being. For example, McCalister et al.'s (2006) research showed that supervisor support was negatively related to stress. In addition, Fletcher and Hanton (2003), Woodman and Hardy (2001), and Rosenfeld and Richman (1997) confirmed supervisor support as a factor that decreased stress and frustration and increased psychological and emotional well-being among athletes.

Although the majority of studies that examine the consequences of supervisor support have been conducted in business settings, a few studies have been performed in the sport organization context. For example, Sagas and Cunningham (2004) hypothesized that supervisor support would increase intent to seek an athletic director position among senior women administrators in Division I and II universities in the USA. The researchers also speculated that perceived supervisor support would be significantly associated with decreased occupational turnover intent. The results revealed that supervisor support was significantly and negatively related to senior women administrators' occupational turnover intent. However, supervisor support was not significantly associated with their intent to seek an athletic director position.

Organizational support

Organizational support has been investigated in conjunction with organizational commitment (e.g., Eisenberger, Armeli, Rexwinkel, Lynch, and Rhoades, 2001; Harris, 1995; Settoon, Bennett, and Liden, 1996; Shore and Tetrick, 1991), job satisfaction (e.g., Pack et al., 2007; Shore and Tetrick, 1991), in-role behavior (e.g., Eisenberger et al., 2001; Settoon et al., 1996), turnover intention (e.g., Eisenberger et al., 2001; Harris, Harris, and Harvey, 2007), extra role performance (e.g., Chen, Eisenberger, Johnson, Sucharski, and Aselage, 2009), organizational citizenship behavior (e.g., Masterson, Lewis, Goldman, and Taylor, 2000; Moorman, Niehoff, and Organ, 1993; Shore and Wayne, 1993), and performance (e.g., Tasi and Lau, 2004). The notion is that when employees perceive that the organization cares about their welfare and provides support, they are likely to return favors to the organization by exhibiting positive feelings, job attitudes, and behavioral intentions (Harris et al., 2007).

Many studies regarding the consequences of different sources of support have been conducted in business settings. For example, regarding organizational support, Eisenberger et al. (2001) examined the reciprocity nature of employees' perceived organizational support and affective commitment and job performance among postal employees. They proposed that perceived organizational support will increase positive mood and felt obligation, and these will have significant impact on affective commitment, organizational spontaneity, in-role performance, and withdrawal behavior. The results showed that the hypotheses were confirmed. In particular, perceived organizational support explained 16 percent of the variance in affective commitment, and the relationship between perceived organizational support and affective commitment was partially mediated by felt obligation and positive mood.

Settoon, Bennett, and Liden (1996) proposed that perceived organizational support would be a predictor for organizational commitment and in-role behavior while the quality of leader–member exchange would be a predictor for in-role behavior and citizenship behavior. As an alternative model, the researchers hypothesized that perceived organizational support would influence citizenship behavior and the quality of leader–member exchange would influence organizational commitment. The researchers tested these hypotheses with non-supervisory hospital employees. All the hypotheses were confirmed except the influence of perceived organizational support on in-role behavior. It was revealed that perceived organizational support explained 49 percent of the variance in organizational commitment, which was measured by an organizational commitment questionnaire. They also found that the quality of leader–member exchange predicted organizational commitment, but the researchers noticed that when they are examined at the same time, perceived organizational support dominates leader–member exchange in explaining variance in organizational commitment.

Choi (2006) investigated group-level predictors and individual-level predictors that had an impact on Korean employees' interpersonal helping behavior. The participants were recruited from a large electronics company in Korea. At the group level, trust among members was included as a factor influencing interpersonal helping behavior. On the other hand, at the individual level, perceived organizational support and perceived fairness were used as the predictors influencing interpersonal helping behavior. Yet, it was assumed that the links between perceived organizational support and perceived fairness and interpersonal helping behavior would be mediated by affective commitment to the organization. The results showed that perceived organizational support and perceived fairness significantly predicted interpersonal helping behavior. In addition, it was found that affective commitment partially mediated the relationship between perceived organizational support and interpersonal helping behavior while it fully mediated the relationship between perceived fairness and interpersonal helping behavior. This study supports the positive relationship between perceived organizational support and affective commitment.

In sport settings, Pack et al. (2007) examined the effects of perceived organizational support on affective commitment, normative commitment, and job satisfaction. The subjects of the study were student employees who worked at a large university recreation center. It was found that employees' perceived organizational support explained 46.2 percent of the variance in affective commitment while it explained 39 percent of the variance in normative commitment. Further, perceived organizational support explained 53.3 percent of the variance in student employees' job satisfaction. The results showed that there was no group difference based on gender, tenure, and type of supervision.

Dixon and Sagas (2007) found that organizational support has a positive direct impact on job satisfaction among female college head coaches. In this study, the strength of the relationship between organizational support and job satisfaction ($r = .63$) was similar to those reported in meta-analysis results ($r = .59$; Rhoades and Eisenberber, 2002) and in other coaching investigations ($r = .60$; Kim and Cunningham, 2005). Taken together, these results add up to show the importance of organizational support also in athletic contexts.

Organizational support also has been suggested as a predictor of athletic performance. For example, Tasi and Lau (2004) investigated the factors related to the success of the Hong Kong wheelchair fencing team in the 2000 Sydney Paralympics. The results indicated that the athletes' perceived positive outcomes, organizational support, and family support were the biggest contributors to the performance of the athletes.

In addition to the attitudes and behavioral outcomes discussed as consequences of organizational support, researchers have also found that organizational support has psychological benefits. For instance, Fletcher and Hanton (2003) and Woodman and Hardy (2001), in their qualitative studies, found that support given to elite athletes from the organization was significantly related to reduced levels of frustration and stress.

Practical implications of studying support

As previous studies have shown, employees' perception of support is both a desirable outcome and a valuable antecedent in organizational models. Assuming perceptions of support as a desirable outcome, the more managers know about its antecedents, the better they can promote it. For example, organizational justice has been largely accepted as an important antecedent of perceived organizational support (Fasolo, 1995; Moorman et al., 1998; Pack, 2005; Wayne et al., 2002). Considering justice as a discretionary action taken by the organization or its agents (supervisors or coworkers), it plays an axiomatic role in the degree of support employees perceived from their organization, supervisors and coworkers (Moorman et al., 1998; Wayne et al., 2002). Thus, a fitness center administrator who desires to improve her instructors' perceptions of support could start displaying justice in her policies.

Supervisor support has also been accepted as an important antecedent of organizational support. Eisenberger et al. (2002) observed that supervisor support was positively related to temporal change in organizational support, suggesting that the former leads to the latter. Additionally, they noted that this relationship rose with supervisor status, suggesting that the higher the perceived standing of a supervisor within the organization, the more likely it would be that an employee perceived his or her supervisor as the organization representative. In this sense, athletic coaches' perceptions of organizational support are directly related to their perceptions of support from the athletic director.

Considering support as a valuable antecedent of other organizational outcomes, previous studies have shown that support could predict job satisfaction, affective commitment, intention to leave, and work effort (Kim and Cunningham, 2005; Pack, 2005; Woo, 2009). Kim and Cunningham (2005) emphasized the importance of perceived organizational support in contributing to the job satisfaction of head coaches. From a practical point of view, the authors proposed that athletic directors should provide feedback to their coaches, in order to show that the organization considers the head coaches' well-being, and to demonstrate that the organization supports their contributions. Coaches who feel the support of their organizations tend to be more satisfied with their jobs.

In a similar vein, Pack (2005) and Dixon and Sagas (2007) found positive relationships between organizational support and job satisfaction. Pack (2005) added that organizational support is also a good predictor of affective commitment. Finally, Woo and Chelladurai (in review) showed that different sources of support (coworker, supervisor, and organization) were significant predictors of intention to leave and work effort.

Taken together, these results have serious practical implications. Job satisfaction, affective commitment, intention to leave, and work effort are all very important organizational outcomes for sport organizations (Kim and Cunningham, 2005; Pack, 2005; Turner and Chelladurai, 2005). Therefore, managers of recreational sport centers who need to increase the job satisfaction or affective commitment of their instructors should give personal support and establish environments where coworkers' support could be felt. Managers of large sports events could retain a great number of volunteers if they understand that supported workers tend to show less intention to quit (Strigas and Jackson, 2003). Fitness center employees tend to put forward a greater work effort when they feel support from coworkers, supervisors, and the organization (Woo and Chelladurai, in review). To sum up, in different sport contexts, perceptions of support have shown a great potential to promote diverse organizational outcomes.

Future studies

Although many studies have been performed in the area of coworker support, supervisor support, and organizational support, there are many needs for further studies in this topic. First of all, as discussed in this chapter, many studies have been conducted in relation to three different sources of support. However, not many studies have been conducted in the context of sport organizations. In fact, many studies have been conducted in business settings. The outcomes of these studies may be replicated in sport settings because many sport organizations are also considered as businesses (Jones, 2002). Yet, the sport management area is in dire need of empirical studies to test relationships between support and other organizational variables.

Secondly, future studies should compare the applicability of the relationships between antecedents and support and the relationships between support and outcome variables among different occupations, such as fitness employees, coaches, and administrators. Though no direct evidence exists, indirect evidence indicates that the relationships between constructs could be different based on occupation. For example, previous studies have shown that the relationships between antecedents and organizational commitment and the relationships between organizational commitment and consequences of it differ based on occupations (e.g., Chelte and Tausky, 1986; Cole and Bruch, 2006).

Thirdly, the relationships among coworker support, supervisor support, and organizational support should be investigated. As discussed earlier, previous studies indicated that supervisor support and organizational support are highly correlated (e.g., Eisenberger et al., 2002; Woo and Chelladurai, in review). In addition, coworker support was also found to be related to supervisor support (e.g., Yoon and Thye, 2000; Woo and Chelladurai, in review).

Fourthly, the relationships between support and its antecedent and consequence variables should be examined in a cross-cultural context. According to Hofstede (2001), culture shapes an individual's beliefs, attitudes, and behaviors in a certain way through collective learning. Therefore, it is possible that the relationships between the variables may be moderated based on the cultural values held by an individual. The moderating effect of culture should be investigated both at national and individual levels. In fact, studies have found that both national culture (e.g., Yao and Wang, 2006) and individual culture (e.g., Ramamoorthy, Kulkarni, Gupta, and Flood, 2007) have a significant impact on work attitudes and behaviors of an individual.

Lastly, more research is needed on the antecedents of perceived support in sport organizations. Although many studies have been performed about the consequences of support in a sport organization context, there have been few studies on the antecedents of support in sport settings. In particular, regarding the antecedents of coworker support, to the authors' knowledge, no studies have been conducted in sport organizational settings. Since coworker support is also a crucial source of support that has an impact on employees' organizational behaviors, studies that identify the factors influencing coworker support are much needed.

References

Anderson, S. E., Coffey, B. S., and Byerly, R. T. (2002) 'Formal organizational initiatives and informal workplace practices: Links to work-family conflict and job-related outcomes', *Journal of Management*, 28, 787–810.

Beehr, T. A., Jex, S. M., Stacy, B. A., and Murray, M. A. (2000) 'Work stressors and coworker support as predictors of individual strain and job performance', *Journal of Organizational Behavior*, 21, 391–405.

Bhanthumnavin, D. (2003) 'Supervisor and group members' psychological and situational characteristics as predictors of subordinate performance in Thai work units', *Human Resource Development Quarterly*, 14, 79–97.

Blau, P. M. (1967) *Exchange and power in social life*, New York, Wiley.

Bowling, N. A., Beehr, T. A., Johnson, A. L., Semmer, N. K., Hendricks, E. A., and Webster, H. A. (2004) 'Explaining potential antecedents of workplace social support: Reciprocity or attractiveness?', *Journal of Occupational Health Psychology*, 9, 339–50.

Chelte, A. F., and Tausky, C. (1986) 'A note on organizational commitment: Antecedents and consequences among managers, professionals, and blue-collar workers', *Work and Occupations*, 13, 553–61.

Chen, Z., Eisenberger, R., Johnson, K. M., Sucharski, I. L., and Aselage, J. (2009) 'Perceived organizational support and extra-role performance: Which leads to which?' *The Journal of Social Psychology*, 119(1), 119–24.

Chiaburu, D. A., and Harrison, D. A. (2008), 'Do peers make the place? Conceptual synthesis and meta-analysis of coworker effects on perceptions, attitudes, OCBs, and performance', *Journal of Applied Psychology*, 93, 1082–1103.

Choi, J. N. (2006) 'Multilevel and cross-level effects of workplace attitudes and group member relations on interpersonal helping behavior', *Human Performance*, 19, 383–402.

Cole, M. S., and Bruch, H. (2006) 'Organizational identity strength, identification, and commitment and their relationships to turnover intention: does organizational hierarchy matter?', *Journal of Organizational Behavior*, 27, 585–605.

Dean, A., and Ensel, W.M. (1982) 'Modelling social support, life events, competence, and depression in the context of age and sex', *Journal of Community Psychology*, 10, 392–408.

Dixon, M. A., and Sagas, M. (2007) 'The relationship between organizational support, work–family conflict, and the job-life satisfaction of university coaches', *Research Quarterly for Exercise and Sport*, 78, 236–47.

Dornbusch, S. M., and Scott, W. R. (1975) *Evaluation and the exercise of authority*, San Francisco, Jossey-Bass.

Ducharme, L. J., and Martin, J. K. (2000) 'Unrewarding work, coworker support, and job satisfaction: A test of the buffering hypothesis', *Work and Occupations*, 27, 223–43.

Eisenberger, S., Armeli, S., Rexwinkel, B., Lynch, P. D., and Rhoades, L. (2001) 'Reciprocicaton of perceived organizational support', *Journal of Applied Psychology*, 86, 42–51.

Eisenberger, R., Cummings, J., Armeli, S., and Lynch, P. (1997) 'Perceived organizational support, discretionary treatment, and job satisfaction', *Journal of Applied Psychology*, 82, 812–20.

Eisenberger, R., Huntington, R., Hutchison, S., and Sowa, D. (1986) 'Perceived organizational support', *Journal of Applied Psychology*, 71, 500–07.

Eisenberger, S., Stinglhamber, F., Vandenberghe, C., Sucharski, I. L., and Rhoades, L. (2002) 'Perceived supervisor support: Contributions to perceived organizational support and employee retention', *Journal of Applied Psychology*, 87, 565–73.

Ellis, B. H., and Miller, K. I. (1994) 'Supportive communication among nurses: Effects on commitment, burnout and retention', *Health Communication*, 6, 77–96.

Fasolo, P. (1995) 'Procedural justice and perceived organizational support: Hypothesized effects on job performance', in R. S. Cropanzano and K. M. Kacmar (eds.) *Organizational politics, justice, and support: Managing the social climate of the workplace*, Westport, CT, Quorum, pp. 185–95.

Fletcher, D., and Hanton, S. (2003) 'Sources of organizational stress in elite sport performers', *The Sport Psychologist*, 17, 175–95.

Gouldner, A. W. (1960) 'The norm of reciprocity', *American Sociological Review*, 25, 165–67.

Graen, G. B., and Uhl-Bien, M. (1995) 'Relationship-based approach to leadership: Development of leader–member exchange (LMX) theory of leadership over 25 years. Applying a multi-level multi-domain perspective', *Leadership Quarterly*, 6, 219–47.

Harris, K. A. (1995) 'Variables related to supervisory confrontation and referral of employees to Employee Assistance Programs', unpublished doctoral dissertation, Wayne State University.

Harris, R.B., Harris, K.J., and Harvey, P. (2007) 'A test of competing models of the relationships among perceptions of organizational politics, perceived organizational support, and individual outcomes', *The Journal of Social Psychology*, 147, 631–56.

Hofmann, D. A., and Morgeson, F. P. (1999) 'Safety-related behavior as a social exchange: The role of perceived organizational support and leader–member exchange', *Journal of Applied Psychology*, 84, 286–96.

Hofstede, G. (2001) *Culture's consequences: Comparing values, behaviors, institutions, and organizations across nations*, Thousand Oaks, CA, Sage Publications.

Holahan, C. J., and Moos, R. H. (1981) 'Social support and psychological distress: A longitudinal analysis', *Journal of Abnormal Psychology*, 90, 365–70.

Johnson, J. V. (1991) 'Strategies for survival in the workplace, in: The psychosocial work environment, work organization, democratization and health', in B. Gardell, J. V. Johnson and G. Johansson (eds.) *Essay in Memory of New York*, New York, Baywood Publishing Company.

Jones, G. (2002) 'Performance excellence: a personal perspective on the link between sport and business', *Journal of Applied Sport Psychology*, 14, 268–81.

Karasek, R. A., and Theorell, T. (1990) *Healthy work: Stress, productivity and the reconstruction of working life*, New York, Basic Books.

Kidd, J. M., and Smewing, C. (2001) 'The role of the supervisor in career and organizational commitment', *European Journal of Work and Organizational Psychology*, 10, 25–40.

Kim, J., and Cunningham, G. B. (2005) 'Moderating effects of organizational support on the relationship between work experiences and job satisfaction among university coaches', *International Journal of Sport Psychology*, 36, 50–64.

Ko, J. W., Price, J. L., and Mueller, C. W. (1997) 'Assessment of Meyer and Allen's three-component model of organizational commitment in South Korea', *Journal of Psychology*, 82, 961–73.

Lee, K. S., and Gao, T. (2005) 'Studying organizational commitment with the OCQ in the Korean retail context: Its dimensionality and relationship with satisfaction and work outcomes', *International Review of Retail, Distribution and Consumer Research*, 15, 375–99.

Liden, R. C., and Maslyn, J. M. (1993) 'Scale development for a multidimensional measure of leader–member exchange'. Paper presented at the Annual Meeting of the Academy of Management, Atlanta, GA.

Luszczynska, A., and Cieslak, R. (2005) 'Protective, promotive, and buffering effects of perceived social support in managerial stress: The moderating role of personality', *Anxiety, Stress, and Coping*, 18, 227–44.

McCalister, K. T., Dolbier, C. L., Webster, J. A., Mallon, M. W., and Steinhardt, M. A. (2006) 'Hardiness and support at work as predictors of work stress and job satisfaction', *Stress Management*, 20, 183–91.

Masterson, S. S., Lewis, K., Goldman, B. M., and Taylor, M. S. (2000) 'Integrating justice and social exchange: The differing effects of fair procedures and treatment on work relationships', *Academy of Management Journal*, 43, 738–48.

Meyer, J. P., and Allen, N. J. (1991) 'A three-component conceptualization of organizational commitment', *Human Resource Management Review*, 1, 61–89.

Moorman, R. H., Blakely, G. L., and Niehoff, B. P. (1998) 'Does perceived organizational support mediate the relationship between procedural justice and organizational citizenship behavior?', *Academy of Management Journal*, 41, 351–57.

Moorman, R. H., Niehoff, B. P., and Organ, D. W. (1993) 'Treating employees fairly and organizational citizenship behavior: Sorting the effects of job satisfaction, organizational commitment, and procedural justice', *Employee Responsibilities and Rights Journal*, 6, 209–25.

Pack, S. (2005) 'Antecedents and consequences of perceived organizational support for NCAA athletic administrators', unpublished doctoral dissertation, Ohio State University.

Pack, S. M., Jordan, J. S., Turner, B. A., and Haines, D. (2007) 'Perceived organizational support and employee satisfaction and retention', *Recreational Sport Journals*, 31, 95–106.

Pastore, D. L., Goldfine, B., and Riemer, H. A. (1996) 'NCAA college coaches and athletic administrative support', *Journal of Sport Management*, 10, 373–87.

Poulin, J.E. (1995) 'Job satisfaction of social work supervisors and administrators', *Administratrion in Social Work*, 19, 35–49.

Price, J. L. (2000) 'Reflections on the determinants of voluntary turnover', *International Journal of Manpower*, 22, 600–24.

Rahim, A., Magner, N. R., and Shapiro, D. L. (2000) 'Do justice perceptions influence styles of handling conflict with supervisors?, What justice perceptions, precisely?', *The International Journal of Conflict Management*, 11, 9–31.

Ramamoorthy, N., Kulkarni, S. P., Gupta, A., and Flood, P. C. (2007) 'Individualism-collectivism orientation and employee attitudes: A comparison of employees from the high-technology sector in India and Ireland', *Journal of International Management*, 13, 187–203.

Rhoades, L., and Eisenberger, S. (2002) 'Perceived organizational support: A review of literature', *Journal of Applied Psychology*, 87, 698–714.

Rhoades, L., Eisenberger, S., and Armeli, S. (2001) 'Affective commitment to the organization: The contribution of perceived organizational support', *Journal of Applied Psychology*, 86, 825–36.

Rook, K. S. (1992) 'Detrimental aspects of social relationships: Taking stock of an emerging literature', in H. O. F. Veiel and U. Baumann (eds.) *The meaning and measurement of social support*, New York, Hemisphere Publishing, pp. 157–69.

Rosenfeld, L. B., and Richman, J. M. (1997) 'Developing effective social support: Team building and the social support process', *Journal of Applied Sport Psychology*, 9, 133–53.

Rousseau, D. M. (1989) 'Psychological and implied contracts in organizations', *Employee Responsibilities and Rights Journal*, 2, 121–39.

Sagas, M., and Cunningham, G. B. (2004) 'The impact of supervisor support on perceived career outcomes of the senior woman administrator', *International Journal of Sport Management*, 5, 229–42.

Scandura, T. A., and Graen, G. B. (1984) 'Moderating effects of initial leader-member exchange status on the effects of a leadership intervention', *Journal of Applied Psychology*, 69, 428–36.

Settoon, R. P., Bennett, N., and Liden, L. C. (1996) 'Social exchange in organizations: Perceived organizational support, leader-member exchange, and employee reciprocity', *Journal of Applied Psychology*, 81, 219–27.

Shanock, L. R., and Eisenberger, S. (2006) 'When supervisors feel supported: Relationships with subordinates' perceived supervisor support, perceived organizational support, and performance', *Journal of Applied Psychology*, 91, 689–95.

Sherony, K. M., and Green, S. G. (2002) 'Coworker exchange: Relationships between coworkers, leader-member exchange, and work attitudes', *Journal of Applied Psychology*, 87, 542–48.

Shore, L. M., and Tetrick, L. E. (1991) 'A construct validity study of the survey of perceived organizational support', *Journal of Applied Psychology*, 76, 637–43.

Shore, L. M., and Wayne, S. J. (1993) 'Commitment and employee behavior: Comparison of affective commitment and continuance commitment with perceived organizational support', *Journal of Applied Psychology*, 78, 774–80.

Shore, T., Sy, T., and Strauss, J. (2006) 'Leader responsiveness, equity sensitivity, and employee attitudes and behavior', *Journal of Business and Psychology*, 21, 227–41.

Simons, K. V., and Jankowski, T. B. (2008) 'Factors influencing nursing home social workers' intentions to quit employment', *Administration in Social Work*, 32, 5–21.

Smith, P. C., Kemdall, L. M., and Hulin, C. L. (1969) *The measurement of satisfaction in work and retirement: A strategy for the study of attitudes*, Chicago, Rand McNally.

Strigas, A. D., and Jackson Jr., N. (2003) 'Motivating volunteers to serve and succeed: Design and results of a pilot study that explores demographics and motivational factors in sport volunteerism', *International Sport Journal*, 7, 111–23.

Sundin, L., Bildt, C., Lisspers, J., Hochwalder, J., and Setterlind, S. (2006) 'Organizational factors, individual characteristics and social support: What determines the level of social support?', *Work*, 27, 45–55.

Susskind, A. M., Kacmar, M., and Borchgrevink, C. P. (2007) 'How organizational standards and coworker support improve restaurant service', *Cornell Hotel and Restaurant Administration Quarterly*, 48, 370–79.

Tasi, E., and Lau, S. (2004) 'Factors associated with achievements of the Hong Kong wheelchair fencing team', *Journal of Physical Education and Recreation*, 10, 27–30.

Turner, B. A., and Chelladurai, P. (2005) 'Organizational and occupational commitment, intention to leave, and perceived performance of intercollegiate coaches', *Journal of Sport Management*, 19, 193–211.

Wayne, S. J., Shore, L. M., and Liden, R. C. (1997) 'Perceived organizational support and leader-member exchange: A social exchange perspective', *Academy of Management Journal*, 40, 82–111.

Wayne, S. J., Shore, L. M., Bommer, W. H., and Tetrick, L. E. (2002) 'The role of fair treatment and rewards in perceptions of organizational support and leader-member exchange', *Journal of Applied Psychology*, 87, 590–98.

Wikaningrum, T. (2007) 'Coworker exchange, leader-member exchange, and work attitudes: A study of coworker dyads', *Gadjah Mada International Journal of Business*, 9, 187–215.

Woo, B. (2009) *Cultural Effects on Work Attitudes and Behaviors: The Case of American and Korean Fitness Employees*. Ohio State University. [Online] Retrieved 7 September 2011 from <http://rave.ohiolink.edu/etdc/view?acc_num=osu1241612067>.

Woo, B., and Chelladurai, P. (in review) 'Influence of support available at work on the attitudes of fitness club employees'. Manuscript submitted for publication.

Woodman, T., and Hardy, L. (2001) 'A case study of organizational stress in elite sport', *Journal of Applied Sport Psychology*, 13, 207–38.

Yao, X., and Wang, L. (2006) 'The predictability of normative organizational commitment for turnover in Chinese companies: A cultural perspective', *International Journal of Human Resource Management*, 17, 1058–75.

Yoon, J., and Lim, J. C. (1999) 'Organizational support in the workplace: The case of Korean hospital employees', *Human Relations*, 52, 923–45.

Yoon, J., and Thye, S. (2000) 'Supervisor support in the work place: Legitimacy and positive affectivity', *Journal of Social Psychology*, 140, 295–316.

14

PSYCHOLOGICAL CONTRACT IN THE CONTEXT OF SPORT ORGANIZATIONS

Gonzalo Bravo, David Shonk and Doyeon Won

Introduction

The central tenets in psychological contract theory posit that employees create expectations about what the organization owes to them and what they owe to their organization (Robinson, 1996). As a result, the psychological contract at work is understood as an exchange relationship about the belief of implicit agreements between employees and employers (Herriot and Pemberton, 1997; Kotter, 1973; Rousseau, 1990, 1995). It is this perceptual nature of the psychological contract that makes it different from a working or legal contract (Robinson, Kraatz and Rousseau, 1994). The psychological contract is essentially subjective, personal and idiosyncratic (Turnley and Feldman, 1999a), or, as noted by Rousseau (1989: 123), "[it lies] in the eye of the beholder."

In spite of the subjective nature of the psychological contract, its importance is seen in its capacity to serve as an analytical framework in human resource practices to observe and predict employees' behavior by focusing on the less explicit deals of the relationship between employees and their organizations (Guest, 2004). This premise holds particularly true in times of dramatic change and work instability. Economic downturns during the 1990s and the proliferation of global competition have been responsible for the significant changes occurring across industries and certainly the sport industry has not been immune to these changes. Downsizing, mergers, increased outsourcing of labor and part-time jobs have created new scenarios and have transformed the traditional form of employment relationships (Chartered Institute of Personnel Development, 2005; Cooper, 2002; Coyle-Shapiro and Kessler, 2000; Robinson, 1996; Sims, 1994). The need for efficiency, cost-cutting and leaner organizations, and a decline in trade union membership, have produced uncertainty and instability in the workplace, which, in turn, has had a severe effect on the dynamics of relationships at work with "the collapse of trust and [the] assumed changes in the psychological contract" (Sparrow and Cooper, 1998: 359). As a result, both organizational scholars and practitioners have re-evaluated traditional human resource practices in order to provide better answers as to how to reduce the level of tension that commonly exists between employees and employers, but most importantly to retain and motivate employees, and keep them committed to and productive for their organizations (Sims, 1994).

During the past 20 years, a vast amount of literature has been published on the psychological contract. These studies have examined the psychological contract from an array of disciplines, including, but not limited to, human resource management, occupational psychology, information technology, sociology and legal studies (Kalleberg, 2000; Koh, Ang and Straub, 2004; Roehling 2004; Rousseau, 1989, 1990, 1995, 2001; Turnley and Feldman, 1999a, 1999b). The literature on the psychological contract within the context of sport organizations is relatively new. Interest in the psychological contract has flourished more recently as a number of studies have been conducted since the early 2000s (e.g., Bravo and Won, 2009; Kelley-Patterson and George, 2002; Kim, Trail, Lim and Kim, 2009; Nichols and Ojala, 2009; Owen-Pugh, 2007; Taylor, Darcy, Hoye and Cuskelly, 2006; Won and Pack, 2010). The interest in the psychological contract research comes from the recognition that in highly competitive environments, or during times of turmoil, human resource capital is one of the most critical resources available to organizations in gaining competitive advantage (Barney and Wright, 1998).

Although the study of the psychological contract within sport is still in its infancy, the issue should receive an increasing amount of interest as a line of research inquiry in the years to come. Over the past twenty years, many sport-related organizations have experienced great changes as the result of macroeconomic turmoil and globalization trends that have seriously impacted the industry (Maguire, Jarvie, Mansfield and Bradley, 2002; Smith, 2008). For example, changes in ownership in European Football (Kelly, 2008; Kelly and Harris, in press; Malcolm, 2000); player–agent relationships in the NHL (Mason and Slack, 2001), inclusion of liquidated–damages clauses in American college coaching contracts (Greenberg, 2006; Greenberg and Smith, 2007; Wasserman, 2008), and the growth of media moguls and their influence on the structure of professional sporting leagues (McGaughey and Liesch, 2002) represent industry changes that have significantly affected sport organizations' structures and operations and the functioning of their working relationships.

While the study of the psychological contract continues to expand and attract the attention of specialists from various disciplines, the theory in itself does not constitute a panacea to fully explain an employee's behavior at work. Other theoretical frameworks, such as employee engagement (Kahn, 1990), organizational citizenship behavior (Organ, 1988), organizational commitment (Meyer and Allen, 1991), and perceived organizational support (Eisenberger and Huntington, 1986) also remain critical to explaining how people behave at work. Regardless, psychological contract theory emerges as an important concept to explain less overt and explicit exchange relationships that occur at work. In this regard, Coyle-Shapiro and Kessler (2000: 908) noted:

> Clearly, the state of the psychological contract in terms of fulfillment or breach is of interest to the extent that the theoretical prediction holds true; organizational desired outcomes will result from contract fulfillment by the employer whereas contract breach by the employer is likely to lead to negative responses.

The purposes of this chapter are twofold: (a) to provide an overview of what we know about psychological contract theory; and (b) to examine psychological contract within the context of sport organizations. Our goal is not only to illustrate the current research, but also to stimulate discussion on the topic, thus advancing both theoretical and empirical research and enhancing our knowledge of working relationships within the context of sport organizations. This chapter is organized in four sections. First, it provides a theoretical background of the psychological contract construct as examined by management and organizational scholars.

Next we review the current research on psychological contract as applied to sport organizations. The third section focuses on methodological issues employed in the extant literature. The chapter ends with a discussion of future research, managerial challenges and, finally, perspectives of the psychological contract as an analytical framework to managers and scholars interested in examining working relationships within the sport industry.

Psychological contract in the management literature

Most authors acknowledge Blau's (1964) social exchange theory as the core pillar of psychological contract theory. Social exchange theory posits that a contractual formal relationship is essentially steered by an economic interest but also influenced by the nature of its social exchange (Aggarwal, Datta and Bhargava, 2007). Other theories have also contributed to explain the foundations of this concept, among these Barnard's equilibrium model (1938), March and Simon's (1958) inducement-contribution model, and Gouldner's (1960) norm of reciprocity (Roehling, 1997).

The development of psychological contract theory can be divided into two main periods: from 1958 to 1989, and from 1990 until today. Most of the theoretical and empirical progress has been made during the last twenty years (Conway and Briner, 2005). While the term psychological work contract was coined by Argyris in 1960, Makin, Cooper and Cox (1996) noted that the roots of the concept can be traced back all the way to the seventeenth and eighteenth century days of the social contract and the writings of Thomas Hobbes, John Locke and Jean-Jacques Rousseau.

During the early period of the psychological contract theory, implicit agreements in the context of working relationships were recognized in the work of Menninger (1958), who observed that patients and therapists needed to establish such agreements in order to succeed with treatment. Furthermore, Argyris (1960) recognized that employees and supervisors built mutual understanding relationships in their attempt to advance their objectives and goals. On the other hand, Levinson, Price, Munden and Solley (1962) noted that the root of the psychological contract lies in unconscious needs. The satisfaction of and attention to those needs becomes critical for the well-being of the parties involved in the exchange relationship. Schein (1965) extended this idea by stating that satisfaction and commitment can only be achieved when expectations of both sides are met. While these studies helped to advance the literature and revealed the complexity of the psychological contract theory, Denise Rousseau (1989), a scholar from Carnegie Mellon University, was responsible for reinvigorating scholarly inquiry on the psychological contract.

Conway and Briner (2005) identified four distinguishing prospects in Rousseau's work that made her ideas novel from previous research. First, Rousseau argues that a psychological contract is based on a belief about promises and obligations and not just about merely expectations. For Rousseau, promises and obligations presuppose a sense of urgency, a condition that does not apply for expectations. Second, Rousseau argues that the target of the psychological contract process must focus on the employee and not the organization. For Rousseau, the organization is where the psychological contract takes place. Third, Rousseau suggested that psychological contract occurs under two conditions: (a) employees' own perceptions about the belief of promises made to them, and (b) the organization's actions in regards to implicit or explicit agreements made to their employees. Thus, according to Rousseau, it is "an individual's perceptions of observable behavior that constitute psychological contracts" (Conway and Briner, 2005: 14). As a result, Rousseau concluded the psychological contract is not explained by the individual's motives or needs as was previously suggested by Levinson

et al. (1962). Finally, for Rousseau, the violation of the psychological contract is what critically influences and triggers an individual's behavior. For Rousseau, a violation of the psychological contract denotes a much more distressful emotion than merely the breach of a perceived
agreement. Thus, when perceived agreements are violated, various employee-related
outcomes, such as a decreased level of satisfaction or lower level of trust and commitment to
the organization, will arise as a behavioral response to this violation (e.g., Coyle-Shapiro and
Kessler, 2000; Robinson, 1996; Robinson and Rousseau, 1994; Tekleab, Takeuchi and
Taylor, 2005).

Transactional and relational psychological contracts

Drawing on MacNeil's (1974, 1985) typology of contracts, Rousseau (1990) noted that
psychological contracts can be organized under two main categories: transactional and relational. Transactional contracts focus on specific and short-term inducements involving
primarily economic and/or monetary exchanges. Relational contracts, on the other hand,
involve long-term, broader exchanges concerned with personal and socio-emotional matters
that are characterized by trust, good faith and fairness (Robinson, Kraatz and Rousseau,
1994; Rousseau, 1995; Rousseau and McLean Parks, 1993; Shore and Tetrick, 1994).

Arnold (1996) argues that, in spite of empirical evidence that supports the existence of
these two dimensions, the distinction between transactional and relational is not clear cut.
Conway and Briner (2005) noted that transactional inducements can also be seen as relational
depending upon the context of the exchange. A pay raise that is granted under a fairness
criterion, that takes into account the employee's welfare, will represent both a transactional
and a relational exchange. As a result, other dimensions have also been recognized like
Rousseau's (2000) balanced contract, Arnold's (1996) training obligations, and Bunderson's
(2001) administrative and professional aspects, dimensions that can be seen as variants of the
traditional transactional–relational distinction.

Breach, violation and fulfillment of the psychological contract

In the psychological contract literature, breach and violation are commonly used as inter-
changeable terms (Conway and Briner, 2005). However, Morrison and Robinson (1997)
made an important distinction between the two. A violation is seen as a more intense reaction
that results when a promise has been broken or an obligation has not been met. In contrast, a
breach is seen as a less distressful emotion and more as a "cognitive assessment of contract
fulfillment that is based on an employee's perception" (Morrison and Robinson, 1997: 230).

The majority of the empirical studies that have examined the outcomes of psychological
contract on employment relationships have been conducted from the employee's perspective
(Guest, 2004; Tekleab and Taylor, 2003). Fewer studies have been conducted from the
employer's perspective (Tsui, Pearce, Porter and Tripoli, 1997). Some studies reporting
outcomes resulting from a psychological contract breach or violation reveal decreased levels
of organizational trust (Deery, Iverson and Walsh, 2006; Robinson, 1996); lower levels of job
satisfaction (Kickul, Lester and Finkl, 2002; Sutton and Griffin, 2004; Tekleab et al., 2005);
lower organizational commitment (Restubog, Bordia and Tang, 2006); employees' lower
level of obligation to their jobs (Robinson, Kraatz and Rousseau,1994); and turnover intention (Robinson and Rousseau, 1994; Turnley and Feldman, 1999a, 1999b). Studies examining psychological contract fulfillment have found a positive influence on employee affective
commitment (Thompson and Heron, 2006); employee perceived organizational support

(Tekleab et al., 2005); employee organizational citizen behavior toward the organization (Turnley, Bolino, Lester and Bloodgood, 2003); and employee perceptions of adequate human resource practices (Guest and Conway, 2002). According to Conway and Briner, breach and violation of the psychological contract lead to unwanted or negative outcomes because these involve "unmet expectations, a breakdown of trust, a loss of inducements, feelings of inequality and an impediment to goal progression" (2005: 71).

Psychological contract processes and model

Psychological contract has been defined as "reciprocal exchange" (Rousseau, 1989: 23), "reciprocal expectation" (McLean Parks, Kidder and Gallagher, 1998: 698), and "reciprocal obligations" (Morrison and Robinson, 1997: 229). These words suggest that a psychological contract occurs within a dyadic relationship. Most empirical research on psychological contract has focused on the employee in terms of fulfillment and/or breach of their contract, in contrast to approaching the subject from the organization's perspective (Cullinane and Dundon, 2006; Guest 2004). Thus, Conway and Briner (2005) call for re-examining the psychological contract from a unilateral and single cross-sectional perspective to a more expanded process approach. In this regard, the primary question then focuses on unfolding not only the type of outcomes, but also the multiplicity of events that lead to such outcomes. As noted by Conway and Briner, "a process approach is also more likely to capture a fuller representation of the experience of being party to a psychological contract" (2005: 132).

The dynamics in which psychological contracts are formed requires researchers and practitioners to focus attention on the many events that shape these relationships. One event that significantly influences the direction and outcomes of the psychological contract is *the state* of how these relationships are negotiated and the level of trust and perception of fairness of these deals (Guest, 2004). Rousseau (2001) identified employment deals as *standard, position-based* and *idiosyncratic*. Standard deals are explicit agreements that do not make distinctions among employees sharing similar responsibilities. Contrarily, position-based and idiosyncratic deals make distinctions and special concessions based on an employee ranking or status (e.g. certain advanced managerial positions or high-profile head coaches in the context of college athletics in America), and are also based on an individual's special employment features, such as having a unique set of skills that gives these employees an advantage over other workers in similar roles (Rousseau, 2001: 261). Rousseau noted that idiosyncratic deals can significantly affect perceptions of psychological contracts of employees working on similar responsibilities. Furthermore, idiosyncratic deals are more challenging to employment relations as they center around the issue of trust and fairness with a direct impact on *the state* of the psychological contract (Guest, 2004).

A critical challenge in psychological contract theory has been integrating the many theoretical as well as empirical findings into a coherent model that reflects the complex dynamics in which the psychological contract takes place. In response to this challenge and following the above argument, Guest (2004) developed an analytical framework of the psychology of employment relationships that includes not only the *context*, the *content* and the *outcomes*, but also *the state of the psychological contract* (see Figure 14.1). In terms of *context*, Guest recognized the influence of the individual (e.g., age, gender, education, etc.) as well as organizational influences (e.g., type of industry, business strategy, human resource, key policies and practices, organizational culture, etc.). According to Guest, "the context helps not only to shape the content of the exchange that forms the psychological contract but also the responses to it"

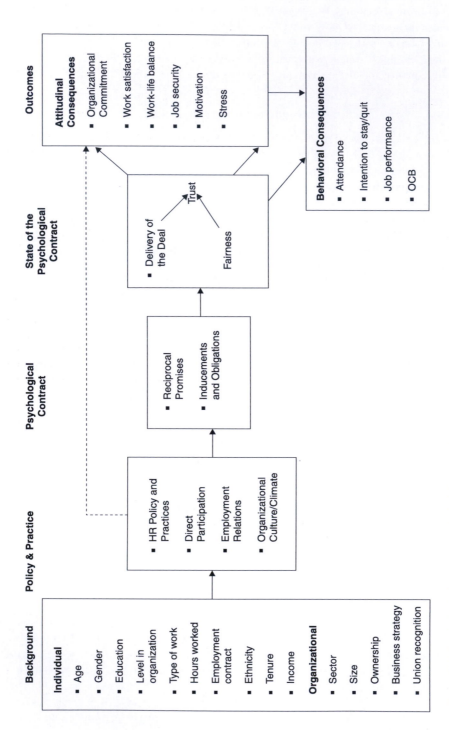

Figure 14.1 Psychological contract analytical framework

Reprinted by permission of *Applied Psychology: An International Review.* From "The psychology of employment relationship: An analysis based on the psychological contract," by D. Guest (2004), 53(4), 541–55. Copyright © 2004 John Wiley and Sons.

(2004: 549). The next pillar of the model is illustrated by (a) the *content*, and (b) the *state* of the psychological contract. The *content* refers to the inducements and promises that are exchanged. Typically these inducements are classified as transactional, relational, training, and administrative and/or professional type. On the other hand, the *state* of the psychological contract relates to what Rousseau calls *the deals*, which according to Guest are highly influenced by the notion of fairness and trust existing between the parties involved. The final pillar corresponds to the *outcomes*, which Guest divided into attitudinal (e.g., organizational commitment, job motivation, etc.) and behavioral consequences (e.g., intention to stay or quit, organizational citizenship behavior).

Both Guest (2004) and Conway and Briner (2005) provide us with important frames of reference that need to be considered in future studies on psychological contract research. Guest's model, built on a "system framework" (2004: 551), presents an organic way of looking at the psychological contract phenomenon. Conway and Briner remind us that psychological contracts are dynamic and outgoing processes that are in constant change and evolution. These two perspectives, we believe, will influence the way psychological contract research in sport will be conducted in the years to come.

Psychological contract in sport organizations

During the last 20 years, hundreds of articles have addressed the psychological contract. However, within the sport studies literature, our search has revealed only eight empirical articles on this issue. When considering these few articles related to sport, it should be noted that all but one of them have been written since 2002. The exception is an unpublished doctoral dissertation completed in 1994. In this respect, the study of the psychological contract is still in its infancy. The existing literature is reviewed below under four broad types of exchange relationships: sport administrators and volunteers; sport administrators and coaches; coaches and players; and managers and graduates.

Sport administrators and volunteers

As many sport organizations are dependent upon volunteer labor, the exchange between sport administrators and their volunteers is important in respect to meeting the needs of the organization and volunteers and their intention to continue in their voluntary role. Taylor et al. (2006) conducted focus groups with 98 community sport club administrators and interviews with volunteers associated with the Australian Rugby Union's (ARU) community sport club network. The focus groups asked administrators to discuss the methods used to manage the volunteers, whereas volunteers were asked to comment on expectations and perceptions of the organization's volunteer management practices.

The findings from the Taylor et al. (2006) study suggested that volunteers and sport club administrators attached differing emphasis to the transactional, assurance of good faith and intrinsic job components of the psychological contract. Club administrators placed greater emphasis on transactional obligations than volunteers. In this regard, local administrators felt that national and state rugby bodies provided little assistance to community sport clubs. In terms of good faith and fair dealing, the differing expectations related not so much to fair treatment, but rather to volunteer expectations of good faith. Volunteers expected to be consulted by management regarding their positions and task, but rarely did this happen. Volunteers and administrators also differed in terms of intrinsic job components. In this regard, volunteers struggled with an increased workload, not being able to leave their jobs without a replacement, and increasing administrative responsibilities.

Using a web-based survey instrument, Kim et al. (2009) collected data from a sample of 224 volunteers who worked for the 2007 State Summer Games of Special Olympics in the United States. Two conceptual frameworks (person–environment fit and empowerment) were employed in this study utilizing the theory of planned behavior, the theory of work adjustment and psychological contract theory. The researchers proposed and tested three models used to explain intention to continue volunteering. The results indicated that empowerment fully mediates the relationship between person–environment fit and intention to continue volunteering and that psychological contract fulfillment moderated the relationship between fit and empowerment. The researchers suggest that it is critical that volunteers perceive a fit with organizational attributes when the psychological contract is not fulfilled. When this does not occur, volunteers will not feel empowered and will be less likely to continue volunteering with that particular organization. They also point out that an organization should provide a detailed description of volunteer duties when the relationship between fit and empowerment for a volunteer is weak.

Using psychological contract theory, the purpose of the Nichols and Ojala (2009) study was to contrast the expectations of event managers and sport event volunteers in an effort to show implications for the management of volunteers and the application of the psychological contract framework. Nichols and Ojala used qualitative methods to interview event managers and conduct focus groups with volunteers in the United Kingdom. Interviews were conducted with six event managers who used volunteers for their events. The volunteer program was set up by the Newham Borough Council and had the purpose of recruiting and training volunteers for the 2012 London Olympic Games. A total of twelve volunteers were interviewed using focus groups, which reflected the collective experience of volunteering in events such as a charity bike ride, children's painting event, a set of walks to inform visitors about the Olympic site, health promotion walks, a triathlon, and a set of events promoted through Newham Council. Results from the study suggested that event managers are vitally concerned about the reliability of volunteers. Volunteers are important to event managers because they are enthusiastic, exhibit a strong and empathetic relationship with the public, and provide a less expensive labor force than paying full-time employees. In contrast, volunteers expect a certain level of flexibility, quality personal relationships, a level of recognition for their contributions, and clear communication regarding the expectations of what they are to do.

The Nichols and Ojala study suggests that when examining and contrasting the expectations between volunteers and managers, the application of qualitative methods is a more appropriate methodological approach and allows researchers to better explore the numerous nuances that exist in a socially constructed phenomenon like the psychological contract. Nichols and Ojala noted that while quantitative methods are quite common in psychological research, these are derived from studies conducted in traditional working relationships. Consequently, quantitative methodology will be of limited use when exploring the relationship between managers and volunteers, as these two groups typically show significant differences in their balance of obligation and power as compared to managers and paid staff.

Sport administrators and coaches

Using a synchronous Web-based survey, Bravo and Won (2009) collected data from 439 coaches employed in athletic departments competing in the National Collegiate Athletic Association (NCAA) in the United States. Athletic departments were stratified based on their

NCAA divisional affiliation: D–IA, D–IAA, D–IAAA, D–II and D–III. Similar to Kim et al. (2009), this study sought to examine psychological contract fulfillment or the breach of fulfillment; however, this time in relation to intercollegiate athletic coaches. Results of the study suggested that respondents perceiving an intentional breach in their psychological contract reported significantly lower job satisfaction, affective commitment and trust. In addition, these coaches also reported significantly higher levels of turnover intention in comparison to those who perceived an unintentional breach or whose contract was fulfilled.

Won and Pack (2010) used paper and pencil surveys which were mailed to high-school athletic directors and coaches with the purpose of understanding the relative impact of psychological contract violations on employees' outcomes. The results are based on 145 respondents from a midwestern state in the United States. The findings suggest that transactional, training and relational psychological contract items had been violated and the violations explained a substantial amount of variance in employee-related consequences such as organizational trust, affective commitment, job satisfaction and turnover intention. Trust was explained most by perceived contract violation, followed by affective commitment and job satisfaction. Another finding from this study suggested well-trained employees may be satisfied and committed to their job, but consider leaving for more lucrative opportunities due to a belief they are well trained for the next job.

Coaches and players

Owen–Pugh (2007) conducted a qualitative study which explored the psychological contracts between coaches and players in British commercial basketball. Using a retrospective case study methodology, players and coaches were asked to explore their professional interdependency and its influence on their career development. The study employed face-to-face semi-structured interviews with coaches and players in the British Basketball League (BBL) and England's National Basketball League (NBL). The findings from the Owen–Pugh study suggest that commercial changes in the game have led to newly emerging forms of psychological contract between coaches and players. The study highlighted the general frustrations felt by British players of being second-class citizens in relation to their North American counterparts and the derogatory comments on the part of coaches and American players about the skills of British players. The study found that American players take primary responsibility for winning games and thus receive more money, playing time, career development and respect from management; whereas the essential support functions performed by British players are not rewarded and these players receive less money, court time and career development than the American players.

Antunes de Campos (1994) examined the strength of the psychological contract as measured by the overall agreement to fulfill the level of expectation and fulfillment between soccer coaches and players. This study was unique since it did not use the traditional theoretical psychological contract distinction of transactional versus relational. It examined the matched contract, which refers to both parties in the exchange relationship knowing the expectation of each other, thus assuming that the need expectation is equal to expectation fulfillment. The sample included 104 female soccer players and four coaches, representing four Division I NCAA teams in the United States. Respondents answered a 25–question paper and pencil questionnaire. Coaches were asked to answer in regard to the players, and players in regard to their coaches. The questionnaire included items regarding expectations and fulfillment of those expectations. Results showed a statistically significant mean difference between teams regarding the strength of the psychological contract. Levels of expectation between coaches and players were found to be different. However, no differences were found between players and coaches in their level of fulfillment.

Managers and graduates

Kelley-Patterson and George (2002) examined the various elements that comprise the initial psychological contract of graduate employees within the hospitality, leisure and tourism industries in the United Kingdom. A small sample was drawn in this study comprising 21 recent graduates with a degree in hospitality, leisure and tourism and 15 managers employed in management or human resource roles who were responsible for graduate employee development. Respondents were asked to complete an eight-page questionnaire that measured background characteristics, organizational attitudes and psychological contract expectations. The findings from this study suggest that graduates view the initial contract in transactional terms, whereas manager expectations of the initial contract are viewed from both a relational and transactional perspective. Graduate employees were more concerned with short-term issues related to equity, job variety and human resource issues pertaining to pay and job conditions in contrast to longer term career development opportunities that managers may believe are more important.

Other studies which discuss psychological contract

Other non-empirical studies within the literature have touched on the psychological contract within the context of sport. For example, Taylor, Doherty and McGraw (2008) provide a brief review of the psychological contract in relation to their discussion of role management in human resources, which is the process of socializing or fine-tuning one's expectations. This socialization process suggests that "individuals are likely to enter the workplace with preconceived ideas about their new job, the organization, the sport, and the industry" (Taylor et al., 2008: 89).

Another study has used the psychological contract to explain the monopolistic tendencies of professional sport leagues. Drawing on the literatures from sport economics, resource-based view and psychological contract, McGaughey and Liesch (2002) examined how the emergence of Australia's Super League challenged the contractual and fiduciary relationship between teams, players and the New South Wales Rugby League (NSWRL). The authors suggest that officials from the NSWRL failed to understand the impact of the psychological contract, as they required their team members to sign a loyalty agreement to stay in the league. This loyalty agreement aimed to safeguard the existing league from competitors. While this might be perceived as legitimate in the minds of NSWRL officials, this might not hold true for players, who, according to McGaughey and Liesch, might have had a different expectation of their psychological contract and commitment to the existing league.

Kim and Chelladurai (2006) presented a conceptual framework which outlines the dynamics of the psychological contract in volunteering. The concept postulated within the study suggests volunteer perceptions of keeping the psychological contract are dependent upon individual difference variables of volunteer motivation, gender and education as well as various human resource practices. Their model suggests that the extent to which volunteers perceive that the organization is abiding by the psychological contract influences volunteer satisfaction and commitment, which leads to a volunteer's intention to continue volunteering.

Methodological issues in psychological contract studies

Psychological contract as a multi-dimensional construct

As mentioned earlier in this chapter, the most conventional way to view a psychological contract is composed of two broad dimensions – the transactional and relational psychological contract (Robinson and Rousseau, 1994). Alternatively, scholars have suggested additional psychological contract dimensions. Coyle-Shapiro and Kessler (2000) suggested that "training" is a distinct psychological contract component independent from transactional and relational components. De Vos and her colleagues (De Vos, Buyens and Schalk, 2003; De Vos, De Stobbeleir and Meganck, 2009; De Vos and Meganck, 2009) claimed that there are five types of employer inducements: career development, job content, social atmosphere, financial rewards, and work-related balance. Similarly, Lester, Turnley, Bloodgood and Bolino (2002) specified the six possible dimensions of psychological contract including benefits, pay, advancement opportunities, work itself, resource support, and employment relationship. On the other hand, some scholars have used a global or composite psychological contract measure when a distinction between psychological contract items is a least concern (e.g., Coyle-Shapiro and Kessler, 2002a; Lewis-McClear and Taylor, 1998; Turnley and Feldman, 1999b). As McLean Parks et al. (1998: 700) mentioned, it is a very challenging task to develop a universal psychological contract measure applicable to all types of employee–employer relationships. The authors cautiously suggest using a two-dimensional model that includes transactional and relational contracts as a starting point.

Among the empirical studies in sport management, Bravo and Won (2009) used a more traditional two-dimensional PC measure in the collegiate sport setting and Won and Pack (2010) utilized a three-dimensional PC measure in the interscholastic athletic setting. On the other hand, Kim et al. (2009) used a global PC measure for sport volunteers. Further sport management studies may develop more sophisticated PC measures that are more relationship or content specific.

Prior research indicates that perceived breach or fulfillment of the psychological contract is related to employee reactions including both work attitudes and behaviors (De Vos and Meganck, 2009; Hamel, 2009; Zhao et al., 2007). Specifically, breach of the psychological contract is negatively related to job satisfaction, organizational commitment, in-role performance and organizational citizenship behavior while it is positively related to turnover intention, job search behavior and actual turnover behavior (Coyle-Shapiro and Kessler, 2000; De Vos and Meganck, 2009; Lester et al., 2002; Zhao et al., 2007). Similarly, some scholars have explored the impact of psychological contract violations (PCV) on employees using an exit, voice, loyalty and neglect (EVLN) typology. In this regard, Hamel (2009) found that PCV in terms of barriers to career advancement influenced employee's EVLN behaviors.

Among the empirical sport management studies, both Bravo and Won (2009) and Won and Pack (2010) examined the impact of PCV on job satisfaction, affective commitment, organizational trust and turnover intention and found meaningful relationships. While those four dependent variables examined are very critical in understanding the exchange relationships between employees and employers, further sport management studies should also consider the impact of PCV on in-role and extra-role performance and actual turnover behaviors which might be more directly related to organizational effectiveness.

Contextual variables: moderators or control variables

Pate (2006) suggested that contextual factors influence the formation of the psychological contract at the macro (business and labor conditions), meso (workplace characteristics; HR systems) and micro level (individual characteristics). From a different perspective, these factors can be considered moderating variables on the relationship between psychological contract breach and outcome variables (Turnley and Feldman, 1999a).

Recent studies have examined the possible moderation or controlling effects of such variables as personality (Tallman and Bruning, 2008), demographic variables such as gender (Tallman and Bruning, 2008; Turnley et al., 2003) organizational tenure (Turnley et al., 2003), protean and boundaryless career orientations (Granrose and Baccili, 2006), professional identification (Hekman, Bigley, Steensma and Hereford, 2009), equity sensitivity (Kickul and Lester, 2001; Restubog, Bordia and Bordia, 2009), procedural justice (Restubog et al., 2009), employment status (Ainsworth and Purss, 2009; Coyle-Shapiro and Kessler, 2002b; Hekman et al., 2009; Liao-Troth, 2001), and labor market situation (Hekman et al., 2009).

In this age of globalization, psychological contracts can be largely influenced by the cultural profiles of individuals (e.g., collectivism vs. individualism) through motivational and cognitive processing in terms of (a) formation of psychological contract, (b) perception and attribution of PCV, and (c) behavioral responses to PCV (Thomas, Au and Ravlin, 2003: 457). The influence of cultural profiles should be considered not only for comparative studies but also for studies on expatriates.

In terms of the empirical sport management studies, there has been a lack of effort to investigate the impact of various contexts or contextual variables that might influence the formation of psychological contract or the consequences of PCV. If any, the previous two empirical studies (Bravo and Won, 2009; Won and Pack, 2010) used such demographic background variables as age, gender and organizational tenure as control variables that influence the perception of PC. Further sport management studies should investigate the role of various contextual factors (e.g., job status, type of work, cultural profile) in understanding PC in sport. In addition, as mentioned earlier, further research about the cultural consequences on psychological contract will be very promising.

Studying mutuality

One of the main issues in psychological contract studies is the bidirectional nature of the psychological contract (Tekleab and Taylor, 2003), also known as mutuality and reciprocity in the psychological contract (Dabos and Rousseau, 2004). That means that in order to fully understand the psychological contract one should realize that there are two parties in an employment relationship such as organization–employee or supervisor–subordinate (Lester et al., 2002; Tekleab and Taylor, 2003). However, as noted by Guest (2004) and Tekleab and Taylor (2003), previous studies have focused more on the employee's perspective and paid less attention to an organization's perspective or perceptual gaps between employer and employee with regard to psychological contract.

In studying psychological contract in working relationships, most studies have paid little attention to understanding the organization's perspective on the psychological contract. While Taylor et al. (2006), Owen-Pugh (2007), Kelley-Patterson and George (2002), and Nichols and Ojala (2009) explored the perceptual discrepancies in terms of psychological contracts between employer and employee in the context of sport organizations, those investigations were mostly qualitative studies with limited samples, and as a result no generalization can be drawn from these studies. Thus, while there is no doubt that qualitative methods contribute to providing a more detailed picture of the phenomenon being studied, large-scale, quantitative, cross-sectional and longitudinal studies would better contribute to the generalizability of the results. Notwithstanding, Nichols and Ojala (2009) suggest that quantitative methods are of limited use when examining and contrasting psychological contract between volunteers and managers, since the nature of their relationships is significantly different as compared to managers and paid employees. Consequently, when examining the psychological contract between volunteers and managers the use of a qualitative approach seems more appropriate.

Measuring psychological contract violation

There are several methods to research the psychological contract including questionnaire surveys, scenario methodologies, critical incident techniques, interviews, diary studies and case studies (Conway and Briner, 2005: 90). Of these six methods, questionnaire surveys have been most utilized in psychological contract studies. There are three approaches in measuring psychological contract breach, namely (a) a composite measure, (b) a global measure, and (c) a weighted measure (see Zhao et al., 2007: 655–56). A composite measure is different from a global measure in terms of whether it asks about specific contract items (a composite measure) or overall psychological contract perceptions (a global measure). A weighted measure is different from a composite measure since it asks also about the importance of each contract item (Zhao et al., 2007). While a composite approach can provide more detailed psychological contract-related information, this approach may not be appropriate for unconventional or complex employment settings (McLean Parks et al., 1998; Zhao et al., 2007).

Due to the dynamic nature of psychological contract, Conway and Briner (2005) suggest using both longitudinal and cross-sectional designs. With these research designs, another key issue when measuring the psychological contract is about when and how often we need to measure PCV (Conway and Briner, 2005). Thus, further studies should consider advantages and disadvantages associated with each research design.

In measuring PCV using questionnaire surveys in sport, as mentioned, Kim et al. (2009) used a global measure while two other empirical studies (Bravo and Won, 2009; Won and Pack, 2010) used a composite measure. None of the sport management studies have utilized a weighted measure approach and a longitudinal study design. Further studies in sport management should be more aware of different measurement strategies and also consider advantages and disadvantages associated with each of the measurement strategies.

Understanding job specifics

Across the countries, there have been more contingent employments in various sectors including sport-related industry (Ainsworth and Purss, 2009). Due to the nature of the contingent employment (voluntary vs. involuntary) and the various types of employment modes (part-time, seasonal, temporary, or fixed-term), contingent workers' psychological contracts can be different from those of traditional employment. In sport, various contingent employment arrangements exist. For example, many professional teams hire ticket sales personnel on a fixed-term basis and sport teams and clubs hire seasonal coaches. Thus, various employment conditions should be considered in studying the psychological contract in sport.

Due to sport globalizations through player trades and joint ventures, there are more people working in countries other than their own (i.e., expatriates). Thus, expatriates' psychological contract should be more carefully understood for their adjustment during and after international assignments (Haslberger and Brewster, 2009).

Managerial challenges and future directions in psychological contract research in sport organizations

What do we know and where do we go from here?

While a scarcity of research on psychological contract within sport currently exists, we believe the focus on the psychological contract within the literature will continue to expand. An unrealistic and almost cultish fascination with the sport industry continues to permeate American culture. King (2009) suggests that approximately 24,000 undergraduate and 6,000 graduate students are currently studying sport management in the United States. Thus, there is an increased competition for employment within the industry, which naturally leads to an enhanced emphasis on human resources and human resource practices. At the same time, current barriers to entry into the industry such as budgetary restrictions within many sport organizations and a continued saturation of the North American market present some serious challenges. With both the current demand and enhanced competition for employment, an increasingly interesting topic of inquiry will be how this socialization process between employers and employees will play out in the sport industry. As noted by Taylor et al., individuals enter the workplace with "preconceived ideas about their new job, the organization, the sport, and the industry" (2008: 89). However, the success of the exchange relationships between the many stakeholders in sport will be based on the development and implementation of successful human resource practices.

From a theoretical and conceptual perspective, the literature suggests that both transactional and relational viewpoints play significant roles within sport. In particular, we have learned that expectations between employees and managers differ, with new employees viewing the contract from more of a transactional perspective than hiring managers (Kelley-Patterson and George, 2002). In the Owen-Pugh (2007) study we also learned that psychological contracts between coaches and players can lead to conflict. We also learned that violation of the psychological contract can have significant consequences within sport. Research by Won and Pack (2010) suggests that such contract violations impact the trust between parties, including commitment, satisfaction and turnover intention. To avoid violations, it is important for hiring managers and new employees to develop mutual understandings as to the contract which are based on realistic expectations (Taylor et al., 2006). However, often what occurs is exemplified in the Kelley-Patterson and George (2002) and the Nichols and Ojala (2009) studies whereby parties view the psychological contract from differing points of view.

The existing research on the psychological contract in sport also highlights the importance of volunteers and volunteer management within the industry. In a similar manner to new employees, volunteers also place differing emphasis on the psychological contract in comparison to hiring managers. The Taylor et al. (2006) study suggests that volunteers and sport club administrators attach differing emphasis to the transactional assurance of good faith and intrinsic job components of the psychological contract. Moreover, Kim et al. (2009) highlighted the importance that volunteers perceive a fit with organizational attributes when the psychological contract is not fulfilled. Finally, Nichols and Ojala (2009) noted that while the primary expectation of event managers is about the reliability of volunteers, volunteers are primarily concerned with their level of flexibility, the quality of their personal interactions and the level of recognition for their contributions.

The literature on psychological contract in sport has implications for sport managers which are important to consider. Managers must be cognizant of any violations of the psychological contract because a violation can lead to lower amounts of trust, job satisfaction, loyalty and performance and can often lead to employee turnover. Managers also need to understand and balance the differing perceptions of employees in terms of transactional items such as compensation in comparison to hours worked, workplace safety and relational components like job security, training and socio-emotional concerns such as the culture of the workplace. While sport managers may acknowledge the importance of volunteers, a systematic plan for incorporating managers into the workplace is an important component of success. Strategic planning must incorporate volunteers as important human resources. National sport governing bodies should consider the need to provide better assistance to local sport organizations in terms of recruitment and retention of volunteers. At all levels, sport managers need to provide better training for volunteers and to more fully integrate volunteers into organizational decision-making, especially in relation to the tasks they are performing. Finally, volunteers must feel empowered and perceive that they fit within the organization in order to continue volunteering.

Research avenues on psychological contract in the context of sport organizations

We have learned that little has been done to develop the literature on psychological contract within sport. However, the handful of empirical studies which have been conducted have focused on exchanges related to administrators, coaches, players and graduates. While most of the studies have focused on higher-level administrators and either volunteers or coaches, future research may focus on mid-level staff. In addition, future studies may take into account the expectations of new entrants into the industry such as interns. While some studies have focused on volunteers, the perceptions of volunteering with an industry that has expectations for long work hours and low pay would be an interesting topic. Other studies may consider how the psychological contract differs between differing segments (e.g., recreational sport, professional teams, non-profits, etc.) of the industry and differing levels (e.g., minor league, major league, collegiate) of sport. Scholars within sport should consider undertaking research in this area as the extant literature is fragmented and covers the subject from a variety of different angles. While managerial practices within sport continue to evolve, there is a need to focus more attention on the psychological contract. Since employees may face different transactional contracts (e.g., fixed vs. commission-based pay) and working conditions based on their occupational areas, further study may explore how the psychological contract differs across various occupational areas (e.g., finance, marketing, ticketing, facilities, operations, etc.) within the same industry.

Another research avenue on psychological contract could be about how the psychological contract is influenced by such individual or organizational factors as careerism and work centrality (De Vos et al., 2009), organizational culture (Richard, McMillan-Capehart, Bhuian and Taylor, 2009), working overseas (Morgan and Finniear, 2009), and merger and acquisition in sport. Additionally, the dynamic nature of employer–employee dyads including gender and ethnicity on the psychological contract should be further examined in sport.

Conclusions

For the past 20 years, organization and management scholars have given significant attention to the study of the psychological contract and its impact on the dynamics of exchange relationship at work. The growth in attention to this construct has been partly attributed to the increase and dramatic changes affecting the workplace. In this regard, as working environments have gone through significant changes, so have the exchange relationships that have occurred between employees and their organizations. It is in this context that our under-standing of the psychological contract becomes critical if organizations are to better manage and/or predict employees' behavior under these conditions of great uncertainty.

The vast amount of psychological construct literature within the past two decades has provided us with a solid background of the complexity of this contract. However, as noted by Conway and Briner (2005), additional research is needed as psychological contract studies should be explored not only as a one-shot attempt but more as an outgoing and dynamic process that evolves over time.

In the context of sport organizations, the study of the psychological construct is still in its infancy and is focused mostly on a few contextual exchange relationships. Future studies should include other contextual settings, such as professional sport and the relationship between coaches/owners, and players/coaches. Particular attention should be focused on understanding how idiosyncratic factors like organizational culture or nationality influence the psychological contract. In addition, future studies should examine not only the employee perspective but also the employers' point of view. Finally, there is a need to expand the methods of research to include not only cross-sectional studies but also longitudinal ones.

The adequate management of the non-contractual agreements and expectations being made between the organization and their employees can have a significant impact on both sides. As noted throughout the chapter, there are a number of studies which provide empirical evidence that the breach and violation of these non-contractual agreements and expectations generate negative outcomes to both sides, and the opposite occurs when these beliefs or agreements have been met. In the context of sport organizations, there is also empirical evidence that supports similar findings to those reported in other organizational settings.

The relevancy of the psychological contract in sport organizations can be attributed to the macroeconomic changes that have affected the structure and dynamic in the workplace, but also to reasons that can be more specifically related to the way the sport industry operates. One of these is the heavy dependency of many sport services on voluntarism (Chelladurai, 1999; Cuskelly, Boag and McIntyre, 1999). Thus, it is possible to argue that volunteers that are attached and committed to give their time in exchange for inducements other than purely transactional (e.g. money) would constitute the prototypical cases in which the adequate management of psychological contract could result not only in their retention but also in their willingness to come back to volunteer (Kim et al., 2009).

Another reason for the importance of the psychological contract in sport organizations is the rapid professionalization of the industry. As sport management education becomes a formal and accepted area of study, sport organizations are increasingly hiring and recruiting professionals and experts specifically trained to work in the sport marketplace. This means that many more organizations today have changed their traditional structure and mode of operation from the "kitchen table design" (Kikulis, Slack and Hinings, 1992) to become highly bureaucratic and formalized. In this context, it is suggested that the working relation-ships in these bureaucratic sport organizations have also experienced changes along with the expectations of employers and employees and the way they build their exchange relationships.

The psychological contract in sport organizations can be observed through the lens of the culture in which most sport organizations operate. In spite of the rapid professionalization of most organizations, one may argue that the sport marketplace still operates very differently from the traditional business. The high visibility of many sport organizations (e.g., profes-sional teams) and the emotional attachments formed in relation to the products and services they produce (e.g., winning or losing teams) cause them to function in a different manner. In many cases decision-making processes influenced by emotions will supersede rationality (Heinemann, 1998); as a result, these can exert a profound impact on the exchange relationship between employers (e.g., owners) and employees (e.g., coaches).

Finally, the relevance of understanding the psychological contract can be seen not only from the perspective of human resource management practices, but also from the overall impact that failing can have across the entire organization. Sport organizations are for the most part service organizations targeted to cater for the needs of people (Chelladurai, 2005). As a result, it is possible to claim that the greatest assets of sport organizations lie in their own human capital. In this context, the psychological contract emerges as an important analytical framework that provides organizations with tools to better understand behaviors regarding what constitutes their most precious and critical resource. This is true regardless of whether these are exchange relationships between volunteers and staff, players and coaches, or professional staff and owners.

In this chapter, we have provided a snapshot of psychological contract theory. We have integrated a vast amount of literature from an array of disciplines. Nonetheless, we recognize that no overview is always fully complete, particularly when reviewing and interpreting such a complex subject as the psychological construct. As a result, it is possible that we have omitted some studies. In addition, as we write and edit this chapter, additional studies of which we are not aware may be in the process of being written. While we have striven to present a complete overview of research on the psychological contract in sport organizations, this may not be possible at this time. But on the other hand, and as stated early in our introduction, this confirms our assertion that the study of psychological contract in sport continues to flourish as the concept becomes more familiar to researchers interested in explaining attitudinal and behavioral responses emanating from exchange relationships in working environments.

References

Ainsworth, S. and Purss, A. (2009) 'Same time, next year? Human resource management and seasonal workers', *Personnel Review*, 38, 217–35.

Aggarwal, U., Datta, S. and Bhargava, S. (2007) 'The relationship between human resource practices, psychological contract and employee engagement. Implications for managing talent', *IIMB Management Review*, 19, 313–25.

Antunes de Campos, P. (1994) 'The relationship between coaches and athletes: the strength of the psychological contract in sport', unpublished doctoral dissertation, Alliant International University, San Diego, CA.

Argyris, C. (1960) *Understanding Organizational Behavior*, Homewood, IL, Dorsey Press, Inc.

Arnold, J. (1996) 'The psychological contract: a concept in need of closer scrutiny?', *European Journal of Work and Organizational Psychology*, 5, 511–20.

Barnard, C.I. (1938) *The function of the executive*, Cambridge, MA, Harvard University Press.

Barney, J.B. and Wright, P.M. (1998) 'On becoming a strategic partner: The role of human resources in gaining competitive advantage', *Human Resource Management*, 37, 31–46.

Blau, P. (1964) *Exchange and power in social life*, New York, Wiley.

Bravo, G. and Won, D. (2009) 'Giving and receiving: An examination of the psychological contract in NCAA coaches', poster session presented at the 24th annual conference of the North American Society for Sport Management, Columbia, SC, June 2009.

Bunderson, J.S. (2001) 'How work ideologies shape psychological contracts of professional employees: Doctor's responses to perceived breach', *Journal of Organizational Behavior*, 22, 717–41.

Chartered Institute of Personnel Development (2005) *Managing change. The role of the psychological contract*, [online] available HTTP: <http://www.cipd.co.uk/hr-resources/research/managing-change-psychological-contract-role.aspx> (accessed 12 August 2009).

Chelladurai, P. (1999) *Human resource management in sport and recreation*, Champaign, IL, Human Kinetics.

—— (2005) *Managing organizations for sport and physical activity: A systems perspective*, Scottsdale, AZ, Holcomb Hathaway.

Conway, N. and Briner, R.B. (2005) *Understanding psychological contract at work. A critical evaluation of theory and research*, New York, Oxford University Press.

Cooper, C.L. (2002) 'The changing psychological contract at work', *Occupational Environmental Medicine*, 59, 355.

Coyle-Shapiro, J.A.-M. and Kessler, I. (2000) 'Consequences of the psychological contract for the employment relationship: a large scale survey', *Journal of Management Studies*, 37, 903–29.

—— (2002a) 'Exploring reciprocity through the lens of the psychological contract: Employee and employer perspectives', *European Journal of Work and Organizational Psychology*, 11, 69–86.

—— (2002b) 'Contingent and non-contingent working in local government: Contrasting psychological contracts', *Public Administration*, 80, 77–101.

Cullinane, N. and Dundon, T. (2006) 'The psychological contract: A critical review'. *International Journal of Management Reviews*, 8, 113–29.

Cuskelly, G., Boag, A. and McIntyre, N. (1999) 'Differences in organizational commitment between paid and volunteer administrators in sport', *European Journal for Sport Management*, 6, 39–61.

Dabos, G.E. and Rousseau, D.M. (2004) 'Mutuality and reciprocity in the psychological contracts of employees and employers', *Journal of Applied Psychology*, 89, 52–72.

De Vos, A., Buyens, D. and Schalk, R. (2003) 'Psychological contract developing during organizational socialization: Adaptation to reality and the role of reciprocity', *Journal of Organizational Behavior*, 24, 537–59.

De Vos, A., De Stobbeleir, K. and Meganck, A. (2009) 'The relationship between career-related antecedents and graduates' anticipatory psychological contracts', *Journal of Business and Psychology*, 24, 289–98.

De Vos, A. and Meganck, A. (2009) 'What HR managers do versus what employee value: Exploring both parties' views on retention management from a psychological contract perspective', *Personnel Review*, 38, 45–60.

Deery, S., Iverson, R. and Walsh, J. (2006) 'Towards a better understanding of psychological breach: A study of customer service employees', *Journal of Applied Psychology*, 91, 166–75.

Eisenberger, R. and Huntington, R. (1986) 'Perceived organizational support', *Journal of Applied Psychology*, 71, 500–507.

Gouldner, A. (1960). 'The norm of reciprocity: A preliminary statement', *American Sociological Review*, 25, 161–78.

Granrose, C.S. and Baccili, P.A. (2006) 'Do psychological contracts include boundaryless or protean careers?', *Career Development International*, 11, 163–82.

Greenberg, M.J. (2006) 'Termination of college coaching contracts: When does adequate cause to terminate exist and who determines its existence?' *Marquette Sport Law Review*, 17, 196–257.

Greenberg, M.J. and Smith, J.S. (2007) 'A study of Division I assistant football and men's basketball coaches' contracts'. *Marquette Sport Law Review*, 18, 25–99.

Guest, D.E. (2004) 'The psychology of the employment relationship: An analysis based on the psychological contract', *Applied Psychology: An International Review*, 53, 541–55.

Guest, D.E. and Conway, N. (2002) 'Communicating the psychological contract: An employer perspective', *Human Resource Management Journal*, 12, 22–38.

Hamel, S.A. (2009) 'Exit, voice, and sensemaking following psychological contract violations: Women's responses to career advancement barriers', *Journal of Business Communication*, 46, 234–61.

Haslberger, A. and Brewster, C. (2009) 'Capital gains: Expatriate adjustment and the psychological contract in international careers', *Human Resource Management*, 48, 379–97.

Heinemann, K. (1998) 'El comportamiento económico como toma de decisiones racionales', in Heinemann, K., *Introducción a la economía del deporte*, Barcelona, Paidotribo.

Hekman, D.R., Bigley, G.A., Steensma, H.K. and Hereford, J.F. (2009) 'Combined effects of organizational and professional identification on the reciprocity dynamic for professional employees', *Academy of Management Journal*, 52, 506–26.

Herriot, P. and Pemberton, C. (1997) 'Facilitating new deals', *Human Resource Management Journal*, 7, 45–56.

Kahn, W. (1990) 'Psychological conditions of personal engagement and disengagement at work', *Academy of Management Journal*, 33, 692–724.

Kalleberg, A.L. (2000) 'Nonstandard employment relations: part-time, temporary and contract work', *Annual Review of Sociology*, 26, 341–65.

Kelley-Patterson, D. and George, C. (2002) 'Mapping the contract: An exploration of the comparative expectations of graduate employees and human resource managers within the hospitality, leisure and tourism industries in the United Kingdom', *Journal of Services Research*, 2, 55–74.

Kelly, S. (2008) 'Understanding the role of the football manager in Britain and Ireland: A Weberian approach', *European Sport Management Quarterly*, 8, 399–419.

Kelly, S. and Harris, J. (in press) 'Managers, directors and trust in professional football', *Soccer and Society*.

Kickul, J. and Lester, S.W. (2001) 'Broken promises: Equity sensitivity as a moderator between psychological contract breach and employee attitudes and behavior', *Journal of Business and Psychology*, 16, 191–217.

Kickul, J.R., Lester, S.W. and Finkl, J. (2002) 'Promise breaking during radical organizational change: Do justice interventions make a difference?', *Journal of Organizational Behavior*, 23, 469–88.

Kikulis, L., Slack, T. and Hinings, B. (1992) 'Institutionally specific design archetypes: A framework for understanding change in national sport organizations', *International Review for the Sociology of Sport*, 27, 343–70.

Kim, M. and Chelladurai, P. (2006) 'Retention of volunteers: The role of psychological contract', paper presented at the 21st annual conference of the North American Society for Sport Management Conference, Kansas City, MO, June 2006.

Kim, M., Trail, G.T., Lim, J., and Kim, Y.K. (2009) 'The role of psychological contract in intention to continue volunteering', *Journal of Sport Management*, 23, 549–73.

King, B. (2009) 'A degree of uncertainty', *SportBusiness Journal*, August 24.

Koh, C., Ang, S. and Straub, D.W. (2004) 'IT outsourcing success: a psychological contract perspective', *Information Systems Research*, 15, 356–73.

Kotter, J.P. (1973) 'The psychological contract: Managing the joining up process', *California Management Review*, 15, 91–99.

Levinson, H., Price, C.R., Munden, K.J. and Solley, C.M. (1962) *Men, management and mental health*, Cambridge, MA, Harvard University Press.

Lester, S.W., Turnley, W.H., Bloodgood, J.M. and Bolino, M. (2002) 'Not seeing eye to eye: Differences in supervisor and subordinate perceptions of and attributions for psychological contract breach', *Journal of Organizational Behavior*, 23, 39–56.

Lewis-McClear, K. and Taylor, S. (1998) 'Psychological contract breach and the employment exchange: Perceptions from employees and employers', in S.J. Havlovic (ed.), *Academy of Management Best Paper Proceedings*, 58.

Liao-Troth, M.A. (2001) 'Attitude differences between paid workers and volunteers', *Nonprofit Management and Leadership*, 11, 423–42.

McLean Parks, J., Kidder, D. and Gallagher, D. (1998) 'Fitting square pegs into round holes: Mapping the domain of contingent work arrangements onto the psychological contract', *Journal of Organizational Behavior*, 19, 697–730.

MacNeil, I.R. (1974) 'The many futures of contracts', *Southern California Law Review*, 47, 691–816.

—— (1985) 'Relational contract: What we do and do not know', *Wisconsin Law Review*, 483–525.

Maguire, J., Jarvie, G., Mansfield, L. and Bradley, J. (2002) *Sport worlds. A sociological perspective*, Champaign, IL, Human Kinetics.

Makin, P.J., Cooper, C.L. and Cox, C.J. (1996) *Organizations and the psychological contract: Managing people at work*, Westport, CT, Greenwood Press.

Malcolm, D. (2000) 'Football business and football communities in the twenty-first century', *Soccer and Society*, 1, 102–13.

March, J.E. and Simon, H.A. (1958) *Organizations*, New York, Wiley.

Mason, D.S. and Slack, T. (2001) 'Industry factors and the changing dynamics of the player–agent relationship in professional ice hockey', *Sport management Review*, 4, 165–91.

McGaughey, S.L. and Liesch, P.W. (2002) 'The global sport-media nexus: Reflections on the 'Super League Saga' in Australia', *Journal of Management Studies*, 39, 383–416.

Menninger, K. (1958) *Theory of psychoanalytic technique*, New York, Basic Books.

Meyer, J.P. and Allen, N.J. (1991) 'A three-component conceptualization of organizational commitment', *Human Resource Management Review*, 1, 61–89.

Morgan, A. and Finniear, J. (2009) 'Migrant workers and the changing psychological contract', *Journal of European Industrial Training*, 33, 305–22.

Morrison, E.W. and Robinson, S. (1997) 'When employees feel betrayed: a model of how psychological contract violation develops', *Academy of Management Review*, 22, 226–56.

Nichols, G. and Ojala, E. (2009) 'Understanding the management of sport events volunteers through psychological contract theory', *Voluntas: International Journal of Voluntary and Nonprofit Organizations*, 20, 369–87

Organ, D.W. (1988) *Organizational citizenship behavior*, Lexington, MA, Lexington Books.

Owen-Pugh, V. (2007) 'The commercialising of British men's basketball: Psychological contracts between coaches and players in the post-Bosman game', *Journal of Contemporary European Research*, 3, 255–72.

Pate, J. (2006) 'The changing contours of the psychological contract: Unpacking context and circumstances of breach', *Journal of European Industrial Training*, 30, 32–47.

Restubog, S.L.D., Bordia, P. and Tang, R.L. (2006) 'Effects of psychological contract breach on performance of IT employees: The mediating role of affective commitment', *Journal of Occupational and Organizational Psychology*, 79, 299–306.

Restubog, S.L.D., Bordia, P. and Bordia, S. (2009) 'The interactive effects of procedural justice and equity sensitivity in predicting response to psychological contract breach: An interactionist perspective', *Journal of Business Psychology*, 24, 165–78.

Richard, O.C., McMillan-Capehart, A., Bhuian, S.N. and Taylor, E.C. (2009) 'Antecedents and consequences of psychological contracts: Does organizational culture really matter?', *Journal of Business Research*, 62, 818–25.

Robinson, S.L. (1996) 'Trust and breach of the psychological contract', *Administrative Science Quarterly*, 41, 574–99.

Robinson, S.L., Kraatz, M.S. and Rousseau, D.M. (1994) 'Changing obligations and the psychological contract: a longitudinal study', *Academy of Management Journal*, 37, 137–52.

Robinson, S.L. and Rousseau, D.M. (1994) 'Violating the psychological contract: not the exception but the norm', *Journal of Organizational Behavior*, 15, 229–45.

Roehling, M.V. (1997) 'The origins and early development of the psychological contract construct', *Journal of Management History*, 3, 204–17.

—— (2004) 'Legal theory: contemporary contract law perspectives and insights for employment relationship theory', in J. Coyle-Shapiro, L. Shore, M.S. Taylor, and L. Tetrick (eds.) *The employment relationship: Examining psychological and contextual perspectives*, Oxford, Oxford University Press.

Rousseau, D.M. (1989) 'Psychological and implied contract in organizations', *Employee Responsibilities and Rights Journal*, 2, 121–39.

—— (1990) 'New hire perceptions of their own and their employer's obligations: a study of psychological contracts', *Journal of Organizational Behavior*, 11, 389–400.

—— (1995) *Psychological contracts in organizations. Understanding written and unwritten agreements*, Thousand Oaks, CA, Sage.

—— (2000) *Psychological contract inventory. Technical report* (Version 3), Heinz School of Public Policy and Graduate School of Industrial Administration, Pittsburgh, PA, Carnegie Mellon University.

—— (2001) 'The idiosyncratic deal: flexibility versus fairness', *Organizational Dynamics*, 29, 260–73.

Rousseau, D.M. and McLean Parks, J.M. (1993) 'The contracts of individuals and organizations', *Research in Organizational Behavior*, 15, 1–43.

Schein, E.H. (1965) *Organizational psychology*, Englewood Cliffs, NJ, Prentice Hall.

Shore, L. and Tetrick, L.E. (1994) 'The psychological contract as an explanatory framework in the employment relationship', in C.L. Cooper and D.M. Rousseau (eds.) *Trends in organizational behavior*, New York, Wiley.

Sims, R.R. (1994) 'Human resource management's role in clarifying the new psychological contract', *Human Resource Management*, 33, 373–82.

Smith, A. (2008) 'A casualty of the financial crisis: Sport sponsorships', *Time Magazine*, 16 September, [online] available HTTP: <http://www.time.com/time/printout/0,8816,1841701,00.html> (accessed 10 August 2009).

Sparrow, P. and Cooper, C. (1998) 'New organizational forms: the strategic relevance of future psychological contract scenarios', *Canadian Journal of Administrative Sciences*, 15, 356–71.

Sutton, G. and Griffin, M. (2004) 'Integrating expectations, experiences and psychological contract violations. A longitudinal study of new professionals', *Journal of Occupational and Organizational Psychology*, 77, 493–514.

Tallman, R.R.J. and Bruning, N.S. (2008) 'Relating employee's psychological contracts to their personality', *Journal of Managerial Psychology*, 23, 688–712.

Taylor, T., Darcy, S., Hoye, R. and Cuskelly, G. (2006) 'Using psychological contract theory to explore issues in effective volunteer management', *European Sport Management Quarterly*, 6, 123–47.

Taylor, T., Doherty, A. and McGraw, P. (2008) *Managing people in sport organizations. A strategic human resource management perspective*, Burlington, MA, Butterworth-Heinemann.

Tekleab, A.G., Takeuchi, R. and Taylor, M.S. (2005) 'Extending the chain of relationships among organizational justice, social exchange, and employee reactions: the role of contract violations', *Academy of Management Journal*, 48, 146–57.

Tekleab, A.G. and Taylor, M.S. (2003) 'Aren't there two parties in an employment relationship? Antecedents and consequences of organization-employee agreement on contract obligations and violations', *Journal of Organizational Behavior*, 24, 585–608.

Thomas, D.C., Au, K. and Ravlin, E.C. (2003) 'Cultural variation and the psychological contract', *Journal of Organizational Behavior*, 24, 451–71.

Thompson, M. and Heron, P. (2006) 'Relational quality and innovative performance in R&D based enterprises', *Human Resource Management Journal*, 16, 28–47.

Tsui, A., Pearce, J., Porter, L. and Tripoli, A. (1997) 'Alternative approaches to the employee–organization relationship: does investment in employees pay-off?', *Academy of Management Journal*, 40, 1089–1121.

Turnley, W.H. and Feldman, D.C. (1999a) 'A discrepancy model of psychological contract violations', *Human Resource Management Review*, 9, 367–86.

—— (1999b) 'The impact of psychological contract violations on exit, voice, loyalty and neglect', *Human Relations*, 52, 895–921.

Turnley, W.H., Bolino, M.C., Lester, S.W. and Bloodgood, J.M. (2003) 'The impact of psychological contract fulfillment on the performance of in-role and organizational citizenship behaviors', *Journal of Management*, 29, 187–206.

Wasserman, H.M. (2008) 'West Virginia University v. Richard Rodriguez: The legal perspective', West Virginia University College of Law. Sport and Entertainment Law Society, [online] available HTTP: <http://richrodriguezlaw.blogspot.com> (accessed 28 April 2009).

Won, D. and Pack, S.M. (2010) 'Violations of the psychological contracts in interscholastic athletics', *International Journal of Sport Management*, 11, 284–303.

Zhao, H., Wayne, S.J., Glibkowski, B.C. and Bravo, J. (2007) 'The impact of psychological contract breach on work-related outcomes: A meta-analysis', *Personnel Psychology*, 60, 647–80.

15

MANAGING CONTINGENT WORKERS IN SPORT

Kyungro Chang

With increasing economic uncertainty and rapidly changing technologies, many organizations have attempted to change their management strategies, and the majority of strategies targeted toward adjusting to this changing economic environment and enhancing competitiveness are associated with human resources management practices such as downsizing, restructuring, and flexible employment arrangements. Organizations in several industries, in particular, are increasingly turning to non-standard employments such as part-time employees as a way to maximize staffing flexibility while lowering personnel costs (Barker 1995; Barling and Gallagher 1996; Brewster, Mayne and Tregaskis 1997; Gallagher 2002). Sport organizations are no exception to this trend and this chapter discusses this phenomenon.

Using non-standard employment is emerging as an increasingly commonplace practice for today's cost-conscious companies striving to improve workplace productivity and profitability, while minimizing costs and overheads. With a number of employees working with a non-standard employment status in most industries, there has been growing academic interest in non-standard employments. Non-standard employments in sport industries, however, have received little scholarly attention even though they perform a widespread and traditional line of work.

Non-standard employments are commonly referred to as "contingent employments," a label which was first used by Audrey Freedman in 1985, and the term came to be applied to a wide range of employment practices including part-time work, temporary employment, employee leasing, self-employment, contracting out, and home-based work, and it is defined as any job in which an individual does not have an explicit or implicit contract for long-term employment (Polivka and Nardone, 1989). Organizations that hire employees on a contingent basis enjoy the freedom and flexibility of using staff resources as needed rather than investing in employees on a permanent and full-time basis. Many employees, too, enjoy this flexibility – such as individuals with other personal or professional pursuits, those who want a bridge to a permanent job placement, or others who want to embark upon a new career path, without making a long-term commitment to the employer.

The market for a contingent labor force has grown rapidly in recent years. According to a 1997 US Department of Commerce report, during the ten years between 1986 and 1996, total employment grew by 1.7 percent; in the same period, employment in temporary services grew 10.3 percent. Contingent workers have historically been higher in service industries than in manufacturing and they were more likely to be female, black, young, and enrolled in school (Polivka, 1996; Sightler and Adams, 1999). Although some contingent workers were found in every industry, contingent workers were much more likely to be concentrated in the service industry than were noncontingent workers. One reason might be that the growth of the service industry has fueled an increasing demand for expanded hours of service. Workforce scheduling in the service industry is much more complicated than in other industries because consumer demand spans 24 hours a day, 7 days a week. The sport industry is also known for its use of nonstandard scheduling, in that sport consumers participate in sport and/or leisure activities outside of daytime and/or weekday hours after they finish their work during standard hours.

More than 53 percent of contingent workers were employed in the service industry. In fact, the proportion of non-standard workers in manufacturing has remained relatively stable while the use of non-standard workers in service industries has risen dramatically, such that 87 percent of non-standard workers are now employed in service industries (Mabert and Showalter, 1990). Contingent work should be especially attractive to individuals with family responsibilities (frequently and traditionally women) who require flexible work hours. Contingent work should also be attractive to professionals who are attending school (typically, younger individuals) to improve their skills or to obtain advanced degrees.

Although the need for flexible manpower strategies leads organizations to prefer contingent employment, contingent employment can also be introduced in order to weaken the power of a labor union or keep it out altogether since the features of irregular jobs, whose work hours and places are different from those of regular jobs, make it difficult to build up strong organizing ability. However, this is also eventually part of efforts to insure the flexibility of business and manpower management.

Organizations have pursued flexibility in two ways (Kalleberg, 2001). The first is functional flexibility. Functional flexibility, a management strategy mainly applied to core labor, is embodied in practice in various forms such as job enlargement, job enrichment, quality circle, self-managed team, and inventory management technique. For this strategy to succeed, it should be preceded by the devotion of core labor, continuous training, and accumulated technology and experience. Through this functional flexibility, the distinction between core and peripheral labor continues to be reinforced and specialization of the labor market becomes fixed. The second approach is numerical flexibility. This management strategy, which can be found in both external and internal labor markets, achieves flexibility in external labor markets by adjusting employment in tandem with changes in economies or management, and this results in various forms of layoffs and contingent employments such as temporary, contract, and part-time labor. Numerical flexibility as a management strategy applied to peripheral labor inside a company causes instability of employment by generalizing an employment contract different from the traditional employment type and thus channeling the risk that employers used to bear into individual labor.

When organizations seek to achieve labor flexibility, they adopt both the above management strategies at the same time. Atkinson (1984) explained the flexibility of the labor market, assuming the "core–peripheral model" as the labor strategy of companies. According to him, the target of functional flexibility strategy is mainly core labor. Companies make investments in core labor like providing a high level of education programs while engaging in flexible labor systems and practices. Core labor means full-time regular and long-term employment whereas peripheral labor means contingent employment such as part-time, temporary, short-term, and externally employable jobs.

Increased reliance on contingency workers results in an economy divided into core and peripheral workers by income, job security and access to human resource development opportunities. Others hold that contingent work provides greater workforce flexibility and reduces wage and benefits costs while creating job opportunities for a diverse workforce.

Some have argued that being part of a contingent work arrangement consigns a person to the bottom of the economic ladder, where the worker experiences frequent job changes and has little economic security and no hope of economic advancement. Further, proponents of this position argue that, as a result of the apparent growth in the number of contingent workers, the economic hardship associated with these types of jobs is increasing. Others argue, by contrast, that contingent employment offers individuals pathways into the labor market that they otherwise would not have, as well as flexibility that helps them balance work with other, non-labor-market obligations. Without contingent work arrangements, these observers insist, individuals with poor access to jobs or with conflicting needs would either be unemployed or drop out of the labor force altogether. Proponents of contingent work arrangements also go so far as to argue that some contingent work arrangements, such as temporary help service employment, offer individuals more stable employment and greater chances for upward job mobility than they would be able to obtain on their own. Implicit in the discussion of the growth of contingent work arrangements and their effect on individuals' labor market prospects is the notion that the job market has undergone a fundamental shift in the last several years. The importance of internal labor markets, it is argued, has declined, and employers have altered the ways they hire and fire workers.

Pros and cons of contingent employment

The reason why organizations came to prefer contingent employment is that the need for cheap and flexible manpower has increased. Reduction of labor costs and flexibility of employment are the main reasons why organizations employ contingent workers. In some cases, however, contingent employment is exploited to avoid personnel control or weaken the labor union and to protect core personnel or secure professional personnel of whom the supply is insufficient in the labor market.

Maintaining and cultivating regular manpower generates significant costs, which include not only wages but also fringe benefits and expenses for recruiting, hiring, training, and socializing. Thus by employing contingent workers, organizations can reduce such expenses. And also contingent workers do not entail an automatic labor cost increase from continuous service, providing another cost-reducing factor. The compensation for contingent employees who perform the same jobs as regular ones is generally lower. This compensation difference is not only from wages but also from various fringe benefits and retirement payments which are generally not available or are lower for contingent workers.

It is often difficult for organizations to hire professional manpower in the labor market because the supply of professional manpower is not enough since it takes a long time to train employees, while the types of manpower needed frequently change due to changes in technology or technological strategy. Therefore, with its less-restricted work hours and places, contingent employment is used to insure professional manpower. Contingent employment is also adopted by companies which are seeking professional manpower as companies recognize that the types of professional manpower needed can easily change. Technological development and change often requires new technology professionals rather than the existing ones, so simple training for newly required professional technology cannot keep up with ever-changing markets or technologies.

There are many studies on the positive effects of contingent employment from various perspectives. Matusik and Hill (1998) argued that contingent employment was adopted for cost reduction but it can play a positive role in introducing people into the organization, forming them, and accumulating new knowledge. According to them, contingent employment allows companies to have easy access to professional or ever-changing knowledge that they do not possess in-house, giving them a competitive advantage that would not be available otherwise. Storey et al. (2002) similarly argued that contingent employment can have a positive effect on innovation. According to them, contingent employment can bring about novel progress and innovation by stimulating the desire for change among already-hired employees as well as opening the door to up-to-date knowledge and technology.

Other scholars, on the other hand, have directly mentioned the possible negative effects of contingent employment on organizational efficiency. They all pay attention to the possibility that cost reduction or efficiency improvement may not be realized in practice, contrary to expectations. Nollen (1996) suggested that employers overestimate the merits of contingent employment while underestimating its demerits. Allan (2000) pointed out the possibility that employers may not be able to consider mid- and long-term hidden costs caused by contingent employment, which became common for cost reduction. According to him, contingent employment can negatively affect work relations, motivation of employees, and quality of products. Analyzing the psychological effect of contingent employment on work relations of existing employees, Pearce (1993) empirically proved that the introduction of contingent manpower generates a higher workload for existing employees and thus decreases their organizational loyalty.

Critics of engagement in diverse employment types present the following points for their arguments. First, contingent employment alone is the tip of an iceberg because as it is expanded it can generate much more serious problems compared with regular employees, including employment instability and worsening pay and work conditions. When organizations adopt contingent workers while holding back new hiring of regular employees, pay and work conditions naturally worsen and employment instability increases. Second, there will be many problems with protecting contingent workers. The existing employee protection schemes were designed for regular workers, thus contingent workers generally remain outside the schemes. Consequently contingent workers tend to suffer inferior conditions to their regular counterparts in terms of labor intensity, pay level, and employment instability. Furthermore, staying outside the labor union, contingent workers cannot be protected by union action either. Third, the spread of contingent employment is highly likely to weaken the labor movement. Contingent employment, whose status is unstable and which is difficult to organize, tends to lower the negotiation power of the union for wage and work conditions.

Fourth, it is a false argument that contingent employment is a voluntary choice accompanying the pattern change of labor supply. Assisting their household incomes, most contingent workers, suc as housewives or juveniles, accept low wages, poor work conditions, and unstable employment. Though it is true that there is a change in the pattern of labor supply, it is doubtful whether this can fully explain the "voluntary" rise of contingent employment. Most contingent workers involuntarily maintain their status due to their lack of chances in the labor market. Fifth, the argument that the expansion of contingent employment is helpful in improving the productivity of companies and national economies does not ring true. By and large, contingent employment represents lower productivity, more training costs, and more supervision costs. Contingent workers are prone to be less bonded to their organizations, less self-motivated, and less skilled. Therefore, even with its low direct labor costs, contingent employment is not necessarily advantageous to companies given its low productivity.

Outsourcing

Another phenomenon, which stands out in the labor market and employment since the 1980s along with the flexible labor market, is outsourcing. Recent reports of organizational down-sizing, the growth of temporary help agencies, and the phenomenon of outsourcing have fueled the perception that the number of contingent workers and workers in alternative work arrangements is increasing. The term outsourcing can be traced back to the information system jobs that Electric Data Systems used to perform on its own inside the company but consigned to the outside from the end of the 1970s to the beginning of the 1980s. Companies use outsourcing because from the transaction expense perspective it is more cost-effective to consign specialized activities to the outside rather than carrying them out in-house due to the development of scientific and information technologies.

Outsourcing originated in information technology (IT), where technology advances fastest at the outset, and was put to use as a restructuring method with a view to slashing information systems expenses until the mid 1980s (Deavers, 1997). The purpose of outsourcing, however, has changed from decreasing costs to taking a strategic position for competitive advantage as the range of outsourcing works has expanded from information systems to accounting, personnel management, and peripheral jobs with insignificant values from the end of the 1980s. Recently outsourcing has spread rapidly even in direct production facilities and manpower.

Organizations now consider outsourcing an efficient way to raise their productivity (Quinn and Hilmer, 1994; Deavers, 1997; Kessler et al., 1999). The concept of strategic outsourcing was created when the American economy launched large-scale employment adjustment and restructuring such as selling businesses in the period of long-term recession in the 1980s. The concept is an attempt to restructure organizational resources and organization centering around core competency by integrating core competency theory, which came into the spotlight as a new strategic theory at the time along with traditional outsourcing.

Quinn and Hilmer (1994), who broadened the theoretical foundation of strategic outsourcing, argued that technology and resources for other strategies will become available to organizations by combining the two approaches and methods, core competency and outsourcing. According to them, firstly, companies should create a competitive advantage that can continuously provide unique values to customers by focusing on technology and knowledge rather than on function or product; and secondly, companies should outsource minor jobs that do not require important strategy or special capacity even though such jobs were traditionally executed in-house.

As can be seen from the existing studies on outsourcing of manpower, outsourcing of peripheral functions does not necessarily have only positive effects even if it arises from a strategic judgment. It can lead employees who are used to traditional production systems to confusion, and can have serious effects on the morale and work desire of constituents. Thus, expenses and risks associated with outsourcing should be carefully pondered (Quinn and Hilmer, 1994). In addition, analyzing the effect of global outsourcing strategy on organizational efficiency for multinational companies, Elmuti and Kathawala (2000) empirically proved that methodical and appropriate outsourcing can improve organizational efficiency.

References

Allan, C. (2000) 'The hidden organizational costs of using non-standard employment', *Personnel Review*, 29(2), 188–206.

Atkinson, J. (1984) 'Manpower strategies for flexible organizations', *Personnel Management*, 16(8), 28–31.

Barker, K. (1995) 'Contingent work: Research issues and the lens of moral exclusion', in L. Tetrick and J. Barling (eds.) *Changing Employment Relations: Behavioral and Social Perspectives*, Washington, American Psychological Association, pp. 31–61.

Barling, J., and Gallagher, D.G. (1996) 'Part-time employment', in C.J. Cooper and I.T. Robertson (eds.) *International Review of Industrial and Organizational Psychology*, Vol. 11, London, John Wiley and Sons.

Brewster, C., Mayne, L., and Tregaskis, O. (1997) 'Flexible workings in Europe', *Journal of World Business*, 32(2): 133–51.

Deavers, K.L. (1997) 'Outsourcing: A corporate competitiveness strategy, not a search for low wages', *Journal of Labor Research*, 18(4), 503–19.

Elmuti, D., and Kathawala, Y. (2000) 'The effects of global outsourcing strategies and organizational effectiveness', *International Journal of Manpower*, 21(2), 112–28.

Feldman, D.C., Doerpinghaun, H.L., and Turnley, W.H. (1994) 'Managing temporary workers: A permanent HRM challenge', *Organizational Dynamics*, 23, 49–63.

Gallagher, D.G. (2002) 'Contingent work contracts: Practice and theory', in C.L. Cooper and R.J. Burke (eds.), *The New World of Work: Challenges and Opportunities*, Oxford, Blackwell Publishers.

Kalleberg, A.L. (2001) 'Organizing flexibility: The flexible firm in a new century', *British Journal of Industrial Relations*, 39(4), 479–504.

Kessler, I., Coyle-Shapiro, J., and Purcell, J. (1999) 'Outsourcing and the employee perspective', *Human Resource Management Journal*, 9(2), 5–19.

Mabert, V.A., and Showalter, M.J. (1990) 'Measuring the impact of part-time workers in service organizations', *Journal of Operations Management*, 9, 209–29.

Matusik, S.F., and Hill, C.W. (1998) 'The utilization of contingent work: Knowledge creation and competitive advantage', *Academy of Management Review*, 23(4), 680–97.

Mayne, L., Tregaskis, O., and Brewster, C. (1996) 'A comparative analysis of the link between flexibility and HRM strategy', *Employee Relations*, 18(3), 5–24.

Nollen, S.D. (1996) 'Negative aspects of temporary employment', *Journal of Labor Research*, 17(4), 567–82.

Pearce, J.L. (1993) 'Toward an organizational behavior of contract laborers: Their psychological involvement and effects on employee co-workers', *Academy of Management Journal*, 36(5), 1082–96.

Polivka, A.E. (1996) 'Contingent and alternative work arrangements defined', *Monthly Labor Review*, October, 3–9.

Polivka, A.E., and Nardone, T. (1989) 'On the definition of contingent work', *Monthly Labor Review*, December, 9–16.

Quinn, J.B., and Hilmer, F.G. (1994) 'Strategic outsourcing', *Sloan Management Review*, 35(4), 43–55.

Sightler, K.W., and Adams, J.S. (1999) 'Differences between stayers and leavers among part-time workers', *Journal of Managerial Issues*, 11(1), 110–25.

Storey, J., Quintas, P., Taylor, P., and Fowle, W. (2002) 'Flexible employment contracts and their implications for product and process innovation', *International Journal of Human Resource Management*, 13(1), 1–18.

Wong, M.L. (2001) 'The strategic use of contingent workers in Hong Kong's economic upheaval', *Human Resource Management Journal*, 11(4), 22–37.

PART III

The marketing of sport

Edited by Guillaume Bodet

16

CONTEMPORARY ISSUES IN SPORT MARKETING

Guillaume Bodet

From sport changes to sport marketing

The question of whether sport marketing is unique and clearly distinct from mainstream marketing has been a long-lasting debate and will probably be an ongoing one for many years in the future. It is, however, likely that the reader of this book and this marketing section might be convinced that sport marketing represents a distinctive field of practice and research, and that textbooks such as those of Mullin, Hardy and Sutton (2000), Desbordes, Ohl and Tribou (2004) and Beech and Chadwick (2007), academic journals such as *Sport Marketing Quarterly, International Journal of Sport Marketing and Sponsorship* and *International Journal of Sport Marketing and Management*, as well as the tremendous number of sport marketing publications, represent enough justifications for such a distinction. This is also an opinion we share and for this reason we are glad to propose to the reader an up-to-date presentation of the level of knowledge of the field.

However, acknowledging a uniqueness of the sport object in relation to marketing should not eclipse the fact that it is an evolving field, with evolving boundaries, and that it might be more appropriate to talk about sport objects, in the plural. Sport marketing cannot be reduced to the marketing of sport fans and its mix marketing component. As sport is a complex and sometimes elusive phenomenon – the definition of what a sport is and what its boundaries are is a perilous exercise – therefore sport marketing should mirror it. Specifically, it seems that all the traditional sport landmarks have been blurred in our rapidly changing societies. For instance, sport fans are no longer only local people supporting only local athletes. As an illustration, we can evoke the case of Arsenal FC, which was the first English Premier League football club, in 2005, to name a completely non-English 16-man squad for a domestic game. Moreover, the globalization phenomenon associated with the development of new media and technology has allowed satellite fans to intensively follow and support their favorite professional club or franchise although they may have never physically attended one of their live games.

We can finally cite the example of the Stade Français rugby club, which can break attendance records a few times a year by attracting between 70,000 and 80,000 spectators to the Stade de France although its 20,000 regular stadium is never sold out for the other regular home fixtures (Bodet, 2009a). Some explanations about this surprising situation are provided in Chapter 17. All these examples indicate that sport has changed and so should sport marketing. The meanings of sport have also changed (Bodet, 2009b; Seippel, 2006), which strongly influences the relation sport participants and sport consumers can have with sport organizations and sport brands. For example, sport participants are not only oriented towards sport performance and sport organizations, and not-for-profit sport organizations in particular, so these no longer represent the automatic and natural place and setting for the practice of sport. This issue is also discussed in Chapter 17.

Looking at another aspect, sport goods brands and sport clothing and footwear brands are no longer bound to sporting fields and arenas, and are passively and actively investing other public spaces. Passively because many of their products are diverted from their original function and purpose by consumers (how many sport shoes have ever seen a changing room?) and actively because they now purposely compete with non-sporting brands within other markets. For example, we can wonder who knows or remembers that René Lacoste nicknamed "the crocodile" (or "the alligator") was a French tennis champion in the 1920s, who created the namesake tennis brand. For many people Lacoste is seen as a fashion brand although it is a tennis and golf clothes supplier as well as the sponsor of many renowned tennis and golf athletes and tournaments. Some explanations of such perceptions are provided in Chapter 18.

Finally, marketing practices implemented by sport organizations have also changed a lot, either driven by internal motives and pressures to better achieve organizational objectives or driven by changes and pressures coming from the external socio-cultural, economic and legal environments. Sport sponsorship is a typical example of such changes in practices (Chapter 22). Facing an increased and globalized competition, sponsors are forced to better rationalize their sponsorship activities and integrate them as much as possible into their overall communication strategy. Moreover, the proliferation of ambush marketing practices has indirectly encouraged sport organizations and sponsors to redefine in depth the nature of their relationship in order to fully support and exploit their investment to achieve their sponsorship objectives and their return on investment while protecting their rights from the sponsor perspective, helping sponsors to capitalize on their investment and creating long-term relationships from a sport organization perspective. These elements are further discussed in Chapters 18 and 23.

From marketing trends to sport marketing

Nevertheless, despite the specificities of the sport marketing field, it should not be ignored that many changes in sport marketing trends and practices also happen in other marketing fields and that the analysis of their evolution should help us to identify the future stakes of the sport marketing field. In this regard, several issues can be identified.

Historically, marketing practices have focused on mass markets and transactions in order to attract and seduce the highest number of consumers and make them spend the highest possible amount of money. Such an approach does not fit any more with the level of competition in specific markets or consumers' behaviors and expectations. Indeed, due to increasing numbers of offers and competitors, firms and organizations cannot afford not to satisfy their consumers as they can easily switch to an alternative offer. Moreover, consumers are no longer (if they were ever) solely rational and logical thinkers driven by rationality and problem-solving strategies (Holbrook and Hirschman, 1982). Consumption is not only an activity fulfilling utilitarian benefits but also a vehicle for hedonic gratifications, sensations and emotions, symbolic identity roles (Holbrook and Hirschman, 1982) and social links

(Cova and Cova, 2002). Sport consumption does not seem to be excluded from this mutation.

From this observation several marketing streams have been developed. The first marketing approach relies on the concept of relationship and "refers to all marketing activities directed toward establishing, developing, and maintaining successful relationship exchanges" (Morgan and Hunt, 1994: 22). At the heart of the relationship approach lies the concept of loyalty, which is thought to produce many positive organizational outcomes and management of which is seen as costing less than recruiting new partners or consumers. The loyalty issue seems increasingly important for both spectator and participation organizations with maybe a more crucial aspect for the latter as the lack of consumers and participants directly questions the sustainability and the survival of these organizations. For this reason, Chapter 17 aims to identify how consumer loyalty is formed in sport participation services. In Chapter 18, the relationship marketing approach is also discussed from a business–to–consumer perspective for sporting spectatorship organizations, as well as from a business–to–business perspective.

The second marketing approach relies on the production of experiences and is highly relevant for sporting events which, by nature, hold a strong experiential dimension (Holbrook and Hirschman, 1982). It is therefore crucial for these sporting organizations to identify who their consumers are and what kind of experience they are looking for in order to provide them the adequate service offer which will satisfy them. This is the purpose of Chapter 19. As mentioned in Chapter 22, the concept of experience also represents an important challenge for sponsors and sport organizations in order to create sufficient emotions to favor the achievement of the sponsors' objectives.

Another field of application of the experiential marketing approach concerns the sporting goods market. Indeed, sporting goods brands have now realized that shops and retail stores are more than just transaction places and that they could benefit from using different point of sale designs and layouts and from creating dramatizing atmospheres. The potential benefits of such strategies and the managerial levers sporting good brands can manipulate are for these reasons analyzed in Chapter 20.

The third marketing approach, which can be seen as an extension of the relationship marketing one, focuses on the social bonds and relationships consumers try to create in their consumption activities, in order to identify, segment and satisfy them. The social dimension of consumption is discussed in relation to sport participation in Chapter 17, to sport spectatorship in Chapter 19 and to sporting good retail brands in Chapter 20.

Regarding the previously mentioned increase of competition worldwide, a last major significant contemporary trend relies on the globalization phenomenon and the development of new technologies and media that are thought to reshape consumer behaviors and management practices as well as simultaneously creating opportunities in new foreign markets and threats from competition intensification. On this specific issue, sport is certainly not excluded from these changes but constitutes a particular case for analysis due to its unique link with mass media and communication. This is the purpose of Chapter 21, which covers both traditional and new media. Therefore, as a popular communication technique, mainly due to its efficiency and the limitations of traditional communication techniques such as advertising, sponsorship's objectives and strategies are analyzed in Chapter 22, whereas the ambush marketing issue which is now the sponsorship correlate is treated in Chapter 23.

As illustrated in the two previous sections, a complete overview of current sport marketing knowledge requires the analysis of the specificities of the sport objects (i.e. services, events and brands) as well as a deep understanding of the major trends which drive the marketing field, and we hope that the following contributions will highlight both components to provide the most up-to-date and diverse picture of the contemporary sport marketing field.

References

Beech, J. and Chadwick, S. (2007) *The marketing of sport*, Harlow, England, Pearson Education Limited.

Bodet, G. (2009a) ' "Give me a stadium and I will fill it". An analysis of the marketing management of Stade Français Paris rugby club', *International Journal of Sport Marketing and Sponsorship*, 10(3), 252–62.

—— (2009b) 'Sport participation and consumption and post-modern society: From Apollo to Dionysus?', *Loisir et Société/Society and Leisure*, 32(2), 223–41.

Cova, B. and Cova, V. (2002) 'Tribal marketing: the tribalisation of society and its impact on the conduct of marketing', *European Journal of Marketing*, 36, 5/6, 595–620.

Desbordes, M., Ohl, F. and Tribou, G. (2004) *Marketing du sport* (3rd edn) Paris, Economica.

Holbrook, M., and Hirschman, E. (1982) 'The experiential aspects of consumption: Consumer fantasy, feelings and fun', *Journal of Consumer Research*, 9(2), 132–40.

Morgan, R.M., and Hunt, S.D. (1994) 'The commitment-trust theory of relationship marketing', *Journal of Marketing*, 58 (July), 20–38.

Mullin, B., Hardy, S., and Sutton, W. (2000) *Sport marketing*, Champaign, IL, Human Kinetics.

Seippel, O. (2006) 'The meanings of sport: Fun, health, beauty or community?', *Sport in Society*, 9(1), 51–70.

17

CONSUMER LOYALTY IN SPORT PARTICIPATION SERVICES

Guillaume Bodet

Introduction

Although it is central in the mainstream marketing literature and the sport marketing literature dealing specifically with sport spectatorship, consumer loyalty has probably not received the attention this concept deserves in the field of sport participation organizations. As an illustration, we can notice the interesting and relevant article of Heere and Dickson (2008), who analyzed the nature of the concept of loyalty in sport marketing but only through the lens of sport fanship and spectatorship and only acknowledged in the conclusion of their study that the analysis could also matter to membership organizations. Not only does it apply to sport participation organizations but it also represents a crucial element for the development and the continuity of these organizations. As noticed by Robinson (2006), consumer expectations in sport participation services have been increasing whereas for other authors, such as Bodet (2009) and Seippel (2006) for instance, the nature of these expectations has also changed, creating a growing mismatch between participants' demands and sport organizations' offers. The mismatch created represents a serious threat for these sport organizations from a long-term perspective. Consumer loyalty appears then an almost necessary aim for sport participation organizations to maintain steady financial revenues and ensure a sustainable development.

As the specific sport marketing literature dealing with consumer or member loyalty is limited, it appears necessary to explore the mainstream marketing literature about services and the literature dealing with leisure activities as well to define the nature of the concept and identify its antecedents. The study of these different streams of literature allows the identification of different but complementary antecedents which represent potential levers of action for sport managers. On one hand, the mainstream marketing literature and the limited specific sport marketing literature mainly focus on the nature of the services offered and the way they are consumed and experienced, emphasizing the importance of the concepts of consumer satisfaction, perceived value and perceived service quality. On the other hand, the leisure literature focuses on the link between individuals and their leisure activities and the concepts of involvement and commitment in particular (some mainstream marketing studies have focused on the concept of commitment but in a business-to-business context for the majority of them). The lack of a clear understanding of how loyalty is formed in services in general and sport participation organizations in particular cries out for the association of the various variables identified in order to address the process of consumer loyalty in all its complexity. Specifically, the most recent frameworks tend to praise conceptualizations focusing on a mediating role of psychological commitment between consumer loyalty and its antecedents.

After having defined and presented the managerial importance of consumer loyalty, the chapter considers the different antecedents of the concept identified in the various streams of literature. These are then integrated into more comprehensive frameworks articulated around consumer psychological commitment.

Members' loyalty in sport participation organizations

Historically, consumer loyalty has been conceptualized from a behavioral perspective, using indicators such as repeat purchase, proportion and frequency of purchase over time (Homburg and Giering, 2001). This vision, centered on the behavioral dimension of the concept, was later criticized by authors such as Day (1969) and Dick and Basu (1994), for whom sole behavioral loyalty only represents a spurious loyalty as no attachment is expressed to the brand, the service or the service provider which could make a consumer switch easily to another alternative or competitor. For these authors, an attitudinal dimension should be added to the behavioral dimension to fully understand the phenomenon of consumer loyalty. This bi-dimensional vision integrating both repeated purchase or retention and a positive attitude seems to have reached a consensus among the researchers on the topic (Homburg and Giering, 2001).

The reason why organizations in general and sport participation ones in particular should concentrate their efforts on increasing the loyalty of their consumers or members relies on the fact that it produces many positive organizational consequences. The primary argument relies on the fact that attracting and recruiting new consumers or members costs more than keeping the current ones loyal (Rosenberg and Czepiel, 1984). Furthermore, for Dick and Basu (1994: 99), consumer loyalty "represents an important basis for developing a sustainable competitive advantage . . . that can be realized through marketing efforts." These authors also estimated that motivation to search for information, resistance to counter persuasion and positive word-of-mouth could be identified as consequences of consumer loyalty (Dick and Basu, 1994). Other authors (e.g. Ganesh, Arnold, and Reynolds, 2000; Hallowell, 1996; Iwasaki and Havitz, 2004; Reichheld and Teal, 1996; Jacoby and Chesnut, 1978) have also linked consumer loyalty to steady revenues, profitability, positive reputation, increases in price premiums and decreasing costs. From a sporting perspective, maintaining the number of participants also helps to achieve further social and political objectives such as enhancing citizens' quality of life, developing community involvement and increasing participation rates (Iwasaki and Havitz, 2004). Moreover, from an individual perspective, Iwasaki and Havitz (2004) also noted that loyal participants can achieve personal goals such as improved skills, health, quality of life and self-expression as well as social rewards such as satisfying social relationships, experiencing a sense of belonging and enhancing their social identity. Nevertheless, despite its demonstrated managerial importance, consumer loyalty's formative process is still misunderstood by both academics and practitioners, even if various antecedents of loyalty have been identified. The most important ones are presented in the following section.

The antecedents of consumer loyalty in sport participation

Five main antecedents are identified in the mainstream marketing, sport marketing and leisure literature and are presented as follows: consumer satisfaction, perceived value, perceived service quality, psychological commitment and enduring involvement.

Consumer satisfaction

The first antecedent of consumer loyalty identified in the mainstream marketing literature is consumer satisfaction, which relies on the assumption that consumers satisfied by an offer would stay loyal to it. Many authors have considered the concept of satisfaction as the necessary premise for the retention of consumers (see Henning-Thurau and Klee, 1997 for a review). Consumer satisfaction has been classically defined as a post-choice evaluative judgment concerning specific purchase decisions (Oliver, 1980). This judgment is considered to integrate both cognitive and affective dimensions with a decrease of the affective dimension in the profit of the cognitive dimension over time following the consumption. A distinction is further made about the basis of satisfaction (Bitner and Hubbert, 1994; Olsen and Johnson, 2003). When consumer satisfaction deals with all the previous past experiences and interactions with a specific service or product, it is defined as overall or cumulative satisfaction, whereas when it only concerns a specific encounter or experience (often the most recent one) then it is defined as transaction-specific satisfaction (Bitner and Hubbert, 1994; Olsen and Johnson, 2003).

From an individual level of analysis, many studies found a positive link between consumer satisfaction and repurchase intentions (Henning-Thurau and Klee, 1997), for both overall and transaction-specific types of satisfaction. In the context of sport participation organizations, and most of the time in the health and fitness clubs context, authors such as Bodet (2008), Cronin, Brady and Hult (2000), De Barros and Gonçalves (2009), Ferrand, Robinson and Valette-Florence (2010), Howat, Murray and Crilley (1999), Murray and Howat (2002) and Pedragosa and Correia (2009) also supported this relationship. However, few studies have focused on the link between consumer satisfaction and repurchase behavior, and those which have studied it found this link to be weak or nonexistent (Henning-Thurau and Klee, 1997). In the case of sport participation, Bodet (2008) could not find a positive and significant relationship between both transaction-specific and overall satisfaction and membership renewal. Nevertheless, Ferrand et al. (2010) and Pedragosa and Correia (2009) found a positive and significant link between consumer satisfaction and frequency of participation. These results confirm the importance of taking into account both dimensions of consumer loyalty but also different types of behavioral loyalty as the status of the relationships strongly depends on the measures of the concepts considered.

Besides the broad majority of studies which focused on adult participation, it has been shown that parents' negative attitudes towards the sport service organization and the service provided were significantly correlated with switching behavior in youth participation (Ferreira and Armstrong, 2002). Even if consumer satisfaction has not been systematically identified as a relevant antecedent of consumer loyalty in sport participation organizations, it still represents an important element for managers, for its own sake or for its positive organizational outcomes such as loyalty. Nevertheless, consumer satisfaction is not sufficient as it cannot predict the behavioral dimension of consumer loyalty and repurchase behavior in particular. Other determinants or antecedents of loyalty have to be identified (Oliver, 1999).

Finally, although the marketing literature has essentially focused on consumer satisfaction towards a sport provider, some authors (e.g. Boiché and Sarrazin, 2009; Iwasaki and Havitz, 2004) have focused on the general level of satisfaction towards a sport activity and Boiché and Sarrazin (2009) even found that participants' level of satisfaction within the activity should be taken into consideration to prevent dropout from organized sport.

Consumer perceived value

Following Oliver's (1999) observation regarding the need to find additional antecedents besides satisfaction, Cronin et al. (2000) theoretically and empirically demonstrated the importance of consumer perceived value alongside consumer satisfaction in the explanation of consumer behavioral intentions. Specifically, their model was validated within the participation sport industry. The underlying assumption is that satisfaction can only significantly influence consumer loyalty if the service is perceived to be of value, defined as a ratio between consumer costs and benefits (Zeithaml, 1988). In this context, if the various financial, psychological and social costs are not counterbalanced by the various perceived benefits associated with the sport practice in a specific organization then it is unlikely that consumer satisfaction would become sufficient to drive consumers' behavior towards loyalty. Murray and Howat (2002) also supported the role of consumer perceived value in combination with customer satisfaction in the context of an Australian public sport and leisure center. These authors also identified that a positive perceived value could lead to satisfaction, which in turn would influence consumer future intentions. In line with this perspective, Boiché and Sarrazin (2009) found the value sport participants put on their activity appears to be an antecedent, when it is perceived as low, of dropout behavior from organized sport.

Even if several authors (e.g., Cronin et al., 2000; McDougall and Levesque, 2000; Murray and Howat, 2002) have called for study of both consumer value and satisfaction in the explanation of consumer post-experience intentions and behavior, few studies have dealt with both concepts simultaneously, and none have investigated the specific link between consumer perceived value and the behavioral dimension of loyalty.

Perceived service quality

Besides the question about its measurement (see for instance Ko and Pastore (2004) for a review of the measurements used in the recreation sport industry), the mainstream marketing literature mainly considers service quality to influence consumer loyalty through consumer satisfaction and consumer value. However, some authors have also supported a direct relationship between service quality and consumer loyalty (Cronin et al., 2000). In the sport participation sectors, researchers such as Alexandris, Zahariadis, Tsorbatzoudis and Grouios (2004), Lentell (2000) and Murray and Howat (2002) have mainly focused on the link between consumer perceived service quality and satisfaction, which was often found to be significant but to explain limited amounts of variance.

One of the potential explanations relies on the linearity of the relationship between the two concepts, which was not automatic for Bartikowski and Llosa (2004) and Llosa (1997). These authors considered that some service quality attributes have a linear or proportional contribution to consumer satisfaction (i.e. secondary and key elements) whereas some are performance-related (i.e. basic and plus elements), which means that their contribution to satisfaction will depend on how these elements are perceived to have performed. This framework was used by Bodet (2006) in a health and fitness context and this author confirmed the existence of the four different types of service attributes' contribution to consumer satisfaction.

Nevertheless, few studies have tested the direct link between perceived service quality and consumer loyalty. Among the few, Alexandris, Dimitriadis and Kasiara (2001) looked at the link between perceived service quality and behavioral intentions in fitness clubs and found for instance that service quality dimensions were positively and significantly associated with purchase intentions but that some variations could be observed between the clubs investigated. Specifically, only the tangible dimension of service quality was positively and significantly associated with purchase intentions in all the three clubs surveyed, although the responsiveness dimension was never found to have a significant influence (Alexandris et al., 2001).

In the same vein, Cronin et al. (2000) empirically tested this relationship and found a positive link between perceived service quality and consumer behavioral intentions in several service industries and in participation sport. In relation with youth participation the quality of the service offered by sport organizations and in particular the guidance role of sport instructors have also been shown to have a noticeable influence on children' switching behavior (de Martelaer, van Hoecke, de Knop, van Heddegem and Theeboom, 2002). Therefore, on the basis of these results it seems justified to postulate a direct link between perceived service quality and the attitudinal dimension of loyalty, even if the potential link with the behavioral dimension of the concept has yet to be proven.

Consumer psychological commitment

In their search for understanding the "psychology" behind the development of consumer loyalty, Pritchard, Havitz and Howard (1999) estimated that consumer psychological commitment to service organizations could be seen as an important determinant of consumer loyalty. Based on a conceptualization of consumer psychological commitment relying on resistance to change as its main evidence, the authors empirically found a positive and significant link with loyalty. The authors used a composite measure of loyalty, made up of attitudinal items and a ratio proportion of purchase. This relationship was later tested and supported by Iwasaki and Havitz (2004) in a health and fitness context. Unlike Pritchard et al. (1999), Iwasaki and Havitz (2004) used two behavioral indicators to measure consumers' loyalty, which were frequency of attendance and proportion of participation in their fitness club in comparison with all the hours dedicated to their recreational and social activities per week.

In their conceptualization, both Iwasaki and Havitz (2004) and Pritchard et al. (1999) considered other factors, named commitment's antecedent processes or formative processes, to directly influence resistance to change, the main evidence of psychological commitment, but also to theoretically have a direct influence on consumer loyalty. These antecedent processes were informational, identification and volitional. The informational processes comprise informational complexity, cognitive consistency and confidence, which means that the more individuals hold complex, consistent and trustful information about the sport participation organization, the more they will be committed and loyal to it (Pritchard et al., 1999). Identification processes refer to position involvement,[1] which relates to the link and the consistency between consumers' personal values and self-images and their sport organization preference, from their own point of view but also from a public perspective (Pritchard et al., 1999). According to Pritchard et al. (1999), the more consumers perceive this consistency, and believe that the public perceives it as well, the more they will be committed and loyal to the sport organization.

Last, volitional processes refer to the level of responsibility consumers have in the decision to consume a specific object (Pritchard et al., 1999), and thus to be part of a specific sport participation organization. Pritchard et al. (1999) supported several of the relationships between these commitments' antecedents and loyalty but the results varied depending on the processes and the types of industry involved. As for Iwasaki and Havitz (2004), the relationship between commitments' formative processes and behavioral loyalty towards a recreation agency was not found to be significant. Even if these studies provided mixed results, it seems premature to provide a definitive judgment about the direct influence of consumer informational, identification and volitional processes on loyalty and more empirical results are therefore needed. It therefore seems relevant at this stage to make the managers of sport participation organizations aware of these processes because they seem to play an active role in the loyalty formation process.

For Heere and Dickson (2008), the conceptualization of consumer attitudinal loyalty and commitments is, however, often characterized by confusion and overlap, which may explain why the relationship between the two concepts is frequently validated although the relationship between consumer psychological commitment and behavioral loyalty has not been so often supported. Although developed in the sport spectatorship sector, Heere and Dickson's (2008) critical analysis and definition propositions appear to be useful to apply in sport participation contexts.

Enduring involvement

Moving from the exchange or relationship approaches between a service provider – the sport participation organization – and its consumers – the participants – the leisure literature has widely studied the link between participants and their recreational activities in order to understand their loyalty towards both activity and recreation agencies. Adapting a definition from Rothschild (1984), Havitz and Dimanche (1999: 123) defined the concept of enduring involvement as "an unobservable state of motivation, arousal or interest toward a recreational activity or associated product" which is related to a specific object, activity or situation and which has drive properties. It seems that the researchers studying the concept (e.g. Funk, Ridinger and Moorman, 2004; Kerstetter and Kovich, 1997; Kyle et al., 2007) have reached a consensus over a multidimensional definition of involvement based on the framework developed by Laurent and Kapferer (1985). In this perspective, involvement comprises five facets or dimensions: importance, pleasure, sign, risk probability and risk importance.

The name and the nature of some of the dimensions were further discussed and sometimes modified in the contexts of leisure and sport activities (e.g. Funk et al., 2004; Iwasaki and Havitz, 1998, 2004; McIntyre and Pigram, 1992; Kyle et al., 2007), but these amendments still provide support for a multidimensional vision of involvement. In an extended review, Havitz and Dimanche (1999) identified some of the properties of involvement such as purchase decisions, search behavior and participation patterns, and recreation service promotion, some of which can be considered to be manifestations of loyalty. Moreover, for many authors high and enduring activity involvement levels are considered to be a precondition of consumer loyalty (Park, 1996). Specifically in the context of adult fitness programs, Park (1996) found a positive correlation between activity involvement and attitudinal loyalty profiles. The author then tested the relationship between enduring involvement and different indicators of behavioral loyalty. No significant relationship was found between enduring involvement and the duration of participation (i.e. length of relationship with this specific club), although a significant relationship was found between attitudinal loyalty and both intensity and frequency of participation. On the contrary, Iwasaki and Havitz (2004) could not find a significant direct relationship between consumer enduring involvement and frequency of attendance and proportion of participation although this was in a similar context of investigation. In conclusion, although many authors support the theoretical idea that high enduring involvement is a precondition to consumer loyalty the empirical results do not clearly support a direct relationship between the concepts.

It is, however, worthwhile to note that the nature of the influence of leisure activity and enduring involvement might be closely linked to the type and the number of offers in a specific sport market. If very few sport participation organizations are perceived to offer a certain kind of sport activities in a specific geographical area, it is likely that enduring involvement would play a significant role as practicing such activities would almost systematically be associated with a single service provider. This is probably the case for not-for-profit organizations in low-populated areas and when sport organizations have strongly differentiated positions and provide very different types of offers (e.g. local gym versus upmarket fitness center).

On the contrary, if consumers perceive many alternative offers for the same sport activity, it is likely that the role played by enduring involvement in loyalty would decrease as the pursuit of the sport activity would not depend on a single organization. If consumers decided to leave a specific sport organization they would still be able to maintain their involvement with their sport in another organization. It is nevertheless important to mention that a gap may exist between the consumers' perceptions of the offers available in a specific market and the reality of it as consumers' levels of awareness are extremely heterogeneous and the marketing promotion actions used by sport participation organizations are often limited, particularly for not-for-profit clubs.

Towards a mediating role of consumer psychological commitment

Although many antecedents to consumer loyalty have been identified in the literature, the exact nature of its formation process is still misunderstood. Specifically, many of these antecedents have been found to have direct influences on the attitudinal dimension of loyalty but few have been shown to have a clear direct influence on its behavioral dimension. It therefore appears necessary to analyze simultaneously both dimensions of loyalty to formulate a definitive judgment. Moreover, the previous conceptualization of consumer loyalty and its antecedents did not seem to grasp the dynamic at stake for such psychological processes. For these reasons, Iwasaki and Havitz (1998) proposed a sequential model where the formation of high levels of enduring involvement in an activity influences the development of psychological commitment(s) to various sport and recreation organizations which, in turn, influences both dimensions of loyalty. In this sequence, the authors conceptualized psychological commitment as composed of the commitment's formative factors (i.e. informational, identification and volitional processes) and resistance to change. The overall model was later tested and supported by Iwasaki and Havitz (2004) in a health and fitness context. However, despite a significant relationship, the amount of variance of commitment's formative factors explained by enduring involvement was very weak (i.e. 8 percent), which seems to call for another conceptualization.

Based on the results obtained by Iwasaki and Havitz (2004) and the antecedents of consumer loyalty identified in the marketing literature, Bodet (in press) has proposed a model focusing on the mediating role of consumer psychological commitment. Specifically, the model postulates that consumer satisfaction, perceived value, enduring involvement and the commitment's formative factors (i.e. informational, identification and volitional processes) would influence resistance to change, considered as the main evidence of psychological commitment, which in turn would influence both attitudinal and behavioral loyalty. The model has been empirically tested in a health and fitness context and, even if the direct relationships were found significant when attitudinal loyalty was analyzed, the overall model could not be fully supported (Bodet, in press). Moreover, no significant relationship was found between resistance to change and the different measures of behavioral loyalty which were length of relationship, frequency of participation and repurchase behavior (i.e. membership renewal) (Bodet, in press). Even if not fully satisfactory, these results tend to support the mediating role of consumer psychological commitment in consumer loyalty's formation process in sport participation organizations and call for further improvements and/or replications in different sport participation contexts.

Another parallel route for investigation relies on the underestimated influence of personal and socio-situational factors on the formation process of loyalty. Iwasaki and Havitz (1998) reviewed many personal characteristics which were found or suggested in the literature to have an influence on enduring involvement, such as values or beliefs, attitudes, motivations, needs or goals, initial formation of preference, initial behavioral experiences, competence and skills, intrapersonal constraints and anticipation of personal benefits. Regarding the social-situational factors, Iwasaki and Havitz (1998) theoretically identified for instance social support from significant others, situational incentives, social and cultural norms, interpersonal and cultural constraints and anticipation of social benefits.

In their study, Iwasaki and Havitz (2004) tested the moderating influence of skill and competence, motivation, social support, social norms, satisfaction (with the leisure activity and not the organization) and side bets/sunk costs, and found that skill, motivation, social support and side bets all significantly moderated the effects of enduring involvement on commitment's formative factors. Specifically, when individuals had low skills, low motivation, low social support and low side bets, the relationship was not found significant. These results could potentially explain why in some studies some relationships have been found significant whereas some have not, and highlight the importance of such moderating effects in the full understanding of consumer loyalty in sport participation organizations.

Conclusion

A core element of the relationship marketing approach, consumer loyalty is or should be the primary objective of sport participation organizations for all its organizational, sport and individual positive consequences. Unfortunately the literature dealing specifically with sport participation organizations is not rich enough, in comparison for instance with the sport spectatorship field, to provide a clear understanding of consumer loyalty's formation processes, even if some antecedents have been identified. One explanation for such scarcity may be the fact that the majority of the sport organizations concerned are not-for-profit and show far less consumer orientation than their commercial counterparts. These sport organizations therefore probably need first to realize the importance of consumer loyalty and to put it at the center of their managerial strategies, which would in turn generate an increasing interest from academics and researchers.

This issue of consumer loyalty is increasingly important for sport managers as the demand for sport participation has been changing (e.g. Bodet, 2009; Heino, 2000; Loret, 1995; Seippel, 2006), which forces sport participation organizations to understand these new consumers' expectations and desires before eventually adapting their offers. Historically, not-for-profit sport participation organizations have been mainly focused on the performance side of sport, often because sport managers and board members were former performance-oriented participants, which did not make the service offers well adapted to recreation-oriented participants. The objective of a marketing approach for not-for-profit sport organizations is not necessarily to make them target recreation-oriented and less-committed sport participants, but to make them aware of the plurality of consumers' expectations and that their service offers might not be adjusted to all of them. Based on their identity, culture and organizational objectives, not-for-profit sport participation organizations may want – or not – to target these segments, but if they do so they need to understand that sport involvement is no longer the main driver for consumer loyalty and that, in increasingly competitive markets, they also need to focus on variables such as consumer satisfaction and perceived service quality, perceived value, identification, knowledge and commitment to keep their consumers loyal.

Commercial organizations are traditionally more consumer-oriented and thus more focused on the issue of consumer loyalty and its formation process, but the level of academic knowledge does not seem advanced enough to provide them with accurate answers about how they should practically proceed. For the moment, no consumer model has been able to predict consumer loyalty and it is difficult to determine whether it is due to inaccurate conceptualizations and methodologies or due to unpredictable behavior. Therefore, sport participation managers probably need to accept the fact that, despite their efforts and focus on loyalty's antecedents, some consumers will still switch or defect. The crucial point for managers and academics, then, is to determine how many consumers correspond to this type and to clarify the levels of responsibility for and control of this behavior to determine if all their managerial efforts are worthwhile or not.

Note

1   Position involvement is different from sport and activity enduring involvement, which is analyzed later in this chapter.

References

Alexandris, A., Zahariadis, P., Tsorbatzoudis, C., and Grouios, G. (2004) 'An empirical investigation of the relationships among service quality, customer satisfaction and psychological commitment in a health context', *European Sport Management Quarterly*, 4(1), 36–52.

Alexandris, K., Dimitriadis, N., and Kasiara, A. (2001) 'The behavioral consequences of perceived service quality: An exploratory study in the context of private fitness clubs in Greece', *European Sport Management Quarterly*, 1(4), 280–99.

Bartikowski, B., and Llosa, S. (2004) 'Customer satisfaction measurement: Comparing four methods of attribute categorisations', *The Service Industries Journal*, 24(4), 67–82.

Bitner, M. J., and Hubbert, A. R. (1994) 'Encounter satisfaction versus overall satisfaction versus quality', in R. T. Rust, and R. L. Oliver (eds.), *Service quality: New directions in theory and practice*, Thousand Oaks, CA, Sage, pp. 72–94.

Bodet, G. (2006) 'Investigating customer satisfaction in a health club context by an application of the tetraclass model', *European Sport Management Quarterly*, 6(2), 149–65.

—— (2008) 'Customer satisfaction and loyalty in service: Two concepts, four constructs, several relationships', *Journal of Retailing and Consumer Services*, 15, 156–62.

—— (2009) 'Sport participation and consumption and post-modern society: From Apollo to Dionysus?' *Loisir et Société/Society and Leisure*, 32(2), 223–41.

—— (in press) 'Loyalty in sport participation services: An examination of the mediating role of psychological commitment', *Journal of Sport Management*.

Boiché, J. C. S., and Sarrazin, P. G. (2009) 'Proximal and distal factors associated with dropout versus maintained participation in organized sport', *Journal of Sport Science and Medicine*, 8, 9–16.

Cronin, J. J., Brady, M. K., and Hult, G. T. (2000) 'Assessing the effects of quality, value, and customer satisfaction on consumer behavioral intentions in service environments', *Journal of Retailing*, 76(2), 193–218.

Day, G. S. (1969) 'A two-dimensional concept of brand loyalty', *Journal of Advertising Research*, 9, 29–35.

De Barros, C., and Gonçalves, L. (2009) 'Investigating individual satisfaction in health and fitness training centres', *International Journal of Sport Management and Marketing*, 5(4), 384–95.

de Martelaer, K., van Hoecke, J., de Knop, P., van Heddegem, L., and Theeboom, M. (2002) 'Marketing in organized sport: Participation, expectations and experiences of children', *European Sport Management Quarterly*, 2(2), 113–34.

Dick, A., and Basu, K. (1994) 'Customer loyalty: Toward an integrated conceptual framework', *Journal of the Academy of Marketing Science*, 22, 99–113.

Ferrand, A., Robinson, L., and Valette-Florence, P. (2010) 'The intention-to-repurchase paradox: A case of the health and fitness industry', *Journal of Sport Management*, 24, 83–105.

Ferreira, M., and Armstrong, K. L. (2002) 'An investigation of the relationships between parents' causal attributions of youth soccer dropout, time in soccer organization, affects towards soccer and soccer organization, and post-soccer dropout behaviour', *Sport Management Review*, 5(2), 149–78.

Funk, D. C., Ridinger, L. L., and Moorman, A. M. (2004) 'Exploring origins of involvement: Understanding the relationship between consumer motives and involvement with professional sport teams', *Leisure Sciences*, 26, 35–65.

Ganesh, J., Arnold, M. J., and Reynolds, K. E. (2000) 'Understanding the customer base of service providers: An examination of the differences between switchers and stayers', *Journal of Marketing*, 64, 65–87.

Hallowell, R. (1996) 'The relationships of customer satisfaction, customer loyalty, and profitability: An empirical study', *International Journal of Service Industry Management*, 7(4), 27–42.

Havitz, M. E., and Dimanche, F. (1999) 'Leisure involvement revisited: Drive properties and paradoxes', *Journal of Leisure Research*, 31(2), 122–49.

Heere, B., and Dickson, G. (2008) 'Measuring attitudinal loyalty: Separating the terms of affective commitment and attitudinal loyalty', *Journal of Sport Management*, 22, 227–39.

Heino, R. (2000) 'New sport: What is so punk about snowboarding?', *Journal of Sport and Social Issues*, 24(2), 176–91.

Henning-Thurau, T., and Klee, A. (1997) 'The impact of customer satisfaction and relationship quality on customer retention: A critical reassessment and model development', *Psychology and Marketing*, 14(8), 737–64.

Homburg, C., and Giering, A. (2001) 'Personal characteristics as moderators of the relationship between customer satisfaction and loyalty – an empirical analysis', *Psychology and Marketing*, 18(1), 43–66.

Howat, G., Murray, D., and Crilley, G. (1999) 'The relationships between service problems and perceptions of service quality, satisfaction and behavioral intentions of Australian public sport and leisure centre customers', *Journal of Park and Recreation Administration*, 17(2), 42–64.

Iwasaki, Y., and Havitz, M. (1998) A path analytical model of the relationships between involvement, psychological commitment, and loyalty', *Journal of Leisure Research*, 30, 256–80.

—— (2004) 'Examining the relationship between leisure involvement, psychological commitment and loyalty to a recreation agency', *Journal of Leisure Research*, 36(1), 45–72.

Jacoby, J., and Chesnut, R. (1978) *Brand loyalty measurement and management*. New York, John Wiley and Sons.

Kerstetter, D. L., and Kovich, G. M. (1997) 'The involvement profiles of Division I women's basketball spectators', *Journal of Sport Management*, 11, 234–49.

Ko, Y. J., and Pastore, D. L. (2004) 'Current issues and conceptualizations of service quality in the recreation sport industry', *Sport Marketing Quarterly*, 13, 158–66.

Kyle, G., Absher, J., Norman, W., Hammitt, W., and Jodice, L. (2007) 'A modified involvement scale', *Leisure Studies*, 26, 399–427.

Laurent, G., and Kapferer, J. N. (1985) 'Measuring consumer involvement profiles', *Journal of Marketing Research*, 22, 41–53.

Lentell, R. (2000) 'Untangling the tangibles: "physical evidence" and customer satisfaction in local authority leisure centres', *Managing Leisure*, 5, 1–16.

Llosa, S. (1997) 'L'analyse de la contribution des éléments du service à la satisfaction: Un modèle tétraclasse. [The contribution of service features to satisfaction: a tetraclass model]', *Decisions Marketing*, 10(1), 81–88.

Loret, A. (1995) *Génération glisse* [Sliding generation] (Série Mutations ed.) Paris, Autrement.

McDougall, G. H., and Levesque, T. (2000) 'Customer satisfaction with service: Putting perceived value into the equation', *Journal of Services Marketing*, 14(5), 392–410.

McIntyre, N., and Pigram, J. J. (1992) 'Recreation specialization reexamined: The case of vehicle-based campers', *Leisure Sciences*, 14, 3–15.

Murray, D., and Howat, G. (2002) 'The relationships among service quality, value, satisfaction, and future intentions of customers at an Australian sport and leisure centre', *Sport Management Review*, 5, 25–43.

Oliver, R. L. (1980) 'A cognitive model of the antecedents and consequences of satisfaction decisions', *Journal of Marketing Research*, 17, 460–69.

—— (1999) 'Whence consumer loyalty?', *Journal of Marketing*, 63, 33–44.

Olsen, L. L., and Johnson, M. D. (2003) 'Service equity, satisfaction, and loyalty: From transaction-specific to cumulative evaluation', *Journal of Service Research*, 5, 184–95.

Park, S. H. (1996) 'Relationships between involvement and attitudinal loyalty constructs in adult fitness programs', *Journal of Leisure Research*, 28, 233–50.

Pedragosa, V., and Correia, A. (2009) 'Expectations, satisfaction and loyalty in health and fitness clubs', *International Journal of Sport Management and Marketing*, 5(450), 464.

Pritchard, M. P., Havitz, M. E., and Howard, D. R. (1999) 'Analysing the commitment–loyalty link in the service contexts', *Journal of the Academy of Marketing Science*, 27(3), 333–48.

Reichheld, F. F., and Teal, T. (1996) *The loyalty effect: The hidden force behind growth, profits, and lasting value*. Boston, MA, Harvard Business School Press.

Robinson, L. (2006) 'Customer expectations of sport organizations', *European Sport Management Quarterly*, 6(1), 67–84.

Rosenberg, L. J., and Czepiel, J. A. (1984) 'A marketing approach for customer retention', *Journal of Consumer Marketing*, 1(2), 45–51.

Rothschild, M. L. (1984) 'Perspectives on involvement: Current problems and future directions', in T.C. Kinnear (ed.) *Advances in consumer research*, Provo, Utah, Association for Consumer Research, pp. 216–17.

Seippel, O. (2006) 'The meanings of sport: Fun, health, beauty or community?' *Sport in Society*, 9(1), 51–70.

Zeithaml, V. (1988) 'Consumer perceptions of price, quality and value: A means–end model and synthesis of evidence', *Journal of Marketing*, 52(2), 2–22.

18

RELATIONSHIP MARKETING

From theoretical issues to its application by sport organizations

Alain Ferrand

Introduction

Relationship marketing is a popular topic in the marketing literature. Analysing the early literature, Coote (1994) identified three broad approaches to relationship marketing: the American approach (e.g. Berry, 1983; Jackson, 1985a; Levitt, 1983), the Nordic approach (e.g. Grönroos, 1989, 1990; Grönroos and Gummerson, 1985; Gummerson, 1987) and the Anglo-Australian approach (e.g. Christopher, Payne and Ballantyne, 1991). From these early works until now, thousands of papers and books have dealt with this issue from either a practical or a theoretical point of view. As an illustration, 3,861 references can be counted in the EBSCO database with the subject terms 'relationship + marketing'.

In the sport industry, Bee and Kahle (2006: 102) observed that

> recently, relationship marketing has received considerable attention in practice. Sport organizations are focusing on long-term consumer retention and incorporating a variety of database-management techniques to maintain and enhance customer relationships.

This mainly testifies to customer relationship management, which is the best-known relationship marketing issue. There are other orientations such as collaboration in a network, and sport organizations could share resources with their partners in a joint program. Bühler and Nufer (2009: 3) stressed the fact that 'many sport organizations always knew the value of a deep and good relationship with their stakeholders and practical relationship marketing without being aware of it'. There is therefore a gap between the application of relationship marketing in the sport industry and the related managerial frameworks. According to Tower, Jago and Deery (2006: 167), 'all sport marketing transactions, in fact, involve some type of relationship marketing. In some cases the efforts are explicit. In other cases they are hidden or even unrecognized.'

Despite the growing importance of relationship marketing in the sport industry it has been ignored by the sport marketing literature (Bühler and Nufer, 2009). There are only 17 references in the EBSCO database corresponding to the following subject terms: 'relationship + marketing + sport'. The first book dedicated to this topic was published in 2008 (i.e. Ferrand

and McCarthy, 2008), followed by a second in 2009 (i.e. Bühler and Nufer, 2009). Consequently, there is a gap between the importance of relationship marketing within the sport industry and the literature and academic research investigating it.

This chapter on relationship marketing aims to provide an overview of the development of the relationship marketing approach in the fields of business and sport, and to present, in an innovative way, a framework for implementing relationship marketing. This framework includes network and market-oriented methods and tools that enable sport organizations to design and develop offers that provide greater value to targeted stakeholders.

The chapter is structured as follows. The first section analyses the literature in order to encompass the various conceptions of relationship marketing in the business and sport sectors. A special focus will define the core concept of relationship and then provide an integrated relationship marketing framework. The second section illustrates this framework with the BNL sponsorship strategy related to the 'Internazionali BNL d'Italia' ATP tennis tournament.

Relationship marketing: conception, definition and application to sport

Relationship marketing is generally associated with consumer relationship management (CRM). However, it covers various practices based on different foundations. This section aims to define relationship marketing in relation to the various approaches, specifying the relationship concept and analysing the relationship literature in sport management. An operational framework will be presented in order to facilitate an efficient implementation of relationship marketing by the sport organizations.

Definition of relationship marketing

Relationship marketing has been defined in a variety of ways by different authors. In order to find a way through the maze based on the three approaches (i.e. the American, Nordic and Anglo-Australian approaches) we analysed the definitions which have gained wide acceptance. These definitions are presented in Table 18.1.

The American approach is rooted in both services marketing and business-to-business marketing streams. It focuses on buyer–seller relationships and emphasizes the development of a lifetime relationship with the customer. Jackson (1985a, 1985b) was among the first authors to differentiate transaction marketing from relationship marketing. With a consumer focus, it refers to a long-term customer retention, which is ultimately reflected in repeat purchasing behavior and moving toward certain levels of psychological attachment and relational attitude positions. According to Coote (1994), the Nordic approach is based on the interactive network theory in the context of industrial marketing, services marketing concepts and customer relationship economics. The Anglo-Australian approach emphasizes 'the integration of quality management, service marketing concepts and customer relationships economics' (Christopher et al., 1991: xi).

Berry (1983) focuses on the supplier–customer dyad, although scholars consider multiple stakeholders. Christopher et al. (1991), Morgan and Hunt (1994) and Gummerson (1999) have gone beyond simple supplier–customer interactions or the supplier–customer–competitor triangle to consider marketing relationships as being embedded in a network of multiple relationships. Marketing strategies could then be conceived and implemented based on a stakeholder dyad or multiple stakeholders. Gummerson's (2006: 3) definition of relationship marketing illustrates the shift from a view of relationship marketing based on a one-to-one

Table 18.1 Definitions of relationship marketing

Authors	Definition	Approach	Key words
Berry (1983: 25)	'Relationship marketing is attracting, maintaining and – in multi service organizations – enhancing customer relationships.'	American	Long-term customer retention.
Morgan and Hunt (1994: 22)	'Relationship marketing refers to all marketing activities directed toward establishing, developing, and maintaining successful relationship exchanges.'	American	Relationship development.
Christopher et al. (1991: 5)	The fundamentals of relationship marketing are 'maximising the lifetime value of a customer', the 'concept of focusing action on multiple markets' and that 'it must be cross functional'.	Anglo-Australian	Customer lifetime value, multiple market, cross functional.
Grönroos (1994: 9)	'Relationship marketing aims to identify and establish, maintain and enhance and, where necessary, terminate relationships with customers and other stakeholders, at a profit, so that the objectives of all the parties involved are met; and this is done by mutual exchange and fulfilment of promises.'	Nordic	Relationship development, customers, stakeholders, objectives, mutual exchange.
Gummerson (2006: 3)	'Marketing based on interaction within networks of relationships.'	Nordic	Interaction, networks, relationships.

relationship to a relationship marketing view developing valuable relationships in the network of stakeholders. These relationships occur within groups of stakeholders.

In a multi-stakeholder perspective, relationship marketing refers to an ongoing cooperative behaviour aimed at establishing, developing and maintaining successful relationship exchanges. Little and Marandi (2003: 24) stressed the fact that relationship marketing 'is not advocated in all situations and with all customers; only where it would be profitable for the company and with those customers who wish to engage in such a relationship'. It means that, in some situations, relationship marketing could be inappropriate for some stakeholders. Specifically, Grönroos (2000: 36) defined three types of customer–supplier relationships: the transactional mode (customers are not looking for any contact), the active relational mode and the passive relational mode. The combination of the fundamental differentiating axis (i.e. transactional versus relational) with the stakeholder's axis (i.e. stakeholders dyad versus multiple stakeholders) allows us to define four types of marketing (see Figure 18.1).

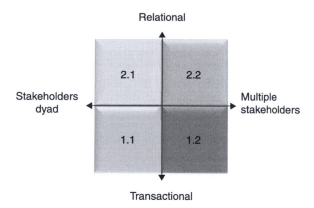

Figure 18.1 Marketing strategies typology

Transactional marketing occurs in a stakeholder dyad (buyer–seller) to achieve a valuable exchange between the two parties involved (quadrant 1.1). Transactions could occur in a network (quadrant 1.2) created by multiple transactions (e.g. provider–organization, organization–customer). Relationship marketing could aim to create a valuable long-term relationship between the buyer and the seller (quadrant 2.1) and a value constellation (Normann and Ramirez, 1993). The partners are co-producing value in the network.

What is a relationship?

The concept of relationship, which lies at the heart of relationship marketing, is quite large and requires definition. The following section outlines the various concepts of relationship which are presented in Table 18.2.

These approaches demonstrate the multidimensionality of the concept of relationship in the fields of business and marketing. In summary, relationships are based on the following characteristics.

- A relationship is a series of interactions between parties with each interaction contributing to the evolution of the relationship.
- A relationship involves reciprocal exchanges between entities that are both active and interdependent (interaction). Hence, this concerns all the stakeholders that interact within the organization's network. Hinde (1979) highlights the mutual dependence of the parties involved and their willingness to act jointly.
- A relationship has an end goal, and this end goal gives purpose to the people and the organizations involved. Marketing actions are finalized and relationships are meaningful and based on arrangements between parts (Sheth and Parvatiyar, 2000).
- Relationships can represent varied realities because they concern different dimensions and they take different forms, thereby procuring a variety of benefits for the participants. Relationships develop through mutually beneficial exchanges (Bhattacharya and Bolton, 2000).
- A relationship is a process-based phenomenon that evolves through a series of interactions and in response to fluctuations in the environment (temporality). The importance of the relationship development during episodes of interaction has been stressed by many authors such as Dwyer et al. (1987), Barnes (2003) and Hakansson and Snehota (1995).

Table 18.2 Definitions of relationship

Author(s), year	Definition	Key words
Hakansson and Snehota (1995)	Relationship is an interaction of mutually committed sides. Relationship develops during a particular time and is a chain sequence of particular actions.	Interdependence, commitment, interactions.
Dwyer, Schurr and Oh (1987)	A mutual dependence is a must, but it is not the only sufficient condition for a relationship to exist. Relationships are defined as long-lasting, dynamic and continuous interactions.	Interdependence, long-lasting, continuous, dynamic interactions.
Barnes (2003)	Relationship is a succession of continuous and long-lasting interactions. However, successful interactions may not necessarily end up with a relationship, as mutual understanding should exist, signifying a special status, valued by both sides.	Long-lasting interactions, mutual understanding, value.
Grönroos (2000: 33)	'A relationship has developed when a customer perceives that a mutual way of thinking exists between customer and supplier or service provider.'	Customer, mutual way of thinking.
Bhattacharya and Bolton (2000: 329)	'A relationship develops between a customer and an organization when there are benefits to both from one or more exchanges.'	Development, benefits, exchanges.
Sheth and Parvatiyar (2000)	Relationships describe arrangements where two or more agencies enter into agreements to work with each other at any point along a continuum from pure transactions to total integration.	Two or more agencies, agreement, total integration.

- Relationships develop in a stakeholders' system which creates a network. We stress the fact that relationship marketing (RM) encompasses dyadic and multiple stakeholder relationships. Sheth and Parvatiyar's (2000) definition encompasses multiple stakeholders. Relationships are not only characterized by the connections and relations between the stakeholders involved but also by the interactions between this system and its larger social environment.
- The existence of a true relationship needs an apparent mutual dependence, meaning that both sides have to act, form and reform relationships (Hinde, 1979).

Relationship marketing in the sport management literature

Originally developed in business, relationship marketing (RM) strategies are increasingly being adopted by sport organizations to implement their actions through their networks of stakeholders. We stressed earlier the gap between the importance of RM in the sport industry and the lack of references on this topic. This attempt to summarize all the literature on relationship marketing in sport has involved some decisions regarding what to include and what to exclude. These decisions have been made based on their impact in the academic literature. This analysis enables the identification of two perspectives: market and network.

Relationship marketing in sport from a market perspective

Most of the studies regarding relationship marketing in sport have focused on customer capture and retention. From the sport customer perspective, McDonald and Stavros (2007) investigated the motivations and future intentions of recently lapsed members (i.e. season ticket holders) of professional sport organizations and the marketing responses of those organizations to the issue of customer retention. Bee and Kahle (2006) examined how and why consumers develop, enter into, and maintain relationships in a sport marketing context.

From the sport organization perspective, Stavros, Pope and Winzar (2008) examined six major Australian sport industries and suggested an empirical advancement of Shani's (1997) framework for relationship marketing implementation (RMI) by sport organizations. Judson, Aurand and Karlovsky (2007) conducted research validating the relationship marketing strategy within higher education, and marketing within intercollegiate athletics. Blatter, Fritschi and Oberhoizer (2000) analysed customer loyalty programmes which are designed to encourage Swiss soccer fans to attend more games and to get season ticket holders to renew their subscriptions. Burton and Howard (2000) provided conceptual tools to better prepare managers for the inevitable recovery process. McDaniel and Moore (2005) described a unique type of RMI, one that can be used prior to product or service production. Lachowetz, McDonald, Sutton, and Clark (2001) applied the work of McDonald and Milne (1997) on customer lifetime value and noted that the National Basketball Association (NBA) utilized relationship marketing strategies to stop the erosion of its consumer base. Kelley, Hoffman and Carter (1999) used Berry and Parasuraman's (1991) three-level process of relationships in examining the impact of a new ice hockey franchise attempting to establish consumer adoption.

Sponsorship is another important issue related to relationship marketing in sport. Lings and Owen (2007) analysed the effect of sponsorship on consumers' purchase intentions and behaviors. Cousens, Babiak and Bradish (2006) provided a framework for assessing inter-organizational relationships between sport organizations and corporate sponsors. Farrelly and Quester (2005) empirically examined the effects of trust and commitment on two critical relationship outcomes, namely economic and non-economic satisfaction.

Relationship marketing in sport from a network perspective

The articles looking at relationship marketing (RM) from a network perspective cover various marketing issues. Relationship marketing acceptance by sport organizations was analyzed by Cousens, Babiak, and Slack (2001), who explored the adoption of a relationship marketing paradigm by the National Basketball Association (NBA) and provided insights into relationship marketing and organizational change for sport managers. Sponsorship in a network perspective was also subject to analysis. Nufer and Bühler (2010) presented a frame-work for relationship marketing with a market and a network focus. They identified and discussed the main factors for successful relationships in the context of sport sponsorship. Olkkonen (2001) discussed the inter-organizational network approach for the development of sponsorship research in Europe. The development of partnership was analyzed by Tower, Jago, and Deery (2006), who identified influences on relationships and determinants of successful and unsuccessful partnerships. Lapio and Speter (2000) used NASCAR stock car racing in the USA as an example of successful relationship marketing strategies to develop partnership with media, sponsors and a more loyal customer base. Territorial marketing related to hosting a mega sport event is another issue. Specifically, O'Brien and Gardiner (2006) investigated how relationship marketing, and networking in particular, was used to create sustainable event impacts in the context of pre-event training for the Sydney 2000 Olympic Games.

The academic literature focuses mainly on market relationships aimed at customer capture and retention. Customers can be fans and spectators, season ticket holders or sponsors. Besides, collaborative relationships in the network is a second important issue and sport organizations' stakeholders, such as sponsors, fans, local authorities and media, are all involved in a triangle of relationships or in a larger network. Surprisingly the internal issue is, however, shaded. Berry's (1983) early work drew attention to the importance of internal marketing as it plays an important role in supporting the external marketing activities. The internal perspective is an important research stream in business (e.g. Ballantyne, 1997; Gummerson, 2006) and an issue in management (e.g. Dunmore, 2002), and this perspective must be considered in sport marketing.

An integrated relationship marketing framework

Relationship marketing relates to a long-term and mutually trusting and committed relationship between the organization and its stakeholders. Research has focused on drawing up a typology of relationships. Morgan and Hunt (1994) outlined ten discrete forms of relationship marketing grouped into four categories: buyers, internal, suppliers and lateral partnerships; Christopher et al. (1991) developed the five markets model (i.e. referral, internal, influence, supplier and employee recruitment); and Gummerson (2006) identified 30 types of relationships in the marketing field (the 30Rs), grouped into market relationships (i.e. suppliers, customers, competitors, other actors in the market) and non-market relationships, which have an indirect impact on market relationships. In sport, Bühler and Nufer (2009) considered the network from various stakeholders' perspectives: sporting organization, fan, sponsor, media, external and external stakeholder.

Developing valuable relationships in three sub-systems

Relationship marketing is complex and complexity is linked to the stakeholders' network and their relationships. Therefore, a relevant marketing framework should be implemented by sport organizations. From this point of view it is important to find a proper balance between the complexity of the theoretical framework and its implementation. Ferrand and McCarthy (2008) developed a framework categorizing the relationship according to three sub-systems: market, network and inside the organization. This categorization encompasses the relationships included in the typologies of Morgan and Hunt (1994), Christopher et al. (1991) and Gummerson (2006), reducing the complexity in order to simplify its implementation. This typology is consistent with the 'how to think, what to do' principle presented in the introduction. According to Ferrand and McCarthy's (2008) framework, sport organizations' relationships with key stakeholders should be developed through market and network-oriented actions that are supported by an internal (organization-based) marketing process involving the creation and exchange of value. This requires a strategy for managing all three sub-sectors – market, network and internal – as illustrated in Figure 18.2.

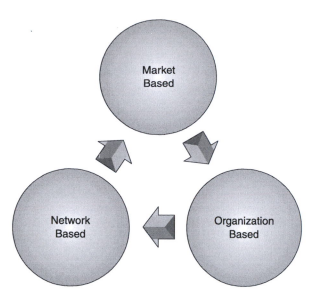

Figure 18.2 The three categories of relationship

Source: Ferrand and McCarthy, 2008

Relationships in the market sub-sector constitute the classical type of relationships between a sport organization and each of its stakeholders. These relationships provide the foundation for commercial and non-profit exchanges and interactions. They are stimulated by competitors and other parties operating in the market. Most sport organizations focus their relationship marketing actions on the market sub-sector. Furthermore, the recruitment of new consumers, users and volunteers often monopolizes efforts and resources to the detriment of the loyalty-building process. Palmer (1994: 573) summarized this strategic issue as follows:

> Successful marketing should focus attention not just on how to gain new customers, but also on how to develop loyalty from those that an organization has previously and expensively gained. It is about seeing a relationship from the customers' perspective and understanding just what they seek in a relationship.

Relationships in the network sub-sector form the platform on which market relationships are based. These relationships focus on stakeholders' alliances, competition and institutional regulations in the sport organization environment. They go much further than the horizontal and unidirectional relationships contained within the notion of a value chain. Normann and Ramirez (1993) referred to the creation of a 'value constellation' and recognized that 'instead of "adding" value one after the other, the partners in the production of an offer create value together through varied types of "co-productive" relationship' (cited in Normann and Ramirez, 1998: 29). Designed in accordance with this idea, collaborative programs involve the co-production of value. When designing this type of offer, it is imperative to ask 'how different actors' activities are to be configured for optimum value creation: who does what, when, where, and with whom?' (Normann and Ramirez, 1998: 53). Hakansson and Snehota (1995) identified three important characteristics: 'activity links', which concern a group of activities on which the partners work together (i.e. marketing, technical and administrative aspects); 'resource ties', which are related to the provision and sharing of technical, human, financial and knowledge-related resources; and 'actor bonds', which are linked to the relationships between the people and stakeholders who work together.

Relationships in the internal sub-sector are intra-organizational. Relationship marketing strategies for the market and network sub-sectors can only be designed and implemented if an organization manages its internal relationships effectively. Managing organizations' internal relationships according to marketing principles has led to the development of internal marketing, which has been defined as

> a relationship development process in which staff autonomy and know-how combine to create and circulate new organizational knowledge that will challenge internal activities which need to be changed to enhance quality in marketplace relationships.
>
> *(Ballantyne, 1997: 44)*

Internal marketing sets the stage for the implementation of marketing actions in the market and network sub-sectors. It is an ongoing process that occurs within organizations that have introduced functional processes that align, motivate and empower employees at all levels. Internal marketing includes recruitment, training, motivation and productivity. Sophisticated marketing relationships with employees, members, fans, and all other stakeholders are essential to maximize productivity in any sport organization. A managerial framework should be theoretically founded and applicable in the field of sport marketing, which is the case of Ferrand and McCarthy's (2008) framework which fits with these criteria.

A three-step process to build valuable relationships

The principles of relationship marketing should be applied step by step. Ferrand and McCarthy (2008) suggest a three-step process as presented in Figure 18.3.

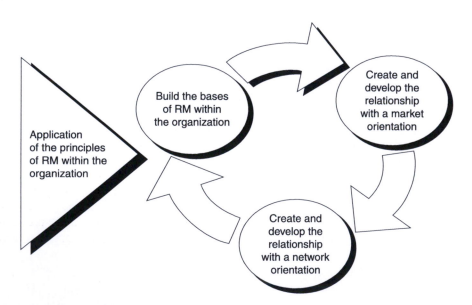

Figure 18.3 The steps in implementing the principles of relationship marketing in a sport organization

Source: Ferrand and McCarthy, 2008

The first step of the method concerns the organization itself, within which the foundations of the marketing action must be built. This essential starting point is often overlooked, resulting in many sport organizations attempting to implement a CRM system without taking into account the fact that this also requires introducing internal changes first. Implementing relationship marketing involves much more than installing the relevant software. It requires modifying relations with stakeholders, as well as changing the behaviour, skills, resources and internal organization of the body. Internal marketing is the major issue allowing management of the resistance to change.

The second step concerns the creation and development of relationships with targeted end-users, which involves a second challenge: that of improving loyalty. Many sport organizations favour offensive marketing, concentrating on recruitment, and neglecting less costly and more effective defensive marketing strategies. The third step is to introduce the changes needed to allow the implementation of a network-oriented relationship marketing approach, as it is more difficult to manage the relationships within a network than to manage a one-on-one relationship. It is only when a sport organization has learned to manage market-based relationships that it will be able to build a collaborative network with its stakeholders.

The procedure must be seen as an iterative process because it is only when a sporting organization has established the foundations of relationship marketing, created a relationship with targeted end-users and built a collaborative network that it will be able to define the improvement objectives for the three phases.

Summary

According to Coote (1995), there are three broad approaches to relationship marketing: the American, Nordic and Anglo-Australian approaches. These approaches are based on different theoretical frameworks but can be encompassed by the combination of two axes corresponding to the transactional versus relational nature of the link and the number of stakeholders concerned. According to this typology, relationship marketing aims to create a valuable long-term relationship between the buyer and the seller (stakeholder dyad) and to create a value constellation (multiple stakeholders) as well. Furthermore, Möller and Halinen (2000) distinguished two basic types of relationship marketing theory; market-oriented and network-oriented.

The analysis of the academic literature related to relationship marketing in sport demonstrates the importance of the market focus to achieve customer and sponsor capture and retention. Besides, the network perspective relates to marketing issues such as relationship marketing adoption, sponsorship, partnership and territorial marketing. However, the internal perspective has been ignored in the sport marketing literature.

Considering the complexity of the existing relationships typologies, we support Ferrand and McCarthy's (2008) relationship marketing framework. It will lead a sport organization to combine its network, market and internal marketing strategies in order to create competitive advantages based on its resources and relationships. The BNL/BNP Paribas sponsorship strategy for the 'Internazionali BNL d'Italia' in the following section illustrates the implementation of relationship marketing in the three internal, network and market sub-systems.

Application of the relationship marketing framework: BNL sponsorship strategy for the 'Internazionali BNL d'Italia'

The first section of this chapter was focused on 'how to think' and this second section will deal with 'what to do'. Specifically, this section illustrates the processes and tools sport organizations can use to improve the constellation value for their stakeholders through relationship marketing. This case study relates to corporate sponsorship with a market, network and internal focus.

The 'Internazionali BNL d'Italia' is one of the nine Masters 1000 tennis events, the second most prestigious ATP event category behind the four Grand Slams. It is part of the WTA (Womens' Tennis Association) season's Top 20 and, in 2010, presented nine of the world's top ten players. The French bank BNP Paribas took control of the Italian bank BNL in 2006 and the following year this bank became the event title sponsor. Since then the event has carried the name of 'Internazionali BNL d'Italia'. With this sponsorship strategy the BNL chose a communication territory which enables it to promote its identity as a large Italian bank recently integrated into BNP Paribas Group, which constitutes a large international bank.

In the tournament press kit, the BNL justified this choice with two main reasons. The 'Internazionali BNL d'Italia' is one of the major annual sporting events in Italy, and one of the most important international events held in Rome. This partnership 'makes it possible for BNL to demonstrate its dynamism by associating its name with an important appointment of the sport which each year involves a large enthusiastic and passionate public. In addition, BNL has always maintained close relationships with Italian sport and its main clubs. BNL has been the Italian National Olympic Committee (CONI) bank for 70 years. In addition, tennis is one of the few sports benefiting from a truly world popularity. Since 1973, tennis has been part of BNP Paribas group's "genetic code". The bank relies on it to raise its awareness, starting from France and then worldwide. In addition to Roland Garros French Tennis Open, the group is today one of the first partners of international tennis: the Davis Cup by BNP Paribas, the Fed Cup by BNP Paribas, BNP Paribas Paris Masters, Monte Carlo Masters Series. BNP Paribas is also associated with thousands of events covering all levels of tennis (i.e. local, family, training and social). Following the acquisition of BNL, Italy became the second domestic market of the BNP Paribas group. It is thus natural that its Italian component became the title sponsor of the most important tennis tournament in the peninsula.'

BNL aims to reinforce the following values: reactivity, creativity, commitment and ambition, which are part of the tennis DNA, and to benefit from the public enthusiasm for tennis to create a competitive advantage on the business to business, business to consumer and recruitment markets. It is also an opportunity to support their corporate social responsibility (CSR) project. The BNP Paribas group intends to fully integrate this event in its strategy to exploit synergies with the other sponsored international events.

BNL sponsorship with a market focus

Customer relationship management constitutes an important objective for BNL. Within the framework of this tournament, the bank aims to capitalize on the interest in this event and tennis in general, to develop an emotional bond with its customers (i.e. individuals and firms). The title sponsor status provides the opportunity of being closely associated with the event. The bank intends to create a common identity. A new logotype was launched for the 2008 tournament which is closely associated with the name of the event: 'Internazionali BNL d'Italia'. BNL benefits from exceptional media exposure during the two-week tournament. As the exclusive sponsor on the tennis court backdrop, the bank logo is visible for 48 per cent of the airtime on television. It runs a traditional activation plan based on TV, radio and poster advertising, posters in the bank's agencies and banners on its website. This plan allows BNL to be the first sponsor quoted, with a 35 per cent unprompted awareness after the first year.

BNL organizes a major promotion and public relations initiative for the event in Foro Italico, the tournament facility, where the bank has a large commercial area in which it carries out promotional events (in partnership with Sony Playstation in particular) and sets up a banking agency. The BNL also manages four 300 square metre private spaces for public relations and a VIP lounge. BNL will welcome nearly 400 customers and prospects each day.

The BNL invited 5,000 people in 2008, of which 78 per cent attended the tournament. It should be stressed that it is the private customers who participated the most with a 90 per cent rate of participation. This strategy aims at customer capture and retention.

Sponsorship with a network focus

The development of a partnership with the event's stakeholders is another important objective for the bank. This strategy is implemented on the basis of a triangular relationship with the Italian Tennis Federation (FIT) and the Italian National Olympic Committee (CONI), via its commercial branch the CONI Servizi SpA. These organizations constitute the primary stakeholders of the tournament. Since 2006, it has been managed as a joint venture between the Italian Tennis Federation (the owner of the tournament) and the CONI Servizi SpA., which is the owner of the Foro Italico facilities. This agreement was supported by the fact that the BNL has been the CONI's bank for 70 years as well as providing banking for the FIT. These relationships are represented by the arrows numbered '1' in Figure 18.4. BNL is part of the BNP Paribas group. Consequently this tournament is fully integrated into the set of events and programs sponsored by the company which include Roland Garros (arrow number 2 in Figure 18.4).

Other essential relationships in this stakeholders' network relate to the ATP and the WTA. We previously stressed that the men's tournament is part of the ATP Masters Series (arrows numbered 3 in Figure 18.4). It is the fourth Masters Series of the season, organized the week after Monte Carlo. It is considered by the top players as a preparation for the French Open in Roland Garros. The women's competition is integrated into the Sony Ericsson WTA Tour (arrows numbered 4 in Figure 18.4). The control of these two organizations creates an

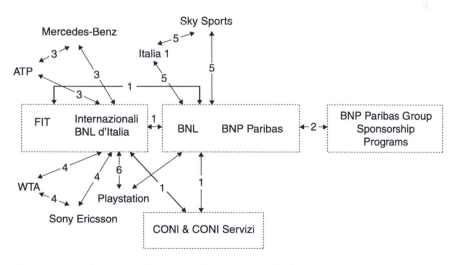

Figure 18.4 Direct and indirect relationships between BNL and Internazionali BNL d'Italia primary stakeholders

indirect relationship with Sony Ericsson WTA, title sponsor and Mercedes-Benz ATP's main partner. The German firm is also a partner of the tournament and provides the official cars.

Contractual agreements with television channels are essential for the mediatization of the event and the promotion of the BNL sponsorship at a national and international level. TV rights are owned by Sky Sports. At a national level, the private channel Italia 1, which belongs to the Mediaset group, is in charge of the production and the diffusion of the tournament (arrows numbered 5 in Figure 18.4). In addition BNL is sponsor of the diffusion of the tournament at the Italian level within the framework of its activation plan. These agreements ensure a world diffusion of the event which exceeds 280 hours of live and delayed coverage. Lastly, BNL has carried out co-marketing actions with event partners such as Sony Playstation, which provided an entertainment system for the promotional and public relations areas (arrow numbered 6 in Figure 18.4).

Figure 18.4 presents a map of the BNL relationships within the tournament. If we consider both contractual and non-contractual relationships, it appears that BNL implements a reticular sponsoring which enables them to develop relationships within the event-driven system (i.e. event rights owner, players, public, media, other sponsors and other sponsored tournaments), the sporting system (i.e. ATP, WTA, FIT and Italian tennis clubs), the territorial system (i.e. local authorities, citizens, business sector, politicians and culture) and extra-territorial (i.e. public opinion, business sector, policies and cultural).

Sponsorship with an internal focus

The BNP Paribas group has one of the largest international networks. It develops its business in more than 85 countries and it employs 162,700 collaborators. Of these, 126,600 are located in Europe (19,900 are in Italy and 64,100 in France), 15,000 in North America and 8,800 in Asia. This company thus operates in a large territory and employs people from different cultures. In this context, the involvement of its employees is an important issue.

The BNP Paribas Group sponsorship is based on tennis 'professionals', 'rising stars', 'amateurs', 'competitions' and 'goodwill tennis', which allows the bank to develop synergies involving its employees worldwide. The internal cohesion of the company is reinforced based on collaborative programs involving the staff with their clients and partners. These actions give substance to the bank's values and its socially and environmentally responsible approach, which is one of the key factors behind their employees' commitment to the group.

Lastly, the sponsorship allows BNL to be active in the recruitment market. The Foro Italico complex also serves as the theatre for EduCare days, where BNL professionals provide training to young people about the bank's different businesses. BNL has centred its sponsorship campaign on the transfer of knowledge and invited forty students from the Aquila Science School, as well as students from a school in Rome which collected the most donations during the Italian Telethon, to take part in the event.

Lessons learned

The sponsorship business is based on the marketing rights management and the collaboration of primary stakeholders, such as the event rights owner, media, sport organizations and main sponsors. Farrelly, Quester and Smolianov (1998), Erickson and Kushner (1999), Chadwick (2002) and Ferrand, Torrigiani and Camps i Povill (2006) demonstrated that sponsorship is based on a network. BNL, in association with the main event stakeholders, implement a relationship marketing strategy in order to create a competitive advantage link to their resources association.

BNP Paribas Group and BNL use this long-term collaborative network to develop actions to ramp up initiatives for both current and prospective customers and internal marketing. This case demonstrates the relevance of the bank's sponsorship strategy, which exploits synergies between and within the three sub-systems: network, market and internal.

It also demonstrates the importance of the construction of collaborative relationships between stakeholders. Peppers and Rogers (2004: 36) have pointed out that the relational dynamic leads to changes in behavior by the parties involved. The process is an iterative one that leads to the establishment of a relationship of trust based on the reliability, durability and integrity of the other party and the belief that one's actions serve the common good, which in turn produces the desired positive effects. This requires a commitment to the relationship that progressively increases the importance of the relationship for both partners.

Conclusion

According to Egan and Harker (2006: 230), 'as a paradigm, relationship marketing is now at the stage of converting theory into tools and guidelines for practice directly relevant to consumer marketing'. Scholars agree on the fact that relationship marketing is based on the notion 'that it is not exchanges per se that are the core of marketing, but that exchanges take place in ongoing relationships between parties in the marketplace – and now also in the virtual marketplace facilitated by the internet' (Grönroos, 2000: 22). Relationships between parties or stakeholders are the core phenomenon; therefore, managing the relationships between the organizations, customers, suppliers and other partners that form a network is a central issue of sport marketing.

This chapter was written according to the 'how to think, what to do' principle. Consequently, a literature review on relationship marketing was performed with a specific focus on sport in order to highlight the various approaches. Relationship marketing is a growing force in the sporting world. As there are no 'one size fits all' solutions in management, the goal of this chapter was to provide a theoretical background as well as a case study to allow the reader to develop an informed and progressive plan to harness the power of the relationship in its many forms in the sporting environment.

References

Ballantyne, D. (1997) 'Internal networks for internal marketing', *Journal of Marketing Management*, 13, (5), 343–66.

Barnes, J.G. (2003) 'Establishing meaningful customer relationships', *Managing Service Quality*, 13 (3), 178–86.

Berry, L.L. (1983) 'Relationship marketing', in L.L. Berry, G.L. Shostack and G.D. Upah (eds.) *Emerging Perspectives on Services Marketing. Proceedings of Services Marketing Conference*, Chicago, American Marketing Association, pp. 25–28.

Berry, L.L. and Parasuraman, A. (1991) *Marketing services – Competing through quality*, New York, Free Press.

Bhattacharya, C.B. and Bolton, R.N. (2000) 'Relationship marketing in mass markets', in J.N. Sheth and A. Parvatiyar (eds.) *Handbook of Relationship Marketing*. Thousand Oaks, CA, Sage Publications Ltd, pp. 327–54.

Bee, C.C. and Kahle, L.R. (2006) 'Relationship marketing in sport: a functional approach', *Sport Marketing Quarterly*, 15, 102–10.

Blatter, P., Fritschi, P. and Oberhoizer, M. (2000) 'Kick-starting soccer', *The McKinsey Quarterly*, 4, 6–8.

Bühler, A. and Nufer, G. (2009) *Relationship Marketing in Sport*, Oxford, Butterworth-Heinemann.

Burton, R. and Howard, D. (2000) 'The NBA's recovery marketing program', *Marketing Management*, Spring, 49–50.

Chadwick, S. (2002) 'The nature of commitment in sport sponsorship relations', *International Journal of Sport Marketing and Sponsorship*, 4(3), 4–14.

Christopher, M., Payne, A. and Ballantyne, D. (1991) *Relationship Marketing: Bringing Quality, Customer Service and Marketing Together*, Oxford, Butterworth-Heinemann.

Coote, L. (1994) 'Implementation of relationship marketing in an accounting practice', in J. N. Sheth and A. Parvatiyar (eds.) *Relationship Marketing: Theory, Methods and Applications*, Atlanta, GA, Emory University.

Cousens, L., Babiak, K. and Slack, T. (2001) 'Adopting a relationship marketing paradigm: The case of the National Basketball Association', *International Journal of Sport Marketing and Sponsorship*, Dec/Jan, 331–55.

Cousens, L., Babiak, K. and Bradish, C.L. (2006) 'Beyond sponsorship: Re-framing corporate–sport relationship', *Sport Management Review*, 9(1), 1–23.

Dunmore, M. (2002) *Inside-out Marketing: How to create an internal marketing strategy*, London, Kogan Page.

Dwyer, F.R., Schurr, P.H. and Oh, S. (1987) 'Developing buyer–seller relationships', *Journal of Marketing*, 51(April), 11–27.

Egan, J. and Harker, M.J. (2006) 'The past, present and future of relationship marketing', *Journal of Marketing Management*, 22(1/2), 215–42.

Erickson, G.S. and Kushner, R.J. (1999), 'Public event networks: an application of marketing theory to sporting events', *European Journal of Marketing*, 33 (3), 348–65.

Farrelly, F. and Quester, P.G. (2005) 'What drives renewal of sponsorship principal/agent relationships?' *Journal of Advertising Research*, December, 353–60.

Farrelly, F., Quester, P. and Smolianov, P. (1998) 'The Australian Cricket Board (ACB): mapping corporate relations', *Corporate Communications: An International Journal*, 3(4), 150–55.

Ferrand, A. and McCarthy, S. (2008) *Marketing the Sport Organizations: Building networks and relationships*, Abingdon, Routledge.

Ferrand, A., Torrigiani, L. and Camps I Povill, A. (2005) *Routledge Handbook of Sport Sponsorship: Successful strategies*, Abingdon, Routledge.

Grönroos, C. (1989) 'Defining marketing: A market-oriented approach', *European Journal of Marketing*, 23(1), 52–60.

—— (1990) *Service Management and Marketing: Managing the moment of truth in service competition*, Lexington, MA, Lexington Books.

—— (1994) 'Quo Vadis, marketing? Toward a relationship marketing paradigm', *Journal of Marketing Management*, 10, 347–60.

—— (2000) *Service Management and Marketing*, Chichester, UK, Wiley.

Grönroos, C. and Gummerson, E. (1985) *Service Marketing – Nordic School Perspectives*. Stockholm, Stockholm University, School of Business, Research Report.

Gummerson, E. (1987) 'The new marketing – developing long-term interactive relationships', *Long Range Planning*, 20(4), 10–20.

—— (1999) *Total Relationship Marketing*, Oxford: Butterworth-Heinemann.

—— (2006) *Total Relationship Marketing* (2nd edn), Oxford, Butterworth-Heinemann.

Hakansson, H. and Snehota, I. (1995) *Developing Relationships in Business Networks*, London, Routledge.

Hinde, R.A. (1979) *Towards Understanding Relationships*, London, Academic Press.

Jackson, B.B. (1985a) *Winning and Keeping Industrial Customers: The dynamics of customer relationships*, Lexington, DC, Hearth.

—— (1985b) 'Build customer relationships that last', *Harvard Business Review*, 63(6), 120–28.

Judson, K.M., Aurand, T.W. and Karlovsky, R.W. (2007) 'Applying relationship marketing principles in the university setting: An adaptation of the exchange relationship typology', *The Marketing Management Journal*, 17(1), 184–97.

Kelley, S.W., Hoffman, K.D. and Carter, S. (1999) 'Franchise relocation and sport introduction: A sport marketing case study of the Carolina Hurricane's fan adoption plan', *Journal of Services Marketing*, 13(6), 469–80.

Lachowetz, T., McDonald, M., Sutton, W. and Clark, J. (2001) 'The National Basketball Association: Application of customer lifetime value', *Sport Marketing Quarterly*, 10(2), 181–84.

Lachowetz, T., McDonald, M., Sutton, W. and Hedrick, D.G. (2003) 'Corporate sales activities and the retention of sponsors in the National Basketball Association (NBA)', *Sport Marketing Quarterly*, 12(1), 18–26.

Lapio, R. and Speter, K.M. (2000) 'NASCAR: A lesson in integrated and relationship marketing', *Sport Marketing Quarterly*, 9(2), 85–95.

Levitt, T. (1983) *The Marketing Imagination*, New York, The Free Press.

Lings, I.N. and Owen, K.M. (2007) 'Buying a sponsor's brand: the role of affective commitment to the sponsored team', *Journal of Marketing Management*, 23(5/6), 483–96.

Little, E. and Marandi, E. (2003) *Relationship Marketing Management*. London, Thomson.

McDaniel, S.W. and Moore, S.B. (2005) 'Pre-production relationship marketing: A lesson from sport marketing', *Journal of Relationship Marketing*, 4(1/2), 73–91.

McDonald, H. and Stavros, C. (2007) 'A defection analysis of lapsed season ticket holders: A consumer and organizational study', *Sport Marketing Quarterly*, 16, 218–29.

McDonald, M.A. and Milne, G.R. (1997) 'A conceptual framework for evaluating marketing relationships in professional sport franchises', *Sport Marketing Quarterly*, 6(2), 27–32.

Möller, K. and Halinen, A. (2000) 'Relationship marketing theory: its roots and direction', *Journal of Marketing Management*, 16, 29–54.

Morgan, R.M. and Hunt, S.D. (1994) 'The commitment-trust theory of relationship marketing', *Journal of Marketing*, 58(July), 20–38.

Normann, R. and Ramirez, R. (1993) 'From value chain to value constellation: designing interactive strategy', *Harvard Business Review*, 71(July/August), 65–77.

—— (1998) *Designing Interactive Strategy: From value chain to value constellation*, Hoboken, John Wiley and Sons.

Nufer, G. and Bühler, A. (2010) 'Establishing and maintaining win-win relationships in the sport sponsorship business', *Journal of Sponsorship*, 3(2), 157–68.

O'Brien, D. and Gardiner, S. (2006) 'Creating sustainable mega-event impact: Networking and relationship development through pre-event training', *Sport Management Review*, 9, 25–47.

Olkkonen, R. (2001) 'Case study: The network approach to international sport sponsorship in the sport industry', *Sport Marketing Quarterly*, 6(2), 9–16.

Palmer, A. (1994) *Principles of Services Marketing*, London, McGraw-Hill.

Peppers, D. and Rogers, M. (2004) *Managing Customer Relationships: A strategic framework*, Hoboken, John Wiley and Sons.

Shani, D. (1997) 'A framework for implementing relationship marketing in the sport industry', *Sport Marketing Quarterly*, 6(2), 9–16.

Sheth, J.N. and Parvatiyar, A. (2000) *The Handbook of Relationship Marketing*, Thousand Oaks, Sage Publications.

Stavros, C., Pope, N.K. and Winzar, H. (2008) 'Relationship marketing in Australian professional sport: An extension of the Shani framework.' *Sport Marketing Quarterly*, 17, 135–45.

Tower, J., Jago, L. and Deery, M. (2006) 'Relationship marketing and partnerships in not-for-profit sport in Australia', *Sport Marketing Quarterly*, 15, 167–80.

19

SPORT SPECTATORS' SEGMENTATION

Guillaume Bodet and Iouri Bernache-Assollant

Introduction

For many observers, the importance of sport in our modern or postmodern societies has significantly increased in people's everyday lives, in terms of either participation or spectatorship, which is characterized by a general trend towards a diversification of sport activities but also of its public. As for sport viewership, times have changed and sport crowds are no longer only composed of local sport fans – individuals who have a special attachment or bond to a team or an athlete – but are now full of consumers looking for extraordinary experiences (Holbrook and Hirschman, 1982), in these re-enchanted sporting arenas that are called "cathedrals of consumption" (Ritzer, 2010). According to Ritzer (2010), individuals are now disenchanted about society and try, through consumption in general and consumption of sporting events in particular, to escape from everyday life and its hyper-rationalized and standardized environments.

If all sport fans are spectators – this statement can even be challenged as being a fan cannot be reduced to attendance – all spectators are not fans, and the terms should not be used interchangeably (Gantz and Wenner, 1995). Sport fans represent a particular type of emotionally committed and strongly identified spectators for whom the issue of the game or the competition is of a high importance, although "sport spectators" designates all viewers of live and mediated sport. Acknowledging this basic distinction is the first step in acknowledging that sport crowds are not homogenous, which has huge implications for sport managers and marketers. Indeed, sport crowds cannot be treated as monolithic; they are composed of numerous individuals who consume sporting events in different manners, to fulfill different goals and needs, which means that they have different expectations (Stewart, Smith, and Nicholson, 2003). Therefore, the satisfaction of these expectations, which should be a priority goal for sport managers both for its own sake and because it represents a powerful trigger for favorable organizational outcomes such as consumer loyalty, can only be achieved by strategically and operationally adjusting the service offer to customers' demands.

From a strategic marketing point of view, it is essential that sport managers identify which kinds of individuals make up their crowds of spectators, who they are, what they look for and how they can accurately be clustered based on common characteristics. This is the purpose of segmentation which is defined as the process of dividing a large, heterogeneous market into more homogeneous groups of people who have similar wants, needs, or demographic profiles, to whom a product may be targeted.

(Mullin, Hardy, and Sutton, 2000: 102)

When different groups are identified, managers have then to decide which segments they should target based on their organization's identity, their organizational capacity and the potential profit each segment could generate, but also on the consistency and the degree of fit between these segments, in terms of both characteristics and expectations.

In the case of sport spectatorship, two different but complementary approaches can be used (Liu, Taylor, and Shibli, 2008). The first one relies on the identification of existing observable groups among the population and explains *a posteriori* why and how they differ (i.e., from the segments to the variables) whereas the second consists in the identification and the use of one or several relevant variables which help managers to cluster the spectator population (i.e., from the variables to the segments). The first approach tends to use observed segments which are close to the reality of a specific situation which is highly relevant for managers of similar sporting events. However, these results can hardly be generalized to other situations and do not always provide a comprehensive analysis of how they differ. On the contrary, the second approach relies on variables that have generally been recognized as relevant in different sporting contexts allowing generalizations and comparisons. Nevertheless, some of these segments can appear artificial or too reductionist and stereotypical. The number of groups (i.e., two, three or four) created from a single variable, especially when psychological, is an example of this shortcoming. Nonetheless, no best approach can be identified as it depends on the use of the segmentation, the characteristics of the sporting contexts and the final use (i.e., knowledge-oriented *versus* practice-oriented).

Observation-driven segments

As mentioned in the introduction of this section, one segmentation approach consists in identifying visible groups based on common patterns. As reality is complex, the first step of the process often consists in identifying extreme cases alongside a continuum, which corresponds to what Stewart et al. (2003) named dualistic approaches. These authors reviewed several studies conducted in a dualistic way (e.g., Bristow and Sebastian, 2001; Ferrand and Pages, 1996; Lewis, 2001; Nash, 2000) and identified that fans had been previously categorized as *old/new, genuine/corporate, traditional/modern, expressive/submissive, irrational/rational, symbolic/civic* and *die-hard/less-loyal*. These kinds of typologies represent a first step to segment but they oversimplify the reality. Specifically, even if extreme cases on a continuum are easy to identify, the differences and then the boundaries between the categories are not so clear-cut.

Another and a more elaborate example of this approach is illustrated by the work of Tapp and Clowes (2002), who distinguished British supporters of English Premier League (EPL) clubs based on matchday activities and behavior – before, during and after the game:

- *Mine's a pint* segment gathers people who come for a drink or two and meet casual acquaintances;
- *Juggling the kids* segment gathers families;
- *Thermos at row D* segment gathers lonely and regular supporters;
- *Season ticket friendlies* segment gathers regular social supporters;

- *Loyal cash and chanters* segment gathers regular and committed supporters;
- *Dads and sons* who are generally loyal and quiet.

Interestingly, Tapp and Clowes (2002) tried to characterize these segments in relation to the consumers' level of attendance and life stage, creating a two–dimension classification. Even if this classification may only describe supporters and not all English Premier League spectators, there is no doubt that it might be relevant for EPL managers as it closely fits the reality. However, the main limitation of such a classification is that it cannot be directly applied to other sporting contexts such as other sports in the same country (e.g., rugby union, cricket) or the same sport but in different countries (e.g., in Spain or Italy). Some may even argue that it may not be applicable to all clubs from the EPL. Finally, the main challenge from a marketing perspective is to estimate the level of differences or commonalities between each segment in terms of socio–demographic characteristics but also in terms of expectations in order to adjust both strategic and mix marketing.

In a similar vein and in relation to English football, Giulianotti (2002) created a classification of football fans based on two dualistic dimensions which relate to the type of identification spectators can express towards a specific club. The *traditional/consumer* dimension reflects the relationship spectators have with their club, ranging from a local and popular cultural identification (*traditional*) to a market-centered type of relationship (*consumer*). The second dimension, the *hot/cool* axis, reflects "the different degrees to which the club is central to the individual's project of self-formation" (Giulianotti, 2002: 31); *hot* forms of loyalty characterizing an intense identification and a strong solidarity with the clubs, and *cool* forms being the contrary. The combination of these two dimensions creates four types of spectators: supporter (*traditional* and *hot*), fan (*consumer* and *hot*), follower (*traditional* and *cool*) and flâneur (*consumer* and *cool*) (Giulianotti, 2002). This framework can be seen as a mixed approach as it is both practically and theoretically driven, relying on spectators' football identities and the types of relationship they have with their club – creating the four profiles of the classification, but also linking them to the specific motivations and the spatial relationships of these spectator identities. As for the previous frameworks, the clear allocation of a spectator to a specific group is not based on clear and specific indicators.

Adopting a similar approach using sport spectator profiles or group identification based on the observation and the interviewing of sport spectators, Bourgeon and Bouchet (2001) identified four spectator profiles.[1] These authors based their framework on the work of Holt (1995), who identified four metaphors of sporting event consumption classified upon two dimensions which are the purpose of action (i.e., hedonistic versus instrumental actions) and the structure of action (i.e., object actions versus interpersonal actions). *Consuming as experience* characterizes the consumers' subjective and emotional reactions; *consuming as integration* refers to how consumers acquire and manipulate objects' meanings and symbols to "enhance the perception that a valued consumption object is a constitutive element of their identity" (Holt, 1995: 6); *consuming as play* refers to how consumers use the consumption object to interact with fellow spectators; *consuming as classification* refers to how consumers use the objects to classify themselves to create and shape their social identity. For Holt (1995), each metaphor can be found in each individual but is expressed at various levels, which does not allow the identification of specific groups or profiles of spectators.

However, this work was further extended by Bourgeon and Bouchet (2001), who created a four-profile model based on spectators' representations and expectations towards sporting events and the values they associate with them. These authors identified the *supporter* profile based on non–existential values such as performance and efficiency and which corresponds to a partisan consumption pattern as supporters essentially look for a victory of the team or athlete they support. The *aesthete* profile is based on existential values such as the beauty of display, the drama and athletes' achievement, and corresponds to a contemplative consumption pattern. The *interactive* profile is based on non–utilitarian values such as entertainment, hedonism and shared emotions and corresponds to a play consumption pattern. Finally, the *opportunist* profile is based on utilitarian values such as interest and image, corresponding to a pragmatic consumption pattern. This last profile is interesting because many researchers have focused on the experiential dimension of sporting events in line with the work of Holbrook and Hirschman (1982) but have omitted the fact that some sport spectators can also consume for instrumental reasons. Even if these *opportunist* individuals rarely represent the majority of spectators they are worthy of note to fully grasp the spectators' heterogeneity. Interestingly, this framework theoretically identifies the relationships (i.e., complementarity, discordance and contradiction) between the profiles which are very useful to inform the targeting strategy, especially when looking at several segments.

Although Bourgeon and Bouchet (2001) partly defined the profiles based on these theoretical semantic relationships, it seems that they might not be as exclusive as theoretically suggested and that, as for Holt (1995), some segments may combine several consumption patterns (Bouchet et al., 2011). Some parallels can be drawn between these profiles and the types of fans (i.e., *super, social, experiential* and *contextual* fans) identified by Richelieu and Pons (2005), but the ways they are theoretically defined and practically measured are significantly different. Specifically, the Richelieu and Pons (2005) fan types were created thanks to a typological analysis using spectators' behavioral characteristics (e.g., attendance, purchase and viewership) and their orientation towards sporting events. In this sense, this approach represents a multidimensional segmentation strategy initially based on theoretical concepts which will be covered later in this chapter. Nevertheless, it is worth noticing that two different segmentation strategies can present outcomes with similarities. This tends to prove the relevance of both approaches.

After reviewing some sport spectator segmentation approaches driven by the observation of sport crowds to identify several relevant segments, the following section deals with the reverse approach, which consists in identifying relevant theoretical variables upon which further segments will be created.

Theory-driven segments

Socio-demographic segmentation

The most used segmentation variables are socio–demographic and describe extrinsic facts about consumers which are then easy to measure, such as their gender, age, income, education and social class (Tapp and Clowes, 2002). Furthermore, it seems relevant to add cultural and ethnic backgrounds to this list because of their influence on consumer behavior.

The gender issue regarding sport spectating has received quite a lot of interest but, as was noticed by Ridinger and Funk (2006), a clear picture is difficult to draw because many of these studies were limited to college students or to a single-gender team as the object. Regarding the long-lasting question of the difference in sport involvement as spectators between men and women, Adams (2003) observed that the proportions of women fans in major North American Leagues were close to those of men (e.g., women represented 49 percent for Major League Soccer, 47 percent for Major League Baseball, 46 percent for National Basketball Association, 43 percent for National Football League, 41 percent for

National Hockey League and 41 percent for NASCAR) but strong variations exist between sport, leagues, levels, countries and cultures which hinder the possibility of a universal answer. Nevertheless, many authors such as Gantz and Wenner (1991), Ridinger and Funk (2006) and Sargent, Zillmann and Weaver (1998) found that differences can be observed between women and men spectators in terms of motives, which strongly supports the use of gender as a segmentation variable.

The second important demographic variable is age, and here mixed results have been found. For instance Thrane (2001) and White and Wilson (1999) found that younger individuals were more likely to attend professional sporting events. The relationship between age and sport spectating, especially with live attendance, may not be as simple and linear as expected, as it can be thought that some age effects will be linked with the income and lifestyle variables.

Among the traditional socio-demographic characteristics, income has been shown to influence sport spectating, especially live attendance. For instance, Thrane (2001) and White and Wilson (1999) found that high-income groups are more likely to attend sporting events than lower income groups. Beyond income, the levels of education and cultural capital have also been found to impact sport spectatorship. White and Wilson (1999) estimated that education was a predictor of sporting event attendance and Mehus (2005) found a negative relationship between education and live attendance although Thrane (2001) found a positive relationship in Norway, a negative relationship in Sweden and no significant relationship in Denmark. These results highlight the importance of this variable but also highlight the variations between cultural and sport contexts. Also for Thrane (2001), the results regarding cultural capital, measured by the cultural events' and activities' frequency of attendance, were not consistent and varied between countries. Following Bourdieu (1978, 1984), these variables were also shown to influence tastes and preferences for some sport. For instance, White and Wilson (1999) and Wilson (2002) found that highly educated and high cultural capital holders tend to dislike "prole" sport such as auto and motorcycle races. The exact nature of the relationship between economic and cultural capital on sporting event attendance is, however, highly dependent on the cultural context, which highlights the importance of these variables to the segmentation of spectators.

Another significant variable in relation to sport spectator segmentation identified in the literature is the concept of ethnic identity or background, which can be extended to other concepts such as national, regional, local or group identity. For Harney (1985) the choice of a specific sporting event carries a strong cultural meaning and allows individuals to identify themselves with a specific group and a particular culture. In this regard, Pons, Laroche, Nyeck and Perreault (2001) found differences in terms of sporting events orientation and consumption patterns among Italian and French Canadians, with French Canadians being more oriented toward ice hockey and Italian Canadians being more oriented toward soccer. Similarly, Armstrong (2002) estimated that race and ethnicity could represent relevant variables to be considered by marketers to better understand sport consumption. On some occasions, and for international events (e.g., Olympic Games, FIFA World Cup) in particular, nationality can also represent an obvious relevant segmentation variable.

Finally, some other variables such as lifestyle, often measured by family status and family size, and which are related to age, can also be used to segment fan spectators (Mullin et al., 2000).

The purpose of this section was not to provide an exhaustive presentation of the analysis of these variables in relation to sport spectating but to highlight the fact that they all represent important elements for consideration to understand the heterogeneity of sport crowds. It also aims to emphasize the fact that, despite being almost universally important, it is almost impossible to establish universal conclusions regarding the influence of these variables as it strongly depends on the sport and the historical, economic and cultural contexts considered. Therefore, they should systematically be taken into consideration.

Psychographic segmentation

As noted by Tapp and Clowes (2002), segmentation profiles often aggregate socio-demographic (or geodemographic) and psychographic variables because the latter capture people's activities, interests and opinions, which allows more subtle segmentations. They can use either one- or multi-dimensional variables. Among the approaches using one-dimensional variables, the concept of team identification has received considerable attention in the field of sport spectatorship and fanship, and will be reviewed within this section. Regarding the multi-dimensional approaches, the majority of the studies have focused on the concept of motivation. The segmentation strategies using both concepts – team identification and motivation – do not appear in opposition but rather complement each other.

One-dimensional psychographic variable: team identification

From the perspective of contemporary social psychology, a sport fan's identity is conceptualized using a social identity framework (Haslam, 2004; Tajfel and Turner, 1986; Turner, Hogg, Oakes, Reicher, and Wetherell, 1987). According to this perspective, social identity refers to the groups with which individuals feel connected, together with the emotional importance and the value they attach to these groups. In this sense, social identity is self-defined and for sport fans is thought of as rooted in the identification with a team. According to Branscombe and Wann (1992: 1017), sport team identification reflects "the extent to which individuals perceive themselves as fans of the team, are involved with the team, are concerned with the team's performance, and view the team as a representation of themselves."

Since the early 1990s, the role of team identification has taken on a central role in the study of sport fans' feelings, thoughts and behaviors (see Wann, 2006 for a complete review) and is perhaps the most used variable in the sport psychology literature on sport fans (Bernache-Assollant, 2010). In regard to sport consumption, research has revealed that team identification is a good predictor of the length of team fanship (Bernache-Assollant, Bouchet and Lacassagne, 2007; Wann and Branscombe, 1993), money spent on the team and related merchandise (Fisher and Wakefield, 1998; Schurr, Wittig, Ruble and Ellen, 1987; Trail, Fink, and Anderson, 2003), actual attendance at games (Murrell and Dietz, 1992; Wakefield, 1995; Wann, Bayens and Driver, 2004), intention to attend the team's future games (Matsuoka, Chelladurai and Harada, 2003; Wakefield, 1995), and time spent following the team on TV or on radio (Fisher, 1998; Melnick and Wann, 2004).

Traditionally, team identification has been examined as a one-dimensional construct. In line with this conception, Wann and Branscombe (1993) developed a single-factor instrument called the Sport Spectator Identification Scale (SSIS). According to Wann and Pierce (2003), this scale has been used successfully in more than 100 studies and in different countries such as the United States (Gayton, Coffin, and Hearns, 1998), Germany (Straub, 1995), Japan (Uemukai, Takenouchi, Okuda, Matsumoto and Yamanaka, 1995), and more recently in England (Jones, 2000), Sweden (Antolovic and Ardby, 2003), Australia (Wann, Dimmock and Grove, 2003), Norway (Melnick and Wann, 2004), Greece (Theodorakis, Vlachopoulos,

Wann, Afthinos and Nassis, 2006), France (Bernache-Assollant, Bouchet and Lacassagne, 2007) and Portugal (Theodorakis, Wann, Carvalho and Sarmento, 2010).

From a segmentation point of view, researchers generally choose to create two categories of spectators using a median split procedure separating the least identified ones – spectators, for whom fanship identity is only a peripheral component of their self-concept – from the highly identified spectators who are extremely identified with their team, which represents a strong component of their identity (Tajfel and Turner, 1986; Wann and Branscombe, 1990). In short, less identified sport spectators have an interest in sporting events and can sometimes demonstrate allegiance to a specific team but they mainly tend to consume mediated sporting spectacles (e.g., TV viewing at home) because they are particularly sensitive to live events' constraints (e.g., ticket prices, uncomfortable settings, bad weather; see Trail, Robinson, Dick and Gillentine, 2003). For highly identified sport spectators the team can become an extension of themselves and lead them to possess a great level of knowledge about their team (Wann et al., 2001). In line with this social identity, they tend to talk and read a lot about their team and to have a direct consumption of sport which implies live attendance and the will to have an impact on their environment. It can be noted that some researchers occasionally choose to create three categories of spectators and fans using for instance a tripartite split (e.g., Wann and Branscombe, 1993), or tertile split procedure (e.g., Hillman et al., 2000). These different methods provide a more subtle and probably less stereotypical description of the reality in comparison with bi-category approaches. However, the choice of three categories still needs to be theoretically justified in comparison with four or five categories for instance.

Although Branscombe and Wann's (1992) definition of team identification has been widely used, recent research in the sport science literature has proposed to rethink this concept in two main ways. First, some authors in the social psychology literature of intergroup behaviors (e.g., Cameron, 2004; Dimmock, Grove and Eklund, 2005; Ellemers, Kortekaas and Ouwerkerk, 1999; Jackson, 2002) follow Tajfel's (1981) original conception of social identification and suggest that social identification with a group is multi-dimensional and contains a cognitive component representing the knowledge of group membership, an affective component representing the emotional significance of the membership, and an evaluative component representing the value of that membership to the self. This new theoretical frame seems interesting to analyze whether specific dimensions of team identification contribute to particular spectators' behaviors and could then be used to create homogeneous groups of spectators. Second, Trail and collaborators (e.g., Kwon, Trail and Anderson, 2005; Robinson and Trail, 2005; Trail et al., 2003) have proposed to study other sources of identification or points of attachment than the team such as specific players, coaches, university, community, sport and specific level of sport to better understand spectators' behaviors. As outlined by these authors, specific sources of identification can be more or less relevant in regard to the types of spectators and to the specific context where sport fanship takes place. For instance, Kwon et al. (2005) found in their study that community identification was considered as inappropriate because the city was small and known to be a university town. Finally, these authors proposed that the different points of attachment could be linked to different types of motivation to attend games and events.

Another psychometric measure of team identification, the Psychological Commitment to Team (PCT) scale (Mahony, Madrigal and Howard, 2000), has been developed in the sport science literature. However, because the SSIS and PCT scales are highly correlated and both predict a number of spectator behaviors (Wann and Pierce, 2003), the PCT scale is not further developed in this section.

Multi-dimensional psychographic variables: motivation and involvement

In the sport spectatorship context, since the seminal work of Sloan (1989), several scientists have paid attention to spectators' motives for watching sport. Although the specific labels given to these motives change according to the particular theory used, it seems widely accepted in the sport science community that at least eight categories of motivation may exist: entertainment (i.e., the desire to be entertained by sporting events), eustress (i.e., the need for positive stress), self-esteem (i.e., the personal enhancement individuals obtain from their team's good performances), group affiliation (i.e., the need to belong to a specific group), escape (i.e., an opportunity to escape personal problems), aesthetic (i.e., enjoying the beauty and grace of sport), economic gains (i.e., benefits offered by activities such as gambling), and family needs (i.e., opportunities to spend time with one's family or spouse).

Researchers have generally classified the relative importance of these different motives using the Sport Fan Motivation Scale (SFMS), a 23-item instrument developed by Wann (1995) and validated by Wann, Schrader and Wilson (1999). From a segmentation point of view, the research that has been done on motives has focused on different theoretical variables. First, some have examined how different demographic characteristics such as gender (Dietz-Uhler, Harrick, End and Jacquemotte, 2000; Fink, Trail and Anderson, 2002; James and Ridinger, 2002; Wann, 1995; Wann, Schrader and Wilson, 1999), race (Bilyeu and Wann, 2002; Wann, Bilyeu, Brennan, Osborn and Gambouras, 1999), age (Pan, Gabert, McGaugh and Branvold, 1997), house income (Wann, 1995), educational level (Wann, 1995, 2002) and family structure (Wann, 1995) are related to sport fan motivation. Others have studied how sport fan motivation is linked to the type of sport attended (individual versus team sport, aggressive versus non-aggressive sport; James and Ridinger, 2002; Wann et al., 1999; Wenner and Gantz, 1989) and to the stadium and home town size and location (Nakazawa, Mahony, Moorman and Hirakawa, 2000; Wann, 1995). Finally, the relationships between team identification and fans' motives have also been studied. For instance, Wann (1995) found that team identification was positively and significantly related to each subscale and particularly to eustress, self-esteem, and entertainment, contrary to the economic and family ones.

As evoked above, Trail and collaborators recently proposed a much more complex view of the identification–motivation link by taking into account different sources of identification or point of attachment (e.g., team, specific players, coaches, university, community, sport and specific level of sport), and other fans' motives than those proposed by the SFMS (i.e., vicarious achievement, acquisition of knowledge, aesthetics, social interaction, drama/eustress, escape, family, physical attractiveness and physical skill). Trail et al. (2003), using the Motivation Scale for Sport Consumption (MSSC; Trail and James, 2001) and the Point of Attachment Index (PAI; Robinson and Trail, 2005), revealed for instance that the aesthetics, acquisition of knowledge, drama and skill motives were linked to the points of attachment of type of sport and level of sport in the US football context. They also demonstrated that the motive of vicarious achievement was linked with attachment to the team, coach, community, and university.

Another multi-dimensional concept widely used in the literature in relation to sport spectatorship is the concept of involvement. Specifically, the Psychological Continuum Model (PCM) developed by Funk and James (2001) aims to distinguish different stages of psychological connection between a spectator and a sporting team, event or athlete based on involvement levels. Adapting a definition from Rothschild (1984), Havitz and Dimanche (1999) defined the concept of enduring involvement as "an unobservable state of motivation, arousal or interest toward a recreational activity or associated product" (p. 123) which presents drive properties. Numerous researchers (e.g., Funk, Ridinger and Moorman, 2004; Kerstetter and

Kovich, 1997; Kyle et al., 2007) have reached a consensus towards a multi-dimensional conceptualization of involvement based on the framework developed by Laurent and Kapferer (1985), which comprised five facets: importance, pleasure, sign, risk probability and risk importance. Some of the dimensions were further developed or modified in the contexts of leisure and sport activities (see for instance Funk et al., 2004; McIntyre and Pigram, 1992; Kyle et al., 2007), but these improvements still support a multi-dimensional vision of the concept, allowing an understanding of different patterns of involvement linked to each facet which is useful for spectator segmentation (Funk et al., 2004). For instance, Kerstetter and Kovich (1997) observed that the rating of the enjoyment facet of involvement varied based on the number of games attended whereas for Funk et al. (2004), spectators' attendance was related to all facets of involvement.

Funk et al. (2004) developed the Team Sport Involvement (TSI) model designed to assess the relationships between 18 antecedents (e.g., entertainment value, family bonding, community pride and drama) and four facets (attraction, self-expression, centrality and risk) of involvement with a professional sport team. The first testing of the model identified several relevant relationships between some facets of involvement and some of their antecedents. This model shows how the concepts of motivation and involvement can be related and how their links can vary among spectators.

Conclusion

The objective of this chapter was to highlight the importance of sport spectators' and fans' segmentation based on homogeneous desires and expectations in adjusting sporting event offers. The different segmentation approaches reviewed demonstrated that there is no "best strategy" as they often depend on the objectives pursued, being more oriented either towards practice or towards theory. Nevertheless, the various approaches identified underline the necessity to combine different types of variables in order to fit as much as possible the reality of specific sport audiences. Specifically, the association of socio-demographic and psychographic variables appears highly relevant. However, even if consumer segmentation represents a strategic step of the marketing approach, academics and practitioners should not forget that it only constitutes a necessary step to understand how sporting event organizations can use the elements of the service experience to market to sport spectators and fans (Greenwell, Fink and Pastore, 2002).

For instance, Greenwell et al. (2002) investigated how the demographic variables age, gender, income and family size, and the psychographic variable of team identification influenced spectators' perceptions of three service elements (the physical facility, the core product and the service personnel) in American minor league ice hockey whereas Bodet and Bernache-Assollant (2009) analyzed the contributions of sport service elements to French ice hockey spectators' level of satisfaction based on their level of team identification. These studies are highly relevant and constitute the logical consequence of segmentation as they allow sport managers to specifically identify which type of offer would attract or satisfy a specific segment and provide useful information to target multiple segments, which in turn would allow sport managers to capture the heterogeneity of sport audiences and crowds.

Note

1 See also Bouchet, Bodet, Bernache-Assollant and Kada (2011) for a description of the framework in English.

References

Adams, R. (2003) 'League works to build diverse crowds', *Sport Business Journal*, 6(8), 19–24.

Antolovic, E., and Ardby, J. (2003) *Mapping out and analyzing athletic support: Identification and underlying motives from a social psychological perspective.* Paper presented at the XIth European Congress of Sport Psychology, Copenhagen, 22–27 July 2003.

Armstrong, K.L. (2002) 'Race and sport consumption motivations: A preliminary investigation of a black consumers' sport motivation scale', *Journal of Sport Behavior*, 25(4), 309–30.

Bernache-Assollant, I. (2010) 'Stratégies de gestion identitaire et supportérisme Ultra: une revue critique selon la perspective de l'identité sociale [Identity management strategies and ultra sport fandom: A critical review based on the tenet of the social identity perspective]', *Sciences et Motricité*, 69, 3–22.

Bernache-Assollant, I., Bouchet, P., and Lacassagne, M.F. (2007) 'Spectators' identification with French sport teams: A French adaptation of the sport spectator identification scale', *Perceptual and Motor Skills*, 104, 83–90.

Bilyeu, J.K., and Wann, D.L. (2002) 'An investigation of racial differences in sport fan motivation', *International Sports Journal*, 6, 93–106.

Bodet, G., and Bernache-Assollant, I. (2009) 'Do fans care about hot dogs? A satisfaction analysis of French ice hockey spectators', *International Journal of Sport Management and Marketing*, 5, 15–37.

Bouchet, P., Bodet, G., Bernache-Assollant, I., and Kada, F. (2011) 'Segmenting sport spectators: Construction and preliminary validation of the sporting event experience search (SEES) scale', *Sport Management Review*, 14, 42–53.

Bourdieu, P. (1978) 'Sport and social class', *Social Science Information*, 17, 819–40.

—— (1984) *Distinction: A social critique of the judgement of taste* (R. Nice Trans.), (8th edn), Cambridge, MA, Harvard University Press.

Bourgeon, D., and Bouchet, P. (2001) 'La recherche d'expériences dans la consommation du spectacle sportif', [Experience seeking in the sporting event consumption], *Revue Européenne de Management du Sport*, 6, 1–47.

Branscombe, N.R., and Wann, D.L. (1992) 'Role of identification with a group, arousal, categorization processes, and self-esteem in sport spectator aggression', *Human Relations*, 45, 1013–33.

Bristow, D., and Sebastian, R. (2001) 'Holy cow! Wait 'til next year! A closer look at the brand loyalty of Chicago Cubs baseball fans', *Journal of Consumer Marketing*, 18(3), 256–75.

Cameron, J.E. (2004) 'A three-factor model of social identity', *Self and Identity*, 3, 239–62.

Dietz-Uhler, B., Harrick, E.A., End, C., and Jacquemotte, L. (2000) 'Sex differences in sport fan behavior and reasons for being a sport fan', *Journal of Sport Behavior*, 23, 219–31.

Dimmock, J.A., Grove, J.R., and Eklund, R.C (2005) 'Re-conceptualizing team identification: New dimensions and their relationship to intergroup bias', *Group Dynamics: Theory, research and practice*, 9, 75–86.

Ellemers, N., Kortekaas, P., and Ouwerkerk, J.W. (1999) 'Self-categorization, commitment to the group and group self-esteem as related but distinct aspects of social identity', *European Journal of Social Psychology*, 29, 371–89.

Ferrand, A., and Pages, M. (1996) 'Football supporter involvement: Explaining football match loyalty', *European Journal of Sport Management*, 3(1), 7–20.

Fink, J.S., Trail, G.T., and Anderson, D.F. (2002) 'An examination of team identification: Which motives are most salient to its existence?', *International Sports Journal*, 6, 195–207.

Fisher, R.J. (1998) 'Group-derived consumption: The role of similarity and attractiveness in identification with favourite sport team', *Advances in Consumer Research*, 25, 283–88.

Fisher, R.J., and Wakefield, K. (1998) 'Factors leading to group identification: A field study of winners and losers', *Psychology and Marketing*, 15, 23–40.

Funk, D.C., and James, J.D. (2001) 'The Psychological Continuum Model (PCM). A conceptual model for understanding an individual's psychological connection to sport', *Sport Management Review*, 4, 119–50.

Funk, D.C., Ridinger, L.L., and Moorman, A.M. (2004) 'Exploring origins of involvement: Understanding the relationship between consumer motives and involvement with professional sport teams', *Leisure Sciences*, 26, 35–65.

Gantz, W., and Wenner, L.A. (1991) 'Men, women, and sport: Audience experiences and effects,' *Journal of Broadcasting and Electronic Media*, 35(2), 233–43.

—— (1995) 'Fanship and the television sport viewing experience', *Sociology of Sport Journal*, 12, 56–74.

Gayton, W.F., Coffin, J.L., and Hearns, J. (1998) 'Further validation of the Sport Spectator Identification Scale', *Perceptual and Motor Skills*, 87, 1137–38.

Giulianotti, R. (2002) 'Supporters, followers, fans, and flâneurs: A taxonomy of spectator identities in football', *Journal of Sport and Social Issues*, 26(1), 25–46.

Greenwell, C.T., Fink, J.S., and Pastore, D.L. (2002) 'Perceptions of the service experience: Using demographic and psychographic variables to identify customer segments', *Sport Marketing Quarterly*, 11, 233–41.

Harney, R.F. (1985) 'Homo ludens and ethnicity', *Polyphony: The Bulletin of the Multicultural History Society of Ontario*, 7(1), 4–12.

Haslam, S.A. (2004) *Psychology in organizations: The social identity approach* (2nd edn), London, Sage.

Havitz, M.E., and Dimanche, F. (1999) 'Leisure involvement revisited: Drive properties and paradoxes', *Journal of Leisure Research*, 31(2), 122–49.

Hillman, C.H., Cuthbert, J.C., Cauraugh, J., Schupp, H.T., Bradley, M.M., and Lang, P.J. (2000) 'Psychophysiological responses of sport fans', *Motivation and Emotion*, 24, 13–28.

Holbrook, M., and Hirschman, E. (1982) 'The experiential aspects of consumption: Consumer fantasy, feelings and fun', *Journal of Consumer Research*, 9(2), 132–40.

Holt, D.B. (1995) 'How consumers consume: A typology of consumption practices', *Journal of Consumer Research*, 22(June), 1–16.

Jackson, J.W. (2002) 'Intergroup attitudes as a function of different dimensions of group identification and perceived intergroup conflict', *Self and Identity*, 1, 11–33.

James, J.D., and Ridinger, L.L. (2002) 'Female and male sport fans: A comparison of sport consumption motives', *Journal of Sport Behavior*, 25, 260–278.

Jones, I. (2000) 'A model of serious leisure identification: the case of football fandom', *Leisure Studies*, 19, 283–98.

Kerstetter, D.L., and Kovich, G.M. (1997) 'The involvement profiles of Division I women's basketball spectators', *Journal of Sport Management*, 11, 234–49.

Kwon, H.H., Trail, G.T., and Anderson, D.F. (2005) 'Are multiple points of attachment necessary to predict cognitive, affective, conative, or behavioral loyalty?' *Sport Management Review*, 8, 255–70.

Kyle, G., Absher, J., Norman, W., Hammitt, W., and Jodice, L. (2007) 'A modified involvement scale', *Leisure Studies*, 26, 399–427.

Laurent, G., and Kapferer, J.N. (1985) 'Measuring consumer involvement profiles', *Journal of Marketing Research*, 22, 41–53.

Lewis, M. (2001) 'Franchise relocation and fan allegiance', *Journal of Sport and Social Issues*, 25(1), 24–31.

Liu, Y.D., Taylor, P., and Shibli, S. (2008) 'Utilizing importance data to identify customer segments for English public sport facilities', *Managing Leisure*, 13(3), 189–206.

Mahony, D.F., Madrigal, R., and Howard, D.R. (2000) 'Using the psychological commitment to team (PCT) scale to segment sport consumers based on loyalty', *Sport Marketing Quarterly*, 9, 15–25.

Matsuoka, H., Chelladurai, P., and Harada, M. (2003) 'Direct and interaction effects of team identification and satisfaction on intention to attend games', *Sport Marketing Quarterly*, 12, 244–53.

McIntyre, N., and Pigram, J. J. (1992) 'Recreation specialization reexamined: The case of vehicle-based campers', *Leisure Sciences*, 14, 3–15.

Mehus, I. (2005) 'Distinction through sport consumption', *International Review for the Sociology of Sport*, 40(3), 321–33.

Melnick, M.J., and Wann, D.L. (2004) 'Sport fandom influences, interests, and behaviors among Norwegian university students', *International Sport Journal*, 8, 1–13.

Mullin, B., Hardy, S., and Sutton, W. (2000) *Sport marketing*. Champaign, IL, Human Kinetics.

Murrell, A.J., and Dietz, B. (1992) 'Fan support of sport teams: The effect of a common group identity', *Journal of Sport and Exercise Psychology*, 14, 28–39.

Nakazawa, M., Mahony, D.F., Moorman, A.M., and Hirakawa, S. (2000) 'The relationship between stadium size and location and spectator characteristics: Implications for marketing strategies', *International Sports Journal*, 4, 9–25.

Nash, R. (2000) 'Contestation in modern English football', *International Review for the Sociology of Sport*, 35(4), 439–52.

Pan, D.W., Gabert, T.E., McGaugh, E.C., and Branvold, S.E. (1997) 'Factors and differential demographic effects on purchases of season tickets for intercollegiate basketball games', *Journal of Sport Behavior*, 20, 447–63.

Pons, F., Laroche, M., Nyeck, S., and Perreault, S. (2001) 'Role of sporting events as ethnoculture's emblems: Impact of acculturation and ethnic identity on consumers' orientation toward sporting events', *Sport Marketing Quarterly*, 10(4), 231–40.

Richelieu, A., and Pons, F. (2005) 'Reconciling managers' strategic vision with fans' expectations', *International Journal of Sport Marketing and Sponsorship*, 6(3), 150–63.

Ridinger, L.L., and Funk, D.C. (2006) 'Looking at gender differences through the lens of sport spectators', *Sport Marketing Quarterly*, 15(3), 155–66.

Ritzer, G. (2010) *Enchanting a disenchanted world: Continuity and change in the cathedrals of consumption* (3rd edn), Thousand Oaks, CA, Pine Forge Press.

Robinson, M., and Trail, G.T. (2005) 'Relationships among spectator gender, motives and points of attachment in selected intercollegiate sport', *Journal of Sport Management*, 19, 58–80.

Rothschild, M.L. (1984) 'Perspectives on involvement: Current problems and future directions', in T.C. Kinnear (ed.) *Advances in consumer research*, Provo, UT, Association for Consumer Research, pp. 216–17.

Sargent, S.L., Zillmann, D., and Weaver, J.B. (1998) 'The gender gap in the enjoyment of televised sport', *Journal of Sport and Social Issues*, 22(1), 46–64.

Schurr, K., Wittig, A., Ruble, V., and Ellen, A. (1987) 'Demographic and personality characteristics associated with persistent, occasional, and non-attendance of university male basketball games by college students', *Journal of Sport Behavior*, 11, 3–17.

Sloan, L.R. (1989) 'The motives of sports fans', in J.J. Goldstein (Ed.) *Sports, games and play: Social and psychological viewpoints* (2nd edn), Hillsdale, NJ, Erlbaum, pp. 175–240.

Stewart, B., Smith, A.C.T., and Nicholson, M. (2003), 'Sport consumer typologies: A critical review', *Sport Marketing Quarterly*, 12(4), 206–16.

Straub, B. (1995) 'Die Messung der Identifikation mit einer Sportmannschaft: Eine deutsche adaptation der "Team Identification Scale" von Wann und Branscombe ['A measure of identification with a sport team: A German adaptation of the "Team Identification Scale" by Wann and Branscombe']. *Psychologie und Sport*, 4, 132–45.

Tajfel, H. (1981) 'The attributes of intergroup behaviour', in H. Tajfel (Ed.), *Human groups and social categories*, Cambridge, Cambridge University Press, pp. 228–53.

Tajfel, H., and Turner, J.C. (1986) 'The social identity of intergroup behavior', in S. Worchel and W.G. Austin (eds.) *Psychology of intergroup relations*, Chicago, IL, Nelson Hall, pp. 7–24.

Tapp, A., and Clowes, J. (2002) 'From "carefree casuals" to "professional wanderers". segmentation possibilities for football supporters', *European Journal of Marketing*, 36(11/12), 1248–69.

Theodorakis, N.D., Vlachopoulos, S.P., Wann, D.L., Afthinos, Y., and Nassis, P. (2006) 'Measuring team identification: Translation and cross-cultural validity of the Greek version of the Sport Spectator Identification Scale', *International Journal of Sport Management*, 7, 506–22.

Theodorakis, N.D., Wann, D.L., Carvalho, M., and Sarmento, J.P. (2010) 'Translation and Initial Validation of the Portuguese Version of the Sport Spectator Identification Scale', *North American Journal of Psychology*, 12, 67–80.

Thrane, C. (2001) 'Sport spectatorship in Scandinavia: A class phenomenon?' *International Review for the Sociology of Sport*, 36, 149–63.

Trail, G.T., and James, J.D. (2001) 'The motivation scale for sport consumption: Assessment of the scale's psychometric properties', *Journal of Sport Behavior*, 24, 108–27.

Trail, G.T., Fink, J.S., and Anderson, D.F. (2003) 'Sport spectator consumption behavior', *Sport Marketing Quarterly*, 12, 8–17.

Trail, G.T., Robinson, M.J., Dick, R.J., and Gillentine, A.J. (2003) 'Motives and points of attachment: Fans versus spectators in intercollegiate athletics', *Sport Marketing Quarterly*, 12, 217–27.

Turner, J.C., Hogg, M., Oakes, P.J., Reicher, S., and Wetherell, M. (1987) *Rediscovering the social group: A self-categorization theory*, Oxford, Basil Blackwell.

Uemukai, K., Takenouchi, T., Okuda, E., Matsumoto, M., and Yamanaka, K. (1995) 'Analysis of the factors affecting spectators' identification with professional football team in Japan', *Journal of Sport Sciences*, 13, 522.

Wakefield, K.L. (1995) 'The pervasive effects of social influence on sporting event attendance', *Journal of Sport and Social Issues*, 19, 335–51.

Wann, D.L. (1995) 'Preliminary validation of the Sport Fan Motivation Scale', *Journal of Sport & Social Issues*, 19, 377–96.

—— (2002) 'Preliminary validation of a measure for assessing identification as a sport fan: The Sport Fandom Questionnaire', *International Journal of Sport Management*, 3, 103–15.

—— (2006) 'Understanding the positive social psychological benefits of sport team identification: The team identification–social psychological health model', *Group Dynamics: Theory, Research and Practice*, 10, 272–96.

Wann, D.L., and Branscombe, N.R. (1990) 'Die-hard and fair-weather fans: Effects of identification on BIRGing and CORFing tendencies', *Journal of Sport and Social Issues*, 14, 103–17.

—— (1993) 'Sport fans: Measuring degree of identification with the team', *International Journal of Sport Psychology*, 24, 1–17.

Wann, D.L., and Pierce, S. (2003) 'Measuring sport team identification and commitment: An empirical comparison of the sport spectator identification scale and the psychological commitment to team scale', *North American Journal of Psychology*, 5, 365–72.

Wann, D.L., Bayens, C., and Driver, A.K. (2004) 'Likelihood of attending a sporting event as a function of ticket scarcity and team identification', *Sport Marketing Quarterly*, 13, 209–15.

Wann, D.L., Bilyeu, J.K., Brennan, K., Osborn, H., and Gambouras, A.F. (1999) 'An exploratory investigation of the relationship between sport fans' motivation and race', *Perceptual and Motor Skills*, 88, 1081–84.

Wann, D.L., Dimmock, J.A., and Grove, J.R. (2003) 'Generalizing the team identification – Psychological health model to a different sport and culture: The case of Australian rules football', *Group Dynamics: Theory, Research, and Practice*, 7, 289–96.

Wann, D.L., Melnick, M., Russell, G., and Pease, D.G. (2001) *Sports fans: The psychology and social impact of spectators*, New York, Routledge.

Wann, D.L., Schrader, M.P., and Wilson, A.M. (1999) 'Sport fan motivation: Questionnaire validation, comparisons by sport, and relationship to athletic motivation', *Journal of Sport Behavior*, 22, 114–39.

Wenner, L.A., and Gantz, W. (1989) 'The audience experience with sports on television', in L.A. Wenner (Ed.) *Media, sports, and society*, Newbury Park, CA, Sage, pp. 241–68.

White, P., and Wilson, B. (1999) 'Distinctions in the stands: An investigation of Bourdieu's "habitus", socioeconomic status and sport spectatorship in Canada', *International Review for the Sociology of Sport*, 34, 245–64.

Wilson, T.C. (2002) 'The paradox of social class and sport involvement: The roles of cultural and economic capital', *International Review for the Sociology of Sport*, 37, 5–16.

20

SPORTING GOODS BRANDS AND RETAIL STORE DRAMATIZATION

Patrick Bouchet

Introduction

The context of in-store shopping has recently been subject to special attention from sporting goods brands' managers who are looking at changing the environment and atmosphere of their stores in order to encourage consumer shopping behaviors. Despite all the advertising investment made to reach the greatest possible numbers of consumers, just over 50 percent of product purchases are decided in retail outlets in most western countries. Similarly, it appears that about 58 percent of purchases in supermarkets are not planned in advance and about 12 percent of products originally provided on shopping lists don't have pre-defined brands.[1] If one adds the percentage of substitution purchases (about 6 percent), the rate of purchase decisions made within a store is about 70 percent to 80 percent (e.g. 70 percent in the USA and 76 percent in France).[2] Such factors as sensory elements, interior design and in-store advertising favor impulsive purchases, change the types of consumer visits, and influence the volume of purchases as well as improving brand loyalty.

Several trends in the research on the store atmosphere (e.g. Baker, 1998; Barrey, Cochoy and Dubuisson-Queillier, 2000; Chebat and Michon, 2003; Donovan and Rossiter, 1982; Michon, Chebat and Turley, 2005) have perfectly highlighted the importance of the functions involved in the development of products to consumers (e.g. packagers, designers, merchandisers), whether it concerns the luxury industry or the hard discount trade. The retail store dramatization is definitely becoming a new trend affecting the forms of shopping as traditional retailing is fiercely challenged by e-commerce. To properly present their products and brands, sporting goods makers tend to prefer developing their own network of thematic stores such as skiing or surfing brands, or developing sales through the internet, as well as staging regular flash promotional sales.

The evolution of commercial spaces that is taking place should also be understood in regards to the changes of functions and status of brands in our societies. Whereas they were originally used to identify and distinguish goods, brands have become symbolic engines which have the function of staging and scripting the universe of goods. This shift of paradigm about the functions of brands is due to various factors including the retail stores' changes of role and physical places. These retail stores have become cultural spectacles displaying places of lifestyles and myths (Goss, 1993). It is therefore logical that retail spaces have been transformed, by a mirror effect, into places of dramatization and expression for brands. This is shown in the West Edmonton Mall in Canada, which is organized in an extraordinary and grandiose manner with numerous thematic stores such as Quiksilver and Lacoste (Andrieu, Badot and Macé, 2004). Commercial places such as entertainment malls and airport or railway station stores invite consumers to different types of visit (e.g. weekend, evening, with family, for fun shopping) and then to purchase less-needed and more spontaneous products and brands.

Behind the retail stores' dramatization that is needed to increase the value of products, sporting goods brands have an obligation to differentiate themselves from the competition. Specifically, sporting goods brands (i.e. manufacturers and retailers) must establish and maintain an intimate relationship with consumers to enable them to appropriate the products and places where they are sold, even if it means altering their original uses or meanings. This trend is leading to an increasing blurring of the distinction between private and commercial space. Therefore, major retailers try to artificially recreate special atmospheres likely to set up close relationships with the consumer, giving the impression that "here is like home." One of the first brands to have explored this concept is Ralph Lauren in the USA in the late 1960s with its shops comprising parts identified by a color, an odor, a musical background, recreating the consumer's home. However, what is in question is the purpose of these new store concepts, whose primary function is no longer only transactional, but serves also to provide a multi-sensory spectacle. By transforming the retail spaces in this way, marketers are using what brands refer to as "places of spectacles", "consumption temples" and "cathedrals of consumption" (Firat and Venkatesh, 1995; Ritzer, 1999).

With the development of TV shopping and online shopping consumers should logically go less and less often into retail stores However, beyond advertising, it appears that a lot of purchases are influenced by the in-store environment. This also applies to those consumers who use shopping lists and those who purchase following their affect and emotions. To this end, aisles and shelves were widened in many supermarkets to encourage consumers to stroll in front of goods with higher profit margins. Conversely, the opposite phenomenon is observed in discount stores: the low-margin items or items in competition with retailers' own brands are piled up in narrower aisles. The differences of aisles and shelf settings are then better understood, as in the case of Decathlon (Oxylane Group), which favors its own sport brands by displaying them at eye level to its consumers, or Intersport, which places value sport brands in specific corners or areas.

If the models of Kotler (1973) and Mehrabian and Russell (1974) take into account internal variables, affective and cognitive, for Bitner (1992) the actions to enhance the store atmosphere have an impact not only on consumer behaviors but also on their emotions and cognitions. The effects of atmosphere on consumers' physical behaviors, their purchases and intentions result in attraction or avoidance behaviors towards the point of sale. In other words, the store atmosphere influences the way people interact with the layout of the retail space. Bellizzi, Crowley and Hasty (1983) showed that consumers were more attracted by warm colors than soft colors. Rieunier and Daucé (2002) presented a research synthesis on the influence of each factor linked to atmosphere on consumers' behavior. For instance, Sibéril (1994) and Yalch and Spangenberg (1993) observed in a clothing store that consumers spent more and made unexpected purchases when they liked the music played.

Consumers were also found to buy more and spend more with classical music than popular music (Ben Dahmane Mouelhi and Touzani, 2003). However, some results also showed that too much sensorial stimulation hinders consumer focus which is unfavorable to purchase

(Rieunier, 2002). Studies (e.g. Bloch, Ridgway and Nelson, 1991; Falk and Campbell, 1997; Kowinski, 1985) seem to converge in considering that the time spent shopping by western consumers comes in third position after their working and domestic activities. Therefore, managers have been increasingly trying to manipulate one or more store internal variables to increase this time and make it more profitable. Attracting new consumers in retail stores also represents a significant objective of such strategies.

The different forms and evolutionary landmarks which have characterized chain store brands since the late 1990s will be presented first. Historically, the brands' differentiation factors within a competitive market mainly relied on classical variables such as price, benefits, quality, types and broadness of range of products, and location, but the intangible dimensions of the service offers were progressively integrated, mainly using consumer imagination and the symbolic and experiential components of consumption (Filser, 2002; Holbrook and Hirschman, 1982). Then, it appears important to understand how the dramatization of sport stores can be implemented and what kind of variables or themes can be used. This discussion first focuses on both structural and architectural aspects and then highlights the innovative aspects of the flagship stores and other concept stores in the current context of sporting goods markets.

The evolution of the sport brands' distribution in a hypercompetitive market

The development of retail spaces has evolved considerably over the past twenty years, hence it is necessary for sport brands to determine their scope of actions to optimize the marketing of entry (i.e. attracting more consumers), the marketing of transformation (e.g. changing visitors into buyers) and the marketing of consumer loyalty.

The transformations of retail sales

The distribution sector is marked by a series of transformations which have forced companies to engage in major reformulations of their strategies: the emergence of world groups, the increased influence of retailers on sales channels, and the emergence of new forms of sales (Filser, 2002). Under pressure from international sport brands which gradually develop downstream strategies of integration, both specialized and generalist distributions of sporting goods have diversified since the late 1980s. This dynamic is not specific to the sport and leisure market, but is part of an evolution of all the distribution forms, of retailer–consumer relationships, and consequently of the modes of sales spaces management. The store chains are not only the place of encounter between the consumer and the products, but have also become objects of attraction, retention and consumer loyalty. The distribution sector is now characterized by a wide variety of formats: cash and carry, variety stores, franchises, hard-discount, supermarkets, hypermarkets, grocers, traditional stores, department stores, specialist department stores and factory outlets (Filser, Des Garets and Paché, 2001). The current number of retail forms involves the emergence of a heterogeneous range of sale areas, each with its own specific method of management. Some innovative concepts of stores have appeared all over the world. Most of the time, they present original layouts (i.e. interior or external) like the Art Deco surf shop of the brand Ron Jon in Cocoa Beach (Florida), as well as new commercial positioning like the surf shop concept of Quiksilver dedicated to the board-riding culture in Anglet (France).

Apart from the forms of distribution which have the ability to control the performances of each category of products, the store merchandising is often treated in a totally different way as it is more than the addition of the merchandising of all the product categories. For this reason, more and more generalist and clothing store chains are opening spaces and shops dedicated to international sporting goods brands. We can also observe the creation of specific sport universes and areas in already established stores and the development of their own sport brands by retail store chains such as Walmart with its brand Starter, developed in collaboration with Nike. In this new commercial environment, international sport brands are now forced to deal simultaneously with the specialized and generalist distribution channels. Indeed, mass-market retailing remains the principal vector of sales, even if all models of the same brand cannot be displayed; it determines pricing policies and is becoming more and more a direct competitor because of the development of the store brands. To compete with the store chains on their own ground, international sporting goods brands have chosen to develop their own networks of stores in order to better defend their products and also to make their consumers live various brand experiences (e.g. Dorotennis, Oxbow and Columbia). Others reinforce their distribution network, such as Billabong which in 2008 acquired one of its partners in the United States, the chain Quiet Flight based on the east coast and including 13 points of sale.

The development of the design and layout and the valorization of traditional retailing are due to the increasing competition to attract new consumers who are subject to multiple stimulations from retailing environments. For instance, some shopping malls have become huge leisure parks or entertainment centers, where it is now common to find merry-go-rounds, playgrounds or mini golf courses, such as in Sawgrass Mills in Fort Lauderdale in the USA or in the West Edmonton Mall in Canada. The development of outlets and malls is strongly related to the consumers' desire to be distracted and entertained, which leads stores to imagine thematic environments which make them dream (Ritzer, 1999). These new thematic environments promote all kinds of sensory stimulations which are supposed to have direct effects on the size of the consumer shopping basket in both the medium and long term. In shopping for fun, which considers the frequenting of a store as a regular cultural activity, the design of commercial centers must have the function to re-enchant the shopping experience that was perceived as boring and repetitive. Among all the major criteria to take into account in building a sales area, elements such as the location, the shop fronts and windows, and the suitability of the products, as well as the competence and the friendliness of its shop assistants appear important (El Aouni, 2006). As for manufacturer brands, these elements shape the consumers' images of a store and store chains. Depending on consumer tastes and shopping motives, it is easy to determine if a shop or store is adopted or avoided. This is illustrated, for example, by sport store chains such as Made in Sport and Sport Leader (two European chains) which are very popular among young people whereas they are avoided by adults and seniors. Similarly, we can understand why the small specialized downtown or corner shops such as cycles, racquet sports or jogging stores are frequented the most by adults and seniors rather than young people.

The sale space's management depends on the physical and technical features of the point of sale (e.g. surface, profit margins, product ranges, price and turnover), on the specific stores' role in relation to consumer behavior (e.g. convenience, comparison and decision stores), and on the characteristics of each family or category of products (Filser et al., 2001). However, its purpose remains to satisfy two basic functions which are the logistic function – to make sure that the consumer has access to the product – and the commercial function – to facilitate the transactional exchange. A third important function should now be added: the recreational or entertainment function which makes sure the store represents a source of hedonic gratification (Babin, Darden and Griffin, 1994).

Valuing stores for competitive advantage

However, this evolution of the retail environment does not solely explain the cases of store valorization implemented by international sporting good brands, and the development of their own network of stores and store chains. The observable changes in sporting goods distribution are also explained by an increasingly fierce competition they are facing from store chains. According to its location and its abilities, a consumer wishing to buy a sporting good has the opportunity to go to many different places, physically or virtually. Basically, the role of a point of sale has changed and the stores have become participating agents of sport brands communication (Kozinets et al., 2002). It now has a direct influence on consumer behavior. This explains why the specialized store chains in the distribution of sporting goods have developed more and more positioning and image strategies aimed at creating a strong distinction from their competitors. In this context, the management methods of the points of sale appear at the intersection of two components: the functional component related to the commercial relation on one hand, and the sensory and entertainment component which transforms the need to buy in a visit and a relaxing moment on the other hand.

Regarding the recreational and entertainment function, the implementation of a store dramatization is often the basis of a point of sale's identity. Firat and Venkatesh (1995) used the terms "Disneyfication" and "thematisation" to describe the intense development of the discursive spaces which are the shopping malls. However, as this dramatization accelerates the ageing process of these stores, the frequency of renewal of these themes, layouts and design has also been accelerated (Daucé, 2000). The trend towards the dramatization of sporting goods' specialized sale spaces is founded on a will to enhance the products and the stores with an obvious aim to influence consumer choices, frequency of visit, purchase and loyalty (Bouchet and El Aouni, 2004). Several studies have attempted to model this trend by either focusing on a specific dimension (e.g. Chebat and Michon, 2003; Rémy, 2002; Trottier, 2000) or synthesizing the basis of a dramatized offer (El Aouni, 2006). From these studies, we can identify two distinct strategies in the market of sporting goods. In both cases, we are dealing with a form of sale space "re-enchantment" which aims to create a particular atmosphere which in turn can positively influence consumer behavior.

The first strategy follows in its design and its operation the strategies implemented by recreation and leisure parks, whereas the second one relies on the play and hedonic component (Holbrook and Hirschman, 1982; Holt, 1995) to enhance the store's attractiveness. That was the original purpose of the concept store "Village La Forme," invented by the store chain Decathlon during the 1990s and implemented in several French cities.[3] This concept-store relies on the gathering within the same area (i.e. the village) of a Decathlon store, several leisure products' partner stores, several commercial sport participation providers (e.g. fitness, diving and golf) and outdoor activities areas. Decathlon has, however, progressively abandoned this concept store, which was not cost-effective because of the important costs of labor and maintenance of the playground areas. Since then, this store chain has changed its strategy. In its store in Mulhouse (France) for example, Decathlon contributed to the construction of a water ski facility adjacent to the store to offer a sport activity to the inhabitants of the region. Now managed by a commercial partner, this sport facility enhances the store chain image, makes profitable the costs of maintenance and operation, and increases the consumer traffic near its point of sale.

In a socio-economic competitive and globalized context, specialized store chains as international sport brands are involved in the optimization process of supplier costs, transport and storage costs and human resources costs, as well as other costs which impact their strategies.

The comparison between different types of store chains such as Citadium (France) and Starter (USA), for example, shows a significant profitability difference in relation to the floor surface. Ultimately, the profitability targets and the store design and layout are heavily dependent on the field of activity and participate in the differentiation of sporting goods brands' strategic positioning. These strategies often rely on the control of the front-side elements (e.g. decor and staff) in a commercial context as well as non-commercial context (e.g. certification and label), such as the shop "Mountain Equipment Co-op" (MEC) built in 2003, in Montreal (Canada). This ecological building uses geothermal energy and is 65 percent more efficient than a traditional store of a comparable size. In the field of eco-design, the Timberland brand is also at the forefront with the openings of stores using recycled furniture and wood panels and in which some shoes are made of ecological constituents. In these examples, these store elements do not directly aim to influence in-store consumer behavior but participate in the creation of a strong environmentally friendly image for the brands.

Although many marketing experts and researchers agree that the new stores aim to produce an "internal differentiation" through a better staging of goods and services, special attention is also given to the creation of pleasant shopping environments and atmospheres likely to be associated with store chains. This is the case with Quiksilver's Boardriders Clubs, relying on the concepts of "into-store shops" such as Quiksvilles and Roxyvilles (for women), which allow the brand to implement its marketing methods and strengthen its identity by providing advertising into the sale space of its independent distributors. The construction of a new retail space no longer relies on simple intuition and results from in-depth exchanges with the sector's practitioners. Beyond the main sensory components, the relational and transactional in-store elements positively influence the consumers' affective, cognitive and physiological reactions. Despite this shift in the distribution of sporting goods, it should not be forgotten that consumers do not have access to the same type of shops because of their geographical location and it would be naive to believe that outlets are homogeneous around the world. Similarly, not all consumers are subject, in their daily lives or during their holidays, to the same influences from sport brands' strategies. For example, it is possible to observe an important difference between sporting goods retailers in North America and in Europe. For instance, the French leader of sport store chains, the Oxylane Group, was unable to export its selling format to North America although it has been successful in many European countries, Russia and China.

North American sporting goods distribution is structured differently because of the sport leagues and franchises system (e.g. NHL, NBA, MLB and NFL), meaning that all merchandised products (e.g. jerseys, shorts, caps) are sold at the same prices within independent stores and store chains. Another specificity is perhaps the presence of manufacturer brands' stores; a trend that is now increasingly noticeable in Europe. Finally, three groups dominate sporting goods distribution and have a huge diversity of store chains spread throughout the continent (and beyond): the Forzani Group, the Foot Locker Group Inc. and Sport Authority. The Foot Locker Group Inc. had, in 2005, nearly 4,000 stores (Foot Locker, 1428; Footaction, 349; Lady Foot Locker, 567; Kids Foot Locker, 346; Foot Locker International, 707; Champs Sport, 570). The Forzani Group has a variety of specific stores (nearly 400 franchises in 2006) as SportChek, SportMart Coats Mountain Sport, Sport Experts, National Sport, Econosport, Nevada Bob's Golf, RnR, Atmosphere, Gen-X, North American Intersport (the only similarity with Europe). The Sport Authority group is one of the largest American retailers, with nearly 400 stores in its name. Unlike most sport store chains, one of its features is to have many own brands: Alpine Design (clothing and accessories for outdoor sport), Aspire (women's sportwear), Golf Day (golf accessories), Tour Collection (clothing and golf accessories), Estero (hardware and accessories for football), Parkside (trampolines and outdoor games) and Bodyfit by Sport Authority (fitness accessories).

In Europe, and in France in particular, the sporting goods market is represented by 75 percent specialists (47 percent are integrated, 24 percent are associated, and 4 percent are single-brand and independent) and 25 percent non-specialists. As an example, the cycles market accounts for nearly 16 percent of the total sales of sporting goods in France. Within this specific sector, 66 percent of the share is due to specialized (e.g. Bouticycle, Culture Bike, Mondovélo and Véloland) and multisport (e.g. Oxylane Group, Intersport, GO Sport and Sport 2000) sport store chains. The rest of the share is split between independents (22.2 percent) and generalist megastores (11.8 percent). Another particular aspect, in the world of specialized and generalist sport store chains in France, is the development of brands owned by large store chains, but whose name is different. For instance Decathlon, which is present across Europe, distributes its own brands such as Tribord (water sport), Quechua (outdoor and hiking activities), B'Twin cycle (cycling) and Kipsta (team sport). All products bearing the names of these brands are exclusively sold in Decathlon's stores.

After having presented the differences in terms of retail store functions and the specificities of distribution networks, the next section focuses on the architectural dimensions of the sport store chains.

The diversity of sport store chains' architectural styles

In response to the saturation of the specialized distribution market, we can observe a trend towards the improvement of existing sale spaces, their renovations and their reinvention. In an intense competitive sector, one's success produces others' failures, and lacks of perceived image or quality are quickly punished. In this context, the mixing of architectural styles responds to a need for fashion and lifestyle associated with a search for aesthetic references. Prinz (2005) identifies ten architectural styles of stores which can be applied to the sporting goods market. However, many of these styles can be used simultaneously by store chains according to their points of reference and to the main role of the sales space.

The traditional style

This type of development is the expression of an era and integrates into a patrimonial logic. Stores are designed as urban markers and faces of the streets. Their architecture and their decor are then a testimony of the past. They are frequented by an accustomed clientele which has its guides and its brands. A comparative study of sporting goods stores in the area of Dijon (France) has shown that "traditional stores" have managed their sale space very heterogeneously but the majority of them considered it a secondary marketing option (Bouchet, 2005). This trend seems to be mainly due to the specificity of the products, often targeting segments with relatively specific and seasonal needs. Several formats of layout can characterize these stores based on the products sold (e.g. running shoes, sport equipments and apparel), the status of the store chains (i.e. independent or franchised retailers) and on the store itself.

The new baroque style

In a world that has lost its mysteries, the new baroque is a ritual and relational expression (Prinz, 2005). This style has been retrieved from the architecture of eighteenth-century baroque art by contemporary architects and designers. However, some retailers have stopped using this style because it is too much attached to fashion or without any notable developments. This style is motivated by the search for new symbolic objects and new commercial shapes. The clientele of this type of point of sale look for emotions and exotic and aesthetic landmarks. As for sporting goods brands, Puma installed in 2010 in New York a shipping container sport store with an interior converted into a soccer shop and with a soccer pitch nearby. This red container gave Puma a new baroque, urban, port or traveler identity.

The rational style

Based on a marketing and merchandising approach linked to a rational, functional, ergonomic and efficient presentation of the products, this style is the result of a process of standardization, normalization and efficiency, and relies more on the valorization of the products than the decor and the settings. In this type of store, the organization, the number of references and their hierarchy are more important than the general atmosphere. The loyal consumers who frequent these stores often find inside their roots, culture and myths. As examples, we can cite chains such as Hema in Amsterdam, Gap, Levis' Store or Dockers in the USA. In the French market, the sporting goods stores chain Au Vieux Campeur fits into this architectural style that focuses on products for consumers who are generally experts in mountain sport.

The classical style

This kind of store can be classical either by the use of classical codes and styles from a past period or by the use of a contemporary style. With the classical style, quality, comfort and design are predominant with a meticulous choice of materials, lighting and furniture. This is the world of good taste and chic. A few examples illustrate perfectly this style of stores: Hermès, Chanel, Dior, Lanvin and Louis Vuitton. The consumers of these store chains are deemed to be difficult and demanding. In the sporting goods market, some brands have used this style in some of their stores, such as Ralph Lauren with locations in the most prestigious places like Madison Avenue in New York, Bond Street in London and La Madeleine in Paris. Ralph Lauren is a very American brand that has its roots in old Europe. For aristocratic and social elites, choosing the brand is choosing classical and immutable values. Nowadays, Ralph Lauren, in particular in the sportwear market, is radically opposed in terms of values to brands such as Gotcha, another sportwear brand (Hetzel, 2002).

The thematic style

The thematic style is inspired by the great success of store chains such as The Nature Company. This style brings together several types of products around a theme or a value. With this thematic style, the store is closer to a "ready to live" philosophy that generates an atmosphere, an imaginary and a lifestyle. The consumers of these outlets are very flexible, changeable, always looking for novelty and innovation, unexpected and exotic. In the sporting goods market, many store chains have adopted this architectural style partly because of their outdoor positioning. It offers a multitude of opportunities for interior designs with a "natural" touch. International brands positioned in mountain sport like Patagonia, in surfing sport like Rip Curl and in rugby with Canterbury or Ruckfield are trying to capitalize on this trend in their own distribution network.

The show style

The show or spectacle style used by some megastores is very close to the dramatization used in theatrical or cinema productions. They evoke worlds and atmospheres where the decor is of considerable importance and provides a strong scenic dimension. Consumers are primarily young, changing, moving, ephemeral; people who compare and travel a lot. As examples, we can cite stores like Original Levis in London, Morgan Puett or Virgin in New York, Caesar's World Retail in Las Vegas and Nike Town in Europe and the USA. The Adidas Originals store opened in 2006 in the Champs-Elysées (Paris), with its space dedicated to customized shoes, is also a very good example of the show style. Another emblem of the show style is the shop Citadium (a contraction of city and stadium), a concept invented in 2000 in Paris, which mixes sport and fashion embedded in urban cultures such as skateboarding and hip-hop practices.

The fun shopping style

The fun shopping style, also called "retailtainment," which is a term used to describe retail marketing as entertainment (Ritzer, 1999), is a trend that is already well known in the USA. As examples, large stores can offer nutrition advice and patisserie lessons, installations by artists, radio broadcasts, or food and wine tastings. In these places, everything is done to pleasantly surprise consumers. These stores are primarily places to live experiences and to stroll. They are places where people meet and where the emotional dimension is predominant over the purchase. In the sporting goods market, we can cite the case of store chains that have chosen to open huge areas dedicated to sport practices, such as the megastore Globetrotter (7,000 square meters) in Cologne (Germany). This is a point of sale where consumers can test a kayak in a large indoor swimming pool and compare scuba diving equipment at four meters deep. Three brands (Columbia, Jack Wolfskin and The North Face) are gathered in an area of 1,000 square meters and 20,000 articles are devoted to outdoor products on four floors.

The trendy style

With this style, shops are impregnated with a fashion spirit. They are unique stores which innovate and which make people talk about them through the fame and the personality of their creators (i.e. stylists or designers). These stores reveal new needs and they make people dream. Consumers of these places are experts and fashion connoisseurs. The store chain Abercrombie and Fitch is a very good example of this trendy style. The musical background is carefully chosen and allows the store chain to highlight certain lifestyles and community and self-fulfillment values as elements to seduce consumers. In the sport market, this type of trendy shop is a booming trend because of store brands such as Puma, Converse and Champion.

The minimalist style

This trend of stores was launched in the 1980s by the Japanese and magnified by top fashion designers Calvin Klein, Jil Sander, Prada and Armani. In this store style, austerity, sobriety and purity of architectural lines are the key words. Only a small selection of products is presented but they are very well valorized. A clean, sober and elegant atmosphere emerges from this type of store. Their consumers are seen as sophisticated, demanding, and at the forefront of fashion design. On the sporting goods market, the minimalist style is reflected, in some way, in the stores of brands located in the premium or ultra-premium segment such as Lacoste. This minimalist style can also concern stores that offer the products of professional sport clubs such as the Manchester United and Barcelona FC stores.

The nomadic style

This style is one of the latest trends in commercial architecture. These are mainly mobile shops which move from town to town and can be found in a mall, in a public place or in a small pedestrian alley. In this type of point of sale, consumers stop by or pass through them. In the sporting goods market, this type of concept is generally not a special layout adopted by specialized brands. However, many of them can be found during time-bound sporting events such as the Olympic Games and FIFA World Cups. For example, a Rugby Park was installed in the Paris subway (Auber station) during the 2007 Rugby World Cup and then visited by more than 250,000 potential consumers per day. These nomadic points of sale can also be found in other places such as open markets, sport stadia and major tourist attractions. Products can come from official channels but counterfeit or illegal products can often also be found in these temporary stalls.

Flagship stores and other concept stores

In the marketing literature dealing with goods distribution, a few researchers (e.g. Sherry, 1998; Filser, 2003) have analyzed the new forms (i.e. flagship and concept) of store layouts and the tendency to "dramatize" the points of sale, designed to enhance competitive differentiation. These new stores have also become the emblems of specialized store chains and international brands that have chosen to develop their own shops. The pioneering aspect of flagship stores in sporting goods consumption is presented below and followed by a discussion on the future of the concept stores in the sporting goods sector beyond the ten architectural styles previously identified.

Flagship stores are the showcases of international brands or some store chains (Kozinets et al., 2002). Through their exceptional or unique character, their purpose is to communicate and display the image that brands and store chains want to project to their targeted audiences. Two orientations are identified in the design of a flagship store brand: the re-enchantment through extraordinary experiences (Ritzer, 1999) and the re-enchantment of everyday life (Cova and Cova, 2001). These two forms of re-enchantment aim to create a unique atmosphere much more attractive than the prices or the products offered. Ultimately, flagship stores have to display two specific characteristics: first, they have to show uniqueness and exceptionality to feed consumer imagination; second, they have to bear a dimension of rationality and utilitarianism to create massive flows of consumers to be transformed in their purchase of products.

They can be developed by the brands themselves or by retailers (Filser, 2001). In the first case, selling products is not imperative as the place is primarily to help in the construction of the brand image, spirit and promise, such as in the Nike Town store for Nike. We are here very close to the finality of this concept in the role of brands museums. In the second case, the flagship stores must illustrate the positioning of the store chains and help them in their external communication. The positioning role of flagship stores is based on the values promoted by the firm, its personality, its philosophy, its culture and its products. Ultimately, the flagship store restores a direct relationship with consumers (Filser, 2001). It also allows the staff to interact with the consumers in a less transactional manner, but also the consumers to interact with each other to create a brand community (McAlexander, Schouten and Koenig, 2002). In the sporting goods market, new flagship store concepts have been developed by store chains which favor more and more the relational dimension of the point of sale, such as the Quiksilver flagship store "three in one" which also involves the brands Andaska and Café Ono.

According to Prinz (2005), there are eight keys to the creation of a concept store in a specialized distribution sector:

- strategic positioning and marketing;
- communication;
- selected products;
- a good location;
- a space big enough to express oneself, to stroll, to manipulate, to appropriate;
- competent staff;
- efficient merchandising;
- innovating, identifiable and memorizable decor.

For this author, the new concept stores should also be oriented towards the following elements: time management, education, support, comfort, tolerance, citizenship, health, well-being, safety and recreation. Even if they do not adopt a flagship store strategy, there is a need for store chains to renew and improve their sales space: more clarity and comfort, bigger spaces, new products, increasing valorization of the products and communication change. As recent examples in the sportswear market, we can cite Onitsuka Tiger, which blends the arts and traditions of authentic Japan with seductive urban design styles, and Adidas, which opened a new concept-store "SLVR" (pronounced "silver"), in the Marais district (Paris) deemed to be a generator of trends, to confirm the company's foray into the world of fashion with an offer of clothes in a trendy and minimalist architectural style.

In a globalized and competitive environment, many store chains, such as Walmart in the USA and Costco in Canada, are now engaged in a dynamic to reduce and optimize their suppliers, transport, storage, and staff management costs. However, the question is no longer one of trying to make the maximum number of products available to the consumers in tightly organized spaces, but rather to develop the product valorization using a store dramatization claiming that it is cheaper (Badot, 2005). There is nowadays a growing success of hard discount which dramatizes the stores in creating a simulation of factory and warehouse. The particular arrangement of products (e.g. bulk pallets, surplus of cardboard boxes, in a dimly lit room) and their positioning now seem to produce among consumers a perception of func-tionality and a "cheap prices" story. Walmart stores appear as the archetype of minimalist and popular points of sale (Badot, 2005). From this trend is born the Starter brand, a collaboration between Nike and Wal-Mart. Even if it is worthy of note, this specific dramatization strategy in the sporting goods market does not seem to record a real success probably because consumers mainly frequent specialized sport stores and because they perceive sporting goods as high-value products.

Conclusion: the influence of in-store shopping contexts on consumers

The physical and social environments of consumers significantly influence their product choices, uses and evaluations. However, the general atmosphere of a point of sale also produces favorable and unfavorable consumer behaviors. In some cases, the presence of other consumers may even constitute a key element of a store chain offer. For example, a small and less frequented sport shop can have a deterrent effect but a dense crowd could also have the same effect on frequentation in a big shopping mall. Impacts are not the same with consumers in a hurry or with low mobility, with young consumers looking for "retailtainment" or with consumers looking for social interactions. For all these reasons, store chains must now integrate multiple settings to optimize their sales and satisfy their consumers, who experience shopping as a constraint or an amusement, a pleasure or an anxiety, an excitement or a nightmare.

To remain competitive, the sporting goods brands are now sold via all distribution channels. In particular, online sales of international sporting good brands are increasingly popular, particularly when they are sold at the cheapest prices in destocking operations. These marketing operations generate tremendous enthusiasm among consumers, which seems to significantly reduce shopping constraints such as time and travelling costs. However, this does not appear to fully apply to clothing, footwear and sport equipment as consumers seem to develop mixed strategies which combine trying the products in stores before ordering them online.

To compete with e-commerce, many store chains have tried to increase the time consumers spend in stores. The sporting goods brands have then focused on more diverse and sophisticated shopping motivations, beyond the simple utilitarian dimension of the product. They have created worlds and environments where consumers primarily go to live a social experience, share common interests, enjoy a pleasant moment, find a good deal or a rare and original model. Studies on the shop atmosphere and its influence on consumers have aroused growing interest from managers of store chains (Michon, Chebat and Turley, 2005). In the sporting goods market, the objective of some of them is to create an atmosphere that can favorably modify the attitudes and behaviors of consumers. Building a specific ambiance is achieved by manipulating specific visual, olfactory, tactile, auditory and social variables around the products. Thanks to stores' architecture and layout, this atmosphere is a vector of additional positioning and differentiation.

It should be remembered that sporting goods brands have objective characteristics, including sensory ones, based on which consumers can make comparison (Bouchet and Hillairet, 2008, 2009). In stores, the impacts of sensory emissions on consumers are highly topical because they are thought to play an important role in the consumer evaluation, selection and buying processes, and sporting goods brands hope that the transformation of the store environment will increase purchases and simultaneously improve consumer loyalty. More empirical results are, however, needed to legitimate such assumptions.

Among all sporting good brands that have created or used a new concept store, it is indeed not easy to identify those which have really enhanced their sales figures and have really innovated and explored some promising tracks. A concomitant question is whether the evolution of in-store dramatization will also be accompanied by a transformation in the relationships between consumers and their sporting goods and retail brands.

Notes

1 'Through the looking glass', *Lifestyle Monitor*, 16, autumn–winter 2002.
2 'La PLV, moteur d'achat', *Marketing Magazine*, 30, May 1998.
3 In French, *la forme* refers simultaneously to body fitness and shape.

References

Andrieu, F., Badot, O. and Macé, S. (2004) 'Le West Edmonton Mall: un échafaudage sensoriel au service d'une cosmogonie populaire?' *Revue Française du Marketing*, 196, 53–66.

Arnold, S., Kozinets, R. and Handelman, J. (2001) 'Hometown ideology and retailer legitimation: the institutional semiotics of Wal-Mart flyers', *Journal of Retailing*, 77, 2, 243–71.

Babin, B., Darden, W.R. and Griffin, M. (1994) 'Work and/or fun: measuring hedonic and utilitarian shopping value', *Journal of Consumer Research*, 20, 644–56.

Badot, O. (2005) 'L'autre raison du succès de Wal-Mart: une rhétorique de l'infraordinaire', *Revue Française du Marketing*, 203, 97–117.

Baker, J. (1998) 'Examining the informational value of store environments', in *Servicescapes: The concept of place in contemporary market*, Chicago, AMA, 55–79.

Baker, J., Grewal, D. and Parasuraman, A. (1994) 'The influence of store environment on quality inferences and store image', *Journal of the Academy of Marketing Science*, 22(4), 328–39.

Barrey, S., Cochoy, F. and Dubuisson-Queillier, S. (2000) 'Designer, packager et merchandiser: trois professionnels pour une même scène marchande', *Sociologie du travail*, 42, 4, 457–82.

Bellizzi, J.A., Crowley, A.E. and Hasty, R.W. (1983) 'The effects of color in store design', *Journal of Retailing*. 59, 1, 21–45.

Ben Dahmane Mouelhi, N. and Touzani, M. (2003) 'Les réactions des acheteurs aux modalités de la musique d'ambiance: cas de la notoriété et du style', *Revue Française du Marketing*, 194, 4/5, 65–82.

Bitner, M.J. (1992) 'Servicescapes: the impact of physical surroundings on consumers and employees', *Journal of Marketing*, 56, 2, 57–71.

Bloch, P.H., Ridgway, N.M. and Dawson, S.A. (1994) 'The shopping mall as consumer habitat', *Journal of Retailing*, 70(1), 23–42.

Bloch, P.H., Ridgway, N.M., and Nelson, J.E. (1991), 'Leisure and the shopping mall', in R.H. Holman and M.R. Solomon (eds.) *Advances in Consumer Research*, Vol. 18, Provo, UT, Association for Consumer Research, pp. 445–52.

Bouchet, P. (2005) 'L'analyse de la "sensorialité" des magasins. Approche exploratoire dans la distribution d'articles de sport', Actes du 21ème Congrès International de l'Association Française de Marketing, Nancy, CD ROM.

Bouchet, P. and El Aouni, H. (2004) La théâtralisation des magasins d'articles de sport: Du discours à la réalité. 20ème Congrès International de l'Association Française de Marketing, Saint Malo, CD ROM.

Bouchet, P. and Hillairet, D. (2008) *Les Marques de sport*, Paris, Economica.

—— (2009) *Les Marques de sport: Approches stratégique et marketing*, Louvain, De Boeck.

Chebat, J.C. and Michon, R. (2003) 'Impact of ambient odors on mall shoppers' emotions, cognition, and spending: A test of competitive causal theories', *Journal of Business Research*, 56, 7, 529–39.

Cova, B. and Cova, V. (2001) *Alternatives marketing*, Paris, Dunod.

Crowley, A.E. (1993) 'The two-dimensional impact of color on shopping', *Marketing Letters*, 4, 1, 59–69.

Daucé, B. (2000) 'La diffusion des senteurs d'ambiance dans un lieu commercial: intérêts et tests des effets sur le comportement', Thèse de Doctorat en Sciences de Gestion, IGR, Université de Rennes 1.

Donovan, R.J. and Rossiter, J.R. (1982) 'Store atmosphere: an environmental psychology approach', *Journal of Retailing*, 58(1), 34–57.

El Aouni, H. (2006) *'La théâtralisation des points de vente: évaluation du décalage entre les intentions stratégiques des détaillants et les perceptions des clients'*, Thèse de doctorat de sciences de gestion, Université de Bourgogne.

Falk, P. and Campbell, C. (1997) *The shopping experience*, London, Routledge.

Filser, M. (2001) 'Le magasin amiral: de l'atmosphère du point de vente à la stratégie relationnelle de l'enseigne', *Décisions Marketing*, 24, 7–16.

—— (2002) 'Le marketing de l'expérience: statut théorique et implications managériales', *Décisions Marketing*, 28, 13–21.

—— (2003) 'Le marketing sensoriel: la quête de l'intégration théorique et managériale', *Revue Française de Marketing*. 194, 4/5, 5–11.

Filser, M., Des Garets, V. and Paché, G. (2001) *La distribution: organisation et stratégie*, Paris, Editions Management et Société.

Firat, F. and Venkatesh, A. (1995) 'Libratory postmodernism and the re-enchantment of the consumption', *Journal of Consumer Research*, 22, 239–67.

Goss, J. (1993) 'The "magic of the mall": an analysis of form, function, and meaning in the contemporary retail built environment', *Annals of the Association of American Geographers*, 83, 1, 18–47.

Greenland, S.J. and McGoldrick, P.J. (1994) 'Atmospherics, attitudes and behavior: modelling the impact of designed space', *International Review of Retail, Distribution and Consumer Research*, 4, 1, 1–16.

Grossbart, S., Hampton, R., Rammohan, B. and Lapidus, R.S. (1990) 'Environmental dispositions and consumer response to store atmospherics', *Journal of Business Research*, 21, 225–41.

Hetzel, P. (2002) *Planète conso. Marketing expérientiel et nouveaux univers de consommation*, Paris, Editions d'Organisation.

Holbrook, M. and Hirschman, E. (1982) 'The experiential aspects of consumption: Consumer fantasy, feelings and fun', *Journal of Consumer Research*, 9(2), 132–40.

Holt, D.B. (1995) 'How consumers consume: A typology of consumption practices', *Journal of Consumer Research*, 22(June), 1–16.

Kotler, P. (1973) 'Atmospherics as a marketing tool', *Journal of Retailing*, 49(4), 48–64.

Kowinski, W.S. (1985) *The malling of America*, New York, William Morrow and Co.

Kozinets, R.V., Sherry, J.F., DeBerry-Spence, B., Duhachek, A., Nuttavuthisit, K. and Storm, D. (2002) 'Themed flagship brand stores in the new millennium: theory, practice, prospect', *Journal of Retailing*, 78(1), 17–29.

McAlexander, J.H., Schouten, J.W. and Koenig, H.F. (2002) 'Building brand community', *Journal of Marketing*, 66, 38–54.

Mehrabian, A. and Russell, J.A. (1974) *An approach to environmental psychology*, Cambridge, MA, MIT Press.

Michon, R., Chebat, J.C. and Turley, L.W. (2005) 'Mall atmospherics: the interaction effects of the mall environment on shopping behavior', *Journal of Business Research*, 58(5), 576–83.

Miller, D. (1998) *A theory of shopping*, Ithaca, NY, Cornell University Press.

Milliman, R.E. (1982) 'Using background music to affect the behavior of supermarket shoppers', *Journal of Marketing*, 46, 86–91.

Prinz, J-C. (2005) 'Quel style d'architecture pour quel type de distribution?', *Admirable Design*, [online] available at: <http://www.admirabledesign.com/Quel-style-d-architecture-pour> (accessed 1 September 2011).

Rémy, E. (2002) 'Comment thématiser le point de vente?', in *Le marketing sensoriel du point de vente*, coord. by S. Rieunier, Paris, Collection Dunod LSA.

Rieunier, S. (2002) *Le marketing sensoriel du point de vente*, Paris, Collection Dunod LSA.

Rieunier, S. and Daucé, B. (2002) 'Marketing sensoriel du point de vente', *Recherches et Applications en Marketing*, 17, 4, 46–65.

Ritzer, G. (1999) *Enchanting a disenchanted world: revolutionizing the means of consumption*, Thousand Oaks, CA, Pine Forge Press.

Sherry, J. (1998) *Servicescapes: The concept of place in contemporary markets*, Chicago, NTC Business Books.

Sibéril, P. (1994) 'Influence de la musique sur les comportements des acheteurs en grandes surfaces de vente', *Thèse de Doctorat en Sciences de Gestion*, IGR, Université de Rennes 1.

Spangenberg, E.R., Crowley, A.E. and Henderson, P.W. (1996) 'Improving the store environment: do olfactory cues affect evaluations and behaviors?' *Journal of Marketing*, 60, 67–80.

Trottier, J.G. (2000) 'La théorie proxémique dans l'aménagement des espaces de distribution: l'exemple du luxe'. Actes du 16ème Congrès International de l'Association Française de Marketing, Montréal, 275–89.

Yalch, R. and Spangenberg, E. (1993) 'Using store music for retail zoning: a field experiment', *Advances in Consumer Research*, 20, 632–36.

21

SPORT PROMOTION THROUGH COMMUNICATION

A mass media perspective

Daniel C. Funk and Kevin Filo

Introduction

Sport promotion has a profound impact on the way sport products and services are communicated and consumed. Promotion represents only one aspect of the sport marketing mix but it receives considerable attention both internally and externally. Internally, sport managers can use promotion as an integrated strategy to develop content and distribute information to potential and current customers about product, price, place, sponsorship and service. The strategy is designed to communicate attractive attributes and benefits of products and services to stimulate awareness and interest for new consumers and facilitate stronger emotional connections among existing consumers. Externally, sport organizations have less control over content and distribution of communication and must use intermediaries such as the mass media as a platform for promotion.

Sport organizations receive a great deal of media coverage, which plays a dominant role in shaping opinions about the organization as well as the products and services they offer. This chapter will focus on the external aspect of sport promotion as a mass communication strategy. In other words, sport promotion that utilizes mass media to inform and influence current and potential customers as well as the general public. This perspective links sport promotion with mass communication to help understand how sport managers can use the mass media as a communication vehicle. Topics to be covered within this chapter include promotion as a mass media strategy, sport mass communication as promotion, sport broadcast rights, the influence of sport editorials, the role of media coverage on live sport attendance, new media and sport, and considerations of the future effects of technology on sport promotion.

Promotion as a mass media communication strategy

The external positioning of the sport product or service will rely upon communication strategies that the sport organization employs to spread information to the outside world. The outside world includes a range of stakeholders including consumers and users, members of the community, potential employees, sponsors, suppliers of services and materials, distributors, opinion leaders and media companies. Hence, an important and useful communication strategy that includes a subset of promotion is public relations. Public relations within the marketing mix can include both community and media relations (Mullin, Hardy and Sutton, 2007) and is designed to help shape public opinion and behavior towards brands, services, issues and people (Baskin, Aronoff and Lattimore, 1997). Hence, sport promotion can be viewed as a communication strategy that employs mass communication.

There is widespread acknowledgement that mass communication influences attitudes and behavior because individuals learn and share information through communication. Communication can take various forms, but all involve the sending and receiving of a message. In general, individuals spend considerable amounts of time each day dealing with communication ranging from interpersonal and group exchanges among friends, family and co-workers to mass communication experiences involving electronic and print media, advertising and public lectures. Hence, the communication of ideas and feelings within a culture serve to both educate and persuade at the individual and societal level. Although interpersonal communication is important, the focus of this chapter will be on the role of mass communication and the influence on the individual sport consumer. Mass media operates as an important communication vehicle to directly and indirectly influence both adolescents and adults. In a meta-analysis of media research, Emmers-Sommer and Allen (1999) found that mass media becomes increasingly important in shaping the behavior of children as they mature. In addition, mass media remains an important force in shaping adult consumption activities (Bush, Smith and Martin, 1999; Trevino, Webster and Stein, 2000). As a result, sport informational content conveyed through mass media plays a dominant role in shaping attitudes and behavior among sport consumers from the cradle to the grave (Funk and James, 2001).

Mass communication

In general, mass communication can operate through two pathways: direct and indirect (Bandura, 2001). The direct pathway serves to inform, motivate, persuade and guide individuals to action. This pathway can be viewed as traditional promotions, including advertising, sales, sponsorship and licensing, that form a central part of the marketing mix framework for an organization (Mullin et al., 2007). The indirect pathway is a socially mediated pathway, where intermediaries such as the mass media, social networks and community settings inform and influence individuals.

The indirect pathway is of particular importance as the influence of mass communication on the individual, and by extension the general public, is widely recognized. In most developed technological societies, individuals access information and develop beliefs and opinions about events beyond their direct experience from messages presented to them through mass communication. For example, media coverage of a sport event (e.g., Olympics, World Cup, English Premier League (EPL) match) can influence public opinion by controlling what individuals know about the event in the absence of actual observation or firsthand knowledge (Bartels, 1993; Entman, 1989). Mass media can construct information in such a way that it promotes dominant group interests as normal, and influences what we think and feel about our social and political environment (Eitzen and Sage, 2003). Research indicates that individuals form impressions and opinions from information provided by a variety of sources, but intermediaries such as mass media, most notably television, newspapers, magazines, radio and internet, continue to play a dominant role (Dalton, Beck and Huckfeldt, 1998; Domke, 2001; Emmers-Sommer and Allen, 1999; Spiro, 2001).

Mass media's influence on shaping individual attitudes, opinions and interests occurs through both sociological and psychological processes. The sociological processes account for how various external forces interact with the individual during the process of socialization (e.g., Domke, 2001); in other words, how the individual learns norms, values, opinions and behavior from various socializing agents such as mass media, organizations and institutions, personalities and governmental agencies (e.g., Bush, Smith and Martin, 1999). Mass media operates as an important socializing agent as it can present information in such a manner that it influences how individuals think and feel about the social, cultural and political environment. The potential influence of mass media on the individual is governed by psychological processes that account for how informational content is framed and processed by the individual (Drew and Weaver, 1990; Schmidt, 1993).

This cognitive perspective highlights how the individual processing the mass media communication evaluates the content (e.g., news coverage, editorials, informational cues) based upon his or her current beliefs and opinions. For example, an individual's prior attitude related to a news event (e.g., a sport event, sport team, coach or athlete) and direct experience related to the event would be used to evaluate the message and would determine the potential persuasiveness of the content (Dalton et al., 1998; Erickson, 1976). Taken together, both the sociological and psychological perspectives highlight the notion that "the media do not control what people prefer . . . they influence public opinion by providing much of the information people think about and shape how they think about it" (Entman, 1989: 361). Hence, there are compelling reasons to expect that mass media communication will have a substantial influence on the opinions and behavior of stakeholders and particular end consumers within the sport industry.

The influence of mass media communication on sport within society can also be highlighted by the dual role it has for sport promotion. The first role is the reporting of sport as news. This role involves the gathering of information for the purposes of editorial use and the use of photographs or video images to add context and depth to the reporting. The second role is the broadcasting of sport as entertainment. This role involves the purchase of exclusive rights from a sporting organization that provides some type of commercial benefit to the sporting organization, the broadcaster who holds the rights, and sponsors and advertisers of the sport or event. As a result, sport mass communication can play an important promotional role for a sport organization and must be managed accordingly.

Sport mass communication as promotion

Sport media emerged over 200 years ago as a sport section in daily newspapers was used to augment traditional news (Nichols, Moynahan, Hall and Taylor, 2002). The printed word of sport news dominated early delivery of sport content to large audiences and the sport section remains an important component of newspapers (Funk and Pritchard, 2006). Sport content can be distributed on paper in newspapers and magazines or electronically via the internet and wireless technologies. Sport content can also be broadcast and appeared in the 1920s through radio and later via television. This dramatically changed how sport was covered by the media. Currently, new media technologies are having a pronounced impact on sport mass communication. These developments transcend geographic boundaries, allowing sport fans to follow sport, teams and athletes from around the globe. Correspondingly, sport brands can promote themselves to a global audience through new media. In addition, new media technologies have introduced greater speed of communication as sport fans can now obtain scores, statistics and analysis both during and immediately following games. Sport-induced media companies are now more than ever viewing sport as a mass communication vehicle to increase profits by producing content to attract audiences and develop advertising revenue.

Sport mass communication involves a process whereby media organizations produce and transmit messages which are sought, used and consumed by sport audiences (Hall, Nichols, Moynahan, and Taylor, 2007). In general, sport mass communication is based on four basic characteristics: 1) the commercial nature of the communication in terms of the profit motive of media organizations to produce content which is used to attract audiences to develop advertising revenue; 2) the ability to reach either a heterogeneous and widely dispersed audience or a specific targeted group; 3) the ability to deliver content via written, audio or visual messages; and 4) the organizational source of the content (e.g., McQuail, 2010). These four characteristics determine the use of sport content by media organizations and, by extension, inform the use of sport mass communication as a promotional tool by the sport organization.

Wenner (1989) suggests that sport media provides various stakeholders with a shared sport culture that shapes a picture of what sport is and what it means to the individual and larger society. Mass media can serve to create general awareness of sport and related activities, as well as change existing knowledge and beliefs about the sport (Cavill and Bauman, 2004). The media's coverage of a sport or sport event can provide insight into various sport subcultures that reinforce or change existing stereotypes (Bernstein, 2002; Wheaton and Beal, 2003). Hence, sport media can be used as a promotional vehicle and play an important role in shaping the meaning of sport and related activities to a wide spectrum of society.

The relationship between the media industry and sport industry is often viewed as symbiotic (Hall et al., 2007). In other words, each industry is unique but exists for mutual benefit. The mass media profit from the distribution of sport content as news and entertainment. The media organization receives programming and content to increase the number of viewers, listeners, readers, visitors and users, which ultimately provides advertising revenue (Schultz, 2005). This symbiotic relationship has the potential to create a dangerous liaison between the media and sport organizations. For example, the media can oversell a match between two teams or a potential clash between two opposing marquee players by using controversial and hyped terminology and images to create a fake rivalry in order to generate more attention and attract a larger audience. However, the relationship can also be used to promote the positive benefits and value of sport such as league, team, and player involvement in charities and contributions to communities.

The product of this relationship allows the sport organization to receive free publicity and exposure in the form of news coverage. In addition, the sport organization can receive revenue through the sale of broadcast and print rights and media partnerships. Based on this relationship, sport organizations that emphasize and understand the mass communication approach can utilize a number of promotional activities including news features, interviews, photos, news releases, opinion pieces, speeches, seminars, online forums, talk shows and promotional and special events.

Overall, these promotional activities are designed to utilize the influence of the mass media on the individual and community to educate and guide understanding of the sport organization and generate publicity for commercial products and services. As stated by Helitzer (2000), "the real talent is not the writing of publicity but the creation of publicity" (p. 205). In addition, electronic broadcast and media rights represent a substantial revenue source for sport organizations. Although some professional sport teams and leagues have implemented strategies such as creating their own local TV and radio channels or producing talk shows in-house to avoid or lessen the reliance on media companies (e.g., New York Yankees), the vast majority do not have the capacity to manage the complexity of the mass media process. Hence, sport managers must understand the link between audience, ratings and broadcast functions to better employ promotional tactics.

Sport broadcast rights

A media organization pays a negotiated fee to a sport entity for the right to broadcast a sport or sport event via TV, radio or internet. Media broadcast rights can be sold by a professional or collegiate sport league (e.g., EPL, NCAA), a sport franchise (e.g., Chelsea, New York Yankees) or sport event (e.g., Olympics, French Open) that holds the intellectual property of the content. The broadcast fee can be substantial, from thousands of dollars for a local sport event to billions of dollars for the World Cup and Olympics. The media company then sells advertising slots (e.g., a 30-second commercial) during the broadcast to companies and commercial partners that advertise products and services. Depending upon the size of the sport or event, the media organization may then sell the broadcast rights to affiliate networks in which the affiliate can sell its own advertising time. For each sport broadcast, there are a contractually agreed upon number of advertising slots. The internet operates in a similar manner with the emergence of display ads such as banner ads and rich media/video advertisements.

There is a direct link between advertising sales and programming decisions for broadcast media (Nichols et al., 2002). In other words, a program (e.g., sport event, sitcom, drama, movie) will be broadcast only if the media organization can generate sufficient advertising revenue during that program to be profitable. If not, then the program will not be broadcast. For example, a company such as McDonald's or Nokia will not purchase advertising time during a TV broadcast of a sport event unless there is a sufficient number of viewers and/or a specific target market watches the program. However, a media organization such as a TV network may also purchase sport broadcast rights as a strategic investment to attract viewers to other programs (sitcoms, dramas, movies) the network has that are advertised during the sport broadcast (Leeds and von Allmen, 2005). To the media company, the sport broadcast represents programming content that provides a means to increase ratings, satisfy affiliates, entice advertisers and allow promotion of primetime shows. Hence, the relationship between programming, audience size and advertising revenue can be complex, but is of critical importance to all stakeholders involved.

This complex relationship is most often represented by metrics which represent a measurement of audience size and composition. Metrics of ratings and shares are used by broadcasters, advertisers and sport organizations to determine who is watching, listening or visiting, and ultimately to calculate the value and cost of commercials during the sport broadcast. Most countries have media research companies that provide this data (e.g., BARB, Nielson, OsTam). For TV, a rating is the percentage of homes in a geographical market area tuned to a sport program. A share is the percentage of all homes watching television within a given time frame in that geographical market watching the sport program. Other metrics that can be used for both broadcast and print media include cost per thousand (CPM), cost per point (CPP) and reach (e.g., cume) to calculate value and cost of advertisement and commercials (Mullin et al., 2007). The internet introduces additional metrics to gauge reach and audience size. These metrics include click-through rate, view-through rate, hits, page views and unique visitors. Although television is recognized as a key media source for developing and delivering content related to sport (Eitzen and Sage, 2003; Lobmeyer and Weidinger, 1992), media coverage in the form of printed newspaper and online news content continues to be an important and popular source in the distribution and consumption of sport related information (Nichols et al., 2002; Pritchard and Funk, 2006).

The influence of the printed word

Printed news content delivered through various channels continues to play a vital role in public affairs, particularly at the local level, by stimulating cognitive learning, informing readers and providing in-depth information (Drew and Weaver, 1990; Gamson and Modigliani, 1989). In fact, newspapers are perceived as one of the more credible sources for news, and are rated as more credible than television and online news (e.g., more thoroughly researched, more detailed and critical, better balanced, more competent, more professional) (Schweiger, 2000; Spiro, 2001). In addition, editorial pieces by columnists in newspapers have been found to be quite persuasive due to the credibility recipients attach to the source (Dalton et al., 1998).

Prior research has noted that news editorials can influence respondents' beliefs related to the position advocated by the columnists. Dalton et al. (1998) reported that editorials that favored a specific candidate directly influenced reader preferences for that candidate. The source credibility operates as a peripheral cue related to the message argument, and has an important role in the message's processing, as well as in determining the outcome of a persuasive effort (Chaiken and Maheswaran, 1994). Kaczynski, Havitz and McCarville (2005) reported that beliefs and intentions toward leisure service providers could be altered by how messages were framed in editorials. The authors suggested that leisure organizations should guide and direct public discourse by shaping perception and framing events. Editorials that appear in newspapers are more likely to be perceived as formal or neutral sources (e.g., not-for-profit, consumer report; public service announcements), rather than a paid advertisement which has a profit-oriented motive, giving the reader more confidence in the message. In addition to the credibility, the popularity of the sport section in newspapers increases the ability to deliver content to large audiences as well as niche segments.

In sport-related research, positive editorials supporting a sport franchise can create more favorable attitudes about the team, while negative editorials create less favorable attitudes (Funk and Pritchard, 2006). In addition, research has found that an individual's level of commitment moderates his/her attitudinal response to reading the sport editorial. For example, the prior level of team commitment functioned to stabilize beliefs and feelings as well as determine the evaluation of informational stimuli embedded in the editorial message. In other words, attitude change toward a professional sport team that occurs from being exposed to media content was evident in the less committed, but no change in attitudes was observed for committed individuals. This research illustrates how a sport consumer's prior level of involvement can cue information processing and prompt message elaboration. This can then determine the number of thoughts and facts recalled from the message, while influencing beliefs and feelings about the sport organization.

The credibility of newspapers stems from their operational difference to broadcast media. The production and delivery of news content is not related to the ability to produce advertising revenue (Pritchard and Funk, 2006). In other words, there is no direct link between the news and advertising. Newspapers depend upon circulation rates and the more subscribers and readers a newspaper has the higher the price it may ask for advertising space. However, historically print media organizations have kept the editorial (i.e., news content) side of production separate from the advertising side of production to minimize the influence of content decisions being based on profit (Hall et al., 2007). A company may purchase advertising space in a newspaper and may even request placement in a specific section (e.g., the sport section), but this does not influence the type of news or editorial content being printed. However, newspaper advertising does influence the amount of news content since production cost is related to advertising volume. The volume of advertising determines the number of pages the newspaper produces. Hence, advertising revenue does limit the amount of content, but has little effect on the nature of coverage or content selection decisions.

The production and delivery of sport media have not been immune from criticism levied at the broader media culture about the transmission and construction of social reality. Newspaper publishers continue to emphasize the right to freedom of the press but socio–political and economic pressures often flavor reports given about local sport teams and events (e.g., Schweiger, 2000). Such pressure can lead beat reporters, columnists and feature writers to manipulate editorials and introduce their own biases or follow a specific agenda (Hackett, 1993). Eitzen and Sage (2003) suggest that in many instances "stories are withheld or distorted, and sport news is edited to ensure a favorable public image of the home team" (p. 253). A good example of how mass media can influence public opinion is the funding of new sport venues. In this context, influencing public opinion to support local, state or regional tax referendums for construction projects is most likely to be successful through strategic relationship building with local and regional newspaper columnists to leverage the impact that media has on public sentiment.

The venue "game"

Governments at various levels pledge millions and even billions of dollars in public funding to build sports venues for professional sport franchises and sports events. Public investment of this magnitude legitimately attracts scrutiny, particularly when the commitment directly benefits a privately owned sport club or franchise. An editorial published by one newspaper typifies the arguments of opponents to such an investment:

> [City X] does not yet need, nor can it sustain, a national club of any type. There is no scientific evidence to support the benefits received from an investment such as this. Does the wider community even want one? I think if you asked the average taxpayer; there would be a resounding "no." We need water, security, hospitals, roads, and literate children – not a professional team.

In defending against these criticisms, proponents of the investment facilitated an editorial in a competing newspaper that argued:

> The stadium would be funded from the Major Facilities Fund at no cost to taxpayers. The Major Facilities Fund is derived from a levy applied to the state's most profitable hotel gaming machine venues.

In addition, a series of weekly editorials was run, stating:

> There are important economic and social benefits that the development of a new sport facility and the introduction of a representative team in a national competition could bring to our community. The new team will increase tax revenues, new money from out of town visitors, creation of full-time jobs, new roads and facilities for youth clubs, attract new businesses to the area, encourage recreational participation and active lifestyles, improve our community image and bring people together and bolster civic pride.

Proponents are usually able to generate more publicity in support of their argument via public officials, local businesses leaders, sport leagues, team players, TV and radio stations,

287

newspapers, and internet and social networking sites. Despite the lack of scientific evidence to support the economic and social benefits of sport venues, proponents are usually successful in persuading the general public to publicly fund the sport construction project.

In a sport marketplace that is filled with a wide array of entertainment alternatives, negative publicity can pose a very real threat to a sport organization's market base (e.g., Funk and Pritchard, 2006; Schmidt, 1993). Building strong relationships with local media is critical. A compelling example of publicity gone wrong and the financial impact is evident in recent comments by one professional sport franchise's management about season-long negative editorials in the local newspapers. The CEO publically stated that the negative publicity cost the club millions, in both attendance receipts and sponsor revenues. This example highlights the potential influence that mass media has not only on public opinion, but also on behavior that can influence the sustainability of a sport organization. Of particular interest is the role that mass media plays in live attendance at sport events.

Media and live attendance

The connection between media use and live attendance remains an important issue for professional sport organizations. Scholars have questioned whether media use and event attendance are competitive or symbiotic, but few studies have examined whether these types of relationships exist for spectators and fans. The issue revolves around the notion of symbiosis or substitution. In other words, does media coverage of a live sport event increase (i.e., symbiosis) or discourage (i.e., substitution) individuals from attending a live sport event? The findings of research are useful to understand the nature of the relationship between media and live attendance.

Mass media as a substitute

A number of studies reveal how mass media operates as either a substitute or a competitor for live consumption of sport events. In England, no relationship was found between media usage and live attendance at a one-day cricket test match (Schofield, 1983). Satellite coverage of EPL football matches was reported as reducing live attendance (Baimbridge, Cameron, and Dawson, 1996). In Israel, a decline in sport participation and event spectatorship from 1970 to 1990 has been attributed to television usage (Katz, Haas, Gurevitch, 1997). Zhang and Smith (1997) argue that media coverage often diminishes attendance by offering sport fans an alternate mode of consumption. The emergence of sport news programming, subscription to live webcasts, cable television coverage and dedicated sport pubs provides the means for a form of consumption without being physically present. Overall, there appears to be a negative relationship between the degree that media usage diminishes or competes with live attendance and operates as a recreational substitute. The sport and media industries recognize this relationship when media broadcasts of a professional or amateur match are not shown in the regional television market (i.e., TV blackout) in an attempt to increase spectator attendance (e.g., Bialik, 2004). Despite this evidence, other studies suggest mass media may operate in a more symbiotic way to increase live sport attendance.

Mass media as symbiosis

Research illustrates the symbiotic nature of mass media usage and live sport attendance. In other words, the consumption of one fuels the other. Burnett, Menon and Smart (1993) reported that spectators with higher attendance rates also displayed heavier sport media consumption habits. Mason (1999: 409) comments that "perhaps the single largest cause of the growth in the professional sport industry has been television, which enjoys a symbiotic relationship with sport." In England, Meir (2000) noted that an increase in the number of EPL broadcasts correlated with an increase in live attendance. Armstrong (2002: 267) also reports that frequent attendees of games are also "avid consumers of televised sport." In a similar vein, Mullin and colleagues' (2007) escalator model of behavior suggests that media use is actually a precursor to behavior and increases live attendance at sport events. Overall, these findings suggest that media usage both initiates and coincides with increased live attendance.

Symbiosis and substitution

The preceding discussion illustrates the complex relationship that mass media has with live attendance. Pritchard and Funk (2006) suggest that the relationship between attendance and media is both symbiotic and substitutive. In other words, both work jointly in the consumption of sport. A dual route framework (DRF) is proposed that shows two routes. One route is where both media usage and live attendance work in concert and increase together (i.e., positively correlated behavior). Individuals with light patterns of media usage (limited watching and reading mass media about the team) also have light patterns of attendance (i.e., light consumption). Individuals with heavy patterns of media usage also have high live attendance rates (i.e., heavy consumption). The second route is when an individual substitutes one form of consumption for another (i.e., media dominant consumption vs. sport event dominant consumption). For example, media is used in place of live attendance to create negatively correlated behavior. In other words, substitution takes place where one form of consumption behavior increases without changing the other form of behavior (i.e., increase in attendance unrelated to increase in media behavior creating uncorrelated behavior). The second route also highlights how a media–dominant consumer who does not attend many live games is more likely to purchase team-related merchandise, use the internet, view advertising and promotions, and be as emotionally involved with the sport team as the avid live game attendee. This media dominant consumption group underscores the importance of technology in the delivery of mass sport communication. The next section provides a discussion of sport communication and new media.

Sport communication and new media

The emergence of new media technology has provided an effective and efficient communication vehicle for sport promotion. The internet is a primary source of information for many individuals, and websites represent a low-cost promotional vehicle to communicate with current and potential customers (Filo and Funk, 2005). A large portion of consumers use the internet and destination websites to engage in information search activities during their pre-purchase search of products and services after they recognize the need or desire to attend a sport event.

Filo and Funk (2005) found that the sport product is the marketing mix element most thoroughly communicated on professional sport teams' websites. Hence, sport organizations have placed emphasis on providing product-related information themes through website content to aid information retrieval during a visit. In subsequent research, Filo, Funk and Hornby (2009) developed a Sport Event Information Template (EIT) with fifteen distinct themes that a sport organization should include on a sport event website. These themes include: event ticket procurement, venue site, shopping locations, accommodations, event schedule, local attractions, entertainment opportunities, travel costs, public transport, food and concessions, location of event, parking, safety and security measures, weather forecast and conditions, and traffic conditions. The template can be also modified to reflect the nature of the sport event, including details such as registration, merchandise purchase, fundraising, charity links and sponsor product trials. The authors also suggest the use of a media dedicated link on the website is advisable.

Although the internet is commonly associated with new media, new media is actually the technology that allows communication. Filo and Beaton (2009) provide valuable insight into new media and its role in the sport industry. The authors suggest that communication mediums are generally grouped into traditional and new media forms. Traditional forms are interpersonal communication (i.e., one-to-one) and mass communication (i.e., one-to-many). The second form is prevalent in the sport industry where the sport organization retains control over the content of communication and the many receive the same message. New media refers to a "many-to-many" situation where mass communications become individualized in a way that creates a two-way mass media. This new medium blends the aspects of content control of the traditional media with the individual customization of new media.

New media can be defined as the emergence of digital, computerized or networked information and communication technologies in the later years of the twentieth century. Beyond destination websites, examples of new media technologies include social media platforms, blogs, podcasts, online video streaming and mobile technology (Flew, 2008). These new media technologies share a number of distinguishing characteristics including geographic distance, speed of communication, interactivity, and interconnection and overlap among communication (Croteau and Hoynes, 2003). Each of these characteristics relates to sport promotion.

As noted above, geographic distance refers to how new media technologies transcend geographic boundaries, while speed of communication reflects the immediacy with which new media technologies allow users to access information. Sport organizations can now promote their product to a global market via new media, while new media provides sport fans with endless information on demand. Volume of communication reflects the vast array of connections shared among sport fans, as well as between sport fans and organizations. Sport fans can follow a sport team via Twitter, interact with other fans of that team on Facebook, and watch highlights on YouTube. In addition, reading (or creating) blogs, listening to podcasts, and participating in discussion forums represent additional forms of sport communication via new media.

The interactive characteristic of new media stems from the impacts of geography, speed of communication, and volume of communication. Sport fans can communicate with sport organizations and other sport fans around the world in real time via a wide array of mechanisms. Finally, the interconnection and overlap among communication reflects how the connections shared among sport fans and sport organizations are linked together. A sport organization can promote their brand via Twitter, which can then link to Facebook, as well as direct traffic to their destination website where links to blogs, podcasts and other features can be presented.

New media technologies provide a relatively easy and cost-effective means for sport organizations to promote their product to a wide-reaching, global audience. However, new media also presents a number of challenges to the sport industry. Sport organizations must continue to develop and maintain destination websites that generate traffic, and provide relevant information and resources to consumers.

As social media continues to evolve as an important aspect of consumers' everyday activities, further emphasis is placed on sport organizations developing social media strategies that humanize their brands, while highlighting promotions and deals. Social media can also be utilized to encourage engagement and interaction among consumers through fan polls, fan voting and discussion forums. In addition, social media can strengthen relationships between the organization and fans through compelling content highlighting team, player and competition information. These efforts can channel the collective power of social networks.

Meanwhile, new media resources such as blogs, podcasts and online video streaming need to be understood, distributed and promoted to facilitate providing users with content when they want it, how they want it and where they want it. Finally, ongoing innovation within mobile phone technology challenges sport organizations to develop applications promoting their brand and communicating to consumers via handheld devices.

Future considerations in sport promotion

A significant issue in sport promotion remains the ability to build and sustain volume in response to fluctuating demand within niche segments and sliding demographic populations. This has created a sophisticated sport entertainment market where the sport's communication through the media plays a dominant role. Sport marketers will need to understand how the use of technological advances informs customization of products and services for niche segments whose demographic composition and lifecycle transitions fluctuate more rapidly. In addition, there is an increased concern for security and safety at large, high-profile sport events that will require new means of communication with consumers.

Futurology is a very difficult topic but here are some items for consideration for sport promotion. Product development and technology will drive sport communication practice. Product development and modification will divide consumer attention, creating a greater need for distinct segmentation strategies that increase personal involvement. This will create a bifurcation of supply and demand that focuses on service and consumption experiences for casual spectators versus the traditionalist sport fan. A good example of this is the phenomenon of Twenty20 cricket in the UK and Australia. Sport marketing will need to become more global, creating and meeting demands of emerging markets such as India, China and Brazil. This will require a more in-depth understanding of the social, cultural and spiritual customs insofar as these customs relate to promotion.

Sport promotion will continue to evolve in relationship to changes in consumption behavior due to work–life balance and social engagement. Wireless communication will have a substantial impact on social change and social connections, and by default the practice and understanding of sport communication. Sport communication may help fill the nexus between people and wireless gadgets with hotspots or connected places. Advances in technology have and will continue to alter ways in which sport consumers live, work, relate to one another, organize their needs, and cope as members of society. The sport exchange process will continue to change with live streaming content using broadband, social networking sites, satellite sites, and use of wireless mobile devices such as iPhones and BlackBerrys that create a generation of sport consumers addicted to connectivity and communication.

Media will continue to play an important role in sport, requiring better education of sport marketing professionals and academics to understand the business of media and advertising. A firm understanding of new media will be important, as sport consumers have considerable freedom of choice with levels of interaction and control. Advances in technology to support marketing practice will require attention to control and interactivity. The challenge will be to determine the appropriate medium for communication. These challenges are even more pronounced with the ongoing advances in television broadcasting. Developments such as high-definition (HD) and 3-D television present implications for the promotion of the in-game experience versus promotion of the consumption of sport at home or in sport bars. And as noted above, continued advances in streaming video and mobile technology will continue to enhance user control. Furthermore, the development of Social TV and Direct TV, whereby consumers view and control content while simultaneously interacting with other viewers, as well as content producers, introduces new dimensions with regard to complementary promotions and engagement. Addressing these challenges will entail blending traditional mediums (e.g., one-to-one, one-to-many as in TV, radio, internet and print) with new media (i.e., many-to-many media as in social networking sites). In response to technology, concerns over intellectual property with local media and social media sites will become more prevalent.

Furthermore, increasing emphasis will be placed on reaching consumers through "alternate channels." Podcasts, blogs and wiki technologies will continue to resonate with consumers. With regard to sport promotion, the development of viral marketing campaigns can be critical to success. Viral video refers to video content which gains popularity via internet sharing. Successful viral videos are short and attention-grabbing, and are more subtle in their promotion of the brand, service or product. These characteristics are appealing to the new generation of sport consumers. The success of viral marketing campaigns is not necessarily gauged by the number of products sold, but rather using metrics such as views, reach, user comments and user ratings. Sport brands such as Vitamin Water, NFL.com Fantasy Football, Gatorade, Nike and Sporting Lisbon have enjoyed a great deal of success from carefully crafted viral video campaigns. Sport organizations must strive to develop creative and innovative ways to speak to consumers. In addition, the growing presence and popularity of e-readers and tablets provide another mechanism by which sport organizations will promote their brands. The open source system of devices such as the iPad allows for the development of applications that can deliver content, engagement and interactivity directly to consumers.

One interesting aspect is the emergence of Sport Nomads from the impact of technology and particularly wireless devices. Advances in media technology will be used to shape delivery of sport products and services to consumers. Although motives for sport consumption will not change much, perceived and actual constraints will see a fundamental shift arising from a new flexibility and freedom that creates a new structure of time. This will make it easier to be a sport consumer (consumption of both passive and active forms of sport) and impact the way sport consumers relate to people and place. There is likely to be a change to social norms and rituals that will have a flow-on effect for sport communication. Technology allows family and friends to stay more easily connected (e.g., strong ties) but may also reduce incidental contact with strangers (e.g., soft ties) that can facilitate social cohesion. No longer will you have a spontaneous conversation with a person standing in line at a coffee shop, because the person is using a wireless device to stay connected to a person not present, or is listening to music. The sport venue may become even more like traditional places of worship that bring communities and people together.

Conclusion

This chapter has outlined and described sport promotion as a mass communication strategy. Sport promotion is critical in raising awareness among new consumers; highlighting attractive attributes and benefits of products and services to existing consumers; and fostering emotional connections among consumers and products. A symbiotic relationship exists between the sport industry and the mass media, in which the coverage of sport produces revenue for media companies, while the sport industry benefits from the enormous amounts of publicity generated by the media coverage. For sport organizations, this means that leveraging the media to create publicity is imperative.

This publicity can come from television broadcasts, newspaper coverage or online news and content providers. In showcasing the product via these media platforms, efforts must be made to complement live sport event attendance, rather than cannibalize traditional game consumption. Advancement in new media technologies poses even greater challenges and offers an incredible opportunity for sport organizations to effectively promote products and services. Sport organizations must evolve along with these technological developments to engage consumers across a variety of different platforms including traditional websites, social media, blogs, podcasts and wireless technology. Effective sport promotion via traditional media and new media technologies will assist the sport industry in confronting an era where sport consumers demand the delivery of the communication of content where they want it, when they want it, and how they want it.

References

Armstrong, K.L. (2002) 'An examination of the social psychology of Blacks' consumption of sport', *Journal of Sport Management*, 16, 267–88.

Bialik, C. (2004) 'SportLine to offer webcasts in "March Madness" ' package', *Wall Street Journal*, 16 March, 4.

Baimbridge, M., Cameron, S. and Dawson, P. (1996) 'Satellite television and the demand for football: A whole new ball game?' *Scottish Journal of Political Economy*, 43, 317–33.

Bandura, A. (2001) 'Social-cognitive theory of mass communication', *Media Psychology*, 3, 265–99.

Bartels, L. (1993) 'Messages received: The political impact of media exposure', *American Political Science Review*, 87, 267–85.

Baskin, O., Aronoff, C. and Lattimore, D. (1997) *Public Relations: The Profession and the Practice* (4th edn), Boston, McGraw-Hill.

Bernstein, A. (2002) 'Is it time for a victory lap?: Changes in the media coverage of women in sport', *International Review for the Sociology of Sport*, 37, 415–28.

Burnett, J., Menon, A. and Smart, D.T. (1993) 'Sport marketing: A new ball game with new rules', *Journal of Advertising Research*, 33(3), 21–35.

Bush, A.J., Smith, R. and Martin, C. (1999) 'The influence of consumer socialization variables on attitude toward advertising: A comparison of African-Americans and Caucasians', *Journal of Advertising*, 28, 13–24.

Cavill, N. and Bauman, A. (2004) 'Changing the way people think about health-enhancing physical activity: do mass media campaigns have a role?' *Journal of Sport Sciences*, 22, 771–90.

Chaiken, S. and Maheswaran, D. (1994) 'Heuristic processing can bias systematic processing: Effects of source credibility, argument ambiguity, and tasks performance on attitude judgment', *Journal of Personality and Social Psychology* 66, 460–73.

Croteau, D. and Hoynes, W. (2003) *Media society: Industries, images, and audiences* (3rd edn), Thousand Oaks, CA, Sage Publications.

Dalton, R.J., Beck, P.A. and Huckfeldt, R. (1998) 'Partisan cues and the media: Information flows in the 1992 presidential election', *American Political Science Review*, 92, 111–26.

Domke, D. (2001) 'The press, race relations, and social change', *Journal of Communication*, 51, 317–44.

Drew, D. and Weaver, D. (1990) 'Media attention, media exposure, and media effects', *Journalism and Mass Communication Quarterly*, 67, 740–48.

Eitzen, D.S. and Sage, G.H. (2003) *Sociology of North American Sport* (7th edn) New York, McGraw-Hill.

Emmers-Sommer, T.M. and Allen, M. (1999) 'Surveying the effect of media effects: a meta-analytic summary of the media effects research in human communication research', *Human Communication Research*, 4, 478–97.

Erickson, R. (1976) 'The influence of newspaper endorsements in presidential elections', *American Journal of Political Science*, 20, 207–34.

Entman, R.M. (1989) 'How the media affect what people think: An information processing approach', *Journal of Politics*, 51, 347–70.

Filo, K. and Beaton, A.A. (2009) 'Sport and new media', in D. Shilbury, H. Westerbeek, S. Quick, and D. Funk (eds.), *Strategic Sport Marketing* (3rd edn), Crows' Nest, Allen and Unwin, pp. 229–44.

Filo, K. and Funk, D.C. (2005) 'Congruence between attractive product features and virtual content delivery for Internet marketing communication', *Sport Marketing Quarterly*, 14, 112–22.

Filo, K., Funk, D.C. and Hornby, G. (2009) 'The role of website content on motive and attitude change for sport events', *Journal of Sport Management*, 23, 21–40.

Flew, T. (2008) *New media: An introduction*. Melbourne, Australia, Oxford University Press.

Funk, D.C. and James, J.D. (2001) 'The Psychological Continuum Model (PCM). A conceptual framework for understanding an individual's psychological connection to sport', *Sport Management Review*, 4, 119–50.

Funk, D. and Pritchard, M. (2006) 'Sport publicity: Commitment's moderation of message effects', *Journal of Business Research*, 59, 613–21.

Gamson, W.A. and Modigliani, A. (1989) 'Media discourse and public opinion on nuclear power: A constructionist approach', *American Journal of Sociology*, 1, 1–37.

Hackett, C.H. (1993) 'Images of public relations in the print media', *Journal of Public Relations Research*, 5, 47–61.

Hall, A., Nichols, W., Moynahan, P. and Taylor, J. (2007) *Media Relations in Sport* (2nd edn), Morgantown, WV, Fitness Information Technology.

Helitzer, M. (2000) *The Dream Job: Sport, Publicity, Promotion and Marketing* (3rd edn), Athens OH, University Sport Press.

Katz, E., Haas, H. and Gurevitch, M. (1997) '20 years of television in Israel: Are there long-run effects on values, social connectedness, and cultural practices?' *Journal of Communication*, 47, 3–20.

Kaczynski, A., Havitz, M. and McCarville, R. (2005) 'Altering perceptions through repositioning: An exercise in framing', *Leisure Sciences*, 241–61.

Leeds, M. and von Allmen, P. (2005) *The economics of sport* (2nd edn), New York, Addison-Wesley.

Lobmeyer, H. and Weidinger, L., (1992) 'Commercialism as a dominant factor in the American sport scene: Sources, developments, perspectives', *International Review for the Sociology of Sport*, 27, 309–27.

Mason, D.S. (1999) 'What is the sport product and who buys it? The marketing of professional sport leagues', *European Journal of Marketing*, 33, 402–18.

McQuail, D. (2010) *McQuail's mass communication theory* (6th edn), Newberry Park, CA, Sage Publications.

Meir, R. (2000) 'Fan reaction to the match day experience: A case study in English professional rugby league football', *Sport Marketing Quarterly*, 9, 34–42.

Mullin, B.J., Hardy, S. and Sutton, W.A. (2007) *Sport marketing* (3rd edn), Champaign, IL, Human Kinetics.

Nichols, W., Moynahan, P., Hall, A. and Taylor, J. (2002) *Media relations in sport*. Morgantown, WV, Fitness Information Technology.

Pritchard, M.P. and Funk, D.C. (2006) 'Symbiosis and substitution in spectator sport', *Journal of Sport Management*, 20, 297–320.

Schmidt, D.E. (1993) 'Public opinion and media coverage of labor unions', *Journal of Labor Research*, 14, 151–64.

Schofield, J.A. (1983) 'The demand for cricket: The case of the John Player League', *Applied Economics*, 15, 283–97.

Schultz, B. (2005) *Sport media: Reporting, producing and planning*. Oxford, Elsevier.

Schweiger, W. (2000) 'Media credibility – Experience of image? A survey on the credibility of the World Wide Web in Germany in comparison to other media', *European Journal of Communication*, 15, 37–59.

Spiro, K. (2001) 'Public trust or mistrust? Perceptions of media credibility in the information age', *Mass Communication and Society*, 4, 381–403.

Trevino, L.K., Webster, J. and Stein, E.W. (2000) 'Making connections: Complementary influences of communication media choices, attitudes and use', *Organization Science*, 111, 163–82.

Wenner, L.A. (1989) 'Media, sport, and society: The research agenda', in L.A. Wenner (ed.), *Media, sport and society*. Newberry Park, CA, Sage Publications.

Wheaton, B. and Beal, B. (2003) 'Keeping it real: Subcultural media and the discourses of authenticity in alternative sport', *International Review of the Sociology of Sport*, 38, 155–76.

Zhang, J. and Smith, D. (1997) 'The impact of broadcasting on the attendance of professional basketball games', *Sport Marketing Quarterly*, 6, 23–29.

22

SPORT SPONSORSHIP

Definitions and objectives

Pascale Quester and Charles Bal

Introduction

Sponsorship has become a critical strategic tool as well as an important component of business firms' communication mix (Thompson and Quester, 2000). Meenaghan's (1983) seminal works have contributed to establishing the legitimacy of sponsorship in the marketing literature and spawned many subsequent studies. Yet, despite multiple definitions proposed by scholars, there remains a lack of unanimous definition, each country holding on to its own (Walliser, 2003). Nevertheless, researchers agree that sponsorship involves an exchange between the sponsor and the sponsored entity, also called property, so as to afford to the former access to the communication potential benefit derived from its association with the latter.

Defining sponsorship

Early definitions of sponsorship stressed the relationship between sponsor and property, describing sponsorship as a mutually beneficial business relationship between a firm and an organization operating in the arts, sport or education realm. However, this definition was soon replaced by that put forward by Meenaghan (1991a: 36, who defined it as "an investment, in cash or kind, in an activity [sports, event, festival, fair or art in general] in return for access to the exploitable commercial potential associated with that activity." Such commercial objectives were, at the time of that definition, held to include brand exposure (Otker and Hayes, 1988), so as to attract audiences' attention (d'Astous and Bitz, 1995). Similar definitions have been developed by Cornwell (1995) and Pope (1998b).

Despite its usefulness, Meenaghan's early definition has become obsolete as sponsorship practice has evolved. Contemporary and subsequent definitions, such as those offered by Sandler and Shani (1989) or Desbordes et al. (2004), emphasize that the support offered by sponsors is not restricted to money and may include human resources and technology as well as in-kind contributions. Likewise, the expectation of the sponsor may reach beyond exposure to include corporate image, brand image or even sales, which other communication media may not afford them (Javalgi et al., 1994). Derbaix (1995) and Erdogan and Kitchen (1998) further extended the definition of the concept by describing the property as a cultural object carrying values and images of its own, distinguishing it from others (Ferrand and Pages, 1996), and able to benefit a firm that associates itself with it.

Described by some as a communication technique and by others as a tool, sponsorship appears to have become more than just a component of the promotional mix of business firms. It has evolved into a more strategic communication medium (Meenaghan, 1998b; Berrett and Slack, 1999) operating in a complex manner.

Sponsorship marketing and sponsorship-linked marketing

The notion of association lies at the core of sponsorship. It is indeed critical to sponsorship effectiveness. According to Cornwell (1995), the communication value of sponsorship remains nil until such time as the sponsor can promote the association it has developed with the property, so as to ensure it is known and understood by its target market. This typically requires the broadcast and articulation of the association by a range of leveraging activities (Cornwell and Maignan, 1998; Amis et al., 1999). As a result, the literature and the professional practice of sponsorship reflected the belief that sponsorship must be supported by communication activities, dubbed sponsorship marketing. Hence, sponsorship must be embedded in its own dedicated communication mix (e.g. PR, advertising, direct marketing, merchandising and packaging), to secure the full communication of the association to the target consumer market (Kuzma, Shanklin and McCally, 1993). It follows that the effectiveness of sponsorship depends on the communication mix dedicated to it. Indeed, empirical studies have demonstrated that the impact of sponsorship on recall and brand image is greater when it is fully integrated into a broader communication strategy (Meenaghan, 1991a; Walliser, 2003). Advertising, in particular, has been shown as critical in the articulation of the association message (Cornwell et al., 2005).

Far from competing with each other, therefore, advertising and sponsorship can be complementary (Meenaghan, 1991b). Their interaction may even be synergetic, each reinforcing the other and combining for better outcomes than would be possible with either alone (Pope and Voges, 1995; Levin, Joiner and Cameron, 2001). Both must be used in combination if consumers are to be made aware of the sponsor's role (Vignali, 1997).

More recent research has alluded to a higher purpose for sponsorship, whereby it becomes not only one of the planks of the communication mix, but the very heart of the overall marketing strategy (Fahy, Farrelly and Quester, 2004). Coined "sponsorship-linked marketing" (Cornwell, 1995), this approach implies that the marketing plan should be designed around sponsorship activities, allowing brand differentiation and positioning, and ultimately delivering to the firm an opportunity for competitive advantage. That competitors would want to emulate such outcomes without necessarily spending the same budget has resulted in the rise of ambush marketing, the strategy whereby non-sponsors "pose" as sponsors in the hope of harvesting commercial benefits.

Sponsorship actors

Having defined sponsorship, it is important to understand all the different actors that participate in this process. At the most simple level, sponsorship involves:

- One or more sponsors: While some events are characterized by an exclusive and unique sponsor, many offer varying degrees of exposure to a specific number of sponsors who have acquired sponsorship rights (e.g. VISA and Coca-Cola for the Olympic Games).

- One or more properties: Sponsors may decide to support one event at a time, or to be associated with a repetitive event, a team, or teams involved in one of more competitive events (e.g. Credit Lyonnais sponsors the Tour de France as well as Judo).
- One or more target markets: Sponsors often aim to reach multiple targets, separately or together: consumers, other businesses, shareholders and potential partners (e.g. local or national sponsors are also involved in the Olympic Games, in addition to more global brands).

Research to date has primarily focused on sponsor and property, endorsing the notion of a dual and reciprocal relationship (Thompson and Quester, 2000; O'Reilly and Harrison, 2005), best described as a partnership or a strategic alliance (Farrelly et al., 2005) that benefits all parties: the property secures resources not otherwise available (Cheng and Stotlar, 1999), while the sponsor reaches commercial objectives (Rodgers, 2003) and the audience enjoys an event that would not be possible without the sponsors (O'Reilly and Harrison, 2005). Authors have stressed the mutually beneficial nature of sponsorship (Farrelly and Quester, 1997; Chadwick and Thwaites, 2004), noting that it may be further enhanced when the images of the sponsor and property are congruent (Thompson and Quester, 2000).

Professional practice suggests that sponsorship often involves further actors, with a range of agencies or facilitators assisting sponsors, properties and audiences. For example, Olkkonen (2001) identify sponsorship right holders, consultant agencies and broadcasters as three other relevant categories of actors, as shown in Figure 22.1.

In other words, sponsorship involves a lot more than the mere addition of a brand name on an athlete's shirt (Shannon, 1999). The association between sponsor and property can create real added value, provided a genuine collaboration occurs between the two. Cheng and Stotlar (1999) compared this to a marriage between sport and business, concluding that "if the firms are only attracted by the commercial potential of sport and do not engage in a future relationship, then sport and its very essence are threatened by over-commercialization."

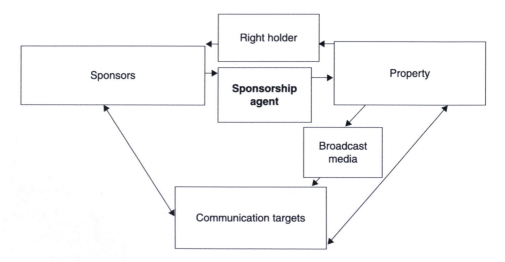

Figure 22.1 The sponsorship actors and their relationships

Sponsorship categories and types

Sponsorship practice demonstrates a wide variety of conceptualizations and manifestations. This variety stems from the many possible contexts in which it can be implemented, the different types of partners and involvements that could exist and the varied approaches to its implementation.

The different contexts of sponsorship

The type of association required to underpin sponsorship is not restricted to the sport arena, although sport tends to be the context of choice for many sponsors (Farrelly and Quester, 1997). Importantly, sponsors increasingly consider a portfolio of properties, as opposed to a single one, to reach a variety of objectives.

Sport sponsorship

Sponsors have long favored sport because of its capacity to deliver exposure (Nichols and Roslow, 1994), convey strong images (Pracejus 2004), transcend cultural and linguistic barriers (Davies, Veloutsou and Costa, 2006), and allow firms to reach audiences, be they broad or narrow (Bennett, 1999). Moreover, because it rests on reality and is subject to the vagaries of athletic pursuits, the spectacle of sport offers thrill and drama, taking audiences on an emotional roller coaster (Johnston and Scherer, 2000).

This combination of exposure, proximity with the target's interest and the richness of the content of the association has made sport the ideal medium to reach a large consumer public (Crowley, 1991). However, researchers have suggested that the effectiveness of sport as a promotional vehicle resides more in its ability to contribute to corporate image than its capacity to increase sales (Javalgi et al., 1994; Thwaites, 1994).

Other types of sponsorship

A different logic seems to be at play when sponsors support the arts (e.g. visual arts, dance, theatre and music). Orientated towards image as opposed to market share (Thwaites, 1995), arts sponsorship tends to be managed by the public relations department rather than the marketing department (Farrelly and Quester, 1997). Arts events attract a qualitatively different audience from that of sport events: older, more affluent, better educated and usually employed in more senior jobs (Meenaghan, 1998b; Quester and Thompson, 2001). As a result, arts sponsorship seems better suited to firms aiming to improve their corporate image and develop or maintain relationships with influential members of networks, by using relationship marketing and corporate hospitality (Farrelly and Quester, 1997; Quester and Thompson, 2001). Consequently, many sport sponsors also engage selectively in art–related activities, in order to broaden their appeal.

Types of partners and partnership levels

In the case of sport sponsorship, partnerships are possible with different types of properties, whether they are organizations (e.g. federations and Olympic committees), events (e.g. Olympic Games, rugby championships or tennis tournaments), teams or individual athletes. An additional proposition has been added with specific locations (e.g. stadium and training centre), through the process of naming, which some have described as more cost effective than traditional advertising (Clark, Cornwell and Pruitt, 2002).

Once the sponsor has selected both the context and type of sponsorship it wants to engage in, a choice remains to be made in relation to the depth of engagement. This can be conceptualized as a continuum. At one extreme, the sponsor may join a long list of companies or brands able to make mention of the property in their communications. At the other extreme, the sponsor may seek total exclusivity, via a naming right contract that all but eliminates others and provides unique access to the property as part of the marketing mix (Quester, 1997a). These increasing levels of engagement are typically reflected in the associated costs of the sponsorship fee and are often subject to protracted and ferocious negotiations, often locking parties into several years of partnership.

- Official supplier: By supplying the property with the product or service it provides to consumers, this type of sponsor seeks to demonstrate its expertise. However, this type of sponsorship, while showcasing the product, remains limited in its ability to deliver meaningful exposure and is usually granted little scope for on-site access for corporate hospitality and relationship building. That Hardy's wines or Cadbury chocolates are partners of the Australian Formula One Grand Prix is more about securing exclusive sales at and around the event than it is about brand awareness or equity building.
- Official sponsor: Despite not contributing directly (beyond financially) to the event, this type of sponsor can often enjoy higher visibility at the event, along with access to corporate boxes and other privileges (such as meeting with athletes or artists). More frequent mentions and inclusion in programs are typical of this type of sponsorship. SingTel, the Singapore telecommunication company, sought and secured the sponsorship of the Singapore Formula One Grand Prix with a view to establishing itself on the world stage, a process enabled by the global audiences of the sport.
- Principal sponsor: Having contributed more than other official sponsors, the principal sponsor can typically claim more benefits. The TOP sponsor scheme put in place by the International Olympic Committee enables brands like VISA, Coca-Cola or General Electric to enjoy a greater status and recognition than other sponsors of the event.
- Naming right sponsor: By paying a premium, the naming sponsor can ensure that its name becomes an integral part of the name of an event or person. This allows the building of a close relationship and longer lasting learning on the part of audiences (Crowley, 1991; Desbordes et al., 2004; McCarthy and Irwin, 2000). This is in addition to all the other benefits already available to the principal sponsor. Commonly associated with stadium and other sport facilities, naming rights can also be attached to specific tournaments, competitions or teams. In Australia, for example, insurance company AAMI has successful earned naming rights in relation to a stadium in Melbourne as well as a Western Australian football team. A dramatic increase in naming rights in recent years has resulted from the realization that sponsorship clutter could restrict the benefit of the approach (McCarthy and Irwin, 2000). Investments in naming rights are often highly expensive, although they are usually associated with greater impact, at least in terms of sponsorship recall (Quester, 1997a).

Implementing sponsorship

The sponsor must now consider how it wants to implement the association and, in particular, what form of exposure it will seek. Several methods are available, depending on the specific sponsorship under consideration:

- On-site signage includes the provision of large logotypes around the field (Walliser, 1997; Lardinoit et al., 1996; Lardinoit and Quester, 2001). Hence, spectators are repeatedly and frequently exposed to the sponsor's brand, whether they are at the event itself or at home watching it on television. However, on-field signage suffers from the very fact that audiences are otherwise engaged, as they follow the on-field performance (Walliser, 1997; Lardinoit and Derbaix, 2001). Hence, only the more involved consumers, those who want to know what the conclusion might be, are highly sensitive to on-field signage (Lardinoit and Quester, 2001).
- Personal display of logo applies to athletes or team whose equipment or clothes will don the sponsor's logo. According to Crowley (1991), this permits the identification of the sponsor at the core of the action but seems restricted in its capacity to make an impact on memory. However, Lardinoit et al. (1996) reported that such on-person logos contributed to a shift in memorization scores greater than that achieved by on-site signage alone.
- Broadcast sponsorship refers to the support of one or more television programs by a sponsor willing to embed its names in the surrounding advertising context. Described in 2005 by Meenaghan, this specific form offers the opportunity to associate a brand to a program without contributing at all to the event broadcast (Meenaghan, 2005). Broadcast has now grown to become one of the most effective and potent forms of sponsorship, given its volume reach.
- Corporate hospitality: Often present yet subtle, sponsors' corporate presence aims at leveraging the investment in the form of clients and partners' entertainment and rewards, recognition of key clients or suppliers, as well as a preliminary stage before signing a contract.

The objectives of sponsorship

Research has now produced a considerable amount of empirical findings in relation to sponsorship objectives (Meenaghan, 1998b; Dolphin, 2003). First equated to advertising (Armstrong, 1988), sponsorship has evolved from a method to simply achieve media exposure to a more sophisticated tool capable of building brand image. The capacity to determine clear objectives is of course at the core of the issue of effectiveness, since no precise evaluation of sponsorship impact can be made in isolation from its initial purpose (Cornwell, 1995; Chadwick and Thwaites, 2004). Despite this, many scholars have lamented the absence of measurable objectives from sponsors' briefs, hampering the opportunity to accurately measure the effectiveness of sponsorship (Farrelly, Quester and Burton, 1997). In this section, therefore, we first identify the different targets which sponsors may seek to influence, before describing two main types of sponsorship objectives: marketing and corporate.

The different targets of sponsorship

One of the advantages of sponsorship lies in its capacity to reach a great variety of existing publics (Pham, 1992; Cornwell and Maignan, 1998). In her synthetic review of sponsorship audiences, Crowley (1991) identified seven potential audiences a firm may wish to reach, including consumer (Thwaites, 1995), suppliers, staff (Meenaghan, 1991a), the general public, local communities, business networks and partners (Meenaghan, 1991a), as well as shareholders. Sport appears particularly suited to reach several types of audiences at once. For example, Quester and Farrelly (2005) described how the Tour de France, one of the longest-running sponsorships in the world, was initially devised to win consumers over, but has evolved into a yearly opportunity to build up the network of Credit Lyonnais branches around the country, firm up connections with the local business community in each of the villages or cities where the Tour stops, and reward and motivate all staff who can participate and experience the Tour (Quester and Farrelly, 2005).

The marketing objectives of sponsorship

Researchers have converged around the notion that sponsorship can contribute to the building of brand equity (Cornwell and Maignan, 1998; Gwinner and Eaton, 1999; Speed and Thompson, 2000; Irwin, Lachowetz, Cornwell and Clark, 2003; Barros and Sylvestre, 2006), most notably by enhancing brand image (Chien et al., 2005). To understand how sponsorship can contribute to brand equity and more broadly to the overall marketing objectives of the sponsor, this section will detail a series of successive steps in brand building, namely brand awareness, brand positioning, brand image and attitudes, and sales.

Brand awareness

By avoiding other communication channels prone to cluttering, sponsorship may offer some degree of exclusivity in relation to key consumers (Kuzma et al., 2003). Hence, the property acts not so much as a communication medium as it does as a supporting platform where the sponsor can display its brand (Nichols and Roslow, 1994). Consequently, the media coverage which the property can generate becomes a key criterion for sponsors to select it (Thwaites, 1995). However, as noted by Meenaghan (1983), such media exposure of the property is a necessary but rarely sufficient step to ensure the awareness of the sponsor. Hence, sponsors must first ensure that they secure appropriate levels of brand exposure as part of the sponsorship to generate desirable levels of brand memorization (Quester, 1997a; Pruitt, Cornwell and Clark, 2004). Brand memorization is often the most cited objective sought by sponsors (Crowley, 1991; Quester, 1997a).

Although Cornwell, Roy and Steinard (2001) suggest that brand awareness follows naturally from sponsorship, any increase in awareness achieved from sponsorship may depend on the awareness enjoyed by the sponsor *prior* to the sponsorship operation. Hence, those sponsors who are already best known will benefit more than less-known ones (Lardinoit and Nagard-Assayag, 2004). Indeed, Walliser (1994) believes that, given consumers' limited capacity to memorize information, any increase enjoyed by one sponsor is achieved at the expense of another, a notion consistent with the idea of "share of mind" (Easton and Mackie, 1998), and endorsed in the case of sponsorship by Lardinoit et al. (1996).

Importantly, the specific choice of sponsorship, related to the type of property or the location of the event, may enable sponsors to create differentiated awareness in specific markets. For example, community-based sponsorships, aimed at the grass-roots level and local areas, can create a strong community-based spirit that benefits a local brand. When Coopers, an Adelaide family brewery, sponsor the Norwood Red Legs, they do so to reinforce their local value to consumers from that specific Adelaide suburb. Likewise, national sponsors, like Australian banking institution Wespac, who become involved in a global event such as the Olympic Games, can often lift their awareness and status in their domestic market.

Brand positioning

The great diversity of sport activities within and across national borders offers sponsors an almost infinite array of positioning options, either by associating their product to the sport itself or by leveraging the values typically associated with the sport (Lardinoit and Nagard-Assayag, 2004). Indeed, the identification of the company as a key sponsor of a sport can be the cornerstone of the brand positioning (Cornwell, 1995; Cousens and Slack, 1996; Cheng and Stotlar, 2000; Farrelly and Quester, 2003), as well as a source of differentiation (Ferrand and Pages, 1996; Quester, 1997a).

Whether it is to reinforce a current positioning or to reposition a brand (Ferrand and Pages, 1999), sponsorship can often help sponsors seeking to align their image with that of the property (Meenaghan, 1994; Fahy et al., 2004). In that sense, such positioning can also be seen as one intermediate objective in the building of a broader brand image, as well as in the fostering of favorable attitudes.

Brand image and attitudes towards the brand

Image transfer from the property to the sponsor's brand is without doubt the most sought after benefit of sponsorship (Javalgi et al., 1994; Meenaghan, 1999, 2001a; Meenaghan and Shipley, 1999; Christensen, 2006). Indeed, empirical evidence has confirmed the occurrence of such image transfers as a result of sponsorship (Otker and Hayes, 1988; Nebenzhal and Jaffe, 1991; Meenaghan and Shipley, 1999). As a social phenomenon, events and properties hold a particular meaning, in terms of associated beliefs, symbols and emotions, in their defined social sphere (Ferrand and Pages, 1999). Hence, each property, just like each brand, projects onto its own audience its own set of values and symbols; in short, its own image.

That image is the sum of all beliefs, ideas and impressions created by the brand, and stored in consumers' memory. Sponsorship, therefore, is a tool that allows the building of an image by activating secondary associations with the brand by linking it with an external party, replete with its own values, symbols and emotions (Roy and Cornwell, 2004). However, while subject to the influence of these secondary associations, this image is far from fully modified or modifiable. The relative permanence of brand image stems in part from consumers' selective perceptions, whereby consumers attend only to the information that "fits" with their pre-existing view. Hence, while it remains one of the most sought after objectives of sponsors, image transfer does not naturally flow from sponsorship. Rather, a set of conditions are required, not least a degree of articulation with the property (Cornwell, 1995; Cornwell et al., 2005), or a congruence or perceived fit between sponsor and property (Johar and Pham, 1999; Fleck and Quester, 2007).

The issue of congruence or fit becomes particularly complex when considering that many properties are sponsored by a collective of brands, just as brands tend to manage an assortment of sponsorships, as previously mentioned. Achieving a coherent set of perceptions requires that additional consideration is given to complementary or at least compatible images and associations. Indeed, some properties, such as the French Federation of Tennis, actively seek to recruit sponsors for whom belonging to a select and highly meaningful network of firms will represent an additional value, a benefit which can only be delivered if long-term relationships, as opposed to opportunistic agreements, are established with sponsors.

Ferrand and Pages (1999) defined an event as a social fact, a "place" where groups gather to celebrate together a sport or cultural spectacle. No event, therefore, can be neutral: it must generate reactive emotional responses and is imbued with meanings from all members of the audience (Grimes and Meenaghan, 1998; Fahy et al., 2004). This is how events develop their own unique sets of attributes that contribute to the formation of attitudes towards them (Chien et al., 2005). Attitudes towards the event are a summary of experiences leading to general favorable or unfavorable predispositions towards the event.

By associating itself with an object valued both symbolically and affectively by the target audience, the sponsor seeks to elicit positive affects and to appeal to consumers' goodwill (Masterton, 2005). Hence, the main benefit of a sponsorship campaign should be able to be measured in terms of attitude change (Crompton, 2004). In other words, the combination of the event image and of the event experience enjoyed by the consumer should result in an attitudinal benefit for the sponsor, in the form of a general cognitive and affective appreciation of the brand by the consumer (Gwinner and Swanson, 2003). Empirical support for increases in attitude scores as a result of a sponsorship activity has been reported in the literature (Speed and Thompson, 2000; Meenaghan, 2001b; Roy and Cornwell, 2004).

Purchase intentions and sales

The ultimate purpose of all marketing endeavor is an increase in sales (Meenaghan, 1983; Crompton, 2004) or an increase in the value of the company's stock (Cornwell et al., 2001). Sport sponsorship offers sponsors very privileged access to a group of consumers who pay attention to what is related to their key focus of interest (Dolphin, 2003). As a result, sport sponsorship is often used to persuade the audience to move from non-consumers or occasional consumers to regular and loyal users of the sponsor's products or services (Garland, MacPherson and Haughey, 2004).

While sponsorship may be valuable to create suitable conditions for future sales (Crompton, 2004), it can also be used to generate sales more directly, as when exclusive rights to sell the product on the site of the event are secured by the sponsor (Meenaghan, 1983). Similarly, offering an opportunity to sample the product on the site of the event can also boost sales by consumers after the event (Meenaghan, 1998b; Crompton, 2004). However, in most instances, it remains difficult to establish a direct causality between sponsorship and sales. Researchers have therefore relied on an intermediate indicator, purchase intentions, to measure the impact of sponsorship on consumers' product choices. Many studies have measured purchase intentions in relation to sponsorship, with mixed results. Some experimental studies have demonstrated a positive link between sponsorship and purchase intentions (e.g. Pham, 1992; Shanklin and Kuzma, 1992; Quester and Farrelly, 1998; Bennett, 1999; Becker-Olsen, 2003) whereas others do not show any relationship between sponsorship and purchase intentions (e.g. Pitts and Slattery, 2004).

The corporate objectives of sponsorship

Beyond the commercial and market-driven considerations, sponsorship can also be conceptualized as the means to engage with various other stakeholder groups, both within and outside the firm, or as a platform to affirm a specific position within society or a variety of community groups. These types of corporate objectives have long been neglected in the sponsorship literature but are becoming more prevalent in justifying ever-increasing sponsorship budgets. This section discusses the three main stakeholder groups which sponsors may wish to communicate with, over and beyond their consumer target markets.

Internal marketing

While research has identified consumers as the prime target of sponsors' efforts, several authors have noted that sponsorship can also be used to enhance staff motivation and job satisfaction (Vignali, 1997; Grimes and Meenaghan, 1998; Pope, 1998b). By building staff engagement around a common project, such as the support of a cause, or the preparation of a boat to be raced in a prestigious competition, or by offering to best-performing staff privileged access to the property, sponsorship can influence staff productivity, decrease absenteeism and improve morale more generally (Irwin and Sutton, 1994; Chadwick and Thwaites, 2004). Hence, as suggested by Gardner and Schuman (1987), sponsorship may help to share or reshape the organizational culture of the sponsor, reinforce its core values and develop a team spirit.

Relationship marketing

A business never operates in isolation from other businesses. Whatever its final consumers, the company must develop and nurture a myriad of relationships in its attempt to design, manufacture and distribute its product or services. In addition to the immediate network of firms with which it must cooperate to deliver to its target market, a firm must also contend with opinion leaders, the media as well as politicians, who all may hold considerable influence or power over the activities a firm engages in. These multiple and diverse relationships must all be developed and maintained, despite the few hard goals that can be measured. Sponsorship can assist in this endeavor, by creating the opportunities for key stakeholders to be invited as special guests to a sport event, a cultural show, or any other property-related performance. Each of these invitations may lead to informal conversations when the sponsor can, at the very least, explain its position on a number of issues, without the risk of being accused of seeking to gain undue influence (Meenaghan, 1983; Quester, 1997b; Vignali, 1997; Pope, 1998b; Farrelly and Quester, 2003).

This practice, also known as corporate hospitality, can become the most beneficial of all elements of a sponsorship campaign, where access to the star athletes or champions, and proximity to the finish line or goal can represent a valued opportunity for the building of the type of relationships both parties can rely on and build upon (Pruitt et al., 2004). Scholars have commented about the potential for sport sponsorship to create social bonds, empathy and complicity, which can lead to solid business collaborations (Cousens, Babiak and Slack, 2001).

Corporate social responsibility

In some industry sectors, such a liquor or tobacco, the image of the firm as a good corporate citizen is one that simply does not appear believable to many consumers. Firms operating in these contexts, and those who have been the subject of adverse criticism before or wish to prepare themselves for the eventuality of a crisis in the future, have been considering sponsorship as the means to build (or rebuild) their battered image.

Meenaghan (1983) was the first to point to the capacity of sponsorship to break through consumers' increasing skepticism towards marketers. As they turned away from advertising and its increasing incapacity to offer an uncluttered voice to consumers, sponsors aimed to illustrate their commitment to causes or communities, to signal their intentions to "give back" and to enter into a dialogue with opinion leaders and secure the goodwill of the public for their activities and behavior. Research in this area has spanned many countries, merging several bodies of literature (Sandler and Shani, 1989; Shanklin and Kuzma, 1992; Javalgi et al,, 1994; Cousens and Slack, 1996; Stipp and Schiavone, 1996; Quester, 1997a; Amis et al,, 1999).

This effect, however, may well be more complex than previously thought: For example, Javalgi et al. (1994) and d'Astous and Bitz (1995) questioned whether sponsorship could provoke such deep change in the corporate social responsibility (CSR) image of the sponsor. For example, they did not find a linear and automatic response in corporate image and the boost in corporate image is, according to these two authors, commensurate with what it was prior to the sponsorship.

One of the most unfortunate outcomes of the potential CSR benefits of sponsorship has been the targeting of sport properties by firms seeking to redress criticism of their negative social impact. Reminiscent of the days when tobacco firms targeted sport as an outlet for conveying advertising messages, fast food brands or firms involved in "unpopular" industries, like pharmaceuticals or genetic engineering, may perceive sponsorship as the means to regain some credit in the minds of consumers. This poses a difficult challenge for sport properties as they contemplate whether such an association may harm their own standing in the minds of consumers.

Conversely, a related issue involves the possible damage done to a brand when the sponsored entity spawns scandals, as when drug taking or corruption occurs, or when a sponsored athlete comes into disrepute for his off-field behavior. Golfer Tiger Woods' womanizing, for example, had more concrete consequences than just tabloid stories: some of his sponsors dropped him while others who had contemplated supporting him withdrew.

Conclusion: the important but forgotten role of emotions

Thirty years of research have transformed sponsorship research into a mature and well-established field of study. Its objectives have evolved, from awareness to image building, trial motivation or CSR manifestation. We now know that sponsorship can be used in a variety of ways, to reach a variety of publics, to fulfill a variety of objectives.

Far from being like advertising, but deprived of a message, sponsorship is seen to be able to work at a more subtle level, creating associations and meanings which, if well conceived by marketers, can benefit the brand. In fact, recent research acknowledges that sponsorship has grown away from a merely tactical tool to a strategic one.

When considering the marketing objectives of sponsorship, McDonald and Shaw (2005) have commented that sponsors no longer seek to build an image with the view of winning their consumers' minds. Rather, sponsors aim to target their hearts, and to communicate emotions before they communicate ideas (Nicholls, Roslow and Dublish, 1999). By addressing consumers through an activity they often relate to with passion, sponsorship offers an opportunity to build an affective bond (Meenaghan, 2001b), by definition less open to direct competition than rational arguments about the merit and attributes of the product or brand.

The connection with the target, via the emotional experience of a game or show, is harder to emulate, longer lasting and resonates better with consumers who are increasingly skeptical about marketing messages and practices. Indeed, in an extensive study undertaken in France and Australia, Bal et al. (2009) showed that both valence and intensity, key emotional dimensions, were related to both memorization and attitudinal responses towards sponsors. Indeed, this research suggested that beyond the actual management of the event itself, it was the experience that needed to be conceptualized and managed for the benefit of both audiences and sponsors. To the extent that greater intensity of emotion can mediate sponsorship effectiveness, experiential marketing would appear to have much to contribute to the sponsorship domain.

Sponsorship offers marketers many opportunities to connect in a unique manner with a multitude of audiences. Research has only just uncovered the tip of the iceberg and much remains to be explored, hypothesized and validated in relation to this highly visible yet only partially understood medium.

References

Amis J., Slack, T. and Berret, T. (1999) 'Sport sponsorships as distinctive competence', *European Journal of Marketing*, 33 (3/4), 250–72.

Armstrong, C. (1988) 'Sports sponsorship: a case-study approach to measuring its effectiveness', *European Research*, 16(2), 97–103.

Barros, C. and Silvestre, A. (2006) 'An evaluation of the sponsorship of Euro 2004', *International Journal of Sport Marketing and Sponsorship*, 7(3), 192–211.

Bal, C., Quester, P. and Plewa, C. (2009) 'Event-related emotions: A key metric to assess sponsorship effectiveness?' *Journal of Sponsorship*, 2(4), 27–41.

Becker-Olsen, K. (2003) 'And now, a word from our sponsor', *Journal of Advertising*, 32(2), 17–32.

Bennett, R. (1999) 'Sport sponsorship, spectator recall and false consensus', *European Journal of Marketing*, 33(3/4), 291–313.

Berrett, R. and Slack, T. (1999) 'Corporate sponsorship and organisational strategy: Bridging the gap', *International Journal of Sport Marketing and Sponsorship*, 1(3), 261–77.

Chadwick, S. and Thwaites, D. (2004) 'Advances in the management of sport sponsorship: Fact or fiction? Evidence from English Professional Soccer', *Journal of General Management*, 30(1), 39–59.

Cheng, P. and Stotlar, D. (1999) 'Success sponsorship: A marriage of sport and corporations for the next millennium', *Cyber-Journal of Sport Marketing*, 3(3), 1–9.

Cheng, P. and Stotlar, D. (2000) 'Analysis of Samsung Electronics' Bangkok Asian Games sponsorship', *Cyber-Journal of Sport Marketing*, 4(2), 1–9.

Chien, P., Cornwell, T. and Stokes, R. (2005) 'A theoretical framework for analysis of image transfer in multiple sponsorships', *Proceedings of the 2005 ANZMAC conference*, Perth, 17–25.

Christensen, S. (2006) 'Measuring consumer reactions to sponsorship partnerships based upon emotional and attitudinal responses', *International Journal of Market Research*, 48(1), 61–80.

Clark, J.M., Cornwell, B.T. and Pruitt, S.W. (2002) 'Corporate stadium sponsorships, signaling theory, agency conflicts and shareholder wealth', *Journal of Advertising Research*, 42(6), 16–32.

Cornwell, T. (1995) 'Sponsorship linked marketing', *Sport Marketing Quarterly*, 4(4), 13–24.

Cornwell, T. and Maignan, I. (1998) 'An international review of sponsorship research', *Journal of Advertising*, 27(1), 1–21.

Cornwell, T., Roy, D. and Steinard, I. (2001a) 'Exploring managers' perceptions of the impact of sponsorship on brand equity', *Journal of Advertising*, 30(2), 21–42.

Cornwell, Y., Weeks, C. and Roy, D. (2005) 'Sponsorship linked marketing: Opening the black box', *Journal of Advertising*, 34(2), 21–42.

Cousens, L. and Slack, T. (1996) 'Using sport sponsorships to penetrate local markets: The case of the fast food industry', *Journal of Sport Management*, 10(2), 169–87.

Cousens, L., Babiak, K. and Slack, T. (2001) 'Adopting a relationship marketing paradigm: The case of the National Basketball Association', *International Journal of Sport Marketing and Sponsorship*, 12(4), 331–55.

Crompton, J. (2004) 'Conceptualisation and alternate operationalizations of the measurements of sponsorship effectiveness in sport', *Leisure Studies*, 23(3), 267–81.

Crowley, M. (1991) 'Prioritising the sponsorship audience', *European Journal of Marketing*, 25(11), 11–21.

d'Astous, A. and Bitz, P. (1995) 'Consumer evaluations of sponsorship programmes', *European Journal of Marketing*, 29(12), 6–12.

Davies, F., Veloutsou, C. and Costa, A. (2006) 'Investigating the influence of a joint sponsorship of rival teams on supporter attitudes and brand preferences', *Journal of Marketing Communications*, 12(1), 31–48.

Derbaix, C. (1995) 'L'impact des réactions affectives induites par les messages publicitaires: Une analyse tenant compte de l'implication', *Recherche et Applications en Marketing*, 10(2), 3–30.

Desbordes, M., Ohl, F. and Tribou, G. (2004) *Marketing du Sport*. Paris, Economica.

Dolphin, R. (2003) 'Sponsorship: Perspectives on its strategic role', *Corporate Communications: An International Journal*, 8(3), 173–86.

Easton, S. and Mackie, P. (1998) 'When football came home: A case history of the sponsorship activity at Euro '96', *International Journal of Advertising*, 17(1), 99–114.

Erdogan, B.Z. and Kitchen, P.J. (1998) 'How to get the most out of celebrity endorsers', *Admap*, 33(4), 17–22.

Fahy, J., Farrelly, F. and Quester, P. (2004) 'Competitive advantage through sponsorship: A conceptual model and research propositions', *European Journal of Marketing*, 38(8), 1013–30.

Farrelly, F. and Quester, P. (1997) 'Sport and arts sponsorships: Examining the similarities and the differences in management practices', *Proceedings of the AMA Conference*, Dublin, Ireland, 874–86.

—— (2003) 'What drives renewal of sponsorship/agent relationships?' *Journal of Advertising Research*, 43(4), 353–60.

Farrelly, F., Greyser, S. and Quester, P. (2005) 'Defending the co-branding benefits of sponsorship B2B partnerships: The case of ambush marketing', *Journal of Advertising Research*, September, 339–48.

Farrelly, F., Quester, P. and Burton, R. (1997) 'Integrating sport sponsorship into the corporate marketing function: An international comparative study', *International Marketing Review*, 14 (2/3), 170–75.

Ferrand, A. and Pages, M. (1996) 'Image sponsoring: A methodology to match event and sponsor', *Journal of Sport Management*, 10(3), 278–91.

—— (1999) 'Image management in sport organization: The creation of value', *European Journal of Marketing*, 33(3/4), 387–401.

Fleck, N. and Quester, P. (2007) 'Birds of a feather flock together . . . Definition, role and measure of congruence: An application to sponsorship', *Psychology and Marketing*, 24(11), 975–1000.

Gardner, M. and Schuman, P. (1987) 'Sponsorship: An important component of the promotion mix', *Journal of Advertising*, 16(1), 11–17.

Garland, M., MacPherson, T. and Haughey, K. (2004) 'Rugby fan attraction factors', *Marketing Bulletin*, 15, 1–12.

Grimes, E. and Meenaghan, T. (1998) 'Focusing commercial sponsorship on the internal corporate audience', *International Journal of Advertising*, 17(1), 51–74.

Gwinner, K. and Eaton, J. (1999) 'Building brand image through event sponsorship: The role of image transfer', *Journal of Advertising*, 28(4), 47–57.

Gwinner, K. and Swanson, S. (2003) 'A model of fan identification: Antecedents and sponsorship outcomes', *Journal of Services Marketing*, 17(3), 275–81.

Irwin, R. and Sutton, W. (1994) 'Sport sponsorship objectives: An analysis of their relative importance for major corporate sponsors', *European Journal for Sport Management*, 1(2), 93–101.

Irwin, R., Lachowetz, T., Cornwell, T. and Clark, J. (2003) 'Cause related sport sponsorship: An assessment of spectator beliefs, attitudes, and behavioral intentions', *Sport Marketing Quarterly*, 12(3), 131–39.

Javalgi, R., Raylor, M., Gross, A. and Lampman, E. (1994) 'Awareness of sponsorship and corporate image: An empirical investigation', *Journal of Advertising*, 23(4), 47–58.

Johar, G. and Pham, M. (1999) 'Relatedness, prominence, and constructive sponsor identification', *Journal of Marketing Research*, 36(2), 81–123.

Johnston, T. and Scherer, K. (2000) 'Vocal communication of emotion', in *Handbook of Emotions* (2nd edn), New York, Guilford Press, pp. 220–35.

Kuzma, J., Shanklin, W. and McCally, J. (1993) 'Number one principles for sporting events seeking corporate sponsors: Meet benefactors' objectives', *Sport Marketing Quarterly*, 2(3), 27–32.

Kuzma, J., Veltri, F., Kuzma, A. and Miller, J. (2003) 'Negative corporate sponsor information: The impact on consumer attitudes and purchase intentions', *International Sport Journal*, 7(2), 140–49.

Lardinoit, T. and Derbaix, C. (2001) 'Sponsorship and Recall of Sponsors', *Psychology and Marketing*, 18(2), 167–90.

Lardinoit, T. and Nagard-Assayag, E. (2004) 'Comment le marketing sportif peut-il contribuer au succès des nouveaux produits?' *Décisions Marketing*, 35, 61–74.

Lardinoit, T. and Quester, P. (2001) 'Attitudinal effects of combined sponsorship and sponsors' prominence on basketball in Europe', *Journal of Advertising Research*, 41(1), 48–58.

Lardinoit, T., Derbaix, C. and Gerard, P. (1996) 'Efficacité mémorielle du parrainage sportif: Une étude de trois modalités de mise en œuvre', *Proceedings of the 12th AFM Congress*, ed. AFM, Poitiers: Saporta, B., 569–82.

Levin, A., Joiner, C. and Cameron, G. (2001) 'The impact of sport sponsorship on consumers' brand attitudes and recall: The case of NASCAR fans', *Journal of Current Issues and Research in Advertising*, 23(2), 23–36.

Masterton, R. (2005) 'The importance of creative match in television sponsorship', *International Journal of Advertising*, 24(4), 504–26.

McCarthy, L. and Irwin, R. (2000) 'An examination of the rationale and motives for corporate purchase of stadia and arena naming rights', *Cyber-Journal of Sport Marketing*, 4(3), 1–9.

McDonald, H. and Shaw, R.N. (2005) 'Satisfaction as a predictor of football club members' intentions', *International Journal of Sports Marketing & Sponsorship*, 7(1), 81–87.

Meenaghan, T. (1983) 'Commercial sponsorship', *European Journal of Marketing*, 17(7), 5–75

—— (1991a) 'The role of sponsorship in the marketing communications mix', *International Journal of Advertising*, 10(1), 35–47.

—— (1991b) 'Sponsorship: legitimizing the medium', *European Journal of Marketing*, 25(11), 5–10.

—— (1994) 'Point of view – Ambush marketing: Immoral or imaginative practice?' *Journal of Advertising Research*, 34(5), 77–88.

—— (1998a) 'Ambush marketing: Corporate strategy and consumer reaction', *Psychology and Marketing*, 15(4), 305–22.

—— (1998b) 'Current developments and future directions in sponsorship', *International Journal of Advertising*, 17(1), 3–28.

—— (1999) 'Commercial sponsorship – The development of understanding', *International Journal of Sport Marketing and Sponsorship*, 1(1), 13–19.

—— (2001a) 'Sponsorship and advertising: A comparison of consumer perceptions', *Psychology and Marketing*, 18(2), 191–215.

—— (2001b) 'Understanding sponsorship effects', *Psychology and Marketing*, 18(2), 95–122.

—— (2005) 'Global sports sponsorship', in Amis. J. and Bettina Cornwell, T. (eds.) *Evaluating Sponsorship Effects*, Oxford, Berg.

Meenaghan, T. and Shipley, D. (1999) 'Media effects in commercial sponsorship', *European Journal of Marketing*, 33(3/4), 328–47.

Nebenzhal, I. and Jaffe, E. (1991) 'The effectiveness of sponsored events in promoting a country's image', *International Journal of Advertising*, 10(3), 223–37.

Nichols, J. and Roslow, S. (1994) 'Sport event sponsorship for brand promotion', *Journal of Applied Business Research*, 10(4), 35–42.

Nicholls, J., Roslow, S. and Dublish, S. (1999) 'Brand recall and brand preference at sponsored golf and tennis tournaments', *European Journal of Marketing*, 33(3/4), 365–87.

Olkkonen, R. (2001) 'Case study: The network approach to international sport sponsorship arrangement', *Journal of Business and Industrial Marketing*, 16(4), 309–17.

O'Reilly, N. and Harrison, M. (2005) 'Sponsorship Management: A Status Report', *The Sport Journal*, 8(4), 34–47.

Otker, T. and Hayes, P. (1988) 'Evaluation de l'efficacité du Sponsoring: Expérience de la Coupe du Monde de Football 1986', *Revue Française du Marketing*, 118, 13–40.

Pham, M. (1992) 'Effects of involvement, arousal, and pleasure on the recognition of sponsorship stimuli', *Advances in Consumer Research*, 19(1), 85–93.

Pitts, B. and Slattery, J. (2004) 'An examination of the effects of time on sponsorship awareness levels', *Sport Marketing Quarterly*, 13(1), 43–54.

Pope, N. (1998a) 'Consumption values, sponsorship awareness, brand and product use' *Journal of Product and Brand Management*, 7(2), 45–67.

—— (1998b) 'Overview of current sponsorship thought', *Cyber-Journal of Sport Marketing*, 2(1), 1–7.

Pope, N.K. and Voges, K. (1995) 'Short term recall and recognition of advertising and signage in telecast stadium sporting events', in Grant, K. and Walker, I. (eds.) *World Marketing Congress*, 7(3), 11-11–1-18, Melbourne, Academy of Marketing Science.

Pracejus, J. (2004) 'Seven psychological mechanisms through which sponsorship impacts consumer', in L.R. Kahle and C. Riley (eds.), *Sport Marketing and the Psychology of Marketing Communications*, Portland, Lawrence Elbraum Associates, pp. 175–89.

Pruitt, S., Cornwell, T. and Clark, J. (2004) 'The NASCAR phenomenon: Auto racing sponsorships and shareholder wealth', *Journal of Advertising Research*, 44(3), 281–96.

Quester, P. (1997a) 'Awareness as a measure of sponsorship effectiveness: The Adelaide Formula One Grand Prix and evidence of incidental ambush effects', *Journal of Marketing Communications*, 3(1), 1–20.

—— (1997b) 'Sponsorship returns: Unexpected findings and the value of naming rights', *Corporate Communications: An International Journal*, 2(13), 101–8.

Quester, P. and Farrelly, F. (1998) 'Brand association and memory decay effects of sponsorship', *Journal of Product and Brand Management*, 7(6), 539–42.

—— (2005) 'Building global alliances: Relationship-marketing and the sponsorship of sport', in B. Cornwell and J. Amis (eds.), *Sport Commerce and Culture: Global Sport Sponsorship*, Oxford and New York, Berg, pp. 225–42.

Quester, P. and Thompson, B. (2001) 'Advertising and promotion leverage on arts sponsorship effectiveness', *Journal of Advertising Research*, 41(1), 33–47.

Rodgers, S. (2003) 'The effects of sponsor relevance on consumer reactions to Internet sponsorships', *Journal of Advertising*, 32(4), 67–76.

Roy, D. and Cornwell, T. (2004) 'The effects of consumer knowledge on responses to event sponsorships', *Psychology and Marketing*, 21(3), 185–207.

Sandler, D. and Shani, D. (1989) 'Olympic sponsorship vs. ambush marketing: Who gets the gold?' *Journal of Advertising Research*, 29(4), 9–14.

Shanklin, W. and Kuzma, J. (1992) 'Buying that sporting image', *Marketing Management*, 1(2), 58–67.

Shannon, J. (1999) 'Sport marketing: An examination of academic marketing publication', *Journal of Services Marketing*, 13(6/7), 517–22.

Speed, R. and Thompson, P. (2000) 'Determinants of sport sponsorship responses', *Journal of the Academy of Marketing Science*, 28(2), 227–38.

Stipp, H. and Schiavone, N. (1996) 'Modeling the impact of Olympic sponsorship on corporate image', *Journal of Advertising Research*, 36(4), 22–38.

Thompson, B. and Quester, P. (2000) 'Evaluating sponsorship effectiveness: The Adelaide Festival of the Arts', in *Proceedings of the ANZMAC Conference*, Gold Coast, 1263–68.

Thwaites, D. (1994) 'Sport sponsorship – Philanthropy or a commercial investment? Evidence from UK Building Societies', *Journal of Promotion Management*, 2(1), 27–44.

—— (1995) 'Professional football sponsorship – Profitable or profligate?' *International Journal of Advertising*, 14(2), 149–64.

Vignali, C. (1997) 'The MIXMAP model for international sport sponsorship', *European Business Review*, 97(4), 187–93.

Walliser, B. (1994) 'Les déterminants de la mémorisation des Sponsors', *Revue Française du Marketing*, 15, 83–95.

—— (1997) 'Le rôle de l'intensité des émotions éprouvées par le téléspectateur dans la mémorisation du parrainage', *Recherches et Applications en Marketing*, 11(1), 5–21.

—— (2003) 'L'évolution et l'état de l'art de la recherche internationale sur le parrainage', *Recherche et Applications en Marketing*, 18(1), 65–94.

23

AMBUSH MARKETING

Benoit Séguin and Dana Ellis

Introduction

Ambush marketing has become an expected part of the marketing and sponsorship landscape that surrounds modern sport events. Its origins are often tied to the 1984 Olympic Games in Los Angeles when Kodak ambushed the official sponsor, Fuji. The proceeding years have seen the cost of staging major sporting events skyrocket and along with this the required investment of sponsors. For instance, the 2010 Vancouver Olympic Winter Games are reported to have cost $1.6 billion USD (Anonymous, 2009) with domestic partners injecting $756 billion US, TOP ("The Olympic Partners") sponsors contributing more than $196 million US and $447 million US coming from the International Olympic Committee (IOC) for television rights (Anonymous, 2009). This level of investment creates an expectation from sponsors that the International Olympic Committee (IOC) and national organizing committee (NOC) will protect their rights to exclusivity in order to ensure they receive maximum value for their money. The biggest threat to sponsorship exclusivity is ambush marketing.

Sandler and Shani (1989: 9) define ambush marketing as "a planned effort (campaign) by an organization to associate itself indirectly with an event in order to gain at least some of the recognition and benefits that are associated with being an official sponsor." While this definition is often cited, it can be argued that there is no clear consensus among academics or practitioners over how to define the practice (Crow and Hoek, 2003; McKelvey and Grady, 2008; Meenaghan, 1994). Much of the disagreement stems from the varying viewpoints of those trying to define ambush marketing. As is often the case with divisive concepts, the position and experiences of the person providing the definition will contribute greatly to the nature and breadth of their description. For example, former marketing executive Jerry Welsh describes ambush marketing as "a marketing strategy with its programmatic outcomes, occupying the thematic space of a sponsoring competitor, and formulated to vie with that sponsoring competitor for marketing pre-eminence" (Welsh, 2002: 1).

On the other hand, those companies who have paid for the right to be a sponsor, and property owners such as the IOC or FIFA (football's governing body) usually take an opposing view. Their definitions tend towards a more negative tone and make statements relating to the perceived ethical issues of such strategies. As Hoek and Gendall (2002) suggest, however, it seems more likely that a true understanding lies somewhere along a continuum with the above viewpoints at either end. Throughout this chapter, we will provide the reader with an objective view by exploring both sides of the arguments and presenting our thoughts on some current issues. We begin with an overview of the research and concerns related to ambush marketing, the various roles and responsibilities of management in dealing with the issue, and finally an examination of where ambush marketing seems to be headed in the future.

Ambush marketing: research and discussion

While marketing and sponsorship are relatively mature fields of study, the area of ambush marketing can be described as comparitively young. As noted above, the most often cited "beginning" of ambush marketing is the 1984 Olympic Games in Los Angeles when Kodak ambushed the official sponsor Fuji by sponsoring the television broadcast of the Games as well as the United States track team (Sandler and Shani, 1989). The practice seemingly took off from there and academic research in the area followed quickly behind. Sandler and Shani's (1989) article "Olympic Sponsorship vs. 'Ambush' Marketing: Who gets the gold?" is viewed as a seminal piece in the area and as a result it can be noted that it has been just over 20 years since the birth of the field. In that time great strides have been made in the practice, management and study of ambush marketing.

Looking at past literature, however, we note five overarching themes in the research including, first, attempts to define and describe the concept of ambush marketing (e.g. Crow and Hoek, 2003; Graham, 1997; Meenaghan, 1998; Payne, 1998; McKelvey and Grady, 2008), and second, investigations of consumer perception/attitude towards a number of sponsorship related issues including ambush marketing (e.g. Meenaghan, 1998; Sandler and Shani, 1993; Séguin, Lyberger, O'Reilly and McCarthy, 2005; Moorman and Greenwell, 2005; Portlock and Rose, 2009; Shani and Sandler, 1998). Third, there is examination of the practice from a legal perspective, including judicial precedence in the area (Batcha, 1998), or a discussion of the legislation which governs intellectual property (i.e. trademarks) generally (e.g. Bean, 1995; Crow and Hoek, 2003; McKelvey, 2003) and ambush marketing legislation specifically (e.g. Bhattacharjee and Roa, 2006; Kendall and Cuthroys, 2001; Scassa, 2008). Fourth is an examination of the ethical issues involved in ambush marketing (e.g. Crompton, 2004; O'Sullivan and Murphy, 1998; Séguin et al., 2005) and finally, various strategies aimed at fighting and preventing ambush marketing (e.g. Burton and Chadwick, 2009).

There is little doubt from the growing literature on the subject that ambush marketing is regarded as a major threat to sponsorship programs. A major part of this threat stems from its contribution to the interconnected issues of sponsorship clutter and confusion. In the context of sport marketing, clutter can be defined as "advertising and/or sponsorship messages vying to get the attention of fans, spectators, and potential consumers, which may cause confusion in the marketplace" (O'Reilly and Séguin, 2009: 226). While sponsorship was originally viewed as the antidote to a cluttered advertising environment, allowing a more focused approach to targeting consumers, currently it is just another factor contributing to the clutter. The environment surrounding sporting events is, by nature, cluttered, particularly in respect of major events like the Olympic Games, Super Bowl and professional sport leagues. Outside of sponsorship itself, multiple channels within broadcast conglomerates showing the event, editorial reporting, in-person spectators as well as television spectators, and also the internet have cluttered the environment. Directly within the sponsorship environment the multiple categories offered (e.g. worldwide partner, national partners, supporters, suppliers, broadcast partners, licensees) add to the clutter. With clutter such an inherent part of the sport sponsorship environment, the addition of ambush marketing is a real concern for property owners and sponsors.

The relationship between high levels of consumer confusion and an increasingly cluttered sponsorship environment is recognized in the literature (Stotlar, 1993; Shani and Sandler, 1998; Séguin et al., 2005; Séguin and O'Reilly, 2008). While clutter itself can be viewed as a negative outcome of ambush marketing it is the consumer confusion resulting from this cluttered environment that is the ultimate threat. It is suggested that companies who partake in ambush marketing seek to create confusion in the minds of consumers with the intention of not just boosting recognition of their own brand, but also weakening the impact of their competitor's sponsorship (McKelvey, 1992; Sandler and Shani, 1989). The most concerning aspect for property owners is that in achieving the aim of weakening their competitor's sponsorship it is argued that ambush marketers devalue the property itself by undermining the property's ability to demand premium sponsorship fees for exclusivity (Payne, 1998; Townley, Harrington and Couchman, 1998). Townley et al. (1998) go even further and suggest that the vitality of entire sport systems and major events could be affected by such practices.

While research seemingly supports the idea that a large amount of confusion surrounds sport sponsorship, attribution of blame for such confusion is much less straightforward. The increasing complexity of sponsorship programs and a lack of consumer understanding related to them are noted to be at least partly at fault for such confusion. For instance, many consumers believe that only official sponsors have the right to advertise during the broadcast of major events, when this is not in fact the case (Lyberger and McCarthy, 2001; Shani and Sandler, 1998).

Ambush marketing strategies

Numerous authors have sought to categorize the various recognized strategies of ambush marketing (e.g. Crompton, 2004; Meenaghan, 1994, 1998). The difficulty is that it can be argued that there are infinite numbers of strategies, limited only by the creativity of marketing professionals. With this in mind only the four most prevalent categories are discussed here.

Sponsoring media coverage

In addition to sponsorship programs the worldwide sale of broadcasting rights is an essential source of revenue for the vitality of major sport events. The broadcast rights for the 2008 Beijing Olympic Games generated more than $1.7 billion US, which was distributed among the organizing committees for the Olympic Games (OCOGs), the NOCs, the international sport federations (IFs) and the IOC (IOC, 2010). However, despite being fundamental facets of an integrated marketing plan, a disconnection between the sale of sponsorship rights and the sale of commercial airtime during broadcasts can lead to difficulties in protecting sponsors from ambush marketing. While sponsors are often offered first right of refusal for commercial airtime during the broadcast of sporting events (e.g. McDonald's during broadcast of Olympic Games), the often premium costs associated with such events may be unreasonable to a sponsor, which in turn may decline the purchase of airtime. This type of ambush is arguably among the most effective as research has indicated that the difference between an advertiser and sponsor is unclear to consumers (Séguin et al., 2005).

Sponsoring subcategories

Athletes, teams and/or national and international sport governing bodies provide sponsors with another way to ambush official sponsors of an event. While an event like the FIFA

World Cup comes around once every four years, athletes and teams compete before and after such events as well, and in doing so develop their own sponsorship agreements. In actively leveraging these associations during a major event, the competitors of official sponsors may cause confusion among consumers, who have difficulty distinguishing a subcategory sponsor from an official event sponsor. For example, while Adidas is the official sponsor of the FIFA World Cup, Nike has sponsorship contracts with many of the biggest players in the game, and in recent years their related commercials have become an eagerly anticipated and much discussed part of the World Cup experience. In fact, in the first week of its release their viral video campaign in the lead-up to the 2010 FIFA World Cup set a record for most views of a viral ad in a week (Engelhart, 2010).[1]

Advertising that corresponds with the event

While they have no right to use official symbols and trademarks, non-sponsors are able to participate in large promotional campaigns in and around a major event which could be classed as ambush marketing. Billboards, television and radio commercials, newspaper advertising, sampling, give-aways, banners and entertainment pavilions are all potential promotional tools to be used. This strategy is particularly effective when the advertising is thematic or uses implied association, which will be discussed below. Partly in an effort to combat this type of ambush, the Olympic Charter sets out specific "clean venue guidelines." The aspects related to ambush marketing require the host city to claim all outdoor advertising space (e.g. billboards, bus advertisements, airport ad space) with only official sponsors being allowed to advertise their product within the areas surrounding the event site. In addition, the IOC has maintained its stance on allowing no form of publicity (e.g. billboards) in and above the sporting venues. The Olympic Games remain the only major sport property to have such a policy and, interestingly, most consumers are not aware of this fact (Séguin et al., 2005).

Thematic advertising and implied association

This type of ambush is closely related to the above strategy of advertising which corresponds to the event. Thematic advertising and implied association refers to an instance where a competitor uses related sport and/or destination (e.g., New Zealand for the 2011 Rugby World Cup) imagery and/or wording in their advertising but does not include restricted trademarks, symbols or words. For example, during the 2006 World Cup in Germany, the nose cones of forty Lufthansa aircraft were painted to resemble a football, raising the ire of FIFA and the official airline sponsor Emirates (Wilson, 2006). While they make no claims about any direct association, corporations who use such strategies do so with the same goal in mind as sponsors: to connect themselves to the event in the consumer's mind.

As discussed above, the four strategies outlined here are only a few of the various ambush strategies used by marketers; others include overextending given sponsorship rights, congratulatory messages, related promotions and the use of disclaimers (Meenaghan, 1998; O'Reilly and Séguin, 2009).

Ambush marketing management roles and responsibilities

While a study by Farrelly, Quester and Greyser (2005) found that some sponsors and property owners believe it is the sole responsibility of the property owner to manage the threat of ambush marketing, it is more accepted that in every sponsorship agreement there are various stakeholders who each have their own integrated role to play in ensuring the success of their partnership. In relation to ambush marketing, each group has specific management responsibilities which they must undertake in order to ensure they do not leave themselves open to ambush attacks. From a property management perspective the relevant stakeholders for most mega-sport events can be identified as the sponsor (e.g. Coca-Cola, McDonald's), the property owner (e.g. IOC, International Cricket Council (ICC)) and the property caretaker (e.g. The London Organising Committee of the Olympic Games and Paralympic Games, the United States Olympic Committee). Using Séguin and O'Reilly's (2008) model as an initial guide, and the Olympic Games as an ongoing example, the following section will discuss various methods of managing ambush marketing and outlining the roles and responsibilities of all stakeholders in relation to each approach.

Managing the event brand

The first strategy to fight ambush marketing is to ensure the proper management and development of the event brand. In the case of the Olympic Games, the event brand is composed of such elements as the five-ring symbol and just as importantly its related associations (e.g. peace, excellence). As the property owner it is the long-term responsibility of the IOC to be proactive in the growth and protection of their brand through various means. Brand management strategies such as defining the brand, establishing a brand identity, positioning the brand, building brand equity and participating in brand research are all important parts of ensuring the brand is strong enough to fight ambush marketing. Such characteristics are fundamental in building and growing a strong brand (Aaker, 1991; Keller, 2003).

Integrated public relations program

By the very nature of this strategy it is the combined responsibility of property owners and caretakers. In the case of the Olympic Games this can refer not just to the IOC and the organizing committee, but also the National Olympic Committee of the host city. It is important that all these groups collaborate on their response to the threat of ambush marketing as the first line of defense is often a public relations move such as "naming and shaming" the offending ambusher. An integrated public relations program involves ensuring that throughout each level of coordination sponsors and ambushers can count on the same public messages and response to ambush activities from the organizers. With this in mind there are four keys to a successful integrated public relations program for mega-sport events. First, the plans must be consistent and seamless, and second, they need to have worldwide scope. Third, they are supported by the marketing plan of each engaged stakeholder, and fourth, they are created through collaboration between stakeholders (Séguin and O'Reilly, 2008).

Education programs

Education programs targeted at specific groups offer a further strategy for managing ambush marketing and are the responsibility of both property owners and caretakers. The main groups to be targeted are likely ambushers, small local businesses, sport federations and consumers. Education programs targeting likely ambushers might ensure they are aware of the legal rights of organizing committees in dealing with ambushers, as well as the committee's promised response to any ambush marketing campaigns. Such programs would hopefully serve as a deterrent. Education programs targeting small local businesses, however, can serve a much more informative purpose. It is often noted that in many cases when a small local business is participating in ambush marketing they are typically unaware their behavior is concerning to event organizers. Ensuring such businesses are aware of formal anti-ambush marketing guidelines as well as the organizing committee's negative stance towards such practices could drastically reduce occurrences of smaller-scale ambush marketing. The sport federations are also the target of educational programs as many times, ambush marketing results from the action of a sport federation, its sponsors or athletes. Finally, consumer education programs have long been suggested as a way to help combat ambush marketing (Sandler and Shani, 1993; Shani and Sandler, 1998) and their importance has not diminished over time.

In the lead-up to the 2010 Vancouver Winter Olympic Games the organizing committee (VANOC) viewed education as the number one tool in fighting and preventing ambush marketing, even with anti-ambush legislation as part of their arsenal. In this instance sponsors, potential ambushers and consumers were all subject to educational programs established by VANOC around this issue. The organizing committee tried to ensure sponsors were in complete understanding about exactly what rights they had purchased, how best to use those rights, the ability of VANOC to protect those rights and the challenges to be expected in this respect. The task of educating consumers and potential ambushers is more complex with a much broader scope. VANOC attempted to do this by creating and publicizing a brochure and website which sought to outline exactly what would be considered ambush marketing in the eyes of the organizing committee. This was accomplished by creating fictional situations and providing an exact framework for how VANOC would assess the threat of ambush marketing in such a situation.

Finally, as demonstrated by many large sport properties such as the IOC and the football governing bodies FIFA and UEFA, among others, education programs for national and local governing bodies and organizing committees covering such areas as general marketing expertise, brand management, ambush protection expectations and symbol registration and protection should be viewed as a vital strategy in managing ambush marketing.

Sponsorship structure

The close control and management of sponsorship structures related to major sport properties is vital. Despite the emergence of product category exclusivity, some sponsorship systems still place too high a value on the amount of money which can be raised over the need to limit clutter and confusion. Four main problems can arise from this:

- Too many companies have access to the brand;
- Ambiguity relating to the rights of different sponsorship categories;
- Uncertainty relating to the broadcast advertising rights;
- Sponsors acting above their purchased rights category.

The major issue with each of these problems is that they serve to further increase confusion and allow ambushers to become just another aspect of sponsorship that is not understood by consumers. In order to successfully manage ambush marketing it is critical that property owners design a sponsorship structure which minimizes such confusion. Three key strategies are suggested. The first is to create a close link between broadcast advertising and sponsorship (Séguin and O'Reilly, 2008; Shani and Sandler, 1998). By linking broadcast advertising and sponsorship, property owners can better control the advertising space surrounding an event. A second strategy would be to ensure there is direct coordination between those stakeholders selling national and international sponsorships (Séguin and O'Reilly, 2008). Taking the Olympics as an example, while the IOC is responsible for selling worldwide sponsorship rights, it is the job of the organizing committee to sell domestic partnerships and form supplier agreements. Ensuring that there is close communication and direct coordination between the two groups helps make certain that the two sponsorship programs complement each other, rather than overlap and create harmful confusion. The final strategy is to ensure that once a sponsorship structure that works is in place, it is largely maintained with few alterations over the long term (Lyberger and McCarthy, 2001; Shani and Sandler, 1998). This gives sponsors and consumers a chance to learn and understand how it works. Such consistency over time should help make education programs like those mentioned above more effective and therefore further limit the confusion.

Sponsorship recognition programs

This strategy is closely related to the education of consumers, and to integrated public relations programs. While most major sport events do have some form of sponsorship recognition program, Séguin and O'Reilly (2008) found that, in relation to Olympic sponsors, the program did not go far enough. It was suggested that once a sponsor has contributed significant funds to support an event and leverage their association they should not be the only party responsible for telling the public of the value they have contributed. In this case it is the responsibility of event organizers to ensure consumers are aware of how important sponsors' contributions are, and what they mean to the vitality of the movement. A highly developed sponsorship recognition program should involve various elements such as:

- International scope: Many sponsors are granted worldwide marketing rights and so it is only logical that their contribution should be recognized and commended on a global scale.
- Integrated approach: The message of thanks and recognition towards sponsors should be not just present, but coherent and consistent among all associated parties. That is, each level from the property owner, the property caretaker and any other governing bodies involved should collaborate on a program rather than trying to construct individual and potentially incongruous programs.
- High level of sophistication. A professional and well-thought-out program of thanks will not only be more likely to impress the sponsor, but will also impress the consumer and therefore hold their attention.

The strategy of ensuring there is a strong sponsorship recognition program is important in managing ambush marketing because, once again, it works towards fighting consumer confusion and can serve as an extension of consumer education programs.

Activation/leveraging of sponsorship

Activation has long been recognized as the fundamental strategy in ensuring successful sponsorship arrangements. It is often said that the initial sponsorship fee really just permits a sponsor to begin spending even more money promoting their new association (Sandler and Shani, 1993). In fact, Séguin, Teed and O'Reilly (2005) note that sponsors may spend anywhere up to a 10:1 ratio of leveraging to sponsorship fee when discussing major sport properties. Ensuring that sponsorships are fully leveraged is frequently discussed as a vital strategy to manage ambush marketing (Farrelly et al., 2005; Lyberger and McCarthy, 2001;

Sandler and Shani, 1993; Séguin and O'Reilly, 2008). In this instance it is a strategy where the focus is on the sponsor to protect themselves rather than on the property owner and care-taker. However, despite the undeniable positive impact on the success of sponsorship and in the fight against ambush marketing, many sponsors are seen to be negligent in this area.

There are three important elements of activation which serve to help combat ambush marketing. The first is the sponsor's use of the full media and promotional mix. That is, their advertising campaigns related to the sponsorship should include, among others, newspaper, internet, radio, billboards, sweepstakes, hospitality and, most importantly, television. An important activation strategy is for the sponsor to make the association with the event long term. In the example of the Olympic Games, sponsors are brought in on contracts many years in advance. It is to the advantage of the sponsors to begin leveraging the association between their own brand and the Olympic brand early on so that consumers build up an awareness of the partnership. Finally, sponsors should participate in brand integration with the property. This means they actively incorporate their own brand and its values with those of the prop-erty using strategies such as co-branding and collaborative messaging (Séguin and O'Reilly, 2008). All of the above strategies for activation will serve to reduce the impact and effective-ness of ambush marketing tactics. It leaves consumers with no doubt as to who is the official sponsor and how they are benefitting the movement. Ultimately it is about ensuring the sponsor has "claimed their space" in the event landscape (Séguin and O'Reilly, 2008) so that no ambusher has the opportunity to intrude.

Legal strategies

Initial legal strategies for the protection of major sporting marks and symbols, such as the Olympic rings, were not created for the purpose of fighting ambush marketing but rather as a way to protect the trademarks from unauthorized use. However, as the dynamic between hallmark sporting events (e.g. Olympic Games, FIFA World Cup) and commercialism has changed, so too have the methods and motivations behind the use of legal strategies to protect their trademarks. While the Olympics offer the most obvious example of this, a similar process has arguably been played out at many other sport organizations and governing bodies as sport sponsorship concerns are added to the reasons for pursuing brand protection.

While the other strategies for fighting ambush marketing discussed in the sections above have not become obsolete, the use of anti-ambush legislation as a last line of defense and a deterrent against the practice has become increasingly prevalent and it could be argued is now a requisite component of any brand protection system. Despite this it was not until the mid 2000s that anti-ambush marketing legislation for hallmark events became commonplace, and in some instances, such as for the Olympic Games and the FIFA World Cup, a requirement for host cities. Examples of such legislation include but are not limited to: the *Melbourne 2006 Commonwealth Games Protection Act 2005*, the *London Olympic Games and Paralympic Games Act 2006*, and *Canada's Olympic and Paralympic Marks Act 2007*, which will be examined in more detail in the following section.

Ambush marketing going forward

Government involvement and anti-ambush legislation

In Canada the *Olympic and Paralympic Marks Act* (OPMA) was passed in 2007 and it "provide[d] for the protection of Olympic and Paralympic marks and protection against certain misleading business associations between a business and the Olympic Games, the Paralympic Games or certain committees associated with those Games" (Olympic and Paralympic Marks Act, 2007). While, like in other countries, Canada's *Trade-marks Act* offers general protection for fundamental Olympic marks, OPMA built on this by covering both those Olympic words and symbols with permanent protection, such as the Olympic rings and the words Canadian Olympic Committee, as well as offering protection for additional words and symbols related specifically to the 2010 Games for a period of time before, during and after the Games, which expired on December 31, 2010.[2]

OPMA also offers event organizers an increased ability to seek resolution though the law in a more timely and undemanding manner. Such a step is viewed by sport event organizers as vital for anti-ambush legislation due to the fact that most major sport events take place over a limited period of time. In the case of a serious ambush attack it may be the case that the event is over, and the damage has been done, before standard court proceedings would have any chance to have an impact.

While OPMA was enacted in 2007 for a specific time period (2007–10), there are instances where such legislation has become permanent. This is the case in New Zealand where the *Major Events Management Act 2007* (MEMA) was passed in preparation for the 2011 Rugby World Cup and the 2015 Cricket World Cup, both of which required a commitment to legislated brand protection in the bid phase. The purpose of MEMA is to "implement the government's decision to enact protections against ambush marketing for major events in a stand–alone, generic piece of legislation" (Major Events Management Act, 2007) and it was explicitly noted that "the availability of ambush protection will be a significant marketing advantage for New Zealand when bidding for future events" (Major Events Management Act, 2007). Under this law there are a set number of criteria that define an event as "major," and if a sporting event meets their requirements and is declared a "major event" it is then subject to the protection offered by MEMA. It seems likely that other countries will follow in the footsteps of New Zealand and such permanent protection will become the next step in the evolution of brand protection.

Looking back on the Vancouver Games and OPMA there seemed to be three obvious benefits of anti–ambush marketing legislation to look towards in the future. The first is its function as a deterrent. The second benefit is arguably the use of the legislation as an educational tool (Ellis, Gauthier and Séguin, 2011a). For instance, when Canadian national sport organizations were interviewed, many noted that OPMA served to help them understand what VANOC would or would not accept (Ellis et al., 2011a). Similarly, businesses, athletes and consumers with little knowledge in this area were able to use the restrictions as a guide to help in understanding the sometimes murky domain of ambush marketing. Finally, the introduction of such legislation provided sponsors with an increasing sense of security from ambushers. It is contended by many that such feelings of security among sponsors are key in allowing major sport events to continue raising the required sponsorship funds.

Going forward, however, there are also some concerns that have been raised about the use of legislation as a tool for combating ambush marketing. Specifically Ellis, Scassa and Séguin (2011b) have noted potential issues from both a legal and a business standpoint. It was noted earlier that the elusive and subjective nature of providing a definition for ambush marketing remains an issue for academics and practitioners. From a legal standpoint this may create a few issues. While on the one hand legislation may be beneficial as a tool for educating people and organizations about what is acceptable or unacceptable in this area, one could equally argue that a practice that consists of so many grey areas is difficult to capture through the black and white realities of legislation. With this in mind the scope of behavior covered under legislation could vary greatly depending on variables such as the wording and the system of government in the legislating country. Another legal concern with anti-ambush marketing legislation is the high cost of access to the legal system. In most countries the cost for a small or medium business to fight against an injunction or other legal judgment would be so prohibitive they would have little choice but to acquiesce even if they feel they are in the right.

With the threat of such measures in mind, such legislation may also run the risk of stifling community engagement in the event. In Vancouver VANOC did an admirable job in enforcing the legislation with enough flexibility to allow community businesses to engage with the Games and take advantage of the event in their city. However, the inherent subjectivity of such legislation, in that it depends on the interpretation of those enforcing it, means that this may not always be the case. There was much public criticism of the 2010 World Cup in South Africa around this issue (Khoabane, 2010; Shikwati, 2010) and with ever more stringent versions of such legislation being enacted it is sure to continue as a talking point in the future.

From a business perspective there are also potential issues raised by anti-ambush marketing legislation. Ellis et al. (2011b) suggest four such issues. The expectation of legislation means there may be some issues for properties to manage increased expectations from sponsors. The second business issue may be the increasing need for legal expertise in sport organizations such as IFs (e.g. ICC, International Ice Hockey Federation (IIHF)), NOCs (e.g. British Olympic Association (BOA), United States Olympic Committee (USOC)), international governing bodies (e.g. IOC, FIFA) and NSOs (e.g. Alpine Canada, British Gymnastics). This may be a particular challenge for smaller federations who could struggle to cope with an increasing need for legal expertise. A third issue which may evolve out of the growing use of ambush marketing legislation is the increasing need for an integrated public relations (PR) structure to handle a potential public backlash.

For example, at the 2010 FIFA World Cup in South Africa a group of women wearing orange dresses given to them by the brewers Bavaria (a competitor to the official sponsor Budweiser) were kicked out of Soccer City Stadium in Johannesburg and two of the group leaders were arrested under the South African anti-ambush legislation. While FIFA refused to back down, the incident created a media storm that brought the attention of the world to the issue of ambush marketing and cast a negative light on FIFA, event organizers and Budweiser while giving Bavaria more exposure then they could ever have foreseen. A clear PR policy on how to deal with similar incidents and the press around them in a way that minimizes negative press and does not put the ambusher in the spotlight will be a challenge for property owners and sponsors in the future.

Challenges of new media

Two major aspects of new media which are making their presence felt in the area of ambush marketing are social media and YouTube. Blogs, Facebook and Twitter are an increasing challenge to the capacity of sport organizations to control the messaging coming from athletes and those involved in an event. Many famous athletes now have their own Twitter accounts and Facebook pages where they interact directly with fans about their day-to-day experiences. While they are usually given strict instruction by event organizers about how they can use these tools during the event, it is often too much of a challenge for organizers to monitor every athlete and ensure compliance. This allows the chance that an athlete will be able to continue associating with their own sponsors, which may be looked upon with distress by event sponsors. Another form of new media creating waves in the area of ambush marketing is the emergence of YouTube and with it the idea of viral videos. When discussing the ambush marketing strategy of sponsoring subcategories, Nike's extremely successful "Write the Future" ambush campaign around the 2010 Football World Cup was discussed. The foundation of this campaign was a three-minute video on YouTube featuring the biggest football stars sponsored by Nike and at the time of writing the video had close to 21 million views on the official Nike channel alone in addition to endless hours of media discussion. Without making any direct reference to the event taking place, Nike was able to create a buzz around their brand which would no doubt have angered official sponsor Adidas.

While many of the large companies that sponsor mega-events like the Olympic Games and the World Cup are becoming ever more adept at using new media to their advantage it seems the property owners such as the IOC, FIFA and event organizing committees are still playing catch-up in regards to stopping ambush marketing. In an age where events such as the Olympic Games are seeking ways to connect to the next generation of consumers, it would seem to be in their best interests to fully engage with and understand the potential of new media as well as the risks.

International perspectives

As with any international phenomena, the unique nature of social norms and legal contexts present in different countries around the world makes for interesting subject matter. While this is also the case in relation to ambush marketing, to date there has been little direct research on how ambush marketing and anti-ambush marketing legislation is understood and perceived differently around the world. Preuss et al. (2008) initiated some discussion in this area when they examined the impact of China's unique culture on their understanding and acceptance of ambush marketing and their approach to protecting the sponsors of the 2008 Olympic Games. It was suggested that the Confucian tradition of copying past creative work and building on it rather than creating new work, the communist ideal of everything belonging to everyone, the limited economic education of medium and small businesses as well as consumers among other elements had an impact on Chinese perceptions and interpretation of ambush marketing and related legislation (Preuss et al., 2008). It was also noted that further study of similar cultural conditions and their effect on ambush marketing perceptions in other countries should be the focus of future research (Preuss et al., 2008). No doubt as ambush marketing legislation continues to evolve as a requirement of host cities this will be a growing area of interest for many stakeholders.

Notes

1   This ad can be found at: <http://www.youtube.com/watch?v=BZtHAVvslQ>.
2   A legislative summary of The Olympic and Paralympic Marks Act can be found at <http://www.parl.gc.ca/Content/LOP/LegislativeSummaries/39/1/c47-e.pdf>.

References

Aaker, D.A. (1991) *Managing Brand Equity*, New York, The Free Press.
Anonymous (2009) 'VANOC releases updated balanced budget', *Sport Business*, February 2. Retrieved September 8, 2011 from <http://www.sportbusiness.com/news/168746/vanoc- releases-updated-balanced-budget>.
Batcha, E.M. (1998) 'Who are the real competitors in the Olympic Games? Duel Olympic Battles: Trademark infringement and ambush marketing harm corporate sponsors – Violations against the USOC and its corporate sponsors', *Seton Hall Journal of Sport Law*, 8(1), 229–59.

Bean, L.L. (1995) 'Ambush Marketing: Sport sponsorship confusion and the Lanham Act', *Boston University Law Review*, (4), 1099–134.

Bhattacharjee, S. and Roa, G. (2006) 'Tackling Ambush Marketing: The need for regulation and analysing the present legislative and contractual efforts', *Sport in Society*, 9(1), 128–49.

Burton, N. and Chadwick, S. (2009) 'Ambush Marketing in Sport: An analysis of sponsorship protection means and counter-ambush measures', *Journal of Sponsorship*, 2(4), 303–15.

Crompton, J.L. (2004) 'Sponsorship ambushing in sport', *Managing Leisure*, 9(1), 1–12.

Crow, D. and Hoek, J. (2003) 'Ambush marketing: A critical review and some practical advice', *Marketing Bulletin*, 14(1), 1–14.

Department of Justice (Canada) (2007) *Olympic and Paralympic Marks Act*, C-47. Retrieved June 28, 2007, from <http://laws.justice.gc.ca/eng/acts/O-9.2/page-1.html>.

Ellis, D., Gauthier, M.E. and Séguin, B. (2011a) 'Ambush Marketing, the Olympic and Paralympic Marks Act and Canadian National Sport Organizations: Awareness, perceptions and impacts', *Journal of Sponsorship*, 4(3), 253–71.

—— (2011b) 'Framing Ambush Marketing as Legal Issue', *Sport Management Review*, 14(3), 297–308.

Engelhart, K. (2010) 'Selling Soccer: The Top 5 Commercials in FIFA History', *Macleans Magazine*, June 3. Retrieved June 3, 2010 from <http://www2.macleans.ca/2010/06/03/selling-soccer>.

Farrelly, F., Quester, P. and Greyser, S.A. (2005) 'Defending the Co-Branding Benefits of Sponsorship B2B Partnerships: The case of ambush marketing', *Journal of Advertising Research*, 45(3), 339–48.

Hoek, J. and Gendall, D. (2002) 'Ambush Marketing: More than just a commercial irritant', *Entertainment Law*, 1(2) 72–91.

Graham, J.J. (1997) 'Ambush Marketing', *Sport Marketing Quarterly*, 6(1), 10–12.

IOC (2010) *Olympic Marketing Fact File*, International Olympic Committee, Lausanne, CH.

Keller, K.L. (2003) *Strategic Brand Management: Building, measuring, and managing brand equity* (2nd edn), Upper Saddle River, NJ, Prentice Hall.

Kendall, C. and Cuthroys, J. (2001) 'Ambush Marketing and the Sydney 2000 Games (Indicia and Images) Protection Act: A retrospective', *Murdoch University Electronic Journal of Law*, 8(2), 1–35.

Khoabane, P. (2010) 'We've Sold Our Flag to FIFA at the Expense of the Poor', *Sunday Times*, April 4. Retrieved September 17, 2010 from <http://www.timeslive.co.za/sundaytimes/article384508.ece/Weve-sold-our-flag-to-Fifa-at-the-expense-of-the-poor>.

Lyberger, M.R. and McCarthy, L. (2001) 'An Assessment of Consumer Knowledge of, Interest in, and Perceptions of Ambush Marketing Strategies', *Sport Marketing Quarterly*, 10(2), 130–37.

McKelvey, S. (1992) 'NHL vs. Pepsi Cola Canada, Uh-huh! Legal parameters of sport ambush marketing', *Entertainment and Sport Law*, 10(3), 5–18.

—— (2003) 'Unauthorized Use of Event Tickets in Promotional Campaign May Create New Legal Strategies to Combat Ambush Marketing: NCAA vs. Coors', *Sport Marketing Quarterly*, 12(2), 117–18.

McKelvey, S. and Grady, J. (2008) 'Sponsorship Program Protection Strategies for Special Sport Events: Are Event Organizers Outmanoeuvring Ambush Marketers?' *Journal of Sport Management*, 22(5), 550–86.

Meenaghan, T. (1994) 'Point of View: Ambush Marketing: Immoral or Imaginative Practice?' *Journal of Advertising Research*, 34(5), 77–88.

—— (1998) 'Ambush Marketing: Corporate strategy and consumer reaction', *Psychology and Marketing*, 15(4) 305–22.

Moorman, A. and Greenwell, C. (2005) 'Consumer Attitudes of Deception and the Legality of Ambush Marketing Practices', *Journal of Legal Aspects of Sport*, 15(2) 183–211.

New Zealand Legislation (2007) *Major Events Management Atc 2007*, Bill 99–1 Retrieved September 23, 2010 from <http://www.legislation.govt.nz/act/public/2007/0035/latest/DLM411987.html>.

O'Sullivan, P. and Murphy, P. (1998) 'Ambush Marketing: The ethical issues', *Psychology and Marketing*, 15(4), 349–66.

O'Reilly, N. and Séguin, B. (2009) *Sport Marketing: A Canadian perspective*. Toronto, Nelson Education Ltd.

Payne, M. (1998) 'Ambush Marketing: The Undeserved Advantage', *Psychology and Marketing*, 15(4), 323–66.

Portlock, A. and Rose, S. (2009) 'Effects of Ambush Marketing: UK consumer brand recall and attitudes to official sponsors and non-sponsors associated with the FIFA World Cup 2006', *International Journal of Sport Marketing and Sponsorship*, 10(4), 271–86.

Preuss, H., Gemeinder, K. and Séguin, B. (2008) 'Ambush Marketing in China: Counterbalancing Olympic sponsorship efforts', *Asian Business and Management*, 7(2), 243–63.

Sandler, D.M. and Shani, D. (1989) 'Olympic Sponsorship vs. Ambush Marketing: Who Gets the Gold?' *Journal of Advertising Research*, 29(4), 9–14.

—— (1993) 'Sponsorship and the Olympic Games: The Consumer Perspective', *Sport Marketing Quarterly*, 2(3), 38–43.

Scassa, T. (2008) 'Faster, Higher, Stronger: The protection of Olympic Marks leading up to Vancouver 2010', *University of British Columbia Law Review*, 41(1), 34–68.

Séguin, B., Lyberger, M., O'Reilly, N. and McCarthy, L. (2005) 'Internationalizing Ambush Marketing: The Olympic Brand and Country of Origin', *International Journal of Sport Marketing and Sponsorship*, 6(4), 216–29.

Séguin, B. and O'Reilly, N. (2008) 'The Olympic Brand, Ambush Marketing and Clutter', *International Journal of Sport Management and Marketing*, 4(1), 62–84.

Séguin, B., Teed, K. and O'Reilly (2005) 'National Sport Organizations and Sponsorship: An Identification of Best Practices', *International Journal of Sport Management and Marketing*, 1(2), 69–92.

Shani, D. and Sandler, D.M. (1998) 'Ambush Marketing: Is Confusion to Blame for the Flickering of the Flame?' *Psychology and Marketing*, 15(4), 367–83.

Shikwati, J. (2010) 'World Cup: How small businesses have lost out', *The Daily Monitor*, June 1. Retrieved September 17, 2010 from <http://www.monitor.co.ug/Business/Business%20Power/-/688616/929698/-/lk1ir9/-/>.

Stotlar, D.K. (1993) 'Sponsorship and the Olympic Winter Games', *Sport Marketing Quarterly*, 2(1), 35–43.

Townley, S., Harrington, D. and Couchman, N. (1998) 'The Legal and Practical Prevention of Ambush Marketing in Sport', *Psychology and Marketing*, 15(4), 333–48.

Welsh, J.C. (2002) 'Ambush Marketing: What it is, What it Isn't', Welsh Marketing Associates. Retrieved September 13, 2011 from <http://welshmktg.com/WMA_ambushmktg.pdf>.

Wilson, B. (2006) 'Protecting sport sponsors from ambush', *BBC News*, February 20. Retrieved May 17, 2010 from <http://news.bbc.co.uk/2/hi/business/4719368.stm>.

PART IV

The economics of sport

Edited by Paul Downward

24

CONTEMPORARY ISSUES IN THE ECONOMICS OF SPORT

Paul Downward

This section of the book presents seven chapters examining the economics of sport. The economic analysis of professional team sports has a long pedigree dating back to seminal articles from Rottenberg (1956) and Neale (1964) in which the unique importance of playing talent (i.e. labor) to the economic activity in sport leagues was identified as well as other unique features of sport. These include the joint production of sporting contests by teams and the consequent hypothesized need for uncertainty of outcome (or its longer term equivalent competitive balance) for the economic viability and growth of leagues. Discussion about how best to theorize about the market structure of sport leagues also developed.

Neale (1964) argued in the US context that sport leagues gravitated towards a natural monopoly, driven by uncertainty of outcome. Subsequent seminal contributions include Sloane (1971), El-Hodiri and Quirk (1971) and Scully (1974). Sloane identified that sport leagues could be viewed as cartels of interdependent teams rather than monopoly structures. Moreover, in the face of sustained financial losses in English football, it was argued that the objectives of clubs might be better understood as utility maximization, connected to the consumption of resources in the pursuit of sporting success, that is wins, as opposed to profit maximization. The latter assumption was implicit in earlier US analysis. It was also assumed in the first formal analysis of sport leagues by El-Hodiri and Quirk (1971). Finally, Scully (1974) provided the first major piece of empirical work examining the players' labor market, identifying the determinants of players' salaries and their weak position relative to clubs, leading to exploitation. In the professional team sport literature, which is now well established, such themes have been revisited extensively, refined, extended and analyzed.

As a developing research base, much of the literature is now available in specialist academic journals such as the *Journal of Sports Economics* and the *International Journal of Sports Finance*, which focus on the economic analysis of sport. Naturally, sport management journals such as the *Journal of Sports Management, European Sport Management Quarterly* and the *International Journal of Sport Marketing and Management* also publish such research. Mainstream economic, management, operational research and sport science journals now also publish sport economics papers and, indeed, textbooks have consolidated this knowledge. For example, in the US key volumes are by Fort (2010) and Leeds and von Allmen (2011).

In Europe, though texts like Szymanski and Kuypers (1999) and Downward and Dawson (2000) provided an economic analysis of professional sport, the seminal contributions in fact came from Gratton and Taylor (1985, 1991, 2000). Two important and distinct features of their work, for which they are often not explicitly given credit, is that they took a much more comprehensive view of the economics of sport. They conceptualized a sport continuum linking amateur participation through to professional sport and major events. Linking and servicing these aspects of the sport economy are public, voluntary and private industries supplying labor, facilities, goods and other services. Connected with this was that they examined sport from an economic perspective that was explicitly concerned with public policy. In this respect, for example, policy aiming to promote participation to meet social welfare goals through the provision of facilities, and the regeneration impacts of public investment in sport, were discussed. Coupled with the differences that the US and European literatures of professional team sport had with respect to the objectives of sport teams, their work introduced the perspective that active public policy through sport may be an appropriate approach in social welfare terms. The US literature and much mainstream economic thinking about sports have tended to emphasize the traditional economics view that freely operating markets are the broadly appropriate policy choice. In my subsequent contribution to the literature I have built upon their framework to try to consider alternative policy positions across the broad spectrum of the sport economy (Downward et al., 2009).

The intention of this section of the book is to echo, but also to develop this sentiment. A major difference, however, is that the arguments are presented by authors who have specialized in research in the respective areas. Each has published widely in their field and, significantly, is known for being able to write economics in a manner that is sensitive to the needs of sport management readers as well as to sport economists. As well as producing good theory and robust empirical analysis, they can also write books, survey articles and policy papers in a comprehensive but accessible way. Of course this is not an exhaustive list of potential contributors and it is hoped that by reading their work and exploring the references to their chapters, readers will find an accessible introduction to the material that is covered. Consequently, in this section of the book, mass participation and consumption in sport are explored. Competitive balance, the demand for professional sport – particularly that emanating from the major driver of TV broadcasts – and the labor market in professional sport leagues are examined. Finally, the role of using investment in sport as a public policy tool, by hosting major events, is discussed.

Two contributions examine the mass participation sport sector. In Chapter 25, Downward, Lera-Lopez and Rasciute provide an introduction to the theoretical and empirical economic literature on sport participation. As well as providing a detailed review of the existing literature, the determinants of sport participation and its frequency in Spain are examined to exemplify the economic approach to empirical analysis. Probit and ordered probit estimators are employed. Results coinciding with the existing literature are identified and show that the likelihood of sport participation is mainly determined by parental participation in sport (particularly by sport participation of fathers), gender, class and educational level. Age affects sport in a nonlinear way. Sport participation also seems to be motivated by socializing and the need for entertainment. Watching sport on television, further, seems to be a complementary activity to practicing sport.

The frequency of participation decreases with age and increases with being male and higher social class, but not with education. Formal membership of sports clubs and federations and participating in sport competitions naturally enhance the frequency of sporting participation. From a policy perspective this might suggest that attracting participants to organized sport may enhance their frequency of participation. However, the largest effect on the frequency of sport participation is connected with solitary sport. This underlies the generalized importance of informal sport activities and their complementary relationship with other physical activities such as walking for fitness. Coupled with the steady decline of sport participation, this could suggest changing tastes of participants and increased difficulties in using the formal sport system to achieve social policy aims.

Pawlowski and Breuer in Chapter 26 focus on a highly neglected feature of mass sport consumption, which is expenditure on sport products and services. The chapter reviews the existing literature exploring the similarities and differences between the findings of these studies. Comparative international data are also presented. The aim is to suggest future research possibilities. Key suggestions include the need to produce much less aggregated analysis, to refine and provide a consistent theoretical underpinning to research and, significantly, to reflect on the econometric strategies used to examine expenditure data.

The next four chapters of the volume address professional sport. Two chapters examine sport leagues and one each the demand for professional sport and the players' labor market. In Chapter 27 Kesenne provides an analysis of sport leagues addressing the question of whether it makes any difference that teams try to maximize profits – which is considered to be commercial enterprises' main objective in microeconomic analysis – instead of trying to pursue maximum sport successes, that is win maximization in (inter)national championships. Crucially it is shown that a different emphasis upon these two objectives can make a substantial difference to insights into the effects of regulations in the market. This is not only in terms of differences in competitive balance, player salaries and total league revenues, but also the imposition of a financial prudence rule. It follows that more detailed empirical research is required to explore and to test these differences to inform sport league governance. At a minimum it suggests that the institutional differences in sport leagues are relevant for policy.

Similarly, Dietl, Fort and Lang in Chapter 28 analyze the impact of regulations on competitive balance in leagues, drawing comparisons between European and North American sport leagues; that is, under the different objectives of utility maximization and profit maximization respectively. League regulation policies such as revenue sharing, talent drafts, payroll caps and reserve systems (the reserve clause in North American leagues and transfer restrictions in European leagues) are examined. A significant contribution of the chapter is that a difference is drawn between the levels of talent in teams and the investment in talent of teams. Whilst the literature, particularly examining profit-maximizing teams in leagues, has generally argued that competitive balance is invariant to league regulation policies, the chapter argues that, moving to any level of generality, this invariance hinges on the interaction between investment in talent and actual talent accumulation to the level put into play during games.

The next two chapters examine the two main sides of professional sport leagues: the primary source of revenues, that is demand, and the primary source of costs, i.e. players. In the first case, in Chapter 29 Buraimo focuses on English football to show how the broadcast demand for football has had a dramatic effect on traditional attendance demand and the way in which football is managed. The chapter argues that league authorities have to manage the dilemma that stadium attendances promote broadcast audiences, but growth in the latter can reduce stadium demand.

In Chapter 30 Frick also uses football to exemplify an analysis of players' labor markets. The scale of the football market is discussed as well as the determinants of footballers' salaries, with particular attention being paid to the inherent risk in the occupation, since players can be cut from their teams and may also suffer long-term injuries. The extent to which forms of discrimination against ethnic minorities persist in modern sport leagues is also discussed, as are issues for future research. These include the need to supplement the existing analysis with ratings of player performance, the extent to which remaining years on a contract affect salaries, a better understanding of the duration of contracts, and the voluntary versus involuntary duration of player careers.

The final chapter of this section examines sport events. In this chapter Gratton charts the historically varying economic rationales for why government (public sector) expenditure on sport has expanded considerably. For example, a transitional emphasis from social welfare to economic regeneration of cities occurred in the UK following rises in unemployment and de-industrialization. The chapter reviews the theory and evidence associated with the potential benefits of hosting major sport events, with a particular focus on the Summer Olympics, and concludes by examining the likelihood of longer-term benefits or legacies being derived from investment in hosting sport events. The chapter concludes by arguing that most evidence relates to the immediate economic impact during and immediately after the event has been held. However, there is a need for research to concentrate on the longer term urban regeneration benefits that sport has the potential to deliver.

References

Downward, P. and Dawson, A. (2000) *The Economics of Professional Team Sports*, London, Routledge.

Downward, P., Dawson, A. and Dejonghe, T. (2009) *Sports Economics: Theory, Evidence and Policy*, London, Butterworth-Heinemann.

El-Hodiri, M. and Quirk, J. (1971) 'An Economic Model of a Professional Sports League', *Journal of Political Economy*, 79, 1302–19.

Fort, R. (2010) *Sports Economics* (3rd edn), London, Prentice Hall.

Gratton, C. and Taylor, P. (1985) *Sport and Recreation: An Economic Analysis*, London, E. and F.N. Spon.

—— (1991) *Government and the Economics of Sport*, Harlow, Longman.

—— (2000) *Economics of Sport and Recreation*, London, E. and F.N. Spon.

Leeds, M. and von Allmen, P. (2011) *The Economics of Sports* (4th edn), London, Prentice Hall.

Neale W. (1964) 'The peculiar economics of professional sport', *Quarterly Journal of Economics*, 78(1), 1–14.

Rottenberg, S. (1956) 'The baseball players labor market', *Journal of Political Economy*, (64)3, 243–58.

Scully, G. (1974) 'Pay and performance in Major League Baseball', *The American Economic Review*, (64)6, 915–30.

Sloane, P. (1971) 'The economics of professional football: the football club as a utility maximiser', *Scottish Journal of Political Economy*, 17(2), 121–46.

Szymanski, S. and Kuypers, T. (1999) *Winners and Losers*, London, Viking Press.

25

THE ECONOMIC ANALYSIS OF SPORT PARTICIPATION

Paul Downward, Fernando Lera-López and Simona Rasciute

Introduction

The 1992 European Sport Charter argues that

> Sport embraces much more than traditional team games and competition. Sport means all forms of physical activity which, through casual or organized participation, aim at expressing or improving physical fitness and mental well-being, forming social relationships or obtaining results in competition in all levels.

As indicated by Downward et al. (2009), however, there are a wide variety of specific activities that can be described as sport, then monitored and promoted as such by public authorities. In this respect, as Gratton and Taylor (2000: 7) note, definitions of sport involve "the criterion of general acceptance that an activity is sporting, e.g. by the media and sport agencies." Recognizing this potential for diversity, between the 1960s and the 1990s there was a significant increase in the number of people taking part in sport and in the frequency of sport participation in Europe (Gratton and Taylor, 2000). In Europe, the "Sport for All" campaign aimed at providing sporting opportunities for the general population. Many European countries developed sport policy programs which aimed to increase levels of mass participation in sport and physical activity (Green and Collins, 2008). Major public investment in new indoor sport facilities led to a striking increase in opportunities for sport (Gratton and Taylor, 1991).

Nevertheless, since the turn of the century, sport participation appears to have reached a stagnation point in many European countries (e.g. Spain, Finland, Belgium, Portugal and Austria), and has actually begun to decline in some countries such as the Netherlands, Italy and England (van Bottenburg, 2005). In England, for instance, sport participation fell from 48 percent in 1990 to 46 percent in 1996, with a further drop to 43 percent by 2002 (Rowe, Adams and Beasley, 2004). In Spain, where traditionally sport participation rates have been below the European average, sport participation seems to have reached a stagnation point. Over the period from 1995 to 2005, sport participation increased by only 1 percent (García Ferrando, 2006).

This decline has not only taken place in European countries, but also in other areas of the world. Sport participation figures for the adult population in Canada, for example, show a decrease from 45 percent to 31 percent between 1992 and 2004 (Bloom, Grant and Watt, 2005). In the United States also, sport participation has either decreased or has grown at a slower rate than the overall population over the past decade (SGMA, 2004).

This decline is of considerable concern for health and social policy. At the same time, surveys show a dramatic increase in the incidence of being overweight and obese in developed societies. There is a large body of scientific evidence regarding the positive impact of sport and physical activity on health and well-being (Scully et al., 1999; Sila, 2003; Biddle and Ekkekakis, 2005; Biddle et al., 2004; Kara et al., 2005; Lafont et al., 2007; Miles, 2007). Contributions are also growing in economics (Rasciute and Downward, 2010; Downward and Rasciute, 2011). Finally, there is also a range of evidence debating the value of sport to other important areas of social policy such as education, community regeneration, community safety (e.g. preventing juvenile crime) and the environment.

Consequently, the negative evolution of sport participation in the last ten years, coupled with evidence of sport's health and social impacts, has resulted in a strong increase in academic interest in sport participation research, although there has been only limited analysis of the economic theories of sport participation (e.g. Downward, 2007; Downward et al., 2009; Gratton and Taylor, 2000; Humphreys and Ruseski, 2007, 2010).

The aim of this chapter is to provide an introduction to this theoretical and empirical literature and also to provide an empirical example by analyzing the determinants of sport participation in Spain. The remainder of the chapter proceeds as follows. The first section reviews the theoretical approaches and the empirical evidence concerning the key determinants of sport participation. This is followed by a description of the data set and the methodology adopted in the study and then a presentation of the main estimation results. The chapter concludes with a summary of the main findings and an indication of the policy implications and opportunities for further research.

Literature review

Theoretical motivation

The theoretical motivation for the economic analysis of sport participation arises from a variety of perspectives (Downward et al., 2009; Downward, 2007; and Downward and Riordan, 2007). For example, a "heterodox" approach draws upon Scitovsky (1976) and Earl (1986, 1983) to explore the psychological underpinnings of consumer choice in lifestyles, emphasizing learning by doing and habits and, as a consequence, maintaining that the preferences of economic agents are endogenous. Post-Keynesian consumer analysis (see, for example, Lavoie, 1994) also draws upon these concepts and combines these with insights from the studies of leisure by Veblen (1925) and Galbraith (1958) and, by implication, the sociological work of Bourdieu (1984, 1988, 1991) to show that preferences and consequent behavior will then be shaped by social values and that sport participation is likely to be linked to income differentials.

In contrast, neoclassical economics has three main theoretical approaches which share the view that preferences are given and fixed to the sport participant. The first approach, which was employed in early US studies such as Adams et al. (1966), applies basic economic consumer demand theory to examine participation, treating sport participation as a commodity demand. An alternative approach is the "income–leisure trade-off" model of labor supply, in which sport is viewed as the consumption of time as discussed by Gratton and Taylor (2000). More recently Wicker, Breuer and Pawlowski (2009), Breuer and Wicker (2008), Downward

(2007), Downward and Riordan (2007), Breuer (2006) and Humphreys and Ruseski (2006) have argued that a more comprehensive foundation for the analysis of sport participation can be constructed with reference to Becker (1965, 1974). In this respect, the participation decision can be understood as an individual choice to commit goods and time to the "production" and then consumption of sport directly, or to the acquisition of personal consumption capital, or social capital that then underpins sport participation. An important feature of this analysis is that it emphasizes that goods and time can be allocated across other activities as well as just sport.

All of these theoretical approaches share common elements. They would predict that prior experience in sport activities is likely to raise participation in any specific activity, and that social interactions, or lifestyles, will also affect participation along with access to income. However, it is equally clear that the explanations for the predictions do differ. In this chapter, no attempt is made to discriminate between the accounts, a task which, it has been argued, is difficult due to data availability and identification issues (Downward, 2007). In contrast, the empirical work that follows seeks to exemplify the literature, which is reviewed next, noting these broad shared insights.

Empirical evidence of the determinants in sport participation

The empirical analysis of sport participation in economics has proceeded by the application of various regression techniques in which measures of sport participation are conditioned on a variety of covariates.[1] In broad terms, the first empirical studies dealing with leisure and sport participation, and considering a wide range of activities, were undertaken in the US. Adams et al. (1966) explored participation in swimming, fishing and boating in the Delaware Estuary. Cicchetti et al. (1969) employed a two-step econometric model to look at decisions to participate as well as their frequency in the US. At the European level, the first evidence was provided by Rodgers (1977). It showed substantial similarities in the pattern of sport participation across different European countries. Later analyses of sport participation in Europe show significant geographical and social differences in European countries, with low rates in South and East European countries on the one hand, and among women, elderly people and individuals living in rural areas and with a lower educational level, on the other hand (Van Tuyckom and Scheerder, 2010). Differences seem to be greater in terms of gender and age (Hovemann and Wicker, 2009; Van Tuyckom et al., 2010).

Over this period the modeling of sport participation decisions has increased in complexity. Rather than applying ordinary least squares, even to binary data measuring participation or not, logistic (Downward, 2007; Hovemann and Wicker, 2009; Van Tuyckom and Scheerder, 2010; Van Tuyckom et al., 2010) and two-step Heckman models as well as multiple classification analysis (Breuer and Wicker, 2008; Downward and Riordan, 2007; Eberth and Smith, 2010; Farrell and Shields, 2002; Humphreys and Ruseski, 2006, 2007; Stratton et al., 2005), and double-hurdle models (Humphreys and Ruseski, 2010) are employed. Logistic regression studies examine the incidence of participation (yes *or* no) for any given activity, or set of activities as an explicitly binary variable.[2] Heckman and Hurdle models employ a further estimate of the frequency of participation. The modeling assumption is that different decisions govern the choice to participate and the frequency of participation in sport. There are differences in interpretation between the models. Essentially the hurdle model treats "zero" values of the frequency of participation as a genuine choice.[3] In Heckman models, the assumption is that the potential to participate is not fully observed because of the participation decision. In this model, therefore, account is taken of any "selection bias" in observing participation frequencies.

Before reviewing the evidence in detail notes of caution should be offered. Firstly, whilst the generic references above are to sport, as noted earlier, it should be remembered that the list of sporting activities varies from one study to another. Secondly, as also noted above, the sport participation variable is measured in different ways. Indeed, relatively few studies consider the time spent on sport participation or the frequency of such participation (e.g. Downward and Riordan, 2007; Eberth and Smith, 2010; García et al., 2010; Humphreys and Ruseski, 2007, 2010; Lera-López and Rapún-Gárate, 2007). Thirdly, the comparability of estimates produced from different statistical approaches may be difficult in both sign and magnitude.[4] Finally, it has been emphasized in different European studies that there are peculiarities about the determinants of sport participation in different European countries (Hovemann and Wicker, 2009; Van Tuyckom and Scheerder, 2010; Van Tuyckom et al., 2010). This suggests the potential for cross-country differences in behavior. Bearing in mind these caveats, it is possible to make some qualitative general assessments concerning the role played by economic, individual and social variables on sport participation. Table 25.1 presents a summary.

Examination of this table reveals that the probability of sport participation decreases with age (Barber and Havitz, 2001; Breuer and Wicker, 2008; Downward, 2007; Downward and Riordan, 2007; Downward and Rasciute, 2011; Eberth and Smith, 2010; Farrell and Shields, 2002; Fridberg, 2010; Hovemann and Wicker, 2009; Humphreys and Ruseski, 2006; Moens and Scheerder, 2004; Scheerder et al., 2005a; Stratton et al., 2005; Wicker et al., 2009). Such differences in sport participation can be attributed to biological and physical limitations and, consequently, to changes in the types of activities preferred by the older age groups (Barber and Havitz, 2001) and it seems to affect males more than females (Bauman et al., 2009). García et al. (2010) report that for Spain sport participation follows a U-shaped curve with two peaks: youth and retirement.

The empirical evidence focusing on sport participation frequency has found a positive relationship between the two variables (García et al., 2010; Humphreys and Ruseski, 2006; Lera-López and Rapún-Gárate, 2007). This could be due to people using sport as a health precaution and because there is a higher level of health awareness among older people. In addition, target-group-specific offers to involve older adults in sport activities seem to be effective (Breuer and Wicker, 2008). In a longitudinal perspective, Stamatakis and Chaudhury (2008) report that trends in adults' sport participation in England between 1997 and 2006 show that sport rates have increased among middle-aged and older adults and have decreased among young men. Nevertheless, there is also empirical evidence that shows that time spent in sport tends to decline with age in Canada (Humphreys and Ruseski, 2010) and Scotland (Eberth and Smith, 2010).

Gender is a highly important influence on sport participation. There is consensus about the fact that men, in general, not only participate in sport more than women (Breuer and Wicker, 2008; Downward, 2007; Downward and Rasciute, 2011; Eberth and Smith, 2010; Fridberg, 2010; Hovemann and Wicker, 2009; Humphreys and Ruseski, 2006, 2007; Lera-López and Rapún-Gárate, 2007; Moens and Scheerder, 2004; Stratton et al., 2005; Wilson, 2002) but they also show a higher frequency of participation (Barber and Havitz, 2001; Eberth and Smith, 2010; Humphreys and Ruseski, 2006, 2007). These differences can be attributed to different variables such as biological factors and cultural and social influences, reflecting differences in family responsibilities as well as differences regarding behavior, social expectations and work. Nevertheless, in a recent study, Humphreys and Ruseski (2010) report that the relationship is more complex. According to their results, women are more likely to participate in five different sports (walking, swimming, cycling, running, home

Table 25.1 Summary of empirical studies on sport participation

Study, country and year	Sample characteristics	Dependent variable (estimator)	Methodology	Evidence/Findings
Downward and Riordan (2007) UK, 2002	2002 General Household Survey N = 14,819 16 years and over General sports participation	1. Sport participation (yes/no) in the last 4 weeks 2. Frequency of sport participation	Two-step Heckman model	1. Membership of sport clubs (+), Skilled manual worker (+), Drinking (+), Age (−), North regions (−), Housekeeper (−), Voluntary work (−), Number of sports (+), Sport lifestyle (−). 2. Health (+), Number of sports (+), Sport lifestyle (+), Recreation lifestyle (+) Leisure lifestyle (−), Number of males in the household (+), Education (−), Employment (−), Income (−), Unpaid work (+), Access to a vehicle (−).
Downward (2007) UK, 2002	2002 General Household Survey N = 14,819 16 years and over	1. Sport participation (yes/no) in the last 4 weeks	Logistic regression modeling	Income (+), Total work hours (−), Education (+), Working (+), Male (+), Housekeeper (−), Children (−), Number of adults in the household (−), Drinking (+), Smoking (−), White (+), Access to a vehicle (+), North regions (−), Volunteering (+), Age (−), Health (+), Leisure activities (+).
Humphreys and Ruseski (2007) US, 1998 and 2000	1998 and 2000 BRDSS N = 275,455 18 years and over 55 Sporting activities, classified into 5 categories	1. Sport participation (yes/no) in the last month 2. Frequency of sport participation (number of times per week)	Two-step Heckman model	1. [1] Age (+), Income (+), Education (+), Female (−), White (+), Married (−), Children (−), Employed (+), Retired (+), Urban (+), Health (+). 2. [2] Age (−), Married (−), Income (+), Female (−), Urban (−), Education (+), Employed (+), Retired (+), White (−).
Humphreys and Ruseski (2006) US, 2000	2000 BRDSS N = 150,648 18 years and over 56 Sporting activities	1. Sport participation (yes/no) in the last month 2. Time in sport participation (minutes per week)	Two-step Heckman model	1. Age (−), Married (−), Children (−), Income (+), Employed (−), Retired (+), Education (+), Female (−) White (+), Health (+). 2. Age (+), Married (−), Income (−), Employed (+), Education (−), Female (−), White (+).

(Continued overleaf)

Table 25.1 Continued

Study, country and year	Sample characteristics	Dependent variable (estimator)	Methodology	Evidence/Findings
Moens and Scheerder (2004) Flanders (Belgium) 1979, 1989, 1999	PF/SBV Flemish Sports Participation Time Lag Survey (1979, 1989, 1999) and TOR 1999 Flemish Time-budge Study N = 39,911 Parents of school-aged children General sport participation	Participation in sport (yes/no)	Logistic regression modeling in two phases	Education (+) Females (−), Age (−), Degree of urbanization (+, no in 1999), Socio-cultural associations participation (+), Watching TV (−).
Scheerder and Breedveld (2004) Flanders and the Netherlands, 1989, 1991 and 1999	SCP Facilities Usage Survey (1991 and 1999) and PF/SBV Flemish Sports Participation Lag Survey (1989 and 1999) N = 32,483 General sport participation in Flanders and 27 sports in the Netherlands	1. Participation in sport (yes/no) 2. Club membership (yes/no)	Binary logistic regressions in two phases	Age (−), Male (+, only in adults and no in adolescents), Education (+).
Stempel (2005) US, 1998	1998 US National Health Interview Survey N = 22,500 25–79 years 15 competitive sports	1. Participation in sports one or more times at least 30 in the last two weeks 2. Frequency and intensity of sports participation over the prior two weeks	Logistic regressions	Education (+). Income (+).
Lera-López et al. (2008) 2006 Spain	2006 Spanish Sport Participation Survey (CSD) N = 640 18–74 years	1. Participation in sports during the previous year 2. Frequency of sport participation	Probit and ordered probit models	Male (+), Age (−), Education (+), Socio-economic level (+), Motivation for health (+), Entertainment (+), Self-reported general health (+).

Study	Data	Dependent variable	Method	Results
Lera-López and Rapún-Gárate (2007) Navarra (Spain), 2003	Primary data N = 700 16–65 years 40 Sporting activities	1. Frequency of sports participation in the previous year (5 categories, from no practice to every day) 2. Frequency of sports participation among regular practitioners (4 categories)	Ordered probit models	1. Female (−), Age (+), Income (+), Entrepreneur (−), Self-employed (−), Farmer (−), Middle manager (−), Skilled worker (−) Unskilled worker (−). 2. Age (+), Income (+), All occupations (−).
Wilson (2002) US, 1993	1993 General Social Survey N = 1,458 Age unspecified Leisure-time activities (sports)	Sport participation in the last year	Multiple classification analysis	Males (+), Education (+), Income (+).
Stamm and Lamprecht (2005) Switzerland, 2002	2002 Swiss Health Survey N = 17,344 15 years and over Physical activities	Degree of physical activity (five categories, from regularly to inactive)	Contingency and gamma analyses	Female (−), Language region (+), Household size (+), Income (+), Nationality (+), Education (+).
Breuer and Wicker (2008) Germany, 1984–2005 period	1984–2005 German Socioeconomic Panel N = 141,129 General sporting activities	Regular sport activity (at least once per week, yes/no)	Multivariate regression	Female (−), Age (−), Income (+), Education (+), Real work time (−), Non-German nationality (−).
Wicker, Breuer, and Pawlowski (2009) Stuttgart (Germany)	Primary data N = 2,054 3 years and over General sporting activities	Regular sport activity (at least once per week, yes/no)	Logistic regression and hierarchical non-linear models	Female (−), Age (−), Nationality (+), Education (+), Time for bringing up children (+), Income (+), Supply of sport infrastructure (+).

(Continued overleaf)

Table 25.1 Continued

Study, country and year	Sample characteristics	Dependent variable (estimator)	Methodology	Evidence/Findings
Barber and Havitz (2001) Canada, 1987 and 1996 years	1987–1996 Print Measurement Bureau N = 13,901; 20,415 18 years and over 10 sporting activities	Frequency of sport participation during the season (ordinal variable with three categories: occasional, regular, avid)	Cross-tabular analyses	Female (−). Age (−).
Scheerder, Vanreusel and Taks (2005a) Flanders (Belgium), 1979–1999 period	1979 Leuven Growth Study of Flemish Girls, 1989/1999 Study on Movement Activities in Flanders N = 38,376 (M+F) 19–77 years (parents of elementary and high school children).	1. General participation in the year (yes/no) 2. Organizational context of sports participation (club-organized and non-organized participation) 3. Participation in six distinct types of sports disciplines	Logistic regression modeling and canonical correlation analysis	Social class (+), Female (−), Age (−), Family size (−), Urbanization (+). Divorced people (−). Sport participation remains socially stratified in the 80s–90s.
Scheerder, Vanreusel and Taks (2005b) Flanders (Belgium), 1979, 1999–2002 period	1979 Leuven Growth Study on Flemish Girls and primary data from the authors (1999–2002) N = 257 females 32–41 years	1. Sports participation for an average of one hour or more per week over a whole year (Adolescence and adulthood). 2. Non-participation in sports (Adolescence and adulthood)	Logistic regression and structural equation modeling	Participation during adolescence (+), Sport practice of the partner (+), Education (+), School program, Age (non-lineal), Parents sport participation (+, only for youth), Parental social class (+, only for youth).
Farrell and Shields (2002) England, 1997	1997 Health Survey of England N= 3,811 households, 6,467 individuals 16–65 years 10 most popular sporting activities	1. Sport participation in the last 4 weeks for more than 15 minutes (yes/no) 2. Participation in every sport in the last 4 weeks for more than 15 minutes (yes/no)	Random-effects probit modeling	Male (+), Age (−), Married (−), Infant (−), Children for males (+), Ethnic minority (−), Education (+), Drinking (+), Smoking (−), Health (+), Income (+), Unemployed (+), Household membership (+).

Study	Data source	Dependent variable	Method	Results
Downward and Rasciute (2010) UK, 2008	2008 DCMS Taking Part Survey N = 7,080 16 years and over 67 sports activities and 24 other leisure activities	1. Ratio of the number of sports activities/number of leisure activities	Tobit model	Age (−), Male (+), Education (+), Income (+), White (+), Number of children (+). Regional effects.
Spinney and Millward (2010) Canada, 2005	2005 Statistics Canada's General Social Survey on Time Use (GSS–TU) N = 14,452 15 years and over 183 physical activities	1. Energy expenditure on physical activities including only moderate and higher intensity	Pearson's conditions and Maun–Withey U technique	Income and time poverty influence on the intensity in physical activity.
Stratton, Conn, Liaw and Conolly (2005) Australia, 2002	2002 General Survey N = 15,500 18 years and over Sports and physical activities	1. Participation in sports and physical activities in the last 12 months	Multiple logistic regression	Proficiency in English (+), Self-assessed health status (+), Age (+), Female (+), Social contact (+), Access to transport (+), Socio-economic status (+), Income (+), Education (+).
Lechner (2009) Germany, 1984–2006	1984–2006 German Socio-economic panel study N = 6,751 18–45 years	1. Frequency of sports participation in the last year. Two samples: participant less than monthly and participant at least monthly	Probit model	Female (−), non-German (−), education (+), income (+), job quality (+), married (−), age (−), number of children (−).
García, Lera-López and Suárez (2010) Spain, 2003	2002–2003 Spanish Time-use Survey N = 27,268 18–65 years Sports and physical activities	1. Likelihood of participation in sports and physical activities 2. Time (hours) spent in sports and physical activities Two samples (female and male)	Probit model and Seeming Unrelated Regression (SUR) method	Likelihood: education (+), children (−), marital status for female (+), for male (−), age (U-shaped curve), size of population (+), health (+, only for male). Time: income (−), age (+), health (−), married (−), number of children (+).

(Continued overleaf)

Table 25.1 Continued

Study, country and year	Sample characteristics	Dependent variable (estimator)	Methodology	Evidence / Findings
Breuer and Wicker (2009) Germany, 1985–2005	1985, 1986, 1988, 1992, 1994, 1996, 1997, 1999, 2001, 2005 German SOEP N = 3,012	1. Dichotomized variable: regular sports participant (yes/no)	Anova	Women's regular sport participation is stable and does not decrease with age while in men, regular sport participation decreases with age.
Stamatakis and Chaudhury (2008) UK, 1997–2006	Health Survey for England (HSfE) Years: 1997, 1998, 2003, 2004 and 2006 N = 27,213 men and 33,721 women	1. Taking part in any of a list of sports in the four weeks before the interview Two samples (female and male)	Multiple logistic regression models	Female: age (−), social class (+), household income (+), education (+), general health status (+), ethnicity (−). Male: age (−), social class (+), household income (+), education (+), general health status (+).
Humphreys and Ruseski (2010) Canada, 2001	2001 Canadian Community Health Survey (CHHS) N = 99,322 Persons aged 12 or older Sport and physical activities	1. Participation in sports and physical activities 2. Time in sports and physical activities	Double hurdle model for only seven sports: swimming, golfing, weightlifting, running, walking, home exercise, cycling	1. Income (+), hourly wage (+), education – college (+), white collar job (−), different effect of age and gender depending of the activity. 2. Income (−), hourly wage (+), education – college (+), white collar job (+), different effect of age and gender depending of the activity, married (−), young children (−).
Eberth and Smith (2010) Scotland, 2003	2003 Scottish Health Survey (SHeS) N = 4,380 16–64 years General sporting activities	1. Decision to participate in sporting activities 2. Duration of time spent undertaking their sporting activities	"Copula approach" for maximum likelihood estimates	Positive association between sport decision and duration. 1. Age (+), male (+), smokers (−), alcohol consumption (+), hours spent watching TV (−), children aged 0–2 (−), children aged 2–15 (+), household income (+), education (+), self-reported general health (+). 2. Female (+), age (−), single (+), watching TV (−), self-reported general health (+), smoking (−).

Study	Data source	Dependent variable	Method	Results
Van Tuyckom, Scheerder and Bracke (2010) EU–25	2005 Eurobarometer Survey 62.0 N = 23,909 Population aged 18 years and older General sporting activities	Dichotomized variable regular and non–regular sports participants	Binary logistic regression	Male (+) and female (−), although with differences among the European countries.
Van Tuyckom and Scheerder (2010) EU–27	2004 Eurobarometer Survey 64.30 N = 26,688 Population aged 15 years and older Physical activities	How much physical activity in the last 7 days?	Bivariate analyses	Male (+), age (+), educational level (+), degree of urbanization (+), South and East European countries (−).
Hovemann and Wicker (2009) EU–25	2004 Eurobarometer Survey 62.0 N = 23,909 Population aged 18 years and older General sporting activities	Dichotomized variable regular and non–regular sports participants	Binary logistic regression	Age (−), married (−), occupation (−), children (−), male (+), degree of urbanization (+), educational level (+).
Fridberg (2010) Denmark, 1964–2004	Surveys on cultural and leisure time activities in 1964, 1975, 1987, 1993, 1998, and 2004 Population aged 15 and above	Regular participants (at least once a week)	Bivariate analysis	Age (−), occupation (−), educational level (+).

(1) For household activities and walking, age, female and married variables/categories are positively associated with sports participation. Urban variable is negatively related to outdoor recreation.

(2) Employed variable is negatively related to household activities, individual sport and walking. White is positively associated with group and individual sports participation.

exercise and weightlifting) and spend more time in three out of five than men (walking, exercise at home and swimming). Also, these differences are less marked among older adults in physical activity participation (Bauman et al., 2009) and it seems that the gap in sport participation between men and women has narrowed in some countries in the last ten years (Fridberg, 2010; Stamatakis and Chaudhury, 2008).

Sport participation requires consumption of some sporting goods and services, and/or the ability to have the time available to pursue sport whilst not crowding out other consumption requirements needing income. Many studies, therefore, include the influence of economic variables, such as household or individual annual income. The literature provides evidence that lower income may act as a barrier to sport participation (Breuer and Wicker, 2008; Downward and Rasciute, 2011; Eberth and Smith, 2010; Farrell and Shields, 2002; Humphreys and Ruseski, 2006, 2007, 2010; Lera-López and Rapún-Gárate, 2007; Spinney and Millward, 2010; Stempel, 2005; Stratton et al., 2005; Wicker et al., 2009; Wilson, 2002). Nevertheless, among regular practitioners, income has no influence on the frequency of their sport participation (Gratton and Taylor, 2000) or the influence is negative (Downward and Riordan, 2007; García et al., 2010; Humphreys and Ruseski, 2006, 2010). This could be explained because the higher the income, the higher the opportunity cost of time spent on any leisure activity (García et al., 2010). In addition, some studies have analyzed the role played by professional status in sport participation. This is likely to be correlated to income. Less sport participation in general has been found among certain occupational segments in the lower socio-economic groups and non-skilled workers (García Ferrando, 2006; Lechner, 2009; Lera-López and Rapún-Gárate, 2007; Stratton et al., 2005). It seems that this gap between high and low socio-economic groups has not been narrowing in the last ten years (Stamatakis and Chaudhury, 2008). Additionally, Humphreys and Ruseski (2010) show that people in white-collar jobs are less likely to participate in sport, but when they are engaged they spend between 4.7 and 33.5 minutes more per week than people in other types of jobs.

From an economic point of view, and linked to the role of income for the theoretical reasons noted above, another important component in the analysis of the demand for sport is the availability of time. Since time is finite, any increase in the time devoted to sport will always be constrained by competing demands for time from other leisure, work and other uses. The influence of the time constraint could be analyzed indirectly thorough different variables such as income and occupation, as above, as well as some variables related to the family structure. In some analyses working and employment is negatively related to sport participation (Breuer and Wicker, 2008; Downward, 2007; Eberth and Smith, 2010; Hovemann and Wicker, 2009).

The household influence on individual sport participation is commonly analyzed by considering the effect of marital status and size of the household on sport participation rates. Married people participate less in sport and physical activities and dedicate less time to it (Eberth and Smith, 2010; García et al., 2010; Hovemann and Wicker, 2009; Humphreys and Ruseski, 2006), although there are significant differences according to the type of activity (Humphreys and Ruseski, 2010), gender (Eberth and Smith, 2010) and the frequency of sport participation (Humphreys and Ruseski, 2007, 2010). In addition, there are significant differences between men and women (Eberth and Smith, 2010).

The size of a household, according to Downward (2007), Humphreys and Ruseski (2006, 2007) and Scheerder et al. (2005a), was negatively associated with sport participation. In Downward (2004) and Farrell and Shields (2002) the effect was not clear and varied according to the type of sport considered. Children may limit the time available for adult sporting activities such as aerobics and running while increasing participation in child-oriented sport such as football or swimming (Downward, 2004). In fact, Humphreys and Ruseski (2010) show that people with young children dedicate more time in family-oriented sport activities like riding bikes and swimming. Stratton et al. (2005) report that families where there are dependent children have the highest rate of sport participation whereas Lechner (2009) reports that young children in the household are negatively associated to sport participation. In Downward and Rasciute (2011) households of a greater number of adults and children are more likely to participate in sport activities than other leisure activities. Finally, García et al. (2010) report that in general children decrease the likelihood of being involved in sport and physical activities but when people with little children decide to participate, they allocate more time to sport than people without children. In addition, in the analysis of the household impact, the parental influence on sport participation has been included in different empirical studies. Children and adolescents who perceive parents to be active report the highest sport participation rates (Berger et al., 2008; Dollman and Lewis, 2010; Taks and Scheerder, 2006).

Traditionally, educational level has been included in the analysis of sport participation. A higher level of education might lead to a greater awareness of the benefits and importance of sport as well as being associated with higher hourly wages and more available resources to take up sporting activities. Also, higher education is more likely to be associated to a sedentary occupation (Fridberg, 2010). Finally education includes habits developed as a student, when access to sports facilities is easy and relatively inexpensive. Indeed, a positive relationship between education and sports participation has been reported in different studies (Breuer and Wicker, 2008; Downward, 2007; Downward and Rasciute, 2011; Eberth and Smith, 2010; Fridberg, 2010; Hovemann and Wicker, 2009; Humphreys and Ruseski, 2006, 2007, 2010; Lechner, 2009; Stempel, 2005; Stratton et al., 2005; Wicker et al., 2009; Wilson, 2002). In terms of the frequency of sport participation and time spent, some authors report a negative relationship with educational attainment (Downward and Riordan, 2007; Humphreys and Ruseski, 2006). Nevertheless, for participation in seven different sports in Canada, Humphreys and Ruseski (2010) show that people with a high school or college education spend between 9 and 43 minutes more per week playing sport than people with less than a high school education.

Many studies include variables measuring the influence of the availability of sport facilities in sport demand. Generally speaking, a degree of sport supply should induce sport demand and participation. For example, Downward and Rasciute (2011) report that sport facilities do promote participation in sport relative to leisure. Wicker et al. (2009) show that a poor supply of sport facilities reduces the regularity of sport activities. Other studies have included the size of population as a proxy variable to measure the availability of sport facilities. On the one hand, the empirical evidence might lead us to expect less access to certain types of sporting facilities in rural areas than in the suburbs or cities (Andreff and Nys, 2001; Hovemann and Wicker, 2009). On the other hand, in large cities there would be more availability of a wider range of entertainment options and consequently more substitute leisure activities for sport activities. This could have a negative effect on the general level of sport participation, as demonstrated by Moens and Scheerder (2004), García et al. (2010) and Scheerder Vanreusel and Taks (2005a).

A large set of studies has focused on the motivations for getting involved in sport. A better understanding of people's motivations for sport involvement offers significant opportunities to develop more effective sport management and marketing strategies to attract new participants. The empirical evidence shows that the most relevant benefits of, and motivations for, sport participation are physical fitness and health, entertainment, relaxation, sense of achievement and skill development and socialization (Bloom et al., 2005; European Commission, 2004; Fridberg, 2010; García Ferrando, 2006). For example, to 78 percent of citizens in 25 European countries, improvement of health is the major benefit of playing sport. In addition, 31 percent of Europeans find that a major benefit of playing sport is to meet with friends and 39 percent identify the major benefit as entertainment and having fun (Fridberg, 2010). Finally, from an economic perspective, participation in other sports also strongly affects participation in any given sport, and the types of sport undertaken. This can be viewed as resulting from the accumulation of personal consumption and social capital (Downward and Riordan, 2007).

Data, variables and method

Data set

In this section, an analysis of sport participation in Spain is presented, to illustrate the empirical approach and theoretical arguments made earlier. The main characteristics of the database drawn upon, as well as the variables included in the analysis, are presented first.

The database is based on a survey developed by the Centro de Investigaciones Sociológicas (CIS), an independent entity established to study Spanish society, mainly through public opinion tools. This survey was financed by the Spanish High Council for Sport (CSD), a Spanish public institution in charge of sport, with the goal of obtaining detailed information about Spanish sport habits. The survey was conducted during the period between March and April 2005 in face-to-face interviews and it generated a sample of 8,170 individuals aged between 18 and 74 years. The sampling method is based on stratified sampling of municipalities and random sampling of addresses within municipalities, following gender and age proportions of the population. In each of the selected sampling points (municipalities), a starting address was drawn at random. Further addresses were selected by standard "random route" procedures from the initial address, commonly used in the European surveys developed by Eurostat, for example. The survey was developed in 389 different towns and villages in the 17 Spanish regions. The confidence level is estimated at 95.5 percent with a sampling error of +/−1.11 percent.

The questionnaire consists of four parts. The first part includes questions concerning the frequency with which the individual performs sporting activities, what types of sport have been practiced, the motivation for this participation, types of sporting facilities available and if club sports are undertaken. The second part includes questions to non-participants to study their motives. The third part investigates opinions concerning public financial support for mass sport participation and professional team sport, and the quality of sporting facilities in the municipalities. The fourth includes questions about the problem of doping. The fifth part of the questionnaire focuses on passive sport participation, defined as attendance at amateur and professional sporting events, watching sport events on television, and reading sport newspapers. The final part of the questionnaire measures the socio-demographic characteristics of respondents such as their gender, age, educational level, employment status and socio-economic status.

Variables

To model sport participation, a number of variables are used in this study. The key dependent variables that are investigated in this chapter are ANYSPORT and SPORTFREQUENCY.

These variables are derived respectively from questions that ask first, "Do you practice any sport?" where a binary "yes/no" answer is required; and second, "What is the frequency of your sport participation: three or more times/1–2 times/less/only on holidays?" This is an ordered variable. In this study, the answer "no" to the first question was taken as a possible outcome for the ordered variable. As discussed earlier, this essentially treats the "no" response as a credible choice by respondents.

The variable ANYSPORT takes the value zero if the person is a non-participant and value one if the respondent has participated in sporting activities. It can be seen as an aggregate measure of sport participation and is modeled using a probit estimator. The second variable, SPORTFREQUENCY, is an ordinal variable measuring the frequency of sport participation. The value zero is given to people who don't practice sport, value one if the sport participation is only on holidays, value two if the frequency of sport participation is less than once per week, value three if participation is at least once or twice per week, and value four if the frequency is three times or higher. As an ordered relationship, increasing participation is noted, but the increases are not uniformly calibrated.

The use of these two dependent variables loosely corresponds to examining a potentially twofold decision made with respect to participation. This includes whether or not to participate in sport and, subsequently, what intensity of participation is undertaken. As noted earlier, such data could lend itself to a variety of estimators such as the Heckman sample selection model, or other hurdle models. The important thing about these models is that the occurrence or not of sampling units for a given set of variables is implied by a given sampling rule (see, for example, Cameron and Trivedi, 2005; Wooldridge, 2002). In the current context, the value of zero has the character of a real limit to behavior. Further, the dependent variable is ordered rather than continuous. It is these circumstances that lead to the choice of the ordered model in exploring frequency.

The covariates employed in the analysis are given in Table 25.2, along with their mean values and descriptions. In addition, column 4 indicates whether or not the variable was included in the ANYSPORT probit equation (P) or the SPORTFREQUENCY ordered probit equation (O).

The first set of variables in the analysis comprises basic socio–demographic characteristics, which are included in both regressions and have been broadly considered in the empirical evidence. These include the age of the respondent, and their sex, class and education. Age is included linearly as well as in a squared form as it is possible that both participation and its frequency might vary in a nonlinear way with age. For example, one might expect a rapid decline in competitive sport with age but, perhaps, less so with more leisurely sport.

As discussed above, it is a standard finding in the literature that males participate more than females and such a prediction is evident in the unconditional proportion of the sample given by the mean value of the sex dummy variable. As no direct income variable could be employed in the analysis due to missing values, social class variables are used as proxies, with the expectation that positive signs will be generated. The same is true for the education variables. The sample characteristics show that higher levels of education are rarer, and it would be expected that these would promote more sport participation because of the generation of relevant tastes and higher incomes as discussed in the literature.

The remaining variables investigated comprise elements of the formation of tastes for sport, that is, the human and social capital required to consume sport, as well as the opportunity costs involved in practicing sport. Consequently, in general terms, in the former case it is to be expected that parental involvement in sport, the membership of a sport association or federation, or participation in an organized group or alone would affect participation in a

Table 25.2 Variable description

Variable	Mean	Type	Model	Label
NUMFREET	7.87047	Count	O	Number of free time activities other than doing/watching sport
AGE	41.4079	Cardinal	P/O	Age in years
AGESQ	1981.01	Cardinal	P/O	Age squared in years
SEX	.513896	Nominal	P/O	Male =1 Female = 0
FATHERSP	.217866	Nominal	P	Has father practiced sport? 1 = yes, 0 = no
MOTHERSP	.113896	Nominal	P	Has mother practiced sport? 1 = yes, 0 = no
UPPERCLA	.744417E-01	Nominal	P/O	Upper class? 1 = yes, 0 = no (base = other class)
MIDDLECL	.361290	Nominal	P/O	Middle class? 1 = yes, 0 = no (base = other class)
PRIMARYS	.554839	Nominal	P/O	Primary School? 1 = yes, 0 = no (base = no study)
SECONDST	.286600	Nominal	P/O	Secondary School? 1 = yes, 0 = no (base = no study)
UNIVERSI	.972705E-01	Nominal	P/O	University? 1 = yes, 0 = no (base = no study)
CLUBMEMB	0.230273	Nominal	O	Member of a sport club? 1 = yes, 0 = no
ADEQFAC	.367990	Nominal	P	Adequate facilities nearby? 1 = yes, 0 = no
SPORTFIT	.986600	Nominal	P	Sport keeps you fit? 1 = yes, 0 = no
SPORTESC	.902978	Nominal	P	Sport is an escape valve? 1 = yes, 0 = no
SPORTSIB	.935484	Nominal	P	Sport allows social interaction? 1 = yes, 0 = no
SPORTLFB	.884367	Nominal	P	Sport allows living life to the full? 1 = yes, 0 = no
SPORTPDB	.837965	Nominal	P	Sport produces personal development? 1 = yes, 0 = no
SPORTCOM	0.049876	Nominal	O	Participates in sport competitions? 1 = yes, 0 = no
SPORTFED	0.073697	Nominal	O	Belongs to a sport federation? 1 = yes, 0 = no
SPORTALO	0.093052	Nominal	O	Plays sport alone? 1 = yes, 0 = no
SPORTORG	0.90323	Nominal	O	Plays sport in an organized way? 1 = yes, 0 = no
HEAVYJOB	.538462E-01	Nominal	P	Has a heavy job? 1 = yes, 0 = no
WALKMOVE	.123573	Nominal	P	Walk and move a lot at work? 1 = yes, 0 = no
WALKBIN	.592060	Nominal	P/O	Walks for fitness? 1 = yes, 0 = no
SPORTWAT	.378412	Nominal	P/O	Watches sport in free time? 1 = yes, 0 = no

N = 4030

positive way. However, it is theorized that parental involvement would affect the decision to participate, by shaping tastes, whereas membership of a sport club and a form of participation will be linked to the frequency of the practice of sport. In the latter case, opportunity costs of sport are more likely to apply when it is likely that other non-sport free time activities are undertaken, that adequate sport facilities are not available, or that work involves physical demands or much walking; therefore, these factors might reduce participation. The same could be the case for walking as a fitness activity, or watching sport, rather than practicing it. Of course, it may well be that watching and practicing sport are complementary rather than substitute activities (Dawson and Downward, 2011).

More specifically, because the number of free time non-sport activities measures the extent of other leisure activities this is included in the frequency equation. The same is true of walking for fitness and watching sport on TV. However, these two variables are also included in the probit equation as substitutes because of their binary nature. The same is true of the characteristics of work. In contrast, all of the motivational aspects of sport participation investigated are employed in the probit equation only as they are concerned with the likely desire to practice sport *per se*. These variables can also be theorized as measuring the human and social capital arising from sport participation.

Method

As noted in the previous section a twofold empirical strategy is adopted in this chapter. The foundation of the approach can be an underlying random utility, or latent variable, in which continuous latent utility y_i^*, as given in equation 25.1, is observed in a discrete form (Greene and Hensher, 2010).

$$y_i^* = \beta' x_i + \varepsilon_i, i = 1,..., N. \tag{25.1}$$

The vector x_i is a set of K covariates that are assumed to be strictly independent of ε_i; x_i is a vector of K parameters. In the probit estimator used to explore the likelihood of ANYSPORT participation or not, observations of the latent continuous utility in discrete form are given by

$$y_i = 0....if .... y_i^* \leq 0. \tag{25.2(a)}$$

and (25.2)

$$y_i = 1....if ....y_i^* > 0. \tag{25.2(b)}$$

This implies that utility from any form of sport participation is captured by a discrete binary indicator. In the ordered probit estimator, to model the SPORTFREQUENCY the continuous latent utility y_i^* is observed in a discrete form through the censoring mechanism:

$$
\begin{aligned}
y_i &= 0 \; if \; \mu_{-1} < y_i^* \leq \mu_0, \\
&= 1 \; if \; \mu_0 < y_i^* \leq \mu_1, \\
&= 2 \; if \; \mu_1 < y_i^* \leq \mu_2, \\
&= ... \\
&= J \; if \; \mu_{J-1} < y_i^* \leq \mu_J.
\end{aligned}
\tag{25.3}
$$

The thresholds μ divide the range of utility into cells that are then identified with the observed frequencies of sport participation. An important feature of the ordered choice model is that the threshold parameters have no obvious interpretation, though they can indicate something about the distribution of preferences of individuals (Greene and Hensher, 2010).

In these models, the effect of a change in one of the variables in the model depends on all the model parameters, the data, and which probability (cell) is of interest. Therefore, one possibility is to compute partial effects to give the impacts on the specific probabilities per unit change in the covariate. The partial effects in the probit model are given by Equation 25.4.

$$\frac{\partial \Pr ob[y_i = 1 | x_i]}{\partial x_i} = \phi(\beta' x_i)\beta \tag{25.4}$$

where the first term on the right-hand side is the derivative of the standard normal cumulative distribution function.

For the ordered choice model, they are expressed as

$$\delta_i(x_i) = \frac{\partial \Pr ob(y = j | x_i)}{\partial x_i} = [f(\mu_{j-1} - \beta' x_i) - f(\mu_j - \beta' x_i)\beta] \tag{25.5}$$

In this case, under certain conditions it might be regarded that a positive (negative) coefficient is connected with a reduction (increase) in the probability in the lowest cell and an increase (reduction) in the probability in the highest cell. With the single crossing feature of the model, such that some probabilities fall and some rise, one can imply that probabilities have shifted in a particular direction. In this respect a positive sign on the coefficient implies that probabilities have shifted in favor of the higher ordered values of the variable. In fact, the same form of logic applies to the probit model, in which the appropriate marginal effects capture the actual changes in the probability of the outcome scored "1" as the dependent variable, giving uniquely scaled magnitudes.

Results

Table 25.3 lists the regression results for the probit and ordered probit analysis with statistically significant values denoted by ***, ** and * referring to significance at 1, 5 and 10 percent respectively. The marginal effects are noted in the third column for each model, for statistically significant coefficients.

Taking the probit model first, and the analysis of participation in ANYSPORT or not, the age variables suggest that there is a nonlinear effect on participation and, in particular. the decline takes place steeply at first, but then it slows down as higher age is reached.[5] This result could be explained by the increasing awareness of sport participation and health among the elderly, or their "sport literacy" as compared to earlier generations. As indicated by the literature reviewed earlier, males are more likely to participate in sport than females and, as revealed by the marginal effects, this is the dominant influence on participation. However, parental participation in sport is the next largest effect, particularly stemming from the sport activity of fathers. This indicates a strong household influence on tastes, and it is a unique result in the literature, which has tended to only analyze the effect of the number of other adults and children in the household.

As is also expected from the literature, higher social class and education are associated with an increase in the probability of participating in ANYSPORT which, as discussed earlier, can be associated with an increase in human and social capital. Similarly, the results indicate that the motivations to participate in sport, which can be associated with human and social capital, are also likely to raise participation in ANYSPORT. Significantly, just doing sport to stay fit is not a significant determinant of the probability of participation. This might suggest that policy simply promoting the health benefits of sport may be unsuccessful. Socialization and entertainment motivation seems to be statistically relevant to the explanation of the probability of participating in sport. Finally, the availability of sport facilities is not statistically significant in explaining the decision to participate in sport activities. This result might also

Table 25.3 Regression results

Covariates	Probit model			Ordered probit model		
	Coefficient	t-stats	ME	Coefficients	t-stats	ME
Constant	−.92756★★★	−3.09		−0.13097	−0.64	
NUMFREET				−0.00436	−0.74	
AGE	−.04364★★★	−5.52	−0.0152	−.04539★★★	−5.62	−0.00479
AGESQ	.00030★★★	3.28	0.0001	.00033★★★	3.48	0.00003
SEX	.43975★★★	9.07	0.15178	.29936★★★	5.76	0.03158
FATHERSP	.35550★★★	6.11	0.12924			
MOTHERSP	.24262★★★	3.24	0.08816			
UPPERCLA	.22151★★	2.49	0.08054	.18185★★	2.00	0.02175
MIDDLECL	0.0659	1.36		.11355★★	2.27	0.01231
PRIMARYS	.29567★★	2.33	0.10183	−0.11406	−0.86	
SECONDST	.45975★★★	3.43	0.16651	−0.07643	−0.55	
UNIVERSI	.54212★★★	3.75	0.2043	0.02634	0.17	
CLUBMEMB				.87686★★★	16.06	0.13617
ADEQFAC	0.02111	0.47				
SPORTFIT	0.08738	0.4				
SPORTESC	.17347★★	2.04	0.05806			
SPORTSIB	.24604★★	2.48	0.08045			
SPORTLFB	.23329★★★	2.73	0.07712			
SPORTPDB	.15804★★	2.25	0.05342			
SPORTCOM				.59678★★★	5.05	0.09533
SPORTFED				.51902★★★	5.87	0.07752
SPORTALO				1.83952★★★	27.33	0.47924
SPORTORG				.96681★★★	11.72	0.18337
HEAVYJOB	−0.01637	−0.16				
WALKMOVE	−0.07882	−1.16				
WALKBIN	0.01744	0.38		.15829★★★	3.24	0.01634
SPORTWAT	.21444★★★	4.55	0.07557	.17310★★★	3.23	0.01894
Mu(1)				1.04621★★★	28.83	

suggest that policy simply promoting new sport facilities could have a very little effect on sport participation rates in Spain.

In the ordered probit model investigating the frequency of participation, the significant variables suggest that age reduces the frequency of participation in a nonlinear way and that being male will increase the frequency of sport participation, as well as the human capital consequences of social class. Unexpectedly, educational level is not a statistically significant factor explaining the frequency of participation, although it is a relevant factor explaining the probability of sport participation.

The variables associated with the more formal aspects of sport such as sport club membership, belonging to a sport federation, participating in sport competitions or participating in sport in an organized way are, more naturally, associated with increased probabilities of greater sporting frequency. However, the largest effect is associated with playing sport alone. This is probably associated with either endurance activities such as running, swimming or cycling or the fact that they may act as training inputs to other sport activities, such as team sport. Some indirect evidence for this conjecture might be implied from the fact that walking for fitness is also positively associated with increases in the frequency of sport participation, suggesting that they are complementary activities. In addition, this result could be a consequence of the increasing importance of unorganized sport participation to the detriment of organized participation. Finally, and consistent with Dawson and Downward (2011), it appears that watching sport on television is a complementary activity to practicing sport.

Conclusions

In this chapter the determinants of sport participation and its frequency in Spain have been studied using probit and ordered probit estimators, respectively. Results broadly similar to the existing literature, which is also extensively reviewed in the chapter, are produced.

The results show that the likelihood of sport participation is mainly determined by parental participation in sport (particularly by sport participation of fathers), gender, class and educational level. Age affects sport in a nonlinear way. Sport participation also seems to be motivated by socializing and the need for entertainment. Watching sport on television, further, seems to be a complementary activity to practicing sport.

The frequency of participation decreases with age and increases with being male. Whereas social class is positively associated with higher frequency of sport participation, educational level is not statistically significant. The variables associated with the more formal aspects of sport, such as sport club and sport federation membership, or participating in sport competitions or in an organized way, are logically associated with greater sporting frequency. This suggests that attracting participants to organized sport may enhance their frequency of participation. However, the largest effect on the frequency of sport participation is associated with playing sport alone, emphasizing the importance of sport activities developed in an unorganized way and the complementary relationship with other physical activities such as walking for fitness. Coupled with the steady decline in sport participation, generally, this could suggest changing tastes of participants and increased difficulties of using the formal sport system to achieve social policy aims, an issue noted in the UK by Downward (2011).

Notes

1　In the review that follows, emphasis is upon large-scale data analysis.
2　The logistic function is used to generate the probabilities of outcomes. Farrell and Shields (2002) use a comparable Probit model, which draws on the cumulative normal distribution. They use a panel-data equivalent of this model to identify shared intra-family preferences (see also Downward and Riordan, 2007).
3　Theoretically this identifies a "corner solution." The Hurdle model can be seen as generalizing the TOBIT model in which only one equation is used to model the data.
4　For a literature review on sport participation see Downward et al., 2009 and Breuer et al. (2010). For a review of participation in physical activities following medicine and health approaches see Sallis et al. (2000) for children and adolescents, and Trost et al. (2002) and Humpel, Owen and Leslie (2002) for adults' participation. Finally, for an international comparative analysis among countries in physical participation see Bauman et al. (2002, 2009) and Haase et al. (2004).
5　This is actually inferred from plotting age against participation. In probit and ordered probit models the marginal effects of non-linear terms cannot be inferred from their separate components.

References

Adams, F.G., Davidson, P., and Seneca, J.J. (1966) 'The social value of water recreational facilities resulting from an improvement in water quality in an estuary.' reprinted in Davidson, L. (ed.) (1991) *The Collected Writings of Paul Davidson, 2, Inflation, Open Economies and Resources*, London, Macmillan.

Andreff, W., and Nys, J.F. (2001) *Economie du sport* [Economics of sport]. Paris, PUF.

Barber, N., and Havitz, M.E. (2001) 'Canadian participation rates in ten sport and fitness activities', *Journal of Sport Management*, 15, 51–76.

Bauman, A., Bull, F., Chey, T., Craig, C., and Ainsworth, B. (2009) 'The international prevalence study on physical activity: results from 20 countries', *International Journal of Behavioral Nutrition and Physical Activity*, 6(21), 1–11.

Bauman, A., Sallis, J., Dzewaltowski, D., and Owen, N. (2002) 'Toward a better understanding of the influences on physical activity', *American Journal of Preventive Medicine*, 23(2S), 5–14.

Becker, G.S. (1965) 'A theory of the allocation of time', *The Economic Journal*, 75, 493–517.

—— (1974) 'A theory of social interactions', *Journal of Political Economy*, 82, 1063–91.

Berger, I.E., O'Reilly, N., Parent, M.M., Seguin, B., and Hernandez, T. (2008) 'Determinants of sport participation among Canadian adolescents', *Sport Management Review*, 11, 277–307.

Biddle, S.J.H., and Ekkekakis, P. (2005) 'Physical Active Lifestyles and Well-being' in Huppert, F.A., Baylis, N. and Keverne, B. (eds.) *The Science of Well-Being*, Oxford, Oxford University Press.

Biddle, S.J.H, Gorely, T., and Stensel, D.J. (2004) 'Health-enhancing physical activity and sedentary behavior in children and adolescents', *Journal of Sport Sciences*, 22, 679–701.

Bloom, M., Grant, M., and Watt, D. (2005) 'Strengthening Canada. The socio-economic benefits of sport participation in Canada', *The Conference Board of Canada Report* August 2005. Retrieved September 5, 2011, from <http://vancouver.ca/parks/activecommunity/pdf/SportsParticipation.pdf>.

Bourdieu, P. (1984) *Distinction: a social critique of the judgment of taste*, Cambridge, MA, Harvard University Press.

—— (1988) 'Program for a Sociology of Sport', *Sociology of Sport Journal*, 2, 153–61.

—— (1991) 'Sport and Social Class', in Mukerji, C. and Schudson, M. (1991) (eds.) *Rethinking Popular Culture, Contemporary Perspectives in Cultural Studies*, Berkeley, University of California Press.

Breuer, C. (2006) 'Sport Participation in Germany – a demo-economical model', German Sport University Cologne, Discussion paper 01–06.

Breuer, C., and Wicker, P. (2008) 'Demographic and economic factors influencing inclusion in the German sport system. A microanalysis of the years 1985 to 2005', *European Journal for Sport and Society*, 5(1), 33–42.

—— (2009) 'Decreasing sport activity with increasing age? Findings from a 20-year longitudinal and cohort sequence analysis', *Research Quarterly for Exercise and Sport*, 80(1), 22–31.

Breuer, C., Hallmann, K., Wicker, P., and Feiler, S. (2010) 'Socio-economic patterns of sport demand and ageing', *European Review Aging Physical Activity*, 7, 61–70.

Cameron, A.C., and Trivedi, P.K. (2005) *Microeconometrics: Methods and Applications*, New York, Cambridge University Press.

Cicchetti, C.J., Davidson, P., and Seneca, J.J. (1969) *The demand and supply of outdoor recreation: An econometric analysis*. Washington, DC, Bureau of Outdoor Recreation.

Commission of European Union (2007) *White Paper on Sport*, COM (2007).391 final Brussels, European Commission.

Council of Europe (1992) *European Sport Charter*, Strasbourg, European Union.

Dawson, P., and Downward, P.M. (2011) 'Participation, Spectatorship and Media Coverage in Sport: Some initial insights' in Andreff, W. (ed.) *Contemporary Issues in Sport Economics, Participation and Professional Sport*, Cheltenham, Edward Elgar.

Dollman, J., and Lewis, N. (2010) 'The impact of socioeconomic position on sport participation among South Australian youth', *Journal of Science and Medicine in Sport*, 13, 318–22.

Downward, P. (2004) 'On leisure demand: a post Keynesian critique of neoclassical theory', *Journal of Post Keynesian Economics*, 26, 371–94.

—— (2007) 'Exploring the economic choice to participate in sport: Results from the 2002 General Household Survey', *International Review of Applied Economics*, 21, 633–53.

—— (2011) 'Market segmentation and the role of the public sector in sports development', in B. Houlihan (ed.) *International Handbook of Sports Development*, Abingdon, Routledge.

Downward, P., and Rasciute, S. (2010) 'The relative demands for sport and leisure in England', *European Sport Management Quarterly*, 10(2), 189–214.

—— (2011) 'Does sport make you happy? An analysis of the well-being derived from sports participation', *International Review of Applied Economics*, 25(3), 331–48.

Downward, P., and Riordan, J. (2007) 'Social interactions and the demand for sport: An economic analysis', *Contemporary Economic Policy*, 25, 518–37.

351

Downward, P., Dawson, A., and Dejonghe, T. (2009) *Sport economics: theory, evidence and policy*, Oxford, Elsevier.

Earl, P. E. (1983) *The Economic Imagination*, Brighton, Wheatsheaf.

—— (1986) *Lifestyle Economics*, Brighton, Wheatsheaf.

Eberth, B., and Smith, M. (2010) 'Modeling the participation decision and duration of sporting activity in Scotland', *Economic Modeling*, 27, 822–34.

European Commission (2004) *The citizen of the European Union and sport. Special Eurobarometer 213*. Brussels, European Commission.

—— (2007) *White paper on sport*, Brussels, Commission of the European Communities.

Farrell, L., and Shields, M.A. (2002) 'Investigating the economic and demographic determinants of sporting participation in England', *Journal of the Royal Statistics Society*, A(165), 335–48.

Fridberg, T. (2010) 'Sport and exercise in Denmark, Scandinavia and Europe', *Sport in Society*, 13(4), 583–92.

Galbraith, J.K. (1958) *The Affluent Society*, Harmondsworth, Penguin.

García Ferrando, M. (2006) *Posmodernidad y deporte: Entre la individualización y la masificación*, Madrid, Consejo Superior de Deportes.

García, J., Lera-López, F., and Suárez, M.J. (2010) 'Estimation of a structural model of the determinants of the time spent on physical activity and sport: Evidence for Spain', *Journal of Sport Economics* (in press).

Gratton, C. and Taylor, P. (1991) *Government and the Economics of Sport*, Harlow, Longman.

—— (2000) *Economics of Sport and Recreation*, London, Spon Press.

Green, M., and Collins, S. (2008) 'Policy, politics and path dependency: sport development in Australia and Finland', *Sport Management Review*, 11, 225–51.

Greene, W.H., and Hensher, D.A. (2010) *Modeling Ordered Choices*, Cambridge, Cambridge University Press.

Haase, A., Steptoe, A., Sallis, J. and Wardle, J. (2004) 'Leisure-time physical activity in university students from 23 countries: association with health beliefs, risk awareness, and national economic development', *Preventive Medicine*, 39, 182–90.

Hovemann, G., and Wicker, P. (2009) 'Determinants of sport participation in the European Union', *European Journal for Sport and Society*, 6(1), 51–59.

Humpel, N., Owen, N., and Leslie, E. (2002) 'Environmental factors associated with adults' participation in physical activity', *American Journal of Preventive Medicine*, 22(3), 188–99.

Humphreys, B.R., and Ruseski, J.E. (2006) 'Economic determinants of participation in physical activity and sport', *IASE Working Paper* No. 06–13.

—— (2007) 'Participation in physical activity and government spending on parks and recreation', *Contemporary Economic Policy*, 25, 538–52.

—— (2010) 'The economic choice of participation and time spent in physical activity and sport in Canada', *Working Paper No 2010–14*, Department of Economics, University of Alberta.

Kara, B., Pinar, L., Ugur, F., and Oguz, M. (2005) 'Correlations between aerobic capacity, pulmonary and cognitive functioning in older women', *International Journal of Sport Medicine*, 26(3), 220–24.

Lafont, L., Dechamps, A., and Boudel-Marchasson, I. (2007) 'Effects of Tai Chi exercises on self-efficacy and psychological health', *European Review of Aging and Physical Activity*, 4(1), 25–32.

Lavoie, M. (1994) 'A post Keynesian approach to consumer choice.' *Journal of Post Keynesian Economics*, 16 (4), 539–62.

Lechner, M. (2009). 'Long-run labor market and health effects of individual sport activities', *Journal of Health Economics*, 28, 839–54.

Lera-López, F., and Rapún-Gárate, M. (2007) 'The demand for sport: Sport consumption and participation models', *Journal of Sport Management*, 21, 103–22.

Lera-López, F., Rapún-Gárate, M., and Aguirre-Zabaleta, J. (2008) *Análisis y evaluación económica de la participación deportiva en España*, Madrid, Consejo Superior de Deportes.

Miles, L. (2007) 'Physical activity and health', *British Nutrition Foundation Nutrition Bulletin*, 32, 314–63.

Moens, M., and Scheerder, J. (2004) 'Social determinants of sport participation revisited. The role of socialization and symbolic trajectories', *European Journal of Sport and Society*, 1, 35–49.

Rasciute, S., and Downward, P.M. (2010) 'Health or happiness? What is the impact of physical activity on the individual', *Kyklos*, 63(2), 256–70.

Rodgers, B. (1977) *Rationalizing sport policies: sport in its social context: international comparison*, Strasbourg, Council of Europe.

Rowe, N., Adams, R., and Beasley, N. (2004) 'Driving up participation in sport: The social context, the trends, the prospects and the challenges', in Sport England (2004) *Driving up participation: the challenge for sport*, 6–13. London, Sport England. Retrieved November 15, 2008, from <http://www.sportengland.org>.

Sallis, J., Prochaska, J., and Taylor, W. (2000) 'A review of correlates of physical activity of children and adolescents', *Medicine and Science in Sport and Exercise*, 32, 963–75.

Scheerder, J., and Breedveld, K. (2004) 'Incomplete democratization and signs of individualization. An analysis of trends and differences in sport participation in the Low Countries', *European Journal for Sport and Society*, 1(2), 1–20.

Scheerder, J., Vanreusel, B., and Taks, M. (2005a) 'Stratification patterns of active sport involvement among adults: Social change and persistence', *International Review for the Sociology of Sport*, 40, 139–62.

—— (2005b) 'Leisure-time sport among physical education students: A time trend analysis of sport participation styles', *European Sport Management Quarterly*, 5(4), 415–41.

Scitovsky, T. (1976) *The Joyless Economy*, Oxford, Oxford University Press.

Scraton, S., and Watson, B. (1999) *Sport, Leisure Identities and Gendered Spaces*, Eastbourne, LSA Publications.

Scully, D., Kremer, J., Meade, M., Graham, R., and Dudgeon, K. (1999) 'Physical exercise and psychological well-being: a critical review', *British Journal of Sport Medicine*, 32, 11–20.

Sila, B. (2003) 'People's estimation of their state of health in relation to frequency of their sport activity', *Kinanthropologica*, 39(1), 99–108.

Spinney, J., and Millward, H. (2010) 'Time and money: A new look at poverty and the barriers to physical activity in Canada', *Social Indicators Research*, DOI 10.1007/s11205-010-9585-8.

Sporting Goods Manufacturers Association (SGMA) (2004) *Sport participation in America*, North Palm Beach, SGMA. Retrieved February 22, 2007 from <http://www.sgma.com>.

Stamatakis, E., and Chaudhury, M. (2008) 'Temporal trends in adults' sport participation patterns in England between 1997 and 2006: the Health Survey for England', *British Journal of Sport Medicine*, 42, 901–8.

Stamm, H., and Lamprecht, M. (2005) 'Structural and cultural factors influencing physical activity in Switzerland', *Journal of Public Health*, 13, 203–11.

Stempel, C. (2005) 'Adult participation sport as cultural capital: A test of Bourdieu's theory of the field of sport', *International Review for the Sociology of Sport*, 40, 411–32.

Stratton, M., Conn, L., Liaw, C., and Conolly, L. (2005) 'Sport and related recreational physical activity. The social correlates of participation and non-participation by adults', Conference proceedings, Sport Management Association of Australia and New Zealand, 11th Annual Conference, Canberra, 2005.

Taks, M., and Scheerder, J. (2006) 'Youth sport participation styles and market segmentation profiles: Evidence and application', *European Sport Management Quarterly*, 6(2), 85–121.

Trost, S., Owen, N., Bauman, A., Sallis, J., and Brown, W. (2002) 'Correlates of adults' participation in physical activity: review and update', *Medicine and Science in Sport and Exercise*, 34 (2), 1996–2001.

Van Bottenburg, M. (2005). *Sport participation in the EU: trends and differences*, Retrieved August 23, 2008, from <http://www.mulierinstituut.nl>.

Van Tuyckom, C., and Scheerder, J. (2010) ' "Sport for all?" Insight into stratification and compensation mechanisms of sporting activity in the 27 European Union member state', *Sport, Education and Society*, 15 (4), 495–512.

Van Tuyckom, C., Scheerder, J., and Bracke, P. (2010). 'Gender and age inequalities in regular sport participation: A cross-national study of 25 European countries.' *Journal of Sport Sciences*, 28(10), 1077–84.

Veblen, T. (1925) *The Theory of the Leisure Class*, London, George Allen and Unwin.

Wicker, P., Breuer, C., and Pawlowski, T. (2009) 'Promoting sport for all age-specific target groups. The impact of sport infrastructure', *European Sport Management Quarterly*, 9, 103–18.

Wilson, T.C. (2002) 'The paradox of social class and sport involvement. The roles of cultural and economic capital', *International Review for the Sociology of Sport*, 37, 5–16.

Wooldridge, J.M. (2002) *Econometric Analysis of Cross Section and Panel Data*. Cambridge, MA, MIT Press.

26
EXPENDITURES ON SPORT PRODUCTS AND SERVICES

Tim Pawlowski and Christoph Breuer

Introduction

This chapter provides an overview of the empirical evidence of the analysis of expenditures on sport products and services. Although the empirical analysis of expenditure in sport is much less developed in the literature than the analysis of participation in sport (Downward, Dawson, and Dejonghe, 2009), several studies from all around the world exist. The main objectives of this chapter are to explore the similarities and differences between the findings of these studies and to serve as a basis for further studies in the field of private expenditures on sport. The chapter is structured as follows. The first section provides an overview of the different studies, their research objectives, and the data employed. This is followed by a comparison of the portion of households/individuals that spend resources on sport. There is then a focus on the monetary value of sport in the different countries before discussing the factors that have been identified to influence sport spending behavior. The chapter closes with a short summary of the need for further research in this area.

Literature, research objectives and data

Of the research that has been conducted on expenditures on sport products and services, in this chapter a distinction is made between studies with a microeconomic focus and studies with a macroeconomic focus. This distinction relates to the underlying data examined rather than the objective of the research. This means, for example, that studies based on disaggregated data (e.g. individuals or households) are classified as microeconomic. In contrast those that examine nations or regions are classified as macroeconomic. As shown in Table 26.1, the macro data studies are based primarily on National Accounting Frameworks and tend to focus on the economic importance of sport. Most of them provide descriptive statistics and only a few apply multivariate analysis techniques, i.e. regression analysis.

Tables 26.2 and 26.3 provide an overview of studies of sport expenditures based on disaggregated data in Europe or Asia, America and Oceania, respectively. Most of the studies try to explain expenditure patterns, i.e. factors influencing the amount of money spent by households or individuals on sport products and services. Therefore, in most instances, multiple

Table 26.1 Macroeconomic oriented studies on sport expenditures

Country	Year[1]	Authors	Research objective	Data	Analysis
B	1987	Késenne and Butzen	EI sport	IP	descriptive
D	1986	Kops and Graff	EI sport	NAF	descriptive
D	2000	Meyer and Ahlert	EI sport	IP	descriptive
D	2002	Winde	inter alia EI leisure	NAF	descriptive
DK	1986	Riiskjaer	EI sport	NAF	descriptive
FIN	1988	Rissanen	amongst others EI sport	NAF	descriptive
GB	2003	LIRC	EI sport (England)	NAF	descriptive
GB	2004a	LIRC	EI sport (North Ireland)	NAF	descriptive
GB	2004b	LIRC	EI sport (Scotland)	NAF	descriptive
GB	2004c	LIRC	EI sport (Wales)	NAF	descriptive
I	1986	Tirelli	inter alia EI sport	NAF	descriptive
IS	1989	Magnusson et al.	EI sport	OT	descriptive
J	1990	Matsuda	EI sport	OT	descriptive
J	1997	Papanikos and Sakellariou	expenditures on vacations	OT	RA
NL	1988	Van Puffelen et al.	inter alia EI sport	GAS, OT	descriptive
P	1986	Tenreiro	EI sport	OT	descriptive
ROK	1996	Lee et al.	expenditures on vacations	OT	RA
TR	1997	Mudambi and Baum	expenditures on vacations	OT	RA
USA	1982	Wagner and Washington	expenditures on leisure	NAF	RA
USA	1983	Loy and Rudman	expenditures on leisure	NAF	descriptive
USA	1991	Pyo et al.	expenditures on leisure	OT	RA
USA	1991	Blaine and Mohammed.	expenditures on leisure	OT	RA
USA	1997	Meek	EI sport	GAS	descriptive
USA	2001	Nelson	expenditures on leisure	OT	RA

[1] Year of publication.
Country: (B): Belgium, (D): Germany, (DK): Denmark, (FIN): Finland, (I): Italy, (IS): Iceland, (J): Japan, (NL): The Netherlands, (P): Portugal, (ROK): South Korea, (TR): Turkey, (GB): Great Britain, (USA): United States of America. Research objective: (EI): Economic impact. Data: (GAS): Official public statistics, (IP): Input–Output Analysis, (NAF): National Accounting Framework, (OT): Others or different data. Analysis: (RA): Regression Analysis.

regression analysis is conducted with expenditures or budget shares as dependent variables. Interestingly, while most of the European studies are based on primary data that were collected for the specific study, most of the non-European studies are based on data from the national family/household or consumer expenditure surveys provided by the national statistical offices.

The portion of individuals with expenditures on sport[1]

There is relatively little empirical evidence on the proportion of individuals with sport expenditures. One of the few studies that specify the rate, among respondents with private consumer expenditures on sport, is Weagley and Huh (2004). They identify that there are 71.9 percent of the sample with expenditures on *active leisure* (e.g. membership fees in sport clubs) and 96.9 percent with expenditures on *passive leisure* (e.g. entrance fees at cinemas, theatres or museums) in the USA. However, their sample only contains households with heads of the household aged older than 49 years. Dardis et al. (1994) undertook a similar study but on a more representative sample of the USA. The portion of households with expenditures on *active leisure* (where spending

Table 26.2 Microeconomic oriented studies from Europe

Country	Year[1]	Authors	Research objective	Data[2]	Analysis
B	1985	IISOP	EI sport	OS (n=4,000)	descriptive
B	1994a	Taks et al.	expenditures on sport	OS (n=900)	MD
B	1994b	Taks et al.	expenditures on sport	OS (n=118)	MD
B	1995	Taks et al.	expenditures on sport	OS (n=900)	CA
B	1999	Taks et al.	expenditures on sport	OS (n=900)	CA, REG
B	2000	Taks and Késenne	EI sport	OS (n=512)	descriptive
D	1989	Rittner et al.	sport development	OS (n=1,138)	MD
D	1990	Euler	EI leisure	LWR	descriptive
D	1993	Fiebiger	EI leisure	LWR	descriptive
D	1993	Gundlach	expenditures on services	EVS	REG
D	1995	Schäfer	EI leisure	LWR	descriptive
D	1995	Weber et al.	EI sport	OS (n=2,866)	MD
D	2002	Breuer and Hovemann	expenditures on sport	OS (n=1,091)	CA
D	2002	Winde	EI leisure	EVS	descriptive
D	2003	Schröder	expenditures on sport	OS (n=1,023)	MD
D	2006	Opaschowski et al.	expenditures on leisure	OT	MD
D	2009	Pawlowski	expenditures on leisure	LWR (n=7,591/ 7,724)	REG
E	2000	Pedrosa	EI sport	OT	MD
E	2001	Redondo-Bellón et al.	expenditures on sport	FES	MD, VA
E	2005	Lera-López and Rapún-Gárate	expenditures on sport	OS (n=700)	CA, REG
E	2005	Nicolau and Más	expenditures on vacation	OT	REG
E	2007	Lera-López and Rapún-Gárate	expenditures on sport	OS (n=700)	CA, REG
F	1987	Michon et al.	expenditures on sport	OS (n=2,200)	MD
F	1998	Legohérel	expenditures on vacation	OS (n=410)	AID
F	1999	Desbordes et al.	expenditures on sport	OT	MD
F	2002	Andreff and Nys	expenditures on sport	OT	MD
GB	1980	Martin and Mason	expenditures on leisure	OT	descriptive
GB	1992	Lamb et al.	expenditures on sport	OS (n=1,364)	ANOVA
GB	1994	Blundell et al.	expenditures on services	FES	REG
GB	2002	Davies	expenditures on sport	OS (n=250)	MD
NL	1994	van Ophem and de Hoog	expenditures on leisure	OS (n=739)	CA, REG
NL	1996	Melenberg and van Soest	expenditures on vacation	CES	REG
N	2001	Thrane	expenditures on sport	OT	REG

[1] Year of publication.
[2] Data and sample size (if available).
Country: (B): Belgium, (D): Germany, (E): Spain, (F): France, (GB): Great Britain, (NL): The Netherlands, (N): Norway. Research objective: (EI): Economic impact. Data: (CES): Consumer Expenditure Survey, (EVS): Einkommens- und Verbrauchsstichprobe, (FES): Family/Household Expenditure Survey, (LWR): Laufende Wirtschaftsrechnungen, (OS): own survey, (OT): others or different data. Analysis: (AID): Automatic Interaction Detector, (ANOVA): Analysis of Variance, (CA): Correlation analysis, (MD): Mean differences, (RA): Regression Analysis.

Table 26.3 Microeconomic oriented studies from Asia, America and Oceania

Country	Year[1]	Authors	Research objective	Data[2]	Analysis
AUS	1988	DASETT	EI sport and recreation	FES	REG
AUS	1991	Veal	expenditures on sport	FES	descriptive
AUS	1998	TAPEY	EI sport	OS	descriptive
AUS	1999	Bittman	expenditures on leisure	FES	REG
AUS	2000	NSWSR	EI sport and recreation	FES	descriptive
AUS	2008	ABS	EI sport	FES	descriptive
CDN	1983	Zalatan	EI sport	OT	descriptive
CDN	1998	HCSCCHSC	EI sport	OS	descriptive
CDN	2004	CBC	EI sport	OT	MD
CH	2001	Zhao et al.	expenditures on sport	OS	MD
CH	2006	Legohérel and Wong	expenditures on vacation	OS (n=2,124)	REG
NZ	1991	Lawson	expenditures on vacation	OT	MD
NZ	1998	Hillary Commission	EI Sport	OT	descriptive
J	1993	Oga and Kimura	expenditures on sport	FES	descriptive
USA	1979	Thompson and Tinsley	expenditures on sport	OS	REG
USA	1981	Dardis et al.	expenditures on recreation	CES	REG
USA	1983	Sobel	expenditures on leisure	CES	SEM
USA	1986	Walsh	expenditures on vacation	CES	MD
USA	1990	Paulin	expenditures on leisure	CES	MD
USA	1990	Pitts	expenditures on leisure	CES	MD
USA	1990	Moehrle	expenditures on leisure	CES	MD
USA	1991	Soberon-Ferrer and Dardis	expenditures on services	CES	REG
USA	1991	Spotts and Mahoney	expenditures on vacation	OS (n=2,613)	MD
USA	1993	Abdel-Ghany and Shwenk	expenditures on leisure	CES	REG
USA	1993	Taylor et al.	expenditures on vacation	OS (n=325)	REG
USA	1994	Dardis et al.	expenditures on leisure	CES	REG
USA	1994	Rubin and Nieswiadomy	expenditures on leisure	CES	REG
USA	1995	Cai et al.	expenditures on vacation	CES	REG
USA	1995	Nieswiadomy and Rubin	expenditures on leisure	CES	REG
USA	1995	Wilkes	expenditures on leisure	CES	MD
USA	1996	Fish and Waggle	expenditures on vacation	CES	CA, REG
USA	1997	Fan	expenditures on leisure	CES	REG
USA	1998	Fan	expenditures on leisure	CES	CL, REG
USA	1998	Leones et al.	expenditures on vacation	OS (n=835)	REG
USA	1999	Agarwal and Yochum	expenditures on vacation	OS (n=1,118)	REG
USA	1999	Costa	expenditures on leisure	CES	REG
USA	1999	Hong et al.	expenditures on vacation	CES	REG
USA	2000	Costa	expenditures on leisure	CES	REG
USA	2002	Cannon and Ford	expenditures on vacation	OS (n=2,488)	REG
USA	2004	Weagley and Hugh	expenditures on leisure	CES	REG
USA	2005	Hong et al.	expenditures on vacation	CES	REG

[1] Year of publication.
[2] Data and sample size (if available).
Country: (AUS): Australia, (CAN): Canada, (CH): China, (NZ): New Zealand, (USA): United States of America. Research objective: (EI): Economic Impact. Data: (CES): Consumer Expenditure Survey. (FES): Family/Household Expenditure Survey, (OS): Own survey, (OT): others or different data. Analysis: (AID): Automatic Interaction Detector, (ANOVA): Analysis of Variance (CA): Correlation Analyse, (CL): Cluster Analysis, (MWU): Mean Differences, (RA): Regression Analysis, (SEM): Structure Equation Model.

on activities needs some physical effort, such as sport, photography or fishing) is 70 percent, on *passive leisure* (where spending on activities that do not necessarily need physical effort, such as television watching or the use of radios) is 47 percent and in the category *social entertainment* (where spending is on spectator activities such as going to sport events, theatres or museums), it is 53 percent. The Household Expenditure Survey by the Australian Bureau of Statistics (ABS, 2008) states that about 28 percent of Australians spend money on sport and recreation services.

Besides these studies, four European surveys are worth noting. Lera-López and Rapún-Gárate (2007) discovered that between 90 percent of their sample and 88.5 percent of people doing sport in their sample incur expenditures on sport-related goods and services. However, Thrane (2001) found a considerably lower rate of 73 percent for Norway. For Germany, Opaschowski et al. (2006) surveyed 2,000 people aged older than 13 years and detected that 53 percent spend money on the cinema, 20 percent on musicals and 20 percent on concerts (including rock, pop and open-air events) For Germany Pawlowski (2009) identified that 70 percent of households spend money on sport and recreational services. Table 26.4 provides a detailed overview of the findings in this study.

Table 26.4 Households with expenditures on specific sport and recreational services

Category	2005	2006
Expenditures on sport and other events and venues	3.516 (46.4)	3.492 (45.2)
Sport events	1.240 (16.4)	1.146 (14.8)
Fairs	2.108 (27.8)	2.043 (27.3)
Entrance fees for swimming pools	1.552 (20.5)	1.667 (21.6)
Training and lessons	1.297 (17.1)	1.343 (17.4)
Music	541 (7.1)	584 (7.6)
Dancing	296 (3.9)	275 (3.5)
Other sport	493 (6.5)	482 (6.2)
Other courses	242 (3.2)	299 (3.9)
Membership fees for fitness centers	645 (8.5)	643 (8.3)
Rental fees for sport and recreational products and services	1.266 (16.7)	1.321 (17.1)
Access to sport facility (e.g. tennis)	973 (12.8)	1.043 (13.5)
Caravans	19 (0.3)	16 (0.1)
Sport and camping products	406 (5.4)	389 (5.0)
Other sport and recreational services	2.937 (38.8)	2.974 (38.5)
Transportation with ski lifts (not during vacation)	149 (2.0)	120 (1.6)
Transportation with ski lifts (during vacation)	258 (3.4)	245 (3.2)
Fees for the usage of alpine slopes	19 (0.3)	22 (0.3)
Fees for the usage of gaming machines	77 (1.0)	49 (0.6)
Guided tours	160 (2.1)	161 (2.1)
Other recreational services	145 (1.9)	168 (2.2)
Membership fees for sport clubs	2.515 (33.2)	2.572 (33.3)

Source: Pawlowski (2009).

In brackets: percentage share of total sample.

The monetary value of sport

In order to give an effective comparison of the monetary value of sport across countries' expenditures, data from previous studies were collected from three different levels: *individuals, households* and the *total population*. Focusing on total population values is useful for macro-economic comparisons. However, in order to allow for differences in the scale of countries expenditures per capita are more appropriate. To do this appropriately means that cross-national distinctions regarding currencies and price levels have to be taken into account. A conversion only using exchange rates would neglect disparities because of different levels of purchasing power. According to the theory of purchasing power parity, a monetary unit everywhere should deliver the same purchasing power. However, as a result of non-tradable goods (as services) or imperfect substitutes (Mankiw, 2004), reflected in price differences, it is possible that a basket of commodities is not valued the same in all countries. Hence, a modified exchange rate (purchasing power parities: PPP) accommodates different levels of purchasing power and eliminates disparities in price levels. The PPP is given by the amount of national currency per unit of US$ (OECD, 2008b). Following Jones (1989) and Andreff et al. (1995) it seems reasonable to compare the given expenditures after converting them into the country-specific PPP-US$$_{2005}$, which are provided by OECD (2008b).

A further complication is that besides the *inter*-national differences of price levels, *intra*-national differences of price levels exist over time. To measure these changes over time, the monetary value of a basket of commodities is valued in the form of the consumer price index (Baßeler et al., 2006). Subsequently, the intra-national differences of price levels can be determined (Cooke, 1994).

To ensure the comparability of surveys from differing years, and across countries, therefore, expenditures are transformed into prices from 2005, using the given national indices of consumer price (OECD, 2008a), and PPP as follows:

$$\text{Expenditures}_{2005} = \text{Expenditures}_Y/(\text{PPP-US\$}_{2005}) \star (\text{CPI}_{2005}/\text{CPI}_Y) \qquad (26.1)$$

Expenditures$_Y$, obtained from a study from the year (Y), are converted to PPP-US$2005 and multiplied by the ratio of the consumer price index of country A in 2005 (CPI_{2005}) to the consumer price index of country A in year Y (in the following indicated as PPP-US$$_{2005}^{2005}$).

The surveys of Weber et al. (1995), Meyer and Ahlert (2000), as well as Veltins (2001) give first impressions concerning the amount of private consumer spending on sport in Germany. Meyer and Ahlert (2000) suggest an amount of 20.1 bn PPP-US$$_{2005}^{2005}$ of expenditures on sport in general, whereas Weber et al. (1995) estimate 28.3 bn PPP-US$$_{2005}^{2005}$. It is likely that divergences in approach of investigation and classification of the categories, rather than varying consumption patterns over time, are responsible for those large variations. This thought is supported by some of the results of the specific categories that they investigate. For example spending on sport travel is estimated to be 0.38 PPP-US$$_{2005}^{2005}$ by Meyer and Ahlert (2000), 4.00 bn PPP-US$$_{2005}^{2005}$ by Weber et al. (1995) and 10.12 bn PPP-US$$_{2005}^{2005}$ by Veltins (2001). For sport insurance the same studies estimate values of 59.81 m PPP-US$$_{2005}^{2005}$ (Meyer and Ahlert, 2000) and 282.59 m PPP-US$$_{2005}^{2005}$ (Weber et al., 1995) However, similar results are found for expenditures on attending sport events. The gap between 0.69 bn PPP-US$$_{2005}^{2005}$ (Veltins, 2001), 1.05 PPP-US$$_{2005}^{2005}$ (Meyer and Ahlert, 2000) and 1.18 bn PPP-US$$_{2005}^{2005}$ (Weber et al., 1995) is notably smaller. Pawlowski (2009) provides an updated overview of specific consumer expenditures on sport and recreational services for Germany (see Table 26.5) The estimates (per person) for total expenditures on sport *services* (117.6 PPP-US$$_{2005}^{2005}$ as well as subcategories

Table 26.5 Private households' expenditures on sport and recreational services in PPP

Category	total (in 1.000) (US$)	per H	per P1	pro P2
Expenditures on sport and other events and venues	2.858.543	80.4	38.1	91.9
Sport events	817.410	23.0	10.9	80.7
Fairs	1.233.285	34.7	16.5	66.1
Entrance fees for swimming pools	740.927	20.8	9.9	53.8
Training and lessons	2.801.181	78.8	37.3	267.7
Music	1.352.789	38.1	18.0	310.9
Dancing	396.755	11.2	5.3	176.0
Other sport	798.289	22.4	10.6	202.8
Other courses	243.789	6.8	3.2	121.9
Membership fees for fitness centers	1.357.568	38.2	18.1	271.9
Rental fees for sport and recreational products and services	1.167.482	32.8	15.6	114.8
Access to sport facility (e.g. tennis)	654.883	18.4	8.7	84.1
Caravans	181.647	5.2	2.5	1.371.7
Sport and camping products	325.052	9.2	4.4	100.0
Other sport and recreational services	4.285.147	120.6	57.1	174.9
Transportation with ski lifts (not during vacation)	205.548	5.8	2.8	177.4
Transportation with ski lifts (during vacation)	449.336	12.7	6.0	243.8
Fees for the usage of alpine slopes	4.781	0.1	0.1	41.9
Fees for the usage of gaming machines	14.341	0.4	0.2	19.6
Guided tours	38.242	1.1	0.6	34.6
Other recreational services	124.285	3.5	1.7	89.7
Membership fees for sport clubs	3.388.392	95.3	45.2	161.4

per H: average value per household, per P1: average value per person, per P2: average value per person of households with expenditures in the particular category.
(*Source*: Pawlowski, 2009)

like sport *events* (10.9 PPP-US$$_{2005}^{2005}$ and *services for active sport consumption* (106.7 PPP-US$$_{2005}^{2005}$) are in the midrange compared to other international studies.

For instance, Figure 26.1 provides an overview of the estimates in PPP-US$$_{2005}^{2005}$ based on data of the second survey for the Council of Europe (Andreff et al., 1995). With about 306 PPP-US$$_{2005}^{2005}$ Finland shows the highest private per capita consumer spending on sport, close to the United Kingdom. This value is around 10 percent higher than the value according to Germany (279 PPP-US$$_{2005}^{2005}$). Regarding private per capita expenditures on sport services, a similar ratio applies. Again German expenditures (173 PPP-US$$_{2005}^{2005}$) are lower than in Finland. Hungary shows the lowest expenditures with 51.7 PPP-US$$_{2005}^{2005}$ for consumer spending and 18.9 PPP-US$$_{2005}^{2005}$ for sport services. Later studies indicate consistently higher values. The expenditures in England, Northern Ireland, Wales and Scotland amount to 567 PPP-US$$_{2005}^{2005}$ (LIRS, 2003), 521 PPP-US$$_{2005}^{2005}$ (LIRS, 2004a), 478 PPP-US$$_{2005}^{2005}$ (LIRS, 2004c) and 625 PPP-US$$_{2005}^{2005}$ (LIRS, 2004b). Lera-López and Rapún-Gárate (2005) calculates expenditures of about 408 PPP-US$$_{2005}^{2005}$ for Spain, and in Norway the spending amounts to 335 PPP-US$$_{2005}^{2005}$ (Thrane, 2001). However, for France, Andreff and Nys (2002) estimate that

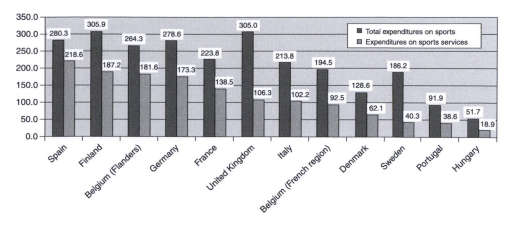

Figure 26.1 Results of the second survey for the Council of Europe (data per capita and in purchasing power parities; US$ at 2005 prices)

Source: Andreff et al., 1995; authors' own calculations

values of private consumer spending on sport that are similar to the survey for the Council of Europe (232 PPP-US$$_{2005}^{2005}$). Van Ophem and de Hoog (1994) provide estimates for the Netherlands which exceed the average expenditures by a per capita spending of 790 PPP-US$$_{2005}^{2005}$. This range of difference suggests different categorizations of expenditure.

Outside of Europe, data from Australia, Canada, New Zealand and the United States exist. TAPEY (1998) estimates that expenditures on sport in Australia are 3.1 bn PPP-US$$_{2005}^{2005}$, which is about 171 PPP-US$$_{2005}^{2005}$ per capita. The Australian Bureau of Statistics (2008) calculates a similar value; about 233 PPP-US$$_{2005}^{2005}$, 104.3 PPP-US$$_{2005}^{2005}$ being allocated to per capita expenditures on sport and recreational services. Following Veal (1991), consumer spending on sport services amounts to 51.5 PPP-US$$_{2005}^{2005}$ per capita. Canada exhibits consumer spending on sport of about 9.4 bn PPP-US$$_{2005}^{2005}$ (Zalatan, 1983), which corresponds to 410 PPP-US$$_{2005}^{2005}$ per capita and is consistent with estimates of 416.9 PPP-US$$_{2005}^{2005}$ per capita and 13.3 bn PPP-US$$_{2005}^{2005}$ (CBC, 2004) 20 years later. The survey of the Hillary Commission (1998) estimates that private consumer spending on sport per capita is 203.7 PPP-US$$_{2005}^{2005}$ in New Zealand. Finally Meek (1997) estimates private consumer spending of 185.6 bn US$ (price level of 2005) and 687.7 US$ per capita (price level of 2005) in the US.

While the difference between total expenditures on sport and expenditures on sport services (see Figure 26.1) might give us an initial idea concerning consumer spending on sport products, the following are examples of direct studies. In France, expenditures on sport products (Andreff and Nys, 2002: 140 PPP-US$$_{2005}^{2005}$) somewhat exceed the expenditures in the United Kingdom (Lamb et al., 1992: 120.5 PPP-US$$_{2005}^{2005}$) and Japan (Oga and Kimura, 1993: 125 PPP-US$$_{2005}^{2005}$). All of these values are by far smaller than the expenditures in the USA with 544 PPP-US$$_{2005}^{2005}$ (Nelson, 2001).

In addition to the data of private consumer spending on sport and the subcategories of sport services and sport products, there are further insights regarding specific categories and types of private consumer spending on sport. Concerning the category *entrance fees for sport events*, with 45.9 PPP-US$$_{2005}^{2005}$ per capita, Spain has very high spending compared to international levels (Andreff et al., 1995). Just below Spain is the USA with 25.2 PPP-US$$_{2005}^{2005}$

per capita (Meek, 1997); after the USA is England (LIRS, 2003: 25.1 PPP-US$$^{2005}_{2005}$), then Scotland (LIRS, 2004b: 24.4 PPP-US$$^{2005}_{2005}$) and Flanders (Taks and Késenne, 2000: 19.0 PPP-US$$^{2005}_{2005}$). Japan (Oga and Kimura, 1993: 7.8 PPP-US$$^{2005}_{2005}$), New Zealand (Hillary Commission, 1998: 2.7 PPP-US$$^{2005}_{2005}$), Sweden (Andreff et al., 1995: 3.6 PPP-US$$^{2005}_{2005}$) and France (Andreff et al., 1995: 4.7 PPP-US$$^{2005}_{2005}$ and Andreff and Nys, 2002: 5.0 PPP-US$$^{2005}_{2005}$) follow. With values between 8.4 PPP-US$$^{2005}_{2005}$ (Veltins, 2001) and 14.8 PPP-US$$^{2005}_{2005}$ (Weber et al., 1995) per capita, Germany exhibits midrange estimates. Figure 26.2 shows the results of several international comparison studies. For a clear view, different results of the same countries are bordered with a white frame.

Besides *entrance fees for sport events*, several studies describe expenditures on *services for active sport consumption*, which contain expenditures like *visiting indoor or outdoor pools, dancing classes, other sport classes, fees and charges for gyms and other facilities, passenger transportation on ski-lifts, or membership fees for sport institutions*. For comparability reasons, the results on subcategories of different international studies are combined in the auxiliary category *services for active sport consumption*.

With private expenditures on services for active sport consumption of 151.9 PPP-US$$^{2005}_{2005}$ per capita, the USA exhibits the highest expenditures (Meek, 1997). England (LIRS, 2003: 117.4 PPP-US$$^{2005}_{2005}$), Scotland (*LIRS, 2004b*: 109.5 PPP-US$$^{2005}_{2005}$) and Flanders (Taks and Késenne, 2000: 99.6 PPP-US$$^{2005}_{2005}$) are far behind. However, the lowest per capita expenditures are to be found in France (Andreff et al., 1995: 22.3 PPP-US$$^{2005}_{2005}$) and Sweden (Andreff et al., 1995: 36.5 PPP-US$$^{2005}_{2005}$). However, using another classification, Andreff and Nys (2002) calculate a value of 61.2 PPP-US$$^{2005}_{2005}$ of annual per capita spending in France. Figure 26.3 summarizes the comparisons.

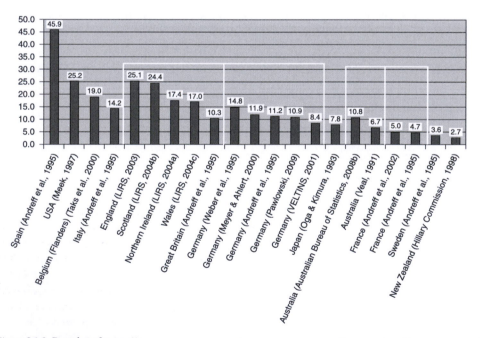

Figure 26.2 Results of miscellaneous surveys on private consumer spending on attending sport events (data per capita and in purchasing power parities)

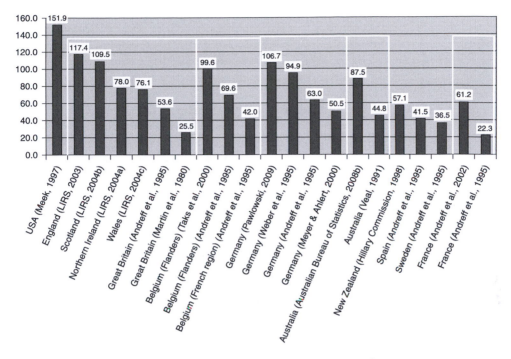

Figure 26.3 Results of miscellaneous surveys on private spending on services for active sport consumption (data per capita and in purchasing power parities)

Factors influencing sport expenditure

As mentioned earlier, most of the studies try to explain expenditure patterns, i.e. factors influencing the amount of money spent by households or individuals on sport products and services. The studies can be differentiated by the definition of the expenditure category to be explained, i.e. sport club membership fees (*club*), expenditures for sport events (*event*), expenditures on entrance fees for swimming pools (*pool*), expenditures on sport and recreational services (*SAR services*), as expenditures on sporting goods (sport goods), total expenditures on sport (*sport total*) as well as expenditures on sport and recreational goods and services (*SAR*).

Regarding the factors that were analyzed as determinants of expenditure categories, income has an unambiguously positive impact. Furthermore, men tend to spend more money than women. Interestingly, age tends to have a significant curvilinear effect on the amount of expenditure, being at first positive, then, with increasing age, negative. Table 26.6 provides an overview of the factors most often analyzed and the revealed signs of the estimates, either positive or negative, in the different studies. The studies are generally difficult to compare since some studies examined population surveys (e.g. Pawlowski, 2009) while other asked only sport-active people (e.g. Wicker, Breuer, and Pawlowski, 2009). As most studies are also based on highly aggregated data (e.g. Lera-López and Rapún-Gárate, 2005; 2007), an ecological fallacy might affect these estimates since it is likely that consumers show different consumption patterns for different subcategories (Robinson, 1950).

This situation is shown in the detailed analysis provided by Pawlowski (2009) addressing a total of 18 budget share categories of sport, leisure and cultural services in Germany, i.e.

Table 26.6 Most frequently analyzed factors influencing consumer expenditure on SAR services

Category	Year	Author(s)	Country	S	A	M	PH	L	E	I	P
SAR	1988	DASETT	AUS	+/−	+	+/−	+/−		+		
Sport total	2005	Lera-López and Rapún-Gárate	E	+	n.s.		n.s.	n.s.	+	+	
Sport total	2007	Lera-López and Rapún-Gárate	E	+	−			n.s.	+	+	+
Sport goods	2001	Nelson	USA							+	
Sport goods	1990	Euler	D		+/−		−	+/−		+	
Sport goods	1983	Sobel	USA					−	+	+	
Sport goods	1995	Wilkes	USA								
SAR services	1987	Késenne and Butzen	B		+/−	+/−	+/−			+	−
SAR services	1989	Jones	B								
SAR services	1989	Rittner et al.	D	+	+/−						
SAR services	1992	Lamb et al.	GB	+	+/−			+			
SAR services	1994a	Taks, Renson and Vanreusel	B								
SAR services	1994	van Ophem and de Hoog	NL		n.s.		+	n.s.	n.s.	n.s.	
SAR services	1995	Taks, Renson and Vanreusel	B					n.s.	n.s.	+	
SAR services	1995	Weber et al.	D	+	−			+	+	+	
SAR services	1999	Taks, Vanreusel and Renson	B		n.s.			n.s.	n.s.	+	
SAR services	2000	Taks and Késenne	B								
SAR services	2001	Thrane	N	+	−	n.s.	n.s.		+	+	
SAR services	2002	Breuer and Hovemann	D		+/−						
SAR services	2002	Davies	GB								
SAR services	2004	CBC	CDN				+/−			+	
SAR services	2009	Løyland and Ringstad	N	+	−		+			+	−
Pool	1987	Késenne and Butzen	B							+	−
Event	1985	IISOP	B	+	+/−						
Event	1994b	Taks, Vanreusel and Renson	B								
Event	2000	Pedrosa	E	+	+/−					+	
Event	2000	Taks and Késenne	B								
Event	2002	Cannon and Ford	USA			n.s.	−		n.s.	+	
Event	2002	Davies	GB								
Club	1994b	Taks, Vanreusel and Renson	B								
Club	1999	Desbordes, Ohl and Tribou	F						+	+	
Club	2000	Pedrosa	E	−	+/−					+	
Club	2000	Taks and Késenne	B								

| Club | 2001 | Veltins | D | | +/− | |
| Club | 2009 | Wicker et al. | D | + | +/− | + |

Category: Club: Sport club membership fees, Event: expenditures for sport events, Pool: expenditures on entrance fees for swimming pools, SAR: expenditures on sport and recreational goods and services, SAR services: expenditures on sport and recreational services, Sport goods: expenditures on sporting goods, Sport total: total expenditures on sport. Factors: (A): age, (E): educational level, (I): income, (L): labour, (M): marital status (reference category: married), (P): price, (PH): number of persons living in the household, (S): sex (reference category: men). States: (AUS): Australia, (B): Belgium, (CDN): Canada, (D): Germany, (E): Spain, (F): France, (GB): Great Britain, (N): Norway, (NL): Netherlands, (USA): United States of America. Impact: (n.s.): not significant, (+): positive, (−): negative.

leisure services (*leisure*), sport and recreational services (*SAR*), cultural services (*culture*), sport events (*event*), swimming pools (*pool*), music lessons (*music*), dancing lessons (*dance*), fitness centre fees (*fitness*), ski lift ticket fees (*ski*), sport club membership fees (*club*), entrance fees to opera (*opera*), theatres (*theatre*), cinemas (*cinema*), circuses (*circus*), museums (*museum*), zoos (*zoo*) as well as costs for pay TV (*paytv*) and the rental of video films (*film*).

To explain the consumption patterns of German households, different factors were used as explanatory variables in the models. The logarithm of total household expenditure (*logto*) serves as an income proxy variable in the model. In order to take leisure specific demand factors into account, the degree of urbanization (fewer than 20,000 inhabitants: *city1*, 20,000–99,999 inhabitants: *city2*, 100,000 and more inhabitants: *city3*) and the area (northwest: *northw*, northeast: *northo*, south: *sued*) where the household is located are included in the model. Furthermore, the reported quarter (January–March: *q1*, April–June: *q2*, July–September: *q3*, October–December: *q4*) and the age (*age, age2*), the social status (public official: *pofficial*, white-collar worker: *wcollar*, blue-collar worker: *bcollar*, unemployed person: *unempl*, retired person: *retired*, student: *stud*), the level of education (high-school diploma and higher: *hedu*), the marital status (married: *married*, single: *single*) of the head of the household, as well as the structure of the household (children aged 6 years and under: *childu6*, children aged 6–18 years: *child618*, children aged 18 years and above: *child1827*, number of people in the household: *person*) are included in the model.

Table 26.7 provides an overview on the signs of the different significant Tobit estimates for each expenditure category based on survey data from 2005 and 2006. Besides some general effects (e.g. households in rural areas tend to allocate a smaller budget share for leisure services in general) some category specific differences could be detected (e.g. concerning the region, the reported quarter or the marital status of the head of households).

Conclusions and further research

In conclusion this chapter has examined in detail the analyses of sport products and services expenditures. International evidence exists and draws upon the contexts of Europe, the United States and Canada. The major findings of these studies relate to the portion of households/individuals that spend on sport, the monetary value of sport (and its subcategories) in the different countries and the estimation of factors that might influence sport spending behavior. In general the research implies the following:

- Not all households spend their income on sport-related products and services. Depending on the definition of sport, previous studies have found different portions of expenditures on sport. It appears that the portion of spend on products and services related to *active* sport

Table 26.7 Signs of the significant Tobit estimates for 18 different expenditure categories

	leisure		SAR		culture		event		bath		music		dance		fitness		ski		club		opera		theatre		cinema		circus		museum		zoo		paytv		film		$n_{positive}$	$n_{negative}$	n_{total}
year	5	6	5	6	5	6	5	6	5	6	5	6	5	6	5	6	5	6	5	6	5	6	5	6	5	6	5	6	5	6	5	6	5	6	5	6	5+6	5+6	5+6
logto	+	+	+	+	+	−	+	+	+	+	+	+	+	+	+	+	+	+	+	+	+	+	+	+	+	+	+	+	+	+	+	+	+	+	+	−	30	2	32
city1	+	−	−	−	−	−	−	−			−	−	−	−	−	−			−		−			−	−	−		−	−	−					−	−	1	19	20
city2			−	−		−	−	−			−	−		−	−	−									−	−							−	−	−		0	7	7
city3																																							
northw	−	−		−	−	−		+		−		−		−		−		−		+		−	−	−	−	−		−	−	−	−		−			+	4	20	24
northe	+	+	+	+	+	+	+	+		−		−		−		+		−		+		−	−	−		+	+	+		−	+	+				+	11	5	16
sued																										−													
q1	+	+	+	+										+						+		+		−			−	−								+	10	4	14
q2	+	+	+	+			+	+	+	+								+	+	+	+	+		−		+		+		+	+			−		+	13	5	18
q3	+	+	+	+			+	+	+	+						−		+	+	+		−		−		+			+	+	+					+	12	4	16
q4																																							
age						−								−						+	+	+	+	+	+	−	+	+	+	+		−	−	+		+	6	3	9
age2																				+	−	−	−	−	−		−	−	−			−	−		−	+	1	7	8
pofficial		+																		+	+			+												+	4	0	4
wcollar	+	+	+	+							+								+	+	+	+	+		+		+	+	+	+		−				+	15	0	15
unempl	−	−	−	−	−	−														−			−	−								−	−			−	1	10	11
retired								+												+	+	+	+	+		+		−				+				+	6	1	7
stud			−			−				−								−									+							−			1	4	5
bcollar																																							
hedu	+	+	+	+		−	+	+	+	+	+	+	+	+		+	+	+	+	+	+	+	+	−	+	+	+	+	+	+		−		+	+	+	15	2	17
married	−	−	−	−		−				−		−		−		+		−	−	−	+	+	−	−	−	−		−		−		+			+	−	4	11	15
single	+	+					+	+				+			+	+	+	+	+	+	+	+			+	+	+	+				+				+	9	0	9
child6	−	−	−	−				−										−		−				−		−						+	+			+	1	9	10
child618	+	+	+	+		+	+	+	+	+	+	+	+	+	−	+	+	+	+	+	+	+	+	+	+	+	+	+			+	+	−		−	+	23	2	25
child1827	−		−	−				+	−	−	−	−	+	+	+	+	+	+	+	+				+		+		+		−					+	+	7	7	14
person	+	+	+			−			+	+	+	+																		−		−					6	4	10

Year: 5 = 2005, 6 = 2006, 5 + 6t = 2005 and 2006 together, $n_{positive}$: number of significant positive estimates, $n_{negative}$: number of significant negative estimates, n_{total}: total number of significant estimates.

Source: Pawlowski, 2009; city3, sued, q4 as well as bcollar are reference categories

is higher than the portion of spend on those related to *passive* sport. However, considerable differences between different subcategories of sport-related products and services exist.

- Private households spend (on average) a considerable amount of money on sport-related products and services. However, country-specific differences exist. For instance, Hungary shows the lowest total expenditures on sport with around 52 PPP-US$$_{2005}^{2005}$ while the USA shows the highest total expenditures on sport with around 688 US$ per capita (price level of 2005). Furthermore, considerable differences exist concerning private consumer spending on attending sport events (3 (New Zealand) – 46 (Spain) PPP-US$$_{2005}^{2005}$ per capita) as well as services for active sport consumption (22 (France) – 152 (USA) PPP-US$$_{2005}^{2005}$ per capita)
- Regarding the factors that were analyzed as determinants of expenditure categories, income has an unambiguously positive impact. Furthermore, men tend to spend more money than women. Interestingly, the effect of age tends to have a significant curvilinear effect on the amount of expenditure, being at first positive, then, with increasing age, negative. As discussed earlier, the studies are generally difficult to compare since different data is used and those studies that are based on highly aggregated data face the risk of ecological fallacy.

The chapter also reveals a relative lack of research in this field which might be summarized as follows:

- Most studies are based on highly aggregated data (e.g. Lera-López and Rapún-Gárate, 2005; 2007). Following Robinson (1950) and his theory of ecological fallacies, this might lead to biased management implications for subcategories since it is not unlikely that consumers show different consumption patterns for different subcategories.
- In line with this, only some studies analyzed the expenditures for subcategories, such as event (e.g. Davies, 2002) or club (e.g. Taks and Késenne, 2000) while (so far) only one study exists that analyzes a significant number of sport and leisure related subcategories (Pawlowski, 2009).
- Only very few studies are based on a consistent demand model, which means that the estimated functional form is directly derived from theory (e.g. Késenne and Butzen, 1987; Løyland and Ringstad, 2009; Pawlowski, 2009).
- Some studies that are based on inquiries rather than actual expenditures might be biased. Expenditure data based on inquiries are often biased since many consumers precisely recall neither the time nor the amount they have spent (Legohérel and Wong, 2006).
- Since not all individuals spent their income on all the sport items, numerous zero observations exist in the data, which leads to the fact that advanced estimators should really be applied in regression analysis (e.g. Tobit, Heckman and double hurdle models). Although not wanting to stress this econometric issue here, not all studies considered this so-called censored sample problem with Lera-López and Rapún-Gárate, 2005, 2007 and Pawlowski, 2009 being exceptions.[2]

Notes

1 An interesting feature of the research on sport expenditures is that since not all individuals spent their income on all the sport items investigated, numerous zero observations exist in the data. As discussed in Chapter 25, this suggests that more advanced estimators should be applied to account for the zeros reflecting constraints or choices. For example the Tobit, Heckman or double hurdle models could be applied.

2 Interested readers are invited to follow up with three recently (after completion of this chapter) published papers that pick up and extend theoretical and econometric issues discussed throughout the chapter (Lera-López, Rabún-Gárate and José Suárez, 2011; Pawloski and Breuer, 2011a; 2011b).

References

Abdel-Ghany, M. and Schwenk, F. N. (1993) 'Functional forms of household expenditure patterns in the United States', *Journal of Consumer Studies and Home Economics*, 17(4), 325–42.

Agarwal, V. B. and Yochum, G. R. (1999) 'Tourist spending and race of visitors', *Journal of Travel Research*, 38(2), 173–76.

Andreff, W., Bourg, J. F., Halba, B., and Nys, J. F. (1995) *Les enjeux économiques du sport en Europe: Financement et impact économique* [The economic importance of sport in Europe: financing and economic impact], Paris, France:Dalloz.

Andreff, W. and Nys, J.-F. (2002) *Économie du sport* [The economics of sport] (5th edn). Paris, France: Presses Univ. de France.

Australian Bureau of Statistics (2008) *Sport and recreation: A statistical overview* (2nd edn). Australia: Australian Bureau of Statistics.

Baßeler, U., Heinrich, J., and Utecht, B. (2006) *Grundlagen und Probleme der Volkswirtschaft (18., überarb. Aufl.)* [Economics. Basics and problems]. Stuttgart: Schäffer-Poeschel.

Bittman, M. (1999) 'Social participation and family welfare: The money and time costs of leisure', (Social Policy Research Centre (SPRC) *Discussion Paper*, No. 95) Sydney, Australia: SPRC.

Blaine, T. W. and Mohammad, G. (1991) 'An empirical assessment of U.S. consumer expenditures for recreation-related goods and services: 1946–88', *Leisure Sciences*, 13(2), 111–22.

Blundell, R., Browning, M., and Meghir, C. (1994) 'Consumer demand and the lifecycle allocation of family expenditures', *Review of Economic Studies*, 61(206), 57–80.

Breuer, C. and Hovemann, G. (2002) *Individuelle Konsumausgaben als Finanzierungsquelle des Sport* [Consumer spending on sport as finance possibility]. In H.-D. Horch, J. Heydel and A. Sierau (Hrsg.), *Finanzierung des Sport. Beiträge des 2. Kölner Sportökonomie-Kongresses* (S. 61–79). Aachen: Meyer and Meyer.

Cai, L. A., Hong, G. S., and Morrison, A. M. (1995) 'Household expenditure patterns for tourism products and services', *Journal of Travel and Tourism Marketing*, 4(4), 15–40.

Cannon, T. F. and Ford, J. (2002) 'Relationship of demographic and trip characteristics to visitor spending: An analysis of sport travel visitors across time', *Tourism Economics*, 8(3), 263–71.

Chase, S. (2000) 'The economic benefits of sport – a review', *Research Report* No. 3. Hong Kong: Hong Kong Sport Development Board.

Conference Board of Canada (CBC) (2004) *National household survey on participation in sport*. Ottawa, Canada: Conference Board of Canada.

Cooke, A. (1994) *The economics of leisure and sport*. New York: Routledge.

Costa, D. L. (1999) 'American living standards, 1888–1994: Evidence from recreational expenditure', (Working Paper Series, No. 7650), Cambridge, MA: National Bureau of Economic Research.

—— (2000) 'American living standards, 1888–1994: Evidence from consumer expenditure' (*Working Paper Series*, No. 7148), Cambridge, MA: National Bureau of Economic Research.

Dardis, R., Derrick, F., Lehfeld, A., and Wolfe, K. E. (1981) 'Cross-section studies of recreation expenditures in the United States', *Journal of Leisure Research*, 13(3), 181–94.

Dardis, R., Soberon-Ferrer, H. and Patro, D. (1994) 'Analysis of leisure expenditures in the United States', *Journal of Leisure Research*, 26(4), 309–21.

DASETT (1988) 'The economic impact of sport and recreation – household expenditure', (Technical Paper, No. 1). Canberra, Australia: Australian Government Publishing Service.

Davies, L. E. (2002) 'Consumers' expenditure on sport in the UK: Increased spending or underestimation?' *Managing Leisure*, 7, 83–102.

Desbordes, M., Ohl, F., and Tribou, G. (1999) *Marketing du Sport* [Sport marketing]. Paris, France: Economica.

Downward, P., Dawson, A., and Dejonghe, T. (2009) *Sport economics: theory, evidence and practice*. Oxford: Elsevier.

Euler, M. (1990) 'Ausgaben privater Haushalte für Freizeitgüter [Private households' expenditures on leisure goods], *Wirtschaft und Statistik*, 3, 219–27.

Fan, X. J. (1997) 'Expenditure patterns of Asian Americans: Evidence from U.S. consumer expenditure survey, 1980–92', *Family and Consumer Sciences Research Journal*, 26(4), 339–68.

—— (1998) 'Ethnic differences in household expenditure patterns', *Family and Consumer Sciences Research Journal*, 26(4), 371–400.

Fiebiger, H. (1993) 'Ausgaben für Freizeitgüter in ausgewählten privaten Haushalten im früheren Bundesgebiet sowie den neuen Ländern und Berlin-Ost: Ergebnisse der laufenden

Wirtschaftsrechnungen' [Private households' expenditures on leisure goods: Evidence from continuous household budget survey], *Wirtschaft und Statistik*, 1, 125–31.

Fish, W. and Waggle, D. (1996) 'Current income versus total expenditure measures in regression models of vacation and pleasure travel', *Journal of Travel Research*, 35(2), 70–74.

Gundlach, E. (1993) *Die Dienstleistungsnachfrage als Determinante des wirtschaftlichen Strukturwandels* [The demand for services as indicator of the economic development] (Kieler Studien, Institut für Weltwirtschaft an der Universität Kiel, Nr. 252) Tuebingen: Mohr.

Hillary Commission (1998) *The growing business of sport and leisure – an update to 1996*. Wellington, New Zealand: Hillary Commission.

Hong, G. S., Kim, S. Y., and Lee, J. (1999) 'Travel expenditure patterns of elderly families in the U.S.', *Tourism Recreation Research*, 24(1), 43–52.

Hong, G.-S., Fan, J.-X., Palmer, L., and Bhargava, V. (2005) 'Leisure travel expenditure patterns by family life cycle stages', *Journal of Travel and Tourism Marketing*, 18(2), 15–30.

HCSCCHSC (House of Commons Standing Committee on Canadian Heritage, Sport in Canada) (1998) 'Everybody's business – leadership, partnership and accountability'. (English summary: Sanderson, K., Harris, F., Russell, S., and Chase, S. (2000). The economic benefits of sport – a review. Research Report No. 3. Hong Kong: Hong Kong Sports Development Board).

IISOP (1985) *Les Pratique Sportives en Communauté Française*. Brussels, Belgium: IISOP.

Jones, H. G. (1989) *The economic impact and importance of sport: A European study*. Strasbourg, France: Council of Europe.

Késenne, S. and Butzen, P. (1987) 'Subsidizing sport facilities: the shadow price-elasticities of sport', *Applied Economics*, 19(1), 101–10.

Kops, M. and Graff, C. (1986) *Die ökonomische Bedeutung des Sport – ein Untersuchungsrahmen*. Universität zu Köln: Seminar für Finanzwissenschaften.

Lamb, L. L., Asturias, L. P., Roberts, K., and Brodie, D. A. (1992) 'Sport participation – how much does it cost?' *Leisure Studies*, 11(1), 19–29.

Lawson, R. (1991) 'Patterns of tourist expenditure and types of vacation across the FLC', *Journal of Travel Research*, 29(4), 12–18.

Lee, C.-K., Var, T., and Blaine, T. W. (1996) 'Determinants of inbound tourist expenditures', *Annals of Tourism Research*, 23(3), 527–42.

Legohérel, P. (1998) 'Toward a market segmentation of the tourism trade: Expenditure levels and consumer behavior instability', *Journal of Travel and Tourism Marketing*, 7(3), 19–39.

Legohérel, P. and Wong, K. K. F. (2006) 'Market segmentation in the tourism industry and consumer's spending: What about direct expenditures?' *Journal of Travel and Tourism Marketing*, 20(2), 15–30.

Leisure Industries Research Centre [LIRC] (2003) *The economic importance of sport in England*. Report for the Sport Council. London: LIRC.

Leisure Industries Research Centre [LIRC] (2004a) *The economic importance of sport in Northern Ireland*. Report for the Sport Council. London: LIRC.

Leisure Industries Research Centre [LIRC] (2004b) *The economic importance of sport in Scotland*. Report for the Sport Council. London: LIRC.

Leisure Industries Research Centre [LIRC] (2004c) *The economic impact of sport in Wales*. Report for the Sport Council. London: LIRC.

Leones, J., Colby, B., and Crandall, K. (1998) 'Tracking expenditures of the elusive nature tourists of south-eastern Arizona', *Journal of Travel Research*, 36(3), 56–64.

Lera-López, F. and Rapún-Gárate, M. (2005) 'Sport participation versus consumer expenditure on sport: Different determinants and strategies in sport management', *European Sport Management Quarterly*, 5(2), 167–86.

—— (2007) 'The demand for sport: Sport consumption and participation models', *Journal of Sport Management*, 21(1), 103–22.

Lera-López, F., Rapún-Gárate, M. and José Suárez, M. J. (2011) and 'Determinants of individual consumption on sports attendance in Spain', *International Journal of Sport Finance*, 6(3), 204–21.

Loy, J. W. and Rudman, W. J. (1983) 'Social physics and sport involvement. An analysis of sport consumption and production patterns by means of three empirical laws', *South African Journal for Research in Sport, Physical Education and Recreation*, 6(2), 31–48.

Løyland, K. and Ringstad, V. (2009) 'On the price and income sensitivity of the demand for sport: Has Lindner's disease become more serious?' *Journal of Sport Economics*, 10(6), 601–18.

Magnusson, G. K., Valgeirsson, G., and Thorlindsson, T. (1989) *The economic significance of sport in Iceland*. Study undertaken for the Ministry of Education, Reykjavik.

Mankiw, N. G. (2004) *Grundzüge der Volkswirtschaftslehre (An introduction to economics)* (3., überarb. Aufl.) Stuttgart: Schäffer-Poeschel.

Martin, W.H. and Mason, S. (1980) *Broad patterns of leisure expenditure*. London: The Sport Council and Social Science Research Council (a review for the Joint Panel on Leisure and Recreation Research).

Matsuda, Y. (1990) 'The basic policies of sport industry in Japan from the viewpoint of sport marketing', *Sport Science Review*, 13, 35–44.

Meek, A. (1997) 'An estimate of the size and supported economic activity of the sport industry in the United States', *Sport Marketing Quarterly*, 6(4), 15–21.

Melenberg, B. and van Soest, A. (1996) 'Parametric and semi-parametric modelling of vacation expenditure', *Journal of Applied Econometrics*, 11(1), 59–76.

Meyer, B. and Ahlert, G. (2000) *Die ökonomischen Perspektiven des Sport. Eine empirische Analyse für die Bundesrepublik Deutschland* [The economic perspectives of sport: An empirical analysis in Germany], (Schriftenreihe des Bundesinstituts für Sportwissenschaft, Band 100) Schorndorf: Hofmann.

Michon, B., Ohl, F., and Faber, C. (1987) *Le prix de la pratique sportive pour le consommateur [The price of sport for the consumer]*. Strasbourg, France: Laboratoire recommande APS et sciences socials.

Moehrle, T. (1990) 'Expenditure patterns of the elderly: Workers and nonworkers', *Monthly Labor Review*, 113 (May), 34–41.

Mudambi, R. and Baum, T. (1997) 'Strategic segmentation: An empirical analysis of tourist expenditure in Turkey', *Journal of Travel Research*, 36(1), 29–34.

Nelson, J. P. (2001) 'Hard at play! The growth of recreation in consumer budgets, 1959–98', *Eastern Economic Journal*, 27(1), 35–53.

Nicolau, J. L. and Más, F. J. (2005) 'Heckit modelling of tourist expenditure: Evidence from Spain', *International Journal of Service Industry Management*, 16(3), 271–93.

Nieswiadomy, M. and Rubin, R. M. (1995) 'Change in expenditure patterns of retirees: 1972–73 and 1986–87', *Journal of Gerontology: Social Science*, 50B, 274–90.

NSWSR (2000) *Economic impact of sport and recreation*. Sydney, Australia: NSW Sport and Recreation.

OECD (2008a) *Consumer price indices* (MEI), Organisation for Economic Cooperation and Development. [Online] Retrieved 5 September 2011 from <http://stats.oecd.org/wbos/Index.aspx>.

—— (2008b) *Purchasing power parities (PPP)*, Organisation for Economic Cooperation and Development. [Online]Retrieved 5 September 2011 from <http://www.oecd.org/department/0,3355,en_2649_34357_1_1_1_1_1,00.html>.

Oga, J. and Kimura, K. (1993) 'Recent trends in the sport industry in Japan', *Journal of Sport Management*, 7(3), 249–55.

Opaschowski, H. W., Pries, M., and Reinhardt, U. (2006) *Freizeitwirtschaft. Die Leitökonomie der Zukunft (Leisure economy. The leading economy in future)* (Zukunft. Bildung. Lebensqualität, Bd. 2) Hamburg: LIT.

Papanikos, G. T. and Sakellariou, C. (1997) 'An econometric application of the Almost Ideal Demand System model to Japan's tourist demand for ASEAN destinations', *Journal of Applied Recreation Research*, 22(2), 157–72.

Paulin, G. (1990) 'Consumer expenditures on travel, 1980–87', *Monthly Labor Review*, 113(6), 56–60.

Pawlowski, T. (2009) *Die Dienstleistungsnachfrage im Freizeitsektor – Eine Analyse des Ausgabenverhaltens von Privathaushalten in Deutschland [The demand for leisure services – An analysis of private households' expenditures in Germany]*. Saarbrücken: SVH.

Pawlowski, T. and Breuer, C. (2011a) 'Expenditure elasticities of the demand for leisure services', *Applied Economics*, doi:10.1080/00036846.2011.577021

—— (2011b) 'The demand for sports and recreational services: Empirical evidence from Germany', *European Sport Management Quarterly]*, 11(1), 5–34.

Pedrosa, R. (2000) *El impacto económico del deporte en Castilla y León [The economic impact of sport in Castile and Leon]*. Valladolid, Spain: Government of Castilla and León.

Pitts, J. M. (1990) 'Income and expenditures of Hispanic households', *Family Economics Review*, 3(2), 2–7.

Pyo, S. S., Uysal, M., and McLellan, R. W. (1991) 'A linear expenditure model for tourism demand', *Annals of Tourism Research*, 18(3), 443–54.

Redondo-Bellón, I., Royo-Vela, M., and Aldás-Manzano (2001) 'A family life cycle model adapted to Spanish environment', *European Journal of Marketing*, 35(5–6), 612–38.

Riiskjaer, S. (1986) *Den Danske Idraetsforening.* Resultater Frau breddeidraetsudvalgets foreningsunder-sogelse. Ministeriet for Kulturelle angliggender. Denmark.

Rissanen, P. (1988) *Kotitalouksien Liikuntamenot* [Sport expenditure of Finnish households]. *Liikunta ja Tiede*, 25(5), 247–51.

Rittner, V., Mrazek, J., Meier, R., Becker, A., Breuer, G., and Meyer, M. (1989) *Sportinfrastruktur im Kreis Neuss [Sport infrastructure in Neuss]* (Band 1) Cologne: Deutsche Sporthochschule Köln.

Robinson, W.S. (1950) 'Ecological correlation and the behavior of individuals', *American Sociological Review*, 15(3), 351–57.

Rubin, R. M. and Nieswiadomy, M. (1994) 'Expenditure patterns of retired and nonretired persons', *Monthly Labor Review*, 117(4), 10–21.

Schäfer, H. (1995) *Freizeitindustrie. Struktur und Entwicklung [Leisure industry. Structure and development].* Wiesbaden: Gabler.

Schröder, S. (2003) *Sportkonsum in Deutschland auf der Grundlage empirischer Forschung* (Empirical evidence on sport consumption in Germany), in G. Trosien and M. Dinkel (Hrsg.), Grenzen des Sportkonsums. Sportmarketing – Sporttandort – Sporttätte (S. 199–209) Butzbach-Griedel: Afra.

Sobel, M. E. (1983) 'Lifestyle expenditures in contemporary America', *American Behavioral Scientist*, 26(4), 521–33.

Soberon-Ferrer, H. and Dardis, R. (1991) 'Determinants of household expenditures for services', *Journal of Consumer Research*, 17(4), 385–97.

Spotts, D. M. and Mahoney, E. M. (1991) 'Segmenting visitors to a destination region based on the volume of their expenditures', *Journal of Travel Research*, 19(4), 24–31.

Taks, M., Renson, R., and Vanreusel, B. (1994a) 'Of sport, time and money: An economic approach to sport participation', *International Review for Sociology of Sport*, 29(4), 381–94.

Taks, M., Vanreusel, B., and Renson, R. (1994b) 'What does sport really cost? A microeconomic study of the consumer cost of golf and soccer', *European Journal for Sport Management*, 1(1), 22–34.

Taks, M., Renson, R. and Vanreusel, B. (1995) 'Social stratification in sport: A matter of money or taste?' *European Journal for Sport Management*, 2(1), 4–14.

Taks, M., Vanreusel, B., and Renson, R. (1999) 'Consumer expenses in sport: A marketing tool for sport', *European Journal for Sport Management*, 6(1), 4–18.

Taks, M. and Késenne, S. (2000) 'The economic significance of sport in Flanders', *Journal of Sport Management*, 14(4), 342–65.

TAPEY (1998) *Economic impact study of sport.* Canberra, Australia: Confederation of Australian Sport. (English summary: Sanderson, K., Harris, F., Russell, S., and Chase, S. (2000) 'The economic benefits of sport – A review', *Research Report* No. 3. Hong Kong, Hong Kong Sport Development Board.

Taylor, D. T., Fletcher, R. R., and Clabaugh, T. (1993) 'A comparison of characteristics, regional expenditures, and economic impact of visitors to historical sites with other recreational visitors', *Journal of Travel Research*, 32(3), 30–35.

Tenreiro, F. (1986) *Economic significance of sport.* First phase report. Direccao Geral dos Desportos. Lisbon, Portugal.

Thompson, C. S. and Tinsley, A. W. (1979) 'Income expenditure elasticities for recreation: Their estimation and relation to demand for recreation', *Journal of Leisure Research*, 10(4), 265–70.

Thrane, C. (2001) 'The differentiation of personal sport expenditures: The Norwegian case', *International Journal of Sport Management*, 2(3), 237–51.

Tirelli, D. (1986) 'An empirical analysis of Italian households' expenditure on leisure and consumption', *Economic Notes*, 15(2), 17–42.

Van Ophem, J. and de Hoog, K. (1994) 'Differences in leisure behavior of the poor and the rich in the Netherlands', in I. Henry (ed.), *Leisure: Modernity, Postmodernity and Lifestyles* (Leisure in Different Worlds, Volume I, 291–305). The Leisure Studies Association, Chelsea School Research Centre, University of Brighton.

Van Puffelen, F., Reijinen, J., and Velthuijsen, J. W. (1988) *De Macro Economische Betekenis van Sport.* Stichting voor Economisch Onderzoek der Universiteit van Amsterdam (Netherlands).

Veal, A. J. (1991) *Australian leisure futures: Projections of leisure expenditure and participation 1991–2001.* Broadway, Australia: Centre of Leisure and Tourism Studies.

Veltins (2001) *Sporttudie* [Sport study]. Meschede: Drees.

Wagner, R. and Washington, V. R. (1982) 'An analysis of personal consumption expenditures as related to recreation. 1946–76', *Journal of Leisure Research*, 14(1), 37–46.

Walsh, R. G. (1986) *Recreation economic decisions: Comparing benefits and costs.* State College (PA), USA: Venture.

Weagley, R. O. and Huh, E. (2004) 'Leisure expenditure of retired and near-retired households', *Journal of Leisure Research*, 36(1), 101–27.

Weber, W., Schneider, C., Kortläcke, N., and Horak, B. (1995) *Die wirtschaftliche Bedeutung des Sport* [The economic significance of sport]. Schorndorf: Hofmann.

Wicker, P., Breuer, C., and Pawlowski, T. (2009) 'Are sport club members big spenders? Findings from sport specific analyses in Germany', *Sport Management Review*, doi: 10.1016/j.smr.2009.07.001.

Wilkes, R. E. (1995) 'Family life cycle stages, transitions and product expenditures', *Journal of Consumer Research*, 22(1), 27–42.

Winde, M. A. (2002) *Wirtschaftsfaktor Freizeit. Typologie, Beschäftigung, Qualifikation (Leisure economy: structure, labour, qualification)* (Beiträge zur Gesellschafts- und Bildungspolitik, Institut der deutschen Wirtschaft Köln, 257) Cologne: Deutscher Instituts-Verlag.

Zalatan, A. (1983) 'The economic value of physical recreation in Canada', *Physical Education Review*, 6(2), 118–23.

Zhao, S. X., Ren, H., Xing, S. J., and Xu, G. X. (2001) 'Study of family sport consumption of urban inhabitants in Beijing Haidian district', *Journal of Beijing University of Physical Education*, 24(3), 292–93.

27

DO SPORT CLUBS MAXIMIZE WINS OR PROFITS?

And does it make any difference?

Stefan Kesenne

Introduction

Since the rapid growth of revenues and costs in professional sport, modern sport clubs have become full commercial businesses, much to true sport enthusiasts' regret. Although sport contests are still, ultimately, about gaining victory, one could wonder whether the advent of large monetary investments has not made realizing financial returns take precedence over sport successes. This chapter does not aim at evaluating this question from a normative, moral or nostalgic perspective. In contrast, the intention is to present a theoretical economic analysis of the question of whether it makes any difference that soccer clubs try to gain maximum profits – which is considered to be commercial enterprises' main objective in microeconomic analysis – instead of trying to pursue maximum sport successes in (inter)national championships.

At the outset the question could be asked as to whether or not the two objectives are actually that different. Are sport successes not the best way to make more profits given that ticket sales and TV rights, as well as sponsorship deals and marketing licenses, correlate with a club's sport success to a considerable extent? And is gaining greater profits not the best way to fund the club's budget in order to be able to hire the best players? In this chapter it is shown, using the well-known Quirk and Fort fixed-talent supply model (Quirk and Fort, 1992), that differences in emphasis upon these two objectives indeed can make a substantial difference. This is not only in terms of differences in competitive balance, player salaries and total league revenue, but also because of the different impacts of league regulations such as transfer systems, revenue sharing and salary caps. The special case of imposing a maximum wage-turnover ratio is analyzed; that is, the imposition of a financial prudence rule. The conclusion of the chapter argues that differences in the objectives of sport clubs do affect the competitive balance and the level of the average player salaries differently. Moreover, the effects of league regulations by the national federations, such as restrictions on player mobility by means of a transfer system or a redistribution of the clubs' revenues, can vary under such differences in objectives. It follows that more detailed empirical research is required to explore and to test these differences to inform sport league governance.

Profit maximization or win maximization?

A team whose goal is to gain maximum profits will hire talents as long as the extra profits for the club exceed the extra costs – that is, in microeconomic terminology, as long as the Marginal Revenue (MR) of a talent is larger than its marginal cost (MC) or its salary (c). Based on the law of diminishing marginal returns, this marginal revenue will decrease in function of the number of talents. In other words, if a club already has a strong team, an additional player will not add much to club revenue. This implies that, in equilibrium, the marginal revenue of talent equals the unit cost of talent. If all clubs are wage takers, and the unit cost of a talent is determined by supply and demand in a competitive talent market, the equilibrium condition can be written as:

$$MR = c. \tag{27.1}$$

Consequently, the demand curve for talent from a profit-maximizing club will be determined by the marginal revenue of talent. This curve is depicted graphically in Figure 27.1. So, with a unit cost of talent equal to c_0, the club will recruit t_0 talents.

A team that seeks sport successes will recruit as much talent as its budget allows. However, under the assumption that unpaid debts to investors, players, social security or tax authorities are no longer tolerated by established license commissions, a break-even condition should be respected, i.e.:

$$R(t) = C(t) = ct. \tag{27.2}$$

In this scheme, R stands for total season revenue and C stands for the total season costs. Both are a function of the number of talents t, and c is the unit cost of talent. It is assumed here, for simplicity reasons, that the total cost only consists of player salaries. This condition implies that a win–maximizing club will hire talent until the decreasing average revenue of

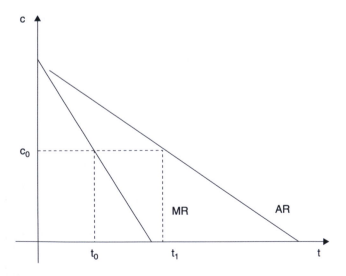

Figure 27.1 Marginal (MR) and average (AR) revenue curves

talent (AR) is equal to the unit cost of talent (c). Assuming that the capital costs are zero, it holds that in equilibrium:

$$AR = R/t = AC = ct/t = c. \qquad (27.3)$$

Consequently, the demand curve for talent of a win-maximizing club is determined by the average revenue curve (AR). In the case of declining average revenues in the number of talents, the marginal revenue will be smaller than the average revenue. Figure 27.1 gives the development of both the marginal revenues (MR) and the average revenues (AR).

When the unit cost of talent is given, the demand for talent from a profit-maximizing club is determined by the curve of the marginal revenues, based on expression (27.1), while the demand for talent from a win-maximizing club is defined by the curve of the average revenues based on expression (27.3). Figure 27.1 shows that, given a unit cost of talent (c_0), the demand of talent from a win-maximizing club (t_1) will be larger than the demand of talent from a profit-maximizing club (t_0).

This is logical indeed, because a win-maximizing club will spend its entire budget on player costs, given its sole objective – to win as many games as possible – while a profit-maximizing club's aim is for the largest positive difference between revenues and costs.

Competition is a fundamental feature of sport, and an attractive league requires a fairly competitive balance among the clubs. Sport will lose its attraction if the winner is known beforehand. We will prove that this *competitive balance* is disturbed to a greater extent in a league where all clubs try to win as much as possible. This can be illustrated by a simple model with only two clubs: a rich team (x) in a big city and a small club (y) with a limited budget in a small town.[1] Here we take it for granted that with a given salary, the large-market club will hire more talents than the small-market club. This is illustrated in Figure 27.2, where the demand curves of both clubs are drawn against each other, each from its own origin O_x and O_y. The distance between the two origins is determined by the total market supply of talent, which is considered a constant in this representation.

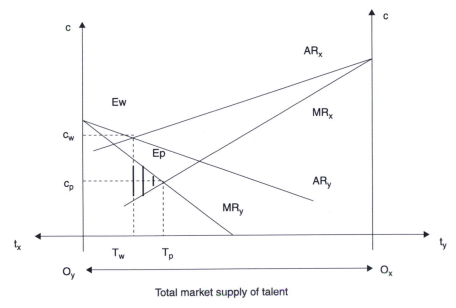

Figure 27.2 Market equilibrium

Figure 27.2 shows both the marginal revenue (MR) curves and the average revenue (AR) curves, so the win maximization and the profit maximization equilibrium can be compared. Notice that talent is more in demand by the large-market club than the small-market club. The equilibrium between the total market demand and the market supply on the talent market can be found at the intersection of the demand curves of the two clubs. Hence this equilibrium simultaneously determines the unit cost of talent or the average salary level of the players. The equilibrium under profit maximization is indicated in Figure 27.2 by the point of intersection of the two MR curves (E_p); the equilibrium under win maximization can be found at the intersection of the two AR curves (E_w). The comparison of these equilibrium points shows on the horizontal axis that the competitive balance is more disturbed in the case of win maximization (T_w). Also, the remuneration of talent will be higher in the case of win maximization ($c_w > c_p$), as can be seen on the vertical axis.

It can also be shown that total league revenue will be higher under profit maximization, implying that win maximization causes a welfare loss, indicated by the shaded triangular area in Figure 27.2. This is due to a misallocation of talents among the clubs; players are not playing in the team where their marginal revenue is highest. All talents between the points T_w and T_p should be playing in the small-market team, where their marginal revenue is higher, but, under win maximization, they are playing in the large-market team.

Based on this analysis, it can already be concluded that it makes a difference whether clubs want to win or to make profits. In the case of win maximization, a larger competitive imbalance can be expected in the league but the players are better paid. Moreover, win maximization causes a welfare loss in terms of total league revenue.

It is also important to note that, in case of a flexible talent supply with an exogenously given unit cost of talent, which is a more realistic description of the economy of the European football leagues since the Bosman verdict in 1995, win-maximizing clubs are willing to invest more in talent which can yield a higher absolute playing quality in a league.

Impact of market regulations

Since the equilibrium allocation of talent in a free talent market can be heavily influenced by market power, and player salaries can rise greatly as there is no natural substitute for playing talent in the sport industry, national sport associations have traditionally regulated their markets. Their main objective was to realize a more balanced spread of talent between the large-market and small-market teams in order to have a more balanced league. In this section it is shown that the effects of these regulations differ substantially, depending on whether win maximization or profit maximization is at stake. The analysis begins again from the equilibrium positions as depicted in Figure 27.2. From this basis successive study of the effects of the transfer system and a system of revenue distribution between the large-market and small-market club are analyzed.

Transfer system

Before 1995 in European football, a transfer system was used with the intention of preventing all talents joining the large-market teams that could afford to pay the highest salaries, which would result in a distorted league. The system stipulated that a player, when his contract had ended, could not move to another club without an official agreement on the transfer fee between the former and the new club. In December 1995, this transfer system was abolished by the Bosman verdict of the European Court of Justice. Restrictions on the free mobility of players in the EU were found to be in violation of the European competition rules.

However, the so-called *Invariance Proposition* of Rottenberg (1956), which was formally proven later by El-Hodiri and Quirk (1971), stated that the transfer system's restriction on the free mobility of playing talent does not have any impact whatsoever on the competitive balance when the clubs' objective is profit maximization. This can be explained by the fact that, in the end, the best players will play for the richest teams anyway. When this does not happen in a free player market, it will be achieved by a free transfer market. Only by forbidding transfers altogether can the distribution of talent be kept more balanced.

One could argue here that it does make a difference if a player is transferred by means of the transfer market or in the free player market. In the first case, the poor small-market club will receive a transfer fee, and this money can be used to hire more talent, which results in a more balanced competition. However, the profit-maximizing poor club will not use the received transfer fees to hire more talent, but will consider this money as extra profits, since the demand for talent, in the case of profit maximization, is determined by the marginal revenues. And these marginal revenues of talent are not affected by the received or paid transfer fees. Hence, the demand for talent by the large-market club and the small-market club will not change and so neither will the competitive balance in the league. Nevertheless, a transfer system may enhance the financial viability of small-market clubs.

In the case of win maximization, the small-market club will use the received transfer fees to hire more talent and the large-market club will necessarily hire less talent due to the transfer fees that were paid, which results in a more balanced competition in the league. This is depicted in Figure 27.3, where the market equilibrium shifts from E_{w1} to E_{w2}.

It should be noted here that this positive effect on competitive balance will be minimal because, in a small market, a poor club cannot find many talents that can be sold to the rich club. Consequently the European Court of Justice abolished a system that not only was

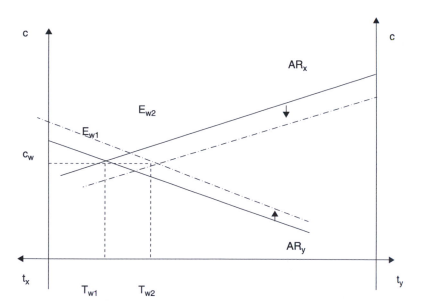

Figure 27.3 Transfer system under win maximization

ineffective, but also violated the fundamental right of an employee to freely choose his employer. Up to the present day, the world of sport still tends to develop laws and rules of its own that are in manifest violation of social laws.

Another important question is how a transfer system affects the level of player salaries. In order to analyze this, it is necessary to comprehend that a transfer system reduces the player market to a *monopsony*, i.e. a market with only one buyer of talent, which is his current club or the national sport federation or association. This association – as a cartel of clubs – deploys strict transfer rules as a result of which in the end there is only one employer for a player. After all, if a player does not yield to these rules, he will not be able to be a professional player in a league organized by the sport federation that holds a monopoly position. Thus, the sport federation, being the professional players' sole employer, is facing an increasing supply curve of talent, because the higher the salary, the more athletes will seek to become professional. In order to attract one more player or talent, the association will need to offer that player or that talent a higher salary. In this case, a non-discriminating monopsonist will have to pay this higher salary to all employed talents. This does not mean that all players are paid the same salary level, because some players have many talents and others have few talents. Consequently the marginal cost curve of talent will increase much more than the talent supply curve, as depicted in Figure 27.4.

A profit-maximizing monopsonist will hire talent until MR = MC, that is: t_p talents. Yet the salary that will be paid will not exceed c_p. A profit-maximizing monopsonist will not pay a higher salary than c_p if he needs only t_p talents to reach profit maximization. So the powerful position of the monopsonist, being the sole employer of professional players, results in under-paying and exploiting players, because $c_p < mr_p$.

Again, a different picture can be seen when win maximization is concerned: now the monopsonist will hire talent until the average revenue (AR) of talent equals the salary (AR = c). This is the point where the AR curve intersects the supply curve of talent so that t_w talents are hired. The salary is now as high as c_w and that is clearly above the marginal revenue (mr_w) so players are now rather overpaid. This point of intersection is at the same

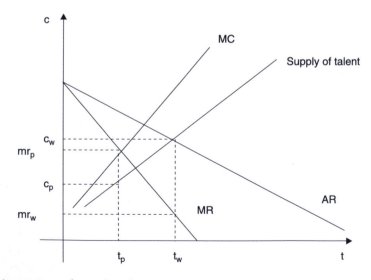

Figure 27.4 Monopsony under profit and win maximization

time also the free market equilibrium so the transfer system does not affect the players' salaries. When it is the clubs' objective to maximize winning, players are overpaid both in a free market and in a monopsony market ($c_w > mr_w$). Empirical research supports such predictions (Scully, 1974, 1989; Forrest and Simmons, 2006; Szymanski and Kuypers, 1999).

The consequences of the Bosman verdict

In order to comprehend the effects of the Bosman verdict the contemporary soccer scene in Europe can be analyzed. To begin with, it should be noted that, apart from the abolition of the transfer system, the Bosman ruling also meant that UEFA's "3+2" rule was in violation of the free mobility of goods and services, capital and labor within the EU. This 3+2 rule stated that a club was allowed to field a maximum of three foreign players plus two semi-foreign players who had played in the country for more than five years. It is the abolition of this rule that reshuffled the talent distribution in Europe. It should be noted, however, that clubs tried to evade the impact of the ruling. After the verdict, clubs extended the length of the player contracts, so buying and selling contracted players on the transfer market simply continued. Only out-of-contract players were free. Another evasion trick was to put heavy pressure on players to sign a new contract before the current one had expired. This way, a player can never reach the end of their contract with a club.

Nevertheless, the abolition of the 3+2 rule has caused a real exodus of all soccer talent toward the major soccer leagues with their vast budgets, resulting in a huge performance gap in international competitions between the top teams in the large and wealthy countries such as England, Spain, Italy, Germany and France, on the one hand, and the top clubs in smaller countries such as the Netherlands, Portugal and Belgium, as well as in the poorer Eastern-European countries, on the other hand. The budget gaps between these clubs were already large before the Bosman verdict, mainly as a result of the increasing broadcast rights during the last few decades. The large revenues from broadcast rights do not depend so much on the size of a club's local market – Brussels or Amsterdam are not smaller cities than Manchester or Liverpool – but on the size of the national market. England is simply much bigger than Belgium or Holland, and so Manchester United and Liverpool have more broadcast rights than Anderlecht or Ajax. The performance gap increased dramatically after the Bosman verdict (see Kesenne, 2007).

Revenue sharing

In all countries, professional sport federations have established some kind of revenue sharing arrangement between the large-market and small-market clubs. In most cases, the broadcasting rights are redistributed because they make up an ever-growing part of the clubs' budget. In a number of North American leagues, such as the National Football League (NFL) and the National Baseball Association (NBA), gate receipts are also distributed between the home team and the visiting team.

Economic research has shown that, under profit maximization, these revenue-sharing arrangements do not have a positive effect on competitive balance; they only lower player salaries. This can be explained by the reduction of the demand for talent by both the large-market and small-market clubs if they have to share the extra revenue of a new talent with the other club. Hence, as is depicted in Figure 27.5, the competitive balance will not change: both clubs will reduce their demand and so the new market equilibrium (E_{p1}) is to be found at exactly the same distribution of talent as the former one.

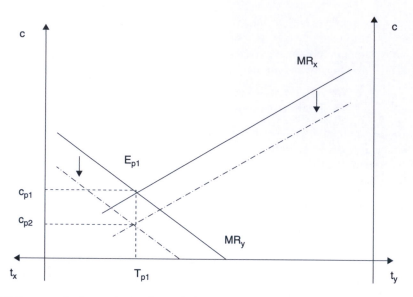

Figure 27.5 Revenue sharing under profit maximization

We also see on the vertical axis that the average player salary comes down from c_{p1} to c_{p2}, which is a logical consequence of a declining market demand and a constant market supply.

Once again the effects of revenue sharing in the case of win maximization are quite different. The small-market club will use the extra money that it receives from sharing to invest in talent and hence its demand for talent will go up. The demand for talent of the large-market team will come down because the large club loses money from sharing with the small club.

Figure 27.6 shows that these shifts of the demand curves move the equilibrium from T_{w1} to T_{w2}, which is a more balanced talent distribution. We also see on the vertical axis that the average player salary has risen after the distribution, caused by the fact that the increase of a small-market club's demand curve is larger than the decrease of the large-market club's demand curve. A simple numerical example will illustrate this situation.

Assume that the large-market club has 100 talents and the small-market club has 50 talents; if a total amount of 1,000 euro goes from the large-market club to the small-market club through the revenue sharing system, then the Average Revenues of the large-market club (AR_x) would decline with $1000/100 = 10$, while the Average Revenues of the small-market club (AR_y) would increase with $1000/50 = 20$. Hence, also, the unit cost of talent will increase by this increasing market demand.

The conclusion is that only in a win–maximization league will revenue sharing have a positive impact on the competitive balance. In a profit-maximization league, revenue sharing will lower player salaries; in a win–maximization league, it will raise player salaries.

Monopolizing broadcast rights

The most popular revenue sharing system, in the US major leagues and in European football, is the redistribution of television rights. The collective sale and distribution of media rights is

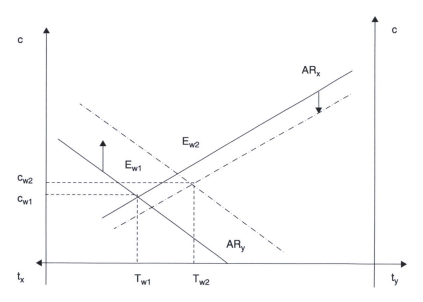

Figure 27.6 Revenue sharing under win maximization

common practice in the US major leagues and in most European national football leagues. As was the case with the transfer system, this monopolization of the broadcast rights turned out to be in violation of European competition laws. Europe advocates revenue sharing and more solidarity in European football, but is opposed to a monopoly in the market of the broadcast rights, created by the national football federations (see the "White Paper on Sport," European Commission, 2007). In most countries, the TV rights are sold by the national federations in a package deal, containing all league games. The collected money is then distributed among all clubs based on specific distribution rules.

It is a widespread misunderstanding that a monopoly of the broadcast rights is necessary for a distribution of the TV money (see Andreff and Bourg, 2006). A distribution is perfectly possible without creating a monopoly. However, the monopoly is probably lucrative for the national federations and the clubs, because more television money can be obtained this way, but it disadvantages football fans who pay too high a subscription fee for too small a number of games that are broadcast. In economic theory, it can be shown that monopolies cause a welfare loss, by reducing market supply and increasing prices. It is also important to know that, in a number of court cases, judges have concluded that the clubs, and not the national federation, are the legal owner of a game's broadcast rights. Consequently, the clubs can individually sell the broadcasting rights for their home games to the highest bidding TV company. However, this does not exclude the fact that the national federation can take measures for a fair redistribution afterwards. This will probably increase transaction costs by more complex administrative procedures. Furthermore, empirical research has shown that there is no correlation between collective or individual selling and competitive balance (see Peeters, 2009). Moreover, some theoretical research has indicated that decentralized selling, combined with a performance-related redistribution of the money, is the best guarantee for a more balanced competition in the case of profit maximization (Kesenne, 2009).

US salary cap

If neither the transfer system nor revenue sharing have any impact on the competitive balance in a profit-maximization league, is there nothing a national federation can do to make the competition more attractive? In North America, some large major leagues, the NBA (basketball) and the NFL (American Football) have adopted the so-called *salary cap*, which is actually a misleading term. It is not the individual player salaries that are capped but the club's payroll; the total expenditures of a team on player salaries, which is in fact a *payroll cap*. The amount of the cap, which is the same for each team, is determined by a negotiated percentage of the previous season's average club budget. In most cases, this cap is relevant only for the large and rich clubs; the small clubs cannot even afford to pay the amount of the cap on player salaries. This salary cap can be depicted graphically as an hyperbolic function, because the product of the number of talents (t_x) and the unit cost of talent (c) can maximally equal the amount of the cap (*cap*) fixed by the federation, i.e.:

$$ct_i \leq cap. \tag{27.4}$$

So, the functional form of the *cap* curve will be:

$$c = cap/t_i. \tag{27.5}$$

In Figure 27.7 this cap curve is drawn for the big club x only. The product of the unit cost of talent and the number of talents must not exceed this *cap* curve. This actually implies that, given the salary level, the large-market club's demand of talent is now defined by this cap curve. Hence the market equilibrium is now at the intersection of the demand curve of the small-market club and the cap curve, that is: at E_2.

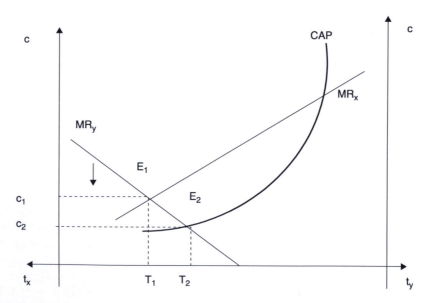

Figure 27.7 Salary cap

We can now derive that the distribution of talent or the competitive balance moves from T_1 to T_2, which is more balanced, and that the unit cost of talent comes down from c_1 to c_2 because of the salary cap.

Obviously, the impact of a salary cap in a win maximization league is similar to this result, but now the new market equilibrium is found at the point of intersection of the cap curve and the small club's average revenue curve (AR), suggesting greater competitive balance still.

Payroll cap of the European Club Association in European football

The European Club Association (ECA), which is an association of the most successful football clubs in Europe, and which was originally called the G–14, has proposed a payroll cap that differs fundamentally from the North American system, discussed above. The proposal, which was to be not more than a kind of gentlemen's agreement, was to impose a maximum wage/turnover ratio to each club or:

$$\frac{ct_i}{R_i} \leq \alpha \quad \text{so that:} \quad cap_i = \alpha R_i \quad \text{with } \alpha < 1 \tag{27.6}$$

where α is a fixed (at 70 percent by the ECA) wage/turnover ratio. Unlike the North American cap, the maximum amount that a club can spend on player salaries is different for each club, so that a different impact on competitive balance and salary level can also be expected.

Starting with profit maximization, this payroll cap has some resemblance to the macro-economic "share economy" proposal of Martin Weitzman (1984) to fight stagflation. An implication of Weitzman's labor compensation system, which grants the employees a percentage of a firm's total revenue, is that the marginal revenue of labor is always higher than the marginal cost. Based on the payroll cap in expression (27.6), $MC_i = \alpha MR_i$ the profit function can be written as:

$$\pi_i = (1 - \alpha)R_i - c_i^0 \quad \text{where } c_i^0 \text{ is the capital cost.} \tag{27.7}$$

So, all profit-maximizing clubs are willing to hire talent until the marginal revenue of playing talent is zero. If all playing talent is looking for the best-paying team, it can be shown that this type of payroll cap worsens the competitive balance. If this payroll cap is binding for both the large- and the small-market club, the new market equilibrium is found at the point of intersection of the AR-curves:

$$\frac{\alpha R_i}{t_i} = c \quad \text{or} \quad AR_i = \frac{c}{\alpha} \quad \text{for all } i. \tag{27.8}$$

It follows that the profit maximization equilibrium under this payroll cap results in the same equilibrium as in a win maximization league. It can be seen in Figure 27.8 that this will cause a more unequal distribution of talent compared with the market equilibrium in a profit maximization league.

However, the salary level that emerges after the introduction of the payroll cap is not found at the point of intersection of the AR-curves, because the payroll is only a fixed percentage α of total revenue. Given the objective of the payroll cap, the parameter α will be

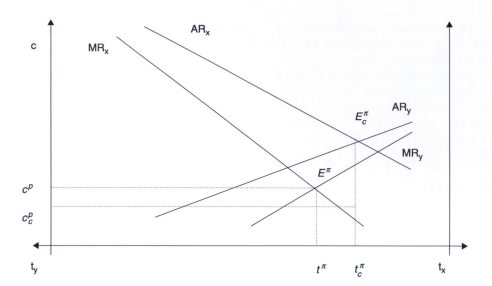

Figure 27.8 ECA payroll cap under profit maximization

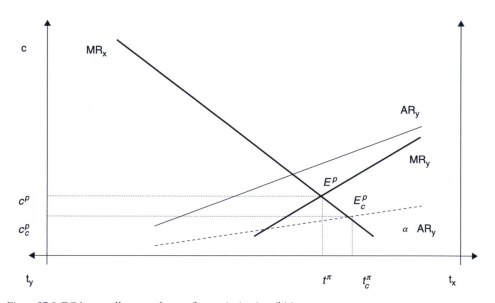

Figure 27.9 ECA payroll cap under profit maximization (bis)

chosen low enough to lower the average player salary level. In Figure 26.8, the new unit cost of talent, or the average salary level, is given by $c_c^p = \alpha \dfrac{R_i}{t_i} = \alpha AR$.

If the payroll cap is not binding for the rich large-market clubs, because they usually have a relatively low wage turnover ratio, this payroll cap still worsens the competitive balance. If the payroll cap is not relevant for the large-market club but only affects the payroll of the small-market club, the result is also a more unbalanced distribution of playing talent as can be seen from Figure 27.9.

The large-market club's demand curve for talent is still given by the marginal revenue curve MRx while the small-market club's demand is given by the curve $\alpha\,ARy$. The new market equilibrium is found at the point of intersection E_c^p, also with a more unequal distribution of talent. The unit cost of talent or the average salary level will then be c_c^p. One can conclude that the proposed ECA payroll cap worsens the competitive balance in a profit maximization league.

In a *win maximization* league, where a club's demand for talent is given by the net average revenue curve (NAR), that is: after subtraction of the capital cost, the free market equilibrium is found where:

$$NAR_i = \frac{R_i - c_i^0}{t_i} = c \qquad \text{for all } i. \tag{27.9}$$

If the G-14 payroll cap is imposed, and if the cap is relevant for both clubs, the market equilibrium is again given by expression (27.8) so that both equilibria can be compared. Different outcomes are possible now, depending on the size of the capital cost.

If the capital cost is assumed to be proportional to total revenue with proportionality factor k:

$$c_i^0 = kR_i \qquad \text{so that:} \qquad AR_i = \frac{1}{(1-k)} NAR_i, \tag{27.10}$$

the distribution of talent, as well as the wage-turnover ratios, will be the same as before, but with a lower salary level.

However, if the wage turnover ratio is lower in the large-market club, the proportionality factor k is larger, the ECA cap worsens the competitive balance in a win-maximization league. This can be seen by considering the shifts of the demand curves of the large- and small-market club in Figure 27.10. If the free market equilibrium is given by E^w, the point of

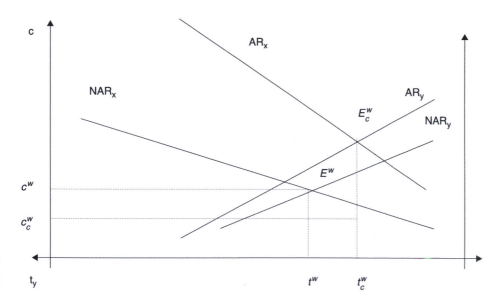

Figure 27.10 ECA payroll cap under win maximization

intersection of net average revenue curves, the distribution of talent after the introduction of the payroll cap is given by point E_c^w with the salary level equal to c_c^w.

Given the higher value of the proportionality factor k in the large-market club, the AR-curve of the large-market club is much steeper. It follows that the ECA salary cap will also worsen the competitive balance in a win maximization league, with an average salary level equal to c_c^w.

Given that the major concern of the ECA was the sound financial structure of the European football clubs, the point of reference for analyzing the impact of a payroll cap should not be the break-even point. If the financial problems of the small-market clubs were, on average, worse than those of the large-market clubs, the reduction in spending on talent would be stronger in the small-market clubs. So, also in this case the ECA payroll cap will worsen the competitive balance (see Kesenne, 2003).

Conclusion

Fairly simple economic theory indicates that the objectives of sport clubs will affect the competitive balance and the level of average player salaries differently. Moreover, the effects of league regulations by the national federations, such as restrictions on player mobility by means of a transfer system or a redistribution of the clubs' revenues, can also be very diverse. Hence it is essential to know what the sport club's objectives are. The empirical research still has not found conclusive answers even though some tests have shown that the hypothesis of profit maximization cannot be dismissed (see Ferguson et al., 1991). However, these tests are all based on the ticket pricing rule, and this rule is identical in the win–maximization and the profit-maximization case; so the tests confirm the hypothesis of win and profit maximization (see Kesenne, 2007). More conclusive tests are needed to answer this fundamental question.

Note

1   The reference to large and small towns refers to traditional catchment areas for fans. Conceptually the important point here is that clubs face different, unbalanced, access to revenue.

References

Andreff, W. and Szymanski, S. (eds.) (2006) *Handbook on the Economics of Sport*, Northampton, MA, Edward Elgar.

Andreff, W. and Bourg, J.F. (2006) 'Broadcasting rights and competition in European football', in C. Jeanrenaud and S. Kesenne (eds.) *Sport and the Media*, Cheltenham UK and Northampton, MA Edward Elgar, pp. 37–70.

Dobson, S. and Goddard, J. (2001) *The Economics of Football*, Cambridge, Cambridge University Press.

El-Hodiri, M. and Quirk, J. (1971) 'An economic model of a professional sport league', *Journal of Political Economy*, 79, 1302–19.

European Commission (2007) *White Paper on Sport*, Brussels, European Commission.

Ferguson, D., Stewart, K., Jones, J. and Le Dressay, A. (1991) 'The pricing of sport events: Do teams maximize profits?' *Journal of Industrial Economics*, 39 (3), 297–310.

Forrest, D. and Simmons, R. (2006) 'New issues in attendance demand: The case of the English Football League', *Journal of Sport Economics*, 7(3), 247–66.

Fort, R. (2003) *Sport Economics*, Englewood Cliffs, Prentice Hall.

Kesenne, S. (2003) 'The salary cap proposal of the G-14 in European football', *European Sport Management Quarterly* 3(2), 120–28.

—— (2007) 'The peculiar international economics of professional football in Europe', *Scottish Journal of Political Economy*, 54(3), 388–99.

—— (2009) 'The impact of pooling and sharing broadcast rights in professional team sport', *International Journal of Sport Finance*, 4(3), 211–18.

Noll, R. (ed.) (1974) *Government and the Sport Business*, Washington DC, The Brookings Institution.

Noll, R. (1999) 'Competition policy in European sport after the Bosman case', in C. Jeanrenaud and S. Kesenne (eds.) *Competition Policy in Professional Sport*, Antwerp, Standaard Uitgeverij.

Peeters, T. (2009) 'Competitive balance and broadcasting rights in European football', *International Journal of Sport Finance* 2011, 6(1), 23–39.

Quirk, J. and Fort, R. (1992) *Pay Dirt, The Business of Professional Team Sport*, Princeton, Princeton University Press.

Rottenberg, S. (1956) 'The baseball players' labor market', *Journal of Political Economy*, 64 (3), 242–58.

Scully, G. (1974) 'Pay and performance in Major League Baseball', *American Economic Review*, 64 (6), 915–30.

—— (1989) *The Business of Major League Baseball*, Chicago, University of Chicago Press.

Szymanski, S. (2003) 'The economic design of sporting contests', *Journal of Economic Literature*, 41 (4), 1137–87.

Szymanski, S. and Kuypers, T. (1999) *Winners and Losers, the Business Strategy of Football*. London, Viking.

Weitzmann, M. (1984) *The Share Economy, Conquering Stagflation*, Cambridge, MA, Harvard University Press.

Zimbalist, A. (ed.) (2001) *The Economics of Sport*, Vols I and II. Northampton, MA, Edward Elgar.

28

INTERNATIONAL SPORT LEAGUE COMPARISONS

Helmut Dietl, Rodney Fort and Markus Lang

Introduction

Comparisons between European and North American sport leagues have occurred over the years. Rather than list the entire literature, we refer the reader to the overviews in Fort (2000), Barros, Ibrahimo, and Szymanski (2002), Fort and Fizel (2004), and Sandy, Sloane, and Rosentraub (2004). The topics have ranged from fan differences across countries, to organizational and business model comparisons, to objective functions of team management, to competitive balance.

As with Chapter 26, we attempt to bring these comparisons down to the essential elements when analyzing what has come to be called Rottenberg's (1956) invariance principle. In other words, the chapter provides theoretical insights into attempts to alter competitive balance using revenue sharing, talent drafts, and payroll caps. Player reserve systems (the reserve clause in North American leagues and transfer restrictions in European leagues) are also examined. However, the so-called "luxury tax" in Major League Baseball (actually titled the competitive balance tax in that league's Collective Bargaining Agreement with players) is not examined as it is specific to that league. In this chapter, however, the differences in invest- ment in talent provide the central focus of analysis. Differences in objective functions are handled similarly, however, as North American leagues are treated as having clubs pursuing profit maximization, while European leagues are treated as having clubs pursuing utility maximization and win maximization.

The focus is on model predictions compared to actual outcomes, and any differences between North America and Europe. The chapter proceeds by specifying a simple general model of talent markets and profit maximization for North American leagues. The recent evolution of utility maximization models in European leagues is extended to that case. A brief overview and assessment of competitive balance arrangements in North America and Europe is presented where relevant.

North American leagues (profit maximization)

The objective in this section of the chapter is to present a simple general model of a league of profit-maximizing teams. The level of generality needs to satisfy that there is an underlying talent market; all outcomes are consistent with a Nash non-cooperative setting,[1] and both closed and open talent markets can be considered.[2] We present the simple general model and then seek theoretical insights about Rottenberg's invariance principle relative to revenue sharing for open and closed leagues. Brief notes on empirical findings about revenue sharing are included, as are extensions to other talent market impositions such as the draft, free agency, and payroll caps.

A simple general model

The intent is to have a model sufficient to include characteristics of the elasticity of talent, that is the degree of its availability for hire, within a Nash non-cooperative setting. A two-team league is modeled to facilitate comparison with the current literature, recognizing the limitations of that choice. An extremely important feature of the model is the additional dimensionality of choice implied in modeling sport league using Nash equilibria. As Winfree and Fort (2011) illustrate, within the literature there has been a traditional focus on fixed talent supply in an essentially perfectly competitive (Walrasian) setting. Whilst Nash equilibria have been introduced into the literature, with the implication that talent choices can be made independently of other teams (i.e. that talent supply is not fixed), this means that the concept of a fixed talent supply is lost to the analysis as talent is viewed as elastically supplied. To resolve this issue, Winfree and Fort (2011) separate out the investment in talent of individual teams and the impact of overall talent in the league on competitive balance. In this sense the authors distinguish between the levels of talent in teams and the investment in talent of teams. Consequently a Nash equilibrium approach to modeling does not have to imply a trade-off with respect to specifying the market for talent. Winfree and Fort (2011) show that this two-dimensional approach, a talent investment leading to team talent levels, follows a strict suggestion in Szymanski (2004), relates to the original work in the area (by Quirk and El Hodiri, El Hodiri and Quirk, Fort and Quirk, summarized and extended in Fort, 2007, and Fort and Quirk, 2007), and is an advance over previous work (Easton and Rockerbie, 2005; Vrooman, 2007; Chang and Sanders, 2009).

In the model, choosing talent is actually an investment in talent either through purchasing talent at a given level in a market or spending resources to develop talent. Let z_1 for team one and z_2 for team two represent investment in talent for each team. This investment may include payroll, minor league development, training facilities or other investments that affect talent. In turn, let $t_1(z_1, z_2)$ and $t_2(z_1, z_2)$ be the actual talent result for the two teams depending on the talent investment across the league. Our interpretation of the Nash insight is that $\frac{dz_2}{dz_1} = \frac{dz_1}{dz_2} = 0$; neither team believes that their talent investment impacts the investment of the other team.

Whether the talent market is closed or open is depicted in the actual talent outcome. In a closed league, talent supply is fixed (completely inelastic), that is, $t_1 + t_2 = T$. In turn, this implies that $\frac{\partial t_1}{\partial z_1} = -\frac{\partial t_2}{\partial z_1}$ and $\frac{\partial t_2}{\partial z_2} = -\frac{\partial t_1}{\partial z_2}$. In an open league (the limiting extreme is a perfectly elastic supply of talent), either team can increase its use of talent without impacting any other team's level of talent, that is, $\frac{\partial t_1}{\partial z_1} = -\frac{\partial t_2}{\partial z_1} = 0$.

Winning, 'w', then depends on the team's own talent as specified in the following contest functions: $w_1 = w_1(t_1(z_1,z_2), t_2(z_1,z_2))$ and $w_2 = w_2(t_1(z_1,z_2), t_2(z_1,z_2))$. Let R_i be team i's revenue. These revenues are modeled dependent on the team's own quality (winning percent): $R_1(w_1(t_1(z_1,z_2),t_2(z_2,z_1)))$ and $R_2(w_2(t_2(z_2,z_1),t_1(z_1,z_2)))$. If α is the proportion of revenue that is shared then team profits are[3]:

$$\pi_1 = (1-\alpha)\,R_1 + \alpha R_2 - z_1,\ \pi_2 = (1-\alpha)\,R_2 + \alpha R_1 - z_2 \tag{28.1}$$

First-order conditions for a profit maximum for team 1 and team 2, respectively, are

$$\frac{\partial \pi_1}{\partial z_1} = (1-\alpha)\left\{ \frac{dR_1}{dw_1}\left[\frac{\partial w_1}{\partial t_1}\left(\frac{\partial t_1}{\partial z_1} + \frac{\partial t_1}{\partial z_2}\frac{dz_2}{dz_1} \right) + \frac{\partial w_1}{\partial t_2}\left(\frac{\partial t_2}{\partial z_1} + \frac{\partial t_2}{\partial z_2}\frac{dz_2}{dz_1} \right) \right] \right\}$$
$$+ \alpha\left\{ \frac{dR_2}{dw_2}\left[\frac{\partial w_2}{\partial t_1}\left(\frac{\partial t_1}{\partial z_1} + \frac{\partial t_1}{\partial z_2}\frac{dz_2}{dz_1} \right) + \frac{\partial w_2}{\partial t_2}\left(\frac{\partial t_2}{\partial z_1} + \frac{\partial t_2}{\partial z_2}\frac{dz_2}{dz_1} \right) \right] \right\} - 1 = 0 \tag{28.2}$$

$$\frac{\partial \pi_2}{\partial z_2} = (1-\alpha)\left\{ \frac{dR_2}{dw_2}\left[\frac{\partial w_2}{\partial t_2}\left(\frac{\partial t_2}{\partial z_2} + \frac{\partial t_2}{\partial z_1}\frac{dz_1}{dz_2} \right) + \frac{\partial w_2}{\partial t_1}\left(\frac{\partial t_1}{\partial z_2} + \frac{\partial t_1}{\partial z_1}\frac{dz_1}{dz_2} \right) \right] \right\}$$
$$+ \alpha\left\{ \frac{dR_1}{dw_1}\left[\frac{\partial w_1}{\partial t_2}\left(\frac{\partial t_2}{\partial z_2} + \frac{\partial t_2}{\partial z_1}\frac{dz_1}{dz_2} \right) + \frac{\partial w_1}{\partial t_1}\left(\frac{\partial t_1}{\partial z_2} + \frac{\partial t_1}{\partial z_1}\frac{dz_1}{dz_2} \right) \right] \right\} - 1 = 0. \tag{28.3}$$

The winning percent adding up constraint must also hold, $w_1 + w_2 = 1$.

Imposing Nash conjectures, $\dfrac{dz_2}{dz_1} = \dfrac{dz_1}{dz_2} = 0$, (28.2) and (28.3) become, respectively:

$$(1-\alpha)\left\{ \frac{dR_1}{dw_1}\left[\frac{\partial w_1}{\partial t_1}\frac{\partial t_1}{\partial z_1} + \frac{\partial w_1}{\partial t_2}\frac{\partial t_2}{\partial z_1} \right] \right\} + \alpha\left\{ \frac{dR_2}{dw_2}\left[\frac{\partial w_2}{\partial t_1}\frac{\partial t_1}{\partial z_1} + \frac{\partial w_2}{\partial t_2}\frac{\partial t_2}{\partial z_1} \right] \right\} - 1 = 0 \tag{28.4}$$

$$(1-\alpha)\left\{ \frac{dR_2}{dw_2}\left[\frac{\partial w_2}{\partial t_2}\frac{\partial t_2}{\partial z_2} + \frac{\partial w_2}{\partial t_1}\frac{\partial t_1}{\partial z_2} \right] \right\} + \alpha\left\{ \frac{dR_1}{dw_1}\left[\frac{\partial w_1}{\partial t_2}\frac{\partial t_2}{\partial z_2} + \frac{\partial w_1}{\partial t_1}\frac{\partial t_1}{\partial z_2} \right] \right\} - 1 = 0 \tag{28.5}$$

and $w_1 + w_2 = 1$. Setting (28.4) and (28.5) equal to one, and then equal to each other, the talent investment equilibrium is:

$$(1-\alpha)\left\{ \frac{dR_1}{dw_1}\left[\frac{\partial w_1}{\partial t_1}\frac{\partial t_1}{\partial z_1} + \frac{\partial w_1}{\partial t_2}\frac{\partial t_2}{\partial z_1} \right] \right\} + \alpha\left\{ \frac{dR_2}{dw_2}\left[\frac{\partial w_2}{\partial t_1}\frac{\partial t_1}{\partial z_1} + \frac{\partial w_2}{\partial t_2}\frac{\partial t_2}{\partial z_1} \right] \right\}$$
$$= (1-\alpha)\left\{ \frac{dR_2}{dw_2}\left[\frac{\partial w_2}{\partial t_2}\frac{\partial t_2}{\partial z_2} + \frac{\partial w_2}{\partial t_1}\frac{\partial t_1}{\partial z_2} \right] \right\} + \alpha\left\{ \frac{dR_1}{dw_1}\left[\frac{\partial w_1}{\partial t_2}\frac{\partial t_2}{\partial z_2} + \frac{\partial w_1}{\partial t_1}\frac{\partial t_1}{\partial z_2} \right] \right\}. \tag{28.6}$$

In addition, $w_1 + w_2 = 1$ implies $\dfrac{\partial w_1}{\partial t_1} = -\dfrac{\partial w_2}{\partial t_1}$ and $\dfrac{\partial w_2}{\partial t_2} = -\dfrac{\partial w_1}{\partial t_2}$. Substituting, we rewrite (28.6) as:

$$(1-\alpha)\left\{\frac{dR_1}{dw_1}\left[\frac{\partial w_1}{\partial t_1}\frac{\partial t_1}{\partial z_1}-\frac{\partial w_2}{\partial t_2}\frac{\partial t_2}{\partial z_1}\right]\right\}+\alpha\left\{\frac{dR_2}{dw_2}\left[\frac{\partial w_2}{\partial t_2}\frac{\partial t_2}{\partial z_1}-\frac{\partial w_1}{\partial t_1}\frac{\partial t_1}{\partial z_1}\right]\right\}$$

$$=(1-\alpha)\left\{\frac{dR_2}{dw_2}\left[\frac{\partial w_2}{\partial t_2}\frac{\partial t_2}{\partial z_2}-\frac{\partial w_1}{\partial t_1}\frac{\partial t_1}{\partial z_2}\right]\right\}+\alpha\left\{\frac{dR_1}{dw_1}\left[\frac{\partial w_1}{\partial t_1}\frac{\partial t_1}{\partial z_2}-\frac{\partial w_2}{\partial t_2}\frac{\partial t_2}{\partial z_2}\right]\right\}.$$

(28.7)

This is clearly a Nash equilibrium since satisfaction of (28.7) has each team taking the talent choice of the other team as given in their independent profit-maximizing choice of talent investment; each plays their best response.

The results in (28.5) are also "general" in the sense that no functional forms are imposed on either revenues or the underlying contest for this non-cooperative portrayal and no reference is made specifically to either open or closed leagues.

Ultimately, one of the distinguishing outcomes for this equilibrium is the presence or absence of Rottenberg's (1956) invariance principle – the distribution of talent in equilibrium is invariant with respect to revenue sharing. Essentially, the invariance principle holds if the equilibrium with revenue sharing in (28.7) with $\alpha > 0$ is the same as the equilibrium without revenue sharing, that is, with $\alpha = 0$. With $\alpha = 0$, (28.7) becomes:

$$\frac{dR_1}{dw_1}\left[\frac{\partial w_1}{\partial t_1}\frac{\partial t_1}{\partial z_1}-\frac{\partial w_2}{\partial t_2}\frac{\partial t_2}{\partial z_1}\right]-\frac{dR_2}{dw_2}\left[\frac{\partial w_2}{\partial t_2}\frac{\partial t_2}{\partial z_2}-\frac{\partial w_1}{\partial t_1}\frac{\partial t_1}{\partial z_2}\right]=0.$$

(28.8)

Expanding and rearranging terms in (28.7) to isolate the left-hand side of (28.8), the invariance principle holds with $\alpha > 0$, when:

$$\frac{dR_1}{dw_1}\left[\frac{\partial w_1}{\partial t_1}\left(\frac{\partial t_1}{\partial z_1}+\frac{\partial t_1}{\partial z_2}\right)-\frac{\partial w_2}{\partial t_2}\left(\frac{\partial t_2}{\partial z_2}+\frac{\partial t_2}{\partial z_1}\right)\right]=\frac{dR_2}{dw_2}\left[\frac{\partial w_2}{\partial t_2}\left(\frac{\partial t_2}{\partial z_2}+\frac{\partial t_2}{\partial z_1}\right)\right.$$

$$\left.-\frac{\partial w_1}{\partial t_1}\left(\frac{\partial t_1}{\partial z_1}+\frac{\partial t_1}{\partial z_2}\right)\right].$$

(28.9)

Further substituting equation (28.8) into equation (28.9), the conditions for the invariance principle are given by

$$\frac{\partial w_1}{\partial t_1}\left(\frac{\partial t_1}{\partial z_1}+\frac{\partial t_1}{\partial z_2}\right)=\frac{\partial w_2}{\partial t_2}\left(\frac{\partial t_2}{\partial z_2}+\frac{\partial t_2}{\partial z_1}\right).$$

(28.10)

Assuming that both teams have identical contest success functions and talent generating functions, we observe the following about the invariance principle, at the level of generality in (28.10). Assume that team 1 is in the larger-revenue market and there are diminishing marginal returns to talent, $\frac{\partial^2 w_i}{\partial t_i^2} < 0$. With team two in the larger-revenue market, these assumptions imply that if both teams increase their investment in talent by one unit, the effect will be larger on team two in the smaller-revenue market, that is $\frac{\partial t_1}{\partial z_1}+\frac{\partial t_1}{\partial z_2}<\frac{\partial t_2}{\partial z_2}+\frac{\partial t_2}{\partial z_1}$. Since it would require a particular $\frac{\partial w_1}{\partial t_1}>\frac{\partial w_2}{\partial t_2}$ to satisfy (28.10) in this case, then the invariance principle will not hold in general. This proposition can also be analyzed with the further restrictions on the elasticity of talent, that is, examining closed versus open talent markets.

Revenue sharing in closed and open leagues

The typical assumption is that North American leagues are "closed," that is, talent supply is fixed (completely inelastic). With the recent increase in the use of imported talent from international leagues in baseball, basketball, and hockey, perhaps this completely closed league idea is most relevant for the NFL. However, since *extensive* talent importing is a fairly recent phenomenon, the closed market remains insightful in all cases.

As noted in the last subsection, the assumption that the talent market is closed implies that $t_1 + t_2 = T$. In turn, this implies that $\frac{\partial t_1}{\partial z_1} = -\frac{\partial t_2}{\partial z_1}$ and $\frac{\partial t_2}{\partial z_2} = -\frac{\partial t_1}{\partial z_2}$. Substituting $\frac{\partial t_1}{\partial z_1} = -\frac{\partial t_2}{\partial z_1}$ and $\frac{\partial t_2}{\partial z_2} = -\frac{\partial t_1}{\partial z_2}$ into (28.10) and rearranging terms yields:

$$\frac{\partial t_1}{\partial z_1}\left(\frac{\partial w_2}{\partial t_2} + \frac{\partial w_1}{\partial t_1}\right) = \frac{\partial t_2}{\partial z_2}\left(\frac{\partial w_2}{\partial t_2} + \frac{\partial w_1}{\partial t_1}\right) \tag{28.11}$$

that is, a Nash, non-cooperative, two-team, closed league equilibrium exhibits the invariance principle if $\frac{\partial t_1}{\partial z_1} = \frac{\partial t_2}{\partial z_2}$. *In equilibrium, the invariance principle holds only if the marginal product* of talent investment *in the actual creation of talent* is the same across teams. Thus, in a closed league, the distribution of talent (and, thus, the invariance principle) depends on the relationship between *the investment in talent* and *the accumulation of talent*. (Winfree and Fort, 2011, show how previous work in the area generated the invariance principle relative to (28.11) and we do not go through that here.)

Open leagues are defined by $\frac{\partial t_1}{\partial z_2} = \frac{\partial t_2}{\partial z_1} = 0$ and (28.10) becomes:

$$\frac{\partial w_1}{\partial t_1}\frac{\partial t_1}{\partial z_1} = \frac{\partial w_2}{\partial t_2}\frac{\partial t_2}{\partial z_2}. \tag{28.12}$$

Now, even if $\frac{\partial t_1}{\partial z_1} = \frac{\partial t_2}{\partial z_2}$ in equilibrium, (28.11) would still require $\frac{\partial w_1}{\partial t_1} = \frac{\partial w_2}{\partial t_1}$ for the invariance principle to hold. This would be true of the trivial case where teams are completely balanced in the first place or for an arbitrary imposition on these marginal products that sets them equal to each other but, generally, the invariance principle does not hold for open leagues.

Interestingly, the data on the distribution of talent, primarily the Noll-Scully "ratio of standard deviation" of end-of-season winning percents, either fail to reject the invariance principle or show that balance worsened in some North American leagues with the imposition of revenue sharing and with any increase in sharing. Fort (2011) shows this for the two North American leagues with extensive sharing, Major League Baseball and the National Football League. The implications for the theory above are pretty clear, sticking with closed leagues since revenue-sharing impositions happened in MLB prior to the modern rise of imported talent and the NFL does not really import any talent. This empirical observation suggests that the relationship between *the investment in talent* and *the accumulation of talent* is really not quite as complex as suggested for closed leagues in (28.11). For the closed talent market, that the invariance principle holds with respect to revenue sharing is consistent with

$\dfrac{\partial t_1}{\partial z_1} = \dfrac{\partial t_2}{\partial z_2}$, that is, equilibrium in the talent investment market is characterized by equal

marginal product of investment in talent across all teams. Of course, it would be preferable to model the talent market more extensively and approach the issue directly in that market.

Other talent market changes and impositions

The theoretical impacts of remaining changes and impositions in the talent market are not derived here. Fort and Quirk (1995) used a somewhat restrictive version of the simple general theory, above, to portray the impacts of the draft, free agency, and payroll caps in the closed market case. While in this chapter analysis is focused on the closed market assessment of these other impositions, the interested reader can also relate the assessment to the open market case using Vrooman (2007). This model is close enough to the general open league case and the two-team league diagram would prove insightful for that case.

Rottenberg (1956) actually only applied the logic of the invariance principle to the draft and free agency (Fort, 2005). The reverse-order-of-finish draft dominates North American professional sport and has the lowest-finishing teams choosing incoming talent first. That talent signs its first contract with the drafting team and must follow the contract for a specific number of years after that (e.g. six years in baseball). Essentially, the owner argument has always been that a reverse-order-of-finish draft should equalize talent across the league since poor teams command better incoming talent than their market revenues should support. Rottenberg's logic, instead, is that as long as player contracts can be bought and sold and players must follow their contracts, then the draft will not change the distribution of talent. The draft itself does not alter the value of talent anywhere in the league so all it does is rearrange the value of talent away from players and toward smaller-revenue market owners. Rottenberg's insight proves insightful with respect to the empirical evidence in the North American case (Fort, 2011, Chapters 29 and 31). Drafts have never improved competitive balance in a statistically significant way.

It is commonly accepted that Rottenberg essentially emphasized the logic of the invariance principle to the case of free agency. Fort (2005) points out that, at least in print, this was the sport version of the weak form of the Coase Theorem a few years prior to its publication by the Nobel Prize winner. Again, as long as contracts can be freely bought and sold and players must follow their contract, then free agency cannot change the distribution of talent. All that happens is the value of talent is reallocated from players to owners and players go to their highest valued use across the league. The evidence supports this case that competitive balance did not change in a statistically significant way with the advent of free agency in any North American league (Fort, 2011, Chapter 31).

Payroll caps were first examined for North American leagues by Fort and Quirk (1995) (the various restrictions in that model are covered in Szymanski, 2004, Fort and Winfree, 2009, and Winfree and Fort, 2011). At that time, the National Basketball Association cap had been in force for quite some time but the National Football League cap was quite new. Since then, the National Hockey League has also added a cap. By forcing a disequilibrium situation, a strictly "hard cap" with equal spending by all teams forces an equilibrium at 0.500 for all teams and, analytically, improves balance. Fort and Quirk (1995) also show that larger-revenue market owners wish to buy more talent than allowed under the cap and smaller-revenue owners want to sell it to them in this disequilibrium so that leagues have an enforcement problem. In addition, leagues have never really embraced the "hard cap" approach and real-world caps are full of exclusions. The data (Fort and Quirk, 1995; Fort, 2011, Chapter 29), however, show that instead of converging to the official cap, actual payrolls have always been highly dispersed around the official cap and balance actually worsened significantly after the imposition of the National Basketball Association cap. Balance also did not change at all in the NFL with its cap, and though balance did improve in the NHL this was only after two years following the imposition of its cap.

European leagues (utility and win maximization)

Organizational structure

European team sports are organized as a pyramid of non-profit amateur clubs with a professional apex. This apex may comprise public or private limited companies, or member-owned collectives. However, the main organizational feature is one of vertical promotion and relegation between leagues based on merit. From a property rights perspective, these member associations in the professional game, or amateur games, differ significantly from the North American professional teams that are usually organized as commercial firms. The owner of such a firm has all decision rights, including the right to sell the team and to make appropriate profits. The only exception in the North American major leagues is the Green Bay Packers, who are governed as a community-owned non-profit organization.

This governance structure is similar to the European clubs that are organized as member associations. These member associations are democratically governed. Each member usually has one vote. Since there are no residual claimants within these member associations, and because in the European leagues there is a need to seek promotion and to avoid relegation for a level of competition, it is usually assumed that the clubs seek to maximize utility rather than profit. This utility maximization may translate into a variety of specific objectives because the clubs are usually open to new members who pursue their own objectives.[4] FC Barcelona, for example, has more than 170,000 members, Bayern Munich more than 150,000 members, and Sport Lisboa e Benfica more than 200,000 members. In addition, as non-profit organizations, the clubs were traditionally subsidized by their communities and therefore responsible to a large number of stakeholders.

In the last few decades, many clubs have changed their governance structures.[5] Some clubs, such as Manchester United, Liverpool and FC Copenhagen, have become more commercially driven and managed like their North American counterparts. Others have incorporated their professionalization and subsequent developments without ceding control by the member associations. Most German clubs have chosen such a hybrid structure due to the so-called "50+1" rule that stipulates that 50 percent plus one vote of an incorporated German football club must be controlled by the club's member association. The logic behind the 50+1 restriction is to ensure the integrity of professional football by avoiding a situation in which anybody could exercise control over more than one professional team. At the same time, however, this restriction results in a rather peculiar governance structure within the football corporations. Even if a business tycoon such as Roman Abramovich acquired all outstanding shares of a German football team, he would still control less than 50 percent of the votes.

The respective national associations organize the pyramid of competitions between the clubs at the national level. These national associations are organized as democratic governing bodies that try to coordinate the objectives of all stakeholders within their constitution. Across national associations, supra-national associations coordinate competition. The European Football Association (UEFA), an association of national associations, organizes international competition within Europe. UEFA organizes European club competitions like the UEFA Champions League and the UEFA Europe League for the teams meeting certain sportive qualification criteria. Teams who qualify for these international competitions continue to compete in their national leagues.

The openness of the European team sport industry has a number of consequences. First, market entry is possible at any time. Through promotion and relegation stronger teams constantly replace weaker teams.[6] Second, the non-profit orientation as well as the absence of residual claimants in many organizations enables the sport to generate revenues from a large variety of sources. For example, the governance structures are highly attractive for sponsors and donors. As a result, top European clubs have generated significantly higher revenues than their North American counterparts in recent years. Third, the sport is responsible to a wide variety of stakeholders, who are able to voice their interests as members of democratically organized governing bodies. Fourth, institutional arrangements, such as revenue sharing, salary caps, and free agency, have to be considered within the heterogeneous context of the European sport pyramid.

Revenue sharing in European sport leagues

Revenue sharing is less common in Europe than in North America. The home team, for example, usually keeps gate revenues. In most leagues, the league markets television rights collectively and the generated income is distributed according to market size or sportive success. In the German Bundesliga, for example, television rights are marketed by the league and distributed according to each club's position in the league table, with the top team earning the largest share. In the Champions League, television revenues are also marketed collectively by UEFA and distributed according to a formula, which includes the club's sportive success as well as the size of the television market of the club's country of origin. In Spain, the two largest clubs, Real Madrid and FC Barcelona, sell the rights to broadcast their home games individually whereas the other clubs market their television rights collectively. Some leagues, such as the Scottish Premier League and the English Premier League, use so-called parachute payments to help clubs which are relegated to a lower league. In 2011, the Premier League, for example, guarantees relegated clubs annual payments of £12 million for four years. The purpose of these parachute payments is to enable clubs to financially survive relegation to the next division. These parachute payments are a special form of revenue sharing, in which top-division clubs share television revenues with relegated clubs.

In addition to these peculiarities, the main difference between European and North American sport leagues with respect to the effect of revenue sharing on competitive balance results from the clubs' objective functions and the elasticity of talent supply. To highlight the effect of revenue sharing in an open league with utility-maximizing clubs and elastic talent supply, we follow Dietl et al. (2011b) and use a standard revenue function from the literature (see Szymanski, 2003; Kesenne, 2005, 2007). It should be noted that in an open league with elastic talent supply, we do not have to differentiate between talent investment and actual talent level because $\frac{\partial t_2}{\partial z_1} = \frac{\partial t_1}{\partial z_2} = 0$, $\frac{\partial t_1}{\partial z_1} = \frac{\partial t_2}{\partial z_2}$ and $\frac{\partial z_2}{\partial z_1} = \frac{\partial z_1}{\partial z_2} = 0$. According to Winfree and Fort (2011) these conditions imply that choosing talent investment is the equivalent of choosing talent.[7]

The revenue of club $i = 1, 2$ is then given by

$$R_i(z_i, z_j) = m_i w_i(z_i, z_j) - \frac{b}{2} w_i(z_i, z_j)^2,$$

(28.13)

where $b > 0$ characterizes the effect of competitive balance on club revenues and $m_i > 0$ represents the market size or drawing potential of club i. The win percentage w_i of club i is characterized by the Tullock contest-success function (CSF), which is the most widely used functional form of a CSF in sporting contests[8]: $w_i(z_i, z_j) = z_i/(z_i + z_j)$. Equation (28.13) shows that club i's revenues initially increase with winning until the maximum is reached for $w_i' \equiv \frac{m_i}{b}$. By increasing the win percentage above w_i' club i's revenues start to decrease because excessive dominance by one team is detrimental to club revenues. This reflects the uncertainty of outcome hypothesis; the higher b is, the more important is competitive balance and the sooner revenues start to decrease due to the dominance by one team.

The objective function of club i is given by a weighted sum of one's own profits and wins:

$$
\begin{aligned}
u_i(z_i, z_j) &= \pi_i(z_i, z_j) + \gamma_i w_i(z_i, z_j) \\
&= (1-\alpha) R_i(z_i, z_j) + \alpha R_j(z_i, z_j) - z_i + \gamma_i w_i(z_i, z_j)
\end{aligned}
$$

(28.14)

where $\gamma_i \geq 0$ is the "win preference," which characterizes the weight club owner i puts on winning in the objective function. A higher parameter γ_i thus reflects that club owner i becomes more win-oriented and less profit-oriented.[9] Note that two dimensions of heterogeneity exist in the model. On the one hand, clubs differ with respect to their market size, and on the other hand, clubs differ regarding their win preference.

Each club $i = 1, 2$ maximizes its objective function u_i yielding the following first-order conditions:

$$
\begin{aligned}
\frac{\partial u_i(z_i, z_j)}{\partial z_i} &= \left((1-\alpha) \frac{\partial R_i}{\partial w_i} - \alpha \frac{\partial R_j}{\partial w_j} + \gamma_i \right) \frac{\partial w_i}{\partial z_i} - 1 \\
&= \left((1-\alpha)(m_i - b) - \alpha m_j + \frac{b z_j}{z_i + z_j} + \gamma_i \right) \frac{z_j}{\left(z_i + z_j \right)^2} - 1 = 0.
\end{aligned}
$$

(28.15)

Regarding the effect of revenue sharing on club revenues, the partial derivative of club i's marginal after-sharing revenue MR_i with respect to the revenue-sharing parameter α is given by $\frac{\partial MR_i}{\partial \alpha} = \frac{z_j}{(z_i + z_j)^2}[b - (m_i + m_j)]$. A higher degree of revenue sharing has a positive effect on club i's marginal revenue if $b > m_i + m_j$, while it has a negative effect on marginal revenue if $b < m_i + m_j$. Revenue sharing has no effect on marginal revenue for $b = m_i + m_j$.[10]

Dietl et al. (2011b) show that if $b > m_i + m_j$, more revenue sharing increases the amount of talent hired by each club and produces a more balanced league if the league is not fully balanced in equilibrium. In the case that revenue sharing has a positive effect on marginal revenue for both clubs, it enhances incentives to invest in playing talent. It follows that both clubs will increase the amount of talent hired in equilibrium. Hence, Dietl et al. (2011b) identify a new effect of revenue sharing, called the "sharpening effect."[11]

In the presence of the sharpening effect, a revenue-sharing arrangement proves to be an efficient instrument for improving competitive balance in an unbalanced league. If the large-market club is the dominant team in equilibrium, then the positive effect of revenue sharing on marginal revenue is stronger for the underdog (i.e. small-market club) than for the dominant team (i.e. large-market club) due to the logit formulation of the CSF. As a consequence, the sharpening effect of revenue sharing is more pronounced for the underdog than for the dominant team, because the marginal impact on the dominant team's revenues of an increase in talent investment by the underdog is greater than the marginal impact on the underdog's revenues of an increase in talent investment by the dominant team. As a result, the small-market club will increase its investment level relatively more than the large-market club such that the league becomes more balanced through revenue sharing.

If, however, the small-market club is the dominant team in equilibrium, then the positive effect of revenue sharing on marginal revenue is stronger for the large-market club than for the small-market club. In this case, the sharpening effect of revenue sharing is stronger for the large-market club. Again, the underdog (in this case, the large-market club) will increase its investment level relatively more than the dominant team (in this case, the small-market club) such that the league becomes more balanced through revenue sharing.

If the league is already perfectly balanced (i.e., both clubs have equal playing strength in equilibrium), the (marginal) sharpening effect of revenue sharing is equally strong for both clubs. As a consequence, both clubs will marginally increase their investment level at an equal rate and competitive balance will not be altered through revenue sharing such that the invariance proposition holds.

If $b < m_i + m_j$, more revenue sharing reduces the amount of talent hired by each club and produces a less balanced league. That is, in this case, the well-known dulling effect of revenue sharing is present. Finally, if $b = m_i + m_j$, more revenue sharing has no effect on equilibrium investments and on competitive balance such that the invariance proposition holds.

Free agency (Bosman ruling)

Traditionally, employment relations in European professional team sport were not only regulated by employment law and by the contracts between clubs and players, but also by a transfer system which was imposed on all employment relations within a team sport by the governing bodies of the respective sports. In football, for example, the European Football Association (UEFA) restricted the number of foreign players per team and the International Football Association (FIFA) prohibited players from signing for a new club without the consent of their former club. This transfer restriction even applied to out-of-contract players until the so-called Bosman ruling of the European Court of Justice in 1995. Jean-Marc Bosman, a Belgian player, went to court after his former club vetoed his transfer to a French club. The court ruled that this transfer restriction does not comply with the principle of free movement of workers within the European Union. As a result, all European sport governing bodies had to change their transfer systems to comply with EU principles. The Bosman ruling had a similar effect to the Seitz decision in Major League Baseball in the USA, which eliminated the reserve clause and led to free agency in American baseball. In addition, the Bosman ruling also prohibited national sport leagues within Europe from discriminating against players form other EU countries by imposing quotas on foreign players.

Players and clubs reacted to the Bosman ruling by significantly extending the average duration of player contracts (Simmons, 1997). This extension of contract durations can be interpreted as an attempt on both sides to opt back into the old transfer system, which applied to all in-contract players. In 2001, the European Union reacted to the contract extensions by limiting the maximal contract durations to five years. In what is known as the "Monti system" after European Commissioner Mario Monti, the football governing bodies further had to adapt their regulatory framework known as the FIFA transfer rules to a whole set of new requirements. The standard interpretation of these restrictions in the application of the transfer system stresses the increased freedom of movement for players, which translates into a relative gain in market power and therefore into higher salaries. While the link between freedom of movement and market power is clear, it can be questioned whether salaries will ultimately be driven up by the reforms. There may be more than one channel of influence between the reforms and the salaries. For example, Antonioni and Cubbin (2000) analyzed the economic effect of the Bosman ruling and found that the Bosman ruling had little effect on player salaries, investment in human capital and transfer activity. They attribute the rise in salaries to increasing television revenues.

Dietl et al. (2008b) looked at the employment relation in football from a different perspective. They developed a model which captures an important and widely overlooked aspect of this employment relation, namely the allocation of risk. Players and clubs alike do not know how the productivity of a player will develop in future periods. Given that players perform in public, and taking into account the importance of reputation effects, pride and career concerns in sport, it seems unlikely that players should shirk on effort. Instead, it seems more appropriate to treat productivity variations as a manifestation of risk. Moreover, on average, the career duration of a professional football player is very short compared with other labor markets. According to Frick et al. (2007), more than one-third of all players "disappear" again after their first season and only one career out of twelve lasts for ten years or more. During this short career duration, the high performance uncertainty creates strong incentives for the player to buy insurance against income uncertainty.

If risk is the key driver behind the performance uncertainty of football players then there is an obvious potential for value creation in this industry. Risk-averse players could buy insurance against future income uncertainty when contracting with risk-neutral clubs, which have the possibility to diversify the risk of productivity variations within their portfolio of players and also through diversified ownership structures. However, if the player turns out to be more productive in the course of time than was assumed when writing down the initial contract, he has incentives to renegotiate the contract. The same holds for the club if the player turns out to be a "bad risk."

De facto labor law in most European countries makes long-term employment contracts asymmetrically incomplete since it is possible to legally bind employers to fulfill long-term contracts but it is practically impossible to bind the employee. There is no "shadow of the law" that prevents players from accepting better job offers. Since "good risk" players would therefore renegotiate the contract and receive wages reflecting their marginal productivity, clubs would be left with all the "bad risks." Given this assumption, clubs cannot offer value creating insurance services. In this context the transfer system imposed by the governing bodies of football works as a surrogate which makes insurance contracts complete. "Good risk" players know that they will have to pay for the insurance, be it through the transfer fee or by continuing to play for a salary below marginal productivity. It is the "shadow of the transfer system" that has allowed players to commit to fulfilling their contracts and enabled the efficient allocation of risk in this industry.

The Bosman verdict restricted the "shadow of the transfer system" to the market for in-contract players. However, it provided freedom for players and clubs to voluntarily position their transactions under the "shadow of the transfer system" by extending the duration of contracts, which is exactly what happened in the industry. The Monti system makes it more difficult to position transactions under the "shadow of the transfer system" by limiting contract durations, thereby making the efficient allocation of risk more difficult. In their model, Dietl et al. (2008b) show that risk-averse players may lose from the reforms because they would benefit from a conversion of risky future income into risk-less current income under the "shadow of the transfer system."

Payroll caps

Although in the last decade European sport leagues have achieved an economic and financial potential comparable to that of the North American major leagues, it has not yet followed those leagues' examples of introducing payroll cap mechanisms. Presumably, this reluctance is not caused by the dangers of competitive imbalance and financial instability being unknown among the stakeholders of European sport leagues. Rather, the opposite seems to be the case. For example, the "Independent European Sport Review" (Arnaut, 2006), an expert report based on a process of intensive consultation with the most important stakeholder groups of European football, leaves no doubt that the general perception is that competitive balance in European club football is declining and that a large number of clubs have stumbled into a massive financial crisis and are accumulating ever-increasing debt.

As Dietl et al. (2011a) have shown, the reasons for this reluctance in Europe to introduce payroll cap mechanisms are structural because the labor relations approach employed by the American major leagues is not feasible within the European association-governed pyramid. Sport associations cannot be compared with the team owners in a North American major league, which represent the demand side of the respective labor market. Instead, associations are conceived as democratic governing bodies, which aim to integrate all of the important stakeholders in a certain geographic region including the players and fans. At the European level, the different political and market conditions of every sport nation create additional stakeholder diversity. It follows that decision-making processes concerning the introduction of payroll caps will be much more complicated in the European association-governed pyramid, as the interests of various stakeholders need to be properly balanced.

A payroll cap system would have to take into account the significant market heterogeneity within the European sport leagues, which encompasses all national and pan-European competitions through a system of promotion and relegation. The American system of an absolute capped payroll amount applicable to all clubs is not discussed in the European model because the revenue differentials between clubs of a certain division in different countries are significant. Taking into account that the cost of administering a specific absolute cap for every league in European would be prohibitive, the only workable solution in the European context seems to be a percentage-of-revenue payroll cap.

Unsurprisingly, all discussions among the stakeholders of European sport leagues focus on this relative capping strategy. For example, a small fraction of European football clubs, known as G–14 and established as an interest group of 18 prominent clubs of European football, brought up the issue of salary cost controls in 2004. The members of G–14 had planned to limit their salary expenditures to 70 percent of audited club turnover from the 2005–6 season onwards. At the same time, the minimum allowable amount for total staff costs of each member was set at €30 million. According to the G–14 plan, their statutory auditors should carry out verification of the clubs' compliance with these principles. However, the G–14 plan has never been put into practice and G–14 dissolved in January 2008, when the new European Club Association (ECA) was founded under the auspices of UEFA.

Representing all stakeholder groups of a particular sport, sport associations perform regulatory functions normally reserved to the state. Because the scope for autonomous regulatory activity by the sport governing bodies is limited by national and EU law, it is *a priori* unclear whether a particular payroll cap mechanism in Europe falls under the margin of discretion granted to the associations by the European Union. As the previous interferences of EU institutions in the regulatory activities of sports associations show, the sports governing bodies will have to prove that their proposal of a salary control system is doing more than, for example, just improving the financial situation of clubs. It is well recognized that sound club financials play an important role in avoiding incomplete seasons and maintaining the integrity of football. Clubs operating on the verge of bankruptcy are more inclined to engage in illegal practices like, for example, money laundering, match fixing, and tax fraud, which harm the image of the whole industry. However, the history of interventions shows that the EU institutions will assess a salary control system from a much broader social welfare perspective, which is not restricted to the improvement of financial stability alone, but at the same time aims to secure fair treatment of players and consumers.

Dietl et al. (2011a) analyzed the effects of a percentage-of-revenue payroll cap δ in an open league with win-maximizing clubs and elastic talent supply. They incorporate the specific European perspective into their model by assuming that a social planner must approve any regulation proposed by the league governing body, taking into account the effect of a payroll cap on all parties in the regulatory scheme: that is, clubs, fans and players. As a result, the objective function of the social planner (social welfare) is given by the sum of player salaries PS and consumer surplus CS that can be written as $W(z_1, \ldots, z_n) = PS(z_1, \ldots, z_n) + CS(z_1, \ldots, z_n)$.[12]

The decision of the league governing body is subjected to approval of the social planner in order to reflect the situation in European football. The social planner will accept a payroll cap proposed by the league governing body only if its introduction does not negatively affect social welfare compared to social welfare $W^\star$ in the benchmark case. The benchmark is an unregulated league, i.e., a league without a payroll cap ($\delta = 1$) and represents the current situation in European soccer, where no payroll caps exist and UEFA demands a balanced budget.[13]

The objective function of the league governing body depends not only on aggregate consumer (fan) surplus, aggregate player salaries and club surplus, but also on aggregate club profits, reflecting the league's concern for financial sustainability. The integration of club profits is motivated by the growing evidence cited by UEFA of a financial crisis spreading throughout the European football leagues. Many European clubs face serious financial difficulties – some have even gone bankrupt. UEFA has repeatedly argued that sound club finances play an important role in avoiding incomplete seasons and maintaining the integrity of football.

It follows that the league governing body has the same objectives as the social planner but in addition has a concern for financial stability in the league. The objective function of the league governing body is defined by $L(\delta) = PS(\delta) + CS(\delta) + \gamma\Pi(\delta) = W(\delta) + \gamma\Pi(\delta)$, where $\gamma \geq 0$ denotes the weight that the league authority puts on club profits. This weight depends on the financial situation of the league and increases with the degree of financial distress.[14] In the case that the league governing body is not concerned with financial stability (i.e. $\gamma = 0$), the objective functions of the league governing body and the social planner coincide.[15] League quality is now defined as $q(z_1, \ldots, z_n) = \theta\Gamma(z_1, \ldots, z_n) + CB(z_1, \ldots, z_n)$, where $\theta > 0$ allows the relative importance of the two components of league quality to shift. Thus, the parameter θ can be interpreted as reflecting the fans' relative preference for aggregate talent.

The problem of the league governing body consists of maximizing $L(\delta)$ under the constraint that social welfare is not lower than in the benchmark W^* without a payroll cap. Formally, the league governing body solves the maximization problem given by $\max\limits_{\delta \in [\delta^{min}, 1]} L(\delta)$ s.t. $W(\delta) \geq W^\star$.

By analyzing the constraint maximization problem of the league governing body, Dietl et al. (2011a) derive the following results:

(i) If the fans' preference for aggregate talent is low with $\theta \in [\theta^{min}, \theta'']$, then no payroll cap will be implemented: that is $\delta^* = 1$. The social planner will never approve a payroll cap set by the league governing body if the fans have a relatively low preference for aggregate talent (i.e. $\theta < \theta''$). In this situation, a payroll cap would inevitably lower social welfare because the beneficial impact of the payroll cap on competitive balance will result in a loss in player salaries and potentially in a loss in consumer surplus, as the unrestricted league is already rather balanced. Nevertheless, the league governing body would propose a payroll cap if financial distress is severe enough, that is, the weight γ on aggregate club profits is sufficiently high. However, the social planner will always veto this proposal. That is, even though the league governing body might want to introduce a payroll cap, the social planner will not tolerate this cap.

(ii) If the fans' preference for talent is sufficiently high with $\theta > \theta''$, then a payroll cap will be implemented according to $\delta^* = \begin{cases} \delta_1^* & \text{if } \theta \in (\theta'', \theta''') \text{ and } \gamma > \gamma', \\ \delta_2^* & \text{otherwise.} \end{cases}$ The proposal of the league governing body to introduce payroll caps can pass the social welfare test if the fans' preference for talent is sufficiently high (i.e. $\theta > \theta''$). In such a situation, the competitive imbalance in the league is so high that the social planner also favors a payroll cap. If the fans' preference for talent increases even more and passes another threshold, i.e., $\theta > \theta'''$, then the social planner always approves the league governing body's proposal and a payroll cap $\delta^* = \delta^*_2$ will be implemented. In this case, the optimal payroll cap from the point of view of the league governing body always lies in the interval of feasible payroll caps that yields a higher social welfare value than in benchmark case. Hence, the objectives of the league governing body and the social planner are sufficiently aligned. The same is true if $\theta \in (\theta'', \theta''')$ and the weight attached to club profits is small. However, if the league governing body puts too much emphasis on club profits (i.e. $\gamma > \gamma'$), the league governing body wants to implement a payroll cap that would be detrimental from a social welfare perspective, as players would suffer unduly. In this case, the league governing body will only be able to introduce the strictest possible payroll cap that still appeases the social planner, i.e. $\delta^* = \delta^*_1 > \delta^*_2$. Even though the objective function of the league governing body increases, social welfare remains unaltered compared with the benchmark case because consumer surplus increases at the expense of player salaries.

Conclusions

As the theory of sport leagues develops, it becomes increasingly clear over time that Rottenberg's (1956) invariance principle only holds in precisely derived situations. Moving to any level of generality, even the simple generality of the models in this chapter, makes the invariance principle a matter of the interaction between investment in talent and actual talent accumulation to the level put into play during games. For revenue sharing, it is interesting that the outcomes in North American leagues typically support the invariance principal, suggesting that those very precisely derived conditions may actually hold. It is also the case in North American leagues that the talent distribution appears invariant with respect to drafts and free agency. Of course, much more work remains to be done before such a statement is even close to definitive.

Perhaps the second overall observation is not so much in the competitive balance outcomes associated with choices made in North American or European leagues, but rather in the observation that the two choose such different approaches to essentially the same problem. By allowing a bit of flexibility in terms of objective function, part of the difference is driven by the North American pursuit of profit and the European pursuit of utility (and in some cases wins). However, clearly the overriding source of the difference in these choices is simply the fundamental difference in organizational structure of the leagues themselves. For example, subject to the rigors of collective bargaining, it is straightforward for North American leagues to choose and institute payroll caps. However, give the wide variety of organizational jurisdiction, as well as the openness of European talent markets compared to those in North America, such caps are administratively simply not possible in Europe.

While form and structure must, therefore, invariably differ in how European leagues pursue competitive balance compared to their North American counterparts, there are at least lessons for each to learn from the others.

Notes

1 This means that the clubs do not form binding commitments to one another in their interactions. Further, equilibrium in the league (market) is based on clubs recognizing that gains cannot be made from further unilateral changes in strategy because of the likely response of other clubs. This approach to modeling sport leagues thus recognizes that clubs engage in a game-theoretic way.
2 In the former case one might think of the talent stock being fixed, such as in the US in which the sports are broadly country specific, with limited international migration. In the latter case, one might think of European soccer, which faces an international labour market. The general theoretical principle, however, concerns the availability of talent, and this might vary across sports, and within countries depending on talent availability and production. These issues are addressed much more fully later in the chapter.
3 Remembering that 'z' represents the cost of talent for teams through their investment.
4 For discussions about the clubs' objective function, see Kesenne (2000), Fort and Quirk (2004) and Vrooman (2007, 2008).
5 At the same time, many European leagues have changed their governance structure and have adopted an organizational form similar to their North American counterparts that have been organized since their beginning in a cooperative-like manner. Based on a comparative institutional analysis, Dietl et al. (2009) explain why European leagues have moved away from a contractual towards a cooperative form of governance.
6 Based on a contest model, Dietl et al. (2008a) show that a system of promotion and relegation enhances the incentives of sport clubs to "overinvest" in playing talent.
7 Note that in an open league with profit-maximizing clubs, even if $\frac{\partial t_2}{\partial z_1} = \frac{\partial t_1}{\partial z_2}$, equation (28.12) would still require $\frac{\partial w_1}{\partial t_1} = \frac{\partial w_2}{\partial t_2}$ for the invariance proposition to hold. This would be true for the trivial case where teams are completely balanced in the first place but, generally, the invariance proposition does not hold for open leagues with profit-maximizing clubs.
8 The logit CSF was generally introduced by Tullock (1980) and was subsequently axiomatized by Skaperdas (1996) and Clark and Riis (1998). See Dietl et al. (2008a) and Fort and Winfree (2009) for studies of the CSF's discriminatory power in sporting contests.
9 As in Rascher (1997) and Kesenne (2007), we refer to this objective function as the utility function of a club. Sloane (1971) was the first to suggest that the owner of a sport club actually maximizes utility, which may include inter alia playing success and profits.
10 Note that the integration of a win preference parameter γ_i for club i allows that the case, in which revenue sharing has a positive effect on marginal revenue, is a feasible equilibrium outcome. Without a win preference parameter, the parameter constellation $b > m_i + m_j$ would not constitute an equilibrium.

11 Note that this "sharpening effect" of revenue sharing has the opposite effect of the "dulling effect." The dulling effect describes the well-known result in sport economics that revenue sharing reduces the incentive to invest in playing talent (see Szymanski and Késenne, 2004).

12 Note that if clubs maximize wins, club surplus depends on the respective win percentages of the clubs. The clubs' wins represent a zero-sum game and therefore enter the objective function of the social planner only as a constant.

13 A cornerstone of the recently approved financial fair play concept is the break-even rule. Beginning in the 2012/13 season, clubs will have to balance their books and operate within their financial means. The new obligation for clubs to break even over a period of time means that they cannot repeatedly spend more than their generated revenues. For the first time in European football, clubs that repeatedly spend more than 100 percent of their revenues will be sanctioned.

14 The degree of financial distress could be measured, for instance, by the ratio of total league debt to aggregate league revenues.

15 However, the objective function of the social planner is defined over the talent investments z_i directly, while the league governing body's objective function is defined over the values of the policy instrument δ.

References

Antonioni, P. and Cubbin, J. (2000) 'The Bosman Ruling and the Emergence of a Single Market in Soccer Talent', *European Journal of Law and Economics*, 9, 157–73.

Arnaut, J.L. (2006) *Independent European Sport Review*, Nyon, UEFA.

Barros, C.P., Ibrahimo, M., and Szymanski, S. (eds.) (2002) *Transatlantic Sport: The Comparative Economics of North American and European Sport*, Cheltenham, UK, Edward Elgar Publishing.

Chang, Y. and Sanders, S. (2009) 'Pool Revenue Sharing, Team Investments, and Competitive Balance in Professional Sport: A Theoretical Analysis', *Journal of Sport Economics*, 10, 409–28.

Clark, D. and Riis, C. (1998) 'Contest Success Functions: An Extension', *Economic Theory*, 11, 201–4.

Dietl, H., Franck, E. and Lang, M. (2008a) 'Overinvestment in Team Sport Leagues: A Contest Theory Model', *Scottish Journal of Political Economy*, 55, 353–68.

—— (2008b) 'Why Football Players May Benefit from the "Shadow of the Transfer System" ', *European Journal of Law and Economics*, 26, 129–51.

Dietl, H., Franck, E., Hasan, T. and Lang, M. (2009) 'Governance of Professional Sport Leagues – Cooperatives versus Contracts', *International Review of Law and Economics*, 29, 127–37.

Dietl, H., Franck, E., Lang, M. and Rathke, A. (2011a) 'Salary Cap Regulation in Professional Team Sport', *Contemporary Economic Policy* (forthcoming).

Dietl, H., Grossmann, M. and Lang, M. (2011b) 'Competitive Balance and Revenue Sharing in Sport Leagues with Utility-Maximizing Teams', *Journal of Sport Economics* (forthcoming).

Easton, S.T., and Rockerbie, D.W. (2005) 'Revenue Sharing, Conjectures, and Scarce Talent in a Sport League Model', *Journal of Sport Economics*, 6, 359–78.

Fort, R. (2000) 'European and North American Sport Differences (?)' *Scottish Journal of Political Economy*, 47, 431–55.

—— (2005) 'The Golden Anniversary of "The Baseball Players' Labor Market" ', *Journal of Sport Economics*, 6, 347–58.

—— (2007) 'Talent Market Models in North American and World Leagues', in P. Rodriguez, S. Kesenne and J. Garcia (eds.), *Sport Economics after Fifty Years: Essays in Honour of Simon Rottenberg*, Oviedo, Spain, Oviedo University Press, pp. 83–106.

—— (2011) *Sport Economics* (3rd edn), Upper Saddle River, NJ, Prentice Hall.

Fort, R., and Fizel, J. (eds.) (2004) *International Sport Economics Comparisons*, Westport, CT, Praeger Publishers.

Fort, R., and Quirk, J. (1995) 'Cross-subsidization, Incentives and Outcomes in Professional Team Sport Leagues', *Journal of Economic Literature*, 33, 1265–99.

—— (2004) 'Owner Objectives and Competitive Balance', *Journal of Sport Economics*, 5, 20–32.

—— (2007) 'Rational Expectations and Pro Sport Leagues', *Scottish Journal of Political Economy*, 54, 377–90.

Fort, R., and Winfree, J. (2009) 'Sports Really Are Different: The Contest Success Function and the Supply of Talent', *Review of Industrial Organization*, 34, 69–80.

Frick, B., Pietzner, G. and Prinz, J. (2007) 'Career Duration in a Competitive Environment: The Labor Market for Soccer Players in Germany', *Eastern Economic Journal*, 33, 429–42.

Kesenne, S. (2000) 'Revenue Sharing and Competitive Balance in Professional Team Sport, *Journal of Sport Economics* 1, 56–65.

—— (2005) 'Revenue Sharing and Competitive Balance: Does the Invariance Proposition Hold?' *Journal of Sport Economics*, 6, 98–106.

—— (2007) *The Economic Theory of Professional Team Sport – An Analytical Treatment*, Cheltenham, UK, Edward Elgar.

Rascher, D. (1997) 'A Model of a Professional Sport League', in W. Hendricks (ed.) *Advances in the Economics of Sport, Vol. 2*, Greenwich, CT, JAI, pp. 27–76.

Rottenberg, S. (1956) 'The Baseball Players' Labor Market', *Journal of Political Economy*, 64, 242–58.

Sandy, R., Sloane, P.J., and Rosentraub, M.S. (2004) *The Economics of Sport: An International Perspective*. New York, Palgrave Macmillan.

Simmons, R. (1997) 'Implications of the Bosman Ruling for Football Transfer Markets', *Economic Affairs*, 17, 13–18.

Skaperdas, S. (1996) 'Contest Success Functions', *Economic Theory*, 7, 283–90.

Sloane, P. (1971) 'The Economics of Professional Football: The Football Club as a Utility Maximiser', *Scottish Journal of Political Economy*, 18, 121–46.

Szymanski, S. (2003) 'The Economic Design of Sporting Contests', *Journal of Economic Literature*, 41, 1137–87.

—— (2004) 'Professional Team Sports Are Only a Game: The Walrasian Fixed-Supply Conjecture Model, Contest-Nash Equilibrium, and the Invariance Principle', *Journal of Sport Economics*, 5, 111–26.

Szymanski, S., and Kesenne, S. (2004) 'Competitive Balance and Revenue Sharing in Team Sport', *Journal of Industrial Economics*, 52, 165–77.

Tullock, G. (1980) 'Efficient Rent-Seeking,' in J. Buchanan, R. Tollison and G. Tullock (eds.) *Toward a Theory of the Rent Seeking Society*, College Station, TX, Texas AandM University Press, 97–112.

Vrooman, J. (2007) 'Theory of the Beautiful Game: The Unification of European Foot-ball', *Scottish Journal of Political Economy*, 54, 314–54.

—— (2008) 'Theory of the Perfect Game: Competitive Balance in Monopoly Sport Leagues', *Review of Industrial Organization*, 31, 1–30.

Winfree, J. and Fort, R. (2011) 'Nash Conjectures and Talent Supply in Sport League Modeling: A Comment on Current Modeling Disagreements', *Journal of Sport Economics* (forthcoming).

29

ATTENDANCE AND BROADCAST DEMAND FOR PROFESSIONAL TEAM SPORT

The case of English league football

Babatunde Buraimo

Introduction

Broadcasting has undoubtedly had and continues to have a profound impact on sport. This is particularly the case for English football. However, this strong link between broadcasting and football has developed over a relatively short period of time, even though both broadcasting and football have much longer histories. The strength of the links between football and broadcasting presents a series of challenges for policy and decision makers. Football authorities and broadcast companies regularly have to deal with issues such as scheduling of matches, bidding for television rights, allocating and selling of broadcast rights, collective versus individual selling of rights, sharing the proceeds among league members, selling rights within secondary markets[1] and dealing with competition authorities.

The importance and relevance of broadcasting is not limited to football clubs and broadcasters. Football broadcasting also has impacts on consumers and it has become the subject of court cases and has attracted the interests of competition authorities. For example, the (then) Monopolies and Mergers Commission (MMC) in 1998 recommended that the proposed merger between Manchester United and British Sky Broadcasting (BSkyB) be prohibited. In 1999, the collective selling of broadcast rights by the English Premier League (EPL) was the subject of a court ruling by the Restrictive Practices Court, a case brought by the Office of Fair Trading. In more recent years, the European competition authorities have taken a continued interest in the collective selling arrangements of broadcast rights in the EPL as well as those of other European football leagues.

One of the main features of broadcasting is its impact on demand for football. Prior to broadcasting, demand for (live) football was limited to stadium attendance. Beyond this, consumption was through coverage in newspapers, on radio, and the transmission of edited highlights on television. However, since the advent of live transmission, consumer demand for football has increased and many more consumers can watch live games on television in the comfort of their homes or in public venues. Broadcast demand for football itself has had a dramatic effect on traditional demand and the way in which football is managed. It is this demand for both live football at stadia and live viewing on television that is the principal focus of this chapter.[2] The chapter examines the emergence of the football broadcast market, and goes on to examine the current situation for both attendance and broadcast consumption. The impact of live broadcasting on attendance demand is investigated, as are the determinants of broadcast demand. This is followed by an examination of the interplay between attendance and broadcast demands. The chapter concludes by noting that league authorities have to manage the dilemma that stadium attendances promote broadcast audiences, but growth in the latter can reduce stadium demand.

The emergence of the football broadcast market

In the early 1980s, there was limited transmission of live English football and much of what was broadcast was limited to a selection of matches from the FA Cup and highlights of league matches. The reluctance of the Football League, who at the time comprised 92 professional football clubs, to expand broadcast coverage was intended to protect its core source of finance, which was matchday revenue; it was thought that having matches televised would reduce revenues for clubs. In contrast, a small number of clubs felt that the Football League could generate more revenue, if only it was willing to engage more with the broadcast market.

The reluctance of the League had dictated the levels of broadcast exposure that the clubs experienced. In 1983, the state broadcaster, the BBC, and the network of independent television broadcasters, ITV, entered into a contract, acting essentially as a cartel, which saw the first broadcast of live games from the Football League. The agreement, which was worth £5.2 million (Baimbridge et al., 1996), meant that the broadcasters would televise ten matches per season; a very small number of games considering the League produced 462 matches per season in Division 1. It is unclear as to whether this small number of televised games had an adverse effect on matchday attendance and revenue, but the Football League sought greater rights fee for the 1985 season and thereafter. Given the lack of competition in the broadcast market for football rights, the broadcasters refused to increase payment and the 1985 season commenced with no agreement. As the balance of power lay with the broadcasters, the Football League eventually settled for a six-month agreement worth £1.3 million to televise six games.

The BBC–ITV cartel was strong enough to exert dominance within the football broadcast market. However, this dominance was challenged with the emergence of satellite broadcasting. While satellite broadcasting was an altogether different broadcast platform (direct-to-home) to that of the incumbent broadcasters, it provided competition within the football broadcast market. Sky Television and British Satellite Broadcasting (BSB) emerged in the late 1980s and while their business models meant that customers were charged directly for programming, their presence, and the mere threat of competition, to the free-to-air broadcasters put a strain on the cartel. This subsequently collapsed when ITV entered into an exclusive agreement with the Football League which foreclosed any involvement by the BBC (Cowie and Williams, 1997). This exclusive long-term agreement meant more broadcast revenue flowed to the Football League and its members.

While ITV enjoyed the exclusive broadcast of live domestic football, further changes were occurring within the broadcast market. Both Sky Television and BSB faced financial difficulties. In order to stem losses, the satellite broadcasters merged to form British Satellite Broadcasting (BSkyB). Another significant change was the growing disquiet among a small number of elite clubs. In the past, the Football League had altered the allocation of broadcast revenues among the four divisions to pacify the bigger clubs, who felt that they should be allocated a greater share of the broadcast revenue. Dobson and Goddard (2001) note that up until 1989 the league had allocated 50 per cent of broadcast income to clubs in Division 1, 25 per cent to clubs in Division 2 and the remaining 25 per cent to clubs in Divisions 3 and 4. With a threat of clubs breaking away from the League, 75 per cent of broadcast revenue was eventually allocated to clubs in the top division, of which 40 per cent was shared among the so-called 'big five' (Arsenal, Everton, Manchester United, Liverpool and Tottenham Hotspur). However, this only served to temporarily halt the inevitable. The big five not only felt that the cross-subsidization policy of the League was inappropriate, they also felt that the League had failed to realize the full commercial potential of the broadcast market. Consequently at the end of the 1991–92 season these clubs, along with 17 others, resigned from the English Football League and formed the English Premier League (EPL).

The start of the EPL coincided with the end of the exclusive ITV–Football League broadcast agreement. In truth, the start of the EPL marked the start of a new broadcast–sport alliance. BSkyB, having struggled with low number of subscribers for its pay service (1.8 million in June 1992), needed a strategy, particularly in light of its direct charge to consumers, to penetrate the UK household market and provide meaningful competition to the incumbent free-to-air broadcasters. Football was to provide what was described as a 'battering ram' approach (Williams, 1994). For the first time in football broadcasting, numerous matches were shown live and the level of payments by BSkyB to the new league was unprecedented. The headline figure was £304 million for five years although not all of this was realized given that BSkyB was unable to penetrate the overseas market; the league did receive approximately £52 million per season (Baimbridge et al., 1996). Table 29.1 shows the contracts for live broadcasting rights before and after the establishment of the EPL.

The football–broadcast alliance proved successful for both parties; BSkyB's finances reverted from losses to profits and clubs in the EPL realized unprecedented levels of revenues, which they were able to spend on better players and improved stadia. The Football League

Table 29.1 Rights fees paid from 1983–84 to 2013–14

Live broadcasting rights for Football League 1985–86 to 1991–92 (all four divisions)

Year	Duration of contract	Broadcaster	Matches per season	Mean annual rights fee (£m)
1983	2 years	BBC/ITV	10	6
1985	6 months	BBC/ITV	6	3
1986	2 years	BBC/ITV	14	6
1988	4 years	ITV	18	19

Live broadcasting rights for EPL 1992–93 to 2013–14

Year	Duration of contract	Broadcaster	Matches per season	Mean annual rights fee (£m)
1992	5 years	BSkyB	60	52
1997	4 years	BSkyB	60	199
2001	3 years	BSkyB	66	371
2004	3 years	BSkyB	88	341
2007	3 years	BSkyB and Setanta★	92 and 46	567
2010	3 years	BSkyB and ESPN	115 and 23	594

★ Setanta's entry into administration saw its final season's rights bought by ESPN.

was now reduced to 70 clubs, which increased to 72 clubs two seasons later. However, it faced weakened revenue streams. The alliance between BSkyB and the newly formed EPL effectively created a monopoly for the broadcast of top-flight domestic football. This monopoly lasted for a number of contract periods from 1992. The first was for five seasons from the 1992–93 season. The subsequent contract period, which spanned the seasons from 1997–98 to 2006–7, saw the continued monopoly, though during this time a competitor in the form of a digital broadcaster, ONDigital (later rebranded as ITV Digital), entered and quickly exited the market as it was unable to compete with BSkyB. ITV Digital's plight was that it tried to compete with BSkyB in the football-broadcast market using an inferior product, live games from the Football League, which it had overvalued. ITV Digital eventually went into administration in 2002 having only paid a fraction of the £315 million owed to the Football League's clubs (Buraimo et al., 2006).

The dominance of BSkyB broadcasting EPL football was scrutinized by the domestic courts, BSkyB having first been prevented from merging with Manchester United in 1998 and the EPL having had to defend its collective selling of broadcast rights. However, it was the European competition authorities that strongly objected to a single broadcaster being able to exclusively broadcast football. By inference, the competition authority's definition of football rights meant that live EPL games were treated as a single market. Therefore the broadcast of matches from, say, the Football League could not be viewed as substitutes for those from the EPL and consequently BSkyB's exclusive contract with the EPL was considered anti-competitive. In fact, disquiet regarding this had been noted for some time and the three-year contract for the 2004–5 season was not sold as a single package but as four. This was to suggest that opportunities existed for competing broadcasters to bid for EPL rights. The four packages were branded as Gold, Silver, Bronze (1) and Bronze (2). Notwithstanding this, BSkyB succeeded in acquiring the rights to all four packages. It is unclear as to whether it outbid all other parties or whether there were simply no competing bids.

For the contract period spanning the three seasons beginning from 2007–8, the BSkyB-Premier League alliance was uneasy about the interest of the European Commission. It had been reported in the media that the European Commission was looking to prevent any single broadcaster from having a monopoly on English Premier League Matches. 'The Commission had insisted that at least two broadcasters must have a viable and meaningful share of football TV rights in England to ensure viewers have more choice' (BBC, 2005). This opportunity allowed Irish broadcaster Setanta to acquire the rights to two of the six packages to show a total of 46 games per season. For the first time, BSkyB's dominance in the EPL rights market had been reduced. Setanta, however, paid a very high price (£392 million) for these two packages but had similar problems to those of ITVDigital. Setanta's broadcast platform had a very low reach and, like ITV Digital, was not able to generate the subscriptions and audience ratings that would allow it to make profits. After all, revenue from advertising depends on viewers. After two seasons of broadcasting EPL football, Setanta went into administration and the broadcast rights for the third season were acquired by ESPN, the American sports broadcaster. The monopoly for live EPL matches that had existed for 15 years is no longer in place and an oligopoly now prevails, with the market dominated by a handful of companies. The extent to which this is good news for consumers depends on the number of televised matches and the price consumers have to pay to watch these.

In the past, the EPL benefited from selling the rights to its matches on an exclusive basis to BSkyB and this has been a key driver in maximizing broadcast revenue. Although the monopoly previously enjoyed by BSkyB has been ended, this does not necessarily mean an end to the substantial sums previously generated by the league. In the present oligopoly, what now matters is the design of the auction and bidding process. With an appropriate design, it is possible for the league to generate demand among broadcasters which should result in increased rights fees. With respect to the broadcast market, the complexities of the market do not preclude a complex monopoly arrangement.

Stadium attendance and audience ratings

The markets for English League football, in the light of the emergence and developments within the football broadcast market, now essentially comprise stadium attendance, the traditional source of revenue, as well as television audiences. A question that will be addressed in the next section is the impact of televised football on stadium attendance. However, before doing so, this section examines the development and state of the two markets.

Revenue from attendance, and by implication the size of matchday attendances, are very important for the League's clubs. This has been and continues to be an important source of revenue for clubs. Matchday attendances have experienced positive growth in the EPL, as shown in Table 29.2. To some extent, the evidence presented in Table 29.2 is not entirely revealing of the positive growth in attendance. In viewing the table, promotion to and relegation from the EPL should be noted. Over the past years, some big city teams have been relegated and replaced by small city teams. For example, over time clubs like Leeds United and Newcastle United, who regularly report average attendances of 35,000 and 44,000 respectively, have been replaced by clubs such as Stoke City and Wigan Athletic, who have a mean attendance of 27,000 and 19,000 respectively. Another important factor to note is that there is a significant number of clubs whose matchday attendances are systematically constrained by the capacities of their stadia. This is the case for nearly all matches of clubs like Arsenal, Chelsea, Liverpool and Manchester United. Furthermore, other clubs from time to time face this problem. Table 29.2 therefore underreports the true level of match day demand for EPL matches.

As matchday attendance and associated revenue have grown, so has revenue from the broadcast market. As noted in Table 29.1, the revenues from the broadcast market have been substantial. Since the 2000–01 season, revenue from broadcasting has dominated that of

Table 29.2 Seasonal EPL attendance

Season	Mean	Standard deviation	Minimum	Maximum
1993–94	23,043	9,891	4,739	45,347
1994–95	24,273	9,026	5,268	43,868
1995–96	27,550	8,835	6,352	53,926
1996–97	28,435	10,070	7,979	55,314
1997–98	29,190	9,930	7,688	55,306
1998–99	30,592	9,841	11,717	55,316
1999–2000	30,756	10,961	8,248	61,629
2000–01	32,906	12,594	14,651	67,637
2001–02	34,469	11,570	15,412	67,683
2002–03	35,466	10,747	14,017	67,721
2003–04	35,020	11,470	13,981	67,757
2004–05	33,917	11,758	16,180	67,989
2005–06	33,888	12,023	16,550	73,006
2006–07	34,357	14,674	13,760	76,098
2007–08	36,076	14,302	14,007	76,013

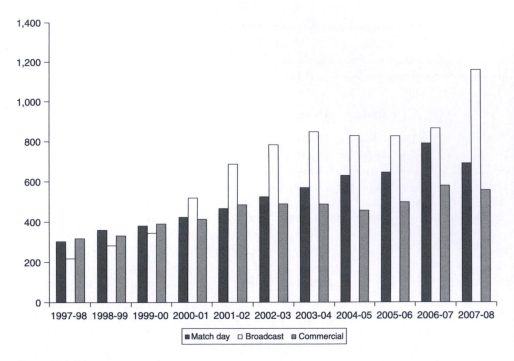

Figure 29.1 Revenue sources by season

matchday takings, as well as other commercial activities (see Figure 29.1). This raises important questions of the relative economic importance of fans who consume EPL games by going to stadia and those who prefer to watch it from the comfort of their homes. The (economic) importance of these two sets of consumers is becoming apparent in the approaches and strategies of football clubs. For many clubs, the revenue they receive from the collective selling of rights is greater than that from matchday attendance. This has prompted some clubs to reduce, in real terms, the price of stadium admission. The revenue that these clubs stand to lose is more than compensated for by the increasing value of broadcast rights fee they receive.

The interplay between the two sets of consumers goes beyond the revenues they generate for the league. Their preferences are somewhat different and this creates complexities within the broadcast market. Fans who prefer to attend matches generally have a preference for weekend fixtures. However, broadcasting normally means rescheduling matches away from the traditional kick-off time of 3.00pm on a Saturday. And while matches are rescheduled at other times during the weekend, the volume of televised matches means that a significant proportion of these are rescheduled on weekday evenings, which is less convenient for those who attend matches. From 1993–94 to 2006–07 inclusive, 24 per cent of matches were played during the week. For the broadcast consumer or 'couch potato', this does not present a problem. It is (in theory at least) conceivable that, as revenue from broadcasting continues to grow faster than that of matchday attendance, football clubs should further subsidize the stadium admission in order to maximize the attendances and makes the product attractive to broadcasters.

For some clubs, the number of their home games that are televised may raise concerns. While broadcasting revenue more than adequately compensates clubs for any losses at the gate, a negative consequence is the disharmony it creates among their core consumers. One means

Table 29.3 Distribution of televised matches in 2006–07 season

Team	Home games	Away games	Total televised games
Arsenal	5	9	14
Aston Villa	4	3	7
Blackburn Rovers	2	3	5
Bolton Wanderers	4	4	8
Charlton Athletic	4	1	5
Chelsea	6	10	16
Everton	6	3	9
Fulham	5	5	10
Liverpool	5	7	12
Manchester City	5	2	7
Manchester United	6	12	18
Middlesbrough	1	3	4
Newcastle United	4	3	7
Portsmouth City	2	5	7
Reading	4	4	8
Sheffield United	4	2	6
Tottenham Hotspur	6	6	12
Watford	4	1	5
West Ham United	7	3	10
Wigan Athletic	4	2	6

of balancing the demands of stadium goers – particularly of those clubs who are likely to generate high television ratings and are therefore more attractive to broadcasters – and those of television audiences is to televise more of the away matches of high-drawing teams. This still allows the broadcaster to show teams which are likely to draw large audiences, but minimizes the disruption to the stadium goers. Consider a rescheduled televised match between two teams, A and B, in which the former is a big-city team and the latter a small-city team. If team A is the home team, the rescheduling of the match to a weekday causes greater disruption as team A has more home fans and team B fewer away (travelling) fans. In contrast, the total disruption is lessened given that the rescheduling will only inconvenience team B's home fans, who are smaller in number compared with team A's, and team A's travelling fans. Table 29.3 shows the distribution of televised matches for the 2006–07 season across home and away teams. From the table it is clear that the four most popular teams have more of their away matches televised compared with home ones. This is necessary if the broadcaster is to maximize audience ratings by showing the most popular teams and, at the same time, not alienate stadium goers even if their economic contribution is less than that of the broadcast market.

Impact of televised games on attendance

There is a growing number of studies assessing the impact that televising sport has on attendance within the stadium. A significant number of these have analysed football. The evidence suggests that the reluctance of the Football League to offer greater numbers of matches for broadcasting was reasonable after all, despite the findings of early research.

Studies that had previously investigated this phenomenon had focused on sport in the US and the results were mixed. For example, stadium attendances at the National Collegiate Athletic Association (NCAA) football have been examined with specific attention placed on broadcasting. Kaempfer and Pacey (1986) examined the relationship between broadcasting and attendance. They examined 72 NCAA teams from 1975 to 1981 and regressed the ratio of average annual attendance to the capacity of the stadium on a number of explanatory variables including the number of appearances by a team on television. They found that rather than adversely affecting attendance, it acted as a complement. Their premise was that television exposure acted as marketing and promotion tools and the more exposure given to a team, the greater its attendance. Fizel and Bennett (1989) also examined the impact of televised matches on NCAA football attendances from 1980 to 1985. They adopted a similar approach to Kaempfer and Pacey by using the ratio of average annual attendance to stadium capacity as their dependent variable. Controlling for a number of explanatory variables, they found that televising matches was detrimental to demand but the number of televised matches over a long-run period had a positive effect. The overall net effect, however, was that televising matches was harmful to attendance. It is interesting that these two studies of the same sport, although over different time periods, should produce contrasting conclusions. This makes decision-making difficult for sport administrators.

With respect to English football, one of the first studies of the impact of televised games on matchday attendance was that of Baimbridge et al. (1996), which was a cross-sectional analysis of the 1993–94 season, the EPL's second season. Controlling for a number of variables, their analysis showed that when matches were televised live on BSkyB's sport channels on Monday, average attendances fell by 15 per cent. Matches televised on Sunday had no significant effect on attendance at normal statistical levels. It would seem that the reservations of the Football League were justified. The financial impact of this decline in attendance, however, was positive. Although televised live matches caused attendance to decline, teams received facility fees which more than compensated for the loss in attendance.

Other studies of football that have investigated the impact of live broadcasting on attendance include Garcia and Rodriguez's (2002) of Spanish football, Allan's (2004) of Aston Villa in the EPL, Forrest et al.'s (2004) of the EPL, Forrest and Simmons' (2006) of the second tier of English league football and, more recently, Allan and Roy's (2008) of Scottish Premier League football, and Buraimo's (2008) and Buraimo et al.'s (2009) of the Championship, the second tier of English league football. All these studies found that live broadcasting of football on television reduced attendance, whether televised on pay television satellite platforms or free-to-air.

When evaluating the impact of television on matchday attendance, the case of the EPL is a special one. Some previous studies have not always acknowledged the capacity constraint problem of the League. Across the 15 seasons from 1993–94 to 2007–08, 40 per cent of matches have been constrained by the capacities of stadia. For this reason special consideration must be given to matchday attendance figures. For example, in the cases of Arsenal, Chelsea, Manchester United and Liverpool, to name four clubs, the reported attendances are not a true measure of demand. The true level of demand is unobserved; these clubs could sell more tickets at current prices. Hence appropriate statistical and econometric approaches are necessary. One approach is to base analysis on those matches whose attendances are not constrained by capacity.

To illustrate this, an analysis of unconstrained matches in the EPL from 1993–94 to 2007–08 (n = 3,305) was undertaken using a fixed effects model[3] for home team and controlling for a number of factors including:

- quality of the home and away teams' players (using wage bills as a proxies);
- the respective performances of the two teams prior to the game;

- whether the match has local or historical significance;
- whether the match is played at the weekend or on a weekday;
- habit persistence of home and away fans.

Matches televised live at the weekend on BSkyB's sport channels reduced attendances on average by 4.8 per cent. For those matches televised live on Monday, attendances fell on average by 8.3 per cent and those televised on other weekdays reduce attendances by 5.4 per cent. During the 2007–08 season, Setanta broadcast 46 matches on its pay television platform. Unlike BSkyB's broadcast, Setanta's had no statistically significant effect on attendance. The main reason for this is that this was Setanta's first season and it had yet to penetrate the market. During the 2007–08 season, BSkyB's mean television audience for EPL games was 1.24 million household viewers while Setanta's was 451,435. Hence Setanta's offering had no substitution effect.

The managerial and financial issues for league administrators are to ensure that revenue generated from the broadcast market compensates for the loss of attendance. In the case of the EPL and BSkyB, the broadcaster has for many seasons compensated the league and its teams. This is principally because the EPL sells its broadcasting rights on a collective basis and the efforts of smaller teams in the league are essentially cross-subsidized. Some European leagues, however, sell their rights on an individual basis, e.g. Spain's La Liga, and while this may suit the bigger teams, smaller teams often find it more challenging to sell their broadcast rights. For such teams, it is vital that they are able to evaluate the negative impact of television on their matchday attendance. It could well be that the rational decision is for their matches not to be televised, assuming there are no additional benefits (besides broadcasting revenue) to having games televised, which is not necessarily the case. The exposure that teams accrue from having their matches televised may itself benefit teams and this is an area for further empirical research.

Television audience demand

The number of studies on television audience demand for sport (and more specifically football) is rather limited compared with stadium demand. One reason is that the market for televised sport is relatively new compared with stadium attendance. Another reason is that data is not widely available. One of the earlier studies of television audience demand in football is by Forrest et al. (2005) in their analysis of the effects of outcome uncertainty on the size of television audiences for EPL matches. Others are Buraimo (2008) on the second tier of English Football and Alavy et al. (2010). A theoretical and empirical understanding of audience demand for football is vital to many of the agents involved in football. In the case of broadcasters, understanding the determinants of the size of television audiences is important. Doing so allows them to select the most appropriate matches for broadcasting in order that revenues from subscription and advertising could be maximized. In the case of leagues, especially where collective selling of rights takes place, at least the minimum value to compensate members should be extracted. For clubs, assessment of audience sizes allows them to determine the market value of their matches.

Forrest et al.'s (2005) analysis of television audience demand in the EPL is interesting for two reasons. Firstly it estimates the likelihood of a match being selected by the broadcaster BSkyB. The broadcaster's role is complex as televising matches is not just a case of selecting the best matches from the schedule. Firstly, there is the constraint that only a proportion of matches may be televised. In the early days of the EPL this was limited to 60. Nowadays it is

138. The selection of matches must be evenly distributed across the number of rounds. It is therefore not possible for the broadcaster to choose an excessive number of matches in one round because the schedule is more attractive and fewer the following round because there are not as many attractive matches. The second constraint is the number of times each team is chosen for broadcast. In practice the broadcaster generally ensures that each team's match is televised live on a minimum number of occasions. It would not be acceptable for the broadcaster to select only the bigger teams for broadcasting for reasons noted earlier. A third constraint is that, to minimize the disruption, during the first half of the season, the broadcaster nominates those matches that are to be televised; during the second half, it can give shorter notice periods to the league and clubs as to which matches are to be featured in its broadcast schedule. Given these constraints, the broadcaster is rational in that it places emphasis on those matches that, *ceteris paribus*, have a greater volume of playing talent on show (as measured using the teams' wage bills) and have a greater level of outcome uncertainty.

The other interesting reason is that Forrest et al. (2005) is one of the first published articles to develop a model for television audience demand. They find in their model that the factors that influence the broadcaster's choice of games to televise are also the factors that influence the demand from television viewers. This suggests that the broadcaster's approach is rational in that its choice of which matches to televise aligns with those which consumers value given the constraints. Television audiences, among other factors, are driven by the talents of the home and away teams and the degree of outcome uncertainty attached to matches. Using the information from the empirical modelling, it would be possible to determine how the determinants of television audience demand might be influenced to maximize television viewers, which is after all one of the main sources of revenue for the broadcaster. The empirical evidence also offers some insight into how the demand for stadium attendance and television could and should be managed; this is now discussed.

The interplay between stadium attendance and TV audiences

To date, the majority of studies of stadium demand and television audience demand have, to a large extent, treated these markets independently in empirical analysis. Given that the demands of stadium goers and television audiences are not independent of one another, the empirical analysis should reflect this. In the above analysis, BSkyB's broadcast of games has an adverse effect on stadium attendance, albeit revenue lost from stadium goers in the EPL is more than adequately replaced by that earned from broadcasting. However, do stadium attendances have an impact on broadcasting? Buraimo's (2008) analysis of the second tier of English league football found that the number of fans in stadia had a positive impact on the size of television audiences. This was also shown to be the case in Spain's Primera Liga (Buraimo and Simmons, 2009). The attractiveness of televised games is not just limited to the players of the two teams. In fact, the (perceived) quality of the televised product is a fusion of the quality of players across the two teams and the atmosphere created by fans in attendance at the stadia. That atmosphere may also impact on the quality of play by the players, which then has an impact on the quality of the game when televised. This is particularly relevant given that television viewers are more easily able to stop their spectatorship if the quality if the game is below expectation. Furthermore, this is also relevant for marketers and advertisers as they are less inclined to promote products and services in empty stadia.

The relationship between stadium demand and television audience demand is also relevant from a financial perspective. In the case of the EPL, and as noted earlier, revenue from broadcasting dominates that from attendance. In other leagues, even major ones, this may not be the case. For example, the revenue generated by clubs in Spain's Primera Liga, although greater than that generated from stadium attendance, does not substantially compensate clubs for the negative impact of broadcasting (certainly not to the same levels as those of the EPL).

What can be made of the relationship between stadium attendance demand and television audience demand? To understand this relationship fully, (some of) the fundamentals of the economics of professional team sport need to be established. Buraimo et al. (2007) in their analysis of market size and competitive outcomes provide empirical evidence of these. They show in a regression analysis that the size of a team's local market and the presence of competing clubs influence performance. However, they also highlight that market size and the presence of competing clubs influence directly the revenues a club generates. Given the levels of revenue generated, this will directly influence the level of playing talent employed by a club. Given the competitive nature of the labor market for players in European football, the best players generally command a higher remuneration and consequently teams' with higher wage bills perform better (see Kuper and Szymanski (2009); Frick (2007); Simmons and Forrest (2004)). Equations 6.1 to 6.3 summarize these relationships. Extending the earlier work Buraimo et al. (2009) and Buraimo and Simmons (2009) provided evidence of the influence of market size and the presence of competing clubs on matchday attendance in the second and first tiers of English League football respectively.

$$\text{revenue} = f(\text{market size, competition}) \tag{29.1}$$

$$\text{wages} = g(\text{revenue}) \tag{29.2}$$

$$\text{performance} = h(\text{wages}) \tag{29.3}$$

Given these fundamentals, what are the impacts of broadcasting and how do they influence the markets for stadium attendance and television audience ratings? The improved performances of teams, as a consequence of acquiring better playing talent, generate better attendances at stadia; this is one of the control variables noted earlier in the model of attendance. The levels of attendance have direct effects on revenue and television audience ratings. As the broadcasters are looking to maximize revenues (and profits), audience ratings are very important, and in turn positively influence advertising revenue. Hence, a high subscription base is not sufficient for a commercial broadcaster; what matters more is the audience ratings for programming generated from this base. Figure 29.2 shows the fundamentals of the market and the role of attendance and television audience demand.

From Figure 29.2, the success of broadcasting as measured by television audience ratings is likely to influence the revenues provided by the broadcasters to the clubs via the league. It is therefore in the interest of league teams to ensure that television audience ratings are maximized, *ceteris paribus*. If clubs do not make a concerted effort to improve the quality of the product for television, this may potentially lead to a fall-out with the broadcaster. For example, Canal Plus, the principal broadcaster of live league matches for France's top-flight domestic league, threatened to withhold payment to the league and its clubs in 2006. The reason was that the quality of football provided by the clubs was deemed by the broadcaster to be generally poor with very few goals (Sport Business, 2006). The quality of football in the EPL, as measured by the amounts spent in the players' labour market, is generally high and consequently creates a sporting spectacle and generates high audience interest. As a result of this and other factors, the broadcasters (BSkyB and others) are willing to pay large sums to the League and its members.

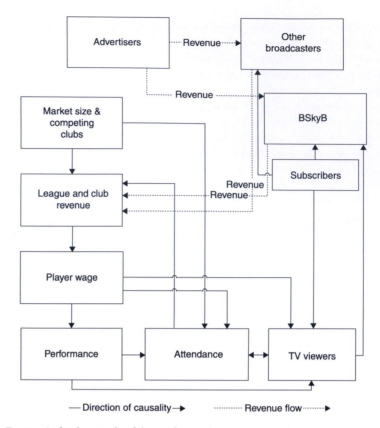

Figure 29.2 Economic fundamentals of the professional team sport market

Conclusions

The broadcast and sport market has evolved over the past years and its developments are typi-fied by those seen within the English Premier League. It is hard to envisage either of these markets functioning independently of each other and their interdependencies have implica-tions for a number of economic agents including leagues, clubs, broadcasters, consumers, players and many others. The developments in these markets have been complex. Competition in the broadcast market has seen major broadcasters in the form of ITV Digital and Setanta enter and exit the market.

Notwithstanding the changes to the supply side of the broadcast market, the developments in English football have coincided with various developments in the broadcast market. In football it is clear that clubs with higher levels of economic power have successfully engaged in regulatory capture and, consequently, this has resulted in the EPL, regarded as the most successful league in Europe and one of the most successful worldwide. The EPL and its clubs have been able to maximize the potential of their offering and monopoly practices have preserved the increases in rights fees that the market has become accustomed to; rights fees have increased over each contract period and clubs have been able to use the proceeds to attract better players and increase player earnings.

There are complexities in the consumption of live sport, however. Traditionally, the demand for football has been dominated by traditional fans visiting stadia on match day. The advent of live broadcasting, while increasing the overall market demand for football, has had an adverse effect on stadium attendance. Clubs, however, have been adequately compensated for matchday revenue losses. While television has had a negative effect on attendances in stadia, stadium attendances have been shown to have a positive effect on television audience ratings. Audiences of the televised product are sensitive to not just the quality of player talent across the two teams involved in the matches, they are also sensitive to the product, that is the size of, and the atmosphere generated by, the crowd. Hence, leagues and clubs need to ensure that the stadium attendances are maximized in order to fulfil the market potential of television. After all, as the scale of television audiences increases, the broadcaster can increase its potential revenue from advertising. The dilemma for those involved in managing consumer demand for football is that stadium attendances are needed to improve television audience ratings; however, televising games reduces stadium attendances. An optimum balance is therefore necessary, particularly given that more and more games are being televised.

Notes

1   Broadcasters often have the option of selling rights to a secondary broadcaster, for example BSkyB in the secondary market buys rights from other broadcasters in addition to those acquired directly from rights owners.
2   This chapter focuses most on the relationship of broadcasting to attendance demand. There is a huge literature examining the determinants of the latter in sport. Interested readers are referred to Borland and McDonald (2003) and Downward et al. (2009), in which recent reviews are provided.
3   This is a regression model applied to data which measures aspects of a set of clubs over time, known as panel data. Qualitative or dummy variables for each club are included in the analysis to capture factors that are specific to the individual clubs.

References

Alavy, K., Gaskell, A., Leach, S. and Szymanski, S. (2010) 'On the edge of your seat: demand for football on television and the uncertainty of outcome hypothesis', *International Journal of Sport Finance*, 5(2), 75–95.
Allan, G. and Roy, G. (2008) 'Does television crowd out spectators? New evidence from the Scottish Premier League', *Journal of Sport Economics*, 9(6), 592–605.
Allan, S. (2004) 'Satellite television and football attendance: the not so super effect', *Applied Economics Letters*, 11(2), 123–25.
Baimbridge, M., Cameron, S. and Dawson, P. (1995) 'Satellite broadcasting and match attendance: the case of rugby league', *Applied Economics Letters*, 2(10), 343–46.
—— (1996) 'Satellite television and the demand for football: a whole new ball game?', *Scottish Journal of Political Economy*, 43(3), 317–33.
BBC (2005) *Football deal ends BSkyB monopoly*, BBC News, 17 November 2005, [online] available at: <http://news.bbc.co.uk/1/hi/business/4444684.stm> (accessed 4 June 2010).
Borland, J. and Macdonald, R. (2003) 'Demand for sport', *Oxford Review of Economic Policy*, 19(4), 478–502.
Buraimo, B. (2008) 'Stadia attendance and television audience demand in English league football', *Managerial and Decision Economics*, 29(6), 513–23.
Buraimo, B. and Simmons, R. (2009) 'A tale of two audiences: spectators, television viewers and outcome uncertainty in Spanish football', *Journal of Economics and Business*, 61(4), 326–38.
—— (2009) 'Market size and attendance in English premier league football', *International Journal of Sport Management and Marketing*, 6(2), 200–214.
Buraimo, B., Forrest, D. and Simmons, R. (2009) 'Insights for clubs from modeling match attendance in football', *Journal of the Operational Research Society*, 60(2), 147–55.
—— (2007) 'Freedom of entry, market size and competitive outcome: evidence from English soccer', *Southern Economic Journal*, 74(1), 204–13.

Buraimo, B., Simmons, R. and Szymanski, S. (2006) 'English football', *Journal of Sports Economics*, 7(1), 29–46.

Cave, M. and Crandall, R. W. (2001) 'Sport rights and the broadcasting industry', *The Economic Journal*, 111, F4–F26.

Cowie, C. and Williams, M. (1997) 'The economics of sport rights', *Telecommunications Policy*, 21(7), 619–34.

Dobson, S. and Goddard, J. (2001) *The Economics of Football*, Cambridge, Cambridge University Press.

Downward, P. and Dawson, A. (2000) *The Economics of Professional Team Sport*, London, Routledge.

Downward, P., Dawson, A. and Dejonghe, T. (2009) *Sport Economics, Theory, Evidence and Policy*, London, Butterworth Heinemann.

Fizel, J. L. and Bennett, R. W. (1989) 'The impact of college football telecast on college football attendance', *Social Science Quarterly*, 70(4), 980–88.

Forrest, D. and Simmons, R. (2006) 'New issues in attendance demand: the case of the English football league', *Journal of Sport Economics*, 7(3), 247–66.

Forrest, D., Simmons, R. and Buraimo, B. (2005) 'Outcome uncertainty and the couch potato audience', *Scottish Journal of Political Economy*, 52(4), 641–61.

Forrest, D., Simmons, R. and Szymanski, S. (2004) 'Broadcasting, attendance and the inefficiency of cartels', *Review of Industrial Organisation*, 24, 243–65.

Frick, B. (2007) 'The football players' labor market: empirical evidence from the major European leagues', *Scottish Journal of Political Economy*, 54(3), 422–46.

Garcia, J. and Rodriguez, P. (2002) 'The determinants of football match attendance revisited: empirical evidence from the Spanish football league', *Journal of Sport Economics*, 3(1), 18–38.

Harbord, D. and Szymanski, S. (2005) 'Restricted view: the rights and wrong of FA Premier League broadcasting', London, Consumers' Association.

Kaempfer, W. H. and Pacey, P. L., (1986) 'Televising college football: the complementarity of attendance and viewing', *Social Science Quarterly*, 67(1), 176–85.

Kuper, S. and Szymanski, S. (2009) *Soccernomics: Why England Lose, Why Germany and Brazil Win, and Why the U.S., Japan, Australia, Turkey and Even India are Destined to Become the New Kings of the World's Most Popular Sport*, New York, Nation Books.

Putsis, W. P. and Sen, S. K. (2000) 'Should NFL blackouts be banned?', *Applied Economics*, 32(12), 1495–1507.

Restrictive Practices Court (1999) *Premier League Judgment*, 28 July, 1999, EandW No. 1.

Simmons, R. and Forrest, D. (2004) 'Buying success: team performance and wage bill in U.S. and European sport leagues', in Fort, R. and Fizel, J. (eds.) *International Sport Economics Comparisons*, Westport, Preager Publishers.

Sport Business (2006) 'French football eyes radical move', [online] available at: <www.sportbusiness.com> (accessed 4 June 2010).

Williams, J., (1994) 'The local and the global in English soccer and the rise of satellite television', *Sociology of Sport Journal*, 11(4), 376–97.

30

THE LABOR MARKET IN PROFESSIONAL TEAM SPORT

The case of football players in Europe

Bernd Frick

Introduction

Since their origin, player labor markets on both sides of the Atlantic – in Europe and in the United States – have been highly regulated. The justifications brought forward by proponents of interventionist measures, that these help to promote competitive balance and financial stability, have always been, and continue to be, welcomed by sport fans as well as the media. While in Europe the situation has changed considerably since the mid 1990s, American labor markets, though subject to modification, have continued to be more highly regulated, a feature that generates market power for team owners and helps hold down the salaries of many players below their contributions to team revenues.[1] In North America these restrictions include:

- A *player draft*, where initial entry into the league is through the organized recruitment of a pool of available players, usually from college;
- A *reserve clause*, where players are tied to their teams until they qualify for free agency; under *restricted free agency* (as e.g. in the National Football League or NFL), players with three years' experience can only negotiate new contracts with rival teams if their existing team has not made an appropriate matching offer comparable to rivals' terms;
- A long period before *free agency* (the freedom to move to any club that makes a suitable salary offer) is achieved. This period is four years in the NFL and six years in Major League Baseball (MLB);
- A *salary cap*, which imposes a ceiling on the total payroll allowed for a team, usually as a percentage of designated revenues (this is applied to teams in the National Basketball Association or NBA, the NFL and the National Hockey League or NHL).

Although none of these restrictions has ever applied in European football, the situation was – for different reasons – quite similar to the one in the US until the mid 1990s.[2] In 1995, however, Belgian footballer Jean-Marc Bosman challenged the "traditional" labor market principles restricting player mobility when his case appeared before the European Court of Justice. Bosman, whose contract with RFC Liège – a Belgian first division club – had expired, was offered a new contract on inferior terms to his previous contract. When Bosman rejected the offer, his club refused permission for him to join US Dunkerque, a French second division club. The player then sued RFC Liège, citing restraint of trade.[3] In December 1995, the European Court of Justice ruled that the provision, whereby out-of-contract players could only move between two clubs in different EU countries if a transfer fee was agreed between the clubs, was incompatible with Article 48 of the Treaty of Rome, which relates to freedom of movement of labor. Moreover, Article 48 was also ruled as incompatible with restrictions on the number of foreign players permitted in a team. Prior to 1995, the European Football Association (UEFA) had set a limit of three for the number of foreign players who were allowed to participate in a European competition match, plus two further players, termed *assimilated*, who had been residents, without interruption, of that country for five years, including three years in junior teams (this was called the *3 plus 2-rule*). This regulation was overturned by the Court's decision because restrictions on the composition of teams on the basis of nationality were deemed a violation of Article 48 of the Treaty of Rome since they discriminated against players from other EU member states and denied free access to employment in EU countries (see Forrest and Simmons, 2000: 20).

The German Football Federation (DFB), for example, decided to expand the right to play professionally in Germany without being considered a foreigner not only to EU residents but to all players living in one of the 51 member states of UEFA. Nevertheless, some restrictions against non-EU players have remained in force until today and are said to be necessary to stop "floods of foreign imports" and to "prevent mediocre foreign players taking the places of domestic players."[4] However, economic theory would suggest that it is difficult to see why clubs should want to employ foreign players who are inferior to domestic players. Since employing foreigners usually incurs extra costs (see Lazear, 1999), foreign players should have some superior ability that makes their employment worthwhile (see Forrest and Simmons, 2000: 21). Obviously, the removal of restrictions on the number of foreign players allowed on a team will lead to an increasing competition for better foreign-born players and a simultaneous decrease in the demand for domestic players. Given these developments, it is clear that labor markets in European football and other sports have far fewer restrictions and opportunities to move are much greater, especially within the European Union countries where freedom of labor to move is a central tenet.

The next section presents data on the economic relevance of European football, which is then followed by basic theory to show how salaries of professional team players might be determined. Some particular issues discussed in player labor markets are then examined. These include the role of player transfers for cash in European football in the former case, and then an assessment of the evidence on the determinants of player salaries in an occupation which is inherently risky, since players can be cut from their teams and may also suffer long-term injuries, in the latter case. The last issue to be considered is the extent to which forms of discrimination against ethnic minorities persist in modern sports leagues. The chapter concludes with a brief summary and some implications for further research.

The economic relevance of football in Europe

For many years football has been a rapidly growing business. Over the period from 1996/97 to 2009/10, annual revenue growth exceeded 20 percent in Italy and Spain and 25 percent in England, France and Germany (see Jones, 2010: 11). In the season 2005/06, average team values in the *Big 5* European leagues varied between €54 and €112 mil., and between €74 and €161 mil. in 2010/11. The most expensive teams (Chelsea in London, Real Madrid, FC Barcelona, Bayern Munich, Juventus in Turin and Inter Milan) have in the meantime reached levels far above €300 mil. each,[5] similar to the team values reported for the most valuable franchises in the US Major Leagues (see Table 30.1).

Table 30.1 Market values of first division teams in the "Big 5" European leagues (2005/06–2010/11)

Country	Season	Aggregated transfer value (in 1.000 €)	Average transfer value per team (in 1.000 €)	Minimum	Maximum
England	2005/06	2.257.600	112.880	36.550 FC Sunderland	366.075 FC Chelsea
	2006/07	2.327.050	116.353	20.800 Watford FC	404.775 FC Chelsea
	2008/09	2.885.175	144.259	34.800 Hull City	403.200 FC Chelsea
	2010/11	3.214.875	160.744	16.050 FC Blackpool	409.750 FC Chelsea
Spain	2005/06	1.653.905	82.695	3.400 FC Cadiz	328.250 Real Madrid
	2006/07	1.938.475	96.924	19.225 Gim. de Taragona	355.850 FC Barcelona
	2008/09	2.450.600	122.530	27.800 Sporting Gijon	399.000 Real Madrid
	2010/11	2.491.750	124.587	15.800 UD Levante	552.300 FC Barcelona
Italy	2005/06	1.726.635	86.332	17.300 Ascoli Calcio	319.500 Juventus Torino*
	2006/07	1.438.420	71.921	14.000 Ascoli Calcio	271.050 Inter Milano
	2008/09	2.268.200	113.410	29.050 US Lecce	325.650 Inter Milano
	2010/11	2.389.285	119.464	20.075 US Lecce	385.200 Inter Milano
Germany	2005/06	1.127.550	62.642	21.800 MSV Duisburg	192.725 Bayern Munich
	2006/07	1.186.075	65.915	16.750 Energie Cottbus	182.150 Bayern Munich
	2008/09	1.410.000	78.333	29.000 Energie Cottbus	254.000 Bayern Munich
	2010/11	1.730.550	96.142	29.400 FC St. Pauli	303.100 Bayern Munich
France	2005/06	1.083.175	54.159	8.100 FC Nancy	156.375 Olympique Lyon
	2006/07	1.100.000	54.991	12.275 AFC Valenciennes	166.425 Olympique Lyon
	2008/09	1.305.200	65.260	25.100 Grenoble Foot	215.800 Olympique Lyon
	2010/11	1.478.550	73.927	14.150 AC Arles-Avignon	195.050 Olympique Lyon

* relegated at the end of the 2005/06 season due to involvement in a league-wide bribery scandal.

Source: <www.transfermarkt.de>, various years

Moreover, the growth rates of the different markets are quite different. While the market value of the average first division club during that five-year period grew by more than 10 percent per year in Germany and in Spain, the growth rate in Italy and France was considerably lower (at 7 percent). Perhaps not surprisingly, the discrepancy in the market values of the top teams from each division (clubs that reach the Champions League regularly) and the market values of the bottom teams in the respective national league has also increased over the five-year interval. Each of the five leagues under consideration includes a number of small-market teams that sometimes do not even reach two-digit figures (such as FC Nancy in France and FC Cadiz in Spain).[6] Since in Europe access to the first division in professional football depends mainly on sporting performance – and not on the size of the market – the variance in team values is considerably higher than in the US Major Leagues, where franchise rights tend to be sold to investors from large metropolitan areas only.[7]

Until recently, however, European football has received less attention from academic economists than any of the *big four* American team sports (football, basketball, baseball and (ice) hockey). The reasons for that lack of interest primarily reflect data availability. This situation is now changing. Szymanski and Kuypers (1999) examined England as an outlier and now in Germany a nationwide Sunday newspaper (*Welt am Sonntag*) and a highly respected football magazine (*Kicker*) have started to collect and publish the data that is required to analyze the (potential) determinants of transfer fees and player salaries.

Thus, the availability of detailed information on player salaries, transfer fees and contract lengths, together with the recent dramatic changes in the regulatory regime governing the football players' now international labor market have convinced an increasing number of economists from all over Europe to devote more attention to that particular market. It is in this context, therefore, that this chapter examines the various dimensions of that market and the forces shaping its operation.[8]

Labor market structure and labor market outcomes

A convenient starting point for an analysis of transfer fee and/or pay determination of sport players in teams is *marginal productivity theory*, which is the workhorse of modern labor economics. In this theory, firms (teams) demand (hire) labor to produce output (team wins). Players are then workers who supply labor services. These players produce team wins in conjunction with other inputs (coaches, training facilities). Players participate in games, viewing of which will be purchased by spectators at the stadium or through television broadcasting. The marginal product price paid by fans is then a weighted average of broadcast fees (for pay TV) and ticket prices for the particular match. If this average price of viewing a particular match is P and matches played are Q then the marginal revenue product of one extra player (L) on a roster is $MRP = P \times dQ/dL$. If total revenue from one match is R and we replace matches played by wins, W, then:

$$MRP = dR/dW \times dW/dL \qquad (30.1)$$

Hence the marginal revenue product of an extra player is the marginal revenue of one more win multiplied by the marginal contribution of the player to wins.[9]

Conventional economics presumes diminishing returns in production. Adding extra players will generate more wins but at a decreasing rate. Then, if the market for players is perfectly competitive without restrictions, market forces will ensure that the wage paid to a player will equal their marginal revenue product. From this principle, it can be deduced that professional sport players are highly paid because their marginal revenue products are high. This could mean that high salaries could be a reflection of high product prices (high marginal revenues from wins) rather than high ability to convert playing effort into wins. This raises the question of whether celebrity players can generate high salaries from their marginal revenue product, independent of their ability to generate wins. For example, a Chinese footballer on an English Premier League team's roster might generate high levels of merchandise sales in Asia. Arguably David Beckham's signing for LA Galaxy might reflect this ability to generate merchandising revenues internationally. However, it is unlikely that players would be selected for teams just because they have high celebrity appeal in mass markets. Celebrity appeal would diminish if the player was revealed to be unsuccessful in helping his team win matches.

It is not surprising that high potential earnings in major sports such as football induce many youngsters to try to gain entry into leagues. Even in lower division football, typical earnings will exceed what players might earn in their next best occupations. In general, increased player earnings will encourage more potential candidates to attempt to join the professional ranks.

At this point, the term "supply" needs further clarification. The number of players on the field at any time in a given sport will be fixed, and team rosters will be fixed in size, either by league rules (as in the NFL) or by convention (as in football). The treatment of supply in sport economics then switches from being number of players to the less easily measured concept of "talent." Many players are available to play professional sport but few have the requisite talent.

In a competitive market, the supply of talent should be upward sloping as wages increase (that is in wage-talent space) while the demand for talent is downward sloping. In market equilibrium, demand for talent should match supply and the resulting salaries should reflect this. The competitive theory does deliver some sensible predictions. If there is an increase in available talent due, for example, to more lenient rules governing work permits for foreign-born players, the supply of talent schedule shifts to the right (in wage-talent space). Player salaries will fall and units of talent (and by implication player quality) will increase, which will be more attractive to fans. Likewise, if there is an increase in the value of broadcasting rights, then the demand for talent schedule, derived from marginal revenue product, will shift to the right. Player salaries will increase and units of talent will also rise. Again this will attract bigger audiences but clubs will face increased player costs.

In major sport leagues, the number of teams or franchises will typically be limited. Premier divisions of European football leagues contain 18 or 20 clubs, although some entry is assured by the system of promotion and relegation. Typically, three clubs are promoted and three are relegated each season. Spain has 42 professional clubs in two divisions and Germany has 56 professional clubs in three divisions, both with a semi-professional tier below this. England's football league is unusually large with a hierarchy of 92 teams in four divisions.

Overall, this means that the number of professional clubs is fairly small and this confers some buying power for teams in the player labor market. But players themselves have some specialized ability. Players are neither completely homogenous nor completely specialized. This creates a situation of bilateral monopoly in which players and teams share a surplus or economic rent. Rent in this context can be viewed as the return to talent above that required to attract it into professional sport. Only a few players who are sufficiently differentiated can shift surpluses (rents) completely into salaries; these players will tend to be the "superstars" of their sport. With bargaining over salaries between team owners and players (or rather their agents) wages will generally fall between marginal revenue product and lowest wage that would induce players to remain professionals. The greater the bargaining power for players, the closer salaries will move towards marginal revenue products. But restrictions on entry into leagues, and a small number of professional teams, will ensure that salaries lie below marginal revenue product.

One plausible rationale for underpayment of players relative to marginal revenue product is that players enjoy rising salaries over their careers as they establish themselves as professionals. But teams may incur costs of training and development. Training tends to be fairly common in style and methods across teams, and only a small proportion could be thought of as specific to the team, i.e. most training is transferable. In the early years of player careers, players implicitly pay for some of the costs of training with salaries that are below marginal revenue product.[10] In later years, assuming they survive in the league, players receive salaries in excess of marginal revenue product both as compensation for earlier underpayment and as an incentive to reject bids for services from rival teams.

The theory of bilateral monopoly is not particularly well suited to European football, since these leagues have a *thick* labor market. This is because players are potentially mobile across many leagues, the number of potential buying teams is quite large and players can sort themselves into hierarchical divisions on the basis of ability.[11] Moreover, in European football free agency is advanced and the barriers to mobility that persist are largely due to culture and language.

Many European football fans will readily identify with an application of the *winners' curse* to their leagues. Teams often seem to hire players without extensive research into their background, attributes, lifestyles and ability to complement existing team members. This is especially the case for imports of players from far-off foreign countries in South America and Africa. Players are sometimes hired largely on the basis of recommendations of agents and video clips. Perfect information on player ability cannot be taken for granted and asymmetric information may have important effects on transfer fees, player salaries and team performance. Mistakes in hiring are often associated with *panic buying* behavior by teams fearing impending relegation and hence substantial losses of revenues. Such vulnerable teams are precisely those which lack the resources and infrastructure to conduct efficient searches for new player talent. But overpayment following such buying is largely due to asymmetric information rather than a winner's curse. Although players' agents like to promote the notion of multiple bidders for player services, the reality is that at most three clubs, and usually just one or two, will be involved in active negotiations over a player's contract.

Summarizing, economic theory predicts that in the absence of labor market restrictions (such as salary caps, reserve clauses and/or draft rules) players will be paid according to their marginal product, i.e. the wage an individual player receives is a function of his talent and his contribution to team revenues (see Rottenberg, 1956). Since the clubs differ with respect to their drawing potential – there are *small market* and *large market* teams – they also differ with respect to their *ability to pay*.

However, since it rests on a number of critical assumptions (such as player mobility, complete information and risk neutrality), the neoclassical model of wage determination has often been rejected not only by sport fans, but also by some highly respected economists, such as "the elementary classical model presents a very poor description of employment relations in advanced economies" (Milgrom and Roberts, 1992: 329).

However, the problems that are characteristic for most – if not all – *real life* labor contracts (information asymmetries, incompleteness, importance of implicit elements) are clearly less important in professional team sport. Here, an individual player's performance can easily be measured, *shirking* can be detected at low cost, and effort and talent can be evaluated not only by a player's current club but also by other teams. It is, therefore, plausible to assume that in professional team sport leagues with an unregulated labor market, players are paid mainly according to their productivity.[12]

Transfer fees in European football

As in any team sport, the trading of players between clubs has always been commonplace in football. Contrary to the major leagues in the US, however, where players are usually traded for other players or for future draft picks, players in European football are usually traded for cash settlements.

Average transfer fees in the German *Bundesliga*, for example, have increased from €350,000–400,000 (in the seasons 1981/82–1986/87) to more than €4 mil. in 2001/02 before they declined again to less than €2 mil. in 2002/03 (see Figure 30.1).[13] In the last five years an upward trend can again be observed. This development, however, seems to be rather volatile, because the standard deviation seems to have increased more than the mean (see Figure 30.2).

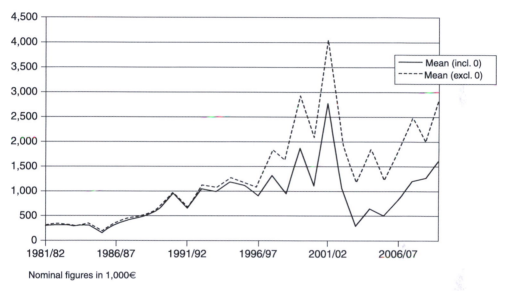

Nominal figures in 1,000€

Figure 30.1 The development of transfer fees in the German Bundesliga (1981/82–2009/10)

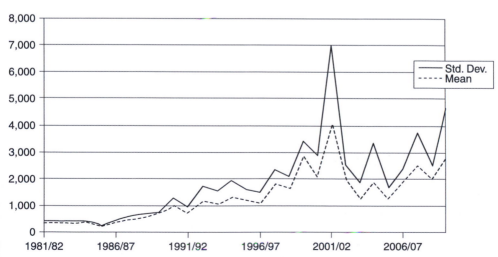

Figure 30.2 Mean and standard deviation of transfer fees in the German Bundesliga (1981/82–2009/10)

This, in turn, indicates that – contrary to the early years of the *post Bosman era* – an increasing percentage of *star players* move from one club to another before their contracts expire. Thus, top clubs bidding for the services of a particularly gifted player do not wait until that player's contract expires but approach that player's current club much earlier than they did a few years ago.

Moreover, the percentage of player moves involving payment of a transfer fee has declined from more than 95 percent in the 1980s and until the mid 1990s to less than 40 percent in 2003/04, before increasing again (to 50 percent over the last couple of years; see Figure 30.3). Clearly, this development is to be attributed to the Bosman ruling stipulating that, for a player who wants to change clubs after his contract has expired, no transfer fee has to be paid. This does not mean, however, that out-of-contract players are "cheaper" than players who still have a valid contract when moving from one team to another. In the former case, the new team usually pays a "signing bonus" to the player. Although these signing fees are usually not disclosed, anecdotal evidence suggests that their level is comparable to the transfer fees that are being paid for observationally similar players still under contract at the time they move from one club to another.

The observable variation in transfer fees can largely be explained by player age, career games played, career goals scored, and international caps, which all have a positive yet decreasing influence on the amount of money paid for the services of a player. Moreover, characteristics of the buying as well as the selling club have also been shown to influence transfer fees: the more successful the buying and/or the selling club is (either in economic or in sporting terms), the higher the transfer fee that the two clubs agree upon (see e.g. Eschweiler and Vieth, 2004; Carmichael, Forrest and Simmons, 1999; Speight and Thomas; 1997a, 1997b; Reilly and Witt, 1995; Carmichael and Thomas, 1993; Frick and Lehmann, 2001; Dobson, Gerrard and Howe, 2000; Dobson and Gerrard, 1999).[14]

There are, however, some extensions to the traditional framework of analysis that deserve to be mentioned in this context. First, since transfer fees are quite often a matter of dispute between the selling and buying club, most European leagues have implemented some kind of arbitration procedure. Controlling for arbitrated settlements (see Speight and Thomas, 1997a,

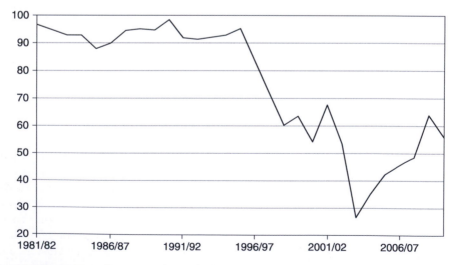

Figure 30.3 Percentage of movers with transfer fee in the German Bundesliga (1981/82–2009/10)

1997b; Reilly and Witt, 1995; Carmichael and Thomas, 1993) produces mixed results. Some studies find that arbitrated fees are higher than those on which buyer and seller agree while others find that they are significantly lower.

Second, since the probability of being traded to a new club is not identical for all players, the estimation procedure employed in almost all of the available studies is likely to produce biased coefficients (see Carmichael, Forrest and Simmons, 1999). Controlling for these individual differences in the probability of transfer via a two-step procedure delivers results that are comparable to the ones produced by simple OLS- or Tobit-estimates. However, it also appears that players who can command higher transfer fees are more likely to be transferred.

Third, particularly since the mid 1990s – since the passage of the Bosman ruling – the number of remaining contract years is likely to be a major determinant of the transfer fees paid (this is due to the fact that under the new regime the old team cannot command a transfer fee any longer when the player's contract has expired). Unfortunately, only one of the available studies has included that variable when estimating a hedonic price equation. Although their results are as expected, the study by Feess, Frick and Muehlheusser (2004) may suffer from a sample selection bias as they have used a rather small sample of transferred players (n = 239). It cannot be ruled out entirely that the cases where contract duration and transfer fee have been published in the popular press are not a random sample of all transfers that have occurred over the period under investigation.

The determinants of player salaries

Contrary to the situation in the US, European football clubs have few incentives to join together to hold down player salaries.[15] Theoretically this is because the individual clubs try to maximize utility (i.e. sporting success) instead of profits (Sloane, 1971; Késenne, 2007).[16] Therefore, increasing revenues from ticket sales, merchandising activities and especially the sale of broadcasting rights have induced a massive increase in player salaries in all of the major European football leagues. In Germany, for example, team wage bills doubled between 1992/93 and 1996/97 and again doubled between 1996/97 and 2000/01 (see Huebl and Swieter, 2002: 111). The increase in individual player salaries mirrors these developments (see Figure 30.4 and 30.5). In 1995/96 and 1996/97 average player salaries reached €550,000. When, in the late 1990s, the league sold the TV rights to the Kirch group, average salaries increased considerably (from €800,000 in 1999/00 to €1.1 mil. in 2002/03). Following the collapse of the Kirch group, salaries went down again (to €900,000 in 2004/05) before they started to increase once more (again following conclusion of a new TV contract). At the end of the period 2009/10 average salaries have stabilized at a level of about €1.2 mil. per year. Thus, the development of players' salaries perfectly mirrors the development of club revenues.

Several empirical studies have examined the remuneration of players in European football. These include Franck and Nüesch (2010), Lehmann and Weigand (1999), Lehmann (2000), Lucifora and Simmons (2003), Huebl and Swieter (2002), Lucifora and Simmons (2003), Lehmann and Schulze (2008), Garcia-del-Barrio and Pujol (2005, 2007), and Frick (2007, 2010). The model structure of these studies is quite similar. In a standard *Mincer-style* earnings function, player salaries are influenced by age, (career) games played, (career) goals scored, international caps, player position, assists and tackles, *superstar status*, and contract duration. While age and experience have a positive, yet decreasing effect, the influence of contract duration is strictly linear. Midfielders and forwards are found to earn a premium relative to

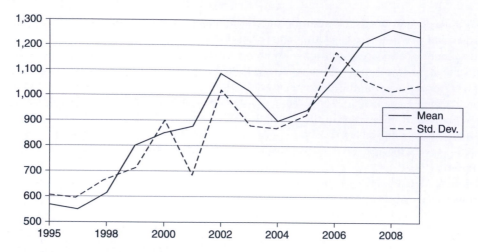

Figure 30.4 The development of player salaries in the German Bundesliga (1995/96–2009/10)

Source: *Kicker* (special issue), 1995–2010; own calculations – figures not available for 1998 – in 1,000€, nominal

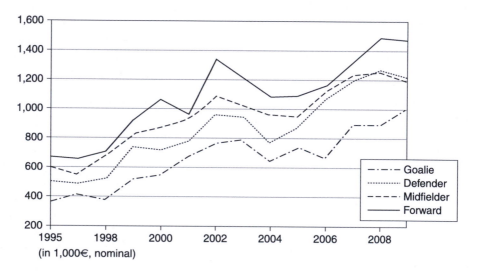

Figure 30.5 The development of player salaries by position in the German Bundesliga (1995/96–2009/10)

Source: as above

defenders. Moreover, presence in the media (measured, for example, by number of Google hits) is also associated with higher salaries.[17] Apart from these individual characteristics, team characteristics (such as attendance, capacity utilization, sponsoring revenues and qualification for international cup competitions) have also been found to affect player salaries positively and statistically significantly.

Recently, three different extensions of the *traditional* estimation framework have emerged in the literature. First, only one of the available studies uses longitudinal data. In this context Frick (2007) demonstrates that player age, career games played and international appearances have a positive, yet decreasing impact on salaries. The distribution of salaries across playing positions is also confirmed. Second, Bryson, Frick and Simmons (2009) also include direct productivity measures, such as the capability of professional football players to control the ball perfectly with both feet, on the individuals' remuneration. They use a large cross–section data set with information on more than 2,500 players who at the beginning of the 2005/06 season were under contract with one of the first division teams in England, France, Germany, Italy or Spain. Controlling for age, height, player position (dummies for midfielder and forward; reference group: defender) and national league (dummies for Serie A, Primera Division, Premier League and Ligue 1; reference league: Bundesliga) it appears that both–feet players enjoy a pay premium of more than 50 percent. Moreover, left–footed players also receive a statistically significant premium of 15 percent. These premiums are identical across the five European leagues (the respective interaction terms are statistically insignificant). This finding is compatible with the idea that due to the liberalization of the national player markets induced by the Bosman ruling in late 1995 a European salary model for players has emerged in the meantime.

Finally, Huebl and Swieter (2002) as well as Feess, Frick and Muehlheusser (2004) find that contract duration has – other things being equal – a significantly positive influence on annual player salaries. This is not surprising as contract length is an increasing function of a player's potential (i.e. better players are signed to longer contracts – which can be termed the *selection effect*). At the same time, however, a player's performance will be lower, the longer his contract (i.e. guaranteed multi-year contracts reduce player effort – a phenomenon that can be termed the *moral hazard effect*). If long-term contracts are indeed used to reward the better players, it remains to be seen whether the selection effect is larger than the moral hazard effect or whether the latter outweighs the former.

The most recent study by Frick (2010) employs a variety of estimators to deal with features of the data. The estimators include an Ordinary Least Squares (OLS) model which is esti-mated with robust standard errors because of heteroscedasticity in the data. This occurs when the variances in the data are not constant and is typical in broadly cross-section data. One possible reason for this is because the data are organized across teams as well as seasons. To potentially control for this a Random Effects panel data model is employed.[18] In addition a Median Regression model, followed by various quantile regressions (.10, .25, .75, .90) with and without bootstrapped standard errors (200 repetitions again to control for any hetero-scedasticity) are employed to explore the possibility that the impact of performance on pay varies across the distribution of pay. A number of studies have employed this approach (Hamilton, 1997; Reilly and Witt, 2007; Berri and Simmons, 2009; Simmons and Berri, 2009; Leeds and Kowalewski, 2001; Vincent and Eastman, 2009). OLS salary regressions are sensitive to the presence of outliers and can be inefficient if the log salary measure has a highly non–normal distribution, as is often the case in professional team sport. In contrast, quantile regression estimates are more robust.[19] The results are comparable to those obtained from OLS as well as RE- and MR-estimation. However, few of the coefficients remain constant over the percentiles.

The estimated model is of the following general form:

$$
\begin{aligned}
\ln\text{PAY} = {} & \alpha_0 + \alpha_1\,\text{AGE} + \alpha_2\,\text{AGE}^2 + \alpha_3\,\text{GPL} + \alpha_4\,\text{CGP} + \alpha_5\,\text{CGP}^2 \\
& + \alpha_6\,\text{CGP}^3 + \alpha_7\,\text{IAL} + \alpha_8\,\text{IAL}^2 + \alpha_9\,\text{IAL}^3 + \alpha_{10}\,\text{IAP} \\
& + \alpha_{11}\,\text{IAP}^2 + \alpha_{12}\,\text{IAP}^3 + \alpha_{13}\,\text{GSL} + \alpha_{14}\,\text{CGS} + \alpha_{15}\,\text{CGS}^2 \\
& + \alpha_{16}\,\text{CGS}^3 + \alpha_{17}\,\text{TEN} + \alpha_{18}\,\text{CAP} + \alpha_{19}\,\text{FDD} + \alpha_{20}\,\text{PD} \\
& + \alpha_{21}\,\text{RD} + \alpha_{22}\,\text{TD} + \alpha_{23}\,\text{YD} + \varepsilon
\end{aligned}
\tag{30.2}
$$

where

- AGE: player age
- GPL: number of appearances in Bundesliga in last season
- CGP: number of career appearances in Bundesliga
- IAL: international appearances last season
- IAP: international appearances in career
- GLS: goals scored last season in Bundesliga
- CGS: career goals scored in Bundesliga
- TEN: tenure with current club
- CAP: captain of team (0 = no; 1 = yes)
- FDD: previous team in first division abroad (0 = no; 1 = yes)
- PD: position dummies (ref.: goalkeeper)
- RD: region of birth dummies (ref.: Germany)
- TD: team dummies (ref.: Borussia Moenchengladbach)
- YD: year dummies (ref.: 2001/02)

Thus, the models distinguish between a player's career performance and his most recent (i.e. last season) performance. The most recent performance (measured by, inter alia, the number of games played, the number of international appearances and the number of goals scored) is, of course, not included in the career performance.[20]

The quantile regression estimates are displayed in Table 30.3.

The main findings from Tables 30.2 and 30.3 can be summarized as follows. First, age, career games played, international appearances over the entire career and international appearances in the last season all have a statistically significant non-linear influence on salaries. The statistically significant coefficient of the cubic term suggests existence of *superstar* effects (Rosen, 1981). A strange result is obtained for career goals scored: the coefficient of the linear and the cubic term are statistically significant and negative, while the coefficient of the squared term is positive and significant.[21]

Second, goals scored last season as well as games played last season have a significantly positive and strictly linear influence on annual income, i.e. there seem to be no decreasing returns to either goals scored or games played. Comparing the returns to career performance and to performance in the last season, it appears that *historical merits* do not count very much, i.e. recent performance is – as expected – far more important than past performance.

Third, defenders, midfielders and forwards earn significantly higher salaries than goalkeepers. The premia for these positions, however, differ considerably across estimations: the effect is most pronounced in the RE estimation and weakest in the MR model. Fourth, region of birth is also important: players from South America and Western Europe receive a considerable pay premium while players from the rest of the world are neither favored nor discriminated against. The pay premium for South Americans and West Europeans is not surprising: other things being equal, players from these regions attract larger crowds (Wilson and Ying, 2003) and contribute more to merchandising revenues (Kalter, 1999). The longer a player has been active for his current club, the lower is his annual salary. Whether this is the result of an adverse selection process (better players are traded while less talented players remain with their old club) or whether some players are willing to forfeit money to stay at home is not yet clear.[22]

Finally, team captains and players who moved from a first division club abroad to Germany are paid a significant premium, too. In the former case this is obviously due to leadership skills

Table 30.2 Estimation results I: various methods

Variable	Random Effects		Robust OLS		Median Regression	
	B	T	B	T	B	T
AGE	.5121	22.43***	.4559	18.99***	.4361	23.71***
AGE^2	−.0092	−21.48***	−.0083	−18.69***	−.0079	−23.12***
GPL	.0191	25.66***	.0240	31.95***	.0226	33.12***
CGP	.0042	7.48***	.0056	11.27***	.0057	12.46***
CGP^2 *100	−.0021	−5.97***	−.0028	−9.18***	−.0030	−10.26***
CGP^3 *10000	.0033	5.46***	.0043	8.07***	.0046	9.06***
IAL	.0848	6.86***	.0903	6.04***	.0909	8.02***
IAL^2	−.0071	−3.56***	−.0081	−2.79***	−.0094	−5.01***
IAL^3	.0002	2.19**	.0002	1.74*	.0003	4.09***
IAP	.0118	4.19***	.0125	5.36***	.0131	5.94***
IAP^2	−.0003	−3.40***	−.0003	4.17***	−.0003	−4.48***
IAP^3 *1000	.0017	2.99***	.0016	3.67***	.0016	3.67***
GSL	.0444	14.24***	.0465	16.28***	.0513	18.26***
CGS	−.0129	−4.71***	−.0114	−4.69***	−.0077	−3.56***
CGS^2	.0002	4.13***	.0002	4.38***	.0001	3.31***
CGS^3 * 1000	−.0011	−3.68***	−.0011	−4.15***	−.0007	−3.11***
TEN	−.0142	−4.43***	−.0187	−6.46***	−.0153	−6.53***
CAP	.2692	6.60***	.3406	10.17***	.3718	10.50***
FDD	.5910	12.46***	.6159	11.41***	.6346	15.11***
DEF	.2113	5.17***	.0990	3.20***	.0539	2.24 **
MID	.2677	6.65***	.1667	5.34***	.0965	4.04 **
FOR	.3157	7.14***	.2167	5.97***	.1020	3.68 **
S_AM	.4494	8.23***	.3778	9.87***	.3824	11.91***
N_AM	−.0822	−0.73 +	−.1785	−1.92 *	−.1510	−2.10 **
W_EU	.2442	6.62***	.1848	7.00***	.1969	8.53***
E_EU	.0774	2.23**	.0329	1.36 *	.0200	0.95 +
AFR	.0654	1.24 +	−.0117	−0.30 +	−.0166	−0.52 +
AS_AU	.0928	1.28 +	.0099	0.20 +	.0185	0.42 +
CONST	5.8725	19.30***	6.8245	21.14***	7.1631	29.21***
Team dummies			included			
Season dummies			included			
N of observations			6,147	6,147	6,147	
Obs. per player			1–13	—	—	
N of players			1,993	—	—	
R^2*100			61,7	62,7	40,5	
F-value			—	164.5***	—	
Wald Chi^2			6,672.0***	—	—	
LM-Test			392.0***	—	—	
Raw sum of dev.			—	—	4,656.6	
Min sum of dev.			—	—	2,772.6	

+ not significant; * p < .10; ** p < .05; *** p < .01

Table 30.3 Estimation results II: quantile regressions

Variable	.10 quantile	.25 quantile	.75 quantile	.90 quantile
AGE	.5415***	.5485***	.3660***	.2829***
AGE^2	−.0097***	−.0099***	−.0068***	−.0055***
GPL	.0347***	.0271***	.0173***	.0124***
CGP	.0050***	.0058***	.0047***	.0030***
CGP^2 *100	−.0027***	−.0034***	−.0021***	−.0001 **
CGP^3 * 10000	.0042***	.0057***	.0030***	.0013 +
IAL	.0340 **	.0568***	.1241***	.1129***
IAL^2	−.0003 +	−.0034 *	−.0149***	−.0114***
IAL^3	.0000 +	.0000 +	.0006***	.0004***
IAP	.0108***	.0119***	.0126***	.0122***
IAP^2	−.0002 **	−.0003***	−.0002***	−.0002 *
IAP^3 *1000	.0014 **	.0019***	.0013***	.0009 +
GSL	.0453***	.0511***	.0486***	.0425***
CGS	−.0094 **	−.0038 +	−.0132***	−.0077 *
CGS^2	.0002***	.0000 +	.0003***	.0002 **
CGS^3 * 1000	−.0014***	.0000 +	−.0001***	−.0009 **
TEN	−.0134***	−.0181***	−.0201***	−.0177***
CAP	.3662***	.3742***	.3114***	.3296***
FDD	.7485***	.6895***	.5848***	.4772***
DEF	.2154***	.1049***	−.0002 +	−.1560***
MID	.2414***	.1458***	.0756***	−.0537 +
FOR	.2832***	.1634***	.1111***	−.0170 +
S_AM	.3010***	.3086***	.3863***	.4230***
N_AM	−.1989 +	−.0509 +	−.2002***	−.2519 *
W_EU	.1999***	.1992***	.1637***	.1627***
E_EU	.0635 *	.0690***	−.0344 +	.0085 +
AFR	−.0153 +	.0538 +	−.0389 +	−.0320 +
AS_AU	.1296 +	.1042 **	−.2022***	−.1494 *
CONST	4.6571***	5.1341***	8.6862***	10.4911***
Team dummies		included		
Season dummies		included		
N of cases	6,147	6,147	6,147	6,147
Pseudo R^2*100	43.6	42.4	39.2	39.2
Raw sum of dev.	2,196.5	3,891.5	3,577.2	1,934.0
Min sum of dev.	1,239.1	2,240.8	2,139.6	1,175.5

+ not significant; * $p < .10$; ** $p < .05$; *** $p < .01$

that are required for the job and that are, therefore, particularly rewarded in the market (Kuhn and Weinberger, 2005; Deutscher, 2009).

Few of the coefficients retain their magnitude across the different quantiles of the salary distribution[23]:

- Generally, the maximum income is reached at an age of about 27 or 28 years. The age-earnings profile, however, is much flatter for the players with the highest incomes.
- The impact of games played last season as well as career games played on annual salaries is much stronger for players at the bottom of the income distribution.

- International appearances (past as well as current) seem to have a much stronger influence on the salaries of the players at the top of the income distribution.
- Goals scored (past as well as most recent season), tenure with the current club and being a team captain seem to have a more or less constant impact on player salaries, i.e. the coefficients are quite similar for the different quantiles.
- The coefficients of the position dummies change considerably across the income distribution, indicating that goalkeepers are the "real superstars" in the business.[24]
- The pay premium enjoyed by players from South America increases across the pay distribution while the premium of players from Western Europe decreases.[25]

Is discrimination an issue in European football?

Especially since the mid 1990s, the percentage of foreign-born players has been increasing in most, if not all, of the European football leagues (today, even Russian teams hire players from Brazil or from Africa). In the German Bundesliga, for example, the percentage of German-born players has dropped from more than 95 percent in the 1960s to less than 50 percent in the most recent seasons (similar developments have occurred in the English Premier League and, to a lesser extent, in Italy and Spain, too). Although this is prima facie evidence against the hypothesis that managers, domestic players and/or fans are discriminating against foreigners, it is at best a necessary, but certainly not a sufficient condition. Discrimination is said to occur when individual characteristics of a player (such as his race or nationality) that are clearly irrelevant for his productivity have an influence on pay, transfer fees, playing time, and career duration.

A number of studies have analyzed various aspects of discrimination. Although the evidence is not completely conclusive, discrimination is apparently not a problem in European football: Pedace (2008) finds that in the English Premier League an increasing percentage of players from South America is detrimental to team performance, but at the same time increases attendance. Preston and Szymanski (2000) corroborate this finding with respect to black players: the number of appearances by black players has a significantly positive influence on team performance, but no effect on gate attendance (with similar results, see Wilson and Ying, 2003).

Moreover, foreign players in the Bundesliga are not paid less, but very often are paid more than otherwise similar German players: Frick (2007, 2010), for example, finds that players from Eastern Europe earn salaries about 15 percent higher than comparable German athletes while players from Western Europe have a 30 percent higher pay and the "ball artists" from South America enjoy a 50 percent premium. These findings are not only in accordance with the argument that in a highly competitive (labor) market discrimination is unlikely to persist; they also suggest that all the players are paid according to their marginal product: players attracting additional spectators and inducing these additional spectators to buy merchandising products have a higher remuneration – even after their contribution to the performance on the pitch has been controlled for.

Similarly, country of origin usually has no influence on the transfer fees paid once individual player characteristics are controlled for. Neither Frick and Lehmann (2001) nor Reilly and Witt (1995), who explicitly address the question, find any evidence of discrimination against, for example, black players or players from Eastern Europe.

Finally, Frick, Pietzner and Prinz (2007, 2009) suggest that there is no discrimination against players from specific areas of the world with regard to the duration of their individual careers. The positive and statistically significant coefficients for Eastern Europeans, Western

Europeans and South Americans may at first suggest that players from these regions face a higher risk of being eliminated from the Bundesliga. This, however, is certainly not necessarily indicative of discrimination in the sense that either managers or spectators prefer players of German origin. Rather, especially players from Western Europe and South America often leave the Bundesliga because they sign more lucrative contracts with teams in Spain, Italy, England and France. This explanation, however, does not apply in the case of players from Eastern Europe, who may indeed suffer from discrimination: Kalter (1999), for example, has recently shown that the number of replica shirts sold is significantly influenced by the players' origin: while shirts with the names of players from Eastern Europe do not sell well, those with the names of South American players are bestsellers.

Thus, the finding that teams may discriminate against players from Eastern Europe should be subject to further research. The most pertinent question in this context is whether teams pay a penalty for their management's or their supporters' taste for discrimination (for empirical evidence on this point see, for example, Szymanski, 2000).

Conclusions

Since the mid 1990s, the labor market for football players has been subject to an already large and still increasing number of empirical studies. That growth can be attributed to a number of different, yet closely related developments. First, the football industry has in the last 15 years enjoyed unprecedented growth, which has turned it into an economically relevant part of the service sector in general and the entertainment industry in particular. Second, the labor market for football players has experienced changes in its regulatory framework that are unparalleled in other labor markets. Starting with the Bosman ruling of the European Court of Justice and subsequent developments, the labor market has liberalized, encouraging economists to examine it. Third, the increasing availability of detailed information on player salaries, transfer fees, contract lengths and career durations has made thorough empirical analyses feasible in Europe that, until recently, could only be conducted by economists working with data from the Major Leagues in the US. This chapter has reviewed those developments.

These developments notwithstanding, a number of questions have not yet been dealt with adequately:

- In principle, a large number of additional measures to explain the observable variance in player salaries are available to the researcher, but have not yet been used in empirical analyses: each player appearing in a regular season match in the German Bundesliga for at least thirty minutes is graded by the journalists of a highly respected football magazine (*Kicker*) with a *school grade*. Given the relative paucity of individual performance measures, such a composite index should be used in further analyses.
- With only one exception, none of the available studies on the determinants of transfer fees takes into account the fact that remaining contract duration is likely to be of major importance. This deficit is certainly due to the fact that the duration of individual player contracts is usually not disclosed. Assembling that information for a representative sample of players is very time-consuming and, therefore, costly.
- The duration of individual player contracts apparently varies with the peculiarities of the regulatory regime. Following the Bosman ruling, average contract length increased by about 20 percent. It is very likely, that under the new *Monti regime*, which stipulates a maximum contract length of five years, the average has declined again. Since contract

duration is an important part of an incentive-compatible remuneration package, the behavioral consequences of alternative contract lengths deserve closer investigation.

- The empirical analysis of individual career durations is still in its infant stage. Although most of the required information is easily accessible, more elaborate models that distinguish between *voluntary* and *involuntary* separations have yet to be estimated. Moreover, since that data is usually available for rather long periods of time (several decades), it is also possible to analyze changes in the relative importance of player and team characteristics as well as the impact of changes in the regulatory regime.

- Although the high (and still increasing) shares of foreign players seem to suggest that discrimination is not an issue in European football, several findings warrant further investigation. If, for example, players from Eastern Europe have – other things being equal – shorter careers and sell fewer replica shirts while having no adverse effects on ticket demand, discrimination may or may not exist. Clearly, further analyses using additional data (such as *player of the match* or *team of the day* information) are required.

- Finally, we certainly need more comparative studies that carefully control for the peculiarities of the national labour markets.[26] However, given the liberalization of the player market and the internationalization of the individual teams in each of the leagues under consideration one would expect virtually identical coefficients in hedonic salary and/or transfer fee equations using data from different leagues.

Notes

1 Moreover, American labor markets are characterized by closed structures with few imports from overseas until today. Finally, the small number of professional franchises in major North American leagues (generally just over 30 in any league) also contributes to buyer power in the player labor market.

2 The English Football League (comprising tiers two through four) operates a voluntary restraint on ratios of payroll to turnover of less than 70 percent while a hard salary cap is imposed in English rugby league and rugby union.

3 The details of Bosman's old contract, the new contract offered to him by RFC Liège and the offer made by US Dunkerque are discussed in more detail in Campbell and Sloane (1997).

4 Subsequent changes to labor markets since the Bosman ruling have also occurred. The Kolpak ruling from the European Court of Justice in 2003 declared that it was ineligible to remove Maroš Kolpak, a Slovak handball player, from his German team beacuse a quota of two non-EU players was met. The ruling declared that citizens of certain countries, which have signed agreements with the European Union, have the same right to freedom of work and movement within the EU as EU citizens. The Kolpak ruling has been particularly influential in increasing the mobility of foreign players in rugby and cricket to and from the UK from Commonwealth countries, as well as North African football players to France and throughout Europe.

5 The Russian "Premier Liga" is number six in terms of the aggregated market value of its teams. Their value, however, is half of that of the French teams. In terms of sporting performance in the Champions League and in the UEFA Cup (now called "Europa League"), the Russian league is again ranked sixth in Europe. However, during the last five years the Russian teams have been considerably less successful on the pitch than the French clubs (for the development of the five-year-moving average of club performances see UEFA, 2010).

6 It is no accident that the names of the poor *teams* change while those of the rich *teams* remain the same. Given the close relationship between market values and sporting performance (see e.g. Szymanski and Kuypers 1999), the poor teams are very likely to be relegated at the end of the season.

7 Individual player salaries and endorsement contracts for football celebrities are now on a par with the incomes of American Basketball, Baseball and Football stars. Top players such as Cristiano Ronaldo, Zlatan Ibrahimovic, Lionel Messi, Samuel Eto'o and Kaka are all earning between 10 and 20 mil. € per year (these are base salaries not including bonus payments, signing fees and/or income from endorsement contracts). The five-year contract that David Beckham signed in January 2007

with Los Angeles Galaxy of the US Major League Soccer is estimated at 250 mil. € (including endorsements). This is by far the most lucrative contract that has even been agreed upon in professional football.

8 Although closely related to the players' labor market the chapter does not examine the existing literature on head coaches (see e.g. Audas, Dobson and Goddard, 2002; Bruishoofd and ter Weel, 2003; Dawson, Dobson and Gerrard, 2000; Barros, Frick and Passos, 2009; Barros, Frick and Prinz, 2010; Breuer and Singer, 1996; Dios Tena and Forrest, 2007; Frick and Simmons, 2008; Hautsch, Frick, Lehmann and Warning, 2001; Koning, 2003; Poulsen, 2000; ter Weel, 2006). Moreover, the literature on team wage bills and playing success (see e.g. Frick, 2005; Forrest and Simmons, 2002, 2004; Hall, Szymanski and Zimbalist, 2004; Lehmann and Weigand, 1997; Szymanski and Kuypers, 1999; Szymanski and Smith, 1997) is not discussed as it is only indirectly related to the labor market issues discussed here.

9 Note that this makes revenues a function of wins and not matches; losses do not count towards revenue.

10 Unfortunately, estimates of training costs and associated comparisons of salary and marginal revenue product are not available for European football. It is notable, though, that top division teams have expanded their training facilities over the last decade and have simultaneously begun to use "nursery teams."

11 In North American leagues, buyer power is observed partly because the number of teams is small but also because there are considerable restrictions on free agency.

12 Contrary to the findings reported by Horowitz and Zappe (1998) for baseball veterans, this suggests that *nostalgia effects* will be of minor importance only.

13 The development was (and continues to be) very similar in, for example, the United Kingdom (see Dobson and Gerrard, 1999).

14 The available econometric analyses differ considerably with regard to sample size: While Dobson and Gerrard (1999) as well as Frick and Lehmann (2001) use information on more than 1,200 transfers, the remaining studies use between 100 and 250 observations.

15 This also applies to other team sports, such as handball, basketball, volleyball and ice hockey.

16 The ensuing rat race has, in turn, led to massive financial problems in most, if not all, of the European leagues (with regard to the five leagues under consideration in this chapter see Baroncelli and Lago, 2006; Buraimo, Simmons and Szymanski, 2006; Gouget and Primault, 2006; Ascari and Gagnepain, 2006; Frick and Prinz, 2006).

17 Significant impacts of experience, performance and peer reputation on salary can also be found in studies of North American sport: see Hamilton (1997) on basketball, Kahn (1993) for baseball, Berri and Simmons (2009) and Simmons and Berri (2009) on American football and Idson and Kahane (2000) for hockey. These papers show that the salaries of professional sport players are influenced systematically by factors such as age, experience and performance in very similar ways to those found in other occupations. Where sport teams differ is in the distribution of salaries, which is even more highly skewed than in standard occupations. Also sport teams apply more stringent selection procedures into occupations. For example, poor performance by a player results in his being dropped from the team squad and very quickly being discarded; there are high levels of mobility within the industry (between teams) and into and out of the industry, with shorter careers than in most occupations. The large skewness of the salary distribution and high degree of player mobility appear to apply to all team sport, including North American major leagues as well as European football.

18 Although the Hausman Test suggests using the results from the fixed effects estimation, the findings of the random effects estimation are reported. The problem is that region of birth is a constant for each player and cannot be used in a fixed effects estimation. However, the differences between the remaining coefficients in the RE and the FE estimations are negligible.

19 Presence of non-normality is indicated by a large kurtosis value and the D'Agostino et al. (1990) test is performed by the sktest command in the econometric software program Stata 10.1. In the panel used by Frick (2010), the p-value for the test statistic of the null hypothesis that kurtosis does not depart from the value associated with a normal distribution is 0.000 and hence the log salary data depart from normality, which justifies the use of these methods.

20 Contrary to the situation in most American team sport leagues with their abundance of performance figures, measurement of individual player performance in (European) football can be problematic, especially for defenders, whose task it is to prevent the opposing team's forwards from

scoring goals. While counting the number of goals scored, shots on goal and assists is straightforward, it is far more difficult to assess the performance of defensive players. In future work the models should, therefore, be estimated separately for the different groups of players.

21 This unexpected result survives a number of different specifications: interacting the number of career goals with the position dummies leaves the finding virtually unaffected. Moreover, estimating the model separately by position yields the same result for forwards and midfielders, but not for defenders. Estimating the model only for position players (i.e. without the goalkeepers) again yields the strange coefficients.

22 Anecdotal evidence seems to support the argument that some players suffer from homesickness once they are traded to another club.

23 Estimating the models with the lagged annual salary to control for unobserved heterogeneity reduces the same size considerably (from 6,100 player-year-observations to 4,700). Although most of the coefficients retain their statistical significance, their magnitudes are somewhat reduced.

24 This term was first used by Alan Krueger (2005), who analyzes the revenues generated by particularly successful rock bands and musicians.

25 In further research subjective evaluations of a player's performance (e.g. school grades) will also be used to estimate the hedonic wage equations.

26 Most of the foreign players in each of the five leagues under consideration tend to come from rather homogeneous regions: in Germany, a large portion of foreign players come from Eastern Europe, while in France players from Africa are over-represented among the foreign-born athletes. In England, it is players from the Scandinavian countries while in Italy and Spain South American players occupy a dominant position.

References

Antonioni, P. and J. Cubbin (2000) 'The Bosman Ruling and the Emergence of a Single Market in Soccer Talent', *European Journal of Law and Economics*, 9, 157–73.

Ascari, G. and P. Gagnepain (2006) 'Spanish Football', *Journal of Sports Economics*, 7, 76–89.

Audas, R., S. Dobson and J. Goddard (2002) 'The Impact of Managerial Change on Team Performance in Professional Sport', *Journal of Economics and Business*, 54, 633–50.

Baroncelli, A. and U. Lago (2006) 'Italian Football', *Journal of Sports Economics*, 7, 1328.

Barros, C., B. Frick and J. Passos (2009) 'Coaching for Survival: The Hazards of Head Coach Careers in the German Bundesliga', *Applied Economics*, 41, 3303–11.

Barros, C., B. Frick and J. Prinz (2010) 'Analyzing Head Coach Dismissals in the German Bundesliga with a Mixed Logit Approach', *European Journal of Operational Research*, 200, 151–59.

Berri, D.J. and R. Simmons (2009) 'Race and the Evaluation of Signal Callers in the National Football League.' *Journal of Sports Economics*, 10, 23–43.

Breuer, V. and R. Singer (1996) 'Trainerwechsel im Laufe der Spielsaison und ihr Einfluss auf den Mannschaftserfolg', *Leistungssport*, 26, 41–46.

Bruinshoofd, A. and B. ter Weel (2003) 'Managers to Go? Performance Dips Reconsidered with Evidence from Dutch Football', *European Journal of Operational Research*, 148, 233–46.

Bryson, A., B. Frick and R. Simmons (2009) 'The Returns to Scarce Talent: Footedness and Player Remuneration in European Soccer', *Discussion Paper No. 339*, London, National Institute of Economic Research.

Buraimo, B., R. Simmons and S. Szymanski (2006) 'English Football', *Journal of Sports Economics*, 7, 29–46.

Campbell, A. and P.J. Sloane (1997) 'The Implications of the Bosman Case for Professional Football', *Discussion Paper 97–02*, University of Aberdeen, Department of Economics.

Carmichael, F. and D. Thomas (1993) 'Bargaining in the Transfer Market: Theory and Evidence', *Applied Economics*, 25, 1467–76.

Carmichael, F., D. Forrest and R. Simmons (1999) 'The Labour Market in Association Football: Who Gets Transferred and for How Much?' *Bulletin of Economic Research*, 51, 125–50.

D'Agostino, R.B., A. Balanger and R.B. D'Agostino (1990) 'A Suggestion for Using Powerful and Informative Tests of Normality', *The American Statistician*, 44, 316–27.

Dawson, P., S. Dobson and B. Gerrard (2000) 'Estimating Coaching Efficiency in Professional Team Sport: Evidence from English Association Football', *Scottish Journal of Political Economy*, 47, 299–421.

Deutscher, C. (2009) 'The Payoff to Leadership in Teams', *Journal of Sports Economics*, 10, 429–38.

Dilger, A. (2001) 'The Ericson Case', *Journal of Sports Economics*, 2, 194–97.

Dios Tena, J. and D.K. Forrest (2007) 'Within-Season Dismissal of Football Coaches: Statistical Analysis of Causes and Consequences', *European Journal of Operational Research*, 181, 362–73.

Dobson, S. and B. Gerrard (1999) 'The Determination of Player Transfer Fees in English Professional Soccer', *Journal of Sport Management*, 13, 259–79.

Dobson, S., B. Gerrard and S. Howe (2000) 'The Determination of Transfer Fees in English Nonleague Football', *Applied Economics*, 32, 1145–52.

Ericson, T. (2000) 'The Bosman Case: Effects of the Abolition of the Transfer Fee', *Journal of Sports Economics*, 1, 203–18.

Eschweiler, M. and M. Vieth (2004) 'Preisdeterminanten bei Spielertransfers in der Fußball-Bundesliga', *Die Betriebswirtschaft*, 64, 671–92.

Feess, E. and G. Muehlheusser (2003a) 'The Impact of Transfer Fees on Professional Sport: An Analysis of the New Transfer System for European Football', *Scandinavian Journal of Economics*, 105, 139–54.

—— (2003b) 'Transfer Fee Regulations in European Football', *European Economic Review*, 47, 645–68.

Feess, E., B. Frick and G. Muehlheusser (2004) 'Legal Restrictions on Outside Trade Clauses – Theory and Evidence from German Soccer', *Discussion Paper No. 1140*, Bonn, Institut Zukunft der Arbeit.

Forrest, D. and R. Simmons (2000) 'Employment Rights in Team Sport: Towards Free Agency'. *Mimeo*, Centre for Sport Economics, University of Salford.

—— (2002) 'Team Salaries and Playing Success. A Comparative Perspective', *Zeitschrift für Betriebswirtschaft*, Ergänzungsheft 4, Sportökonomie, 72, 221–37.

—— (2004) 'Buying Success: Team Performance and Wage Bills in U.S. and European Sport Leagues', in Fort, R. and J. Fizel (eds.), *International Sport Economics Comparisons*, Westport, CT, Praeger, pp. 123–40.

Franck, E. and S. Nüesch (2010) 'Talent and/or Popularity – What does it Take to Be a Superstar?' *Economic Inquiry* (forthcoming).

Frick, B. (2005) 'und Geld schießt eben doch Tore: Die Voraussetzungen sportlichen und wirtschaftlichen Erfolges in der Fußball-Bundesliga', *Sportwissenschaft*, 35, 250–70.

—— (2007) 'Salary Determination and the Pay-Performance Relationship in Professional Soccer: Evidence from Germany', in Rodriguez, P., S. Késenne and J. Garcia (eds.), *Sport Economics After Fifty Years: Essays in Honour of Simon Rottenberg*, Oviedo, Ediciones de la Universidad de Oviedo, pp. 125–46.

—— (2010) 'The Football Players' Labor Market: Recent Developments and Econom(etr)ic Evidence', *mimeo*, Department of Management, University of Paderborn.

Frick, B. and E. Lehmann (2001) 'Die Kosten der externen Rekrutierung qualifizierten Personals: Empirische Evidenz aus dem professionellen Fußball,' in Backes-Gellner, U. et al. (eds.), *Entlohnung, Arbeitsorganisation und personalpolitische Regulierung*, München, Rainer Hampp Verlag, pp. 243–63.

Frick, B. and J. Prinz (2006) 'Crisis? What Crisis? Football in Germany', *Journal of Sports Economics*, 7, 60–75.

Frick, B. and R. Simmons (2008) 'The Impact of Managerial Quality on Organizational Performance: Evidence from German Soccer', *Managerial and Decision Economics*, 29, 593–600.

Frick, B., G. Pietzner and J. Prinz (2007) 'Career Duration in a Competitive Environment: The Labor Market for Soccer Players in Germany', *Eastern Economic Journal*, 33, 429–42.

—— (2009) 'Team Performance and Individual Career Duration: Evidence from the German Bundesliga', in Andersson, P., P. Ayton and C. Schmidt (eds.), *Myths and Facts about Football: The Economics and Psychology of the World's Greatest Sport*, Cambridge, Cambridge Scholars Press, pp. 327–48.

Garcia-del-Barrio, P. and F. Pujol (2005) 'Pay and Performance in the Spanish Soccer League: Who Gets the Expected Monopsony Rents?' *Working Paper No. 05/04*, Faculty of Economics, University of Navarra.

—— (2007) 'Hidden Monopsony Rents in Winner-Take-All Markets: Sport and Economic Contribution of Spanish Soccer Players', *Managerial and Decision Economics*, 28, 57–70.

Gouget, J.-J. and D. Primault (2006) 'The French Exception', *Journal of Sports Economics*, 7, 47–59.

Hall, S., S. Szymanski and A. Zimbalist (2002) 'Testing Causality between Team Performance and Payroll: The Cases of Major League Baseball and English Soccer', *Journal of Sports Economics*, 3, 149–68.

Hamilton, B.H. (1997) 'Racial Discrimination and Basketball Salaries in the 1990s', *Applied Economics*, 29, 287–96.

Hautsch, N., B. Frick, E. Lehmann and S. Warning (2001) 'Shirking or Mismatch? Coach-Team Separations in German Soccer', *mimeo*, University of Konstanz.

Huebl, L. and D. Swieter (2002) 'Der Spielermarkt in der Fußball-Bundesliga', *Zeitschrift für Betriebswirtschaft*, Ergänzungsheft 4, Sportökonomie, 72, 105–25.

Horowitz, I. and C. Zappe (1998) 'Thanks for the Memories: Baseball Veterans' End-of-Career Salaries', *Managerial and Decision Economics*, 19, 377–82.

Idson, T. and L.H. Kahane (2000) 'Team Effects on Compensation: An Application to Salary Determination in the National Hockey League', *Economic Inquiry*, 28, 345–57.

Jones, D. (2010) *National Interest: Annual Review of Football Finance*, Manchester, Deloitte Sport Business Group.

Kahn, L.H. (1993) 'Free Agency, Long-Term Contracts and Compensation in Major League Baseball', *Review of Economics and Statistics*, 75, 157–64.

Kahn, L.M. (2000) 'The Sport Business as a Labor Market Laboratory', *Journal of Economic Perspectives*, 14, 75–94.

Kalter, F. (1999) 'Ethnische Kundenpräferenzen im professionellen Sport? Der Fall der Fußballbundesliga', *Zeitschrift für Soziologie*, 28, 219–34.

Késenne, S. (2007) 'The Peculiar International Economics of Professional Football in Europe', *Scottish Journal of Political Economy*, 54(3), 388–99.

Kicker (1995–2005) *Sonderheft Bundesliga*, published annually at the beginning of the season, Nürnberg, Olympia-Verlag.

Koning, R. (2003) 'An Econometric Evaluation of the Firing of a Coach on Team Performance', *Applied Economics*, 35, 555–64.

Krueger, A.B. (2005) 'The Economics of Real Superstars: The Market for Rock Concerts in the Material World', *Journal of Labor Economics*, 23, 1–30.

Kuhn, P. and C. Weinberger (2005) 'Leadership Skills and Wages', *Journal of Labor Economics*, 23, 395–436.

Lazear, E.P. (1999) 'Globalisation and the Market for Team-mates', *Economic Journal*, 109, F15–F40.

Leeds, M. and S. Kowalewski (2001) 'Winner Take All in the NFL. The Effect of the Salary Cap and Free Agency on the Compensation of Skill Position Players', *Journal of Sports Economics*, 2, 244–56.

Lehmann, E. (2000) 'Verdienen Fußballspieler was sie verdienen?' in Schellhaaß, H.-M. (ed.), *Sportveranstaltungen zwischen Liga-und Medieninteressen*, Karl Hofmann, Schorndorf, pp. 97–121.

Lehmann, E. and G. Schulze (2008) 'What Does it Take to be a Star? The Role of Performance and the Media for German Soccer Players', *Applied Economics Quarterly*, 54, 59–70.

Lehmann, E. and J. Weigand (1997) 'Money Makes the Ball Go Round: Fußball als Ökonomisches Phänomen', *Ifo-Studien*, 43, 381–409.

—— (1999) 'Determinanten der Entlohnung von Profifußballspielern – Eine empirische Analyse für die deutsche Bundesliga', *Betriebswirtschaftliche Forschung und Praxis*, 51, 124–35.

Lucifora, C. and R. Simmons (2003) 'Superstar Effects in Sport: Evidence from Italian Soccer', *Journal of Sports Economics*, 4. 35–55.

Milgrom, P. and J. Roberts (1992) *Economics, Organization and Management*, Englewood Cliffs, NJ, Prentice Hall.

Pedace, R. (2008) 'Earnings, Performance, and Nationality Discrimination in a Highly Competitive Labor Market as an Analysis of the English Professional Soccer League', *Journal of Sports Economics*, 9, 115–40.

Poulsen, R. (2000) 'Should He Stay or Should He Go? Estimating the Effect of Firing the Manager in Soccer', *Chance*, 13, 29–32.

Preston, I. and S. Szymanski (2000) 'Racial Discrimination in English Football', *Scottish Journal of Political Economy*, 27, 342–63.

Reilly, B. and R. Witt (1995) 'English League Transfer Prices: Is there a Racial Dimension?' *Applied Economics Letters*, 2, 200–22.

—— (2007) 'Determinants of Base Pay and the Role of Race in Major League Soccer: Evidence from the 2007 League Season', Department of Economics, University of Surrey, *Discussion Paper*, D19/07.

Rosen, S. (1981) 'The Economics of Superstars', *American Economic Review*, 71, 845–58.

Rosen, S. and A. Sanderson (2001) 'Labour Markets in Professional Sport', *Economic Journal*, 111, F47–F68.

Rottenberg, S. (1956) 'The Baseball Players' Labor Market', *Journal of Political Economy*, 64, 242–58.

Simmons, R. (1997) 'Implications of the Bosman Ruling for Football Transfer Markets', *Economic Affairs*, 17, 13–18.

Simmons, R. and D. Berri (2009) 'Gains from Specialization and Free Agency: The Story from the Gridiron', *Review of Industrial Organization*, 34, 81–98.

Sloane, P.J. (1971) 'The Economics of Professional Football: The Football Club as a Utility Maximizer', *Scottish Journal of Political Economy*, 18, 121–46.

Speight, A. and D. Thomas (1997a) 'Arbitrator Decision-Making in the Transfer Market: An Empirical Analysis', *Scottish Journal of Political Economy*, 44, 198–215.

—— (1997b) 'Football League Transfers: A Comparison of Negotiated Fees with Arbitration Settlements', *Applied Economics Letters*, 4, 41–44.

Szymanski, S. (1999) 'The Market for Soccer Players in England after Bosman: Winners and Losers', in Jeanrenaud, C. and S. Késenne (eds.), *Competition Policy in Professional Sport: Europe after the Bosman Case*, Antwerp, Standard Editions, pp. 133–60.

—— (2000) 'A Market Test for Discrimination in the English Professional Soccer Leagues', *Journal of Political Economy*, 108, 590–603.

Szymanski, S. and T. Kuypers (1999) *Winners and Losers: The Business Strategy of Football*, London, Viking.

Szymanski, S. and R. Smith (1997) 'The English Football Industry: Profit, Performance, and Industrial Structure', *International Review of Applied Economics*, 11, 135–53.

Tervio, M. (2006) 'Transfer Fee Regulations and Player Development', *Journal of the European Economic Association*, 4, 957–87.

ter Weel, B. (2006) 'Does Manager Turnover Improve Firm Performance? New Evidence Using Information from Dutch Soccer, 1986–2004', *Discussion Paper No. 2483*, Bonn, Institut Zukunft der Arbeit.

UEFA (2010) *UEFA Champions League Zugangliste*, [online] available at: <http://de.uefa.com/uefachampionsleague/accesslist/index.html> (accessed 6 September 2011).

Vincent, C. and B. Eastman (2009) 'Determinants of Pay in the NHL: A Quantile Regression Approach', *Journal of Sports Economics*, 10, 256–77.

Wilson, D. and Y.-H. Ying (2003) 'Nationality Preferences for Labour in the International Football Industry', *Applied Economics*, 35, 1551–59.

31

THE ECONOMIC BENEFITS TO CITIES FROM HOSTING MAJOR SPORT EVENTS

Chris Gratton

Introduction

In the UK, in the 1970s and early 1980s, government expenditure on sport expanded considerably. The rationale for this increased expenditure was that sport made a considerable contribution to local communities in welfare terms. Following the publication of the White Paper on Sport and Recreation (Department of the Environment, 1975), it was established that sport should be regarded as part of the general fabric of the social services. Most of this additional expenditure was made by local government on indoor sports centres and swimming pools. In 1971, there were 12 indoor sports centres and 440 swimming pools in Britain. By 1981, there were 461 indoor sports centres and 964 swimming pools (Gratton and Taylor, 1991). This growth in expenditure came to an end in the mid–1980s with the public expenditure cuts of the then Conservative government.

At the same time as the investment in sport for welfare reasons started to decline, a second wave of sport investment began, but this time the rationale was economic regeneration. Investment in sport infrastructure in cities was not primarily aimed at getting the local community involved in sport but was instead aimed at attracting tourists, encouraging inward investment, and changing the image of the city. The first example of this new strategy was seen in Sheffield with the investment of £147 million in sporting facilities to host the World Student Games of 1991. There were also the Olympic bids of Birmingham and Manchester in the 1980s and 1990s. These did not immediately result in investment in facilities since the bids were unsuccessful, but substantial expenditure was required just to mount the bids. More recently, Manchester spent over £200 million on sporting venues in order to host the 2002 Commonwealth Games, with a further £470 million expenditure on other non-sport infrastructure investment in Sportcity in East Manchester.

In the British context, most of the cities following this strategy of using sport for economic regeneration were industrial cities, not normally known as major tourist destinations. The driver of such policies was the need for a new image and new employment opportunities caused by the loss of their conventional industrial base. In the USA, cities such as Indianapolis and Cleveland had adopted a similar strategy in the 1970s and 1980s, again following increased unemployment due to deindustrialization. However, in the USA sport-related regeneration strategies have tended to be focused on facilities for domestic professional team sport rather than on hosting major international sports events. In the rest of Europe and Australia, we have seen similar strategies, most notably in Barcelona with the hosting of the 1992 Olympics, in Athens with the 2004 Olympics, and in Sydney with the 2000 Olympics. The difference between these cities and the British and American ones is that they were already major tourist destinations in their own right prior to hosting the Olympics and were not facing the same problems of industrial decline. The objective here was to transform the image of these cities and turn them into major world cities.

This chapter analyses the justification for such investments in sport in cities and assesses the evidence on the success of such strategies. The next section begins the discussion by examining the context of sport being used as a tool of economic regeneration. The remaining sections then critically review the theory and evidence associated with the potential benefits of hosting major sport events. There is an analysis of the summer Olympic Games, as the largest single major sporting event, followed by an examination of the impacts of investment in sport infrastructure more generally in both the US and UK respectively. The chapter then reviews the likelihood of longer-term benefits or legacies being derived from investment in hosting sport events.

Sport and urban regeneration

As Downward et al. (2009) argue, a variety of characteristics have been used to characterize what is meant by a sport event; including their regularity, scale, and their sporting and economic significance. Specific taxonomies also exist as, for example, those developed by the Sport Industry Research Centre at Sheffield Hallam University (see Gratton et al., 2000; Gratton and Taylor, 2000). However, because of their prestige and/or scale respectively, the study of hallmark events or mega-events initiated interest and became an important part of the tourism literature in the 1980s. Since then the economics of sport tourism at major sport events has become an increasing part of this event tourism literature.

Many governments around the world have adopted national sport policies that specify that hosting major sports event is a major objective. A broad range of benefits has been suggested for both the country and the host city from staging major sports events, including urban regeneration legacy benefits, sporting legacy benefits, tourism and image benefits and social and cultural benefits as well as the direct economic impact benefits which will be the main focus of this chapter. It is well known that cities and countries compete fiercely to host the Olympic Games or the football World Cup. However, over recent years there has been increasing competition to host less globally recognized sport events in a wide range of other sports where spectator interest is less assured and where the economic benefits are even less clear cut. In this chapter, we will analyse the benefits generated across a wide range of sport events from large spectator events staged as part of domestic professional team sport to World and European Championships. We will concentrate on the economic benefits generated but will also consider the broader benefits outlined above. To begin, we discuss the literature associated with hosting major sport events.

The literature on the economics of major sport events is relatively recent. One of the first major studies in this area was the study of the impact of the 1985 Adelaide Formula 1 Grand Prix (Burns, Hatch and Mules, 1986). This was followed by Brent Ritchie's in-depth study of the 1988 Calgary Winter Olympics (Ritchie, 1984; Ritchie and Aitken, 1984, 1985; Ritchie and Lyons, 1987, 1990; Ritchie and Smith, 1991). In fact, immediately prior to these studies it was generally thought that hosting major sport events was a financial liability to host cities following the large debts faced by Montreal after hosting the 1976 Olympics. There was a general change in attitude following the 1984 Los Angeles Olympics which made a clear profit. For a specific event or organizing body simply to make its own profit or loss is, however, not the central issue in evaluating the hosting of sport events.

Mules and Faulkner (1996) point out that even with such mega-events as Formula 1 Grand Prix races and the Olympics, it is not always an unequivocal economic benefit to the cities that host the event. They emphasize that, in general, staging major sport events often results in the city authorities losing money even though the city itself benefits greatly in terms of additional spending in the city. Thus the 1994 Brisbane World Masters Games cost the city A\$2.8 million to organize but generated A\$50.6 million of additional economic activity in the state economy. Mules and Faulkner's basic point is that it normally requires the public sector to finance the staging of the event and incur these costs in order to generate the subsequent benefits to the local economy. They argue that governments host such events and lose taxpayers' money in the process in order to generate such multiplier effects as spillover effects or externalities.[1] Consequently, the hosting of major sport events is often justified by the host city in terms of long-term economic and social consequences, directly or indirectly resulting from the staging of the event (Mules and Faulkner, 1996). These effects are primarily justified in economic terms, by estimating the additional expenditure generated in the local economy as the result of the event, in terms of the benefits injected from tourism-related activity, known as economic impacts (Roche, 1992).

It is not a straightforward job, however, to establish this for a specific event. There are practical issues to consider such as delineating the area and timescale over which impacts are to be measured. For example, major sport events require investment in new sport facilities and often this is paid for in part by central government or even international sport bodies. Thus some of this investment expenditure represents a net addition to the specific local economy since the money comes in from outside this area. Of course, this may mean that within countries some localities may benefit at the expense of others if resources are transferred nationally. Expenditures from international sources, of course, may benefit one area specifically, but by implication this benefits the country as a whole. Also facilities remain after the event has finished and can act as a platform for future activities that can generate additional tourist expenditure (Mules and Faulkner, 1996). The life cycle of the investment thus needs to be considered. There are also technical issues to address, including how best to calculate the multiplier effects and other accounting qualifications such as allowing for inflation and changing interest rates on the value of monetary flows (for a discussion of these issues see Downward et al., 2009).[2]

Sport events are also increasingly seen as part of a broader tourism strategy aimed at raising the profile of a city and therefore success cannot be judged on simply economic criteria. Often the attraction of events is linked to a re-imaging process, and in the case of many cities is invariably linked to strategies of urban regeneration and tourism development (Bianchini and Schwengel, 1991; Bramwell, 1995; Collins and Jackson, 1996; Loftman and Spirou, 1996; Roche, 1994). Cities staging major sport events have a unique opportunity to market themselves to the world. Increasing competition between broadcasters to secure broadcasting rights to major sport events has led to a massive escalation in fees for such rights, which in turn means broadcasters give blanket coverage at peak times for such events, enhancing the marketing benefits to the cities that stage them.

Such benefits might include a notional value of exposure achieved from media coverage and the associated place marketing effects related to hosting and broadcasting an event that might encourage visitors to return in future, or alternatively have sport development impacts, which may encourage young people to get more involved in sport. Collectively these

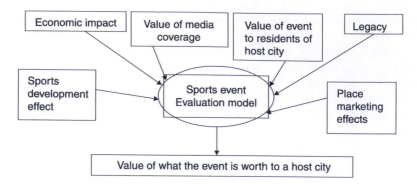

Figure 31.1 Towards an event evaluation model

additional benefits could be monitored using a more holistic approach to event evaluation as outlined in Figure 31.1.

The economic impact of the summer Olympic Games

Despite the huge sums of money invested in hosting the summer Olympics there has never been an impact study of the type described in Figure 31.1 to assess the economic benefits of hosting the event, and the economic impact studies that have been done have dubious characteristics.

Kasimati (2003) analysed all economic impact studies of the summer Olympics from 1984 to 2004 and found, in each case, that the studies were done prior to the Games, were not based on primary data, and were, in general, commissioned by proponents of the Games. It was found that the economic impacts were likely to be inflated since the studies did not take into account supply-side constraints such as investment crowding out existing economic activity, price increases due to resource scarcity, and the displacement of tourists who would have been in the host city had the Olympics not been held there. It is also a common error to include residents' expenditures in the analysis (see also Crompton, 2006).[3]

Although no proper economic impact study using primary data has ever been carried out for the summer Olympics, Preuss (2004) has produced a comprehensive analysis of the economics of the summer Olympics for every summer Olympics from Munich 1972 using secondary data, and employing a novel data transformation methodology which allows comparisons across the different Olympics.

Despite collecting a massive amount of secondary data, Preuss's conclusion on the estimation of the true economic impact of the summer Olympics is the same as Kasimati's:

> The economic benefit of the Games . . . is often overestimated in both publications and economic analyses produced by or for the OCOG [Organising Committee of the Olympic Games]. . . . multipliers tend to be too high and the number of tourists is estimated too optimistically
>
> *(Preuss, 2004: 290)*

Preuss, however, does make some strong conclusions from his analysis. He shows, for instance, that every summer Olympics since 1972 made an operational surplus that the OCOG can spend to benefit both national and international sport. Stories relating to massive losses from hosting the Olympics have nothing to do with the Games operational costs and revenues. Rather they are to do with the capital infrastructure investments made by host cities on venues, transport, accommodation and telecommunications. These are investments in capital infrastructure that have a life of 50 years or more and yet many commentators count the full capital cost against the two to three weeks of the Games themselves. Preuss points out that this is economic nonsense:

> It is impossible and even wrong to state the overall effect of different Olympics with a single surplus or deficit. The true outcome is measured in the infrastructural, social, political, ecological and sporting impacts a city and country receive from the Games.
>
> *(Preuss, 2004: 26)*

This indicates of course the importance of addressing the economic impacts of events properly, though estimating the true economic impact of the summer Olympic Games properly would require a huge research budget in addition to the other costs associated with the Games. Research needs to start several years before the Olympics and continue several years after they have finished. So far nobody has been willing to fund such research. However, there is increasing research output relating to other major sporting events.

Despite a strong theoretical case in favour of urban regeneration benefits from investment in sporting infrastructure in order to host major sport events, then, there are also strong arguments that the negative impacts of such investment may match or even outweigh these benefits. This has been particularly pronounced in US literature.

City sport strategies in North America

Over the last two decades many cities in the United States have invested vast amounts of money in sport stadia on the basis of arguments that economic benefits will accrue to the city from such investment. Most of these strategies have been based on professional team sports, in particular, American football, baseball, ice hockey, and basketball. Unlike the situation in Europe, professional teams in North America frequently move from city to city.

Since the late 1980s, cities have offered greater and greater incentives for these professional teams to move by offering to build new stadia to house them, costing hundreds of millions of dollars. The teams just sit back and let cities bid up the price. They either move to the city offering the best deal or they accept the counter offer invariably put to them by their existing hosts. This normally involves the host city building them a brand new stadium to replace their existing one, which may only be ten or fifteen years old.

Baade (2003) indicates how, since the 1980s, escalating stadium construction costs have increased the size of stadium subsidies:

> the number of stadiums that have been built since 1987 to the present is unprecedented. Approximately 80 per cent of the professional sport facilities in the United States will have been replaced or have undergone major renovation during this period of time. The new facilities have cost more than $19 billion in total, and the public has provided $13.6 billion, or 71 per cent, of that amount. In few, if any, instances have professional teams in the United States been required to open their books to justify the need for these subsidies. Rather, teams have convinced cities that

to remain competitive on the field they have to be competitive financially, and this, teams claim, cannot be achieved without new playing venues.

(Baade, 2003: 588)

This use of taxpayers' money to subsidize profit-making professional sport teams seems to be completely inappropriate and particularly out of place in the North American context. The justification for such public expenditure is an economic one: the investment of public money is a worthwhile investment as long as the economic impact generated by having a major professional sport team resident in the city is sufficiently great.

Baade (1996), Noll and Zimbalist (1997) and Coates and Humphreys (1999), however, showed no significant direct economic impact on the host cities from such stadium develop-ment. Crompton (1995, 2001) also argues that economic impact arguments in favour of such stadium construction using public subsidies have been substantially exaggerated. However, he goes on to suggest (Crompton, 2001, 2004) that there are other possible benefits to cities from such developments: increased community visibility, enhanced community image, stimula-tion of additional development related to the stadium, and psychic income to city residents from having a professional team in the city. The first three of these focus on the ability of such stadium developments to influence external audiences which may lead to inward investment into the host city and generate similar benefits to economic impact. Psychic income relates to the social and psychological benefit local residents may feel by identifying with the resident professional team. Although sport researchers are well aware of such benefits they are notori-ously difficult to measure effectively and no evidence currently exists to suggest these broader benefits justify the high levels of public subsidies to professional sport teams in the USA.

The question that arises therefore is why such subsidies have grown to these massive levels in recent years. Quirk and Fort (1999: 169–70) suggest an answer to this question:

> As monopolies, sport leagues artificially restrict the number of teams below the number that would be in business if there was competition in the sport. By constantly keeping a supply of possible host cities – cities that could support a league team – on line, current host cities are in the unenviable position of being pressured to provide exorbitant subsidies to their teams or risk losing them.

Thus it is simply a problem of supply and demand and the market power lies with the profes-sional sport teams. Most economists are agreed that this phenomenon is not an example of sport contributing substantially to economic regeneration. However, some American cities have gone beyond the professional sport team stadium game and taken a broader approach to using sport for economic regeneration. Indianapolis, Cleveland, Philadelphia, Kansas City, Baltimore and Denver are examples of cities that have adopted broader sport-orientated economic regeneration strategies and Indianapolis is perhaps the best example out of these.

Schimmel (2001) and Davidson (1999) analyse how sport has been used in Indianapolis for economic regeneration of the city. Indianapolis is a midwestern US city that in the mid 1970s was suffering from the decline of its heavy manufacturing base, in particular its car industry. Local politicians were keen to develop a new image for the city. As Schimmel indicates, the problem was not that the city had a bad image, but rather that the city had no image at all. The strategy was to target the expanding service sector economy in an attempt to redevelop the city's downtown area by using sport as a catalyst for economic regeneration. From 1974 to 1984, a total of $1.7 billion in public and private resources was invested in inner-city construction (Schimmel, 2001), in which sporting infrastructure played a major role. The strategy included investment in facilities in professional team sports but added to this a strategy of hosting major sport events in the city.

Between 1977 and 1991, 330 sport events were hosted by Indianapolis. Davidson (1999) attempted to measure the economic contribution of sport to the city in 1991. He found that in that year, 18 sport organizations and nine sports facilities in the city employed 526 employees. In addition, 35 sport events held in the city in 1991 generated additional spending of $97 million. He estimated the total economic contribution of sport organizations, facilities and events in Indianapolis in 1991 to be $133 million. In addition, other studies had shown that the sport strategy aimed at economic regeneration had resulted in other non-economic benefits, including increased sport participation by young people, increased pride in the city, and an enhanced image for the city, resulting in more convention tourism. Although Indianapolis was an early example, the strategy of using sport events as a catalyst for urban regeneration became popular in the UK in the 1980s and 1990s.

Sport and economic regeneration in cities and regions in the UK

Several cities in the UK (e.g. Sheffield, Birmingham and Glasgow) have used sport as a lead sector in promoting urban regeneration and these three cities were awarded National City of Sport status in 1995 partly because of this. They have all invested heavily in their sport infrastructure so that each has a portfolio of major sporting facilities capable of holding major sports events.

In addition to facilities, each city has a supporting structure of expertise in event bidding and management to ensure quality bids with a high probability of success and to guarantee high-quality event management. Events are a major vehicle for attracting visitors to the city and hence contributing to urban regeneration. However, these cities are also involved with developing sport in the cities through performance and excellence programmes (e.g. training, squad preparation, coaching) and in community sport development, so that the local population benefits from the investment in sport infrastructure.

These and other cities have made a specific commitment to public investment in sport as a vehicle for urban regeneration. However, the quantity and distribution of returns to such public sector investment in sport, predominantly from local government, have been largely under-researched and remain uncertain. Often such investment attracts criticism because of media attention on a specific event, such as the World Student Games in Sheffield in 1991, and there has been little research on the medium- and long-term returns on such investment.

In a report commissioned by UK Sport, *Measuring Success 2: the economic impact of major sport events* (UK Sport, 2004), the Sport Industry Research Centre presented an overview of the findings from 16 economic impact studies of major sport events undertaken since 1997, many of which took place in these three cities and all but three of which (Spar Europa Cup, World Cup Triathlon, World Indoor Athletics) were carried out by the Sport Industry Research Centre. This consolidated piece of research builds on the original *Measuring Success* (UK Sport, 1999a) document published by UK Sport in 1999, which recognized and demonstrated the potential of major sport events to achieve significant economic impacts for the cities that host them.

These sixteen studies have been conducted using essentially the same methodology as that published by UK Sport in 1999 entitled *Major Events: the economics – a guide* (UK Sport, 1999b). This therefore provides a dataset in which the events are directly comparable and we concentrate on these comparisons. Key findings from the research are outlined in Table 31.1, commencing with the impact of each event.

Table 31.1 Economic impact of 16 major sport events

Year	Event	Host city	Event days	Impact (£)	Impact per event day (£)
1997	World Badminton	Glasgow	14	2.22m	0.16m
1997	European Junior Boxing	Birmingham	9	0.51m	0.06m
1997	1st Ashes Test – Cricket England v Australia	Birmingham	5	5.06m	1.01m
1997	IAAF Grand Prix 1 Athletics	Sheffield	1	0.18m	0.18m
1997	European Junior Swimming	Glasgow	4	0.26m	0.06m
1997	Women's British Open Golf	Sunningdale	4	2.07m	0.52m
1998	European Short Course Swimming	Sheffield	3	0.31m	0.10m
1999	European Show Jumping	Hickstead	5	2.20m	0.44m
1999	World Judo	Birmingham	4	1.94m	0.49m
1999	World Indoor Climbing	Birmingham	3	0.40m	0.13m
2000	Flora London Marathon	London	1	25.46m	25.46m
2000	Spar Europa Cup – Athletics	Gateshead	2	0.97m	0.48m
2001	World Amateur Boxing	Belfast	8	1.49m	0.19m
2001	World Half Marathon	Bristol	1	0.58m	0.58m
2003	World Cup Triathlon	Manchester	1	1.67m	1.67m
2003	World Indoor Athletics	Birmingham	3	3.16m	1.05m

Overall the findings confirm that major sport events can have significant economic impacts on host communities. These impacts ranged from the £0.18m of additional expenditure attributable to the half-day IAAF Grand Prix Athletics staged on a Sunday in Sheffield in June 1997, to the £25.5m attributable to the Flora London Marathon in April 2000. Moreover, other events, most notably the World Cup Triathlon, World Indoor Athletics and Test Cricket attracted additional expenditure per day in excess of £1m. Junior events (e.g. European Junior Swimming and Junior Boxing) had the least significant daily impacts, mainly because they rarely attract considerable numbers of spectators. It is interesting to note that the two events generating the highest economic impacts, the London Marathon and a cricket Test Match, were domestic events that take place annually, do not need to go through a bidding process and do not require new sporting infrastructure investment.

Economic impact is not UK Sport's rationale for attracting major events to the UK but it is a useful device by which to justify funding an event in economic terms. The evidence suggests that as a general rule it is the expenditure by visitors to an event which contributes the majority of any additional expenditure, rather than spending by the organizers of an event.

Spectators contributed the majority of the additional expenditure at 10 of the 16 events, and such events are termed 'spectator driven'. Further analyses revealed a strong correlation between the number of spectator admissions and the absolute economic impact of an event, which suggests that the absolute number of spectators is the key driver of economic impact.

A typical competitor spends between £55 and £60 per day at an event, of which 82 per cent is spent on subsistence (accommodation, food and drink). Cricketers at the Test Match spent the most per day of all the competitors (£113), compared to athletes at the World Half Marathon who spent the least (£42). Typical daily spend of an official was £70, of which 80 per cent was attributable to expenditure on subsistence. Competitors spend relatively little on items other than subsistence, because their days are characterized by a cycle of preparation, competition and rest, which leaves little time for interaction with the local economy. Similarly, officials work long hours to ensure that events run smoothly, and consequently they too have little time to get out and about locally. By contrast daily spend of a typical media representative was around £100 (and often much more for those on expenses), with 75 per cent of this attributable to spending on subsistence (usually commercial accommodation). Moreover, daily expenditure by media personnel on other items (around £25) almost doubled that spent by the typical competitor or official. Hence, not only do events benefit from the value of media coverage but they also benefit from the relatively high additional daily expenditure of media representatives.

The daily spending of spectators varies considerably across events, ranging from £86 at the European Junior Swimming (where parents spent money on behalf of and supporting their children) to less than £10 per day at the IAAF Athletics Grand Prix. Although the absolute number of spectators is the key driver of economic impact, the average spectator (at a little under £50) spends less per day than the other groups. This is because spectators are most likely to be day-visitors and least likely to make use of commercial accommodation (hotels and guest houses), as evidenced by only 59 per cent of their daily expenditure being attributable to subsistence. However, average daily expenditure of spectators is a function of the proportion staying overnight in the host area.

As discussed above, with such events, much of the economic impact referred to here is actually a redistribution of money around the UK economy, which has no lasting impact on overall GDP. However, expenditure by visitors from overseas is actually 'new' money to the UK economy in the form of invisible exports, as exemplified by the Flora London Marathon, which revealed a net export effect approaching £1.2m. Events that achieve this genuine inflow of funds arguably provide a better quality impact in the national interest than those associated with the recirculation of money within the UK economy. Notwithstanding this, the Local Organizing Committees of events such as the World Half Marathon or World Indoor Athletics are unlikely to worry from where any additional expenditure originates, as long as it is forthcoming. However, they may be interested in evidence suggesting that visitors from overseas stay longer and spend more than the average visitor.

The research has revealed high approval ratings from the public for continued support of events through the National Lottery. Moreover, based on evidence from 10 of the 11 part Lottery funded events, for every £1 of Lottery support, additional expenditure in host economies amounted to £7.23. However, Lottery support rarely covers the total costs associated with hosting an event, and as such the return on investment figure does not allow for the additional costs incurred by Local Organizing Committees. Consequently, the impact in host economies for every £1 invested at an event will be less than £7.23.

Additional benefits have been monitored at more recent events, as organizers look beyond the direct economic impact when evaluating their events following the balanced scorecard approach as indicated in Figure 31.1.

The public profile of the European Short Course Swimming Championships was measured by the analysis of the television coverage for the event. This monitoring of an event's television coverage has revealed some interesting and perhaps unexpected findings. The key finding is that the event achieved television audiences that were greater than those for some sports generally perceived as having larger audiences than swimming. Most notably, audiences for the European Short Course Swimming Championships exceeded those for some rugby union international matches as well as prestigious events in the rugby league and cricket calendars.

The European Short Course Swimming Championships achieved coverage in 18 programmes or programme segments lasting 1,087 minutes, which were broadcast in the UK and mainland Europe (Shibli and Gratton, 1999). A total of nearly eight million viewers across the UK and Europe watched coverage of the event. The highest audience share was achieved in the UK (23 per cent) and the highest TVR (television rating) was achieved in Finland, where 9 per cent of the country's population watched recorded highlights of the event.

The economic impact of the spending of visitors at this event was relatively small (around £300,000). However, the public profile achieved by the television coverage was worth substantially more than this to the host city, Sheffield, the event itself (owned by the international governing body LEN), and the event sponsor (Adidas).

The analysis of these events shows the wide variety of economic impacts generated by different events and how, for some events, other benefits can be greater than the economic impact. Some of the events generate relatively small economic impacts. Just because the event is a World or European Championship does not guarantee that it will be important in economic terms. The difficulty for cities trying to follow an event strategy for regeneration purposes is that it is difficult to forecast the economic impact of any event prior to staging it. However, cities such as Sheffield, Birmingham and Glasgow that now have a history of hosting a wide range of events do acquire the experience of being able to judge those events which generate the most significant benefits.

Case study

Commonwealth Games Manchester 2002

The Commonwealth Games held in Manchester in 2002 involved an investment of £200 million in sporting venues in the city and a further £470 million investment in transport and other infrastructure. This is by far the largest investment related to the hosting of a specific sport event ever to be undertaken in Britain prior to the Olympic Games. It was also the first time in Britain that planning for the hosting of a major sport event was integrated with the strategic framework for the regeneration of the city, in particular East Manchester.

In 1999, three years before the Games were held, the Commonwealth Games Opportunities and Legacy Partnership Board was established to manage the legacy of the Games. Legacy activities were funded under the 2002 North West Economic and Social Single Regeneration Board Programme, which operated from 1999 to 2004. This was the first time in Britain an ambitious legacy programme was designed around a major sport event. The objective was to ensure that the benefits of hosting the event would not disappear once the event was over but that rather there would be a long-term permanent boost to the local economy of East Manchester.

Despite the long-term planning for the Games and the legacy there was one major omission: no economic impact study was carried out during the Games in 2002 and so no primary data is available on the immediate economic benefit of the Games. Cambridge Policy Consultants produced a pre-event estimate of the economic impact in April 2002 and then revised it in November 2003 (Cambridge Policy Consultants, 2003) using secondary evidence available from the Games period. They estimated that the Games generated 2,900 full-time equivalent (FTE) additional jobs in Manchester. However, without any visitor survey data available for the Games themselves there must be serious doubts as to the validity of such an estimate.

A further study of the benefits of the Games was carried out for the North West Development Agency in 2004 by Faber Maunsell, in association with Vision Consulting and

Roger Tym and Partners (Faber Maunsell, 2004). The study used secondary sources and interviews with key stakeholders.

As part of the study they measured employment change in East Manchester between 1999 and 2002 as revealed by the Annual Business Inquiry (ABI) data. This showed a 1,450 increase in jobs (including both part-time and full-time jobs) or a 4 per cent increase over the 1999 level. However, this is annual data and therefore it is difficult to isolate how much of this increase was due to the Games. The distribution of the increase in construction (23 per cent increase), distribution, hotels and restaurants (14 per cent increase), and other services (24 per cent increase) is consistent with the Games having been the main generator of the increase in jobs. Also, out of the 210 new jobs in 'other services', 200 of them were in the 'recreational, cultural, and sporting' category, suggesting again a significant Games effect. However, 1,450 new jobs, which included part-time jobs, is considerably different from the 2,900 FTE jobs estimated by Cambridge Policy Consultants, although this figure relates to the effect on the whole of Manchester and not just East Manchester.

The net additional value of capital investment in the Games was estimated by Faber Maunsell at £670 million, of which £201 million was for the sporting venues, and £125 million was for transport infrastructure. Other major investment included an Asda-Walmart superstore occupying 180,000 square feet and employing 760 FTE staff.

Since no visitor survey was carried out during the Games, actual tourism indicators were difficult to obtain. Using annual tourism data from the UK Tourism Survey (UKTS) and the International Passenger Survey (IPS), Faber Maunsell (2004) indicate a 7.4 per cent increase of overseas residents visitors to Greater Manchester in 2002 compared to 2000. However, there was a 6.4 per cent decrease in UK resident visitors to Greater Manchester over the same period and a 2.2 per cent decrease in the number of nights overseas residents spent in Greater Manchester. Overall, though, there was a 21 per cent increase in UK resident expenditure and a 29 per cent increase in overseas residents expenditure in Greater Manchester in 2002 compared to 2000. Again, because these are annual figures it is impossible to isolate the influence of the Games on these figures but it is reasonable to conclude that they were the most significant factor.

The Faber Maunsell study does not give a detailed media analysis of the Games, indicating only that the opening and closing ceremonies had an 'estimated' worldwide audience of one billion. The Commonwealth Games is an unusual event in that it receives television coverage across most continents but is not a global event in the same way as the Olympics and the football World Cup are. There are key markets where there will be no coverage at all. These include the USA, the whole of the rest of Europe outside the United Kingdom, Japan and China. The event, therefore, is limited in its potential effect on the image and profile of the host city.

Some indication of the public profile benefits of the Games is indicated by Manchester moving up the European Cities Monitor from 19th in 2002 to 13th in 2003. The Monitor is a measure of the best European cities in which to locate a business, compiled by Cushman and Wakefield Healey and Baker. This is constructed from the views of Europe's 500 leading businesses on the top business locations in Europe and is used to indicate aspects affecting business location decisions. For Manchester it is an indicator of an improvement in the city's image from a business perspective and an indicator of greater potential for inward investment.

Despite the lack of hard evidence on the economic impact of the Commonwealth Games on Manchester in 2002, there is enough evidence to indicate that East Manchester has benefited considerably. Manchester City FC now use the City of Manchester stadium as their home ground and other sporting venues in East Manchester have become the English Institute of Sport and are used for the training of elite athletes. Since much of the funding for the new investment for the facilities came from the National Lottery or central government, this is a clear economic boost for the area. We will have to wait and see whether the legacy benefits are as great as were hoped for but the indications are promising.

Longer term benefits of hosting major sport events

Although it is too early to assess the urban regeneration legacy benefits of Manchester 2002, it should be possible to assess the long-term benefits of events held ten or twenty years ago. Unfortunately, there are few research studies that attempt to measure systematically such long-term benefits. Spilling (1998) found he could identify no long-term economic benefits for Lillehammer from hosting the Winter Olympics in 1994. He concluded that:

> If the main argument for hosting a mega-event like the Winter Olympics is the long-term economic impacts it will generate, the Lillehammer experience quite clearly points to the conclusion that it is a waste of money.
>
> *(Spilling, 1998: 121)*

Spilling seems to question whether there can be any long-term effect for an area the size of Lillehammer, a city of 25,000 inhabitants situated 180 kilometres north of Oslo. The two Winter Olympics prior to the Lillehammer Games, in Calgary in 1988 and in Albertville in 1992, had been in larger regions and there was more evidence of a continuing benefit several years after the Games. In the case of Albertville, this was partly due to massive transport infrastructure investment which made access to the region by car substantially easier, although at a severe cost to the alpine environment. It is certainly the case that there is little evidence to support the argument that the Winter Olympics leave a substantial long-term benefit.

There is some evidence, however, that the Summer Olympics do generate a legacy benefit. One example that is often quoted to support the argument that there are long-term benefits of hosting major sport events is the case of the Barcelona Olympics in 1992.

Sanahuja (2002) provided evidence on the longer term economic benefits of hosting the Olympics in Barcelona in 1992. The paper analysed the benefits to Barcelona in 2002, ten years after hosting the games. Table 31.2 shows almost a 100 per cent increase in hotel capacity, number of tourists, and number of overnight stays in 2001 compared to the pre-Games

Table 31.2 Legacy benefits of the Barcelona Olympic Games

	1990	2001
Hotel capacity (beds)	18,567	34,303
Number of tourists	1,732,902	3,378,636
Number overnights	3,795,522	7,969,496
Average room occupancy	71%	84%
Average stay	2.84	3.17
Tourists by origin		
Spain	51.2%	31.3%
Europe	32%	39.5%
Others (USA, Japan, Latin America)	16.8%	29.2%

Sources: Turisme de Barcelona (Barcelona Tourist Board) and Sanahuja (2002)

position in 1990. Average room occupancy had also increased from 71 per cent to 84 per cent. In addition the average length of stay had increased from 2.84 days to 3.17 days. In 1990, the majority (51 per cent) of tourists to Barcelona were from the rest of Spain, with 32 per cent from the rest of Europe, and the remainder (17 per cent) from outside Europe. By 2001, the absolute number of Spanish tourists had actually risen by 150,000 but given the near doubling in the number of tourists overall this higher total only accounted for 31 per cent of the total number of tourists. The proportion of tourists from the rest of Europe went up from 32 per cent to 40 per cent (representing an absolute increase of around 800,000) and from the rest of the world from 17 per cent to 29 per cent (representing an absolute increase of around 600,000).

Overall infrastructure investment prior to the Games was $7.5 billion compared to a budget of around $1.5 billion for the Olympic Committee to stage the games. The Olympics in Barcelona were the most expensive ever staged. However, Barcelona's use of the Games as a city marketing factor is generally regarded as a huge success. This is evidenced by Barcelona's rise in ranking in the European Cities Monitor from 11th in 1990 to 6th in 2002.

Given the scarcity of evidence on the long-term urban regeneration benefits of hosting sporting events, the Department of Culture Media and Sport/Strategy Unit (2002) in their review of sport strategy in England were sceptical over the existence of such benefits:

> Our conclusion is that the economic justifications for any future bids for mega–events must be rigorously assessed. If regeneration is intended as an explicit pay-off from hosting a mega event, then it must underpin the whole planning process to ensure that maximum benefit for the investment is achieved.
>
> *(Department of Culture Media and Sport/Strategy Unit, 2002: 68)*

It is interesting, therefore, that very soon after this review was published in December 2002, the government decided to back the bid for London to stage the 2012 Olympics, which tends to support Roche's (1994) argument that in the end such decisions are political rather than part of a rational planning process.

Conclusions

Sport has the potential to generate substantial economic and social returns to local and regional government investment in the sport industry. The focus of research over the last decade, however, has been the national economic importance of sport. Although some evidence is available on the economic benefits of sport events, and sport tourism, many of the economic benefits to the local community have been poorly researched. Most of the serious gaps in knowledge over the broader economic benefits of sport can best be filled at the local level. Such research would allow more rational investment appraisal in new investments in sport infrastructure and sport programmes by local government.

It is clear from the discussion in this chapter, however, that in both North America and Europe the strategic thinking relating economic regeneration and sport has been dominated by the view that sport can only contribute to economic activity by attracting sport tourists, either spectators or participants, to the city or region. Such strategies have also been relatively easy to sell to taxpayers in the local economy since the economic argument has been rein-forced by the additional generation of social and environmental benefits that such a sport-led economic regeneration can bring to local residents and taxpayers.

In North America, there is increasing questioning of the investment of public money into professional team sports that generate huge profits to their owners and athletes. In Europe, however, economic impact studies over the recent past have shown there is a small number of major sport events (including the Olympics, the World Cup and the European Championship in football) that generate an unequivocal economic benefit to host cities. There is another group of events (such as Wimbledon, the FA Cup Final, Six Nations Rugby Internationals) that also generate significant economic benefits but are not normally 'on the market' for competing cities to bid for (i.e. they always take place in the same venues each year). There are a large number of other events (National, European and World Championships across all sports) that have the potential to generate significant economic impact. The evidence provided in this chapter has shown the wide diversity in economic impacts generated from such events but also that a sport strategy based around events can deliver significant benefits to cities.

Whether such benefits justify the expenditure involved is, however, a difficult question to answer. When the money for sporting infrastructure investment is provided by local taxpayers, as it was for the World Student Games in Sheffield, the question arises of whether other projects might have provided better returns to the local community. When the money for investment comes primarily from outside the local community, as it did for the Commonwealth Games in Manchester, then it is an unequivocal benefit to the local community in economic terms but may not be the best use of the funds from a national perspective. At this point in time we simply do not have adequate evidence to make judgements of this type. The evidence that we do have relates to the immediate economic impact during the event and immediately afterwards. There is a need for research to concentrate on the longer term urban regeneration benefits that sport has the potential to deliver.

Notes

1 In economic language, multiplier effects represent the additional economic activity that is generated from an investment beyond that *directly* connected to the investment. These effects will have geographical and temporal boundaries. Multiplier effects are conceptually different from externalities and spillovers more generally as examples of market failure because the former derive from the re-employment of previously underemployed resources whereas the latter arise because activity directly affects the benefits or costs experienced by others despite their not being party to the economic activity concerned.

2 It should be noted too that, for many economists, focusing on economic impacts – as the *net* benefits – from an investment is inappropriate. The welfare associated with such investments and their evaluation with respect to the opportunity costs of alternatives in a cost–benefit analysis are considered more appropariate (see Downward et al., 2009; Kesenne, 2005).

3 As implied in the discussions above, economic impact refers to the total amount of additional expenditure generated within a host city (or area), which could be directly attributable to the staging of a particular event. Only visitors to the host economy as a direct result of an event being staged are eligible for inclusion in the economic impact calculations (i.e. the expenditure by people resident in the host area is not included, on the basis that they would spend money locally irrespective of whether an event is taking place).

References

Baade, R.A. (1996) 'Professional Sport as Catalysts for Economic Development', *Journal of Urban Affairs*, 18(1) 1–17.

—— (2003) 'Evaluating Subsidies for Professional Sports in the United States and Europe: A Public-Sector Primer', *Oxford Review of Economic Policy*, 19(4), 585–97.

Bianchini, F. and Schwengel, H. (1991) 'Re-imagining the City', in Comer, J. and Harvey, S. (eds.) *Enterprise and Heritage: Crosscurrents of National Culture*, Routledge: London, pp. 214–34.

Bramwell, B. (1995) 'Event Tourism in Sheffield: A Sustainable Approach to Urban Development?' Unpublished paper, Sheffield Hallam University, Centre for Tourism.

Burns, J. P. A, Hatch, J. H. and Mules, F. J. (eds.) (1986) *The Adelaide Grand Prix: the impact of a special event*, Adelaide, The Centre for South Australian Economic Studies.

Cambridge Policy Consultants (2003) *The Commonwealth Games 2002: A Cost and Benefit Analysis: Executive Update*, Cambridge, Cambridge Policy Consultants.

Coates, D. and Humphreys, B. (1999) 'The Growth of Sport Franchises, Stadiums and Arenas', *Journal of Policy Analysis*, 18(4), 601–24.

Collins, M.F. and Jackson, G.A.M. (1996) 'The Economic Impact of a Growing Symbiosis: Sport and Tourism', Fourth European Association for Sports Management (EASM) Conference, Montpelier, France.

Crompton, J. L. (1995) 'Economic Impact Analysis of Sport Facilities and Events: Eleven Sources of Misapplication', *Journal of Sport Management*, 9(1), 14–35.

—— (2001) 'Public Subsidies to Professional Team Sport Facilities in the USA', in Gratton, C. and Henry, I. P. (eds.) *Sport in the City: The Role of Sport in Economic and Social Regeneration*, London, Routledge.

—— (2004) 'Beyond Economic Impact: An Alternative Rationale for the Public Subsidy of Major League Sport Facilities', *Journal of Sport Management*, 18, 40–58.

—— (2006) 'Economic Impact Studies: Instruments for Political Shenanigans?' *Journal of Travel Research*, 45: 67–82.

Davidson, L. (1999) 'Choice of a Proper Methodology to Measure Quantitative and Qualitative Effects of the Impact of Sport', in Jeanreaud, C. (ed.) *The Economic Impact of Sport Events*, Neuchatel: Switzerland, Centre International d'Etude du Sport (CIES).

Department of Culture, Media, and Sport/Strategy Unit (2002) 'Game Plan: a strategy for delivering Government's sport and physical activity objectives', London, UK Sport.

Department of the Environment (1975) 'Sport and Recreation', HMSO, Cmnd 6200.

Downward, P., Dawson, A. and Dejonghe, T. (2009) *Sport Economics: Theory Evidence and Policy*, London: Butterworth-Heinemann.

Faber Maunsell (2004) 'Commonwealth Games Benefit Study: Final Report, Manchester', North West Development Agency.

Gibson, H. J. (1998) 'Sport Tourism: a Critical Analysis of Research', *Sport Management Review*, 1, 45–76.

Gratton, C. and Taylor, P. (1991) 'Government and the Economics of Sport', Harlow, Longman.

—— (2000) 'Economics of Sport and Recreation', London, E. and F.N. Spon.

Gratton, C., Dobson, N. and Shibli, S. (2000) 'The Economic Importance of Major Sport Events: A Case Study of Six Events', *Managing Leisure*, 5, 17–28.

Kasimati, E. (2003) 'Economic Aspects and the Summer Olympics: a Review of Related Research', *International Journal of Tourism Research*, 5, 433–44.

Kesenne, S. (2005) 'Do We Need an Economic Impact Study or a Cost-Benefit Analysis of a Sport Event?', *European Sport Management Quarterly*, 5, 133–42.

Loftman, P. and Spirou, C. S. (1996) 'Sport Stadiums and Urban Regeneration: the British and United States Experience', paper presented to the conference, Tourism and Culture: Towards the 21st Century, Durham.

Mules, T. and Faulkner, B. (1996) 'An Economic Perspective on Major Events', *Tourism Economics*, 2(2), 107–17.

Noll, R. and Zimbalist, A. (eds.) (1997) 'Sport, Jobs and Taxes', Washington, The Brookings Institution.

Preuss, H. (2004) *The Economics of Staging the Olympics: A Comparison of the Games 1972–2008*, Cheltenham, Edward Elgar.

Quirk, J. and Fort, R. (1999) *Hard Ball: The Abuse of Power in Pro Team Sport*, Princeton, Princeton University Press.

Ritchie, J. R. B. (1984) 'Assessing the impact of hallmark event: conceptual and research issues', *Journal of Travel Research*, 23(1), 2–11.

Ritchie, J. R. B. and Aitken, C.E. (1984) 'Assessing the impacts of the 1988 Olympic Winter Games: the research program and initial results', *Journal of Travel Research*, 22(3), 17–25.

—— (1985) 'OLYMPULSE II – evolving resident attitudes towards the 1988 Olympics', *Journal of Travel Research*, 23 (Winter), 28–33.

Ritchie, J. R. B. and Lyons, M. M. (1987) 'OLYMPULSE III/IV: a mid-term report on resident attitudes concerning the 1988 Olympic Winter Games', *Journal of Travel Research*, 26 (Summer), 18–26.

—— (1990) 'OLYMPULSE VI: a post-event assessment of resident reaction to the XV Olympic Winter Games', *Journal of Travel Research*, 28(3), 14–23.

Ritchie, J. R. B. and Smith, B. H. (1991) 'The impact of a mega event on host region awareness: a longitudinal study', *Journal of Travel Research*, 30(1), 3–10.

Roche, M. (1992) 'Mega-event Planning and Citizenship: Problems of Rationality and Democracy in Sheffield's Universiade 1991', *Vrijetijd en Samenleving*, 10(4), 47–67.

—— (1994) 'Mega-Events and Urban Policy', *Annals of Tourism Research*, 21(1), 1–19.

Sanahuja, R. (2002) 'Olympic City – The City Strategy 10 years after The Olympic Games in 1992.' Paper delivered to the conference, Sport Events and Economic Impact, Copenhagen, April 2002.

Schimmel, K. S. (2001) 'Sport matters: urban regime theory and urban regeneration in the late capitalist era', in Gratton, C. and Henry, I.P. (eds.) *Sport in the City: The Role of Sport in Economic and Social Regeneration*, London, Routledge.

Shibli, S. (2001). 'Using an understanding of the behavior patterns of key participant groups to predict the economic impact of major sport events', *Proceedings for the 9th EASM Congress*, Vitoria-Gasteiz, Spain, 294–98.

Shibli, S. and Gratton, C. (1999) 'Assessing the Public Profile of Major Sport Events: A Case Study of the European Short Course Swimming Championships', *Sport Marketing and Sponsorship*, 1(3), 278–95.

Spilling, O. A. (1998) 'Beyond Intermezzo? On the Long-term Industrial Impacts of Mega-events: the Impact of Lillehammer 1994', *Festival Management and Event Tourism*, 5, 101–22.

UK Sport (1999a) *Major Events: the economics*, London, UK Sport.

—— (1999b) *Major Events: the economics – a guide*, London, UK Sport.

—— (2004) *Measuring Success 2: the economic impact of major sport events*, London, UK Sport.

32

THE FUTURE OF SPORT MANAGEMENT

Leigh Robinson, Packianathan Chelladurai, Guillaume Bodet and Paul Downward

The previous four sections have set out issues of contemporary relevance in sport management which are the focus of practitioners and researchers in this field. It is clear that sport management is a diverse and vibrant research area and the organizations that deliver sport are increasingly competitive and effective. However, there are a number of factors in the operating context that will continue to require innovation and the ongoing development of sport management and these will need to be considered by researchers and practitioners alike.

The first of these is globalization, which means that sport markets are increasingly international, subject to diverse and complex laws, policies and cultures and increasingly competitive. Globalization also means that mega-events such as the Olympic Games and World Cups attract worldwide audiences and, consequently, the activities of the organizations that deliver these events are played out on an international stage. This means that the performance of these organizations will need to be acceptable to that international audience. Associated with this are customers who are expecting more for their money (Chapter 5) and are demanding increasingly personal and customized services, which are resource intensive and need to be delivered within a tough economic climate. Finally, sport is perceived to make a key contribution to society in terms of health, politics, social capital and urban regeneration and legacy (Robinson and Palmer, 2011) which are often used to justify state expenditure on sport and sport organizations.

So what does this mean for the future of sport management?

Identifying the future direction of a discipline is always a perilous exercise as we can never be sure that a trend is sustainable. It is also difficult to determine if theoretical research can be transferred to a practical situation and thus become part of the sport management environment. Consequently, it seems easier to identify issues in the context that may drive changes of practice and research and these are set out below under the four key themes of this *Handbook*.

The future of the performance of sport organizations

The principles of accountability, transparency and ethical behavior will continue to be of importance and indeed are likely to become of greater importance. The importance of good governance and thus models of good governance will continue to be a focus for the performance of sport organizations, both theoretical and practical. The challenge will be to identify activities that deliver and demonstrate accountability and transparency which can be incorporated into a framework that can subsequently be proved to guide most sport organizations.

In association with accountability and ethical behavior, human resources will need to become increasingly reflective of the people they deliver services to and staff will need to be managed in an ethical way. As addressed in Chapter 15, the challenge here is to ensure that contingent workers are as much part of a sport organization as any other staff member. However, perhaps most importantly, those who are at the top of the organization, who are perceived to benefit most from the organization, will have to be perceived as deserving of their benefits. Appointments to key positions will need to be transparent, appointees will need to be accountable and the challenge for research in the performance of sport organizations is to provide evidence to support that this is the correct way for organizations to operate.

Second, sport will need to develop mechanisms of becoming integrated into the "health agenda" in order to guarantee the sustainability of sport organizations. The UK has had a number of years of declining participation and sport is not a particularly attractive option for an increasing number of people (Robinson and Palmer, 2011). In order to ensure the ongoing survival of many sport organizations there will need to be a strong link between what they can deliver and the health agenda. Indeed, this is perhaps the biggest challenge as sport per se does not improve health; physical activity does. For managers, this may mean using planning systems and expectations management to repackage their product in a way that is appealing to those who are not committed to sport. It will certainly be necessary to address the rising trend of sport spectating, rather than participation, that is becoming increasingly evident in many societies. Research should also continue to focus on establishing the benefits of sport to society and on how this can be best delivered.

"Evidenced-based" management of performance will become increasingly important and will be needed to justify investment in sport organizations and the activities they undertake. For example, will sponsorship of sport continue to be important unless research can establish measurable benefits? This will place greater emphasis on research that "proves" that management techniques and approaches work, or that develops new ways of managing performance. Performance management techniques, in particularly performance measurement, will continue to underpin the performance of all sport organizations and will be used for demonstrating successes, identifying areas of underperformance and allocating priorities.

The future of human resource management in sport

The first thing that is clear about human resource management in sport is that most of the work under the purview of sport management cannot be outsourced. This is because the sport industry is service-based and services have to be produced in conjunction with the clients. They cannot be produced elsewhere, stored, transported and delivered at a different place, in a different time, as is done in the case of goods such as tennis rackets and basketballs. It means that service workers are the backbone of the sport industry and always will be.

It is also expected that the sport industry will grow in size and stature. For instance, Molitor (1996) has noted that leisure time pursuits will be the primary driving force behind economic growth in the near future, beginning about 2015. As consumption of sport in all its forms is largely a leisure time pursuit, we can expect that the sport industry will also grow and, by implication, the size and significance of the workforce in sport will also increase. Hence, more attention will be paid to managing this group of workers in an effective and ethical manner.

We must also be cognizant of two other forces that exert their influence on human resource management in sport. First, bureaucracy characterized by division of labor, specialization, routinization of jobs controlled by rules, and hierarchy of authority was considered relevant only to the manufacturing sector and the public sector. However, in recent years, service operations have also adopted the bureaucratic tenets of specialization and routinization. The most glaring example is the McDonald's restaurants and their delivery of fast food, although other service operations are also embodying what Ritzer (1996) calls the "McDonaldization" of the workplace. This is the application of the production principles and processes of the fast-food industry to other workplaces.

The essential elements of such a process are (a) efficiency, by choosing the best means for achieving a goal, (b) calculability, which is quantifying everything the worker does, (c) predictability of the products, and services being the same every time they are produced, and (d) control of the behaviors of both workers and customers guided by the technology of the production process. Ritzer (1996) also notes that McDonaldization results in the creation of "McJobs" involving simple and predictable tasks and controlled by non-human technologies. This process is contradictory to the motivational strategies such as job enrichment (Herzberg, 1968) and enhancing the motivating potential of jobs (Hackman and Oldham, 1980). The challenge for future managers of sport is to balance the process of rationality with the need to keep the workers motivated and satisfied. This will also need to be a focus of research in this area.

The other trend is that the workforce in developed and developing countries will be more and more diversified in terms of gender, ethnicity, nationality and language. By the same token, the customers and clients of sport organizations will also belong to diverse groups. As mentioned above, managers of sport organizations need to be attuned to the diversity in their workplace as well as their market and become more efficient and effective in managing such diversity.

The future of sport marketing

The globalization phenomenon is probably one of the most noticeable factors affecting the sport marketing field. Globalization is characterized by the increased free flows of individuals, ideas, goods, services and capital, which creates new opportunities for sport organizations, but also intensifies the competition between these sport organizations and creates more complex performance environments. One challenge for sport marketers will be to understand these environments and adapt their offers to this complexity. To achieve this goal, the role of strategic marketing (identity, segmentation, targeting and positioning) will be more crucial than ever.

For instance, selling replica shirts abroad cannot be the only strategy of a club in new foreign markets given the increasing number of professional clubs and leagues that are now competing for these markets. Professional sports clubs and leagues have to clearly understand who their new satellite fans are, what their characteristics and levels of attachment are, how they have become fans, how they are satisfied, how they become loyal, who they are competing with in their sport and in other sports, who are their local and international competitors and how they are perceived in these new markets, by these new fans. Moreover, they need to have the same strategic thinking with regards to their local fans and spectators, as foreign sport clubs and leagues will increasingly compete with them in their home markets.

The challenge will certainly be for sport marketers to understand the heterogeneity of sport consumers and the organizations they now compete with, but they will also need to determine how far can they go in their activities and quests for new foreign markets because this is not a "neutral" activity. This will impact on their home fans, who appear to be more and more dissatisfied by these commercial practices as they sometimes make them feel less valued and appreciated than high-spending foreign fans.

In the same vein, the intensification of competition between sport organizations will force managers to not consider their customers as a captive audience, as the range of offers can lead them to switch loyalty easily. At every level, it seems crucial for sport organizations to create and maintain individualized relationships with their customers and different stakeholders. Although the massive number of potential new customers may lead sport marketers to focus on customer attraction and recruitment strategies, the new configuration of sport markets and a newly-expressed customer need which emphasizes the social aspect of consumption both support the importance, if not the necessity, of relationship marketing.

Inextricably attached to the relationship marketing approach and the individualization or customization of offers is the other major factor affecting the sport marketing field: information and communication technology. This new technology offers unlimited options for sport organizations that aim to develop and maintain individualized relationships; for example, the development of Customer Relationship Management (CRM) programs by sport clubs, the development of websites such as www.miadidas.com and the increased presence and use of social networks by sport organizations. The communication and technological dimension of sport marketing is probably the most evolving dimension of sport marketing practice and research. Excitingly, the page is blank and sport marketers have the freedom to write on it.

Finally, experiential marketing appears to be another trend of sport marketing in this hyper-rationalized and standardized world where consumers want to be re-enchanted. However, as for other practices and marketing trends, such as relationship or tribal marketing, we can wonder if this trend will be translated into any real changes in the practice of sport organizations. This is a key challenge for research in the sport marketing area.

The future of sport economics

The chapters contained in Part IV cover a fairly narrow range of topics and issues. They are united, however, by the view that the sport economy comprises mass participation, the expenditure on goods and services to support that participation, and upon professional team sport and events.

Within this set of contexts there are many interfaces that need to be further investigated. From the demand side it is clear that the interface between economic theories of demand and marketing needs to be explored to better understand revenue sources for both commercial goods and services providers and professional sport. The role of sponsorship is important likewise. As a source of revenue for professional sport, and indeed amateur sport, it has implications for consumer behavior. In other words the set of interrelated demands in sport needs further investigation.

Supply side issues also need further analysis. This includes examining to what extent access to facilities of different types and organizations underpins participation. The role of the qualities of those facilities in maintaining demand also requires examination. The latter has implications for professional team sport as well as events. It is well known, for example, that different types of stadia can account for variations in demand for professional team sport.

The role of volunteer labor in sport also requires further analysis. Whilst we know that it supports sport-club systems and events, we know less about how volunteering is shaped by the leisure choices of volunteers. What substitute and complementary activities are present?

Further, do events promote volunteering and participation? These are issues that are yet to receive adequate answers. Finally, the role of the financing of sport needs more analysis. There has been some initial work on the role of alternative capital structures for sport. However, it is clear from the current debates concerning financial fair play that this issue is of paramount concern for future research.

Outside of this traditional core of activities are further topics that require elaboration. The globalized nature of sport means that, currently, sports of different types and geographical locations may actually be in competition more than traditional alternatives. This might mean that emergent sport leagues face unique economic obstacles. Sport economics has not examined this possibility and broadly remains focused on traditional geographical boundaries and dimensions of provision and demand. Whilst individual sports are now investigated more than in the past, examining how both their economic organization and sporting results are related through tournament theory remains a fertile avenue for research.

Does competitive balance matter for sets of rolling tournaments between individuals across different geographical domains, or across tournaments with different brand identities and technical features? What gives certain tournaments their status and market power? As the Olympics, for example, begins to extend into competition with existing tournaments, what will be the implication of this? Finally, much more work needs to be done on how talent produces sporting results. Part of the answer here will lie in examination of the interpretation of rules by officials, and the influence of location and other advantages on both these decisions and the efforts of athletes. This is a fertile research area currently; however, as this brief note suggests, there is much more work yet to be done.

Conclusion

The discussion above shows that sport management research and its practice needs to continue evolving and responding to changes in society. Many of the challenges to be faced will impact on all areas of sport management and indeed some of these challenges are fundamental to the way sport has been managed and the way sport organizations perform. As a consequence, the field of sport management is left with a question: is sport, as we know it, appropriate anymore in today's society? Given declining participation in organized sport, particularly among the young; the increasing competition bought about by technological advances for both spectators and participants; and increasing public discontent with the way major sport organizations are managed, it would be relatively easy to suggest that sport has had its golden age. The challenge is for the field to continue to address these major issues and cement the role of sport and its management as a valuable and integral part of society.

References

Hackman, J.R. and Oldham, G.R. (1980) *Work design*, Reading, MA, Addison-Wesley.

Herzberg, F. (1968) 'One more time: How do you motivate people?', *Harvard Business Review*, 46, 53–62.

Molitor, G.T.T. (1996) 'The next thousand years: The "big five" engines of economic growth', in G. T. Kurian and G. T. T. Molitor (eds.), *The 21st century*, New York, Simon & Schuster Macmillan.

Nichols, G., Taylor, P., James, M., Garrett, R., Holmes, K., King, L., Gratton, C. and Kokolakakis, T. (2004) 'Voluntary activity in UK sport', *Voluntary Action*, 6(2), 31–54.

Ritzer, G. (1996) *The McDonaldization of society*, Thousand Oaks, CA, Pine Forge Press.

Robinson, L and Palmer, R. (2011) (eds.) *Managing voluntary sport organisations*, London, Routledge.

INDEX

Bold type indicates Figures or Tables.

Abramovich, R. 394
accountability 3–5, 76
action plans 50
active expectations 58
'activity links' 245
'actor bonds' 246
Administration 8–10
aesthete profile 257
agency theory 27–8
Amateur Swimming Association 4, 64–6; knowledge of ASA work **64**; member expectations 63; overall satisfaction with membership **65**; satisfaction with membership 65
ambush marketing 311–21; activation/leveraging of sponsorship 317–18; advertising that corresponds with the event 314; challenges of new media 320–1; education programs 315–16; going forward 318; government involvement and anti-ambush legislation 318–21; integrated public relations program 315; international perspectives 321; legal strategies 318; management roles and responsibilities 314–18; managing the event brand 315; research and discussion 312–13; sponsoring media coverage 313; sponsoring subcategories 313–14; sponsorship recognition programs 317; sponsorship structure 316–17; strategies 313–14; thematic advertising and implied association 314
American approach: definition of relationship marketing 239
American Sport Education Program (ASEP) 165
Anglo-Australian approach: definition of relationship marketing 239
anticipatory measures 33–4
ANYSPORT 345

Arena swimsuits 117
Arsenal Double Club 101
Athletes Commission 16
attendance demand: professional team sport 405–17
Audit Commission 70, 73–4
auditing 32
Australian football: change agenda 128; governance practice reform 127–32; impact of change 130–1; people and organizational culture 128–9; stakeholder management 129–30
Australian Soccer Association 128, 130
Australian Sport Commission 29

Bank of Credit and Commerce International (BCCI) 27
basic economic consumer demand theory 332
'Basic universal principles of good governance of the Olympic and Sport Movement' 21
'battering ram' approach 407
BBC–ITV 406
Beckham, D. 146
benchmarking 78
Berlioux, M. 8–9
Bernard, A. 88–9
'big five' 407
Blau's social exchange theory 195
BNL sponsorship strategy: direct and indirect relationships between Internazionali BNL of Italia and **249**; 'Internazionali BNL d'Italia' 247–51; lessons learned 250–1; sponsorship with a market focus 248–9; sponsorship with a network focus 249–50; sponsorship with internal focus 250
Bosman, J-M. 397, 419
Bosman ruling 379, 397
Bradley Report 128

Index

brand awareness 302
brand image: and attitudes towards the brand 303–4
brand positioning 302–3
breach 196
Bright Sparks 101
British Satellite Broadcasting (BSkyB) 406, 407–8
broadcast demand: professional team sport 405–17
broadcast sponsorship 301
broadcasting rights 379
BSkyB 102

Cadbury Report 27
Carnegie, A. 102
"cathedrals of consumption" 254, 268
Celtic plc 102
Centro de Investigaciones Sociológicas (CIS) 344
change management: Dunphy and Stace change matrix 125; models of change 122–5; new technologies **117**; reforming football governance practice in Australia 127–32; resistance to change 125–7; Schein/Lewin model **123**; schematic overview of different change issues **119**; theoretical approaches and practical strategies 116–32; types and characteristics 118–22
charismatic transformations 125
citizen satisfaction 72
clutter 312–13
coaching 32
Code of Ethics for Sport 20
coercive pressures 121
commercial organization 74–6; performance ratio **75**
communication: word of mouth 60
community sporting events: recruitment and selection 170–1; retention 171–2; training 171; volunteer management 170–2
competence 140
composite measure 205
Comprehensive Area Analysis 76
Comprehensive Performance Assessment 76
conceptual approach 160
consumer loyalty: antecedents in sport participation 228–33; consumer perceived value 230; consumer psychological commitment 231–2; consumer satisfaction 229; enduring involvement 232–3; members' loyalty in sport participation organizations 228; perceived service quality 230–1; sport participation services 227–35; towards a mediating role of consumer psychological commitment 233–4
consumer perceived value 230
consumer psychological commitment 231–2
consumer relationship management (CRM) 239
consumer satisfaction 229
consuming as classification 256

consuming as experience 256
consuming as integration 256
consuming as play 256
"consumption temples" 268
content analysis 111
contextual approaches 121
contextual/processual change theory 124
contingency theory 146
Contingent and Standards governance framework (CaS) 31–3; contingency model **32**; development 30–1; outline 34–7; partnership and communication standards 35–6; performance standards 37; planning standards 36–7; structural standards 34–5; transparency standards 38–9
contingent employment: advantages and disadvantages 216–17; management in sport 214–18; outsourcing 218
contingent workers 138
continuous latent utility 347
"core-peripheral model" 215
corporate governance 7
corporate hospitality 301, 305
corporate identity 63
corporate social responsibility 5, 101–13, 305–6; activities undertaken by SPL clubs **111**; motives-oriented 108–9; organizations 102–3; other CSR themes 109–13; outcomes-oriented 106–8; review of CSR in sport 105–6; sports organizations 103–5
County Sport Partnerships 122
Court of Arbitration for Sport (CAS) 19–20
Coventry, K. 89–90
coworker exchange scales 179
coworker support: antecedents of support 181; consequences of support 183–4; definition 178–9; measure of support 179–80
Crawford Report 127–8; stakeholder management 129–30
customer education 62–3
customer expectations: Amateur Swimming Association (ASA) 64–6; customer education 62–3; customer needs 60; image 61, 63; influences 59–61; management of expectations 61–3, **63**; market communications 61, 63; past experience 60, 62; service quality and customer satisfaction 57–8; sports organizations 57–66; types 58–9; word of mouth 60
customer needs 60
Customer Relationship Management (CRM) 460
customer satisfaction 57–8, 71–2

data benchmarking 78
de Campos, A. 201
Decathlon 271
developmental transitions 124
direct incentives 151

Direct TV 292
"Disneyfication" 271
"diversification" approach 93
double-hurdles model 333
driving governance role 31; anticipatory
    mechanisms 33; definitions 32–3
dual route framework (DRF) 289

econometric modeling 88
economic analysis: sport participation 331–50
economic benefits: hosting of major sport events
    441–54
economic impacts 443
economics: contemporary issues in sport 327–30
economy 71
education programs 315–16
efficiency 71
efficiency savings 71
egalitarian sport 141
elite sport 141–2; athletic and post-career
    support 92–3; coaching provision and coach
    development 93; factors influencing improved
    performance **98**; financial support 92;
    integrated approach to policy development 92;
    international competition 93; nine pillars used
    in elite sport development systems **91**; output
    93–4; participation in sport 92; performance
    of nations 86–98; scientific research 93; talent
    identification and system development 92;
    training facilities 93
emergent change 120
employees: sources of support in sport
    organizations 178–89
empowerment 140–1; contingency approach to
    HRM practices **141**
enduring involvement 232–3
English Football League 407; attendance and
    broadcast demand 405–17
English Premier League (EPL) 255, 405, 407, 416
entertainment sports 142
Entourage Commission 13
episodic volunteers 166, 170
equity 71
ethical behavior 3–5
Ethics Commission 16–17
European Charter for Sport 20
European Club Association (ECA) 383, 399;
    payroll cap in European football 383–6; payroll
    cap under profit maximization **384**; payroll cap
    under win maximization **385**
European Elite Athletes Association 17
European Football Association (UEFA) 395, 397
European leagues (utility and win maximization)
    394–401; free agency (Bosman ruling) 397–9;
    organizational structure 394–5; payroll caps
    399–401; revenue sharing in European sport
    leagues 395–7

European Short Course Swimming
    Championships 449–50
European Sport Management Quarterly 327
event 303
"evidence-based" management of performance 458
evolutionary change 120
Executive Board 12
exit, voice, loyalty and neglect (EVLN)
    typology 203
expenditures: further research 365–7; households
    with expenditures on specific sport and
    recreational services **358**; influencing factors
    363–5; literature, research objectives and
    data 354–5; macroeconomic oriented studies
    on sport expenditures **355**; microeconomic
    oriented studies from Asia, America and
    Oceania **357**; microeconomic oriented studies
    from Europe **356**; miscellaneous surveys on
    private consumer spending on attending sport
    events **362**; miscellaneous surveys on private
    consumer spending on services for active sport
    consumption **363**; monetary value of sport
    359–62; most frequently analyzed factors
    influencing consumer expenditure on
    SAR services **364–5**; portion of individual
    with expenditures on sport 355–8; private
    households' expenditures on sport and
    recreational services in PPP **360**; second survey
    results for the Council Of Europe **361**; signs of
    the significant Tobit estimate for 18 different
    expenditure categories **366**; sport products and
    services 354–67
experiential marketing 460
explicit expectations 59

FedEx St Jude Classic 107
FIFA 3
"50+1" rule 394
Fiji Swimming Association 52–5; assessment
    development **53**; recommendations **54–5**
finance 72
Finance Commission 13–14
'financial doping' 105
FirstGolf 101
football broadcast market 406–9
Football Federation Australia 130–2
Football for Hope 101
forecasting technique 94–8; China's performance
    in the Olympic Games **94**; extrapolating China's
    gold medals in 2008 based on past performance
    95; forecasted gold medals vs actual **97**; host
    nation performance vs performance prior to
    hosting **96**
formal training 150
Freedman, A. 214
functional flexibility 215
fuzzy expectations 58

parachute payments 295
partnership and community
passive expectations 58

G–14 383, 399
'gap' score 72
geographic distance 290
German Bundesliga: development of player salaries **428**; development of player salaries by position **428**; development of transfer fees **425**; mean and standard deviation of transfer fees **425**; percentage of movers with transfer fee **426**
German Football Federation (DFB) 420
'Gibraltar National Olympic Committee' 19
'Global Coalition for Good Governance in Sport' 18
global measure 205
globalization 457
"good risk" players 398
governance 7, 21, 28; anticipatory mechanisms for governance role 33; Contingent and Standards framework 31–3; contingent and standards framework for national governing bodies 26–39; development of the CaS framework 30–1; five levels of IOC governance **23**; governance and organisational lifecycle **27**; International Olympic Committee 7–23; literature review 27–30; outline of CaS standards 34–7; transparency standards 38–9
governance lifecycle 26

Hawthorne Study 153
"heterodox" approach 332
Hilmer Report 27
horizontal equity 71
hot/cool axis 256
human resource management 145–55; contemporary issues 137–44; future of 458–9; principle of fit 139–42; service-based 147–54; social responsibility 138–9; top 10 Premier League transfers 146; vertical differentiation 142–4
Husin, S. 137

ICC British Company Financial Datasets 74
identification processes 231
idiosyncratic deals 197
image 61, 63
impact 72, 140
implicit expectations 58–9
incentives 151
"income-leisure tradeoff" model 332
informal training 150
information and communication technology 460
informational processes 231
institutional theory 121
integrated public relations program 315
interactive profile 257
internal marketing 304–5
International Charter for Physical Education and Sport 20

International Council of Arbitration for Sport (ICAS) 19
International Journal of Sport Marketing 223
International Journal of Sport Marketing and Management 327
International Journal of Sports Finance 327
International Olympic Committee (IOC) 166; basic universal principles of good governance of the Olympic Movement **22**; daily management and high politics 7–23; five levels of governance of the IOC **23**; five levels of management and governance **8**; harmonizing the regulatory mechanisms 17–20; IOC regulatory mechanisms 15–17; management 8–11; management of IOC management 11–14; meta-governance 20–2; organization chart **10**
International Passenger Survey (IPS) 451
international sport league: comparisons 388–403; European leagues (utility and win maximization) 394–401; North American leagues (profit maximization) 388–94
'Internazionali BNL d'Italia' 247–51
interpersonal communication 290
Invariance Proposition of Rottenberg 377
Investing in Change 29
'IOC 2000' 15
IOC Television and Marketing Services 11
isomorphism 121
ITV Digital 408

Job Descriptive Index 179
Journal of Management and Organization 105
Journal of Sport Management 105
Journal of Sports Economics 327
Journal of Sports Management 327

Key Performance Indicators (KPIs) 50
Key Result Areas 48
King Reports 27
Kotter model 126–7; Kotter's eight-step model **126**

labor market: professional team sport 419–37; structure and outcomes 422–4
leader–member exchange scale 179, 180
Lewin's classic change model 122–3
Lisbon Treaty (2009) 21
live attendance: and mass media 288–9; mass media as substitute 288; mass media as symbiosis 288–9; symbiosis and substitution 289
logistic model 333

Major Events: the economics – a guide 447
Major Events Management Act (2007) 319
major sport events: city sport strategies in North America 445–7; Commonwealth Games Manchester 2002 450–3; economic benefits of hosting to cities 441–54; economic impact of

16 major sport events **448**; economic impact of summer Olympic Games 444–5; legacy benefits of the Barcelona Olympic Games **452**; longer term benefits of hosting 452–3; sport and economic regeneration in cities and regions in UK 447–50; sport and urban regeneration 442–4; towards an event evaluation model **444**
managerialism 122
marginal productivity theory 422
market communications 61, 63
mass communication 282–3, 290
mass media: as substitute 288; as symbiosis 288–9; promotion as communication strategy 281–2
mass sport consumption 329
MASTER 70–1
material incentives 160
Maunsell, F. 451
"McDonaldization" 459
meaning 140
Measuring Success 2: the economic impact of major sport events 447
media: and live attendance 288–9; mass media as substitute 288; mass media as symbiosis 288–9; symbiosis and substitution 289
Median Regression model 429
mega events: recruitment and selection 166–8; retention 169–70; training 168–9; volunteer management 166–70
mimetic pressures 121
Modified Volunteer Function Inventory for Sport (MVFIS) 164
Monopolies and Mergers Commission (MMC) 405
monopsony 378
"Monti system" 398, 399
moral hazard effect 429
Motivation Scale for Sport Consumption (MSSC) 261
motives-oriented 108–9
"Mountain Equipment Co-op" (MEC) 272
multi-dimensional planning 43
multiple regression 88
mutuality 204

naming right sponsor 300
Nash equilibrium approach 389
National Alliance for Youth Sport (NAYS) 165
National Audit Office 87
National Basketball Association cap 393
National Benchmarking Service (NBS) 4, 76, 78–84; benchmarks and quartiles **82**; benefits of benchmarking 83–4; grid analysis of importance and satisfaction scores **82**; performance indicators **79–80**; reasons for using NBS 82–3; uses 83
National Football League cap 393
National Governing Bodies (NGB) 3–4, 43, 46
National Governing Bodies of Sport Success Criteria/ Model Framework 29

National Hockey League 117
National Youth Sport Coaches Association (NYSCA) 165
NBA Cares 107–8
new media technologies: and sport communication 289–91
Nine Steps to Effective Governance 29–30
Noll-Scully "ratio of standard deviation" 392
Nominations Commission 15–16
nonprofit sport organizations: recruitment and selection 160–1; retention 161–3; training 161; volunteer management 160–3
nonstandard employment 214
Nordic approach: definition of relationship marketing 239
normative pressures 122
North American leagues (profit maximization) 388–94; other talent market changes and impositions 393–4; revenue sharing in closed and open leagues 392–3; simple general model 389–92
numerical flexibility 215

Oceania Regional Anti Doping Agency 47
official sponsor 300
official supplier 300
Olympic Advocates Together Honorably (OATH) 17
Olympic and Paralympic Marks Act (2007) 318–19
Olympic Broadcasting Services 11
Olympic Charter 12, 15, 19
Olympic Foundation 11
Olympic Games: actual *versus* predicted gold medals outside the range of +/- 2 **89**; Australia's performance in the summer Olympic Games **90**; Bernard forecast medals vs actual in Beijing **89**; macro-economic measures 87–90
Olympic Museum Foundation 11
Olympic Solidarity Commission 14
on-site signage 301
ONDigital 408
opportunist profile 257
organizational justice 182
organizational support 138; antecedents of support 182; consequences of support 185–7; definition 179; measure of support 179–80
orientation 165
outcomes 72
outcomes-oriented 106–8
output 72
outsourcing 218
Owen, R. 102
Oxylane Group 272

parachute payments 395
partnership and communication standards 35–6
passive expectations 58

passive leisure 358
payroll cap 382; European Club Association in European football 383–6
perceived organizational support scale 180
perceived service quality 230–1
perceived supervisor support 182
performance 71–2
performance indicators 72–7; criteria **73**; private or commercial sector 74–6; public sector 76–7; voluntary sector 77
performance management: benchmarking 78; measure 69–70; National Benchmarking Service 78–84; objectives 70–1; performance 71–2; performance indicators 72–7; sports organizations 69–85; targets 77–8
performance of nations: alternative forecasting technique 94–8; elite sport 86–98; input 92; lessons from the performance of China 98; macro-economic measures of performance 87–90; output 93–4; performance management in elite sport development systems 91; throughput 92–3
performance standards 37
person–organization fit 141–2; sport domains **142**
person–task fit 139–40
personal display of logo 301
PGA Tour 107
"places of spectacles" 268
planned change 120
planned development 42, 43–4; benefits of planning 45–6; implementation of plan 51–5; need for planned development 44–5; planning process 47–51; sports organizations 42–55; vision and mission statement 46–7
planning benefits 45–6
planning process 47–51; diagnosis 47–8; monitoring and evaluation 51; putting into action 49–51; setting the direction 48–9
planning standards 36–7
Point of Attachment Index (PAI) 261
policy governance model 28–9
position-based deals 197
Post-Keynesian consumer analysis 332
precise expectations 59
PricewaterhouseCoopers 13
principal sponsor 300
principle of fit 139–42; empowerment 140–1; person–organization fit 141–2; person–task fit 139–40
printed word 286–7
"priority" ' approach 93
process benchmarking 78
professional sport leagues 329
professional team sport: attendance and broadcast demand 405–17; determinants of player salaries 427–33; development of player salaries by position in German Bundesliga **428**; development of player salaries in German Bundesliga **428**; development of transfer fees in the German Bundesliga **425**; discrimination issue in European football 433–4; distribution of televised matches in 2006–07 season **411**; economic fundamentals **416**; economic relevance of football in Europe 420–2; emergence of the football broadcast market 406–9; estimation results I: various methods **431**; estimation results II: quantile regressions **432**; impact of televised games on attendance 411–13; interplay between stadium attendance and TV audiences 414–16; labor market 419–37; labor market structure and labor market outcomes 422–4; market values of first division teams in the "Big 5" European leagues **421**; mean and standard deviation of transfer fees in German Bundesliga **425**; percentage of movers with transfer fee in German Bundesliga **426**; revenue sources by season **410**; rights fees paid from 1983–84 to 2013–14 **407**; seasonal EPL attendance **409**; stadium attendance and audience ratings 409–11; television audience demand 413–14; transfer fees in European football 425–7
Psychological Commitment to Team (PCT) scale 260
psychological contract 138, 193–209; analytical framework **198**; as multidimensional construct 203; breach, violation and fulfillment of 196–7; coaches and players 201–2; contextual variables 203–4; management literature 195–9; managerial challenges and future directions in research in sport organizations 206–7; managers and graduates 202; measuring psychological contract violation 205; methodological issues in studies 203–6; other studies 202; processes and model 197–9; research avenues in the context of sport organizations 207; sport administrators and coaches 200–1; sport administrators and volunteers 199–200; sport organizations context 199–202; studying mutuality 204–5; transactional and relational psychological contracts 196; understanding job specifics 205; what do we know and where do we go from here 206–7
psychological contract theory 193, 194
psychological contract violations (PCV) 203
psychological empowerment 140
public sector 76–7; national indicators relevant to sport services in the UK **76**
purchase intentions 304
purchasing power parities (PPP) 359
purposive incentives 160

quality management techniques 59
Quirk and Fort fixed-talent supply model 373

Random Effects panel data model 429
rational approaches 120–1
Readiness Assessment Tool (RAT) 48; Fiji Swimming Association 52–5
realistic expectations 59
reciprocity 182–3, 204
reinforcement theory 151
relational psychological contracts 196
relationship marketing 238–51, 305; application of the framework 247–51; BNL sponsorship with market focus 248–9; concept of relationship 241; conception, definition and application to sport 239–44; definition 239–41, **240**; definitions of relationship **242**; developing valuable relationships in three subsystems 244–6; direct and indirect relationships between BNL and Internazionali BNL of Italia **249**; integrated framework 244–7; lessons learned 250–1; marketing strategies typology **241**; sponsorship with a network focus 249–50; sponsorship with internal focus 250; sport from a market perspective 243; sport from a network perspective 243–4; sport management literature 242–3; steps in implementing the principles in sport organization **246**; three categories of relationship **245**; three-step process to build valuable relationships 246–7
'resource ties' 245–6
"retailtainment" 275
revolutionary change 120
reward system 151–2
Rogge, J. 9, 13
Rousseau, D. 195

salary cap 382–3
sales 304
Salt Lake City scandal 15
Samaranch, J.A. 9
Schein, E. 123
Schein/Lewin model 123–4
SCORE 48
Scottish Premier League 110–13; examples of CSR activities **111**
segmentation 254–5; multidimensional psychographic variables 260–2; observation-driven segments 255–7; one-dimensional psychographic variable 259–60; psychographic segmentation 259; socio-demographic segmentation 257–9; sport spectators 254–62; theory-driven segments 257–62
selection effect 429
self-determination 140
semi-structured interviews 112
service-based human resource management 147–54; performance appraisals 153–4; reward system 151–2; sources **149**; supervisory assistance 152; support at work 148–50; training 150–1
service quality 57–8
7-item scale 180
"shadow of the transfer system" 398
"sharpening effect" 396–7
should expectations 58
single-outcome planning 43
six-item scale 180
Sky Television 406
"SMART objectives" 48–9
social entertainment 358
social exchange theory 162, 182–3, 195
social incentives 151
social media 291
social performance 72
social responsibility: human resource management 138–9
Social TV 292
solidary incentives 160
Special Event Volunteer Motivation Scale (SEVMS) 166–7
'spectator driven' 448
SPLISS project 5
sponsorship 243; actors and their relationships **299**; categories and types 299; different contexts of 299; other types 299; sponsorship marketing and sponsorship-linked marketing 297–9; sport sponsorship 299
sponsorship actors 297–9
Sponsorship and International Journal of Sport Marketing and Management 223
sponsorship marketing 297–9
sponsorship recognition programs 317
sponsorship structure 316–17
sport: contemporary issues in the economics of 327–30; corporate social responsibility 101–13; expenditures on products and services 354–67; future of human resource management 458–9; future of management 457–61; future of performance of sport organization 457–8; future of sport economics 460–1; future of sport marketing 459–60; human resource management 145–55; managing contingent workers 214–18; promotion through communication 281–93; volunteer management 159–73
sport and recreational and services (SAR) 363
sport broadcast rights 285
sport clubs 373–86; consequences of Bosman verdict 379; ECA payroll cap under profit maximization **384**; ECA payroll cap under win maximization **385**; impact of market regulation 376–83; marginal and average revenue curves **374**; market equilibrium **375**; monopolizing broadcast rights 380–1; monopsony under

profit and win maximization **378**; payroll cap of the European Club Association in European football 383–6; profit or win maximization? 374–6; revenue sharing 379–80; revenue sharing under profit maximization **380**; revenue sharing under win maximization **381**; salary cap **382**; transfer system 376–9; transfer system under win maximization **377**; US salary cap 382–3

sport economics: future of 460–1

Sport Event Information Template (EIT) 289

sport events 330

Sport Fan Motivation Scale (SFMS) 261

"Sport for All" 331

sport leagues 327, 329

sport marketing: contemporary issues 223–6; from marketing trends to 224–6; from sport changes to 223–4; future of 459–60

Sport Marketing Quarterly 223

sport mass communication as 283–5

sport organization: accountability, transparency and ethical behavior 3–5; antecedents of support 180–2; approaches to managing performance 69–85; benefits of planning 45–6; consequences of support 182–7; definitions 178–9; future of performance of 457–8; future studies 188–9; implementation of plan 51–5; managing customer expectations 57–66; measure of support 179–80; need for planned development 44–5; organizationala competitiveness 5–6; performance issues 3–6; planned development 42–55; planning process 47–51; practical implications of studying sport 187–8; psychological contract 193–209; social responsibility 103–5; sources of support for employees 178–89; vision and mission statement 46–7

sport participation 328–9; consumer loyalty in services 227–35; data, variables and method 344–8; data set 344; economic analysis of 331–50; empirical evidence of determinants 333–44; literature review 332–44; method 347–8; regression results **349**; results 348–50; summary of empirical studies on **335–41**; theoretical motivation 332–3; variable description **346**; variables 344–7

sport promotion: as a mass media communication strategy 281–2; future considerations 291–2; influence of printed word 286–7; mass communication 282–3; media and live attendance 288–9; sport broadcast rights 285; sport communication and new media 289–91; sport mass communication as 283–5; through communication 281–93; venue "game" 287–8

Sport Spectator Identification Scale (SSIS) 259

sport spectators: multidimensional psychographic variables 260–2; observation-driven segments 255–7; one-dimensional psychographic variable 259–60; psychographic segmentation 259; segmentation 254–62; socio-demographic segmentation 257–9; theory-driven segments 257–62

sport sponsorship 224, 296–306, 299; brand awareness 302; brand image and attitudes towards the brand 303–4; brand positioning 302–3; corporate objectives of sponsorship 304; corporate social responsibility 305–6; defining sponsorship 296–7; different targets 301–2; implementing sponsorship 300–1; internal marketing 304–5; marketing objectives 302; objectives 301–6; purchase intentions and sales 304; relationship marketing 305; role of emotions 306; sponsorship actors 297–9; sponsorship actors and their relationships **299**; sponsorship categories and types 299; sponsorship marketing and sponsorship-linked marketing 297–9; types of partners and partnership levels 299–300

SPORTFREQUENCY 345

sporting goods: brands and retail store dramatization 267–78; classical style 274; diversity of sport store chains' architectural styles 273–6; evolution of brands' distribution in hypercompetitive market 269–73; flagship stores and other concept stores 276–7; fun shopping style 275; influence of in-store shopping contexts on consumers 277–8; minimalist style 275–6; new baroque style 273–4; nomadic style 276; rational style 274; retail sales transformation 269–70; show style 275; thematic style 274; traditional style 273; trendy style 275; valuing stores for competitive advantage 270–3

stakeholder management 129–30

stakeholder theory 109–10

standard deals 197

steering 33

"strategic approach to elite sport development" 89

strategic plan 47, 52

strategic thinking approach 45

strengths, weaknesses, opportunities and threats (SWOT) 48

structural standards 34–5

substitution 289

Super Bowl 110

supervising 33

supervisor support: antecedents of support 181–2; consequences of support 184–5; definition 179; measure of support 179–80

supervisory assistance 152

supply 460
Supporters Direct 109
Swiss Civil Code 20
symbiosis 289

targets 77–8
task-focused transitions 124
Taylor, F. 148
Taylorism 125
Taylor's theory 148
team identification 259–60
Team Sport Involvement (TSI) 262
television audience demand 413–14
'The Olympic Movement' 7
thematic advertising and implied association 314
"thematisation" 271
theory of bilateral monopoly 424
theory of organizational authority 181
"3+2" rule 379
Ticketed 117
Ticketmaster 117
Trademarks Act 319
traditional/consumer dimension 256
training 150–1
transactional psychological contracts 196
transfer system 376–8
transparency 3–5
transparency standards 38–9
Treaty of Nairobi (1981) 20
Tullock contest-success function (CSF) 396
turnarounds 125
TV Rights and New Media Commission 14
two-step Heckman model 333

UK Sport 29
UK Sport Good Governance Guide for National Governing Bodies 29

UK Tourism Survey (UKTS) 451
unrealistic expectations 59

'value constellation' 245
Vancouver Winter Olympic Games the organizing committee (VANOC) 316
venue "game" 287–8
vertical differentiation 142–4; three subsystems of an organization **143**
vertical equity 71
"Village La Forme" 271
violation 196
viral video 292
vision and mission statement 46–7
voluntary sector organizations 77
Volunteer Function Inventory (VFI) 164
volunteer labor 460
volunteer management 159–73; community sporting events 170–2; mega events 166–70; nonprofit sport organizations 160–3; stages **173**; youth sport settings 163–6
Volunteer Motivations Scale for International Sporting Events (VMS-ISE) 167
Volunteer Protection Act (1997) 165
volunteers 137–8

weighted measure 205
Weitzman, M. 383
Welsh, J. 311
will expectations 58
World Anti-Doping Agency (WADA) 18, 47
World Anti-Doping Code 18

youth sport settings: recruitment and selection 163–4; retention 165–6; training 165; volunteer management 163–6
YouTube 117